Timetables
of History
for Students
of Methodism

Timetables of History

for Students of Methodism

REX D. MATTHEWS

Abingdon Press
Nashville

TIMETABLES OF HISTORY FOR STUDENTS OF METHODISM

This book is printed on acid-free paper.

Library of Congress Cataloging-in-Publication Data

Timetables of history for students of Methodism / compiled by Rex D. Matthews.
   p. cm.
   ISBN 978-0-687-33387-5 (binding: pbk. with lay flat binding : alk. paper)
   1. Methodist Church—History. 2. World history. I. Matthews, Rex Dale.

BX8231.T56 2007
287.09—dc22

                                                                                    2006035299

07 08 09 10 11 12 13 14 15 16—10 9 8 7 6 5 4 3 2 1
MANUFACTURED IN THE UNITED STATES OF AMERICA

Dedicated to my mother,
Mary Ann Perry Matthews,
my first teacher and finest role model

Preface

Timetables of History for Students of Methodism intends to help its readers more readily and fully understand the significance of important events and developments in the history of Methodism by putting those events and developments into their context and showing their relationship to one another as well as to other happenings in human history. The volume places major events of every year across the period from 1700 to 2005 into eight parallel columns:

A. World History & Politics
B. American History & Politics
C. Science, Medicine & Technology
D. Daily Life, Popular Culture & Entertainment
E. Education, Literature & the Fine Arts
F. Religion, Theology, Philosophy & Psychology
G American & United Methodism
H. British & World Methodism

This tabular arrangement of information enables students to gain a sweeping overview of the past three centuries, allowing them to discern something of what was happening simultaneously in all these different areas of human life and activity at any given point. It helps them "contextualize" significant events, movements, and developments in the history of Methodism, both in North America and in the rest of the world, by placing them into relationship with other historical, political, cultural, intellectual, artistic, and literary currents.

Through the use of this volume, students with a particular interest in the historical development of Methodism can readily see that development taking place in the context of other major trends and developments in human culture and social life. Those who are interested, for example, in the struggle of Methodist women to achieve lay representation and clergy rights can easily perceive how that struggle is related to the larger series of developments involving women's rights and women's suffrage, both in the United States and elsewhere. Major milestones concerning the abolition of slavery and the development of the civil rights movement help to illumine the relationships between racial and ethnic groups within Methodism. The spread of Methodism around the world through the activities and influence of missionaries from Britain and America can be seen to result in the emergence of autonomous Methodist churches in many countries, just as European and American colonialism ultimately led to the formation of numerous independent nation-states.

Sometimes it is both interesting and instructive simply to observe the conjunction of seemingly unrelated events occurring in a given year. For example, The United Methodist Church came into being in 1968. The delegates to the Uniting Conference that year in Dallas lived through a year that also witnessed and experienced all of the following:

- The signature of the Nuclear Nonproliferation Treaty by the US, the USSR, and the UK
- The crushing of the "Prague Spring" democratic movement in Czechoslovakia by Soviet troops
- The capture by North Korea of the USS *Pueblo*, an American intelligence-gathering vessel
- The surprise of the Tet Offensive by the North Vietnamese army
- The rise to power in Iraq of an obscure general named Saddam Hussein
- The report of the National Advisory Commission on Civil Disorders (often called the Kerner Commission) saying that "our nation is moving toward two societies, one black, one white—separate and unequal"
- The assassinations of the Reverend Martin Luther King Jr. and Robert F. Kennedy
- The founding of the American Indian Movement
- The journey of the *Apollo 8* astronauts around the moon and safely back to earth
- The premiere of the rock musical *Hair* on Broadway
- The posthumous release of "Sittin' on the Dock of the Bay" by Otis Redding, his last and biggest hit record
- The imposition of restrictions on the mail-order sale of rifles and shotguns by the 1968 Gun Control Act
- The surprise announcement by President Johnson that he will not seek reelection, due in large measure to increasing protests over the Vietnam War
- The advent of the television news magazine *60 Minutes* on CBS
- The introduction by McDonald's of the double-decker Big Mac hamburger
- The issuance by Pope Paul VI of the encyclical *Humanae Vitae (On the Regulation of Birth)*, which reasserted traditional Roman Catholic opposition to birth control
- The US Supreme Court decision invalidating an Arkansas state law that had prohibited the teaching of evolution in public schools
- The publication of Mary Daly's *The Church and the Second Sex*, Jürgen Habermas's *Knowledge and Human Interests*, Norman Mailer's *Armies of the Night*, and John Updike's *Couples*
- The release of the movies *2001: A Space Odyssey*, *Romeo & Juliet*, *Yellow Submarine*, *The Lion in Winter*, and *Rosemary's Baby*
- The violent confrontations between protesters and police at the Democratic National Convention in Chicago
- The discovery of oil on the North Slope of Alaska
- The ruling of the Equal Employment Opportunity Commission that sex-segregated help-wanted ads in newspapers are illegal
- The signature by President Johnson of the landmark 1968 Civil Rights Act (also known as the Housing Rights Act), which outlawed discrimination in the sale, rental, or financing of housing
- The first public demonstration of a networked computer system at the Stanford Research Institute, marking the public debut of the computer mouse, hypertext, and video teleconferencing
- The election of Richard Nixon to the presidency of the United States

As any historian knows well, the simple conjunction of events does not demonstrate causality, and none of those events, perhaps, had any *direct* bearing or any *specific* influence on the establishment of The United Methodist Church. However, that list of events does serve to give the reader some sense of the complicated nature and character of the world into which The United Methodist Church was born. That list of events does help to describe the historical, political, scientific, technological, and cultural context within which The United Methodist Church came into existence and provides some important clues about the texture of the lives and experiences of the people who brought it into being and to whom it endeavored to be in ministry.

This volume takes its inspiration in large part from Bernard Grun's classic *Timetables of History: A Horizontal Linkage of People and Events*, now in its fourth edition, which is in turn based on Werner Stein's *Kulturfahrplan*, first published in 1946. This important reference work provides a guide to well over 2,000 years of history, enabling its readers to gain some sense of the complexity of human experience and endeavor during those years. As valuable as this massive volume is, it provides relatively little attention to religion in general, even less attention to Christianity in particular, and has no specific concern with or focus on Methodism in any of its incarnations. The same is true of other more recent volumes similar to or inspired by Grun's work, such as Laurence Urdang's *The Timetables of American History* or John B. Teeple's *Timelines of World History*.

Timetables of History for Students of Methodism is much more limited it its scope and ambition and makes no attempt to compete with volumes such as those just mentioned. This work instead takes as its particular focus the historical development of Methodism from its origins in the life and work of John Wesley, including the history of the British Methodist Church and The United Methodist Church and their direct predecessor bodies. It is concerned, however, to present key events and happenings of that history in their larger context and to place them into relationship with relevant developments in other branches of the Methodist and Wesleyan family, both in America and around the world. Despite its particular attention to United Methodism, from its origins through its growth into a denomination that spans much of the globe, the volume should also be of some interest and relevance for those whose primary concern is with other branches of the Methodist family tree.

This volume is, by design and intention, illustrative rather than comprehensive in nature and scope. Due to limitations of time and space, it makes no attempt to include every significant happening that might possibly be mentioned under each category for each year. It is necessarily selective, and sometimes perhaps even idiosyncratic, in its choices of which events or developments it records. As Daniel Boorstin writes in his foreword to the third edition of Grun's work, "except for the more familiar and more obvious items in politics and the arts, the authors' choice has been personal" because "there really is no such thing as a 'correct' or complete selection of items for inclusion in such a volume as this."

The information presented in this volume is drawn from a wide range of readily available standard reference works and resources, a partial list of which is provided at the end of the volume. Limitations of space preclude the citation of specific sources for individual entries. No claim of originality is made for anything other than the selection, organization, arrangement, and form of presentation of this information. While every attempt has been made to ensure the accuracy of this information, is it likely that other scholars may find good reason to question certain dates or quarrel with certain explanatory comments. And it is virtually certain that most readers of this volume will at some point find themselves saying, "Why is that included?" or perhaps even more likely, "Why is that *not* included?" or "If *that* is included, then why in the world is *this* omitted?"

To questions or objections about the inclusion or omission of particular entries—whether relating to historical events or scientific discoveries or technological achievements or works of art or "notable publications" or popular culture—the only honest response is that something is or isn't found here because of the assumptions, perspectives, judgments, biases, and perhaps inexplicable whims that have shaped and informed my work on the project and have necessarily influenced my selections and decisions. Other individuals, in preparing such a volume, would certainly have made other choices at certain points about what should and should not be included. The volume is intended to be starting point for further exploration rather than a destination and should be regarded as a resource for beginning historical research rather than concluding it.

The following comments about some of the major features of the volume, and about the editorial principles or conventions observed in it, may be helpful to the reader.

The categories used in this volume have a degree of fluidity. It is virtually impossible to maintain a rigid separation between religious history and political, social, or cultural history, or between political or cultural history and scientific or technological achievements—or failures. Readers may sometimes find certain events listed under one category that they might expect to find under another category. For example, the 1719 entry noting that "Tsar Peter the Great expels the Jesuit Order from Russia" will be found under the category of Religion, Theology, Philosophy & Psychology rather than under World History & Politics. The 1942 entry noting that "The Grand Coulee Dam on the Columbia River in central Washington, begun in 1931, is completed; it is the largest concrete structure and the largest single producer of electricity in the US" will be found under the category of Science, Medicine & Technology rather than under American History & Politics. The same is true of the 2003 entry noting that "The space shuttle *Columbia* disintegrates on reentry into the earth's atmosphere, killing everyone on board." But the 1832 entry noting that "Public street-car service begins in New York City with horse-drawn trolleys" is placed under the category of Daily Life, Popular Culture & Entertainment.

The titles of major publications, works of art, or musical compositions are generally given in their English forms only unless there seems to be a compelling reason to do otherwise. Works first appearing in languages other than English are noted under the date of completion or first publication unless otherwise indicated. Occasionally the original title of a major work may be given followed by the English title and the date of its English translation when that information is deemed particularly significant or helpful to the reader.

Personal or place names originating in non-Western languages are transliterated using the style recommended in the 15th edition of *The Chicago Manual of Style*, for example, Sergey Prokofiev rather than the older Sergei, Mao Zedong rather than Mao Tse-tung, Beijing rather than Peking. Geographic designations can be tricky because political and military changes sometimes alter the names of states as well as their borders. To avoid the appearance of anachronism, countries or regions are generally given in their modern designations, for example, Tasmania instead of Van Dieman's Land or Tonga instead of the Friendly Islands. Occasionally a parenthetical explanation is provided when an older designation seems necessary or helpful, for example, Bechuanaland (modern Botswana) or Upper Volta (now Burkina Faso).

The births and deaths of individuals are not generally noted except for a few particularly prominent figures from the "founding era," such as John Wesley, Francis Asbury, and Richard Allen in regard to Methodist history; or Benjamin Franklin, George Washington, and Thomas Jefferson in relation to American history; or Johann Sebastian Bach and Wolfgang Amadeus Mozart in relation to the arts. When the death of a particular person is a matter of national or international significance, such as the assassinations of Abraham Lincoln, John F. Kennedy, and Martin Luther King Jr. or the death of President Franklin Roosevelt, Chinese Communist Party Chairman Mao Zedong, or Rosa Parks, the "Mother of the Civil Rights Movement," then it is included.

Unless there is serious risk of confusion, famous individuals are generally identified by last name only after the first occurrence; for example, Napoleon or Stalin in politics, Hegel or Wittgenstein in philosophy, Mozart or Mendelssohn in music, Barth or Bonhoeffer in theology, Wesley or Asbury in Methodist history. When it appears alone, *Wesley* always means John Wesley; other members of the Wesley family are always identified by first name when reference to them is intended.

The elections of all U.S. presidents and vice presidents are noted along with their political party affiliation, as are important changes of reign or rule in the major European countries. The accession of a new monarch to the British throne, for example, is always noted, but not every change in the office of prime minister. Other major changes in government around the world are noted when they seem particularly significant, for example the French Revolution of 1789, the Russian Revolution of 1917, the establishment of the People's Republic of China in 1949, the independence from colonial rule of many African nations in the late 1950s and early 1960s (such as the Belgian Congo, now Zaire, in 1960), the dissolution of the Soviet Union in 1991, and the election of Nelson Mandela as the first black president of South Africa in 1994.

A brief summary is provided of the major decisions or actions of every General Conference of The United Methodist Church and of all the major Methodist bodies that constitute its direct ancestry since the formation of The Methodist Episcopal Church in 1784. Due to limitations of time and space, coverage of comparable decisions and actions taken by the governing bodies of other members of the worldwide Wesleyan and Methodist family of churches is necessarily much more selective.

Events related to the missionary or other overseas activities of various American Methodist church bodies are generally noted in connection with the locus of those activities. For example, the 1856 entry noting that "Clementina Rowe Butler and William Butler establish the first MEC mission work in India" will be found under the category of British & World Methodism rather than under American & United Methodism, even though the Butlers were Americans and were sent to India by the Methodist Episcopal Church in America.

Informational or editorial comments relating to later history are occasionally made in connection with particular entries. Such comments are placed inside square brackets, as in the following example from 1794: "African Zoar Church in Philadelphia, first formed by black Methodists from St. George's Church in 1792, is formally established as a separate congregation; Harry Hosier is its founding pastor [it is now the oldest continuous historically black congregation in the United Methodist tradition]."

Certain benchmark data have been included regularly throughout the volume. For example, population data from the decennial U.S. Census is provided under the American History & Politics category for every decade from 1790 to 2000. Under the same category the increase or (rarely) decrease of the U.S. national debt is regularly noted, as are increases in the level of the U.S. minimum wage after its establishment in 1938. Under the category of Daily Life, Popular Culture & Entertainment, readers can, if they wish, track the changing cost of a U.S. first-class postage stamp beginning in 1863.

In cases where standard sources disagree about the dating or details of particular events, which happens with surprising frequency, the *Encyclopedia of World Methodism* has generally been regarded as authoritative for events related to Methodist history (at least through 1974, the date of its publication), corrected and supplemented by John A. Vickers, ed., A *Dictionary of Methodism in Britain and Ireland,* and Charles Yrigoyen Jr. and Susan E. Warrick, eds., *Historical Dictionary of Methodism.* For other dates, the *Encyclopedia Britannica* is generally regarded as authoritative.

After careful consideration, a decision was reached not to provide a printed index for the volume due to the additional time that would be required to prepare such an index, the additional space that would be required to print it, and the additional cost of the volume that would inevitably be the result. Instead, the full text is provided in searchable electronic form on the CD-ROM that is included with the volume. While this will not take the place of a true subject index, readers will be able to use the electronic form of the volume to search for entries containing specific names or terms in which they may have an interest, for example, (Francis) Asbury, or (Georgia) Harkness, or apartheid, or prohibition, or lay representation, or ordination.

To facilitate easy reference to particular events recorded in this volume, the column heads use capital letters. Readers may find it convenient to employ the following style of citation, combining the row (year) with the column (letter), which will work equally well for both the print and electronic editions:

- The Irish Methodist Conference bans women from preaching as "contrary to the Scriptures and prudence" and expels the very popular and effective evangelist Alice Cambridge when she refuses to quit preaching (*Timetables,* 1802H).
- The Woman's Home Missionary Society (WHMS) is formed by MEC women; Lucy Webb Hayes (wife of former president Rutherford B. Hayes) is elected president (*Timetables,* 1882G).
- The UMC establishes the Baltic Methodist Theological Seminary in Tallinn, Estonia, with instruction in Estonian, Russian, and English (*Timetables,* 1994H).

Despite the effort that has been expended to ensure the accuracy of the information contained in this volume, it will no doubt be found to contain errors. As errors requiring correction are discovered, they will be added to the "List of Errata and Corrections," which will be regularly updated and may be freely accessed at the following URL: https://webdrive.service.emory.edu/users/rmatthe/Timetables/Timetables_Errata.pdf

Much of the initial work on this project was completed during the Summer Wesley Seminar at Duke Divinity School in the summer of 2004, graciously hosted and creatively directed by Richard P. Heitzenrater, William Kellon Quick Professor of Church History and Wesley Studies. The rich resources of the Duke Divinity School Library and in particular the superb collection of the Baker Methodist Research Center, along with collegial engagement with fellow Seminar participants, helped to get the project off the ground, and a return engagement with the Seminar in the summer of 2005 helped to move it toward completion. I greatly appreciate the assistance and support provided through the Seminar, both directly and indirectly. Thanks are due as well to Roger L. Loyd, Director of the Duke Divinity School Library, to M. Patrick Graham, Director of the Pitts Theology Library at Candler School of Theology, and to the superbly helpful staff members of both institutions. Academics all too often take for granted the services and the holdings of such remarkable libraries.

A number of individuals have provided assistance and encouragement to persist in what has seemed at times to be an impossible and endless undertaking. I greatly appreciate and thankfully acknowledge the helpful comments and suggestions made by numerous friends and colleagues, especially Kenneth Cracknell, W. Harrison "Bill" Daniel, Morris L. Davis, Thomas E. Frank, Richard P. Heitzenrater, Randy L. Maddox, Russell E. Richey, and Charles Yrigoyen, Jr. Both Robert A. Ratcliff, a friend of many years and an erstwhile editorial colleague who now has the dubious privilege of serving as *my* editor, and Susan L. Cornell, who tackled the task of copyediting a very complicated manuscript with cheerful competence and careful attention to its myriad details, have my sincere thanks for their efforts to purge this volume of factual errors, questionable judgments, and infelicities of expression. Any that remain are entirely my responsibility.

My largest measure of appreciation and thanks, however, must be reserved for the students in my classes on Methodist theology and history at Candler School of Theology, Emory University. Their positive, even enthusiastic, response to earlier drafts of this work helped convince me that the project might be something more than a curious personal preoccupation and indeed could have some real pedagogical value, and their numerous criticisms, comments, and suggestions for improvement through a series of drafts have greatly strengthened and enriched the volume. For all that they have taught me about Methodist history, I am deeply grateful.

Rex D. Matthews

List of Abbreviations for Methodist Church Bodies

AMEC   African Methodist Episcopal Church (1816–)

AMEZC   African Methodist Episcopal Zion Church (1821–)

BC   Bible Christian(s) (primarily in the UK 1815–1907, but also in Canada, Australia, New Zealand, and elsewhere)

BMK   Bischöfliche Methodistenkirche (in Germany, 1868–1968; also known as the German Annual Conference of the MEC/MC)

CMEC   Christian Methodist Episcopal Church (after 1954; originally the Colored Methodist Episcopal Church, 1870)

EA   Evangelical Association (1807/1816–1922)

EC   Evangelical Church (1922–1946)

EMK   Evangelische-methodistischen Kirche (in Germany after 1968; also known as the Germany Central Conference of the UMC)

EUBC   Evangelical United Brethren Church (1946–1968)

FMC   Free Methodist Church (1860–)

MC   Methodist Church (in the US, 1939–1968)

MC [UK]   Methodist Church (in the UK, 1932–)

MCA   Methodist Church in Australasia (1902–1977)

MCC   Methodist Church in Canada (1874–1925)

MCCA   Methodist Church of the Caribbean and the Americas (1967–)

MCI   Methodist Church in Ireland (1878–)

MCNZ   The Methodist Church of New Zealand/Te Haahi Weteriana o Aotearoa (1913–)

MEC   Methodist Episcopal Church (1784–1939)

MECC   Methodist Episcopal Church of Canada (1834–1884)

MECS   Methodist Episcopal Church, South (1845–1939)

MNC   Methodist New Connexion (in the UK, 1797–1907)

MPC   Methodist Protestant Church (1830–1939)

PHC   Pilgrim Holiness Church (1922–1968)

PM   Primitive Methodism/Primitive Methodist(s) (primarily in the UK after 1811, but also in the US, Canada, Australia, New Zealand, and elsewhere)

PMC   Primitive Methodist Church (in the UK after 1902; originally Primitive Methodist Connexion, 1811)

PMCUSA   Primitive Methodist Church in the USA (after 1889)

UAMEC   Union American Methodist Episcopal Church (after 1865; originally part of the Union Church of Africans, 1813–1865)

UBC   United Brethren Church, or Church of the United Brethren (1800–1946)

UEC   United Evangelical Church (1891–1922)

UMC   United Methodist Church (1968–)

UMC [UK]   United Methodist Church (in the UK, 1907–1932)

UMFC   United Methodist Free Churches (in the UK, 1857–1907)

WM   Wesleyan Methodism/Wesleyan Methodist(s) (primarily in the UK, 1797–1891, but also in Canada, Australia, New Zealand, and elsewhere)

WMC   Wesleyan Methodist Church (in the US, 1947–1968; originally Wesleyan Methodist Connection, 1843–1947)

WMC [UK]   Wesleyan Methodist Church (in the UK, 1891–1932)

WMCC   Wesleyan Methodist Church of Canada (1833–1874)

	A. WORLD HISTORY & POLITICS	B. AMERICAN HISTORY & POLITICS	C. SCIENCE, MEDICINE & TECHNOLOGY	D. DAILY LIFE, POPULAR CULTURE & ENTERTAINMENT
1700	• The Great Northern War breaks out when the young Charles XII comes to the throne of Sweden, the dominant power in the region; King Augustus II of Poland, King Frederick IV of Denmark and Norway, and Tsar Peter the Great of Russia all launch attacks on Swedish territories • The Holy Roman Empire (Austria) signs the Treaty of Sistova with the Ottoman Empire, ceding Belgrade to the Ottomans in exchange for northeastern Bosnia	• The population of the American colonies is about 250,000, including about 28,000 slaves; Boston is the largest city with 7,000; New York is second with 5,000	• The Berlin-Brandenburg Society of Scientists is established; it becomes the Berlin Academy of Science in 1740	• Francisco Romero becomes Spain's first nationally famous bullfighter
1701	• King James II of England, who has been in France since the "Glorious Revolution" of 1689 deprived him of the English throne, dies in exile; his son, James Francis Edward Stuart, is proclaimed by France's King Louis XIV to be the rightful heir and crowned as King James III of England (and VIII of Scotland); he is not recognized as monarch in either country • The Act of Settlement limits succession to the English crown to Protestants, establishing Anne (the daughter of King James II and sister of Queen Mary II) as the heir to the throne, but specifying that if Anne should have no children at the time of her death, the crown after her goes to Sophia of Hanover and her descendents • Prussia becomes an independent kingdom ruled by the Hohenzollern dynasty when Frederick I, Elector of Brandenburg, crowns himself King	• The French establish Fort Ponchatrain at what is now Detroit • William Penn's "Charter of Privileges for the Province of Pennsylvania" establishes complete religious freedom in the colony	• Jethro Tull (England) invents the seed drill, a horse-drawn planter that drops seeds in a neat row • Italian physician Giacomo Pylarini experiments with the inoculation of children in Constantinople against smallpox	• The famous pirate William Kidd is publicly hanged in London before a crowd of thousands, leaving behind persistent stories of buried treasure
1702	• King William III of England dies (Queen Mary II had died in 1694); he is succeeded by Mary's sister, Anne, daughter of James II • The War of the Spanish Succession breaks out when England declares war on France after the death of the King of Spain, Charles II, in order to prevent the union of France and Spain • King Charles XII of Sweden invades Poland and captures Warsaw and Cracow	• The War of the Spanish Succession spills over into America as Queen Anne's War; English and American colonists battle the French, their American Indian allies, and the Spanish for the next eleven years	• French inventor Guillaume Amontons creates an air-pressure thermometer, improving on a design first suggested by Galileo	• The first daily newspaper in the English language, the *Daily Courant*, begins publication in London • Cotton Mather establishes the "Society for the Suppression of Disorders" in Massachusetts to help suppress public swearing, blasphemy, and so on
1703	• The city of St. Petersburg is founded by Russian Tsar Peter the Great • A major earthquake in Tokyo kills over 200,000 people • The Swedish army defeats Russian forces at Rultusk • The "Great Storm of 1703" roars through the English channel, killing thousands along both coastlines	• Three counties of Pennsylvania are detached to become the new colony of Delaware	• Isaac Newton is elected to the presidency of England's Royal Society	• When duties are reduced as the result of a treaty between England and Portugal, Port wine becomes popular in England
1704	• England captures Gibraltar from Spain; the Duke of Marlborough defeats the French-Bavarian army at Blenheim	• A strong French and Indian force attacks the settlement of Deerfield, CT, killing 56 English settlers and taking captive another 109 • British and colonial forces unsuccessfully attack the French settlement of Port Royal in Nova Scotia	• Isaac Newton's landmark work *Optics* is translated from the original Latin into English	• *The Boston News-Letter*, the first successful newspaper in the American colonies, begins publication

E. EDUCATION, LITERATURE & THE FINE ARTS	F. RELIGION, THEOLOGY, PHILOSOPHY & PSYCHOLOGY	G. AMERICAN & UNITED METHODISM	H. BRITISH & WORLD METHODISM	
• Johann Sebastian Bach becomes a chorister at St. Michael's Church, Lüneburg, Germany • Marc-Antoine Charpentier (France) composes his *Te Deum* • Henry Purcell composes his opera *Dido and Aeneas*	• Pope Innocent XII dies; he is succeeded by Pope Clement XI • Count Nicolaus Ludwig von Zinzendorf, founder of the Moravian church, is born in Germany • American jurist Samuel Sewall publishes *The Selling of Joseph*, the first antislavery tract written in America, drawing on both biblical and legal arguments • Quaker leader William Penn begins holding monthly meetings for blacks and advocating emancipation from slavery		• Samuel Wesley establishes a small religious society in Epworth modeled on the Society for Promoting Christian Knowledge (SPCK), which had been founded in London in 1698	**1700**
• Collegiate College, which will become Yale College in 1718, is founded in Killingworth, Connecticut • English musician and publisher Henry Playford establishes a series of free weekly public concerts in Oxford • Daniel Defoe publishes *The True-Born Englishman*	• The Society for the Propagation of the Gospel in Foreign Parts (SPG) is founded in London • Roman Catholic priests are banned from Massachusetts on pain of death or imprisonment for life • The West Street Chapel in London is built for the use of Huguenot refugees		• Tensions between Samuel and Susanna Wesley (who is pregnant at the time) flare over her "nonjuror" doubts about the legitimacy of the monarchy of William and Mary, resulting in a separation when Samuel leaves Epworth for London, declaring that "if we have two kings we must have two beds" • Susanna gives birth to a daughter, whom she names Anne (no doubt to make a point; the child is also called "Nancy")	**1701**
• Defoe's pamphlet *The Shortest Way with the Dissenters* satirizes the attitudes of "high-church" Anglicans and leads to his arrest on charges of blasphemy • George Frideric Handel becomes chapel organist at Halle	• The Church of England is established as the official church in Maryland, financially supported by taxation imposed on all free men, male servants, and slaves • French Protestants known as "Camisards" (from their black shirts) revolt against King Louis XIV because in 1685 he had revoked the religious freedom granted to them by the Edict of Nantes (1598); their rebellion is finally crushed in 1710 • Cotton Mather produces his landmark work *Magnalia Christi Americana: Or, The Ecclesiastical History of New England* • William Penn publishes *Primitive Christianity Revived*		• Queen Anne's accession to the throne resolves the cause of "nonjuror" disagreement between Samuel and Susanna • When the Epworth rectory is seriously damaged by fire, Samuel returns to Epworth from London to care for the family and is reconciled with Susanna	**1702**
• Jonathan Swift publishes his first important satirical work, *The Tale of a Tub*, which burlesques all forms of dogmatic Christianity • English dramatist Nicholas Rowe writes *The Fair Penitent*; the play features the memorable character Lothario	• Jonathan Edwards is born • The *Moral and Religious Aphorisms* of English cleric Benjamin Whichcote appears 10 years after his death • Justus Falckner becomes the first Lutheran minister to be ordained in America		• John Wesley is born; his parents call him "Jacky"	**1703**
• John Harris compiles his *Lexicon Technicum; or an Universal English Dictionary of Arts and Sciences Explaining not only the Terms of Art, but the Arts Themselves*, generally acknowledged to be the first alphabetically arranged encyclopedia in the English language (2nd edition in 2 vols. 1708–10)	• England's Queen Anne introduces "Queen Anne's Bounty," which makes some church funds controlled by the crown available for the support of poor clergy and their families • Gottfried Wilhelm Leibniz publishes his important *New Essays on Human Understanding*		• Samuel Wesley Jr. leaves Epworth to enter the Westminster School in London	**1704**

	A. WORLD HISTORY & POLITICS	B. AMERICAN HISTORY & POLITICS	C. SCIENCE, MEDICINE & TECHNOLOGY	D. DAILY LIFE, POPULAR CULTURE & ENTERTAINMENT
1704 cont.				
1705	• Holy Roman Emperor Leopold I dies; he is succeeded by his son, Joseph I • English forces capture and occupy Barcelona, Spain • Queen Anne grants the royal manor of Woodstock to the Duke of Marlborough and the construction of Blenheim Palace begins (completed 1722)	• Laws banning miscegenation and restricting the travel of slaves are enacted in New York, Massachusetts, and Virginia	• English astronomer and scientist Edmond Halley publishes his *Synopsis on Cometary Astronomy*; it correctly predicts that the 1682 comet now bearing his name will return 76 years later, in 1758	• The *Edinburgh Courant*, Scotland's first newspaper, is founded
1706	• The English army defeats the French at Ramillies, conquers Belgium, and expels French forces from Italy • The Swedish army overruns most of Saxony	• Spanish settlers establish the town of Albuquerque in what is now New Mexico • Benjamin Franklin is born	• English mathematician William Jones introduces the use of the Greek letter pi (π) to represent the ratio of the circumference of a circle to its diameter • English carriage maker Henry Mill creates the first metal springs for carriages	• London's first evening paper, *The Evening Post*, begins publication • Thomas Twining serves tea for the first time at Tom's Coffee House in London, which evolves into London's first teashop called the Golden Lyon; his tea importing business will become Twinings of London • Grace Sherwood (Virginia) is the last person to be tried for witchcraft in America
1707	• England and Scotland unite to form the United Kingdom of Great Britain • Japan's Mount Fujiyama erupts for the last time in modern history	• Settlers in Charlestown, SC, successfully fend off an attack by French and Spanish colonists from Havana and St. Augustine	• English physician John Floyer begins the modern practice of recording the pulse rate of a patient	• The earliest recorded major cricket match in England takes place between sides from London and Kent
1708	• Tsar Peter the Great divides Russia into eight administrative districts • Britain's East India Company ensures continuation of its monopoly on trade with India by merging with a rival company • King Charles XII of Sweden concludes a secret peace agreement with the Ukrainian Cossacks and then invades Russia	• British troops from New England besiege the French settlement at Port Royal, Nova Scotia • French forces and Indian allies destroy the British settlement at Haverhill, MA	• Edmond Halley demonstrates the relative motion of the stars, disproving the notion that their positions are fixed	• Ebenezer Cook satirizes life in colonial Maryland in his poem "The Sot-Weed Factor" [he will later be the main character in John Barth's 1960 novel of the same title]
1709	• King Charles XII of Sweden is defeated by Peter the Great of Russia at Poltova, turning the tide of the Great Northern War • British forces led by the Duke of Marlborough defeat the French at Malplaquet • Austrian forces defeat the Spanish at Zaragoza	• 3000 German refugees from the Palatinate are settled along the Hudson River in New York to produce supplies for the British Navy; when the colony fails, the settlers go first to the Mohawk Valley (in New York) and finally to eastern Pennsylvania	• British metallurgist Abraham Darby devises a process for producing iron in a coke-fired furnace • German chemist Daniel Fahrenheit invents an alcohol thermometer	• The first "cologne water" is produced in Cologne, Germany • Richard Steele begins regular publication of *The Tatler*, with contributions from Joseph Addison
1710	• Native peoples in Brazil revolt unsuccessfully against Portuguese colonial rule in the War of Mescates	• The population of the American colonies is about 332,000 • New Englanders, aided by British ships, capture Port Royal from the French	• An outbreak of bubonic plague kills more than 500,000 people in Austria and Germany (through 1711)	• The hoop skirt becomes fashionable for women in Britain and France • The Messian porcelain factory, the first in Europe, is established in Germany

4

E. EDUCATION, LITERATURE & THE FINE ARTS	F. RELIGION, THEOLOGY, PHILOSOPHY & PSYCHOLOGY	G. AMERICAN & UNITED METHODISM	H. BRITISH & WORLD METHODISM	
• Jonathan Swift publishes his ironic *The Battle of the Books* • Georg Philipp Telemann founds the Leipzig Collegium Musicum				**1704 cont.**
• The young Bach walks 200 miles from • The young Bach walks 200 miles from the southeast German town of Arnstadt to the Baltic port of Lübeck to hear an organ concert by Dietrich Buxtehude	• The Church of England is established as the official church in North Carolina • Samuel Clarke publishes *A Discourse Concerning the Being and Attributes of God* • Edward, Lord Herbert of Cherbury publishes *The Ancient Religion of the Gentiles, and Causes of their Errors Considered*, one of the earliest works to advocate universal principles of "natural religion"			**1705**
• Isaac Watts completes *Horae Lyricae: Poems, Chiefly of the Lyric Kind*, establishing his place in the history of English poetry	• The Church of England is established as the official church in South Carolina • Francis Makemie organizes the first American Presbytery in Philadelphia (ancestor of the PCUSA) • Samuel Clarke publishes *A Discourse Concerning the Unchangeable Obligations of Natural Religion, and the Truth and Certainty of the Christian Revelation*		• Martha ("Patty") Wesley is born	**1706**
• Handel meets Domenico Scarlatti in Venice • Bach composes one of his first notable cantatas, *Christ lag in Todesbanden* (Christ Lay in Death's Bondage) • John Williams, minister of the settlement at Deerfield, CT, publishes his account of the 1704 Indian attack and its aftermath in *The Redeemed Captive Returning to Zion*; it goes through six editions before 1800	• The Philadelphia Association of Regular Baptists is established; it is the first Baptist organization in America • Isaac Watts publishes his *Hymns and Spiritual Songs*; his original compositions for use in worship are a landmark of liturgical innovation in England • Anthony Collins makes an early attack on the evidential value of miracles as proof of the truth of Christianity in *An Essay Concerning the Use of Reason in Propositions the Evidence Whereof Depends on Human Testimony*		• Charles Wesley is born	**1707**
• Bach composes *Toccata & Fugue in D Minor* • Jonathan Swift writes his ironic *Argument Against Abolishing Christianity*	• British philosopher Shaftesbury [Anthony Ashley Cooper, 3rd Earl of Shaftesbury] publishes *A Letter Concerning Enthusiasm*			**1708**
• The British parliament passes the first Copyright Act; it grants owners fourteen years of protection, renewable for another fourteen if the author is still alive • Bartolomeo Cristofori (Italy) replaces the plucking mechanism of the harpsichord with a hammer action that strikes the strings and produces an instrument called *a gravicembalo col piano e forte* (Italian for "harpsichord with soft and loud"), later called the *pianoforte* or simply the *piano* • Antonio Vivaldi composes his *Sonata for Violin and Basso Continuo in C Major*	• The French mystic Madame Guyon (Jeanne Marie Bouvier de la Motte Guyon) completes work on her autobiography, *The Life of Mme. J. M. B. de la Mothe Guyon* [it is first published by her disciple and editor, Pierre Poiret, in 1720] • George Berkeley publishes *An Essay toward a New Theory of Vision* • John Strype begins the publication of his *Annals of the Reformation* (through 1731)		• Fire, probably caused by arson, destroys the Epworth rectory; John Wesley is rescued from the fire as "brand plucked from the burning" • The old wood-frame thatched-roof rectory is replaced by a fine new brick building in the Queen Anne style [which still stands] • The Wesley children stay with neighbors while the rectory is being rebuilt; when her family is reunited in the new rectory, Susanna begins spending "special time" with each child in the evenings; John's night was Thursday	**1709**
• Handel becomes *Kapellmeister* to George of Hanover (who becomes King George I of England in 1714)	• Cotton Mather publishes *Bonifacius* (*Essays To Do Good*)		• The preaching of Griffith Jones begins an evangelical revival in Wales • Keziah ("Kezzie") Wesley is born, the last child of Samuel and Susanna	**1710**

	A. WORLD HISTORY & POLITICS	B. AMERICAN HISTORY & POLITICS	C. SCIENCE, MEDICINE & TECHNOLOGY	D. DAILY LIFE, POPULAR CULTURE & ENTERTAINMENT
1710 cont.	• King Charles XII of Sweden persuades Ottoman Turks to support him by going to war with Russia (to 1711)			
1711	• Holy Roman Emperor Joseph I dies; he is succeeded by his son, Charles VI • French forces capture and sack the Portuguese colony at Rio de Janeiro • The Ottoman Turks defeat Peter the Great of Russia at the Prut River, halting (for a time) Russia's effort to become a Black Sea power • The South Sea Company is incorporated in England	• Tuscarora Indian War begins when Indians kill 200 white settlers in North Carolina • A large British and colonial joint military and naval expedition against Quebec and Montreal ends in failure to dislodge the French	• Italian explorer and scientist Luigi Marsigli demonstrates that corals are formed by animals and are not plants	• *The Spectator* is founded by Joseph Addison and Richard Steele • Queen Anne establishes the horse races at Ascot in England • Newspaper ads for the sale of organs along with other musical instruments indicate their presence in America
1712	• St. Petersburg replaces Moscow as the capital of Russia (until 1918)	• Slave revolt fails in New York; 21 are executed, 6 more commit suicide	• British inventor Thomas Newcomen constructs the first practical working steam engine	• Jane Wenham is the last person convicted of witchcraft in England (last execution was in 1684)
1713	• The Peace of Utrecht, a series of treaties between France, Spain, Britain, and other European powers, brings to a close the War of the Spanish Succession (Queen Anne's War); the separation of the crowns of France and Spain is confirmed; France cedes its Canadian colonies to Britain; Spain cedes Gibraltar to Britain; Britain secures control of the African slave trade to the Spanish colonies in the Americas • Prussia's King Frederick I dies; he is succeeded by his son, Frederick William I	• England's South Sea Company is authorized to transport 4,800 slaves per year into the Spanish colonies of North America • Colonial militia forces defeat the Tuscarora Indians at Fort Nahucke, forcing the Tuscarora out of the Carolinas; they migrate to New York where they become the sixth nation of the Iroquois Confederation	• Greek physician Emanuel Timoni describes to the Royal Society of London the Turkish practice of inoculating young children with smallpox to prevent the development of more serious cases when they get older	• Joseph Addison's comedy *Cato* is first performed in London's Drury Lane Theater
1714	• Queen Anne (UK) dies without an heir; as provided by the 1701 Act of Settlement, George I, son of Sophia of Hanover, is crowned King, establishing the House of Hanover in Britain	• After the Peace of Utrecht, British forces and colonists take control of Newfoundland and Nova Scotia	• Daniel Fahrenheit invents the mercury thermometer and devises the temperature scale that bears his name • The British parliament sets up a prize of £20,000 for the first person who develops and demonstrates a scientifically accurate way to calculate longitude at sea	• Tea is introduced into the American colonies and quickly becomes a very popular drink • The popular musical comedies known as "vaudevilles" appear in Paris for the first time; the term comes to represent the genre of entertainment
1715	• James Edward Stuart ("The Old Pretender") raises a "Jacobite" rebellion in Scotland (with half-hearted French backing) seeking to overthrow George I and claim the British throne but is soundly defeated and forced to return to France	• Yamasee tribes of the Creek Indian Nation, incited by the Spanish, attack and kill several hundred settlers in South Carolina	• Jethro Tull introduces the horseshoe into England from Europe	• An annual rowing race for first-year apprentice watermen is started by Thomas Doggett on the Thames River in London; the winner receives "Doggett's Coat and Badge"

E. EDUCATION, LITERATURE & THE FINE ARTS	F. RELIGION, THEOLOGY, PHILOSOPHY & PSYCHOLOGY	G. AMERICAN & UNITED METHODISM	H. BRITISH & WORLD METHODISM	
	• English philosopher and theologian George Berkeley's *Treatise Concerning the Principles of Knowledge* expounds his conviction that "to be is to be perceived" • Gottfried Wilhelm Leibniz produces his *Theodicy*, in which he tries to deal with the problem of evil by arguing that ours is "the best of all possible worlds" because it was created by a perfect God and that its apparent imperfections are due to the limitations of human perception • Pierre Bayle's *Dictionnaire historique et critique* (1697) is published in English as *Historical and Critical Dictionary*			**1710 cont.**
• Vivaldi composes his *Concerto for 2 Violins and Cello in G Minor* • Alexander Pope publishes his influential *Essay on Criticism*	• Christopher Wren completes the construction of St. Paul's Cathedral, London, including the great Dome (begun 1675) • Passage of the Occasional Conformity Act reinforces restrictions on qualification for offices of public trust by Roman Catholics and Dissenters from the Church of England • Shaftesbury publishes his observations on *Characteristics of Men, Manners, Opinions, Times*		• John Wesley receives Holy Communion for the first time from his father at St. Andrew's Church in Epworth	**1711**
• The Biblioteca Nationale is founded in Madrid, Spain • Alexander Pope completes the first version of his most famous poem, *The Rape of the Lock* (final form 1714) • Italian violinist Archangelo Corelli composes his *12 Concerti Grossi*, which establish the concerto grosso musical form	• The colony of South Carolina passes a law compelling observance of the Sabbath and attendance at church services		• During the winter of 1711–12, while Samuel is in London attending the Convocation of the Church of England, Susanna invites the neighbors in Epworth into her kitchen for evening prayers; soon the crowds grow quite large, provoking Samuel's curate to complain; Susanna resists Samuel's peremptory order that she should stop the practice	**1712**
• Vivaldi completes his opera *Orlando Furioso* • The School of Dance is established at the Paris Opera	• George Berkeley publishes *Three Dialogues between Hylas and Philonous* • Anthony Collins produces *A Discourse of Free-thinking* • William Derham attempts to prove the existence of God in *Physico-Theology; or, A Demonstration of the Being and Attributes of God from His Works of Creation*		• Samuel Wesley Jr. becomes a Master at the Westminster School in London	**1713**
• The first pipe organ in the colonies is installed in King's Chapel in Boston; its use by the Anglican congregation is denounced by the Puritans, who forbid the use of instrumental music • Peter the Great establishes public education for children in Russia • Bach publishes *The Little Organ Book*	• Cotton Mather preaches a sermon indicating his belief in the Copernican theory of the universe, which places the sun at the center and planets in orbit around it; the traditional or Ptolemaic view at that time held that all revolved around the earth • Bernard de Mandeville publishes *The Fable of the Bees, or: Private Vices, Publick Benefits*, describing a complex society in which the pursuit of private interests by individuals leads to the creation of public good		• John Wesley leaves Epworth to enter the Charterhouse School in London • George Whitefield is born • Howell Harris is born	**1714**
• Alexander Pope begins publishing his translation of Homer's *Iliad* (6 vols., 1715–25)	• William Derham continues his proof of God's existence in *Astro-Theology; or, A Demonstration of the Being and Attributes of God, from a Survey of the Heavens*			**1715**

	A. WORLD HISTORY & POLITICS	B. AMERICAN HISTORY & POLITICS	C. SCIENCE, MEDICINE & TECHNOLOGY	D. DAILY LIFE, POPULAR CULTURE & ENTERTAINMENT
1715 cont.	• Louis XIV of France, the "Sun King," dies after 72 years on the throne; he is succeeded by his grandson Louis XV under regency of the Duc d'Orleans			
1716	• The Qing (Manchu) Dynasty emperor, Kangxi, repeals an Edict of Toleration and bans Europeans from China • Scottish financier John Law establishes the private Banque Générale in Paris and begins issuing notes backed by his speculative Mississippi Company • France establishes the first national highway department for the improvement of roads	• South Carolina settlers enlist the Cherokee as allies, and with their aid and assistance from fellow colonists in Virginia, they attack and defeat the Yamasee • The first group of black slaves is brought to the Louisiana territory • Spanish forces occupy parts of Texas in response to westward expansion by the French from the Louisiana territory	• Edmond Halley invents an underwater diving bell with an air replacement system	• The first Italian daily newspaper, *Diario di Roma*, begins publication
1717	• Prussia sells its slavery stations in Africa to the Dutch • Britain, France, and the Netherlands form the Triple Alliance in an attempt to check Spanish expansionism	• A wave of Scots-Irish immigration to America begins, with most of the immigrants settling in western Pennsylvania, later moving into Virginia and the Carolinas and farther south and west	• Lady Mary Montagu initiates smallpox inoculations in England, having her own two children inoculated and winning wide public approval of the practice by 1721	• The Grand Lodge of Freemasons is established in London; it is the "mother" of all other Masonic lodges • School attendance is made compulsory in Prussia
1718	• Philip V of Spain attempts to nullify provisions of the Peace of Utrecht; the Holy Roman Empire (Austria) joins Britain, France, and the Netherlands to form the Quadruple Alliance against Spain • France turns John Law's private Banque Générale into the Banque Royale, meaning its notes and investments are backed by the King • Peter the Great of Russia has his son and heir, Alexis, murdered	• New Orleans is founded by French settlers • Spanish settlers establish San Antonio in what is now Texas	• English gunsmith James Puckle invents the first working machine gun; the revolving flintlock can fire six times per minute • Scottish physician William Douglass settles in Boston and opens one of the first known medical practices in America	• The first paper bank notes are issued by the Bank of England • Porcelain is manufactured for the first time in Vienna
1719	• The British parliament declares that Ireland is inseparable from England • The "South Sea Bubble" bursts in Britain, ruining many investors in the speculative South Sea Company		• The technique of three-color printing is perfected by Jacob C. Le Blon (Germany)	• *The American Mercury* appears in Philadelphia; *The Boston Gazette* begins publication
1720	• The Treaty of the Hague between Spain and the Quadruple Alliance confirms Spanish withdrawal from Sicily and Sardinia • France experiences national bankruptcy as a result of the spectacular financial collapse of John Law's Mississippi Company • China declares protectorate status for Tibet • Dutch and German settlers from Cape Town reach the Orange River in southern Africa	• The population of the American colonies is about 466,000: Boston, 12,000; Philadelphia, 10,000; New York, 7,000; Charleston, 3,500 • The Treaty of the Hague halts skirmishing between French and Spanish forces in Florida and Texas and confirms Spanish possession of Texas • The French build forts on the Mississippi, the St. Lawrence, and the Niagara rivers • The first British colonial settlements are established in Vermont • The Governor's Palace in Williamsburg, VA, is completed; it is considered the finest colonial residence of the time • Edmond Halley becomes the Royal Astronomer in Britain and begins an 18-year study of the moon	• An outbreak of bubonic plague kills over 60,000 people in France	• Wallpaper becomes fashionable in England and soon after in America • Connecticut enacts a very strict Sabbath law: no person may leave home on Sunday except to go to worship services or to do some "essential task"

E. EDUCATION, LITERATURE & THE FINE ARTS	F. RELIGION, THEOLOGY, PHILOSOPHY & PSYCHOLOGY	G. AMERICAN & UNITED METHODISM	H. BRITISH & WORLD METHODISM	
• Domenico Scarlatti composes his *Stabat Mater* • Isaac Watts publishes *Hymns for Children and Divine Songs*				**1715 cont.**
• François Couperin publishes his important work, *The Art of Playing the Harpsichord*, which provides invaluable documentation of early 18th-century performance practice • Vivaldi completes his *Six Violin Sonatas*	• The Bangorian Controversy is sparked when Benjamin Hoadly, Bishop of Bangor, publishes his provocative *Preservative against the Principles and Practices of Non-Jurors* • Madame Guyon publishes her *Discours Chrétiens et spirituels* (Christian and Spiritual Discourses)		• The Wesley family in Epworth is disturbed by the haunting of a ghost to whom they give the name "Old Jeffrey" • Charles Wesley leaves Epworth to enter the Westminster School in London, where elder brother Samuel looks after him	**1716**
• Handel composes his *Water Music Suites*, which is played during a royal party on barges along the Thames	• British theologian William Law enters the Bangorian Controversy with his *Letters to the Bishop of Bangor* • The Bangorian Controversy results in the suspension of the Convocation of the Church of England			**1717**
• Collegiate College (1701), which had been relocated to New Haven in 1716, is renamed Yale College to honor a generous gift by Elihu Yale • The Society of Antiquaries of London is founded; it receives a British royal charter in 1751; the Society's library is the first in England devoted to archaeology	• Cotton Mather publishes a new book of psalms, *Psalterium Americanum*			**1718**
• The Royal Academy of Music is established in London; Handel is appointed as musical director • Defoe publishes his classic *Robinson Crusoe*	• Tsar Peter the Great expels the Jesuit Order from Russia • The British parliament repeals the Occasional Conformity Act (1711) making it easier for Roman Catholics and Dissenters to qualify for offices of public trust • Isaac Watts completes *Psalms of David Imitated*, which includes his immortal paraphrase of Psalm 90, now known (after John Wesley's later editorial tinkering) as "O God Our Help in Ages Past"			**1719**
• The Three Choirs Festival, a British music festival held alternately at the cathedrals of Hereford, Gloucester, and Worcester, takes place for the first time • Bach composes his *Prelude for Lute in C Minor* • Defoe writes *Memoirs of a Cavalier*	• Cotton Mather publishes *The Christian Philosopher: A Collection of the Best Discoveries in Nature, With Religious Improvements* • Bernard de Mandeville produces his *Free Thoughts on Religion*		• John Wesley enters Christ Church College, Oxford	**1720**

	A. WORLD HISTORY & POLITICS	B. AMERICAN HISTORY & POLITICS	C. SCIENCE, MEDICINE & TECHNOLOGY	D. DAILY LIFE, POPULAR CULTURE & ENTERTAINMENT
1721	• The Treaty of Nystadt ends the Great Northern War (1700–21); Russia now controls Estonia, Latvia, and southeastern Finland and has eclipsed Sweden as the great power of the North • France seizes control of Mauritius from the Dutch • Dutch explorer Jacob Roggeveen makes the first European contact with the Polynesian Islands, including Tahiti and Samoa • Robert Walpole becomes the first person generally acknowledged as prime minister in Britain and shapes the nature of the office	• White settlers from North and South Carolina begin to encroach on the ancestral homelands of the Cherokee Indians	• A smallpox epidemic in Boston prompts Cotton Mather and Zabdiel Boylston to experiment with inoculation against the disease	• Flintlock rifles are brought to America by Swiss immigrants; they are lighter, more accurate, and have a greater range than the ubiquitous smooth-bore musket • Regular postal service begins, connecting London with Boston and Philadelphia • *The New-England Courant*, Boston's third newspaper, is established by James Franklin, Benjamin Franklin's elder brother
1722	• Revolution in Afghanistan overthrows the Safavid Dynasty, which had ruled the Persian Empire since 1501	• The Iroquois Confederation of Six Nations (Mohawk, Oneida, Onondaga, Cayuga, Seneca, and Tuscarora) signs a treaty with white settlers in Virginia to end a period of prolonged conflict; each party agrees not to cross the Potomac River or the Blue Ridge Mountains	• French scientist René-Antoine de Réaumur provides the first technical explanation of *The Art of Converting Iron into Steel*	• The British parliament bans newspapers from printing accounts of parliamentary debates • While working for his brother as a printer's apprentice, the young Benjamin Franklin writes a series of satirical essays under the pen name "Silence Dogood" that his brother unknowingly publishes in *The New-England Courant*
1723	• The British Africa Company is established and buys large tracts of land along the Gambia River in west Africa • England and Prussia conclude the Treaty of Charlottenburg; the grandson of George I is pledged to marry a Prussian princess, Prince Frederick is pledged to marry the daughter of the Prince of Wales	• The Abenaki Indian Wars begin in Maine and Vermont; they continue until 1727	• Swiss physician Maurice A. Capeller publishes his *Introduction to Crystallography*, the first known treatise on the subject	• Boston establishes a police department; its twelve members are instructed to "walk silently and slowly, to stand still now and then, and to listen to what is going on" • Massachusetts Colonial authorities find the feisty *New-England Courant* to be "seditious" and ban James Franklin from publishing it
1724	• Spain's King Philip V shocks the world when he abdicates in favor of his oldest son, but his son (Louis I) dies shortly thereafter so Philip resumes the throne • The kingdom of Dahomey becomes the principal supplier of African slaves to European traders	• The French introduce *Le Code Noir* ("The Black Code") in Louisiana, banning Jews from the colony and permitting slaveholders to brand runaways and cut off their ears	• Dutch physician Hermann Boerhaave publishes his landmark work *Elements of Chemistry*	• England experiences a dramatic increase in gin distilling and consumption • The Paris Bourse (stock exchange) opens for business
1725	• Russia's Tsar Peter the Great dies; he is succeeded by his wife, Tsarina Catherine	• The population of black slaves in the American colonies reaches 75,000 • British settlers in northern Maine kill a French Jesuit priest for inciting attacks on their settlements by the Abenaki Indians	• The St. Petersburg Academy of Science is founded by Tsarina Catherine	• The first issue of *The New York Gazette* is published • Nathanael Ames begins publication of *The Astronomical Diary and Almanac* in Boston; it is America's first almanac • The heavy, horse-drawn freight-carrying vehicle that comes to be called the Conestoga wagon originates in the Conestoga region of Pennsylvania
1726	• Persian forces retake Isfahan from the Afghans • Russia and the Holy Roman Empire (Austria) form an alliance against the Ottoman Turks	• A riot erupts in Philadelphia when poor workers protest what they believe to be unjust labor laws; the colonial governor puts down the uprising but not before considerable damage is caused	• British physician Stephen Hales measures human blood pressure for the first time	• The first marriage notice in a newspaper is published (in Manchester, England)

E. EDUCATION, LITERATURE & THE FINE ARTS	F. RELIGION, THEOLOGY, PHILOSOPHY & PSYCHOLOGY	G. AMERICAN & UNITED METHODISM	H. BRITISH & WORLD METHODISM	
• The Hollis Professorship of Divinity at Harvard College is established [it is the first endowed and named professorship in America] • The first modern encyclopedia, the *Allegmeines Lexikon*, is published in Germany by Johann Theodor Jablonski • Bach completes his suite of six *Brandenburg Concerti*	• Peter the Great abolishes the Moscow patriarchate and puts the Russian church under the government-controlled "Holy Synod" • Pope Clement XI dies; he is succeeded by Pope Innocent XIII • Montesquieu [Charles Louis de Secondat, Baron de la Brède et de Montesquieu] writes his hilarious and satirical epistolary novel *Lettres persane* (Persian Letters), consisting of letters to and from two fictional Persians who tour Europe and misunderstand everything they see		• Samuel Wesley becomes the rector of Wroot in addition to Epworth • Charles Wesley is elected a King's Scholar at Westminster, which helps ease the financial pressure of his education	**1721**
• Defoe produces his *Journal of a Plague Year* • Bach becomes *Kapellmeister* at St. Thomas Kirche, Leipzig, and publishes *The Well-Tempered Clavier*, Part 1 (Part 2, 1738) • Jean Philippe Rameau finishes his influential *Treatise on Harmony*	• Zinzendorf allows a small band of Moravians to settle on his estate in Germany; they build a town they call Herrnhut, or "the Lord's Watch"			**1722**
• Bach composes his *Magnificat* • Defoe publishes *The Fortunes and Misfortunes of Moll Flanders*	• The Workhouse Test Act authorizes church parishes in Britain to set up "workhouses" to provide paid employment for the poor who can work and relief for those who cannot • Bernard de Mandeville publishes the second edition of *The Fable of the Bees, or: Private Vices, Publick Benefits*, which is condemned as a "nuisance" by a county grand jury in England • William Law responds to Mandeville in *Remarks on the Fable of the Bees*			**1723**
• Both Oxford and Cambridge Universities establish endowed professorships in history and languages • Defoe writes *A Tour Through the Whole Island of Great Britain* • Bach's *St. John Passion* is first performed at St. Nicolaikirche in Leipzig	• English freethinker Anthony Collins attacks the basis of Christianity as a revealed religion in *A Discourse of the Grounds and Reasons of the Christian Religion* • William Wollaston argues for theism in *The Religion of Nature Delineated* • Pope Innocent XIII dies; he is succeeded by Pope Benedict XIII		• John Wesley earns his BA degree from Christ Church College	**1724**
• Vivaldi composes *The Four Seasons* • Alessandro Scarlatti composes his *Sonatas for Flute and Strings* • Alexander Pope publishes his translation of Homer's *Odyssey* and also his edition of *The Works of William Shakespeare*	• Giambattista Vico publishes *Principles of a New Science Concerning the Common Nature of Nations* • August Hermann Francke writes *A Letter to a Friend Concerning the Most Useful Way of Preaching* • Francis Hutcheson publishes his *Inquiry into the Original of Our Ideas of Beauty and Virtue* • Isaac Watts produces his *Logick, or the Right Use of Reason in the Enquiry after Truth*	• Martin Boehm is born in Pennsylvania	• Wesley is ordained deacon of the Church of England; begins keeping a diary; reads Thomas à Kempis, *The Imitation of Christ*, and Jeremy Taylor, *The Rule and Exercises of Holy Living and Holy Dying*	**1725**
• Jonathan Swift publishes the first edition of *Gulliver's Travels*, which is both a satire on the foibles of human nature and a parody of the "travellers' tales" books of the time • The first public circulating library is established by Allan Ramsay in Edinburgh • London's Church of St. Martin-in-the-Fields, designed by James Gibbs, is completed	• St. John of the Cross is canonized by the Roman Catholic Church • William Law publishes his *Treatise upon Christian Perfection*		• Wesley is elected Fellow of Lincoln College and appointed as Greek Lecturer and Moderator of Classes • Brother Charles enters Christ Church College, Oxford • William Otterbein is born in Germany • Samuel Wesley suffers a stroke which leaves his right hand partially paralyzed	**1726**

	A. WORLD HISTORY & POLITICS	B. AMERICAN HISTORY & POLITICS	C. SCIENCE, MEDICINE & TECHNOLOGY	D. DAILY LIFE, POPULAR CULTURE & ENTERTAINMENT
1727	• King George I (UK) dies and is succeeded by his son, George II • Tsarina Catherine of Russia dies; she is succeeded by Peter II, the grandson of Peter the Great • Spain attacks British forces in Gibraltar, breaking the Peace of Utrecht and provoking war between Britain and Spain, in which France allies with Spain • England employs Hessian mercenary troops in its army for the first time	• New York colonial official Cadwallader Colden publishes *The History of the Five Indian Nations*, an imperialist tract designed to illustrate the importance of Iroquois allegiance to the English	• Isaac Newton's revolutionary *Mathematical Principles of Natural Philosophy*, wherein he describes universal gravitation and the three laws of motion, is translated into English (first published in Latin in 1686) • Newton dies in London and is buried in Westminster Abbey; he is acclaimed as the most influential scientist in history; Alexander Pope composes his famous epitaph: "Nature and nature's laws lay hid in night; God said 'Let Newton be' and all was light"	• The first coffee plantation is established in Brazil
1728	• Spain's 14-month siege of Gibraltar ends unsuccessfully • Vitus Bering, a Dutch explorer employed by Russia, discovers the strait now named for him in Alaska • China and Russia sign the Treaty of Liakhta, resolving a border dispute and regularizing trade relations between them	• William Byrd surveys the boundary between Virginia and North Carolina	• British agriculturalist Charles Townsend develops the four-year crop rotation system; he gains the nickname "Turnip" due to his enthusiasm for the use of that crop • John Bartram establishes the first botanical garden in America, near Philadelphia	• John Gay's lighthearted political satire *The Beggar's Opera* debuts in London • Boston begins to enclose the Commons to preserve the grass from carts and horses
1729	• The Treaty of Seville establishes peace between France, Spain, and England; Spain renounces its claims to Gibraltar • Attacks from Oman force the Portuguese to leave east Africa • Emperor Yung Cheng prohibits opium smoking in China	• North and South Carolina become British crown colonies after giving up their original charters • The town of Baltimore is established in the Maryland colony • The Natchez Indians in upper Louisiana kill over 300 French settlers and soldiers because of encroachment on their holy places and burial grounds	• Isaac Greenwood's *Arithmetic Vulgar and Decimal* is the first mathematics textbook published in America	• Benjamin Franklin, who had left Boston for Philadelphia in 1723, purchases and begins publishing the *Pennsylvania Gazette*, which later becomes *The Saturday Evening Post* • The British parliament passes an act requiring a five-year apprenticeship for attorneys
1730	• Tsar Peter II of Russia dies; he is succeeded by his cousin Anna, the grand-niece of Peter the Great	• The population of the American colonies is about 629,000	• René-Antoine de Réaumur develops an alcohol thermometer and graduated temperature scale	• Freemasonry is established in America with the foundation of the first Masonic Lodge in Philadelphia; Benjamin Franklin is among the first members
1731	• 10 Downing Street, London, becomes the official residence for the British prime minister	• Construction begins on the State House in Philadelphia; designed by Andrew Hamilton, it is completed in 1732 and later named Independence Hall	• English mathematician John Hadley and American inventor Thomas Godfrey independently invent the sextant, enabling the accurate calculation of a ship's latitude	• *The Gentleman's Magazine*, considered the first modern magazine, is published in England; it includes essays, stories, poems, and political commentary • Benjamin Franklin and a group of friends in Philadelphia establish America's first public circulating library
1732	• King Frederick William I of Prussia introduces military conscription, building one of the largest armies in Europe	• A British royal charter is granted for the Georgia colony; it is the 13th British colony in North America • George Washington is born	• Jethro Tull's *Horse-hoeing Husbandry* advocates "modern" agricultural techniques including using manure, pulverizing the soil, growing crops in rows, and removing weeds by hoeing	• Benjamin Franklin begins publishing *Poor Richard's Almanac* • Franklin also begins publishing the *Philadelphia Zeitung*, the first non-English newspaper in America

E. EDUCATION, LITERATURE & THE FINE ARTS	F. RELIGION, THEOLOGY, PHILOSOPHY & PSYCHOLOGY	G. AMERICAN & UNITED METHODISM	H. BRITISH & WORLD METHODISM	
• Handel becomes a naturalized British citizen • Defoe publishes *The Complete English Tradesman* • John Gay publishes his *Fifty-one Fables in Verse* • Benjamin Franklin establishes the "Junto," a society for scientific and philosophical discussions	• Zinzendorf organizes the Moravian religious community at Herrnhut into the "Unitas Fratrum" and becomes its spiritual head • Construction begins on Christ Church, Philadelphia (completed 1744) • Roman Catholic nuns from France arrive in New Orleans and establish the first Catholic charitable institutions in America (a hospital, orphanage, and school for girls) • Thomas Woolston publishes his scurrilous *Discourses on the Miracles of Christ*		• Wesley receives his MA degree from Christ Church College, then leaves Oxford for Epworth to serve for a time as his father's curate at the nearby parish of Wroot	**1727**
• Georg Philipp Telemann completes his *St. John Passion* • Alexander Pope produces the first version of *The Dunciad* • Ephraim Chambers brings out his revolutionary *Cyclopaedia; or An Universal Dictionary of Arts and Sciences*, the first such work to make systematic use of cross-references • James Gibbs, the most important British architect since Wren, publishes his *Book of Architecture*, which influences architecture in Britain and its colonies for the rest of the century	• Peter Browne publishes *The Procedure, Extent, and Limits of Human Understanding* • Hutcheson publishes his influential *Essay on the Nature and Conduct of the Passions and Affections, with Illustrations upon the Moral Sense*		• Wesley travels to Oxford where he is ordained priest of the Church of England by John Potter, Bishop of Oxford, then returns to Epworth	**1728**
• Bach composes his soaring *St. Matthew Passion* • Jonathan Swift's satirical pamphlet *A Modest Proposal* suggests relieving the distress of the poor Roman Catholic children of Ireland by eating them; it is perhaps the best example of sustained irony ever written	• William Law publishes *A Serious Call to a Devout and Holy Life*		• Wesley is recalled to Oxford and resumes his teaching duties as Fellow of Lincoln College; he also begins participating in a study group that has gathered around his brother Charles • John William Fletcher is born in Switzerland • Wesley begins reading William Law's *Serious Call to a Devout and Holy Life* soon after its publication	**1729**
• The earliest known American performance of Shakespeare's *Romeo and Juliet* takes place in New York City	• The Jewish congregation in New York City, which was established in 1654, dedicates the first American synagogue, Shearith Israel, also known as the Mill Street Synagogue • Matthew Tindal argues the case for Deism in *Christianity as Old as the Creation: Or, The Gospel, A Republication of the Religion of Nature* • Pope Benedict XIII dies; he is succeeded by Pope Clement XII		• Wesley preaches "The Image of God" as his first university sermon at St. Mary's, Oxford • Oxford Methodism has its beginning when the study group (John and Charles Wesley, William Morgan, and Robert Kirkham) starts prison visitation, fasting twice a week, and taking communion every week; they are soon labeled as (among other names) the "Holy Club" • Charles Wesley receives his BA degree from Christ Church College	**1730**
• Italian violin maker Antonio Stradivari, who developed the modern violin and created violins of unequaled tonal quality, finishes a violin that will be owned a hundred years later by Nicolò Paganini • Alexander Pope begins publishing his *Moral Essays*	• William Law rebuts Tindal in *The Case of Reason, or Natural Religion, Fairly and Fully Stated, in Answer to a Book, entitled, Christianity as Old as the Creation*		• Samuel Wesley is badly injured when he is thrown from a wagon; he never entirely recovers	**1731**
• The Covent Garden Opera House opens in London • William Hogarth produces his series of engravings *A Harlot's Progress* • Bach's *Kaffee-Kantate* (Coffee Cantata) gives evidence of the increasing popularity of the beverage	• Johann Conrad Beissel founds the Ephrata Cloisters religious community, an offshoot of the German Dunkers, in Lancaster County, PA [the community takes the name Seventh Day German Baptists in 1814] • George Berkeley publishes his *Alciphron, or the Minute Philosopher*		• John Clayton associates with the Oxford Methodists • William Morgan dies; Wesley defends himself and Oxford Methodism against rumors that severely ascetical practices were to blame • George Whitefield enters Pembroke College, Oxford	**1732**

	A. WORLD HISTORY & POLITICS	B. AMERICAN HISTORY & POLITICS	C. SCIENCE, MEDICINE & TECHNOLOGY	D. DAILY LIFE, POPULAR CULTURE & ENTERTAINMENT
1733	• France declares war against the Holy Roman Empire (Austria) beginning the War of the Polish Succession • The Great Northern Expedition of Vitus Bering surveys the coasts of Siberia	• The town of Savannah is founded by James Oglethorpe, leader of the Georgia colony; Oglethorpe establishes defensive fortifications at Augusta, Frederica, and St. Simon's Island and prohibits both liquor and slavery in the colony • The Molasses Act, passed by the British parliament, imposes heavy duties on molasses, rum, and sugar imported from non-British islands in the Caribbean to protect the English planters there from French and Dutch competition	• English weaver John Kay invents the flying shuttle, which greatly increases the efficiency of commercial looms; this marks a major step in the development of the industrial revolution	• St. Andrew's Masonic Lodge is established in Boston; the first members include John Hancock and Paul Revere • The Serpentine Lake in London's Hyde Park is completed • John Peter Zenger launches *The New York Gazette*
1734	• Danzig is occupied by Russian forces • Spain takes over the kingdom of Naples	• French colonists establish their first settlement in what is now Indiana at Vincennes, on the Wabash River	• René-Antoine de Réaumur publishes the first of several volumes on insects that are foundational for the science of entomology	• The first known horse race on American soil is held in South Carolina • British tea merchant Thomas Twining abandons the coffee business to concentrate on tea, establishing Twinings of London
1735	• The Treaty of Vienna concludes the War of the Polish Succession; Austria and Russia begin to dominate Polish affairs; Spain receives Naples and Sicily and cedes to Austria its claims to Parma; Austria retains control of Lombardy	• John Peter Zenger, publisher of *The New York Gazette*, is charged by the colonial government of New York with seditious libel; the case goes to trial and Zenger is acquitted after his lawyer successfully convinces the jury that truth is a defense against libel; the case stands as a landmark ruling for freedom of the press in America • John Adams is born	• Swedish naturalist Carolus Linnaeus develops the binomial system for the classification of biological organisms by genus and species in his landmark *System of Nature*	• The Royal Golfing Society is founded in Edinburgh • *The Boston Evening Post* begins publication
1736	• China begins to expand its empire, which by the end of the century will include Mongolia, Turkistan, Nepal, Tibet, and Burma	• Britain cannot effectively enforce the Molasses Act; colonial merchants continue to import sugar, molasses, and rum from traders on non-British islands in the Caribbean	• French surgeon Claudius Aymand performs the first successful surgical appendectomy in the course of treating a hernia patient	• All remaining English statutes against witchcraft are repealed • The Gin Act of 1736 imposes high duties on gin in England, resulting in street riots

E. EDUCATION, LITERATURE & THE FINE ARTS	F. RELIGION, THEOLOGY, PHILOSOPHY & PSYCHOLOGY	G. AMERICAN & UNITED METHODISM	H. BRITISH & WORLD METHODISM	
• Jean Philippe Rameau composes his opera *Hippolytus and Aricia* • Thomas Arne's opera *Rosamund* debuts at Covent Garden, London • Alexander Pope publishes his *Essay on Man*	• Presbyterian minister Ebenezer Erskine leads the establishment of the Associate Presbytery (later Associate Presbyterian Church) in Scotland, which is transported to America by Scots-Irish immigrants in about 1750 • The first mass is celebrated at St. Joseph's Church in Philadelphia [it is the oldest surviving Roman Catholic church in the US] • A group of Jewish settlers from London establish Congregation Mikve Israel in Savannah, Georgia, five months after the foundation of the colony; it is the third oldest Jewish community in America (after New York and Newport) • A group of Moravians accepts an invitation to establish a settlement in Georgia; they are led by August Spangenberg and follow the teachings of Zinzendorf		• Wesley preaches "Circumcision of the Heart" as the university sermon at St. Mary's, Oxford (not published until 1748) • Wesley publishes his first book, *A Collection of Forms of Prayer for Every Day in the Week* • Benjamin Ingham joins the Oxford Methodists • Charles Wesley receives his MA degree from Christ Church College	**1733**
• The University of Göttingen is established by Britain's King George II, who is also (still) the Elector of Hannover • Bach completes his *Christmas Oratorio* • Handel composes his *Six Concerti Grossi*	• A large group of Salzburger Protestants, followers of August Hermann Francke and grounded in the Halle Pietist tradition of Philipp Jacob Spener, establish a settlement at New Ebenezer in the Georgia colony • Voltaire [François Marie Arouet] writes his *Philosophical Letters*, a thinly-disguised attack on the religious and political institutions of France • George Sale completes his influential English translation of the Qu'ran, based on the 1698 Latin version by Ludovic Maracci; Sale's version is retranslated into Dutch (1742), German (1764), French (1750), and Russian (1792)		• Wesley's sister Mary ("Molly," b. 1696) dies along with her infant child • Wesley preaches the university sermon in St. Mary's, Oxford; his sermon (which has not survived) is called the "Jacobite" sermon because it is critical of the House of Hanover • Samuel Wesley presses John to agree to succeed him as rector at Epworth; John declines to do so	**1734**
• William Hogarth finishes his engravings of *A Rake's Progress* • Handel's opera *Alcina* opens at Covent Garden, London	• The powerful preaching of Jonathan Edwards sparks a religious revival in Northampton, MA, marking the beginning of the Great Awakening in America		• Samuel Wesley dies at the age of 72 and is buried in the Epworth churchyard; John preaches his father's funeral and returns to Oxford; Susanna and her unmarried daughters are forced to leave the Epworth rectory to live with a succession of relatives • George Whitefield experiences evangelical conversion and a call to preach and associates with the Oxford Methodists • Both John and Charles Wesley volunteer and are accepted by the SPG for service as missionaries in Georgia • Charles is ordained deacon and then priest of the Church of England before the brothers sail for America • Howell Harris begins revival preaching in Wales; the revival soon spreads into western England around Bristol	**1735**
• Giovanni Battista Pergolesi composes his *Stabat Mater*, generally considered to be his finest work • Handel's opera *Alexander's Feast* opens at Covent Garden, London	• Joseph Butler publishes *The Analogy of Religion, Natural and Revealed, to the Constitution and Course of Nature* • Freemasonry is condemned by Pope Clement XII	• John and Charles Wesley arrive in Georgia along with Benjamin Ingham and Charles Delamotte (February); John is appointed parish priest in Savannah, Charles in Frederica; Charles serves as Oglethorpe's secretary • The first "Methodist" religious society meeting in America is held at Frederica (June) • Charles Wesley becomes ill and returns to England (July)	• George Whitefield is ordained deacon of the Church of England	**1736**

	A. WORLD HISTORY & POLITICS	B. AMERICAN HISTORY & POLITICS	C. SCIENCE, MEDICINE & TECHNOLOGY	D. DAILY LIFE, POPULAR CULTURE & ENTERTAINMENT
1737	• Russia attacks Ottoman Turk forces in the Crimea; Austria joins Russia by attacking Ottoman possessions in Serbia	• Richmond (Virginia) is founded by William Byrd	• English carpenter John Harrison builds his first marine chronometer, enabling accurate shipboard timekeeping and thus the determination of longitude • John Bevis, working at the Royal Observatory in Greenwich, observes the passage of Venus in front of Mercury, demonstrating their relative distance from the earth	• The British parliament passes the Licensing Act which restricts the number of London theaters and subjects all plays to censorship by the Lord Chamberlain • The *Belfast Newsletter*, Ireland's first newspaper, is founded [it is now the world's oldest surviving general daily newspaper]
1738	• Turkish forces capture Orsova, driving Austrian forces back to Belgrade and following close behind	• Spain and England become embroiled in a dispute about the boundary of the Georgia colony; English troops are sent to Georgia	• Carolus Linnaeus's *Genera of Plants* classifies over 18,000 species of plants and explains his methods of doing so • British engineer Charles Labeyle develops the caisson while attempting to build a bridge over the Thames at Westminster	• The first cuckoo clocks are produced in the Black Forest region of Germany • Samuel Johnson begins to write for *The Gentleman's Magazine*
1739	• The Treaty of Belgrade ends the Austro-Russian War against the Ottoman Empire, which regains control of Serbia • The "War of Jenkins's Ear" breaks out between England and Spain over new world trade • British forces sack the Spanish trading center of Portobelo, Panama • Spain establishes the fortress of New Granada to defend its territories in the Caribbean	• The English colonists in Georgia and South Carolina declare war on the Spanish settlers in Florida • Three separate, violent slave revolts occur in South Carolina • French explorers travel across the plains from the Missouri River to Santa Fe, marking the probable beginnings of the Santa Fe Trail	• London's Foundling Hospital is established • John Winthrop publishes his *Notes on Sunspots*, the first such work published in America • Thomas Clap, President of Yale College, introduces astronomy and "natural philosophy" (science) into the Yale curriculum	• Camellias are first imported to England from the Far East • Strict behavior codes are relaxed somewhat in New England; in Boston, Charles Bradstreet receives permission to teach "French dancing" provided that he keeps "good order" among his students
1740	• King Frederick William I of Prussia dies; he is succeeded by his son, Frederick II "The Great," who introduces freedom of press and freedom of worship in Prussia • Holy Roman Emperor Charles VI dies, ending the male Hapsburg line; his daughter, Maria Theresa, is declared heir to the Austrian crown; Britain, France, Prussia, Russia, and the Netherlands support her accession to the throne, which is opposed by rival claimants in Austria, supported by Spain; Prussia attacks and occupies Silesia, setting off the War of the Austrian Succession (to 1748)	• The population of the American colonies is about 905,000 • Fifty black slaves are hanged in Charleston after plans for another revolt are revealed • A major fire destroys a substantial part of Charleston • French explorers, pressing westward from the Louisiana Territory, reach Colorado	• Frederick the Great reorganizes the Berlin-Brandenburg Society of Scientists into the Berlin Academy of Science • Berlin suffers a major outbreak of smallpox	• Benjamin Franklin organizes the first successful fire insurance company, the "Philadelphia Contributorship"; the company identifies insured properties with "fire marks"

E. EDUCATION, LITERATURE & THE FINE ARTS	F. RELIGION, THEOLOGY, PHILOSOPHY & PSYCHOLOGY	G. AMERICAN & UNITED METHODISM	H. BRITISH & WORLD METHODISM	
• The Imperial Russian Ballet is established in St. Petersburg [later known as the Kirov Ballet] • British composer William Boyce conducts the Three Choirs Festival • James Gibbs begins construction of the Radcliffe Camera in Oxford (completed in 1749)	• Jonathan Edwards publishes an account of the Northampton revival in *A Faithful Narrative of the Surprising Work of God* [also known as *A Narrative of Surprising Conversions*] • The Virgin of Guadalupe is proclaimed patroness of Mexico by the Roman Catholic Church in Mexico	• John Wesley publishes *A Collection of Psalms and Hymns* in Charleston, SC, consisting mostly of his translation of Moravian hymns from German into English; it is his first hymnbook and also the first to be published in America • Benjamin Ingham returns to England (February) • John Wesley returns to England (December)	• George Whitefield launches his preaching career in Bristol, then sails for America	**1737**
• A second volume of John Gay's *Fables* is published posthumously; it is less ironically moral and more indignantly satirical and overtly political than the first volume (1727)	• William Warburton begins publication of his huge work *The Divine Legation of Moses* (through 1741)	• Whitefield arrives in America (February); he succeeds Wesley as pastor in Savannah and decides to establish an orphanage in Georgia • Charles Delamotte returns to England (September)	• Wesley arrives back in England and meets Peter Böhler in London (February); helps to establish the Fetter Lane Society (May); feels his heart "strangely warmed" at Aldersgate (May); preaches "Salvation by Faith" as the university sermon at St. Mary's, Oxford (June); visits the Moravian communities in Germany and meets Nicolaus von Zinzendorf in Herrnhut, travels to Halle, returns to England (July–September); reads Jonathan Edwards's *Faithful Narrative* about the revival in America (October); publishes his extracts from the Homilies of the Church of England (November)	**1738**
• The Royal Society of Edinburgh is established • An American edition of the *Hymns and Spiritual Songs* of Isaac Watts is published in Philadelphia; it strongly influences the development of American music • Handel's opera *Israel in Egypt* premieres at the King's Theater in London	• David Hume publishes *A Treatise of Human Nature* (vols. 1 and 2; vol. 3, 1740), which, in his words, "falls stillborn from the press"	• Whitefield goes back to England (briefly), in part to raise money for his projected orphanage, then returns to America; he preaches his way up and down the East Coast in 1739–40 raising more money for his orphanage project, in the process meeting Jonathan Edwards and Gilbert Tennent, helping to advance the Great Awakening, becoming a friend of Benjamin Franklin, and emerging as an international celebrity	• Whitefield gets involved in the open-air revival around Bristol, then persuades Wesley to start field preaching; Wesley then enlists brother Charles • The first Methodist societies are formed in Bristol and London from people responding to Wesley's preaching • Wesley establishes the Kingswood School outside Bristol • John Cennick, a teacher at the Kingswood School, begins preaching (without Wesley's prior approval) to the miners in the area [he is regarded by some as the first Methodist lay preacher] • The Methodists in Bristol acquire and open the New Room [it is now the oldest Methodist building in the world] • Wesley's "Free Grace" sermon ignites a dispute with Whitefield over predestination, which lasts until 1741 • Selina Hastings, the Countess of Huntingdon, experiences an evangelical conversion, joins the Fetter Lane Society, and becomes a patron of the revival • Wesley begins his publishing operations, planting the seed from which the Wesleyan Book Establishment will grow • Wesley's brother Samuel Jr. (b. 1690) dies	**1739**
• Handel completes his *Twelve Concerti Grossi* • Thomas Arne's masque *Alfred* opens at Covent Garden, London; it includes "Rule, Britannia," which very quickly becomes a favorite patriotic popular song • Samuel Richardson publishes his first major novel, *Pamela* • South Carolina passes a law prohibiting slaves from learning to read or write and specifying penalties both for those who try to educate slaves and for the slaves who seek to learn; several other southern colonies follow suit; these laws will remain in effect until 1865	• A major split occurs among Congregationalists in New England between the "Old Light" (traditionalist) wing, led by Charles Chauncy, and the "New Light" (revivalist) wing, led by Gilbert Tennent; the "New Light" wing develops the evangelical New England theology, while the "Old Light" wing gradually drifts toward Unitarianism • A group of Moravian settlers from Germany arrive in Pennsylvania and establish the town of Nazareth; many of the Georgia Moravians move north to join them and establish the town of Bethlehem	• Whitefield establishes the Bethesda Orphanage in Georgia, near Savannah, and publishes *A Short Account of God's Dealings with George Whitefield* [it is printed by his friend Benjamin Franklin]	• Wesley leases and renovates the Foundery, which becomes the center of Methodist activities in London • Susanna Wesley moves into an apartment in the Foundery • Wesley accepts Thomas Maxfield as his first "son in the gospel" (full-time itinerant lay preacher), followed by Thomas Richards and Thomas Westall • Wesley breaks decisively with the English Moravians, now led by Philip Molther, over their "quietism" and "antinomianism" and withdraws from the Fetter Lane Society along with a group of *(cont.)*	**1740**

	A. WORLD HISTORY & POLITICS	B. AMERICAN HISTORY & POLITICS	C. SCIENCE, MEDICINE & TECHNOLOGY	D. DAILY LIFE, POPULAR CULTURE & ENTERTAINMENT
1740 cont.	• Tsarina Anna of Russia dies and a period of royal instability follows			
1741	• Maria Theresa accepts the crown of Hungary • Sweden declares war on Russia • Vitus Bering surveys the Alaskan coast and the Aleutian Islands for Russia, where he is trapped by bad weather and dies of hunger and cold along with most of his crew	• A slave revolt in New York City results in the execution of 26 and the sale or deportation of 71 more slaves • North Carolina enacts laws to prosecute any person caught assisting runaways • Another significant wave of Scots-Irish immigration to America begins	• Steller's sea cow, named for British naturalist George W. Steller, is discovered living along the coast of the Kamchatka Peninsula; akin to manatees, the sea cow will be hunted to extinction for its highly prized meat and fur in less than 30 years	• Benjamin Franklin plans to publish America's first magazine, *General Magazine*, but is beaten to the punch when *American Magazine* comes out three days earlier
1742	• Prussian forces defeat the Austrian army at Mollwitz and again at Chotisitz; in the ensuing Peace of Berlin, Austria cedes control of most of Silesia to Prussia • Charles VII, Elector of Bavaria, is crowned Holy Roman Emperor	• British and colonial troops in Georgia commanded by Oglethorpe clash with Spanish troops from St. Augustine in the "Battle of Bloody Marsh"	• Swedish scientist Anders Celsius develops the temperature scale that bears his name (the Celsius scale, or the centigrade thermometer)	• The Gin Act of 1736 is repealed in England, resulting in an explosive increase in gin production and consumption • The first known cookbook in America, Eliza Smith's *The Complete Housewife*, a reprint of a British title, is published in New York
1743	• George II becomes the last British monarch to personally lead British troops into battle (at Dettingen in Bavaria) • Austrian forces drive the French out of Bohemia • In the Treaty of Åbo, Sweden is forced to cede southern Finland to Russia	• Oglethorpe's Georgia troops invade Florida but are unable to take St. Augustine from its Spanish defenders • The War of the Austrian Succession ignites conflict between the British and French in North America, where it is called King George's War • French explorers reach the Rocky Mountains, where they give the name "Le Grande Tetons" to one especially impressive mountain range in what is now Wyoming • Thomas Jefferson is born	• Britain's first cotton mills are established in Birmingham and Northampton	
1744	• The family of Saud begins its rise to power in Arabia, guided by a fundamentalist version of Islam called Wahhabism, named for its creator, Muhammad ibn 'Abd al-Wahhab	• British and colonial forces capture the fortress at Louisbourg on Cape Breton Island from the French; the French raid New York • The first white settlements are established in what is now South Dakota	• Benjamin Franklin invents the Franklin stove, which provides more heat with less fuel than a typical fireplace	• The song "God Save the King" is first published in the musical series *Thesaurus Musicus* in London [it will be adopted as the British national anthem in 1825]

E. EDUCATION, LITERATURE & THE FINE ARTS	F. RELIGION, THEOLOGY, PHILOSOPHY & PSYCHOLOGY	G. AMERICAN & UNITED METHODISM	H. BRITISH & WORLD METHODISM	
	• The British parliament passes an act permitting foreign Jews to be naturalized as British subjects in the colonies • Pope Clement XII dies; he is succeeded by Pope Benedict XIV		supporters; they begin meeting at the Foundery • Wesley publishes the first "Extract" from his *Journal*, covering the Georgia period, followed soon after by a second "Extract" which goes through 1738 and includes the account of his Aldersgate experience	**1740 cont.**
• Bach completes his *Goldberg Variations* • David Garrick makes his acting debut in London in the lead role of Shakespeare's *Richard III*	• Jonathan Edwards preaches his famous sermon "Sinners in the Hands of an Angry God" and publishes *The Distinguishing Marks of a Work of the Spirit of God* • Gilbert Tennent's preaching tour with George Whitefield helps make him one of the most influential preachers of the Great Awakening • The revivalism of the Great Awakening provokes a split between "Old Side" (anti-revivalist) and "New Side" (pro-revivalist) Presbyterians in America (to 1758) • Isaac Watts publishes *The Improvement of the Mind* • David Hume publishes his *Essays Moral and Political*	• Whitefield returns to England after a preaching tour with Gilbert Tennent through the middle colonies and New England	• Wesley tightens membership requirements for the societies and begins issuing quarterly "tickets" indicating membership in good standing • Wesley offends many in his audience when he preaches "The Almost Christian" as the university sermon at St. Mary's, Oxford • Wesley's sister Keziah ("Kezzie," b. 1710) dies • Whitefield opens the Moorfields Tabernacle, which becomes his primary preaching station in London • Wesley and Whitefield are reunited and agree to suppress their theological differences over predestination	**1741**
• G. F. Handel's beloved oratorio *Messiah* is performed for the first time in Dublin, Ireland, and receives its London premier soon after in St. Paul's Cathedral • Henry Fielding's first novel, *The History of the Adventures of Joseph Andrews and of His Friend Mr. Abraham Adams*, is a parody of the sentimental moralism of Samuel Richardson's *Pamela* • Edward Young begins publication of *The Complaint, or Night-Thoughts* (through 1746)	• The Philadelphia Association of Regular Baptists adopts the landmark *Philadelphia Baptist Confession of Faith*, which is based on the *London Baptist Confession* of 1689 • Jonathan Edwards, *Some Thoughts Concerning the Present Revival of Religion* • German biblical scholar Johann Bengel completes his *Gnomon Novi Testamenti* (Exegetical Annotations on the New Testament)		• Wesley publishes *The Character of a Methodist* and *The Principles of a Methodist* • Wesley gathers a group of lay preachers for a conference in London, but no minutes are kept • Class meetings begin in Bristol and London; the class soon replaces the band as the basic organizational unit of the Methodist societies • When he is refused permission to preach in St. Andrew's Church at Epworth, Wesley preaches outside standing on his father's tomb • The first Methodist preaching house in Newcastle is opened • Susanna Wesley dies at the Foundery at the age of 73; she is buried in Bunhill Fields, the old Dissenter's burial ground on City Road in London, where she lies in the company of William Blake, Jonathan Swift, Daniel Defoe, and Isaac Watts	**1742**
• Italian instrument maker Guarneri del Gesu builds a violin that will become Nicolò Paganini's favorite instrument, known as "The Cannon" because of its enormous natural sound [it still survives and is now considered an Italian national treasure] • Handel completes his oratorio *Samson* • Alexander Pope produces the final version of *The Dunciad* in four books • Inspired by the earlier "Junto" group, Benjamin Franklin and his associates in Philadelphia establish The American Philosophical Society	• Charles Chauncy writes his *Seasonable Thoughts on the State of Religion in New England* • America's first religious magazine, *The Christian History*, begins publication in Boston		• Wesley publishes *The Nature, Design, and General Rules of the United Societies* and *An Earnest Appeal to Men of Reason and Religion* • Howell Harris and his followers form the Welsh Calvinistic Methodist Conference, which covers Wales and southwestern England; Whitefield presides at the first meeting; this marks the organizational division between the "Calvinistic Methodists" and the "Wesleyan Methodists" • With the approval of John Potter, now Archbishop of Canterbury, Wesley leases the West Street Chapel, which had been abandoned by its Huguenot congregation, and begins holding regular communion services there; it becomes the primary Methodist sacramental center in London	**1743**
• The London Madrigal Society is founded • Moravians in Bethlehem, PA, establish a Collegium Musicum	• Philip Doddridge publishes *The Rise and Progress of Religion in the Soul*	• Whitefield makes his third trip to America	• Wesley preaches "Scriptural Christianity" as the university sermon at St. Mary's, Oxford; his stinging criticism of the university for its spiritual apathy offends many, and he is not again invited to preach there	**1744**

	A. WORLD HISTORY & POLITICS	B. AMERICAN HISTORY & POLITICS	C. SCIENCE, MEDICINE & TECHNOLOGY	D. DAILY LIFE, POPULAR CULTURE & ENTERTAINMENT
1744 cont.				
1745	• Britain withdraws protection from Empress Maria Theresa after heavy defeats by the French • Holy Roman Emperor Charles VII dies; Francis I, the husband of Maria Theresa, is elected to succeed him • Charles Edward Stuart ("Bonnie Prince Charlie" or "The Young Pretender") lands in Scotland, raises support in the Highlands, and launches the unsuccessful Jacobite Rebellion of 1745–46 in Britain	• French forces and their Indian allies attack British settlements on the western borders of New England	• Pennsylvania physician Thomas Cadwalader establishes a link between cases of lead poisoning in America and the use of lead pipes in distilling rum in the Caribbean	• The Quadrille, a formal ballroom dance, becomes popular in France • Louis Debaraz, a Roman Catholic priest, is the last person executed for witchcraft in France
1746	• The Battle of Culloden (the last major battle fought inside Britain) ends with the defeat of Jacobites and the flight of "Bonnie Prince Charlie" back to France • King Philip V of Spain dies; he is succeeded by his son Ferdinand VI • Russia and Austria form a mutual defense alliance, prompting formation of a similar alliance between Sweden and Prussia	• French forces fail to retake Louisbourg and Nova Scotia from the British	• E. G. von Kleist (Germany) discovers a method of storing an electrical charge in a glass jar lined with silver foil; Pieter van Musschenbroek (Netherlands) independently makes the same discovery; the device is the first electrical capacitor and is known as a "Leyden jar" because Musschenbroek first made the discovery known to the world	• In the aftermath of the Jacobite Rebellion, the wearing of Scottish tartans is banned in England
1747	• The kingdom of Afghanistan is founded by Ahmad Kahn Abdali • A British fleet commanded by George Anson defeats the French fleet off Cape Finisterre • Yoruba tribal warriors conquer Dahomey and become the major power in the Niger Delta	• The New York Bar Association is founded in New York City	• British doctor James Lind shows that fresh citrus fruits prevent scurvy, a leading cause of death of British seamen • Andreas Marggraf (Germany) discovers how to extract sugar from beets, establishing the foundation of Europe's sugar-beet industry • British physicist Benjamin Robins demonstrates that guns with "rifled" barrels perform better than smooth-bore muskets	• A carriage tax is introduced in England for the first time; it is the ancestor of later vehicle taxes
1748	• Russian forces invade Bohemia and march toward Prussia • Peace of Aix-la-Chapelle brings an end to the War of the Austrian Succession (King George's War); Prussia wins control of Silesia; Francis I, husband of Maria Theresa, is recognized as Holy Roman Emperor, and the Holy Roman Empire (Austria) remains intact	• King George's War comes to an end with the Peace of Aix-la-Chapelle; Cape Breton is returned to the French; the British retain control of Nova Scotia	• The first archaeological excavations begin at Pompeii, which had been buried by the eruption of Mt. Vesuvius in A.D. 79 • British industrialist John Wilkinson establishes the first blast furnace in England • Benjamin Franklin coins the term *battery* to describe an array of electrically charged glass plates	• The first Parisian salon is opened by Marie-Thérèse Geoffrin as a meeting place reserved for "men of letters"

E. EDUCATION, LITERATURE & THE FINE ARTS	F. RELIGION, THEOLOGY, PHILOSOPHY & PSYCHOLOGY	G. AMERICAN & UNITED METHODISM	H. BRITISH & WORLD METHODISM	
			• Wesley convenes the first formal Conference (with minutes) of his Methodist preachers in London: they consider "what to teach, how to teach, what to do" • Wesley's sister Anne ("Nancy," b. 1702) dies around this date; the actual date is unknown, but there is no reference to her by either John or Charles after 1744	**1744 cont.**
• Johann Stamitz composes his *Mannheim Symphonies* • William Hogarth completes his engravings *Marriage à la Mode*	• David Brainerd begins his missionary work among the American Indians of New Jersey and eastern Pennsylvania		• Wesley publishes *A Farther Appeal to Men of Reason and Religion* (in 3 parts) and (with Charles) *Hymns Upon the Lord's Supper* • Francis Asbury is born • Methodism is first introduced into Scotland through British soldiers stationed near Edinburgh	**1745**
• The College of New Jersey, originally founded by William Tennant in 1726, is formally chartered; it becomes Princeton University in 1896 • Samuel Johnson signs the contract for his *Dictionary of the English Language*, agreeing to deliver it in three years [it takes nine years to complete]	• Jonathan Edwards completes his important *Treatise Concerning Religious Affections*, in which he argues that "the essence of all true religion lies in holy love" that proves its genuineness by its inner quality and practical results • James Hervey publishes his *Meditations and Contemplations* • The hymnody of the Ephrata Colisters community is printed in a series of illuminated songbooks including arrangements for as many as seven parts • The first professorship of divinity is established at Yale College		• As the Methodist movement spreads, Wesley establishes "circuits" for the lay preachers through which they itinerate • Wesley establishes a free medical clinic for the poor at the Foundery; it lasts until 1754 • Wesley publishes the first collection of his sermons, entitled *Sermons on Several Occasions*, vol. 1 • Selina, Countess of Huntingdon, opens her London home to evangelistic services by Calvinistic Methodist preachers	**1746**
• Handel completes his opera *Judas Maccabeus* • Bach composes his *Musical Offering* • Three-year-old Luigi Boccherini goes to Rome to study the cello • Samuel Richardson publishes his novel *Clarissa*	• The German Reformed Church holds its first synod in North America • French philosopher Denis Diderot completes his *Pensées philosophiques* (published anonymously)		• Wesley makes the first of his 21 visits to Ireland and forms the first Irish society in Dublin • Wesley publishes his *Primitive Physic*, a collection of home remedies • Thomas Coke is born	**1747**
• John Cleland publishes his bawdy novel *Memoirs of a Woman of Pleasure* (better known after its main character as *Fanny Hill*) describing the activities of a London prostitute; it is promptly declared to be obscene and is suppressed, and has been many times since • The Bayreuth Opera House opens in Germany	• Henry Muhlenberg establishes the Pennsylvania Ministerium, the first North American Lutheran church organization • David Hume recasts a major part of his *Treatise of Human Nature* (1739–40) as *An Enquiry Concerning Human Understanding* • Montesquieu examines the three main types of government (republic, monarchy, and despotism) in his *On the Spirit of the Laws*	• Whitefield returns to England via Bermuda	• Wesley begins holding watch night services and love feasts • The first circuit quarterly meeting is held by William Grimshaw • Kingswood School is rebuilt and reorganized in Bristol • The New Room in Bristol is thoroughly remodeled • Wesley publishes *Sermons on Several Occasions*, vol. 2, including "The Great Privilege of Those That Are Born of God" • Whitefield associates with Selina, Countess of Huntingdon, and becomes one of her chaplains • The Wesleys meet with Howell Harris and the Welsh Methodist Association to consider possible union of their movements but fail to reach agreement	**1748**

	A. WORLD HISTORY & POLITICS	B. AMERICAN HISTORY & POLITICS	C. SCIENCE, MEDICINE & TECHNOLOGY	D. DAILY LIFE, POPULAR CULTURE & ENTERTAINMENT
1749	• The Qing (Manchu) Dynasty in China begins its conquest of Tibet and Turkestan • Mysore begins its rise to power in southern India • The French East India Company begins aggressive competition against the British East India Company	• British control of Nova Scotia is strengthened by the establishment of Halifax • Georgia becomes a British crown colony, and the ban on slavery in the colony is revoked • The Ohio Company receives a British royal charter and a large grant of land around the Forks of the Ohio, resulting in the establishment of the first permanent white settlements in the region	• Sign language is devised by Jacob Pereire (France) • Benjamin Franklin invents the lightning rod and installs one on his own home in Philadelphia	• *The Monthly Review* begins publication of book reviews and literary criticism in London (through 1845) • The first known European study of the game of chess is published in France • Sarah Fielding's *The Governess; or, The Little Female Academy*, one of the first books published specifically for girls, contains two didactic fairy tales
1750	• The population of Europe is estimated at 140 million • The Treaty of Madrid defines the boundaries between Spanish and Portuguese colonies in South America including Brazil; Portugal renounces its claims to territory in Uruguay	• The population of the American colonies is about 1.2 million • The Iron Act is passed by the British parliament, limiting the growth of the iron industry in the American colonies to protect the British iron industry • Britain and France argue about the boundary between Acadia (Canada) and Nova Scotia • The French build Fort Rouillé (near modern Toronto) to counterbalance growing British trade and influence in the Niagara River region	• British printer John Baskerville develops the typeface named after him • The Westminster Bridge is completed in London; it provides a second crossing of the Thames and relieves some of the pressure on the medieval London Bridge	• Cotton produced by British mills begins to surpass south Asian textiles in Europe • New York City gets its first playhouse; the first performance is John Gay's *The Beggar's Opera* • Samuel Johnson begins *The Rambler* (through 1752) • The English Jockey Club is established in London
1751	• England joins the 1746 alliance of Russia and Austria against Prussia and Sweden • China invades Tibet and establishes control over the Dalai Lama	• The British parliament prohibits the issuance of paper money by the American colonies • Canadian French troops and settlers enter the Ohio Valley region	• The first general hospital in America is founded in Philadelphia • British steel maker Benjamin Huntsman invents the crucible process for casting steel, resulting in the purest and hardest form of steel available at the time	• The first professional theater company established in the colonies, the Virginia Company of Comedians, opens a temporary wooden playhouse in Williamsburg • The Gin Act of 1751 requires distillers to sell gin only to licensed retailers and reintroduces stuff duties, significantly curtailing consumption by the poor in Britain • The first porcelain factory in Worcester, England, is established by John Wall [it will become the Worcester Royal Porcelain Company in 1862]
1752	• Great Britain and her colonies adopt the Gregorian calendar, "losing" 11 days in September	• The Ohio Company increases active British colonization of the Ohio Valley; tensions between British and French settlers and traders in the region increase	• Benjamin Franklin performs his famous kite experiment, proving that lightning is electricity • René-Antoine de Réaumur discovers the role of gastric juices in digestion, proving it to be a chemical and not merely a mechanical process	• *The Halifax Gazette*, the first English language newspaper in Canada, begins publication • A theater troupe called "The American Company" presents a performance of Shakespeare's *The Merchant of Venice* in Williamsburg
1753	• France joins the alliance of Austria, Russia, and England against Prussia and Sweden	• The bell that will become known as the Liberty Bell is hung in the newly completed State House in Philadelphia, later known as Independence Hall • The French begin building a string of forts in Pennsylvania and Ohio to try to stop the spread of British influence	• Carolus Linnaeus's *The Species of Plants* completes his development of the use of binomial nomenclature in botany, which remains the foundation of the science	• The Jockey Club creates England's first permanent horse racing track at New Market • Britain's Marriage Act abolishes "common-law" marriage; it prohibits the marriage of males under 14 and females under 12 and requires parental consent if either

(cont.)

E. EDUCATION, LITERATURE & THE FINE ARTS	F. RELIGION, THEOLOGY, PHILOSOPHY & PSYCHOLOGY	G. AMERICAN & UNITED METHODISM	H. BRITISH & WORLD METHODISM	
• Handel composes his *Royal Fireworks Music* • Bach completes the final form of his majestic *Mass in B Minor* shortly before his death the following year • Henry Fielding publishes *Tom Jones*	• David Hartley's *Observations on Man*, an attempt to interpret the phenomenon of the human mind by the theory of association, is the first work in English to use the term *psychology* • George Lavington, Bishop of Exeter, attacks the Methodists in *The Enthusiasm of Methodists and Papists Compared* • Conyers Middleton produces *A Free Inquiry Into the Miraculous Powers, Which are Supposed to have Subsisted in the Christian Church* • Jonathan Edwards publishes *The Life of David Brainerd*		• Charles Wesley marries Sarah Gwynne; John performs the ceremony; they settle in Bristol with a guarantee from John of £100 a year from the sale of Methodist publications; Charles continues to itinerate and Sarah travels with him • Wesley considers marriage to Grace Murray until Charles intervenes by encouraging her to marry John Bennett and then performing the ceremony in John's absence, causing great strain between the brothers • Conference mandates quarterly meetings for all 12 circuits then in existence; the term *Assistant* is now limited to the head of each circuit • Wesley begins publication of *A Christian Library: Consisting of Extracts From, and Abridgements of, the Choicest Pieces of Practical Divinity Which have been Published in the English Tongue* (50 vols.,1749-55)	**1749**
• Bach dies; his passing is usually taken to mark the end of the Baroque era of classical music; his unfinished work *The Art of the Fugue* is published posthumously in 1751 • Leopold Mozart (the father and teacher of Wolfgang Amadeus Mozart) composes his *Partita for Violin, Cello and Double Bass (The Frog)*	• The Jewish religious renewal movement called Hasidism is established by Rabbi Israel ben Eliezer, known as the Baal Shem Tov ("Master of the Divine Name"); it quickly spreads through eastern Europe • Jonathan Edwards comes to reject the "Halfway Covenant" allowing the admission of baptized but unconverted individuals to the Lord's Supper and is forced to resign from his pastorate in Northampton • Jean-Jacques Rousseau publishes his *Discourse on the Sciences and the Arts*		• Wesley publishes *Sermons on Several Occasions*, vol. 3, and *A Plain Account of the People Called Methodists* • Wesley responds to Bishop Lavington's attacks on Methodism in *A Letter to the Author of "The Enthusiasm of Methodists and Papists Compared,"* followed by a second letter in 1751 • John Cennick, one of Wesley's first lay preachers who had left the Methodist movement several years before, is ordained deacon by the English Moravians	**1750**
• Thomas Gray's *Elegy Written in a Country Churchyard* marks the beginnings of English Romanticism • Henry Fielding's novel *Amelia* provides a chilling account of the contemporary English penal system • William Hogarth's engraving *Gin Lane* lampoons the drunkenness of London's poor • Francesco Geminiani publishes *The Art of Playing on the Violin* in London	• The Charleston Baptist Association is established; it is the second oldest Baptist association in America • Denis Diderot and Jean Le Rond d'Alembert begin publication of the massive *Encyclopédie ou dictionnaire raisonné des sciences, des arts et des métiers*, universally called simply the *Encyclopédie* [17 volumes of text will be completed by 1765, with an additional 11 volumes of supplements and plates added by 1780] • David Hume publishes *An Enquiry Concerning Principles of Morals and Political Discourses*	• Whitefield makes his fourth trip to America	• Wesley begins to employ "local preachers" who have gifts but are unwilling to leave their families or trade to itinerate as traveling preachers • Wesley suffers a fall on the ice-covered London Bridge and is carried to the home of Mary Vazeille, a sailor's widow; within two weeks he marries her without his brother's knowledge or consent; as a consequence he resigns his fellowship at Lincoln College; the marriage is a failure, and they soon separate (1755) • Wesley makes the first of his 15 visits to Scotland • Wesley's sister Mehetabel ("Hetty," b. 1697) dies	**1751**
• William Hogarth completes his engravings of *The Analysis of Beauty* • Jean-Jacques Rousseau's opera *Le devin du village* (The Village Sage) has its first performance	• David Hume publishes his *Political Discourses* • The first English Bible published in America comes off the press in Boston • Jonathan Edwards defends his religious principles and practices in *Misrepresentations Corrected and Truth Vindicated*	• William Otterbein, who had been ordained in Germany in 1749, arrives in America and soon becomes the minister of the German Reformed congregation in Lancaster, PA • Whitefield returns to England	• Howell Harris establishes a religious community at Trevecca, Wales • The first Irish Methodist Conference meets at Limerick • John William Fletcher emigrates to England, joins the Methodist society in London, and quickly becomes a leader in the society and a friend of the Wesley brothers	**1752**
• The British Museum, London, built around the private collection of Sir Hans Sloane, is granted a British royal charter • Carl Philipp Emanuel Bach, the son of Johann Sebastian Bach, publishes his *Essay on the True Art of Playing Keyboard* (cont.)	• Robert Lowth publishes his groundbreaking study of Hebrew poetry, *On the Sacred Poetry of the Hebrews*		• Wesley employs the first Book Stewards to oversee the growing Methodist publishing business • Wesley produces *Minutes of Several Conversations between the Rev. Mr. John Wesley and Others*	**1753**

	A. WORLD HISTORY & POLITICS	B. AMERICAN HISTORY & POLITICS	C. SCIENCE, MEDICINE & TECHNOLOGY	D. DAILY LIFE, POPULAR CULTURE & ENTERTAINMENT
1753 cont.				party is under 21; it also requires that a license be obtained and that the marriage be solemnized in church • Britain allows Jews to become naturalized citizens
1754	• France recalls its colonial governor from India, effectively ceding control of India to Britain	• Benjamin Franklin proposes the "Albany Plan" calling for the British colonies in North America to organize for their common defense against the encroaching French and to supervise Indian relations with new settlements; neither the colonial legislatures nor the royal governors are interested in pursuing the idea • The French and Indian War begins; it will be the final conflict in the ongoing struggle between the British and French for control of eastern North America • The French establish Fort Duquesne at the Forks of the Ohio, where the Monongahela and Allegheny rivers join to form the Ohio River (the site of modern Pittsburgh)	• British chemist Joseph Black discovers carbon dioxide (carbonic acid gas formed through the decomposition of chalk and limestone), anticipating the later work of Antoine Lavoisier • Britain's first iron-rolling mill is established in Hampshire	• The Royal and Ancient Golf Club of St. Andrews, Scotland, is founded
1755	• A massive earthquake and subsequent fires destroy most of Lisbon, Portugal, killing over 30,000 people and producing traumatic effects all across Europe	• British and American forces capture Fort Beauséjour in Canada from the French, but a British and American attack on Fort Duquesne is repelled by the French, and the British commander, Edward Braddock, is mortally wounded; George Washington assumes command • The Cherokee Indians in the Southeast cede control of a large amount of their territory in what is now Tennessee and North Carolina to white settlers	• Immanuel Kant, better known for his later philosophical works, suggests in his *General Natural History and Theory of the Heavens* that observed nebulae are large clusters of stars and that the solar system originated from a cosmic dust cloud	• The first regularly scheduled transatlantic passenger service begins between England and the American colonies
1756	• The French and Indian War widens into the Seven Years War, an international conflict pitting England and Prussia against France, Spain, and Austria • Prussia invades Saxony, captures Dresden, and defeats the Austrian army at Lobositz • France captures Minorca from the British	• The French capture Fort Oswego from the British, restoring French control of Lake Ontario	• Swiss physiologist Albrecht von Haller distinguishes the contraction of muscle fibers from the transmission of nerve impulses	• The first direct stagecoach line is established between New York and Philadelphia
1757	• British forces defeat the army of the Mughal Empire at the Battle of Plassey in Bengal [this is the conventional date for the beginning of the British Raj (Empire) in what is modern India and Pakistan] • Ahmed Shah of Afghanistan occupies Delhi and most of the Punjab region of India • Prussian forces are defeated by the Austrians at Kolin and forced to abandon Bavaria	• French forces capture Fort William Henry in New York; Indian allies of the French massacre many British and American prisoners	• British iron maker John Wilkinson develops a water-powered bellows to increase the flow of air in a blast furnace and thus increase its operating temperature	• The first public music concert in Philadelphia is presented in the Assembly Room in Lodge Alley
1758	• British and Hanoverian forces defeat the French at Krefeld • Prussian forces defeat an invading Russian army at Zorndorf • British forces capture Senegal in west Africa from the French and also defeat French armies in India	• The French repel a British attack in Fort Ticonderoga, New York • British and American troops capture Fort Duquesne from the French and their Indian allies and rename it Fort Pitt • British forces also recapture Louisbourg on Cape Breton Island and Fort Fontenac on Lake Ontario	• Halley's Comet reappears as predicted, 76 years after its original discovery	• The first whale-oil street lamps are lit in Philadelphia

E. EDUCATION, LITERATURE & THE FINE ARTS	F. RELIGION, THEOLOGY, PHILOSOPHY & PSYCHOLOGY	G. AMERICAN & UNITED METHODISM	H. BRITISH & WORLD METHODISM	
Instruments, which provides an important description of the performance practices of his time; a second volume appears in 1762			• Whitefield builds the new Moorfields Tabernacle, replacing the original wooden structure with a larger brick edifice	**1753 cont.**
• King's College, New York, is founded by Britain's King George II [it becomes Columbia University in 1784] • David Hume begins publication of his *History of Great Britain* (completed 1762)	• Jonathan Edwards publishes perhaps his most influential work, *A Careful and Strict Enquiry into . . . Notions of . . . Freedom of Will*, in which he denies the possibility of human self-determination and asserts divine foreknowledge and predestination • Anthony Benezet publishes his *Epistle of Caution and Advice Concerning the Buying and Keeping of Slaves*	• Whitefield makes his fifth trip to America, bringing with him 22 British orphans to be housed at his Bethesda Orphanage in Georgia • In recognition of his preaching ministry and charitable work, Whitefield receives an honorary MA degree from the College of New Jersey	• Wesley draws up the first real "circuit plan" scheduling the itineration of the traveling preachers in and around London; it is soon extended to the rest of England and Ireland • Financial pressures force Wesley to close the free medical clinic at the Foundery and also to shut down his experimental Poorhouse project	**1754**
• The University of Moscow (now Moscow State University) is established by Russian scientist Mikhail Vasilyevich Lomonosov • Samuel Johnson publishes his monumental *Dictionary of the English Language* and is awarded an honorary MA degree from Oxford • William Boyce is appointed Master of the King's Music in England • Leopold Mozart composes his *Divertimento in F Major (Musical Sleigh Ride)*	• Scotts-Irish immigrants have by now established both the Associate Presbytery (later Associate Presbyterian Church) and the Reformed Presbytery (later Reformed Presbyterian Church) in Pennsylvania • Jean-Jacques Rousseau publishes his *Discourse on the Origin of Inequality*, arguing that the natural, or primitive, state is morally superior to the civilized state and that society corrupts human innocence • Francis Hutcheson's complete *System of Moral Philosophy* is published posthumously	• Whitefield returns to England and remains there until 1763, working with what will become the Countess of Huntingdon's Connexion of Calvinistic Methodist congregations	• Conference decides not to permit Methodist preachers to administer the sacraments and resists pressure to separate from Church of England • A semipermanent breach separates Mr. and Mrs. John Wesley after she opens and reads some of his private letters • Wesley publishes his *Explanatory Notes Upon the New Testament*, based on work by Heylen, Guyse, Doddridge, and Bengel's *Gnomon*; Wesley adopts many of Bengel's principles of textual criticism • Wesley holds the first Methodist covenant renewal service in London	**1755**
• Tobias Smollett founds *The Critical Review* (runs through 1817) • Samuel Johnson establishes *The Literary Magazine, or Universal Review*	• Voltaire publishes his *Essay on General History and on the Customs and the Character of Nations* in which he denounces organized religion in general and the power of the clergy in particular	• Martin Boehm becomes a Mennonite preacher (bishop in 1759)	• The first regular Methodist fund at a national level is established to provide annual collections for Kingswood School • Charles Wesley makes his last itinerant preaching tour; after this he remains primarily in Bristol as he and Sarah start a family • Whitefield opens his new Tottenham Court Road Chapel in London	**1756**
• Leopold Mozart composes his *Concerto for Trombone in G Major* • Tobias Smollett begins publication of *A Complete History of England* (through 1765)	• David Hume publishes his *Four Dissertations: The Natural History of Religion, Of the Passions, Of Tragedy, Of the Standard of Taste* • Edmund Burke publishes his *Philosophical Enquiry in the Origin of our Ideas on the Sublime and the Beautiful*		• Wesley publishes his longest single theological treatise, *The Doctrine of Original Sin, According to Scripture, Reason and Experience* • Charles Wesley's son, Charles Jr., is born (d. 1834) • After consultation with Wesley, John William Fletcher is ordained priest of the Church of England	**1757**
• The Royal Library in London is transferred to the British Museum, becoming the foundation of the British Library • William Boyce becomes organist of the Chapel Royal	• Pope Benedict XIV dies; he is succeeded by Pope Clement XIII • Jean d'Alembert resigns from the *Encyclopédie* project but Denis Diderot carries on • Jonathan Edwards publishes *The Great Christian Doctrine of Original Sin Defended* shortly before his death from a failed inoculation against smallpox, which was then epidemic		• Nathaniel Gilbert travels from Antigua to meet Wesley in England; Wesley baptizes two of Gilbert's black slaves, which breaks the color barrier for Methodist societies • Wesley publishes his *Reasons Against a Separation from the Church of England*	**1758**

	A. WORLD HISTORY & POLITICS	B. AMERICAN HISTORY & POLITICS	C. SCIENCE, MEDICINE & TECHNOLOGY	D. DAILY LIFE, POPULAR CULTURE & ENTERTAINMENT
1758 cont.		• British forces also recapture Louisbourg on Cape Breton Island and Fort Fontenac on Lake Ontario		
1759	• The British defeat the French army at Lagos and Quiberon Bay • British and Hanoverian forces combine to defeat the French at Minden • King Ferdinand VI of Spain dies; he is succeeded by his half-brother Charles III	• British forces led by James Wolfe capture Quebec City, the capital of French Canada; Wolfe dies from wounds received during the battle • War erupts between Cherokee Indians, led by Oconostota, and white settlers in the Carolinas; it will last almost without interruption until 1785	• John Smeaton, regarded as the "father of civil engineering," completes construction of the third Eddystone Lighthouse in England, for which he pioneers the use of interlocking blocks of granite held together with water-resistant hydraulic lime mortar	• Edmund Burke and Robert Dodsley begin publication of the political review *The Annual Register*
1760	• Britain's King George II dies; he is succeeded by his son, George III • Austrian forces are defeated at Torgau; Berlin is burned by occupying Russian armies • The Boers, European settlers of Dutch and German descent who had first come to south Africa and established a colony at Cape Town in the 1650s, cross the Orange River and begin settlement of the south African interior • China declares that Canton (Guangahou) is the only port open to trade with Europeans • Ali Bey Al-Kabir becomes the Mamluk Sultan of Egypt	• The population of the American colonies is about 1.6 million • Montreal surrenders to British forces; French resistance in North America ends; Britain effectively controls most of the formerly French territory in North America • Benjamin Franklin publishes *The Interest of Great Britain Considered with Regard to Her Colonies*, urging the annexation of the remaining French territory in Canada • Cherokee warriors massacre the entire garrison at Fort Loudon on the Tennessee River; in reprisal, captured Cherokees being held as hostages at Fort St. George are executed • Governors of frontier colonies are instructed not to honor land grants that trespass on Indian lands; most ignore the order	• The Royal Botanical Gardens at Kew, London, are established • New York begins requiring that all physicians and surgeons pass prescribed tests and receive a license to practice medicine • Jared Eliot publishes *Essays Upon Field Husbandry in New England*, the first significant work adapting British agricultural techniques for American use	• Josiah Wedgwood founds his pottery works in Staffordshire, England • Edmund Hoyle defines the rules of the card game Whist • Tobacco prices fall sharply in Britain; many colonial farmers begin to plant corn and wheat instead
1761	• The Afghans defeat the Marathas, from southwest India, ending their advance into northern India and seriously weakening the Mogul Empire • The British largely eliminate French power in India after they take control of Pondicherry	• Boston attorney James Otis argues in court that "writs of assistance" (general search warrants permitting colonial customs officers to enter homes or businesses looking for contraband goods on which duties have not been paid) violated the "natural rights" of the colonists and that any act of Parliament violating those rights was null and void; John Adams will later cite this moment as "the first scene in the first act of resistance" to oppressive British policies	• The atmosphere of Venus is discovered by Russian scientist Mikhail Lomonosov	• Robert Hinchcliffe (England) creates scissors made of steel
1762	• Britain declares war on Spain, which had been planning to ally itself with France and Austria; the British then successfully attack Spanish outposts in the West Indies and Cuba, capturing Havana • Peter III becomes Tsar in Russia and withdraws Russia from the Seven Years' War	• Ethan Allen establishes an iron works in Salisbury, CT, which will become a major source of weapons in America	• John Roebuck converts cast iron for the first time into malleable iron at the Carron Ironworks in Scotland • Samuel Klingenstierna (Sweden) claims a prize from the Russian Academy of Science for the development of techniques to construct optical instruments that are free of chromatic aberration	• "Springfield Mountain," the earliest known American folk ballad, becomes popular • The Earl of Sandwich is said to have invented the sandwich by placing a slice of meat between two slices of bread so that he could eat without leaving the gaming tables

E. EDUCATION, LITERATURE & THE FINE ARTS	F. RELIGION, THEOLOGY, PHILOSOPHY & PSYCHOLOGY	G. AMERICAN & UNITED METHODISM	H. BRITISH & WORLD METHODISM	
	• The African Baptist or "Bluestone" Church is founded on the William Byrd plantation near the Bluestone River in Mecklenburg, VA; it is the first known black church in North America • The "Old Side" and "New Side" Presbyterians in the colonies reunite, but the rift (from 1741) never entirely heals			**1758 cont.**
• Joseph Haydn's *Symphony No. 1 in D Major* is considered by many to be the first major composition of the Classical era • Samuel Johnson's fable *The History of Rasselas, Prince of Abissinia* satirizes the philosophy of optimism and emphasizes the illusory nature of happiness • The British Museum opens to the public for the first time	• The Jesuit Order is expelled from Portugal and its territories, including Brazil • The *Encyclopédie* is formally suppressed by the Roman Catholic Church in France, but Denis Diderot continues clandestine work on it • Voltaire publishes his philosophical fantasy *Candide*, which ridicules the optimism of Leibniz and insists that this is not "the best of all possible worlds" • Adam Smith publishes *The Theory of Moral Sentiments*	• Jacob Albright is born	• Nathaniel Gilbert returns to Antigua and becomes the first Methodist preacher in the Caribbean • The Methodist chapel opens at Newbiggin-in-Teesdale, England [it is now the oldest Methodist chapel in the world in continuous use for weekly worship] • Wesley publishes *Thoughts on Christian Perfection* • Charles Wesley's daughter, Sarah, is born (d. 1828)	**1759**
• The Royal Society of the Arts is established in England and holds its first exhibition • British composer William Boyce completes his *Eight Symphonies* and begins publication of *Cathedral Music*, the first collection of church music in England to be printed in score (3 vols., 1760–73) • Johann Christian Bach (son of Johann Sebastian) becomes the organist of Milan Cathedral • Michael Haydn (the brother of Joseph) composes his *Concerto for Violin in B Flat Major*	• Denis Diderot begins work on *Rameau's Nephew* (completed in 1774, published posthumously in 1805)	• Richard Allen is born • Philip and Margaret Embury, Paul and Barbara Heck, and Robert Strawbridge, all immigrants from Ireland, are among the first Methodists to arrive in America	• Three Methodist preachers in Norwich administer the Lord's Supper in the Methodist Society there; they are strongly condemned by both John and Charles Wesley and expelled from the Society • Controversy over Christian perfection leads George Bell and Thomas Maxfield to leave the Methodist movement along with their followers • The West Street Chapel in London is remodeled • Selina, Countess of Huntingdon, begins building chapels throughout England, planting the seeds of what will later become her Connexion of Calvinistic Methodist congregations • John William Fletcher, staunch friend of the Wesleys and supporter of the Methodists, becomes vicar of Madeley, Shropshire • The first overseas Methodist Society is formed by John Gilbert in Antigua • Wesley publishes *Sermons on Several Occasions*, vol. 4	**1760**
• J. B. Delaborde (France) invents an electric harpsichord, the world's first electrical musical instrument • Benjamin Franklin perfects the "glassychord," later called the glass harmonica • Christoph Willibald Gluck completes his ballet *Don Juan*	• Jean-Jacques Rousseau publishes his philosophical romance *The New Heloise* • Ezra Stiles publishes his *Discourse on the Christian Union*, advancing the notion that the various church groups ("sects") in America "will unavoidably become a mutual balance upon one another"		• Conference establishes the "General Fund," to which every Methodist in England is expected to contribute; used primarily for paying costs of building preaching houses • Wesley approves the public speaking of Mary Bosanquet and Sarah Crosby but counsels them to avoid assuming the "character" of a preacher • Francis Asbury experiences conversion at the age of 16 and becomes a Methodist local preacher	**1761**
• The Sorbonne Library in Paris is established • Wolfgang Amadeus Mozart, a child musical prodigy, tours Europe at the age of 6, performing on the piano and harpsichord in Paris and London • Christoph Gluck's *Orpheus and Eurydice* transforms opera by emphasizing drama • Georg Philipp Telemann composes his *Christmas Oratorio* • Italian artist Giovanni Pannini completes his sculpture for the Trevi *(cont.)*	• William Warburton, now Bishop of Gloucester, attacks both the Deists and the "enthusiasts" (meaning both Wesley and Whitefield and their respective followers) in *The Doctrine of Grace: Or, the Office and Operations of the Holy Spirit Vindicated from the Insults of Infidelity and the Abuse of Fanaticism* • William Hogarth's engraving *Credulity, Superstition and Fanaticism* is a satirical attack upon Methodism, meaning the followers of both the Wesleys and Whitefield		• Whitefield attends and participates in the conference of Wesley's preachers at Leeds • Wesley responds strongly to Bishop Warburton's attack on Methodism in his *Letter to the Right Reverend The Lord Bishop of London*	**1762**

	A. WORLD HISTORY & POLITICS	B. AMERICAN HISTORY & POLITICS	C. SCIENCE, MEDICINE & TECHNOLOGY	D. DAILY LIFE, POPULAR CULTURE & ENTERTAINMENT
1762 cont.	• Peter III dies after six months on the throne; his wife becomes Tsarina Catherine II and will be known to history as Catherine the Great			
1763	• The Treaty of Paris I ends the Seven Years' War: Britain takes control of all French territory in North America east of the Mississippi River, except New Orleans; Spain acquires the Louisiana Territory of North America (west of the Mississippi River) from France but gives up east and west Florida to Britain in return for Cuba; France concedes India to Britain; Prussia emerges as a major European power • Rio de Janeiro becomes the capital of Brazil	• The French and Indian War also comes to an end; the British and French both abandon the Indian tribes who have been allied with them • Ottawa chieftain Pontiac leads a group of Indian tribes in "Pontiac's Rebellion" against the British and Americans; they capture and destroy eight smaller forts but fail to take Fort Pitt or Fort Detroit, despite besieging the latter for five months • Further British settlement in America is restricted by royal proclamation to the area east of the Appalachian Mountains in order to prevent new wars with the American Indian tribes; American settlers pay no attention to the proclamation	• James Hargreaves (UK) invents the "spinning jenny," which enables one operator to spin several yarns at once	• *St. James' Chronicle* is first published in London
1764	• Stanislaus II becomes King of Poland; Russia and Prussia agree to cooperate in Polish affairs • British military victories in India give them uncontested control of the Bengal and Bihar regions	• Britain passes the Currency Act, which prohibits the use of paper money as legal tender for the payment of debts in America, and the Plantation Act, which reduces the duty on imported foreign molasses but places a high duty on refined sugar and prohibits foreign rum; both measures are intended to raise revenue from the American colonies to pay for the Seven Years' War; both spark colonial protests • James Otis publishes *The Rights of the British Colonies Asserted and Proved*, in which he asserts that "the colonists are by the law of nature free born, as indeed all men are, white or black" • The first permanent white settlement is established at St. Louis, the "Gateway to the West"	• Scottish engineer James Watt develops the condenser, which greatly improves the power and efficiency of the steam engine • Pierre Fournier of France develops the point system to measure type sizes; his system is further refined by François Didot, establishing consistency in type measurement throughout the world	• The practice of giving street numbers to houses is introduced in London
1765	• Holy Roman Emperor Francis I dies; he is succeeded by his son (with Theresa Maria), Joseph II, establishing the Hapsburg-Lorraine dynasty in Austria	• The Stamp Act (requiring the purchase of tax stamps to be affixed to everything from legal documents to newspapers) and the Quartering Act (for housing and feeding British troops in America at colonial expense) are passed by Parliament; both provoke outrage in the American colonies • The Sons of Liberty, a secret patriotic organization led by Samuel Adams and Paul Revere, is formed to oppose the Stamp Act • The Stamp Act Congress, comprised of delegates from 9 of the 13 colonies, convenes in New York City; it denounces "taxation without representation," adopts a "Declaration of Rights and Grievances" to be submitted to the King and Parliament, and recommends a trade boycott of British goods	• The first medical school in America is established at the College of Philadelphia (later the University of Pennsylvania) • Italian biologist Lazzaro Spallanzani first suggests the possibility of preserving food by sealing it into containers that air cannot penetrate ("hermetic sealing")	• English publisher John Newbery brings out a book of *Mother Goose* rhymes and publishes his children's book *The History of Little Goody Two-Shoes* • Boulanger's Restaurant in Paris is the first public place where any diner might order a meal from a menu offering a choice of dishes
1766	• Louis de Bougainville sets out on a voyage across the Pacific on which he discovers Tahiti, the Solomon Islands, and New Guinea	• The Stamp Act is repealed after British merchants complain about their loss of trade as a result of the colonial boycott • The Declaratory Act asserts the full power of Parliament to make laws binding in the colonies "in all cases whatsoever"	• Henry Cavendish discovers that hydrogen is lighter than air • American naturalist George Crogham discovers fossilized mastodon bones at a place called Big Bone Lick on the Ohio River	• The first paved sidewalk in London is laid down in Westminster • Chocolate is manufactured in America for the first time by John Hanin and James Baker in Dorchester, MA, from cocoa beans imported from the West Indies; by 1780 they are marketing "Baker's Chocolate"

E. EDUCATION, LITERATURE & THE FINE ARTS	F. RELIGION, THEOLOGY, PHILOSOPHY & PSYCHOLOGY	G. AMERICAN & UNITED METHODISM	H. BRITISH & WORLD METHODISM	
Fountain (of "three coins in the fountain" fame) in Rome • Robert Lowth publishes his *Short Introduction to English Grammar*, which distinguishes sharply between informal speech and informal writing	• Jean-Jacques Rousseau publishes both *Emile*, expounding a novel theory of education, and *The Social Contract*, which defends the will of the people against divine right of kings			**1762 cont.**
• Joseph Haydn completes his *Symphonies No. 12 and 13* • James Boswell is introduced to Samuel Johnson at Thomas Davies' bookshop in London • British artist Joseph Wright paints the best-known of his "candlelight pictures," *The Orrery*	• The Jewish community of Newport, RI, completes and dedicates the Truro Synagogue [it is the oldest surviving synagogue in the US] • Voltaire publishes his *Treatise on Tolerance*	• Robert Strawbridge begins itinerant preaching and organizes a Methodist society at Sams Creek, MD; John Evans becomes the first known Methodist convert in America • Whitefield makes his sixth trip to America	• Conference establishes the "Preacher's Fund" to pay pensions to "worn out" preachers and their widows and children • The "Large" *Minutes*, which becomes the basic handbook of Methodist discipline, are published for the first time • Wesley creates the Model Deed as the basis for Methodist property deeds; it establishes doctrinal standards for Methodist preachers, who are to preach "no other doctrine than is contained in Mr. Wesley's *Notes Upon the New Testament* and four volumes of *Sermons*" • Wesley publishes *A Survey of the Wisdom of God in Creation; or, a Compendium of Natural Philosophy* (1st edition in 2 vols.; 4th edition in 5 vols., 1777)	**1763**
• Rhode Island College is founded in Warren, RI; in 1770 it moves to Providence, and in 1804 it is renamed Brown University • The eight-year-old W. A. Mozart becomes a pupil of Johann Christian Bach • Johann Winckelmann publishes his *History of Ancient Art* • Horace Walpole creates the gothic novel with *The Castle of Otranto*	• France suppresses the Jesuit Order in the country and all its territories • Voltaire completes his influential *Philosophical Dictionary* • Thomas Reid publishes *An Inquiry into the Human Mind on the Principles of Common Sense*	• A log meetinghouse is built by the Methodist society at Sam's Creek, MD, and used as a preaching station by Robert Strawbridge; it is the first Methodist building erected in America [the building has not survived]	• The octagonal stone preaching houses at Yarm (Northumberland) and Heptonstall (Yorkshire) are completed; Wesley is enthusiastic about the design • Wesley's sister Susanna ("Suky," b. 1695) dies	**1764**
• W. A. Mozart composes his *Symphony No. 1* • C. P. E. Bach composes his *Oboe Concerto in E Flat* • Samuel Johnson completes his edition of *The Works of William Shakespeare* • English jurist William Blackstone begins publication of his classic *Commentaries on the Laws of England* (through 1769)	• Jonathan Edwards's important treatise on *The Nature of True Virtue*, published posthumously, describes true or genuine virtue as disinterested love (benevolence) toward God as "Being in general" and toward other beings in proportion to their "degree of being" • Samuel Hopkins publishes *An Inquiry Into the Promises of the Gospel*	• Whitefield returns to England • Robert Strawbridge organizes his second Methodist society in Leesburg, VA	• Wesley publishes *A Plain Account of Christian Perfection* (first edition) and "The Scripture Way of Salvation," one of his most important sermons • Wesley begins the annual publication of the "Large" *Minutes* • Sarah Crosby, Sarah Ryan, and Mary Bosanquet establish a school and orphanage in Leytonstone, Essex; it moves to Cross Hall in Yorkshire in 1770 • Charles Wesley's health deteriorates, and he basically retires from itinerant preaching and moves with his family from Bristol to Bath • Whitefield participates in dedication of Lady Huntingdon's Chapel in Bath	**1765**
• The first permanent American theater building, Southwark Theater, is erected in Philadelphia • Joseph Haydn composes his *Great Mass in E Flat*	• Tsarina Catherine the Great allows complete freedom of worship in Russia • Gotthold Lessing publishes *Laocoon: An Essay on the Limits of Painting and Poetry*	• Barbara Heck and Philip Embury establish a Methodist society (with class meetings) in New York City; Barbara Heck's black servant, Betty, is one of the members • The United Ministers, a nonsectarian group, is established; it is a forerunner of the United Brethren Church	• Methodism is established in Canada by Laurence Coughlin, one of Wesley's traveling preachers, who immigrates from Ireland to Newfoundland • Charles Wesley's son, Samuel, is born (d. 1837)	**1766**

	A. WORLD HISTORY & POLITICS	B. AMERICAN HISTORY & POLITICS	C. SCIENCE, MEDICINE & TECHNOLOGY	D. DAILY LIFE, POPULAR CULTURE & ENTERTAINMENT
1766 cont.		• "Pontiac's Rebellion" is ended by a peace treaty that pardons the Indians but takes much of their traditional territory		
1767	• Military forces from Burma invade Siam (Thailand) and destroy the capital city of Ayutthaya • James Rennell is appointed Surveyor-General of Bengal and begins the first geographical survey of India	• New York Assembly refuses to pay for quartering British troops and is suspended • Parliament passes the notorious Townshend Acts, which require the colonies to pay import duties on tea, glass, lead, oil, paper, and painters' colors • Philadelphia attorney John Dickinson writes a series of "Letters from a Farmer in Pennsylvania" (1767–68), which are first published in the *Pennsylvania Chronicle*, stating positions that become central for American colonists resisting British policies of colonial taxation • Daniel Boone makes his first exploratory trip through the "wilderness" of the Shawnee and Cherokee Indian homeland, starting from North Carolina going west of the Appalachian Mountains through the Cumberland Gap • Charles Mason and Jeremiah Dixon complete their survey (begun in 1763) of the border between Pennsylvania and Maryland, which comes to be called the Mason-Dixon Line	• Joseph Priestley publishes *The History and Present State of Electricity* • King's College (later Columbia University) in New York opens the second medical school in America	• David Garrick writes and stars in the popular play *A Peep Behind the Curtain*
1768	• James Cook sails on his first attempt to circumnavigate the world [he returns in 1771] • Ali Bey, the Mamluk Sultan of Egypt, overthrows the Ottoman governor of Egypt and in 1769 declares independence from the Ottoman Empire • Civil war erupts in Poland when a group of Polish nobles form the Confederation of Bar to support Polish independence • Tsarina Catherine the Great dispatches Russian troops to restore order in Poland • The Ottoman Turks, alarmed by Russian intervention in Poland and urged on by France, declare war on Russia	• The Iroquois Confederation signs the Treaty of Fort Stanwyx, which establishes a boundary between white and Indian territory but conveys much of the land between the Tennessee and Ohio rivers to white control • All of the colonial Assemblies urge opposition to the Townshend Acts • The Massachusetts Assembly refuses to aid in tax collection and is dissolved by order of the colonial governor • Boston refuses to house British troops, who then occupy the town	• The experiments of Lazzaro Spallanzani (Italy) prove that boiling kills bacteria • Swiss mathematician Leonhard Euler publishes the first volume of his *Integral Calculus* (to 1770)	• Sheet music is first published and sold in Boston • The New York Chamber of Commerce, the first organization of the kind in America, is formed
1769	• James Cook surveys and charts the coastline of New Zealand • Russian forces overrun Moldavia and Wallachia and enter Bucharest • King Frederick II of Prussia and Holy Roman Emperor Joseph II of Austria meet to discuss the partition of Poland • The French East India Company is dissolved	• The Virginia Assembly passes "Virginia's Resolutions," stating that only Virginia's legislature could tax its citizens • The colonial governor of Virginia dissolves the Virginia Assembly • Colonial seaports up and down the coast draw up agreements not to allow the import of British goods • San Diego de Alcala (Mission San Diego), the first in a series of 21 California missions along the coast, is founded by the Franciscan Friars	• Richard Arkwright builds the first completely mechanized, water-powered spinning mill in England, a landmark in Britain's industrial revolution • James Watt patents his design for the reciprocating steam engine • French engineer Nicolas Cugnot designs a steam-powered vehicle that is usually considered to be the first self-propelled car	• Dartmouth College is established in Hanover, NH, with a royal charter authorizing it to provide "education and instruction of Youth and of the Indian Tribes in this Land . . . and also of English Youth and any others" • Boston harpsichord maker John Harris constructs the first spinet made in the colonies
1770	• King Louis XVI of France marries Marie Antoinette of Austria • The Russian fleet destroys a Turkish fleet in the Aegean Sea	• The population of the American colonies is about 2.1 million • Parliament repeals the Townshend Acts, removing tax on glass, paper, and dye in the colonies, but the tea tax remains in place	• John Warren and several other students at Harvard form a society for the secret dissection of animals; it will later become the Massachusetts Medical Society	• Joseph Priestley discovers that caoutchouc (India gum) can be used to erase lead pencil marks; he calls it "rubber" because it "rubs out" the marks

E. EDUCATION, LITERATURE & THE FINE ARTS	F. RELIGION, THEOLOGY, PHILOSOPHY & PSYCHOLOGY	G. AMERICAN & UNITED METHODISM	H. BRITISH & WORLD METHODISM	
• Michael Haydn composes his *Symphony in B Flat Major* • Oliver Goldsmith publishes his classic (and only) novel, *The Vicar of Wakefield*	• Anthony Benezet writes *A Caution and Warning to Great Britain on the Calamitous State of the Enslaved Negroes in the British Dominions*			**1766 cont.**
• Laurence Sterne completes his most important work, *The Life and Opinions of Tristram Shandy* (9 vols., 1759–67), creating a literary sensation • C. P. E. Bach succeeds his godfather, Telemann, as director of church music in Hamburg • Johann Christian Bach gives the earliest known public solo piano concert in London • Jean-Jacques Rousseau publishes his *Dictionnaire de musique* (Musical Dictionary)	• Spain expels the Jesuit Order from the country and all of its colonial possessions	• Thomas Webb forms "The Religious Society of Protestants Called Methodists" in Philadelphia • The New York society rents the "Rigging Loft" for their services • William Otterbein meets Mennonite bishop Martin Boehm and proclaims *"Wir sind Brüder!"* ("We are brothers!")	• Francis Asbury is accepted as a full-time itinerant preacher and becomes a member of Conference	**1767**
• The first edition of the *Encyclopedia Britannica* is published in Edinburgh • The Royal Academy of Arts is founded in London; British painter Joshua Reynolds is elected as its first president • "The Liberty Song," written by John Dickinson, is considered the first American patriotic song • John Singleton Copley completes his portrait of *Paul Revere*, depicting the soon-to-be-famous patriot-silversmith holding one of his silver teapots	• Herman Samuel Reimarus, one of the pioneers of critical biblical scholarship, dies in Germany; his massive *Apology of the Rational Worshipers of God* remains unpublished until portions are published by Gotthold Lessing (1774–78)	• The New York society outgrows the "Rigging Loft" and builds Wesley Chapel on John Street, known as the John Street Church [it survives until 1814 when it is replaced by a larger structure] • American Methodists request that Wesley send them experienced preachers qualified to nourish and supervise the growth of the movement	• Methodism grows to 34 circuits, half of which have over 800 members, requiring the appointment of a General Steward to handle the finances of each circuit • Selina, Countess of Huntingdon, opens Trevecca College in Wales; Whitefield participates in the opening ceremonies • Wesley publishes his *Free Thoughts on the Present State of Public Affairs*	**1768**
• W. A. Mozart composes his *Te Deum in C* • Johann Albrechtsberger composes his *Concerto for Trombone in B Flat Major* • David Garrick organizes the first Shakespeare Festival at Stratford-upon-Avon	• Pope Clement XIII dies; he is succeeded by Pope Clement XIV	• Whitefield makes his seventh trip to America • Wesley sends Richard Boardman and Joseph Pilmore to America; Boardman is designated "chief assistant"; they begin holding quarterly conferences on the British pattern • The Philadelphia society purchases and completes construction of the unfinished St. George's Church, which had been abandoned by a German Reformed congregation [it is now the oldest surviving Methodist church in America and is regarded as the "Mother Church of American Methodism"]	• Hannah Ball begins the first Methodist Sunday school at High Wycombe, near London • Wesley again endorses the public speaking of Sarah Crosby but cautions her to "keep as far from what is called preaching as you can" • The first Methodist preaching house in Canada is constructed near Blackhead in modern Nova Scotia	**1769**
• Johann Wolfgang von Goethe completes the first part of *Faust* • British artist Thomas Gainsborough completes his painting *The Blue Boy* • William Billings, America's first notable composer, produces *The New England Psalm Singer*, which shows the deep influence of Isaac Watts	• Scottish philosopher James Beattie attacks the skepticism of David Hume in *An Essay on the Nature and Immutability of Truth*; he is dismissed by Hume as a "minute philosopher"	• Whitefield dies and is buried in Newburyport, MA • The Methodist society in Leesburg, VA, completes and dedicates the Methodist chapel later known as The Old Stone Church [begun in 1766, the building survives until 1902]	• Wesley preaches the "official" funeral sermon for Whitefield both at the Moorfields Tabernacle and Tottenham Court Road Chapel, then again five days later at Greenwich Tabernacle; he irritates some of Whitefield's followers by failing to *(cont.)*	**1770**

	A. WORLD HISTORY & POLITICS	B. AMERICAN HISTORY & POLITICS	C. SCIENCE, MEDICINE & TECHNOLOGY	D. DAILY LIFE, POPULAR CULTURE & ENTERTAINMENT
1770 cont.	• James Cook surveys and charts the eastern coast of Australia, including Botany Bay and the Great Barrier Reef, formally claiming it for Britain • Scottish explorer James Bruce discovers the source of the Blue Nile at the spectacular Tisisat Falls of Lake Tana in modern Ethiopia	• Five Americans are killed by British troops in the "Boston Massacre," including Crispus Attucks, a free black sailor • Paul Revere publishes his engraving "The Bloody Massacre," which spreads outrage throughout the colonies		
1771	• Russia completes its conquest of the Crimea, in the process destroying an Ottoman fleet and alarming the Austrians and Prussians • Prussia's King Frederick II arranges for the partition of Poland by agreement among Austria, Russia, and Prussia	• Spanish settlers establish Mission San Gabriel Arcángel in what is now California	• The *Transactions of the American Philosophical Society* are published for the first time • The work of Henry Cavendish on electrical force leads to his mathematical "single-fluid" theory of electricity	• "Visiting cards" or "Calling cards" become popular in England • The "tower" becomes a popular hairstyle among wealthy colonial women; the hair is piled high, heavily greased, then decorated with ribbons, lace, feathers, etc.
1772	• William Murray, Britain's Lord Chief Justice, rules in the Somersett case that "as soon as any slave sets foot in England he becomes free"; this effectively ends slavery in Britain, but not throughout the British empire • James Bruce charts the course of the Blue Nile to its confluence with the White Nile • James Cook sails from England on his second voyage to the Pacific; he returns in 1775	• The Boston Assembly threatens secession from Great Britain • The British government decides that colonial officials in Boston will be paid directly, making them independent of the Assembly • The British revenue cutter *Gaspee* is attacked and burned by Americans in Narragansett Bay • Samuel Adams leads an effort to form Committees of Correspondence in all of the colonies to further the protest against British oppression	• Joseph Priestley and Daniel Rutherford independently discover nitrogen • The first carriage road is constructed through the Brenner Pass of the Tyrolean Alps between Austria and Italy	• Joseph Priestley creates carbonated water, popularly called "soda water"
1773	• James Cook is the first European to cross the Antarctic Circle; he charts Tonga and Easter Island during the winter, and discovers New Caledonia • The British parliament passes the Regulating Act, which limits the authority of the East India Company and appoints a Governor-General for India • Cossacks and peasants in southeast Russia unsuccessfully revolt against the government of Catherine the Great • The Ottoman Turks suppress the revolts against their rule in Egypt and Syria; Ali Bey is killed in Cairo	• Passage of the Tea Act by the British parliament allows the East India Company to monopolize the colonial tea trade through its own agents; this provokes the Boston Tea Party, in which colonists disguised as Indians dump $10,000 worth of tea into Boston Harbor • Similar "tea parties" occur in Philadelphia, New York, Maine, North Carolina, and Maryland	• The world's first cast-iron bridge is built by John Wilkinson and Abraham Darby across the Severn River at Coalbrookdale, Shropshire; it has a 100-foot arch, is 52 feet tall and 34 feet wide, and weighs 378 tons; it still stands and is called "The Stonehenge of the Industrial Revolution" • The British government prize for accurate determination of longitude (first offered in 1714) is awarded to John Harrison for his chronometer	• Oliver Goldsmith's boisterous comedy *She Stoops to Conquer* premieres at the Covent Garden Theater in London • The first large-scale street lighting project in America begins in Boston
1774	• Russia and the Ottoman Empire sign the Treaty of Kuchuk Kainarji and end their war (since 1768); Russia annexes most of the Crimea and secures free navigation on the Black Sea; the Ottoman Turks retain control of Moldavia and Wallachia	• The Coercive ("Intolerable") Acts are passed by Parliament in reaction to the Boston Tea Party (and others); British troops close the port of Boston until the East India Company is reimbursed for its tea	• Joseph Priestley discovers oxygen (which he calls "dephlogisticated air") • British iron maker John Wilkinson invents a cannon-boring machine that is safer and more precise than any other in use at the time	• The *Royal American Magazine* begins publication; it is the first magazine to use illustrations regularly, including engravings by Paul Revere attacking British tyranny and oppression

E. EDUCATION, LITERATURE & THE FINE ARTS	F. RELIGION, THEOLOGY, PHILOSOPHY & PSYCHOLOGY	G. AMERICAN & UNITED METHODISM	H. BRITISH & WORLD METHODISM	
• The first known performance of portions of Handel's *Messiah* in America takes place at George Burn's Music Room in the New York City Tavern • Quaker antislavery activist Anthony Benezet establishes the Negro School in Philadelphia for the education of American blacks	• Paul-Henri Dietrich, Baron d'Holbach denies the existence of God, describes the universe as "matter in motion," and grounds morality on happiness in his most important work, *The System of Nature*	• The first Methodist Love Feast service in America is held by Joseph Pilmore at St. George's Church in Philadelphia • Mary Evans Thorne is appointed as a class leader by Joseph Pilmore in Philadelphia; she is probably the first woman in the colonies to hold this position	mention predestination as among those key doctrines that Whitefield had always affirmed • Following Whitefield's death, Wesley and the Conference say that they have "leaned too close to Calvinism," sparking controversy with the Calvinistic Methodists and provoking Augustus Toplady to publish his venomous *Letter to Mr. Wesley* attacking Wesley's Arminianism • John William Fletcher emerges as the champion of the Wesleyan position with his *Checks to Antinomianism* (five separate works, 1770–75) • Wesley's sister Emilia ("Emily" b. 1692) dies	**1770 cont.**
• The Royal Theatre Ballet School in Copenhagen, Denmark, is founded • English instrument maker Robert Stodart takes out a patent using the name "Grand" to describe his piano • Luigi Boccherini composes his *Minuet in G* • Mozart completes his *Symphonies No. 12, 13, and 14* • Tobias Smollett publishes *The Expedition of Humphry Clinker*	• Johann Salmo Semler publishes his revolutionary *Treatise on the Free Investigation of the Canon* (4 vols., 1771–75), one of the foundational works of "higher criticism" of the Bible • Anthony Benezet publishes *Some Historical Account of Guinea, its Produce, and the General Disposition of its Inhabitants, with an Inquiry into the Rise and Progress of the Slave Trade, its Nature and Calamitous Effects*, which has a galvanizing effect on John Wesley	• Wesley sends Francis Asbury and Richard Wright to America; Asbury is designated "chief assistant" and preaches his first American sermon at St. George's Church • The German Evangelical Reformed Church congregation in Baltimore is organized [later called the "Old Otterbein Church"]	• Wesley publishes his *Collected Works* (the "Pine edition," 32 vols., 1771–74) • The Calvinist controversy heats up as Wesley satirizes Toplady's views in *The Consequence Proved* and Toplady responds with the scalding *More Work for Mr. Wesley* • Wesley accepts the preaching of Mary Bosanquet and Sarah Crosby as an exception to the general rule against women preachers because of what he regards as their "extraordinary call," but does not change the "Large" *Minutes* to authorize women as preachers generally • Charles Wesley and his family move from Bath to London • Molly (Mrs. John) Wesley leaves London to live with her married daughter in Newcastle; Wesley declines to call her back to London	**1771**
• Joseph Haydn composes his *Symphony No. 45 (Farewell)* • Charles W. Peale, the most important American painter of the time, produces a life-size portrait of George Washington	• Johann Gottfried von Herder publishes his influential essay *On the Origins of Language*	• William Watters becomes the first native-born American Methodist itinerant preacher, followed by Philip Gatch in 1773 and Freeborn Garrettson in 1776	• Wesley spends several months in Scotland • Thomas Coke is ordained priest of the Church of England	**1772**
• Johann Albrechtsberger composes his *Concerto for Harp in C Major* • The Philadelphia Museum is established, largely due to the efforts of Benjamin Franklin • Phillis Wheatley, generally recognized as the first black writer of consequence in America, publishes her *Poems on Various Subjects, Religious and Moral* with the assistance of Selina, Countess of Huntingdon; it includes her best-known poem "To the University of Cambridge in New England"	• The Jesuit Order is expelled from the Austrian Empire and is then suppressed globally by order of Pope Clement XIV • The important sermon by Isaac Backus, "An Appeal to the Public for Religious Liberty," articulates and defines the Baptist faith in the late colonial period • New England clergyman Samuel Hopkins publishes *An Inquiry Into the Nature of True Holiness*	• Wesley sends George Shadford and Thomas Rankin to America; Rankin is designated "chief assistant"; Rankin and Francis Asbury soon clash • The first conference of American Methodist preachers meets at St. George's Church in Philadelphia; the annual conference now begins in addition to the quarterly conferences on each circuit	• Wesley asks the preachers at Conference to sign "articles of agreement" to adhere to covenant relationship with each other and to uphold "the old Methodist doctrines" and discipline; 43 preachers do so	**1773**
• Antonio Salieri, who will become W. A. Mozart's great rival, is appointed court composer to Holy Roman Emperor Joseph II • Joseph Haydn completes his *Great Organ Mass*	• Pope Clement XIV dies; he is succeeded in 1775 by Pope Pius VI • Mother Ann Lee arrives from England with a group of followers called the United Society of Believers in Christ's Second *(cont.)*	• Wesley recalls Boardman and Pilmore to England and sends James Dempster and Martin Rodda to replace them • The annual conference determines that Wright should be sent back to England	• Wesley's *Thoughts Upon Slavery*, immediately inspired by his reading of Anthony Benezet's 1771 work, condemns slavery, most especially in America	**1774**

	A. WORLD HISTORY & POLITICS	B. AMERICAN HISTORY & POLITICS	C. SCIENCE, MEDICINE & TECHNOLOGY	D. DAILY LIFE, POPULAR CULTURE & ENTERTAINMENT
1774 cont.	• Grigory Potemkin becomes the lover of Tsarina Catherine the Great of Russia and takes effective control of Russian policy, helping to create the "New Russia" • The British parliament passes the Quebec Act, vesting the government of Quebec in a governor and council, preserving the French Civil Code of Law, and establishing the Roman Catholic Church • King Louis XV of France dies; he is succeeded by his grandson, Louis XVI • Mt. Vesuvius, near Pompeii, Italy, erupts	• The first Continental Congress meets in Philadelphia with delegates from all the colonies except Georgia; petitions of grievances are sent to the king of England • Rhode Island becomes the first American colony to pass legislation prohibiting the importation of black slaves		
1775	• Britain hires 29,000 German and Hessian mercenaries for the coming war in North America • Tsarina Catherine the Great reorganizes Russian provincial administration to tighten government control over rural regions	• Patrick Henry addresses the Virginia legislature, encouraging Virginians to arm themselves, saying "give me liberty or give me death" • The Second Continental Congress meets, raises an army, and names George Washington as commander-in-chief of American forces • The Revolutionary War begins: Paul Revere makes his famous ride; "the shot heard 'round the world" rings out when American Minutemen confront British troops at the Battle of Lexington; Ethan Allen and his "Green Mountain Boys" capture Fort Ticonderoga (NY) from the British; the British defeat colonial forces at Bunker Hill in Boston • Congress drafts the "Olive Branch" Petition, outlining the major issues of American concern asking the British government to respond; King George III refuses to accept the petition, believing that the American rebellion can quickly be crushed by military force • Anthony Benezet organizes the forerunner of the Pennsylvania Abolition Society in Philadelphia • Daniel Boone blazes the "Wilderness Road" trail from Virginia through the Cumberland Gap into Kentucky and establishes the settlement of Boonesborough on the Kentucky River; settlers soon begin moving into Shawnee and Cherokee lands in the Ohio Valley region	• Joseph Priestley discovers hydrochloric and sulfuric acids • George Washington observes burning natural gas that escapes from the ground in the Ohio Valley • John Lorrimer invents the dipping needle compass	• Anna Maria Schwiigel is the last person executed for witchcraft in Germany • Colonial government regulations close down theaters and coffee houses and prohibit sporting events throughout America • English inventor Alexander Cummings receives a patent for putting a water trap under a toilet bowl, a major step toward the modern flush toilet
1776	• James Cook leaves England on his third voyage to the Pacific • Russia creates a major naval force in the Black Sea • Siam (Thailand) succeeds in driving Burmese military forces out of the country and restoring the traditional Thai monarchy	• The Virginia Constitutional Convention approves the "Declaration of Rights"; it is widely copied by the other colonies and becomes the basis of the Bill of Rights in 1789 • Congress adopts the Declaration of Independence, formalizing the break with Great Britain • Benjamin Franklin is appointed as Ambassador to France • The Virginia State Constitution is adopted; it becomes a model for all the colonies as they transform themselves into states • The new American states adopt oaths of loyalty, some of which are very harsh in their condemnation of Britain • American troops under Henry Knox use cannons removed from Fort Ticonderoga to force the British to evacuate Boston	• David Bushnell invents a hand-operated, one-man submarine called the American Turtle; it is the first vessel to use propellers for both horizontal and vertical movement; he unsuccessfully uses it to try to blow up a British warship in Boston harbor by attaching time bombs to its hull • Lionel Chambers publishes *An Account of the Weather and Diseases in South Carolina*, advancing the theory that the two are related	• Richard Sheridan's farcical drama *The Rivals* introduces the world to the memorable Mrs. Malaprop • The *Pennsylvania Evening Post* devotes its entire front page and most of the second page to publishing the Declaration of Independence • Thomas Paine's *Common Sense*, which urges and supports American independence from Britain, sells more than 100,000 copies in 3 months • Philip Freneau, called "The Poet of the American Revolution," begins publishing his biting satires of the British

E. EDUCATION, LITERATURE & THE FINE ARTS	F. RELIGION, THEOLOGY, PHILOSOPHY & PSYCHOLOGY	G. AMERICAN & UNITED METHODISM	H. BRITISH & WORLD METHODISM	
• Carl Stamitz composes his *Concerto for Viola in D Major* • William Billings organizes the first known singing school in America in Stoughton, MA • Thomas Jefferson publishes *A Summary View of the Rights of British America* • Goethe's novel *The Sorrows of Young Werther* exemplifies the *Sturm und Drang* ("Storm and Stress") movement in German literature, the forerunner of German Romanticism	Coming (better known as the "Shakers"); they establish a community at New Lebanon, NY • John Woolman's *Journal* is published posthumously • Gotthold Lessing anonymously publishes portions of the manuscript of Reimarus's *Apology* as the "Wolfenbüttel Fragments" (1774–78)	• Lovely Lane Chapel is built in Baltimore • William Otterbein becomes pastor of the German Evangelical Reformed Church in Baltimore • Philip Embury and Barbara Heck move to Montreal	• Toplady publishes his *Historic Proof of the Doctrinal Calvinism of the Church of England*, in which he attempts to show that Wesleyan Methodism has deviated from fundamental Anglican doctrine; Wesley ignores it, choosing not to "fight with chimney sweeps" • Toplady becomes the editor of the *Gospel Magazine* and turns it into a formidable weapon against Wesley and the Methodists	**1774 cont.**
• John Behrent makes and advertises a square piano in Philadelphia; it is the first piano known to be made in America • W. A. Mozart completes his *Violin Concerti No. 3, 4, and 5* • Karl Ditters von Dittersdorf completes his *Concerto for Oboe in D Major*	• Joseph Priestley publishes *Hartley's Theory of the Human Mind*	• Methodists in America begin to experience hostility, in large part because of Wesley's strenuous opposition to revolution against the British monarchy • Many members of the Continental Congress attend services at St. George's Church in Philadelphia • James Dempster is forced to retire from itinerant ministry due to ill health	• Wesley plagiarizes Samuel Johnson's pamphlet *Taxation no Tyranny* and publishes his version as *A Calm Address to Our American Colonies*, which condemns armed revolution • Both Joseph Benson and John William Fletcher propose plans for restructuring the order of Methodism along specifically ecclesiastical lines; neither proposal is ever approved or enacted • Thomas Coke receives his Doctor of Civil Laws degree	**1775**
• The Bolshoi Ballet is founded in Moscow and the Bolshoi Theater hosts its first full concert season • English musicologist Charles Burney publishes his *History of Music* • W. A. Mozart composes his *Haffner Serenade* • Edward Gibbon begins publication of his classic account of *The Decline and Fall of the Roman Empire* (to 1788) • Joseph Wright completes his masterful artistic depiction of *An Eruption of Vesuvius Seen from Portici*	• Adam Smith publishes his *Inquiry into the Nature and Causes of the Wealth of Nations*, the first attempt to analyze the nature of capital and study the historical development of trade and industry • Toplady publishes *Psalms and Hymns for Public and Private Worship*; it includes the hymn "Rock of Ages," written as he sought shelter amid the rocks of the Cheddar Gorge in England during a fierce thunderstorm	• The Church of England is formally disestablished in America, first in Virginia and then throughout the colonies; disestablishment is opposed by most Methodists, who consider themselves part of the Church of England and are dependent on it for the sacraments; Methodist opposition to disestablishment angers Congregationalists, Baptists, and Presbyterians, all of whom are seen by the Church of England as "dissenters" • Methodists, especially the preachers, come to be seen as "Tories," supporters of the British monarchy and opponents of American independence • Francis Asbury is arrested and fined £5 for not having taken an oath of loyalty to the state of Maryland	• Wesley publishes *Some Thoughts on Liberty*, again attacking the cause of American independence • A final, permanent separation takes place between Mr. and Mrs. John Wesley	**1776**

	A. WORLD HISTORY & POLITICS	B. AMERICAN HISTORY & POLITICS	C. SCIENCE, MEDICINE & TECHNOLOGY	D. DAILY LIFE, POPULAR CULTURE & ENTERTAINMENT
1776 cont.		• The British defeat a small colonial fleet commanded by Benedict Arnold on Lake Champlain, but the campaign slows the advance of British troops from Canada long enough to force them into winter quarters • British troops under William Howe capture New York City and defeat the Continental army at White Plains, NY, forcing Washington to retreat into Pennsylvania • A major fire, apparently set by American troops retreating in the face of Howe's advance, destroys much of the older part of New York City • In a surprise winter attack, American forces commanded by Washington cross the Delaware River to defeat British forces at Trenton and then at Princeton, NJ • The British capture Nathan Hale and hang him as a spy: "I regret that I have but one life to give for my country" • Spanish settlers establish missions at San Francisco and San Juan Capistrano in what is now California		
1777	• Spain and Portugal resolve their disagreements concerning their respective colonies in South America through the Treaty of San Ildefonso • Portugal makes a significant investment in Brazil, reorganizing its administration and giving native Brazilians important government positions	• The Continental Congress adopts the Stars and Stripes as the flag of the US and drafts Articles of Confederation for formation of a unified national government • The British army enters and occupies Philadelphia; another British force retakes Fort Ticonderoga from the Americans but fails to capture Albany, NY • American troops inflict a major defeat on the British army at Saratoga, NY, foiling British attempts to cut New England off from the other states • Washington and the American army encamp for the winter at Valley Forge; British forces occupy New York and much of New Jersey • Vermont proclaims itself to be a sovereign and independent republic; its revolutionary constitution prohibits slavery	• Antoine Lavoisier proves that air consists mainly of oxygen and nitrogen • George Washington orders that all his soldiers be inoculated against smallpox • Samuel Miller (England) invents and receives a patent for the circular saw	• Richard Sheridan's satirical comedic masterpiece *The School for Scandal* has its first performance in London's Drury Lane Theater • The first major newspaper in France, the *Journal de Paris*, begins publication
1778	• France signs a Treaty of Amity and Commerce with the US, signaling official recognition of the new republic; France then declares war on Britain and sends military aid to the Americans • The "War of the Bavarian Succession" breaks out between Austria and Prussia; Austria refuses to aid the Americans in their war of independence against Britain; Prussia is more sympathetic to the American cause but provides no direct assistance • The British parliament passes a Catholic Relief Act; it allows Roman Catholics in Britain to own property, inherit land, and join the army but requires an oath disavowing Stuart claims to the British throne and the civil jurisdiction of the Pope	• Virginia abolishes the slave trade, but does not outlaw slavery itself • The Continental Congress rejects a British peace offer and ratifies treaties of alliance with France and the Netherlands • A French fleet arrives off the coast of Delaware, and British forces withdraw from Philadelphia, fearing blockade by the French navy • The American army engages the British and defeats them at Monmouth, NJ, but fails to prevent them from reaching New York • British forces capture and occupy Savannah, GA • The Continental Congress outlaws the importation of slaves into colonies	• John Hunter's *A Practical Treatise on the Diseases of the Teeth* is the first work of modern dentistry; it first classifies teeth into molars, bicuspids, cuspids, and incisors	• English inventor Joseph Bramah patents an improved toilet with flushing water and a bowl encased in wood
1779	• James Cook discovers the Hawaiian Islands, names them the "Sandwich Islands," and is killed there by native Polynesians	• A bid by French and colonial forces to retake Savannah, GA, ends in failure • American troops commanded by Anthony Wayne defeat the British at Stony Point, NY	• Dutch physiologist Jan Ingenhousz discovers that plants give off oxygen when exposed to sunlight; this is a major step toward understanding the process of photosynthesis	• The English Derby horse race is established in Surrey, England • Velocipedes, a type of early bicycle, appear in Paris

E. EDUCATION, LITERATURE & THE FINE ARTS	F. RELIGION, THEOLOGY, PHILOSOPHY & PSYCHOLOGY	G. AMERICAN & UNITED METHODISM	H. BRITISH & WORLD METHODISM	
				1776 cont.
• Samuel Arnold becomes the musical director of the Haymarket Theatre in London • Johann Nikolaus Forkel, widely regarded as the father of the modern science of musicology, publishes his first major work, *On the Theory of Music* • Samuel Johnson begins writing *The Lives of the Poets*, combining biography and literary criticism; it is completed in 10 volumes in 1781	• Construction of the chapel at San Juan Capistrano is completed [it is now the oldest building in California]	• Richard Allen is converted by Methodist preaching while still a slave • Methodist preachers and people are divided by the revolution: Thomas Ware takes up arms against the British; Jesse Lee allows himself to be drafted but refuses to train with a gun and is jailed for a time and then assigned to noncombatant service driving wagons; Freeborn Garrettson is a conscientious objector, as is Francis Asbury; Martin Rodda is an ardent Tory and returns to England • Preparing to return to England, Thomas Rankin appoints a Committee of Five to oversee American Methodist work: Philip Gatch, Edward Dromgoole, Daniel Ruff, William Glendenning, and William Watters (Asbury is not included)	• Thomas Coke is forced to leave his parish and position in the Church of England because of his "Methodistical" leanings; he soon becomes Wesley's chief lieutenant • Wesley's *A Calm Address to the Inhabitants of England* continues his anti-American stance • Construction begins on the New Chapel on City Road in London; Wesley lays the cornerstone and preaches the sermon "On Laying the Foundation of the New Chapel," which reviews (and revises) the history of the Methodist movement	**1777**
• Milan's La Scala Opera, Italy's leading opera house and one of the world's most renowned, is built; its first production is Antonio Salieri's opera *L'Europa riconosciuta* • W. A. Mozart composes his *Concerto in C for Flute and Harp* • William Billings publishes *The Singing Master's Assistant*	• Immanuel Kant publishes *Laws of Universal Motion* • Jean-Jacques Rousseau publishes his meditative *Reveries of the Solitary Walker* • Herman Samuel Reimarus's *On the Intention of Jesus and His Disciples*, published posthumously, disputes the resurrection of Jesus and argues that the disciples stole his body and made up the entire story	• The Church of England basically ceases to function in America, provoking a sacramental crisis for both Anglicans and Methodists • Thomas Rankin and George Shadford return to England; of all of the preachers Wesley had sent to America, only Asbury now remains active • Asbury refuses to take the state oath of loyalty in Maryland that would have committed him to support the use of arms against Great Britain; he takes refuge in the home of Judge Thomas White in Kent County, Delaware, venturing out only occasionally until 1780 • The annual conference does not meet	• The City Road Chapel in London is completed and dedicated; it soon comes to be known as "Wesley's Chapel" • Wesley begins publication of *The Arminian Magazine* as a response to numerous Calvinist periodicals such as *The Gospel Magazine*	**1778**
• Under Thomas Jefferson's leadership, the College of William and Mary creates schools of law, medicine, and modern languages and institutes a system allowing students to choose the courses they wish to take	• John Murray establishes the first Universalist congregation in the US at Gloucester, MA • David Hume's *Dialogues Concerning Natural Religion* are published posthumously	• The annual conference meets in two sessions; the northern session in Kent County, Delaware; the southern session at Fluvanna, VA; the multiple session system remains the norm until 1784	• William Black, "The Apostle of Nova Scotia," begins preaching and establishes Methodism there • Selina, Countess of Huntingdon, forms her Connexion of Calvinistic Methodist congregations when, after losing a court *(cont.)*	**1779**

	A. WORLD HISTORY & POLITICS	**B. AMERICAN HISTORY & POLITICS**	**C. SCIENCE, MEDICINE & TECHNOLOGY**	**D. DAILY LIFE, POPULAR CULTURE & ENTERTAINMENT**
1779 cont.	• Spain recognizes the US and declares war on Britain but does not provide aid to the American and French forces against the British • The Boers battle Bantu tribesmen in southern Africa	• American volunteers from Virginia commanded by George Clark complete their conquest of the Old Northwest, forcing the British to surrender at Vincennes, IN • The US frigate *Bonhomme Richard*, captained by John Paul Jones, defeats the British frigate *Serapis* off the east coast of England	• Lazzaro Spallanzani studies human reproduction and discovers that the sperm must make physical contact with the egg for fertilization to take place	
1780	• Riots erupt in London when Lord George Gordon leads 50,000 members of his Protestant Association in a march on Parliament to protest the Catholic Relief Act of 1778; 285 are killed • Maria Theresa dies; her son, Joseph II, becomes sole ruler of Austria; he introduces numerous reforms including religious toleration of Protestants and Jews and the abolition of serfdom • War between The Netherlands and England hastens the end of the commercial and political influence of the Dutch East India Company • The Masai begin to expand their territory in east Africa	• The population of the US is about 2.8 million • Charleston surrenders and is occupied by British forces • Pennsylvania becomes the first state to prohibit slavery by legislative enactment; Massachusetts bans slavery in its state constitution • US army officer Benedict Arnold is revealed to be a traitor, escapes to England • British forces win the Battle of Camden, SC, but are then defeated by colonial forces at King's Mountain • A contingent of French troops arrives at Newport, RI, to assist the Colonial Army • American troops brutally suppress the Iroquois along the Mohawk River in New York	• Luigi Galvani observes and describes the connection between electricity and muscle movements in a frog • Antoine Lavoisier discovers and describes the role of oxygen in combustion	• The *British Gazette* and the *Sunday Monitor* are published in London; they are the first Sunday newspapers • The *Bengal Gazette*, the first English language newspaper in India, begins publication
1781	• Spanish military forces capture Pensacola from the British and take control of most of Florida • Holy Roman Emperor Joseph II commands religious toleration and freedom of the press throughout Austria and its territories • The British capture and take over Dutch settlements in western Sumatra • Conflict over grazing lands between the Boers and Xhosa tribesmen in south Africa lead to a series of large-scale cattle raids and skirmishes called the First Cape Frontier War	• A strong French fleet defeats the British fleet at Hampton Roads and blocks the Chesapeake Bay • French and American troops trap the British army at Yorktown, forcing it to surrender and effectively ending Britain's hope for defeat of the rebellious colonies • Maryland becomes the 13th state to ratify the Articles of Confederation • John Hanson becomes the first person to hold the position of "President of the United States, in Congress Assembled" under the provisions of the Articles of Confederation • Thomas Jefferson is almost captured by British troops at his home, Monticello • Spanish settlers in what is now California establish El Pueblo de Nuestra Señora la Reina de los Ángeles de la Porciúncula ("The Town of Our Lady Queen of the Angels of the Porziuncola"), now known simply as Los Angeles	• British astronomer William Herschel discovers a previously unknown planet later named Uranus • James Watt patents five different ways to change the power from a steam engine from reciprocating to rotary motion	• A French traveler to Annapolis, MD, reports on its splendor: "fine women, elegant horses and coaches, sumptuous dinners and balls" • The first written reference to Mardi Gras celebrations in New Orleans appears in report of the Spanish colonial government • Thomas Jefferson begins growing tomatoes for food at Monticello using seeds imported from Europe
1782	• The British parliament votes to end the American war • France and the Netherlands recognize the independence of the United States • Spain captures Minorca and Honduras but fails to take Gibraltar from the British	• Benjamin Franklin is appointed Ambassador to Great Britain • Franklin, John Adams, and John Jay begin negotiating a peace treaty with representatives of the British government in Paris • British troops evacuate from Savannah and Charleston • Congress approves the design for the Great Seal of the US, including an eagle with a heart-shaped shield, holding arrows and an olive branch in its claws, with the motto "E Pluribus Unum" appearing on a scroll held in its beak • A massacre of Delaware Indians by colonial militia from Virginia and Pennsylvania at Gnadenhutten in the Ohio territory enrages all the American tribes in the region	• James Watt patents a double-acting steam engine, which operates more efficiently than earlier designs by using steam alternately on each side of the piston	• The first Roman Catholic parochial school in the US is founded by St. Mary's Catholic Church in Philadelphia • A town meeting in Worcester, MA, opposes a state liquor tax because liquor is seen as necessary for the "good morale" of farmworkers

E. EDUCATION, LITERATURE & THE FINE ARTS	F. RELIGION, THEOLOGY, PHILOSOPHY & PSYCHOLOGY	G. AMERICAN & UNITED METHODISM	H. BRITISH & WORLD METHODISM	
• Samuel Johnson begins publishing *The Lives of the Poets*; when it is completed in 1781, Johnson personally gives a set to John Wesley • W. A. Mozart composes his *Sinfonia Concertante*	• Gotthold Lessing produces his fable *Nathan the Wise* promoting religious toleration • John Newton and William Cowper publish *Olney Hymns*, which includes Newton's timeless hymn "Amazing Grace"	• A group of the southern Methodist preachers agree to form a presbytery, ordain themselves, and begin to administer the sacraments; Asbury and the northern preachers strongly oppose this	case, she registers 67 of her chapels under the Toleration Act as "dissenting places of worship" • After preaching in Shropshire, Wesley walks to Coalbrookdale to see the new cast-iron bridge (1773) • Wesley publishes *Popery Calmly Considered*, which supports the newly-formed Protestant Association, headed by Lord George Gordon, in opposing the Catholic Relief Act of 1778	**1779 cont.**
• American Academy of Sciences founded at Boston • Transylvania College (later University) is established in Lexington, KY; it is the first college west of the Allegheny Mountains • Karl Ditters von Dittersdorf composes his oratorio *Job*	• Gotthold Lessing publishes *The Education of the Human Race* • Richard Challoner's *Douay Bible* becomes the standard translation for English-speaking Roman Catholics • Moses Mendelssohn publishes his translation of the Pentateuch into German • The Congregational Church of Connecticut licenses Lemuel Hayes to preach, making him the first black minister to be certified by a predominantly white denomination	• The southern preachers agree to a moratorium on celebration of the Lord's Supper while an appeal is made to Wesley for guidance • Barratt's Chapel is built in Kent County, Delaware, on land donated by Philip Barratt; it is the oldest surviving structure in the US built by and for Methodists • Asbury comes out of seclusion, takes an oath of loyalty, and becomes a citizen of the state of Delaware; as a result he is able to resume his travels openly	• Wesley publishes *A Collection of Hymns for the Use of the People called Methodists*, the definitive collection published during his lifetime and the ancestor of all later Methodist hymnals • Methodist layman Robert Raikes establishes Sunday schools in Gloucester; his account of this work, printed in the *Gloucester Journal* in 1783 and the *Gentleman's Magazine* in 1784, is generally taken to mark the beginning of the Sunday school movement in Britain	**1780**
• Mozart composes *Idomeneo, King of Crete*, arguably the finest *opera seria* ("serious opera," as distinct from *opera buffa*, or "comic opera") ever produced to date • Christian Gottlob Neefe takes on ten-year-old Ludwig van Beethoven as a pupil • Samuel Wesley (son of Charles Wesley) composes his *Concerto for Violin No. 2 in D Major* • Jacques-Louis David secures admission to the French Academy with his memorable neoclassical painting of *Belisarius*	• Kant publishes his revolutionary *Critique of Pure Reason*, arguing that human reason cannot arrive, through pure thought alone, at truths about realities, which, by their very nature, can never be objects of experience, such as God, human freedom, and immortality • Anthony Benezet publishes his *Short Observations on Slavery* • *A Pocket Hymn Book, Designed as a Constant Companion for the Pious: Collected From Various Authors*, compiled by Robert Spence, is published in London	• The annual conference meets in one session in Baltimore; it continues the ban on administration of the sacraments while awaiting guidance from Wesley • Harry Hosier's sermon "The Barren Fig Tree," preached at Adam's Chapel, Fairfax County, VA, is the first known sermon by a black Methodist preacher	• Wesley and the British Conference strongly support the position taken by Asbury against administration of the sacraments by the American preachers • Wesley tries unsuccessfully to secure ordination of some of his preachers by bishops of the Church of England for service in America • Wesley publishes *A Short History of the People Called Methodists* • William Black begins Methodist work in Nova Scotia • Mary Bosanquet marries John William Fletcher, Rector of Madeley, and exercises what is effectively a joint ministry with him until his death in 1785, then continues as the unofficial curate to his successor • Molly (Mrs. John) Wesley dies; Wesley does not hear of it until two weeks after her burial	**1781**
• Mozart completes his operetta *The Abduction from the Seraglio* and composes his *Symphony in D Major (Haffner Symphony)* • Luigi Boccherini completes his *Symphonies No. 1 in D Major, No. 2 in E Flat Major, No. 3 in A Major, No. 4 in F Major*, and *No. 5 in E Flat Major* • William Shield is appointed resident composer to Covent Garden	• Robert Aitken's 1782 Bible (King James Version) is the first English Bible printed in the US and the only Bible ever authorized by the US Congress • Some members of the Associate Presbyterian Church and the Reformed Presbyterian Church join to create the Associate Reformed Presbyterian Synod (later Church) in Philadelphia • Joseph Priestley publishes *The History of the Corruptions of Christianity* • Jean-Jacques Rousseau's autobiographical *Confessions* is published posthumously • Johann Gottfried von Herder publishes *The Spirit of Hebrew Poetry*	• The annual conference meets in two sessions, one in Baltimore, one in Virginia; it continues the ban on administration of the sacraments	• In the wake of the Gordon Riots of 1780, Wesley publishes his short paper "How Far Is It the Duty of a Christian Minister to Preach Politics?" asserting that while their main duty is to "preach Christ," they should certainly also defend the king and his ministers against "unjust criticism" • Wesley relaxes his previous injunctions about church attendance by Methodists and allows Methodist services to extend into "church hours" at the option of local societies	**1782**

	A. WORLD HISTORY & POLITICS	B. AMERICAN HISTORY & POLITICS	C. SCIENCE, MEDICINE & TECHNOLOGY	D. DAILY LIFE, POPULAR CULTURE & ENTERTAINMENT
1783	• The Treaty of Paris II (the Peace of Versailles) ends the Revolutionary War; Britain recognizes the independence of the US with its western boundary at the Mississippi River, retains control of Canada, and cedes Florida back to Spain • American independence is now recognized by all major European powers, including Britain, France, Spain, the Netherlands, Prussia, Austria, and Russia	• Following signature of the Treaty of Paris II, the last British troops leave New York • George Washington resigns as commander of the Continental Army, which is then disbanded	• French brothers Joseph and Jacques Montgolfier launch their first hot-air balloon for a 10-minute flight • French inventor Jouffroy d'Abbans builds the first paddle-wheel steamboat on the river Saône	• The *Pennsylvania Evening Post* is the first daily newspaper in America
1784	• Russian settlers move into the coastal regions of Alaska, which is known as "Russian America" until 1867 • William Pitt becomes Prime Minister in Britain; his India Act gives Britain more direct control in India	• Congress establishes the concept of "public land," declaring that land not included within the boundaries of the original thirteen states is in the public domain, owned and administered by the national government, and implicitly denying any claim by American Indian tribes to ownership or control of land on which they had lived for centuries • The first recorded shipment of cotton from the US to England is exported from New Orleans • The State of Franklin is organized in western North Carolina [now NE Tennessee]; John Sevier is elected governor; it endures for only 4 years, until North Carolina reasserts political control of the region in 1788 • Rhode Island and Connecticut prohibit slavery through legislative enactments, New Hampshire through its new state constitution • The *Empress of China* became the first American ship to sail to China; Salem, MA, becomes the center for New England trade with China	• Henry Cavendish publishes *Experiments on Air* • Andrew Meikle (Scotland) invents a mechanical threshing machine that separates grain from straw and chaff (patented in 1788) • Thomas Jefferson's *Notes on the State of Virginia* is the most influential work of American natural history of the 18th century	• The first school for the blind opens in Paris • The first regular mail coach service in England is established between Bristol and London • James Watt uses steam pipes to heat his office; this is the first recorded use of "steam heat" • Benjamin Franklin invents bifocal glasses
1785	• Russian traders and fur trappers establish outposts in the Aleutian Isles • Prussia signs the Commercial Treaty with the US; this is the first international trade agreement between the US and a major foreign power • Spain and the US quarrel over navigation rights on the Mississippi River and about the boundaries of Florida	• The Land Ordinance of 1785 provides for surveying public land using the township, range, and section method and for the sale of public land in 640-acre (1 square mile) tracts at $1 per acre • The US signs the Treaty of Hopewell with the Cherokee Nation, pledging to respect Cherokee sovereignty and territory • Thomas Jefferson becomes Minister to France; John Adams becomes Minister to Great Britain	• Edmund Cartwright (England) patents the power loom for weaving cloth • William Herschel's *On the Construction of the Heavens* gives the first reasonably correct description of the shape of the Milky Way Galaxy	• *The Times* of London is founded; it is published under the name *Daily Universal Register* until 1788 when it takes its current name [it is Britain's oldest surviving newspaper with continual daily publication] • Amsterdam's Bourse is the first stock exchange in Europe to formally begin public trading in securities rather than currencies and commodities

E. EDUCATION, LITERATURE & THE FINE ARTS	F. RELIGION, THEOLOGY, PHILOSOPHY & PSYCHOLOGY	G. AMERICAN & UNITED METHODISM	H. BRITISH & WORLD METHODISM	
• English piano maker John Broadwood patents a design for "damper" and "soft" pedals on a piano • William Blake publishes his *Poetical Sketches*, his first collection of poetry • Mozart composes his *Mass in C Minor* (*The Great*) • Beethoven composes *Three Sonatas* ("*Kurfuerstensonaten*") in E-flat, F, and D, his first notable works	• Anglican clergy meet in Maryland to establish the Protestant Episcopal Church in America • Kant publishes his *Prolegomena to Any Future Metaphysics* • Johann Gottfried von Herder publishes his *Ideas on the Philosophy of the History of Mankind*	• The annual conference again meets in two sessions, one in Baltimore, one in Virginia; it again continues the ban on administration of the sacraments despite the restiveness of the southern preachers • The Holston Circuit is the first to be organized west of the Allegheny Mountains	• Robert Carr Brackenbury pioneers Methodism in the Channel Islands; from there it spreads to France • The first Methodist chapel in the Caribbean is built in St. John's, Antigua, due to the efforts of John Baxter, a local preacher who had immigrated from England; the wooden structure seats over 2,000 people • Wesley makes a tour of the Netherlands, mostly as a holiday	**1783**
• Joseph Haydn composes his *Symphony No. 76* • Michael Haydn composes his *Symphony in B Flat Major* and *Symphony in C Major* • William Blake completes his partly auto-biographical and satirical *An Island in the Moon*	• Samuel Seabury is consecrated as the first Anglican bishop in America by Scottish bishops of the Church of England; he becomes rector of St. James's Church in New London, CT • Kant publishes his enormously influential essay *What is Enlightenment?* in which he defines *enlightenment* as "man's emergence from his self-imposed immaturity" and states that "the motto of enlightenment is therefore: *Sapere aude!* [Dare to know!] Have courage to use your own understanding!" • Johann Gottfried von Herder begins publication of his *Outlines of a Philosophy of the History of Man* (4 vols., 1784–91)	• Thomas Coke, Richard Whatcoat, and Thomas Vasey arrive in New York and travel through Philadelphia to meet Asbury at Barratt's Chapel; Asbury insists on being elected to office of superintendent by Methodist preachers in America; provokes calling of the Christmas Conference at Lovely Lane Chapel in Baltimore • The Christmas Conference: – formally establishes the Methodist Episcopal Church (MEC) in the US – adopts the Articles of Religion and the *Sunday Service* prepared by Wesley – passes the "binding minute" acknowledging Wesley's authority "in all matters belonging to church government" – adopts a threefold pattern of ministry: deacon, elder, and "general superintendent" or bishop – elects Asbury to be "general superintendent" or bishop along with Coke – elects twelve other elders to serve the societies in the US, one for Antigua, and two for Nova Scotia (fifteen total) • In three successive days, Asbury is ordained deacon, then elder, then "set apart" as bishop by Coke, Whatcoat, and Vasey; William Otterbein, who is attending the conference, also takes part in the ordination • Asbury and Coke, along with Whatcoat and Vasey, then ordain the fifteen newly elected elders • At its establishment, the MEC has some 18,000 members, about 100 traveling preachers and as many local preachers, twice as many licensed exhorters, 60 chapels, and 800 recognized preaching stations • Richard Allen and Absalom Jones become the first black persons licensed to preach as Methodists	• Wesley executes Deed of Declaration, making the "legal hundred" of the Conference (which at the time has 191 members) his legal heir and successor as the governing body of British Methodism, thus ensuring its continuity after his death • Wesley edits and abridges the Book of Common Prayer of the Church of England to create *The Sunday Service of the Methodists in America, with Other Occasional Services*, including his abridgement of the Articles of Religion (from 39 down to 24) • Wesley, with the assistance of Thomas Coke, ordains Richard Whatcoat and Thomas Vasey as deacons and then as elders, and then "sets apart" Coke (who was already an elder) to be "general superintendent" of Methodists in America along with Asbury; instructs Coke to inform Asbury and the American preachers of these decisions and to ordain Asbury • The ordinations of 1784 create a breach between John and Charles Wesley that is never entirely healed; Charles insists that "ordination means separation" of the Methodists from the Church of England; John refuses to acknowledge this as true	**1784**
• Antonio Salieri produces his opera *La Grotta di Trofonio* at La Scala in Milan • Mozart composes his *Concerto No. 20 in D Minor for Piano and Orchestra* • Joseph Haydn composes his *String Quartet in D Minor* • James Boswell publishes his *Journal of a Tour to the Hebrides with Samuel Johnson*	• The national Sunday School Society is founded in England to educate poor children • Charles Wilkins publishes his English translation of the famous Hindu text, the *Bhagavad Gita*, which is influential on Ralph Waldo Emerson and Henry David Thoreau • Other notable publications include: – Kant, *Groundwork of the Metaphysics of Morals*, in which Kant articulates his understanding of the "categorical imperative" – William Paley, *The Principles of Moral and Political Philosophy* – Thomas Reid, *Philosophy of the Intellectual Powers*	• The church now known as Old Otterbein Church is built in Baltimore; it is regarded as the mother church of the United Brethren in Christ [and is the oldest church edifice still standing in that city] • Asbury and Coke meet with George Washington at Mount Vernon to seek his support in bringing about emancipation of slaves in Virginia • The annual conference meets in three sessions (Baltimore, Virginia, and North Carolina) and ratifies decisions of the Christmas Conference	• Wesley ordains John Pawson, Thomas Handy, and Joseph Taylor as elders for service in Scotland • Wesley publishes his important sermon "On Working Out Our Own Salvation" • Wesley prints in the *Arminian Magazine* an original account by Robert Raikes of the Gloucester experiment with Sunday schools, begun in 1780 • Wesley produces *A Pocket Hymn Book for the Use of Christians of all Denominations* • John William Fletcher, whom Wesley had selected as his "designated successor" to lead British Methodism, dies	**1785**

	A. WORLD HISTORY & POLITICS	B. AMERICAN HISTORY & POLITICS	C. SCIENCE, MEDICINE & TECHNOLOGY	D. DAILY LIFE, POPULAR CULTURE & ENTERTAINMENT
1785 cont.		• Traders from the Ohio Valley region (called "Kaintucks") begin floating flatboats and rafts filled with products and crops down the Ohio and Mississippi rivers to Natchez, then returning overland to their homes by a network of Indial trails that comes to be called the Natchez Trace		
1786	• King Frederick II the Great of Prussia dies; he is succeeded by his nephew, Frederick William II • Pirates along the Barbary Coast of north Africa begin raiding US ships in the Mediterranean • The Qajar Dynasty begins in Persia	• Facing bankruptcy and recognizing the inadequacy of the 1777 Articles of Confederation, Congress authorizes a Constitutional Convention "to devise such further provisions as shall appear . . . necessary to render the constitution of the Federal Government adequate to the exigencies of Union"	• American inventor Ezekiel Reed creates a machine that makes nails • Jacques Balmat and Michel-Gabriel Paccard of France make the first successful ascent of Mont Blanc, the highest peak in the Swiss Alps	• The first golf club in America is founded in Charleston, SC
1787	• The Society for Effecting the Abolition of the Slave Trade is formed in London by William Wilberforce and colleagues • Catherine the Great launches Russia into a second war with the Ottoman Turks • Sierra Leone becomes a British territory	• The Constitutional Convention meets in Philadelphia; George Washington is selected as the presiding officer; among the prominent Americans who do *not* attend are Richard Henry Lee, Patrick Henry, Thomas Jefferson, John Adams, Samuel Adams, and John Hancock • After much argument, the "Three-Fifths Compromise" is incorporated into the Constitution; it stipulates that three-fifths of a state's slaves, although they cannot vote, will be counted as citizens for the purposes of representation and taxation, which significantly increases the political power of southern states • The final draft of the Constitution is approved by the Convention, signed, and sent to the states for ratification • The US federal government is established, and the dollar is named official US currency • Delaware becomes the first state to ratify the US Constitution • The Northwest Ordinance creates the Northwest Territory (present-day Illinois, Indiana, Michigan, Ohio, Wisconsin, and part of Minnesota), establishes the process by which new states will be added to the US (with the same powers as the original 13 states), prohibits slavery in the area, and prohibits seizure of Indian lands or property without their consent	• John Fitch demonstrates the first steamboat in the Americas to the Constitutional Convention on the Delaware River at Philadelphia • Benjamin Rush's *Observations on the Causes and Cure of Tetanus* suggests for the first time that some diseases may be psychosomatic in origin	• The Metropolitan Cricket Club is established in London, leading to a codification of the rules of cricket • Prince Hall, a Revolutionary War veteran, organizes the Negro Masonic Lodge in Boston (which now bears his name)
1788	• King Louis XVI of France is presented with a "list of grievances" from French parliament • King Charles III of Spain dies; he is succeeded by his son Charles IV	• The US Constitution is approved when New Hampshire becomes the 9th state to ratify it; Rhode Island is the last of the 13 original states to ratify the Constitution (in 1790)	• James Watt invents the "Watt governor" to regulate the speed of a steam engine based on the servomechanical "feedback" principle that links output to input	• Protests over the dissection of human bodies in medical schools turn into riots in New York and Boston • Fuchsia appears in Europe for the first time, imported from Peru

E. EDUCATION, LITERATURE & THE FINE ARTS	F. RELIGION, THEOLOGY, PHILOSOPHY & PSYCHOLOGY	G. AMERICAN & UNITED METHODISM	H. BRITISH & WORLD METHODISM	
		• The term "presiding elder" begins to be used instead of "assistant" (Wesley's term) for the preachers (ministers) who have charge over the other preachers on a circuit • The first American Methodist *Discipline* is published in Philadelphia: *Minutes of Several Conversations . . . comprising a Form of Discipline* • The rules against slavery in the 1785 *Discipline* are suspended after six months, despite strenuous opposition by Coke • Cokesbury College is established in Abingdon, MD, to train students to be "rational scriptural Christians"; it opens for classes in 1787 • Coke returns to England		**1785 cont.**
• The Stoughton Musical Society is founded in Stoughton, MA; it is America's first singing society • Mozart's opera *The Marriage of Figaro* premieres in Vienna, and he composes his *Symphony No. 38 in D Major (Prague)* • William Parsons succeeds John Stanley as Master of the King's Music in England • Robert Burns publishes his *Poems Chiefly in the Scottish Dialect* • Charles W. Peale opens the first art gallery in the US in Philadelphia	• The (Lutheran) New York Ministerium is established; lay delegates receive the right to vote	• Richard Allen organizes separate class meetings for blacks at St. George's Church in Philadelphia • Asbury organizes the first Sunday school class in America (in Hanover County, VA) • The annual conference meets in three sessions (Baltimore, Virginia, and North Carolina)	• The British Conference allows the administration of the sacraments in Methodist societies under "special conditions" • Four more preachers are ordained ("set apart") by Wesley as elders: Joshua Keighley and Charles Atmore for Scotland, William Warrener for Antigua, and William Hammet for Newfoundland • Thomas Coke lands in Antigua and finds that Methodism is already established in the Caribbean due to the work of Nathaniel Gilbert and John Baxter; when Coke arrives there are 1500 Methodists there, only three of whom are white	**1786**
• British schoolteacher and philosopher Mary Wollstonecraft argues in her controversial (at the time) *Thoughts on the Education of Daughters, with Reflections on Female Conduct in the More Important Duties of Life*, that women are no less capable of intellectual achievement than men • Mozart composes his opera *Don Giovanni* and his sublime *Serenade for Strings in G Major*, better known as *Eine Kleine Nachtmusik (A Little Night Music)* • Beethoven travels to Vienna where he meets and briefly studies with Mozart; the relationship is interrupted after only two months by the death of Beethoven's mother • Joseph Haydn composes his meditation on *The Seven Last Words of Christ* • William Billings publishes *The Psalm Singer's Amusement*	• Bishops of the Church of England in England obtain parliamentary permission to consecrate William White and Samuel Provoost as bishops for the Protestant Episcopal Church in America • King's Chapel in Boston, until then an Episcopal church, removes all references to the Trinity from the Book of Common Prayer and assumes an independent existence; it is generally regarded as the first organized Unitarian church	• Coke makes his second trip to America (March–May) • Wesley provokes Asbury and the American Methodists by instructing them (via Coke) to accept Richard Whatcoat as a third Superintendent in addition to Coke and Asbury • The annual conference meets in three sessions (Baltimore, Virginia, and South Carolina): – refuses to accept or elect Whatcoat as a third Superintendent (Bishop) – rescinds the "binding minute" of 1784 that had acknowledged Wesley's authority over American Methodism – places regulations concerning membership in the *Discipline* in the section on "Class Meetings" • Richard Allen and Absalom Jones lead a walkout from St. George's Church after black worshipers there experience discrimination and abuse; they form the Free African Society and begin to hold their own separate religious meetings • Coke signs an agreement stating that he will refrain from exercising any episcopal power related to the MEC while he is absent from the US, then returns to Britain	• The British Conference requires that all Methodist preachers have "a note from Mr. Wesley or from the Assistant of the circuit from whence he comes" authorizing them to preach and that such notes be renewed yearly • Sarah Mallet receives a note from the Assistant of her circuit authorizing her to preach on the circuit "so long as she preaches the Methodist doctrines and attends to our discipline," thereby becoming the first woman officially approved as an itinerant preacher in Methodism • Five more preachers are ordained as elders for service in Scotland • British Methodist preachers are stationed at St. Vincent and St. Kitts in the Caribbean • After returning from the US, Coke serves as president of the British Conference	**1787**
• William Blake invents "relief etching" in *All Religions Are One* and *There is No Natural Religion* • Antonio Salieri is appointed Imperial Royal Kapellmeister by Emperor <div align="right">(cont.)</div>	• Kant publishes his *Critique of Practical Reason*, arguing that the ideas of God, freedom, and immortality, although they cannot be directly known because they transcend human sense experience, <div align="right">(cont.)</div>	• The annual conference meets in six separate sessions due to the growth of the movement: – restores Wesley's name to the Conference *Minutes*	• Charles Wesley dies and is buried in the graveyard of his parish church in Marylebone, London, rather than at City Road Chapel	**1788**

	A. WORLD HISTORY & POLITICS	B. AMERICAN HISTORY & POLITICS	C. SCIENCE, MEDICINE & TECHNOLOGY	D. DAILY LIFE, POPULAR CULTURE & ENTERTAINMENT
1788 cont.	• Jacques Pierre Brissot founds the Société des Amis des Noirs (Society of the Friends of Blacks) in Paris to campaign for the abolition of the French slave trade • Botany Bay in New South Wales (Australia) is established as a British crown colony; the first colonists (and convicts) arrive there from England on January 26, now celebrated as Australia Day	• Maryland and Virginia agree to give land along the Potomac River to Congress to be used as the site for a federal capital • Tecumseh emerges as major war leader of Shawnee and other Indian tribes in Ohio territory	• The Medical Society of New Haven publishes *Cases and Observations*, the first collection of medical papers in America	
1789	• The French Revolution begins with the storming of the Bastille; the National Assembly adopts the Declaration of Rights of Man and of the Citizen, proclaiming *liberté, égalité, fraternité* • Russian explorers found Odessa on the Black Sea • After mutiny on the HMS *Bounty*, the mutineers settle on Pitcairn Island	• The US Constitution goes into full effect, and the three branches of the new federal government—executive (President), legislative (Congress), and judicial (Supreme Court)—are established • The US Congress, comprising the Senate and the House of Representatives, meets for the first time (in New York City) • After election by Congress, George Washington is inaugurated as the first president of the US under the new Constitution; John Adams becomes vice president • Congress passes the Judiciary Act, establishing the Supreme Court and 13 district courts, one in each state; John Jay becomes the first Chief Justice of the Supreme Court • Congress approves the Bill of Rights (Amendments 1-10 to the US Constitution) and sends it to the states for ratification • Congress establishes the Departments of State, War, and the Treasury • The US War Department creates the nation's first regular standing army	• The first steam-powered steel rolling mill is constructed in England • Antoine Lavoisier publishes his *Elements of Chemistry*, the first modern textbook on the subject	• President Washington proclaims a national Day of Thanksgiving in honor of the ratification of the US Constitution; this is the first time Thanksgiving Day is celebrated as a US national holiday • Christopher Colles publishes *A Survey of the Roads of the United States of America*, the first American road atlas, consisting of a series of strip maps of various routes around the mid-Atlantic states
1790	• Holy Roman Emperor Joseph II dies; he is succeeded by his brother, Leopold II • Louis XVI is forced to accept a new French constitution drafted by the National Assembly creating a limited monarchy with an elected unicameral legislature • Sweden wins a major naval victory over Russia; Sweden and Russia then sign a peace treaty that leaves Finland under Russian control	• The first US census reports that the population is 3,929,214: – whites: 3,172,006 (80.7%) – free blacks: 59,527 (1.5%) – slaves: 697,681 (17.8%) • Five of the thirteen states are "free states" that have abolished slavery (New Hampshire, Massachusetts, Connecticut, Rhode Island, Pennsylvania); eight are "slave states" where slavery remains legal *(cont.)*	• The first patent granted by the US is issued to Samuel Hopkins for a process of making potash, an ingredient used in fertilizer • Samuel Slater builds the first American steam-powered cotton processing factory in Rhode Island, marking the dawn of the Industrial Revolution in the US	• The first American temperance society is organized by a group of farmers in Connecticut who pledge not to drink during farming season • Congress rejects a proposal by Thomas Jefferson to adopt a decimal system of weights and measures • Noah Webster is instrumental in persuading Congress to pass the first US Copyright Act

E. EDUCATION, LITERATURE & THE FINE ARTS	F. RELIGION, THEOLOGY, PHILOSOPHY & PSYCHOLOGY	G. AMERICAN & UNITED METHODISM	H. BRITISH & WORLD METHODISM	
Joseph II of Austria and composes his opera *Il Talismano* (The Talisman) • Mozart composes his majestic symphonic trilogy, his final works in this form: *Symphony No. 39 in E Flat*, *Symphony No. 40 in G Minor*, and *Symphony No. 41 (Jupiter)* • Johann Nikolaus Forkel publishes his pathbreaking *Allgemeine Geschichte der Musik* (General History of Music)	are essential postulates for the moral life and for articulating the "categorical imperative" as the foundation of ethical behavior • *The Federalist Papers* is published, collecting together a series of newspaper articles written by Alexander Hamilton, James Madison, and John Jay under the pen name of "Publius" advocating ratification of the US Constitution	– recognizes three individuals as "exercising the episcopal office in the Methodist Church in Europe and America" (Wesley, Coke, and Asbury) but only two as elected by the Conference to superintend the Methodist connection in America (Coke and Asbury) – extends the probationary period of candidates for membership from two months (as in 1785 *Discipline* and the English "Large" *Minutes*) to six months [unchanged by the MEC until 1908] • Asbury (with Coke's approval) substitutes the term *bishop* for *superintendent* in the *Discipline* and the Conference *Minutes*, provoking Wesley's wrath	• Wesley ordains nine more preachers as elders for Scotland, and "sets apart" (ordains) Alexander Mather to serve as superintendent in England • The British Conference sends preachers to Dominica, Barbados, Nevis, Tortola, and Jamaica • Wesley instructs Asbury to stop using the title bishop, saying that "men may call me a knave or a fool, a rascal, a scoundrel, and I am content; but they shall never, by my consent, call me a bishop"; Asbury ignores him	**1788 cont.**
• Joseph Haydn composes his *Symphony No. 92 in G Major* (Oxford) • Mozart writes to a friend saying that next time they meet, he will tell him about Antonio Salieri's plots "which, however, have completely failed"; this ambiguous letter provides the basis for later legends about Salieri's murderous jealousy of Mozart • Georgetown College is established; it is the first Roman Catholic college in the US • William Blake's volume of poetry *Songs of Innocence* is hand illustrated and printed • William H. Brown writes *The Power of Sympathy*, generally considered to be the first American novel	• The Protestant Episcopal Church in the US is formally organized as the successor to the Church of England in America; Samuel Seabury, William White, and Samuel Provoost are its first bishops; the new church affirms its intention not to depart "in any essential point of doctrine, discipline, or worship" from the Church of England • The first General Assembly of the Presbyterian Church in the USA (PCUSA) meets in Philadelphia • Pope Pius VI appoints John Carroll as the first Roman Catholic bishop in the US • Jeremy Bentham's *An Introduction to the Principles of Morals and Legislation* argues that something is good which produces "the greatest happiness of the greatest number"	• Coke makes his third trip to America (Feb.–June) • The growth and westward expansion of Methodism (e.g., four circuits in Tennessee, three in Kentucky, one in Ohio, and one in Mississippi) requires that the annual conference be held in eleven different sessions; the multisession annual conference plan is becoming unworkable • The annual conference approves the ordination of local preachers as deacons, giving them limited sacramental authority (and thus creating a distinction between the local deacon and the traveling or itinerant deacon who is a probationary member of an annual conference) • Asbury proposes creation of a council, an executive body to be composed of the bishops and presiding elders, to make critical decisions as an alternative to calling together a general conference of the entire church; the plan arouses wide opposition and is not adopted • Asbury and Coke visit President Washington to express the support of the MEC for "the head of the new civil government" • The Methodist Book Concern is established in Philadelphia; John Dickins is appointed first Book Steward; it begins publication of an American edition of *The Arminian Magazine* (until 1791) • William Otterbein organizes the first conference of his followers, who take the name "United Brethren" • Saying "I can never be anything but a Methodist," Richard Allen withdraws from the Free Africa Society due to its increasing tendency to embrace Quaker traditions, leaving Absalom Jones as its leader; Allen and his followers establish separate class meetings	• William Black is ordained by Thomas Coke as Superintendent for Nova Scotia; Black serves there until his death in 1814 and is remembered as "the Apostle of Nova Scotia Methodism" • In conjunction with two other Anglican priests, James Creighton and Peard Dickenson, Wesley ordains Henry Moore and Thomas Rankin as elders; they are empowered to administer the sacraments as Wesley's deputies and to pass that power on to others after Wesley's death • The "Large" *Minutes* are published for the last time during Wesley's lifetime; this edition becomes their final form	**1789**
• William Blake publishes *The Marriage of Heaven and Hell* • Mozart's opera *Cosi fan tutte* (All Women Are Like That) premieres in Vienna • James Bruce publishes the account of his *Travels to Discover the Sources of the Nile, 1768–1773*	• Matthew Carey publishes the first Roman Catholic Bible printed in the US • John Murray plays a primary role in the formal establishment of the Universalist Church of America • Edmund Burke's *Reflections on the Revolution in France* is a passionate denunciation of its excesses and a defense of monarchy	• The annual conference schedules fourteen separate sessions • The annual conference recognizes Sunday schools as a mission of the church and votes to establish them across the denomination • Black persons, slave and free, make up an estimated 20% of American Methodists	• Wesley completes a revised edition of his 1755 translation of the New Testament and writes "On the Wedding Garment," which he thought would be his last sermon [he actually writes 5 more] • An increasingly frail Wesley presides over his last Conference (in Bristol), preaches his last open-air sermon, and makes the last entry in his diary • American Methodists take over the British Methodist work in Canada	**1790**

	A. WORLD HISTORY & POLITICS	B. AMERICAN HISTORY & POLITICS	C. SCIENCE, MEDICINE & TECHNOLOGY	D. DAILY LIFE, POPULAR CULTURE & ENTERTAINMENT
1790 cont.		(New York, New Jersey, Delaware, Maryland, Virginia, North Carolina, South Carolina, Georgia) • Congress convenes for the first time in Philadelphia, then the temporary US capital • Congress creates the District of Columbia to be the location of a permanent national capital and orders construction of the US Capitol building there • Charles L'Enfant designs a plan for the District of Columbia modeled on Versailles, with large public spaces and wide avenues centered on a domed Capitol building • The Revenue Cutter Service, predecessor of the US Coast Guard, is created and charged with enforcing US customs and tariffs • Over the strong objections of Thomas Jefferson, Congress adopts the financial programs of Alexander Hamilton, the first Secretary of the Treasury; the Federal government assumes responsibility for the national debt; revenue is raised by a combination of import tariffs and excise taxes • The Society of Friends (Quakers) presents a petition to Congress calling for the abolition of slavery • Benjamin Franklin dies, and his beloved Philadelphia gives him the most impressive funeral in its history; he is eulogized as the man who "snatched the lightning from the skies and the sceptre from tyrants"	• The monumental statue of the Aztec Earth goddess Coatlicue and the so-called Calendar Stone are discovered beneath the Plaza Mayor in Mexico City; they are the most striking Aztec works ever discovered	
1791	• King Louis XVI of France and his family fail in an attempt to escape from Paris • François-Dominique Toussaint L'Ouverture leads a slave rebellion on the island of Hispaniola; it will be the first successful uprising by nonwhite people against a white colonial power • The British parliament passes the Canada Constitutional Act, dividing Upper Canada from Lower Canada; in mostly French-speaking Lower Canada (present-day Quebec), French civil law and customs prevail and the rights of the Catholic Church are preserved; in mostly English-speaking Upper Canada, Protestant churches (especially the Church of England) are favored, and English civil laws and customs govern • Austria signs the Treaty of Sistova with the Ottoman Empire, returning Belgrade to the Ottomans in exchange for northeastern Bosnia	• The Bill of Rights (Amendments 1-10 to the US Constitution) is ratified • After 14 years as a sovereign and independent republic, Vermont joins the US as the 14th state; it is a free state • The Treaty of Holston reconfirms the 1785 Treaty of Hopewell; portions of Cherokee territory are ceded to the US, but the permanent rights of the nation to its remaining territory are guaranteed by the US [this pledge will be broken by the Indian Removal Act of 1830] • The (first) Bank of the United States is established but with a charter for only ten years • Congress passes the first internal revenue laws, establishing 14 revenue districts and imposing a tax of 30¢ per gallon on distilled spirits • The US national debt, reported this year for the first time, is $75,463,476	• Anthracite coal is discovered in Pennsylvania, marking the start of the American coal mining industry • The first successful sugar refinery in America is built in New Orleans	• The first major "macadamized" turnpike in the US is completed between Philadelphia and Lancaster, PA
1792	• The French Republic is proclaimed; "La Marseillaise," composed by Claude-Joseph de Lisle, becomes the French national anthem • France declares war on Austria and Prussia, who hope to restore Louis XVI to the French throne, and defeats Prussian forces at the Battle of Valmy, seizing the Austrian Netherlands	• The US Postal Service is established • The Coinage Acts establish a decimal currency system for the US; the value of the dollar is defined in terms of both silver and gold (bimetallism) • Kentucky is admitted to the US as the 15th state; it is a slave state	• William Murdock pioneers the use of natural gas for lighting in his home and factory in Scotland • American physician Benjamin Waterhouse publishes *The Rise, Progress and Present State of Medicine*	• The New York Stock Exchange (NYSE) has its beginning when twenty-four stock-brokers in New York sign the "Buttonwood Agreement" [the organization adopts a formal constitution as "The New York Stock & Exchange Board" in 1813 and takes its present name in 1863]

E. EDUCATION, LITERATURE & THE FINE ARTS	F. RELIGION, THEOLOGY, PHILOSOPHY & PSYCHOLOGY	G. AMERICAN & UNITED METHODISM	H. BRITISH & WORLD METHODISM	
	• Mary Wollstonecraft defends the French Revolution in her spirited response to Burke, *A Vindication of the Rights of Men* • Kant publishes his *Critique of Judgment*	• Henry Evans, a black freedman and licensed preacher, establishes a Methodist church in Fayetteville, NC • The *Pocket Hymn Book*, originally published in England by Robert Spence in 1781, is reprinted in Philadelphia with a preface prepared by Asbury and Coke; it serves as the primary hymnbook of American Methodists until 1821, since the 1780 *Collection of Hymns* and the 1784 *Sunday Service* were largely ignored in America		**1790 cont.**
• Benjamin Franklin's unfinished *Autobiography* is published in Paris and in French; the first English edition appears in London in 1793 • Mozart's most popular opera, *The Magic Flute*, has its first performance in Vienna • Mozart also completes his sublime *Ave Verum Corpus*, then dies at the tragically young age of 35, leaving his great *Requiem* unfinished • Joseph Haydn composes his *Symphony No. 94 in G Major (Surprise)* • James Boswell publishes his magisterial *Life of Samuel Johnson, LL.D.* • The Théâtre de St. Pierre, the first opera house in the US, opens in New Orleans	• Thomas Paine's *The Rights of Man* answers Burke's *Reflections* by defending the French Revolution and calling for the overthrow of the English monarchy • John Quincy Adams publishes *An Answer to Paine's Rights of Man*, advancing the Federalist argument for a strong judiciary to defend the rights of the minority against Paine's insistence on the absolute power of the majority	• The annual conference schedules seventeen separate sessions; not all of them actually meet; plans are made to call a true General Conference in 1792 • Jacob Albright experiences an evangelical conversion • Coke makes his fourth trip to America (Feb.–May) • Coke sends a confidential letter to William White, Bishop of the Protestant Episcopal Church, proposing a union between that body and the Methodist Episcopal Church; the overture is not productive • Richard Allen purchases a lot in Philadelphia on which he hopes to build a church for his black Methodist followers	• John Wesley dies at the age of 87 and is buried in the cemetery behind City Road Chapel; his final testimony is "The best of all is, God is with us" • Wesley's sister Martha ("Patty," b. 1706) dies three months after her brother; she is the last member of the Epworth Wesley family • William Thompson calls a meeting of senior preachers to discuss the governance of Methodism after Wesley's death; they issue the "Halifax Circular" to all Methodist preachers and societies, advocating a corporate form of governance to avoid having "another king in Israel" • When Conference meets, it elects Thompson as the first President of Conference and enacts most of the provisions of the "Halifax Circular," including establishment of an annual elected presidency • Conference divides British Methodism into districts, each with a district committee authorized to exercise disciplinary powers between meetings of Conference • France is made a separate circuit of British Methodism	**1791**
• Architect Charles Bullfinch designs the State House in Hartford, CT [it is now the oldest surviving building of the kind in the US] • Beethoven returns to Vienna and becomes a student of Joseph Haydn and composes his *Piano Sonata No. 19 in G Minor* and *Piano Sonata No. 20 in G Major*	• The (Lutheran) Pennsylvania Ministerium grants voting rights to laymen • The Baptist Missionary Society is founded in London; it sends William Carey to India as its first mission; Carey is now considered the father of the English-speaking foreign missions movement	• Coke makes his fifth trip to America (Oct.–Dec.) • The first quadrennial MEC General Conference meets in Baltimore, marking an end of the period of multisession annual conference: – determines that bishops will be elected by and are amenable to the General Conference, which now has sole legislative power for the church	• Controversy about the future direction of Methodism flares between "Church Methodists" (or "Old Planners") who understand themselves as "Methodist Anglicans" and want to retain Methodism's historic connection with the Church of England, and "Conference Methodists" (or "New Planners") who want Methodism to *(cont.)*	**1792**

	A. WORLD HISTORY & POLITICS	B. AMERICAN HISTORY & POLITICS	C. SCIENCE, MEDICINE & TECHNOLOGY	D. DAILY LIFE, POPULAR CULTURE & ENTERTAINMENT
1792 cont.	• The French royal family is imprisoned • Britain forms an alliance with Austria against France • The war between Russia and the Ottoman Turks ends with the Treaty of Jassy and modest territorial exchanges • Holy Roman Emperor Leopold II dies; he is succeeded by his son, Francis II • Denmark abolishes the slave trade within its territories	• Political parties appear for the first time in the US when Thomas Jefferson forms the Democratic-Republican party, and John Adams and Alexander Hamilton form the Federalist party • George Washington is elected to a second term as president and John Adams as vice president		• Benjamin Banneker, a free black farmer and self-taught astronomer and mathematician, begins the publication of *The Pennsylvania, Delaware, Maryland, and Virginia Almanac and Ephemeris*; he sends the manuscript of the first volume to Thomas Jefferson along with a letter disputing Jefferson's claim that blacks are intellectually inferior to whites and protesting against slavery • Robert B. Thomas begins the publication of what will be the most enduring of all American almanacs, *The Old Farmer's Almanack*
1793	• Britain, the Netherlands, and Spain join Austria and Prussia in their coalition against France • The Reign of Terror begins in France under the leadership of Robespierre; the monarchy is abolished, and Louis XVI and Marie Antoinette are executed; Roman Catholicism is proscribed • The Relief Act of 1793 gives Roman Catholics in Britain and Ireland the right to vote, but not to sit in the British parliament • Alexander Mackenzie becomes the first European to cross Canada from coast to coast • The first free settlers migrate from Britain to Australia	• President Washington lays the cornerstone of the US Capitol building in Washington, DC • Washington declares the US to be neutral in the war between France and the other European powers • Congress passes the first Fugitive Slave Act, making it illegal to harbor escaped slaves • Robert Gray establishes the US claim to the Columbia River territory in the Pacific Northwest	• Eli Whitney (US) invents the cotton gin to remove the seeds from cotton fibers • An epidemic of yellow fever kills over 5,000 people in Philadelphia in the worst outbreak of the disease in any American city to date	• France institutes compulsory education for all children beginning at the age of six • Noah Webster establishes the pro-Federalist newspaper *The American Minerva*
1794	• Robespierre falls from power and is executed • The French armies defeat Austrian forces along the Rhine River • Agha Muhammad comes to power in Persia and establishes the Qajar Dynasty, which controls the region until 1925 • Thaddeus Kosciusko leads an unsuccessful revolt against Russian and Prussian domination of Poland	• US Secretary of State John Jay negotiates "John Jay's Treaty" between Britain and the US, which settles disagreements over British violations of the 1783 Treaty of Paris; the British agree to withdraw from the Ohio Valley and stop supplying their Indian allies there with arms • The Neutrality Act prohibits US citizens from serving in the military forces of foreign countries and from servicing or supplying foreign warships in US ports • The American Convention of Abolition Societies is formed in Philadelphia • The "Whiskey Rebellion" in Pennsylvania, protesting the excise tax placed on whiskey in 1791, is crushed when President Washington sends in federal troops • The first US coins are struck at the newly established US Mint in Philadelphia • The US Department of the Navy is formally established when Congress orders the construction and deployment of six frigates • Congress prohibits the export of slaves from the US to any other country	• The École Polytechnique, the first technical college in Europe, is established in Paris • William Bartram's *Travels Through North and South Carolina, Georgia, East and West Florida, the Cherokee Country, the Extensive Territories of the Muscogulges or Creek Confederacy, and the Country of the Chactaws* is a landmark work in American natural history	• Postage costs in the US are paid by the person receiving mail and the rates are set by distance, e.g., 6¢ up to 30 miles; 15¢ up to 200 miles; 25¢ over 400 miles • Robert Burns composes the song "Auld Lang Syne" • The New Theater in Philadelphia opens with a performance of Samuel Arnold's comic opera *The Maid of the Mill* • James Lackington opens the Temple of the Muses in London, the first large book emporium and the pioneer of "remaindering," buying up bulk stock from elsewhere at a bargain price and selling cheap
1795	• The Directory is formed in France; it adopts a new constitution for the country • Bread riots break out in Paris • Poland is partitioned between Austria and Russia and ceases to exist as an independent nation	• The 11th Amendment to the US Constitution limits power of US federal courts in suits arising in the states • Following their defeat by military forces commanded by Anthony Wayne in the Battle of Fallen Timbers (1794), (*cont.*)	• British inventor Joseph Bramah develops the first steam-powered hydraulic press • Robert Fulton patents the first steam-powered mechanical shovel, intended primarily for digging canals	• The Haymarket Theater opens in Boston; it is at the time the largest building in the city • French chemist Nicholas Jacques Conte fires a mixture of powdered graphite and clay in a kiln, producing the "lead" for modern pencils

E. EDUCATION, LITERATURE & THE FINE ARTS	F. RELIGION, THEOLOGY, PHILOSOPHY & PSYCHOLOGY	G. AMERICAN & UNITED METHODISM	H. BRITISH & WORLD METHODISM	
	• Mary Wollstonecraft publishes her feminist classic *Vindication of the Rights of Woman*, arguing for the equal rights of men and women on the basis of their common possession of the faculty of reason • Scottish philosopher Dugald Stewart publishes the first volume of his *Elements of the Philosophy of the Human Mind* (vol. 2, 1814; vol. 3, 1827)	– formally establishes the office of presiding elder and adds a section to the *Discipline* detailing its powers and responsibilities: they are to be appointed by the bishops, and their primary responsibility is supervision of preachers on assigned circuits and chairing quarterly conferences – approves new order of worship and incorporates it into the *Discipline*, effectively setting aside the Sunday Service provided by Wesley • James O'Kelly vehemently opposes Asbury's exercise of "arbitrary power" in the appointment of presiding elders and the stationing of preachers and leads a group of dissident preachers into schism	cut its ties to the Church of England and become an independent "free" church • The Irish Methodist Conference begins meeting annually • Thomas Coke and Henry Moore publish *The Life of the Rev. John Wesley, A.M., Including an Account of the Great Revival of Religion in Europe and America, of Which He Was the First and Chief Instrument*	**1792 cont.**
• The Louvre Museum in Paris opens to the public as the Central Museum of the Arts • Nicolò Paganini makes his debut as violin virtuoso in Genoa at the age of eleven • Joseph Haydn composes his *Symphony No. 100 (Military)* and *Symphony No. 101 (Clock)* • Mary Wollstonecraft publishes her *Historical and Moral View of the Origin and Progress of the French Revolution* • William Blake publishes his *Songs of Experience*, including the memorable "The Tyger," which contrasts powerfully with "The Lamb" from *Songs of Innocence* • William Wordsworth publishes *An Evening Walk and Descriptive Sketches*	• The Reformed Church in the United States, long known as the German Reformed Church, adopts a formal constitution • Samuel Hopkins outlines the theological position that bears his name, "Hopkinsianism," in his *System of Doctrines Contained in Divine Revelation* • Kant publishes *Religion Within the Limits of Reason Alone* • Johann Schiller's *On Grace and Dignity* criticizes Kant's ethical theories	• O'Kelly and his followers establish the Republican Methodist Church • Richard Allen and his followers erect a church building in Philadelphia on the lot he had purchased for that purpose; the church is dedicated by Asbury in 1794 and named Bethel Church [and is now universally known as "Mother Bethel"]	• Conference makes a number of important decisions, which remain in force until 1836: – that Methodist preachers may administer the sacraments when requested by a local society – that there should no longer be any distinction between ordained and unordained preachers – that gowns, cassocks, bands, or surplices should not be worn by the preachers – that the title *Reverend* should not be used by any Methodist preacher – that ordination with "laying on of hands" would no longer be used when accepting preachers into full connexion	**1793**
• Samuel Taylor Coleridge and Robert Southey publish their dramatic account *The Fall of Robespierre* • William Blake produces his famous engraving of *The Ancient of Days* as the frontispiece to his poetic volume *Europe: A Prophecy* • Charles W. Peale organizes the Columbianum, the first society of American artists, in Philadelphia; the society holds its first exhibition the following year	• Anglican priest Samuel Marsden arrives in Sydney and becomes the de facto religious leader of Australia • Notable publications include: – Thomas Paine, *The Age of Reason* – Johann Gottlieb Fichte, *On the Concept of the Science of Knowledge* – William Paley, *A View of the Evidence of Christianity* – Denis Diderot, *Essays on the Progress of the Human Spirit*	• African Zoar Church in Philadelphia, first formed by black Methodists from St. George's Church in 1792, is formally established as a separate congregation; Harry Hosier is its founding pastor [it is now the oldest continuous historically black congregation in the United Methodist tradition] • The African Church of Philadelphia, established by the Free Africa Society in 1791, joins the Protestant Episcopal Church and is consecrated as St. Thomas African Episcopal Church; Absalom Jones becomes the pastor and is the denomination's first black priest [he is ordained deacon in 1795 and priest in 1802]	• Samuel Clapham attacks the Methodist movement in his sermon "How Far Methodism Conduces to the Interests of Christianity and the Welfare of Society"; he is answered anonymously by "a Member of the Church of England" in early 1795 with "Methodism Vindicated From the Charge of Ignorance and Enthusiam"	**1794**
• Charles Bullfinch designs the Massachusetts State House • Construction of the Bank of England building begins in London (not completed until 1827) • Beethoven composes his *Piano Concerto No. 1* • The Paris Music Conservatory is founded	• The ecumenical London Missionary Society is formally established by Anglicans and Presbyterians in Britain • Friedrich Wilhelm Joseph von Schelling writes *On the I as Principle of Philosophy, or on the Absolute in Human Knowledge*	• The Republican Methodist Church (1793) is renamed the Christian Church • Cokesbury College is destroyed by fire; the college is relocated to Baltimore	• A "Plan of Pacification" approved by Conference marks a crucial stage in the separation of Methodism from the Church of England: – stipulates that the Lord's Supper may be celebrated in Methodist chapels where a majority of both the trustees and the leaders and stewards approve	**1795**

	A. WORLD HISTORY & POLITICS	B. AMERICAN HISTORY & POLITICS	C. SCIENCE, MEDICINE & TECHNOLOGY	D. DAILY LIFE, POPULAR CULTURE & ENTERTAINMENT
1795 cont.	• France occupies the Netherlands; Spain and Prussia make peace with France, with Prussia ceding all its lands west of the Rhine River to the French through the Peace of Basel	eleven Indian tribes sign the Treaty of Greenville, which places most of the Ohio Valley under white control		
1796	• Napoleon Bonaparte assumes command of the French army, forms an alliance with Spain, wins several strategic battles against Austria, and marries Josephine • Catherine the Great of Russia dies; her son, Paul I, becomes Tsar and establishes laws concerning regular succession to the throne • Great Britain conquers Ceylon (Sri Lanka) • The Edict of Beijing (Peking) forbids the import of opium into China	• Tennessee is admitted to the US as the 16th state; it is a slave state • The Wilderness Road through the Cumberland Gap is widened enough to permit the passage of wagons, connecting the Ohio Valley region with the East by the Great Valley Road, which ran through the Shenandoah Valley from Pennsylvania • The Boston African Society, one of the first such mutual-aid organizations, is established • Andrew Ellicott surveys the border between Florida and the US • George Washington refuses a third term as president; delivers "Farewell Address" warning against the dangers of US involvement in permanent foreign alliances and a powerful permanent military establishment • John Adams (Federalist Party) is elected president, Thomas Jefferson (Democratic-Republican Party) is elected vice president	• British physician Edward Jenner develops the first effective smallpox vaccine from a cowpox lesion • Alois Senefelder (Germany) develops lithography, a method of printing that produces high-quality images • The first suspension bridge in the US is constructed across Jacob's Creek in Westmoreland, PA • Pierre-Simon LaPlace (France) publishes his *System of the World*, a semipopular exposition of his theory of celestial mechanics including his "nebular hypothesis" that stars and planets are formed by the cooling and contraction of hot, gaseous nebulae	• Amelia Simmons publishes *American Cookery*, the first cookbook by an American • Travelers between Boston and Philadelphia complain of deep holes and ditches in the roads, which sometimes cause carriages to overturn
1797	• Austria and France reach a peace agreement; Austria cedes Belgium to France and receives control of Venice and Dalmatia • Prussia's King Frederick William II dies; he is succeeded by his son, Frederick William III	• The USS *Constitution* ("Old Ironsides") is launched as part of the new US Navy; she will become the most famous ship in US history • France complains that "John Jay's Treaty" of 1794 shows US bias toward Britain, begins interfering with US ships, and threatens to declare war	• Henry Maudslay in England and David Wilkinson in the US independently add a sliding tool carriage geared to the spindle of the lathe, producing the modern carriage lathe • Charles Newbold patents the first cast iron plow in the US	• The first copper pennies are minted in England and the first £1 paper notes are issued

E. EDUCATION, LITERATURE & THE FINE ARTS	F. RELIGION, THEOLOGY, PHILOSOPHY & PSYCHOLOGY	G. AMERICAN & UNITED METHODISM	H. BRITISH & WORLD METHODISM	
	• Marie Jean Antoine Nicholas de Caritat, Marquis de Condorcet, better known simply as Condorcet, publishes his *Sketch for a Historical Picture of the Progress of the Human Mind*		– permits only preachers authorized by Conference to celebrate sacraments – forbids sacramental services at times when the Church of England would be worshiping – restricts the stationing of preachers solely to Conference • Conference sends some local preachers to Sierra Leone but the mission proves a failure and is abandoned in 1796	**1795 cont.**
• The first American edition of *The Complete Works of Shakespeare* is published in Boston • Goethe's novel *Wilhelm Meister's Apprenticeship* becomes a model for later German fiction • American artist Gilbert Stuart paints his famous *Portrait of George Washington*	• Johann Gottlieb Fichte publishes *The Foundation of Natural Right in Accordance with the Principles of the Science of Knowledge* [*Wissenschaftslehre*]	• Coke makes his sixth trip to America (Oct.–Feb. 1797) to attend the General Conference • The MEC General Conference: – establishes six geographically defined annual conferences: New England, Philadelphia, Baltimore, Virginia, South Carolina, and Western; an annual conference now becomes both an *area* and a *meeting* – writes into the *Discipline* the "trust clause" requiring that property deeds be drawn so as to "secure the premises firmly and permanently to the Methodist Episcopal Church," to be held in trust by a board of trustees "for the use of the members of said church in the place where the property is located" – establishes the Chartered Fund for the relief of "distressed preachers" out of the proceeds of the Book Concern – restores to the *Discipline* the section on slavery, suspended since 1785 – makes a traveling deacon eligible for elder's orders and full annual conference membership after two years • Jacob Albright begins his preaching ministry among Germans in Pennsylvania with an MEC exhorter's license • Cokesbury College is again destroyed by fire and is never reestablished • Richard Allen and associates sign the Articles of Association of Bethel African Methodist Episcopal Church in order to secure control of their church property in Philadelphia • Peter Williams, James Varick, and Christopher Rush lead black Methodists in New York in requesting permission from Asbury to form their own separate society, leading to the establishment of Zion Church in 1801 • African Zoar Church in Philadelphia dedicates its first permanent building; Asbury presides over the ceremony	• Alexander Kilham leads protests against the refusal of Conference to allow lay representation and involvement in stationing of preachers, resulting in his expulsion from Conference	**1796**
• Coleridge writes his exotic and mysterious poem *Kubla Khan* (published posthumously in 1816) • Goethe publishes his poetic ballad *The Sorcerer's Apprentice*, based on a story by the ancient poet Lucian of Samosata • William Blake provides the engravings for an illustrated edition of Edward Young's *Night Thoughts* • Joseph Haydn composes his *Emperor String Quartet* • Luigi Cherubini composes his first notable opera, *Médée* (Medusa) • *Pianoforte*, the first magazine devoted to the piano, begins publication in London	• von Schelling publishes *Ideas on the Philosophy of Nature*	• Coke makes his seventh trip to America to meet with Virginia Annual Conference	• Conference publishes the *Form of Discipline* for the first time • Kilham spearheads the formation of the Methodist New Connexion (MNC), resulting in the first schism in British Methodism; the main body (called the "Old Connexion") begins to use the name "Wesleyan Methodist" (WM) to distinguish themselves from the "Kilhamites" and from Welsh Calvinistic Methodism	**1797**

	A. WORLD HISTORY & POLITICS	B. AMERICAN HISTORY & POLITICS	C. SCIENCE, MEDICINE & TECHNOLOGY	D. DAILY LIFE, POPULAR CULTURE & ENTERTAINMENT
1798	• The French capture Rome and proclaim a revolutionary Roman Republic; the Pope moves to southern France • Napoleon names himself Master of Egypt after defeating the native Mamluk army in the Battle of the Pyramids, but his navy is defeated by British forces commanded by Horatio Nelson in the Battle of the Nile; Napoleon returns to France • England introduces a wartime income tax of 10 percent on all annual incomes over £200	• The US Marine Corps is formally established as a separate service within the US Department of the Navy; its roots go back to British Royal Marines and the Continental Marines of 1776 • President Adams signs the Alien and Sedition Acts, which impose harsh restrictions on noncitizens and curtail the freedom of the press, providing for fines or imprisonment for individuals who criticized the government, Congress, or the president in speech or print	• Eli Whitney creates a milling machine that can produce standard and interchangeable gun barrels for muskets • British chemist Humphry Davy discovers the anesthetic effects of nitrous oxide (laughing gas)	• *The Columbian Songster and Free Mason's Pocket Companion*, published in Boston, is perhaps the first collection of strictly secular music to appear in the US
1799	• Austria again declares war on France as Napoleon's armies continue to march throughout Europe • Napoleon's invasion of Syria is turned back by the Ottoman Turks at Acre • Napoleon returns to France, abolishes the Directory, establishes the Consulate, and names himself First Consul of the French Republic • The Combination Acts of 1799 and 1800 outlaw the emerging Trades Union Movement in Britain • German naturalist Alexander von Humboldt begins his exploration of the entire length of the Orinoco River and most of the Amazon River system in South America (to 1803)	• The New York legislature passes an Emancipation Act outlawing slavery within the state • President Adams keeps the US out of war by opening diplomatic negotiations with France • The Kentucky and Virginia resolutions, drafted by James Madison and Thomas Jefferson, protest against the usurpation of states' rights by the federal government through the 1798 Alien and Sedition Acts and argue for the authority of states to nullify objectionable acts passed by Congress • George Washington, the "father of his country," dies at his home in Mount Vernon, VA; he is eulogized as "first in war, first in peace, and first in the hearts of his countrymen"	• The metric system of weights and measures (meter, gram, and liter) is formally implemented in France • A near-perfectly preserved mammoth is found encased in glacial ice in Siberia • Alexander Hamilton publishes *A Report on the Subject of Manufactures*, which despite its dull title provides a good description of the state of American industry	• A strike by shoemakers in Philadelphia produces the first recorded use of the abusive word *scab* for those persons hired to replace striking workers • Josiah Spode (Britain) adds calcined bone to his formula for making porcelain and creates strong, chip-resistant bone china
1800	• Napoleon's armies conquer Italy, defeat the Austrians at the Battles of Marengo and Hohenlinden, seize Munich, and march on Vienna • Under pressure from Napoleon, Spain signs the secret Treaty of San Ildefonso, by which the Louisiana Territory in North America, acquired by Spain from France in 1763, is ceded back to France • The settlement of Ottawa, Canada, is established • The British capture Malta • The British East India Company concludes a trade agreement with the Shah of Persia	• The US census reports that the population is 5,308,483: – whites: 4,306,446 (81.1%) – free blacks: 108,435 (2.0%) – slaves: 893,602 (16.9%) • The US national debt is $82,976,294 • The US capital is moved from Philadelphia to Washington, DC; President Adams moves into the still unfinished White House • The north wing of the US Capitol building, containing the Senate chamber, is completed and Congress convenes there for the first time • Congress divides the Northwest Territory into two new territories, Ohio and Indiana • Thomas Jefferson and Aaron Burr (Democratic-Republican Party) run in the presidential election against incumbent John Adams and his vice president, Charles Pinckney (Federalist Party); because there is at the time no distinction between candidates for president and vice president, Jefferson and Burr each end up with the same number of electoral college votes, throwing the election into the House of Representatives • Gabriel Prosser organizes a slave revolt in Virginia; the conspiracy is uncovered, Prosser and a number of others are hanged, and Virginia's slave laws are consequently tightened • Congress passes the Harrison Land Act, reducing the minimum amount of land that *(cont.)*	• Erasmus Darwin completes his *Phytologia, or the Philosophy of Agriculture and Gardening* • The first zinc/copper battery is developed by Alessandro Volta • William Herschel discovers infrared radiation in the sun's light • The Royal College of Surgeons is founded in London • An epidemic of yellow fever kills over 80,000 people in Spain	• Philadelphia shoemaker William Young for the first time makes shoes shaped differently for the right and left feet • John Chapman, better known as "Johnny Appleseed," travels through the Ohio Valley distributing religious tracts along with apple seeds

E. EDUCATION, LITERATURE & THE FINE ARTS	F. RELIGION, THEOLOGY, PHILOSOPHY & PSYCHOLOGY	G. AMERICAN & UNITED METHODISM	H. BRITISH & WORLD METHODISM	
• Michael Haydn accepts Carl Maria von Weber as a pupil, free of charge • Joseph Haydn completes what is perhaps his greatest oratorio, *The Creation* • Beethoven composes his *Piano Sonata No. 8 (Pathetique)* • Coleridge and Wordsworth publish a joint volume of poetry, *Lyrical Ballads*; it is a milestone of English Romanticism and includes Coleridge's "The Rime of the Ancient Mariner"	• Thomas Malthus publishes his *Essay on the Principle of Population*, arguing that the human population of a region tends to increase in relation to the available food supply and that overpopulation will always be checked by famine, disease, or warfare • Friedrich von Schlegel founds the journal *Athenäem*	• As instructed by the 1796 General Conference, Asbury and Coke publish an annotated version of *The Doctrines and Discipline of the Methodist Episcopal Church in America* • John Dickins begins publication of an American edition of *The Methodist Magazine*; it is not successful in the US, and publication is suspended in 1799 • James O'Kelly publishes *The Author's Apology for Protesting Against the Methodist Episcopal Government*	• The WM sacramental center in London moves from the West Street Chapel (acquired by John Wesley for that purpose in 1743) to the newly constructed Great Queen Street Chapel; the West Street Chapel becomes a "free chapel" of the Church of England under the Bishop of London • The Irish Methodist Conference begins sending Gaelic-speaking missionaries into Roman Catholic areas of the country • *The Arminian Magazine* (1777) is replaced in Britain by *The Methodist Magazine*	**1798**
• French soldiers in Egypt discover the Rosetta Stone, bearing an inscription in Greek, Egyptian hieroglyphics, and Egyptian demotic script; this makes it possible for scholars to decipher hieroglyphic inscriptions reliably for the first time • William Blake's depiction of *The Last Supper* is exhibited at the Royal Academy • Friedrich von Schiller completes his three-part poetic historical drama, *Wallenstein*	• Pope Pius VI dies; he is succeeded in 1800 by Pope Pius VII • The Church Missionary Society is founded in London • Friedrich Daniel Ernst Schleiermacher publishes *On Religion: Speeches to its Cultured Despisers*, in which he defines religion for the skeptical intellectual elite of Germany as being "a sense of the Infinite in the finite" • Other notable publications include: – Johann Gottlieb Fichte, *The System of Ethics in Accordance with the Principles of the Science of Knowledge [Wissenschaftslehre]* – Johann Gottfried von Herder, *Understanding and Experience: A Metacritique on the Critique of Pure Reason*	• Richard Allen is ordained deacon by Asbury; he is the first black person to be ordained in the history of Methodism	• Eccentric American Methodist preacher Lorenzo Dow decides to undertake a preaching mission in Ireland without permission from either American (MEC) or British (WM) Conferences • Jabez Bunting becomes a WM preacher • John Stephenson from the Irish Methodist Conference begins mission work in Bermuda	**1799**
• The Library of Congress is established in Washington, DC • Friedrich von Schiller publishes his dramatic play *Mary Stuart* • Beethoven composes his *Symphony No. 1 in C Major* • Luigi Cherubini's operatic masterpiece *Les Deux Journées* (also known as *The Water Carrier* from its German title, *Der Wasserträger*) debuts at the Salle Feydeau in Paris • Carl Friedrich Zelter becomes director of the Singakademie in Berlin	• The first identifiable camp meeting in America takes place at Mud Creek in Logan County, KY; the leading spirits are brothers John McGee (a Methodist local pastor) and William McGee (a Presbyterian minister), who often held meetings together; inspired by a fiery revival service held by James McGready in 1799 at which they both preached, the McGee brothers organize a meeting that brings thousands of people together to camp in the woods for several days of evangelistic services; the camp meeting movement soon spreads across Kentucky and Tennessee • von Schelling publishes *The System of Transcendental Idealism*	• Coke makes his eighth trip to America (April–May) in time for the General Conference • The MEC General Conference: – limits participation in General Conference to preachers who have traveled for at least four years – declines proposals to establish a delegated General Conference, to approve a Council to aid the bishops in making appointments, and to authorize the election of presiding elders – elects Richard Whatcoat as a third bishop, alongside Coke and Asbury – requires each annual conference to elect a secretary, who is to make an annual report to the General Conference – authorizes ordination of blacks as local deacons to assist with mission work among slaves – makes provision for the support of disabled preachers and the widows and orphans of preachers from the Chartered Fund – requires preachers holding slaves to emancipate them but refuses to exclude slaveholders from office in the church – creates the New York Annual Conference (total now 7) • William Otterbein and Martin Boehm found *Die Vereinigte Brüderschaft in Christo* (The Church of the United Brethren in Christ, a.k.a. United Brethren Church, or UBC) and are elected its first bishops; the *(cont.)*	• The MEC severs its links with Nova Scotia and ceases to support churches there and elsewhere in Canada; the WM Conference takes up responsibility for Canadian churches • The WM Conference sends Welsh-speaking missionaries into Wales • William Turton is sent by the WM Conference as the first official missionary to the Bahamas	**1800**

	A. WORLD HISTORY & POLITICS	B. AMERICAN HISTORY & POLITICS	C. SCIENCE, MEDICINE & TECHNOLOGY	D. DAILY LIFE, POPULAR CULTURE & ENTERTAINMENT
1800 cont.		can be purchased directly from the federal government from 640 to 320 acres, raising the price to $2 per acre and allowing payment over four years		
1801	• The Act of Union joins the kingdoms of Ireland and Great Britain (itself a merger of England and Scotland under the Act of Union of 1707) to create the United Kingdom of Great Britain and Ireland (UK); the "Union Jack" is adopted as the official flag of the UK • Denmark allies itself with France; British naval forces commanded by Horatio Nelson defeat the Danish fleet near Copenhagen • Tsar Paul I of Russia is assassinated; he is succeeded by his son, Alexander I • The US goes to war against the Barbary States along the north coast of Africa, comprising modern Morocco, Algeria, Tunisia, and Libya, which were harboring pirates who preyed on ship traffic in the Mediterranean Sea	• The House of Representatives chooses Thomas Jefferson as president; Aaron Burr becomes vice president • John Marshall is appointed Chief Justice of the US Supreme Court	• Italian astronomer Giuseppe Piazzi discovers the first minor planet, or asteroid, which he names Ceres • Robert Fulton builds the *Nautilus*, a four-man, hand-operated submarine; he demonstrates it successfully in France but is unable to interest either the French or the British in purchasing it	• *The New York Evening Post* begins publication • The American Company of Booksellers, the first such organization in America, is organized in New York • The London Stock Exchange opens as a regulated exchange with formal membership requirements
1802	• France, Spain, and Britain enter into the Treaty of Amiens, leaving France the dominant power on the European continent • Napoleon declares himself President of the Italian Republic • France suppresses the rebellion led since 1791 by Toussaint L'Ouverture on the island of Hispaniola; he is captured, taken to France, and dies in prison in 1803	• Congress repeals portions of the Alien and Sedition Acts of 1798 and allows the other portions to expire • President Jefferson uses the famous phrase "a wall of separation between Church and State" in a letter to the Baptist Association in Danbury, CT • The US Military Academy is established at West Point, NY • Georgia cedes its western territory to the US; it is organized into the Mississippi Territory, embracing most of what is now Alabama and Mississippi	• Johann Ritter discovers ultraviolet radiation (radiation with wavelengths that are shorter than those of light waves) • Humphry Davy demonstrates that metal strips can be heated to incandescence by passing a sufficiently strong electric current through them • Merino sheep are imported into the US from Spain for the first time	• American sailor Nathaniel Bowditch publishes the first edition of his classic work *The New American Practical Navigator*, which becomes a standard sailing text • The British parliament passes The Factory Health and Morals Act, the first important child labor law; it applies primarily, though not exclusively, to young apprentices in cotton and woolen mills
1803	• Responding to Napoleon's usurpation of power, Britain declares war on France • France occupies Hanover, the homeland of the British royal family, and threatens to invade Britain	• In the case of *Marbury v. Madison*, the Supreme Court under Chief Justice Marshall rules that an act of Congress is null and void when it conflicts with provisions of the US Constitution; this is the first important test of the system of checks and balances between the executive, legislative, and judicial branches of government • Ohio, formed in the Northwest Territory, is admitted to the US as the 17th state; it is a free state	• Henry and Sealy Fourdrinier (England) develop a papermaking machine that produces a continuous roll of paper • British artillery officer Henry Shrapnel successfully demonstrates to the British Army the exploding shot cannonball that he had first designed in 1784; his name comes to be used as the term for the fragments that result from any exploding shell or bomb	• British industrialist William Murdock lights his main factory with coal gas, derived from heating coal; it is the first building to be routinely lit in this way

E. EDUCATION, LITERATURE & THE FINE ARTS	F. RELIGION, THEOLOGY, PHILOSOPHY & PSYCHOLOGY	G. AMERICAN & UNITED METHODISM	H. BRITISH & WORLD METHODISM	
		first annual conference session meets at the home of Peter Kemp • Jacob Albright organizes three classes among the Germans in eastern Pennsylvania and the Shenandoah Valley; his followers become known as "Albright's People" • Nicholas Snethen answers O'Kelly's attack on MEC polity with *A Reply to an Apology for Protesting Against the Methodist Episcopal Government* • The Western (Annual) Conference meets for the first time; Asbury and Whatcoat pass through the Cumberland Gap to attend, along with newly appointed presiding elder William McKendree		**1800 cont.**
• Joseph Haydn composes his oratorio *The Seasons* • Beethoven composes his *Piano Sonata No. 14 (Moonlight)*; his first ballet, *Die Geschöpfe des Prometheus (The Creatures of Prometheus)* premieres in Vienna's Burgtheater; and he becomes aware that he is going deaf • Italian pianist Muzio Clementi publishes *The Art of Playing on the Piano Forte*	• A concordat between Napoleon and the Vatican leads to revival of the French Catholic Church • American feminist Martha Meredith Read publishes *A Second Vindication of the Rights of Women*, one of the earliest American feminist treatises, which supports and elaborates on Mary Wollstonecraft's pioneering 1792 work on women's rights • American Deist philosopher Elihu Palmer, founder of the Deistical Society of New York, publishes his *Principles of Nature*, arguing that "the world is infinitely worse" because of Christianity • The Cane Ridge camp meeting begins in Bourbon County, KY, around the church pastored by Presbyterian minister Barton W. Stone, marking the beginning of the "great revival" in the West and fueling the Second Great Awakening in America • German philosophers Georg Wilhelm Friedrich Hegel and von Schelling establish *The Critical Journal of Philosophy*	• Black Methodists in New York incorporate the "African Methodist Episcopal Church (called Zion Church) of the City of New York"; by agreement they are supplied with ministers by the MEC • Peter Cartwright, who will become one of American Methodism's best-known "circuit riders," is converted	• William Myles publishes *A List of Methodist Preachers*; it is the first biographical dictionary in Methodist history	**1801**
• Thomas Bruce, 7th Earl of Elgin, begins sending ancient Greek sculptures to England, including friezes from the Parthenon; the "Elgin Marbles" stir controversy when they are exhibited at the British Museum • The influential literary journal *The Edinburgh Review* begins publishing its blunt critical reviews • Johann Nikolaus Forkel publishes *Johann Sebastian Bach: His Life, Art, and Work*, the first biographical and musicological study of Bach, using information provided by Bach's sons • The American Academy of Fine Arts is established in New York	• William Paley publishes *Natural Theology: Or, Evidences of the Existence and Attributes of the Deity*, in which he formulates the classic version of the teleological or "design" argument for God's existence: if the complexity of a watch does not just "happen" but requires a designer or maker, then the infinitely more complex universe in which we live also requires a designer or maker, i.e., God • François Auguste René, Vicomte de Chateaubriand, writes *The Genius of Christianity*, in which he argues for the aesthetic and moral superiority of Christianity over all other religions	• Ezekiel Cooper revises Wesley's 1785 Pocket Hymn Book and publishes it in New York as *The Methodist Pocket Hymn Book, Revised and Improved: Designed as a Constant Companion for the Pious of All Denominations*; it competes directly with Robert Spence's 1785 collection	• The Irish Methodist Conference bans women from preaching as "contrary to the Scriptures and prudence" and expels the very popular and effective evangelist Alice Cambridge when she refuses to quit preaching	**1802**
• New York's City Hall, a classical example of Georgian architecture, is completed • Beethoven composes his *Sonata for Violin and Piano (Kreutzer)*	• Barton W. Stone and his followers withdraw from the Presbyterian Synod of Kentucky and organize the Springfield (Kentucky) Presbytery; they adopt practically the same theological position as that of the Christian Church (1795)	• Coke makes his ninth and last trip to America (Nov.–June 1804) • The first annual conference of the society called "Albright's People" meets and ordains Jacob Albright as their elder and minister	• The WM Conference effectively restricts women to preaching only to other women and then only under strictly limited conditions; Sarah Mallet ceases to preach as a result • The WM mission in the Caribbean is extended to the Bahamas	**1803**

	A. WORLD HISTORY & POLITICS	**B. AMERICAN HISTORY & POLITICS**	**C. SCIENCE, MEDICINE & TECHNOLOGY**	**D. DAILY LIFE, POPULAR CULTURE & ENTERTAINMENT**
1803 cont.		• James Monroe negotiates and Jefferson approves the Louisiana Purchase from France, which doubles the land area of the US, for $15 million (820,000 square miles for 3¢ an acre) • The 12th Amendment to the US Constitution sets procedure for deciding presidential elections in the House of Representatives when no electoral college majority exists		
1804	• Napoleon proclaims and crowns himself emperor of France, promulgates the Napoleonic Code (a thorough reformation and codification of the French civil laws) • Holy Roman Emperor Francis II assumes the title Emperor of Austria • Denmark becomes the first European country to ban the slave trade • A US expedition commanded by Stephen Decatur enters the harbor at Tripoli and destroys the US frigate *Philadelphia*, which had been captured by the Barbary pirates • Jean-Jacques Dessalines, who served under Toussaint L'Ouverture, succeeds in driving the French out of Hispaniola; he declares the independence of the Republic of Haiti and names himself emperor	• President Jefferson dispatches Meriwether Lewis and James Clark on their epic three-year expedition through the Louisiana Territory; they travel up the Mississippi and Missouri rivers and spend the winter with Mandan and Hidatsa Indians near what is now Bismarck, ND • New Jersey becomes the last northern state to pass legislation outlawing slavery or calling for its gradual abolition; this makes the balance nine free states (New Hampshire, Vermont, Massachusetts, Connecticut, Rhode Island, Pennsylvania, New York, New Jersey, Ohio) against eight slave states (Delaware, Maryland, Virginia, North Carolina, South Carolina, Georgia, Kentucky, Tennessee) • Extreme anti-Federalists led by Aaron Burr plan to separate from the US to form a separate Northern Confederacy; Alexander Hamilton blocks Burr's plan to become governor of New York and lead the breakaway and attacks Burr's character; Burr challenges Hamilton to a pistol duel, and Hamilton is killed • Congress reduces the minimum amount of land that can be purchased directly from the federal government from 320 to 160 acres • President Jefferson is reelected and George Clinton is elected as vice president (Democratic-Republican Party) in the first election in which candidates are separately nominated for president and vice president	• Alexander von Humboldt returns from South America with a wealth of botanical, geological, and geographical information, including samples of guano; soon guano is being mined and shipped to Europe and North America for use as nitrate fertilizer • Cornish engineer Richard Trevithick successfully tests the first steam-powered railway locomotive in Penydarren, Wales • Thomas Bewick completes his beautifully illustrated *History of British Birds*	• Dahlias are imported into England for the first time • "Coonskin Libraries" spring up along the Ohio River as settlers trade coonskins for books from "back east" • Bananas are imported into the US for the first time from Cuba (later from other sources in Central and South America)
1805	• After Napoleon annexes Genoa and declares himself king of Italy, a coalition against him is formed by Britain, Austria, Russia, and Sweden • The British navy under Horatio Nelson defeats the French and Spanish fleets in the Battle of Trafalgar; Nelson is mortally wounded • Napoleon defeats Russian and Austrian armies under Tsar Alexander I and Emperor Francis II at Austerlitz (the battle is described in Tolstoy's *War and Peace*) • US Marines land "on the shores of Tripoli" and capture Derna, a stronghold of the Barbary pirates, forcing a peace agreement with them by which US prisoners are released and US ships receive free passage in the Mediterranean	• Lewis and Clarke with the Corps of Discovery pass the Great Falls of the Missouri and through the country that will become Yellowstone National Park, cross the continental divide in the Bitterroot Mountains, and descend on the Snake and Columbia rivers, reaching the Pacific Coast and building winter quarters there • Toussaint Charbonneau, a French-Canadian fur trader, and his Shoshone Indian wife, Sacagawea, travel with Lewis and Clark to translate and help ease relations with other Indian tribes they encounter • The Michigan Territory is formed in the Northwest Territory • Britain and the US quarrel over trade in the West Indies	• French physician Georges Cuvier completes his *Lessons in Comparative Anatomy* (5 vols., 1801–5), which provide the foundation for that science	• The first shipment of ice from New England to the West Indies arrives in Martinique • The Free School Society (later, Public School Society) is founded in New York to establish an alternative to the current pauper school system
1806	• After Prussia declares war in France, Napoleon defeats the Prussian army at Jena and enters Berlin • Napoleon's Berlin Decree begins the "Continental System," declaring Britain to *(cont.)*	• Lewis and Clarke set out on their return journey in March, pass through the Bitterroots in July, and reach St. Louis in September	• Francis Beaufort devises the wind scale bearing his name for measuring the velocity of wind at sea	• Philadelphia's striking shoemakers go on trial for engaging in "criminal conspiracy" to increase their wages; seen as the first prosecution of a trade union in the US • The first coal gas street lights in the US are installed in Newport, RI

E. EDUCATION, LITERATURE & THE FINE ARTS	F. RELIGION, THEOLOGY, PHILOSOPHY & PSYCHOLOGY	G. AMERICAN & UNITED METHODISM	H. BRITISH & WORLD METHODISM	
				1803 cont.
• Beethoven composes his *Symphony No. 3 in E Flat Major (Eroica)*; the name was originally "Napoleon" but Beethoven changed it in anger after Napoleon crowned himself Emperor • William Blake publishes *Jerusalem*	• The Christian Church (1795) is largely absorbed into a union with the Presbyterian and Baptist followers of Barton W. Stone to form the Christian Connection or Church • The British and Foreign Bible Society is established in London with the goal of translating the Bible into every language spoken by any significant number of people	• The MEC General Conference: – limits participation in General Conference to traveling elders in full connection – authorizes presiding elders to call a quarterly conference composed of official members "and none else," and prohibits them from employing a preacher not approved by the Conference – changes maximum length of appointment of preachers on a given circuit from one to two years [this rule is not changed until 1864] – revises the section of the *Discipline* on slavery to "encourage" but not require slaveholders to emancipate their slaves – permits Coke to return to England provided that he holds himself subject to recall and that he returns for the next General Conference, "if he lives" – approves a rule that "no traveling preacher be permitted to publish any book or pamphlet without the approbation of the annual conference to which he belongs, or a committee chosen by them" – votes to move the Methodist Book Concern from Philadelphia to New York and elects Ezekiel Cooper as Book Steward – declines proposal for election of presiding elders	• Coke returns to England from America and never goes back again, effectively ending his service as bishop of the MEC • Coke, in his capacity as General Superintendent of WM Missions, publishes *An Account of the Rise, Progress and Present State of the Methodist Missions*, the first such general report	**1804**
• The Pennsylvania Academy of Fine Arts is established in Philadelphia • Beethoven completes his *Piano Sonata No. 23 (Appassionata)*, and his opera *Fidelio* has its first performance in Vienna • Franz Krommer composes his *Concerto for Oboe in F Major* • J. M. W. Turner's painting *The Shipwreck* exemplifies a powerful new romanticism in landscape art	• Congregationalism in New England splits into Calvinist (Trinitarian) and Liberal (soon to be Unitarian) branches when the Harvard Board of Overseers appoints the liberal Henry Ware to the long-vacant Hollis Professorship of Divinity; Calvinists conclude that they have lost control of theological instruction at Harvard College • A group of German pietists called "Harmonists" establish a settlement near Pittsburgh, which they name Harmony • Denis Diderot publishes *Rameau's Nephew*	• Peter Spencer leads a group of supporters out of Asbury Methodist Episcopal Church of Wilmington, DE, to form the Union Church of Africans; they worship in their homes until 1813	• Lorenzo Dow visits England again, stimulating the development of the camp meeting movement there • Coke marries Penelope Smith and again serves as president of the WM Conference	**1805**
• Noah Webster publishes his *Compendious Dictionary of the English Language* • Italian composer Gioacchino Rossini produces his first opera, *Demetrio a Polibio*, at the age of 14	• American architect Benjamin Henry Latrobe designs and begins the construction of his greatest work, the neoclassical Basilica of the Assumption of the Blessed *(cont.)*	• Richard Whatcoat dies; with Coke being in England and effectively discontinued from the episcopacy, this leaves Asbury as the sole bishop of the MEC	• A union of Independent Methodists is formed in England, bringing together various groups of Methodist reformers who had broken away from WM or the MNC; each body retains its own name and identity	**1806**

	A. WORLD HISTORY & POLITICS	B. AMERICAN HISTORY & POLITICS	C. SCIENCE, MEDICINE & TECHNOLOGY	D. DAILY LIFE, POPULAR CULTURE & ENTERTAINMENT
1806 cont.	be under blockade and closing continental ports to British shipping • A group of 16 minor German states form the Confederation of the Rhine in alliance with France • The Holy Roman Empire is dissolved by Napoleon and Holy Roman Emperor Francis II of Austria is forced to abdicate; he continues to rule Austria until 1835 as Emperor Francis I • British forces invade and occupy the Cape Colony in south Africa	• Zebulon M. Pike, leading a company exploring the Arkansas and Red rivers in the southern Louisiana Territory, discovers and unsuccessfully attempts to climb the mountain now known as Pike's Peak in modern Colorado • The Federal Road begins when the Creek Indians sign a treaty with the US allowing for the creation of a postal road through their territory in Georgia and Alabama to speed mail delivery between Washington City and New Orleans • Aaron Burr schemes to form and lead an independent republic in the Southwest; Jefferson has him arrested and indicted on charges of treason	• German chemist Friedrich W. A. Sertürner creates morphine, the first medicinal drug to successfully be isolated from a plant, the opium poppy	• Ann and Jane Taylor publish *Rhymes for the Nursery* in London; it includes Jane's rhyme "Twinkle, Twinkle, Little Star"
1807	• Napoleon issues the Milan Decree, ordering that all ships calling on British ports before sailing into French territorial waters are subject to seizure by France • The British frigate *Leopard* attacks the US frigate *Chesapeake* off Hampton Roads, killing and wounding several of her crew; four US seamen, alleged to be British subjects, are impressed into British naval service • The slave trade is abolished throughout the British Empire, but not the institution of slavery • Gambia and Sierra Leone become British crown colonies • Napoleon concludes the Treaties of Tilsit with Russia and Prussia; Russia recognizes the grand duchy of Warsaw (under French control); Prussia loses half of its territory to France	• The south wing of the US Capitol building, containing the chamber of the House of Representatives, is completed • Attempting to force Britain and France to stop interference with US shipping and trade, Congress passes the Embargo Act, which prohibits American shipping bound for foreign ports and prohibits foreign vessels from taking cargo at American ports • After the *Chesapeake* incident, Jefferson orders all British warships out of US waters • Aaron Burr is tried for treason but is acquitted after a six-month trial and leaves the US for Europe	• Robert Fulton builds the *Clermont*, the first reliable steamboat to enter commercial service • Charles Bell's *System of Comparative Surgery*, regarded as the finest textbook of the time, considers surgery almost wholly from an anatomical rather than a medical point of view	• The first coal gas street lights in London appear on Pall Mall, using lamps designed by William Murdock • Charles and Mary Lamb publish *Tales from Shakespeare*, a collection of children's stories based on Shakespeare's plays • The first Ascot Gold Cup horse race is held in England
1808	• Napoleon conquers Spain; King Charles IV is forced to abdicate the throne in favor of Napoleon's brother, Joseph • Napoleon's occupation of Spain encourages the rise of movements toward independence in Spain's colonial possessions in the Americas • Napoleon annexes the Papal States to the French Empire and holds Pope Pius VII prisoner in Savona, Italy, and later in Fontainebleau, France • British forces land in Portugal and defeat the French at Vimerio; the French surrender Lisbon to British control	• The slave population of the US reaches 1 million; Congress prohibits further slave importation into the US but does not prohibit the sale or trading of slaves who are already inside the US, including their children • James Madison is elected as president and George Clinton is reelected as vice president (Democratic-Republican Party)	• John Dalton's *A New System of Chemical Philosophy* builds the foundations of modern chemistry with its theory about atomic particles • British lumberman William Newberry invents the band saw, putting the cutting teeth on a continuous metal loop or band	• American clock maker Seth Thomas begins the mass production of clocks with interchangeable parts

E. EDUCATION, LITERATURE & THE FINE ARTS	F. RELIGION, THEOLOGY, PHILOSOPHY & PSYCHOLOGY	G. AMERICAN & UNITED METHODISM	H. BRITISH & WORLD METHODISM	
• German poets Clemens Brentano and Achim von Arnim publish *Des Knaben Wunderhorn* (The Boy's Magic Horn), an anthology of old German folk or "peasant" songs, which establishes them as among the leaders of the Romantic movement in Germany • Beethoven composes his *Three "Rasumovsky" String Quartets* • Carl Czerny publishes his first piano composition at the age of 15	Virgin Mary in Baltimore, the first Roman Catholic cathedral in the US (completed in 1821) • Schleiermacher explores the meaning of Christian love by depicting a German family's celebration of Christmas in his *Christmas Eve: A Dialogue on the Incarnation*		• Methodism is introduced into southern Africa by British soldiers stationed in the Cape Colony	**1806 cont.**
• The Boston Athenaeum is established; it combines features of a social club, a reference library, and a museum of natural history • Beethoven composes his *Coriolan Overture* and *Leonore Overture No. 3* • British poet Lord George Gordon Noel Byron publishes his first important book of poetry, *Hours of Idleness* • William Wordsworth publishes *Poems in Two Volumes, including Ode: Intimations of Immortality*	• The London Missionary Society sends Robert Morrison to China; he initiates the first Protestant mission work in China • G. W. F. Hegel publishes his *Phenomenology of Mind [Spirit]*, which attempts to solve the subject-object problem of modern epistemology as well as the dichotomy between idealism and realism through his vision of "the dialectical movement of spirit" • First African Presbyterian Church is organized in Philadelphia; it is the first black Presbyterian church in the US • Moravian Theological Seminary is established in Bethlehem, PA • Andover Theological Seminary is established by Calvinist Congregationalists in New England as an alternative to Harvard College [it is the oldest graduate school of theology in the US]	• "Albright's People" create *Der Neuformirten Methodisten Confernez* (The Newly-Formed Methodist Conference, or NFMC, forerunner of the Evangelical Association), elect Jacob Albright as their bishop, and begin holding regular annual conferences • The Pennsylvania Supreme Court rules that the black Methodist congregation at Bethel Church, rather than the MEC, owns the property on which they worship and that they can determine who may preach there	• An English camp meeting at Mow Cop, organized under the inspiration of Lorenzo Dow by Hugh Bourne and William Clowes, prompts the WM Conference to condemn the holding of camp meetings	**1807**
• The *American Law Journal*, the first legal periodical in the US, is founded in Baltimore • Harvard College forms the first student symphony orchestra in the country • Carl Friedrich Zelter establishes an orchestra, the Ripienschule, to accompany the Singakademie in Berlin • Beethoven's *Symphony No. 5 in C Minor* and *Symphony No. 6 in F (Pastoral)* symbolize his role as a transitional figure between Classicism and Romanticism • Goethe publishes the first version of *Faust*	• Johann Gottlieb Fichte speaks about a "national consciousness" in his *Addresses to the German People* • The Roman Catholic Inquisition in Spain and Italy is abolished on the orders of Napoleon	• The MEC General Conference: – adopts six "Restrictive Rules" that place limits on what subsequent General Conferences can do, marking the beginning of the real constitutional development of American Methodism – adopts plans for a *delegated* General Conference beginning in 1812 to help balance membership disparity among the annual conferences – orders that the section on slavery be stricken from copies of the *Discipline* printed for the South, and authorizes each annual conference to make its own rules concerning slavery – approves a resolution that Coke "is not to exercise the office of superintendent among us, in the United States, until he be recalled by the General Conference, or by all the annual conferences respectively" – elects William McKendree as bishop; he is the first native-born American to be elected an MEC bishop and is now effectively the second bishop alongside Asbury • Methodist printer J. C. Trotter produces the "Double Hymn Book" in New York; the formal title is *A Selection of Hymns from various authors, designed as a Supplement to the Methodist Pocket Hymn Book, compiled under the direction of Francis Asbury and published by order of the General Conference* • Jacob Albright dies	• Hugh Bourne is expelled from the WM Conference, followed by William Clowes in 1810, because of their unwillingness to stop leading camp meetings; their respective followers withdraw from the WM Connexion	**1808**

	A. WORLD HISTORY & POLITICS	B. AMERICAN HISTORY & POLITICS	C. SCIENCE, MEDICINE & TECHNOLOGY	D. DAILY LIFE, POPULAR CULTURE & ENTERTAINMENT
1809	• Russia conquers and annexes Finland, then under the control of Sweden • British forces under Arthur Wellesley (later the Duke of Wellington) drive the French out of Portugal and invade Spain, defeating the French at Talavera • Napoleon's forces occupy Vienna; by the Peace of Schönbrunn, Austria loses major chunks of territory to France and Russia	• The Non-Intercourse Act lifts all embargoes on American shipping except for shipments bound for British or French ports • The Illinois Territory is organized from a portion of the Northwest Territory	• The *Phoenix*, built and captained by John Stephens, becomes the first oceangoing steamship when she travels from New York to Philadelphia • Scottish-born American geologist William Maclure completes the first geological survey of the US, begun in 1807, during which he crossed the Allegheny Mountains some fifty times; his survey is published in the *Transactions of the American Philosophical Society* as a memoir entitled *Observations on the Geology of the United States* together with the first geological map of the US	• Nicholas Appert (France) invents a process for preserving food by sealing it in airtight jars and sterilizing it with heat; this is the basis of food "canning" • The first cricket club in the US is organized in Boston
1810	• Napoleon's Rambouillet Decree, issued in retaliation for the American Embargo Act of 1807, orders American ships seized and sold • Having divorced Josephine, Napoleon marries Archduchess Marie Louise of Austria (daughter of Emperor Francis II) and annexes much of Europe • Mixed-race (*creole*) peoples in the Spanish colonies in Central and South America begin to rebel against Spanish rule; Simón Bolívar emerges as a key leader in South America • Mexican priest Miguel Hidalgo y Costilla calls for independence from Spain, racial equality, and redistribution of land, exhorting the people to take up arms for Our Lady of Guadalupe; the event, known as El Grito de Hidalgo, is celebrated as Independence Day in Mexico	• The US census reports that the population is 7,239,881: – whites: 5,862,073 (81.0%) – free blacks: 186,446 (2.6%) – slaves: 1,191,362 (16.4%) • The US national debt is $53,173,217 • US postal services are consolidated under uniform private contracts • After settlers in western Florida protest against Spanish rule, the US annexes the area	• Italian scientist Amadeo Avogadro formulates his theory about the molecular composition of gases; "Avogadro's number," which indicates the number of molecules of any gas present in a specified volume regardless of their chemical nature or physical properties, becomes one of the fundamental constants of chemistry • Yale College (now University) establishes its school of medicine	• Peter Durand (England) receives a patent from King George III for a tin-plated iron can as a food container • Britain's first public billiards parlor opens in Covent Garden, London
1811	• Austria declares bankruptcy due to the Napoleonic Wars • British workers led by Ned Ludd destroy new textile machinery, which they believe threatens their jobs; the name *Luddite* comes to refer to anyone strongly opposed to technological innovation • The Spanish colony of Venezuela declares independence, but fighting persists until 1821 • The "army" of Miguel Hidalgo y Costilla is soundly defeated by Spanish soldiers, and he is captured and executed	• The largest and most powerful series of earthquakes known to have occurred in North America rock the Mississippi Valley near New Madrid, Missouri, reversing the course of the Mississippi River for days and creating Reelfoot Lake in Tennessee • The US decides to widen the Federal Road from Washington to New Orleans to allow the movement of troops and supplies quickly across the Mississippi Territory despite the objections of the Creek Indians, through whose territory the road runs, leading to the Creek Indian War of 1813–14 • Construction begins on the National Road, also called the Cumberland Road, running west from Cumberland, MD, into the Ohio Valley; it will provide an overland route connecting the Potomac and Ohio rivers and serve as a gateway to the Ohio Valley for thousands of settlers • US Army forces commanded by William Henry Harrison destroy the Shawnee Confederation of Tecumseh at Tippecanoe; Tecumseh is not there at the time, but the Confederation is fatally weakened • The charter of the (first) Bank of the United States expires	• Charles Bell's *New Idea of the Anatomy of the Brain* announces his discovery that the nerves corresponding to different parts of the brain have different functions (sensory and motor) • British chemist Humphry Davy publishes his *Elements of Chemical Philosophy* • Caspar Wistar publishes the first important American textbook on anatomy, *A System of Anatomy* (2 vols., 1811–14) • Swiss explorer Johann Mann makes the first ascent of the Jungfrau peak in the Alps	• English architect John Nash designs and builds Regent's Park in London
1812	• British forces commanded by the Duke of Wellington defeat the French at Salamanca, Spain, and enter Madrid • Russia makes peace with the Ottoman Turks at Bucharest	• The British-American War of 1812 begins when the British continue to interfere with American shipping and to impress US sailors • British forces from Canada and allied Indian warriors commanded by Tecumseh capture Detroit	• Philippe Girard invents a machine for spinning flax • The steamship *New Orleans* begins the first regular passenger and freight service between New Orleans and Natchez, charging passengers $18 for the trip downstream and $25 for the trip upstream	• The London Gas Light & Coke Company is formed, leading to the lighting of most of the city of London over the next 20 years • William Monroe begins making lead pencils in Concord, MA

E. EDUCATION, LITERATURE & THE FINE ARTS	F. RELIGION, THEOLOGY, PHILOSOPHY & PSYCHOLOGY	G. AMERICAN & UNITED METHODISM	H. BRITISH & WORLD METHODISM	
• Lord Byron, stung by a critical review of his *Hours of Idleness* in the *Edinburgh Review*, responds with a bitingly satirical reply entitled *English Bards and Scotch Reviewers* • Washington Irving publishes his timeless tale *Rip Van Winkle* • Beethoven composes his towering *Piano Concerto No. 5 (Emperor)* • Caspar David Friedrich completes his romantic and allegorical painting *Abbey in an Oak Forest*	• The International Bible Society (IBS) is founded in New York City • "Mother" Elizabeth Ann Seton establishes the first American community of the Sisters of Charity in Emmitsburg, MD; it is the first Roman Catholic religious order to be established in the US; in 1975 she will become the first native-born American to be made a saint by the Roman Catholic Church • Adam Clarke begins work on his *Commentary on the New Testament* (3 vols.) • F. W. J. von Schelling publishes *Of Human Freedom*	• The NFMC adopts its first *Discipline* and publishes a catechism but decides not to elect a new bishop to succeed Jacob Albright	• The WM mission in the Caribbean is extended to Trinidad	1809
• Sir Walter Scott publishes *The Lady of the Lake* • Beethoven composes his *Egmont Overture* • Rossini's first comic opera, *La cambiale di matrimonio* (The Bill of Marriage), premieres in Venice • Francisco Goya completes his etchings of *The Disasters of War*	• The Cumberland Presbyterian Church (CPC) is formed by pioneers who turn away from the Calvinist Presbyterian doctrine of predestination to embrace the "Whosoever Will" gospel of the new church	• The NFMC holds its first camp meeting • Christian Newcomer and George Geeting organize a second UBC annual conference in Ohio, later named the Miami Conference • Jesse Lee publishes *A Short History of the Methodists in the United States of America*, the first history of American Methodism • John Totten publishes *An Apology for Camp-Meetings, Illustrative of their Good Effects and Answering the Principal Objections Urged Against Them*	• The first Methodist Society in Trinidad is formed by Thomas Talboys from the WM Conference • Samuel Wesley's son and Charles Wesley's grandson, Samuel Sebastian Wesley, is born (d. 1876)	1810
• Carl Maria von Weber composes perhaps his finest instrumental piece, the overture *Der Beherrscher der Geister* (The Master of the Spirits) • Beethoven composes his *Piano Trio No. 7 (Archduke)* • Giacomo Meyerbeer completes his oratorio *Gott und die Natur* (God and Nature) • Jane Austen publishes her first major novel, *Sense and Sensibility*	• Schleiermacher publishes his *Brief Outline of the Study of Theology* • Percy Bysshe Shelley publishes *The Necessity of Atheism*	• Asbury reports in his journal that Methodist folks are involved in over 400 camp meetings annually along the frontier from Michigan to Georgia • The Western Conference (MEC) experiences dramatic membership growth in 1811–12, probably due in part to the effects of the New Madrid earthquakes	• Hugh Bourne's "Camp Meeting Methodists" and the followers of William Clowes unite, creating the Primitive Methodist Connexion (PMC) • The WM Conference approves an "extraordinary resolution" accepting Alice Cambridge as a Conference member and allowing her to preach • The WM Conference authorizes Thomas Coke to organize a mission to Ceylon (Sri Lanka), which he begins to organize • Penelope Smith (Mrs. Thomas) Coke dies (Jan.); Coke marries Anne Loxdale (Dec.) • George Warren is appointed as the first WM missionary to western Africa; when he arrives in Sierra Leone, he finds Methodist laypeople already active there • Welsh Calvinistic Methodists break with the Church of England to establish themselves as an independent church [it will become The Presbyterian Church of Wales in 1864]	1811
• Jacob Ludwig Karl Grimm and Wilhem Karl Grimm, better known as the Brothers Grimm, publish their first collection of *Children's and Household Tales*, commonly called *Grimm's Fairy Tales*; a second volume appears in 1814	• Percy Bysshe Shelley publishes *Declaration of Rights* • The Theological Seminary at Princeton is established by the General Assembly as the first national Presbyterian school for ministers	• The MEC General Conference: – meets as the first delegated General Conference, with 90 delegates elected from the eight annual conferences – approves the ordination of local preachers as elders after four years of service as deacon, (cont.)	• The British parliament passes the New Toleration Act, which repeals all remaining provisions of the Conventicle and Test Acts of 1670; this gives full legal rights and formal recognition to Methodist preachers in Britain as clergy	1812

	A. WORLD HISTORY & POLITICS	B. AMERICAN HISTORY & POLITICS	C. SCIENCE, MEDICINE & TECHNOLOGY	D. DAILY LIFE, POPULAR CULTURE & ENTERTAINMENT
1812 cont.	• Napoleon invades Russia; the Russians are forced to abandon Moscow but they burn the city as they leave; stalled by the brutal winter weather and a lack of supplies, Napoleon is forced to retreat back to France, losing most of his army along the way to cold and starvation • Spaniards who refused to accept Napoleon's brother, Joseph, as the legitimate king of Spain (1808) adopt the Constitution of Cadiz, under which Spain would be a constitutional monarchy, with the power of the king limited by a unicameral legislature (the Cortes), with guarantees of freedom of speech, of assembly, and of universal (male) suffrage	• The US frigate *Constitution* defeats the British frigates *Guerriére* (off Nova Scotia) and *Java* (near Brazil), earning the name "Old Ironsides" • Louisiana is admitted to the US as the 18th state; it is a slave state, bringing the balance to 9 free states and 9 slave states • President Madison is reelected and Elbridge Gerry is elected as vice president (Democratic-Republican Party) • The Federalist Party, having ceased to be a force in national politics, disappears		
1813	• Prussia and Austria join Britain and Russia in the quadruple alliance against Napoleon when they declare war on France • Wellington's British forces again defeat the French army at the Battle of Vitoria in Spain, forcing Napoleon to withdraw from Spain • Ferdinand VII, son of the deposed Charles IV, becomes king of Spain, restoring the Bourbon line • Simón Bolívar assumes control in Venezuela • The British parliament ends the trade monopoly of the East India Company in India but continues it in China	• American ships under Oliver Perry defeat the British flotilla in the Battle of Lake Erie • American forces capture York (Toronto) and reoccupy Detroit • Tecumseh is killed while fighting with British forces at the Battle of the Thames in Ontario; his death ends organized resistance of the Shawnee and other Indian nations in the Ohio Valley region • American forces commanded by Andrew Jackson defeat the Creek Indians at Horseshoe Bend in Alabama, shattering the power of the Creek nation; Jackson is promoted to Major General	• Robert Bakewell's *Introduction to Geology* is one of the first and most important textbooks on the subject • Shaker Sister Tabitha Babbitt is credited with devising the first circular saw used in a saw mill as an improvement to the two-man pit saws that were then used for lumber production	• The last gold guinea coins are issued in Britain • The dice game called "Craps" emerges in New Orleans, adapted from a French dice game called "Hazzards"
1814	• Paris falls to allied troops; Napoleon signs the Peace of Fontainebleau, abdicates as emperor, and is banished to Elba • King Louis XVIII takes the French throne as the monarchy is restored • Pope Pius VII is released from French captivity • The Cape Colony in south Africa is formally ceded by the Netherlands to Great Britain • Spanish forces succeed in putting down revolutionary independence movements in Chile, Venezuela, and Guatemala	• British troops take Washington and burn the US Capitol building, the White House, and the Library of Congress; they then march on Baltimore but withdraw after failing to capture Fort McHenry • Francis Scott Key's poem "The Defense of Fort McHenry" is later set to the tune of "To Anacreon in Heaven" to become "The Star-Spangled Banner" • American Naval forces under the command of Thomas MacDonough destroy the British fleet on Lake Champlain, forcing a 10,000-man British Army column to call off an attack on New York and retreat to Canada • The Treaty of Ghent ends the War of 1812 with no major territorial concessions on either side	• George Stephenson constructs the first practical steam locomotive • In England, a revolutionary steam-powered press prints the *London Times* newspaper at a rate of 1,100 copies per hour	• London's Metropolitan Cricket Club moves to the new grounds of Thomas Lord
1815	• Napoleon returns to France from exile for the "Hundred Days," is defeated by British Army under Wellington at Waterloo, then banished for life to St. Helena • The second Peace of Paris brings a final close to the era of the Napoleonic Wars • The Congress of Vienna deprives France of all the territories conquered by Napoleon and thoroughly rearranges the political landscape of Europe: – reestablishes the monarchies of Prussia and Austria and creates the German Confederation – ratifies the 1809 annexation of Finland by Russia	• American forces commanded by Andrew Jackson defeat the British in the Battle of New Orleans; neither side was aware that the Treaty of Ghent had already been signed, formally ending the War of 1812 • The US and Britain sign a treaty through which each side ends discriminatory tariffs toward the other, restoring normal commerce between them • Black Quaker abolitionist Paul Cuffe begins to advocate for the establishment of a colony in Sierra Leone for freed black slaves from America	• The USS *Fulton* becomes first steam-powered warship • British chemist Humphry Davy invents the miner's safety lamp for use in British coal mines; its use soon spreads to the US and Europe • British geologist William Smith's *Geological Map of England* is the first work to identify rock strata on the basis of fossil evidence, enabling geologists in different parts of the world to know that they are working in the same (or different) time periods	• The Apothecaries Act prohibits unqualified doctors from practicing medicine in Britain • The quadrille, a formal French ballroom dance, becomes popular among the upper classes in Britain and America

E. EDUCATION, LITERATURE & THE FINE ARTS	F. RELIGION, THEOLOGY, PHILOSOPHY & PSYCHOLOGY	G. AMERICAN & UNITED METHODISM	H. BRITISH & WORLD METHODISM	
• J. M. W. Turner completes his painting Snow Storm: Hannibal and His Army Crossing the Alps, depicting human help-lessness in the face of the force of nature • Lord Byron publishes his poetic account of Childe Harold's Pilgrimage • Beethoven completes his Symphony No. 7 in A Major and Symphony No. 8 in F Major	• The American Board of Commissioners for Foreign Missions, founded in 1810, sends the first American missionaries, Adoniram and Ann Judson and Luther Rice, to join British Baptist William Carey in India (since 1792)	giving them full sacramental authority (and thus creating a distinction between the local elder and the traveling or itinerant elder who is a full member of an annual conference) – authorizes the ordination of black preach-ers as elders – creates the Genesee Annual Conference and divides the Western Annual Conference into two: Ohio and Tennessee (total now 9) – authorizes annual conferences to raise a fund for the support of retired or disabled preachers – orders that the Doctrinal Tracts, including Wesley's Plain Account of Christian Perfection, be omitted from the Discipline and printed in a separate volume • Martin Boehm dies	• First Methodist class meeting and service in Australia is held by WM preachers Thomas Bowden and Edward Eagar • Anne Loxdale (Mrs. Thomas) Coke dies almost exactly one year after her marriage	1812 cont.
• McGill University is founded in Montreal • Beethoven composes Wellington's Victory to commemorate the Duke of Wellington's victory over the French at the Battle of Vitoria; it is also known sometimes as "The Battle Symphony" or "The Battle of Vitoria" and features a full orchestra with a large percussion battery including muskets and other artillery sound effects • J. M. W. Turner completes his painting Frosty Morning • Notable publications include: – Johann David Wyss, The Swiss Family Robinson – Jane Austen, Pride and Prejudice	• William Ellery Channing helps to estab-lish the monthly periodical The Christian Disciple to promote the causes of Unitarianism and peace • The Protestant Episcopal Church begins publication of its first important periodical, The Quarterly Theological Magazine and Religious Repository	• Following Martin Boehm's death, the UBC Conference meets at the home of William Otterbein • Otterbein, assisted by MEC elder William Ryland, ordains Christian Newcomer, Joseph Hoffman, and Frederick Shaffer as elders • Following Otterbein's death, Newcomer is elected to serve as bishop for a one-year term • Asbury Church in New York is estab-lished after a split within Zion Church • Peter Spencer and his followers build a church in Wilmington, DE, and formally incorporate as the Union Church of Africans (UCA)	• Coke sails for Ceylon (Sri Lanka) with a missionary party of 9 in two ships, which are part of a much larger merchant fleet • The first WM Missionary Society is organized in the Leeds District; other dis-trict societies soon follow • C. Gottleib Müller begins first Methodist evangelism in Germany, near Stuttgart • Methodist layman Charles Thwaites opens Bethesda School in Antigua; it is the first school in the West Indies for the edu-cation of slaves	1813
• Pioneering American educator Emma Hart Willard begins the Middlebury Female Seminary by holding classes in her own home when she is denied admission to Middlebury College; it is the first academy for the higher education of women in the US • Beethoven's opera Fidelio premieres in Vienna • Notable publications include: – Jane Austen, Mansfield Park – Sir Walter Scott, Waverley	• When he returns to Rome after the fall of Napoleon, Pope Pius VII reestablishes the Jesuit order and revives the Inquisition and the Index Librorum Prohibitum (Index of Forbidden Books) • Anglican priest Samuel Marsden travels from Australia to New Zealand and begins the first Christian missionary work among the Maori there • Luther Rice, returning from India, moti-vates the creation of the General Missionary Convention of the Baptist Denomination in the United States for Foreign Missions (known as the Triennial Convention), the first unified national mis-sionary-sending effort formed in the US [forerunner of the later American Baptist Board of International Ministries]	• The NFMC elects John Dreisbach as its first presiding elder (no bishop is elected until 1839) • The Reformed Methodist Church is established in Vermont by a group of Methodists opposed to episcopacy; it adopts an essentially congregational polity • The UBC reelects Christian Newcomer as bishop for a three-year term	• Coke dies aboard ship en route from Britain to Ceylon (Sri Lanka) and is buried at sea • Australian Methodists write to the WM Conference in Britain requesting that mis-sionaries be sent to Australia	1814
• The Library of Congress is reestablished with the purchase of 6,487 books from Thomas Jefferson's personal library • Boston's Handel and Haydn Society is established and holds its first concert • Johann Maelzel patents the metronome, enabling musicians to keep a regular beat during rehearsals • Francisco Goya publishes his etchings of La Tauromaquia (The Bullfight) • Rossini is appointed as musical and artis-tic director of the Teatro San Carlo in Naples • Franz Schubert composes his Mass No. 2 in G Major	• The Boston Society for the Moral and Religious Instruction of the Poor is estab-lished to promote Sunday school education • In his Essay on the Influence of a Low Price of Corn on the Profits of Stock, David Ricardo articulates what comes to be known as "the law of diminishing returns" • Nathan Bangs publishes The Errors of Hopkinsianism	• The UBC General Conference meets for the first time: – adopts Confession of Faith and Discipline similar to that of the MEC – limits bishops to four-year terms, to which they can be reelected – provides for the election of delegates to General Conference – gives ministers "a large measure of discre-tion and authority" in their work • Black MEC layman John Stewart begins the first organized Methodist mission to the American Indians among the Wyandots	• Samuel Leigh arrives in Sydney as the first WM missionary in Australia; from there, Methodist work in Australia expands to New Zealand (1818), Tasmania (1820), Melbourne (1836), Adelaide (1837), and Perth (1840) • William O'Brien is expelled from the WM Conference and forms his own inde-pendent preaching circuit, which becomes the nucleus of a new group in Britain that takes the name Bible Christians	1815

	A. WORLD HISTORY & POLITICS	B. AMERICAN HISTORY & POLITICS	C. SCIENCE, MEDICINE & TECHNOLOGY	D. DAILY LIFE, POPULAR CULTURE & ENTERTAINMENT
1815 cont.	– transfers Norway from Denmark to Sweden – grants the Austrian Netherlands (Belgium) to the Netherlands – gives control of most of Poland to Russia – confirms British control of Malta and gives Britain control of some former French and Dutch colonial possessions • Britain enacts the Corn Law prohibiting the import of cereal grains and artificially inflating prices • The explosion of Tambora in Indonesia is the largest volcanic eruption in recorded history; over 82,000 people are killed directly or indirectly, and global weather is so affected that, in America and northern Europe, 1816 is called "the year without a summer"			
1816	• King Louis XVIII of France dissolves the reactionary Chamber of Deputies • Prince Metternich of Austria begins his rise to European political power by dominating the German Confederation • The United Provinces of La Plata (modern Argentina) declare independence from Spain • Spain reestablishes its authority and control in Mexico, scattering the rebel forces of José María Morelos y Pavón then capturing and executing him • British forces in northern India defeat the Gurkhas and force them back into Nepal • A massive emigration from England to Canada and the US takes place due to a British economic crisis that produces large-scale unemployment	• Indiana is admitted to the US as the 19th state; it is a free state • The American Colonization Society is formed to resettle freed American slaves in Africa; it is supported both by abolitionists and by prominent slaveholders such as Henry Clay and Francis Scott Key • The Second Bank of the United States is established, with a charter to expire in 1836 • The US Supreme Court affirms the right of federal courts to review the decisions of state courts when cases involve federal law • James Monroe is elected as president and Daniel Thompkins as vice president (Democratic-Republican Party)	• French physician R. T. H. Laënnec invents the stethoscope • John McAdam (UK) publishes his *Remarks on the Present System of Road-Making* in which he documents the techniques he developed in the 1780s for "macadam" road pavement, using a layer of large rocks, then another layer of smaller stones, the whole then covered with finely crushed gravel • An epidemic of typhoid fever breaks out in Ireland; it lasts for three years and kills about 25% of the population	• The waltz is included among the dances at a ball given in London by the prince regent; a few days later a blistering editorial in *The Times* condemns the "obscene display" of that "indecent foreign dance," which should be "confined to prostitutes and adulteresses" and not "forced on the respectable classes of society" • Freakish weather caused by the 1815 eruption of Tambora in Indonesia brings 10 inches of snow to New England in June and a half-inch of ice to New Hampshire and Vermont in August • The first Mutual Savings Banks are established in Boston and Philadelphia to provide banking services and access to credit to people of modest means who were effectively ignored by the large and established banking community
1817	• Chile declares independence from Spain; José de San Martín leads a revolutionary army from Argentina across the Andes Mountains and defeats the Spanish at Chacabuco, Chile • Serbia gains partial independence from the Ottoman Empire • The US and Britain sign a treaty limiting their naval forces on the Great Lakes	• Mississippi is admitted to the US as the 20th state; it is a slave state, making the balance 10 free states and 10 slave states • Sylvanus Thayer, known as the "father of the Military Academy," sharply upgrades academic standards at West Point, instills military discipline, and emphasizes honorable conduct; students begin studying civil engineering as well as Napoleonic military tactics	• David Brewster (Scotland) invents the kaleidoscope • Construction begins on the Erie Canal, which will connect the Great Lakes with the Hudson River and thus the Atlantic Ocean	• The first public fire hydrant is installed in New York City • Gas street lamps are installed in Baltimore

E. EDUCATION, LITERATURE & THE FINE ARTS	F. RELIGION, THEOLOGY, PHILOSOPHY & PSYCHOLOGY	G. AMERICAN & UNITED METHODISM	H. BRITISH & WORLD METHODISM	
		• Due to his failing health, Asbury (for the first time) turns the responsibility for stationing preachers over to McKendree		**1815 cont.**
• Rossini's *The Barber of Seville* debuts in Rome; the audience receives it with hisses, but it later becomes a popular success • Schubert composes his *Symphony No. 5 in B Flat* • Luigi Cherubini composes his *Requiem in C Minor* • Louise Reichardt becomes the first woman known to conduct a major orchestra when she takes charge of a performance of work by Handel in Lubeck, Germany • Jane Austen publishes her novel *Emma* • Coleridge publishes *Kubla Khan* (written in 1797) and *Christabel*	• The American Bible Society (ABS) is established • Harvard Divinity School is established as the first nondenominational theological school in the US [it becomes generally Unitarian after the formation of the American Unitarian Association in 1825] • Hegel publishes *The Science of Logic*	• Francis Asbury, the "Prophet of the Long Road," dies, marking the end of an era in American Methodism • The MEC General Conference: – replaces the term *connection* throughout the *Discipline* with the term *church* – replaces the term *society* with the term *church* in the section of the *Discipline* concerning membership; the term *society* continues as a vestigial elsewhere – elects Enoch George and Robert Roberts as bishops to serve along with McKendree and creates a plan of episcopal supervision – asks the bishops to outline a course of study for the training of preachers – urges individual societies to secure parsonages for the preachers – establishes the Missouri and Mississippi Annual Conferences (total now 11) – removes the provision giving annual conferences the right to regulate on the subject of slavery; slaveholders are made ineligible for church office where the laws of their states will allow emancipation – defeats a proposal to elect presiding elders after nomination by the bishops – authorizes the bishops to form new annual conferences in the interval between General Conferences • The African Methodist Episcopal Church (AMEC) is formally organized as a separate and independent denomination; Richard Allen is elected as its first bishop; Absalom Jones assists in his ordination as elder and consecration as bishop • The NFMC reorganizes itself as *Diese Vereinigte Evangelische Gemeinschaft* (The Evangelical Association, or EA) and adopts Articles of Faith; this is considered the first General Conference of the EA	• The Bible Christians hold their first Quarterly Meeting • The Irish Methodist Conference allows administration of the sacraments in local societies upon request • Barnabas and Jane Shaw are the first WM missionaries sent from Britain to south Africa • MEC missionaries resume work in Canada following the conclusion of the War of 1812	**1816**
• Mendelssohn begins studying composition with Carl Friedrich Zelter at the Singakademie in Berlin • Rossini composes his *Cinderella and Thieving Magpie* • Beethoven composes his *String Quintet*	• Hegel publishes his *Encyclopedia of the Philosophical Sciences* • David Ricardo, in *Principles of Political Economy and Taxation*, proposes a "labor theory of value," which later influences Karl Marx • Wilhelm M. L. de Wette publishes *Manual of Historico-Critical Introduction to the Bible*	• The UBC General Conference: – for the first time since the days of William Otterbein and Martin Boehm, elects two bishops, Christian Newcomer and Andrew Zeller, both to four-year terms – reaffirms the 1815 *Discipline* with few changes – authorizes the printing of the *Discipline* in German and English	• Irish Methodists split between WM and PM branches • James Lynch travels from Ceylon (Sri Lanka) to Madras, India, becoming the first WM missionary on the mainland of India • The first WM society in Tobago is established by John Brown and James Catts from Britain, who begin the first Methodist work in Haiti the same year • Samuel Leigh establishes the first WM society in Tasmania	**1817**

	A. WORLD HISTORY & POLITICS	**B. AMERICAN HISTORY & POLITICS**	**C. SCIENCE, MEDICINE & TECHNOLOGY**	**D. DAILY LIFE, POPULAR CULTURE & ENTERTAINMENT**
1817 cont.		• President Monroe moves back into the White House, but restoration work goes on for years • The Seminole Indians launch attacks on white settlers in Florida and Georgia; the US demands that Spain either control the Indians or cede Florida to the US		
1818	• José de San Martín defeats the Spanish royalist army at Maipú, thus assuring the independence of Chile • The US and Britain agree to establish the border between the US and Canada along the 49th parallel from the Lake of the Woods to the Rocky Mountains; the border is left open in the Oregon Territory • France outlaws the slave trade throughout its colonial territories • Scottish explorer John Ross leads an expedition into the Arctic in hopes of discovering the fabled "Northwest Passage"	• The First Seminole War (1817–18) ends indecisively: American forces commanded by Andrew Jackson inflict much damage but do not capture the Seminole leaders • Illinois is admitted to the US as the 21st state; it is a free state • Congress passes the Flag Act, which states that a star shall be added to the flag for any new state on the Fourth of July following that state's admission to the US • Connecticut abolishes property ownership as a qualification for voting	• Moses Rogers begins the first regular steamship service between Savannah and Charleston with the *Charleston* • American woodworker Thomas Blanchard designs a special lathe for turning irregularly shaped objects such as gun stocks	• British merchant Peter Durand introduces tin cans of food to the American market
1819	• Local militia forces in Manchester, England, attack a large crowd of demonstrators demanding social and political reforms; 11 are killed and 400 injured in what is called the Peterloo Massacre; intense indignation sweeps the country and helps lead to the passage of the Reform Bill of 1832 • Simón Bolívar becomes president of the newly proclaimed Republic of Greater Colombia, a union of New Granada (now Colombia and Panama), Venezuela, and Ecuador • Zulu chief Shaka eliminates the last of his rival chiefs in southern Africa to establish the Zulu Kingdom	• The US acquires Florida from Spain as part of a deal to cancel $5 million of Spanish debts to US citizens • In the landmark case *McCulloch v. Maryland*, the US Supreme Court upholds the power of Congress to establish a national bank, articulating the principle of "implied powers" in the Constitution • Alabama is admitted to the US as the 22nd state; it is a slave state, making the balance 11 free states and 11 slave states	• The *Savannah*, captained by Moses Rogers, is the first steam-powered vessel to cross the Atlantic (though under sails for most of the trip), going from New York to Liverpool in just under 24 days • David Napier constructs the flatbed cylinder press for printing • Hans C. Oersted discovers electromagnetism when he notices that an electric current flowing through a wire affects a magnetized needle	• Britain restricts minors to 12-hour workdays • The pioneer of Swiss chocolate-making, François Louis Callier, opens the first chocolate factory in Switzerland
1820	• Britain's King George III dies; he is succeeded by his son, George IV • The Spanish Revolution leads to the restoration by King Ferdinand VII of the 1812 Constitution of Cortez • The slave trade is outlawed throughout the Spanish Empire • José de San Martín transports his military forces by sea from Chile to Peru; the Spanish viceroy abandons Lima • The American Colonization Society (ACS), founded in 1816, purchases Sherbro Island in Sierra Leone to become a colony for freed blacks from the US and sends 86 colonists from New York to establish a settlement there	• The US census reports that the population is 9,638,453: – whites: 7,866,797 (81.6%) – free blacks: 233,634 (2.4%) – slaves: 1,538,022 (16.0%) • The US national debt is $91,015,566 • Congress approves the Missouri Compromise: the northern part of Massachusetts will become Maine and will be admitted to the US as a free state, while Missouri will be admitted as a slave state, thereby maintaining a balance of 12 slave states and 12 free states; in addition, an imaginary line is drawn at 36°30' north latitude and slavery prohibited in portions of the Louisiana Territory lying north of that line • Congress encourages the rapid sale of public land for farms and homesteads by reducing the minimum land purchase from 160 to 80 acres and the price from $2 to $1.25 per acre, but it eliminates the provision for payment across a four-year period • Maine is admitted to the US as the 23rd state; it is a free state	• Construction is completed on the Regent's Canal in London	• The modern style of men's trousers, cut to follow the lines of the body, becomes the standard form of dress for men in Europe • British botanists, experimenting with the growing of Chinese tea bushes in India, discover the previously unknown native tea bushes of Assam

E. EDUCATION, LITERATURE & THE FINE ARTS	F. RELIGION, THEOLOGY, PHILOSOPHY & PSYCHOLOGY	G. AMERICAN & UNITED METHODISM	H. BRITISH & WORLD METHODISM	
• American artist John Trumbull is commissioned by the US Congress to re-create four of his paintings in large scale in the rotunda of the Capitol: *Washington Resigning His Commission, The Surrender of Cornwallis, The Surrender of Burgoyne,* and, best known of all, *The Declaration of Independence*; he completes the project in 1824 • Coleridge publishes his *Biographia Literaria,* the most significant work of general literary criticism produced in the English Romantic period	• Nathan Bangs publishes *Examination of the Doctrine of Predestination* • The Lutheran and Calvinist Churches of Prussia reunite • The General Theological Seminary is founded in New York City [it is the oldest seminary of the Episcopal Church in the USA]	• UBC and EA representatives meet at the "Social Conference"; discussions about a potential merger do not result in agreement • The first EA publishing house is established in New Berlin, PA • The first *Book of Discipline* of the AMEC is published • Richard Allen gives Jarena Lee (AMEC) permission to exhort and hold prayer meetings, but does not authorize a preaching license for her		**1817 cont.**
• Boston's Handel and Haydn Society gives the first complete American performance of Handel's *Messiah* • Beethoven completes his *Piano Sonata No. 29 (Hammerklavier)* • Mary Wollstonecraft Shelley (daughter of Mary Wollstonecraft and wife of Percy Bysshe Shelley) tells the story of *Frankenstein* • Percy Bysshe Shelley writes *Ozymandias* • Jane Austen publishes her novels *Persuasion* and *Northanger Abbey* • Sir Walter Scott publishes *Rob Roy*	• The Evangelical Lutheran Joint Synod of Ohio and Other States (Joint Synod of Ohio) separates from the Pennsylvania Ministerium • The Christmas carol "Stille Nacht" (Silent Night), written by Josef Mohr and arranged by Franz Grüber, is sung for the first time in the Church of St. Nikolaus in Oberndorf, Austria • Arthur Schopenhauer, *The World as Will and Representation* (2nd ed. 1844; 3rd ed. 1859)	• The MEC begins publication of *The Methodist Review,* the descendant of the American Edition of Wesley's *Arminian Magazine,* which ceased publication in 1791 • The MEC opens Elizabeth Academy in Washington, MS; it is the first church-sponsored school for girls in America (closes in 1845) • The AMEC organizes Bethel Church in Brooklyn, NY, and publishes its first hymnal	• The Wesleyan Methodist Missionary Society (WMMS) is formally established by the WM Conference for the entire Connexion • WM preachers in Britain begin calling themselves "ministers" and referring to each other as "Reverend" • Irish Methodist conservatives, upset by the Conference decision to allow sacraments, withdraw to form the (Irish) Primitive Wesleyan Methodist Society • Walter Lawry arrives from Britain to assist Samuel Leigh, who promptly begins WM mission work in New Zealand	**1818**
• Schubert composes his *Piano Quintet in A (The Trout)* • British landscape artist John Constable paints *Flatford Mill in the River Stour* • Caspar David Friedrich paints *Two Men Contemplating the Moon* • Washington Irving publishes *The Sketch Book of Geoffrey Crayon,* which includes the stories "The Legend of Sleepy Hollow" and "Rip van Winkle"	• Thomas Jefferson publishes *The Life and Morals of Jesus of Nazareth Extracted Textually from the Gospels in Greek, Latin, French and English,* commonly known as *The Jefferson Bible,* in which he tries to separate the ethical teachings of Jesus from the "religious dogma" and "supernatural elements" that he believes are mixed with them in the four Gospels • William Ellery Channing publishes *Unitarian Christianity,* articulating the distinctive tenets of the Unitarian movement, including a belief in human goodness and the subjection of theological ideas to the critical light of reason	• The MEC establishes the Methodist Missionary and Bible Society (a direct ancestor of the later Board of Missions and current General Board of Global Ministries); Nathan Bangs becomes the first secretary	• The Bible Christians in Britain hold their first national Conference, marking their formal separation from the WM Connexion • Methodism spreads from Scotland to the Shetland Islands	**1819**
• Notable publications include: – Sir Walter Scott, *Ivanhoe,* his classic tale of chivalry set in the age of Richard the Lion-Hearted – Alexander Pushkin, *Ruslan and Ludmila* – Robert Burns, *The Songs of Robert Burns*	• The Lutheran Church in the US (General Synod) is established, uniting most Lutheran bodies in the US except the New York Ministerium, which does not join • Notable publications include: – John Stuart Mill, *An Essay of Government* – William Ellery Channing, *The Moral Argument Against Calvinism*	• The MEC General Conference: – admits local preachers to the General Conference for the first time, but only as spectators – passes legislation mandating the election of presiding elders, then suspends that action in deference to Joshua Soule, who refuses election to episcopacy over the matter – urges annual conferences to establish institutions of higher education and alters the *Discipline* to allow preachers to serve as college teachers and administrators without first locating and giving up their orders – authorizes the creation of District Conferences within existing annual conferences to provide an administrative connection for local preachers – elects Nathan Bangs and Thomas Mason as Book Agents in New York, and Martin Ruter as Book Agent for the new branch in Cincinnati	• WM missionaries from Britain begin work in Gambia • Conflict between MEC and WM missionaries in Canada leads to an agreement whereby the MEC withdraws from Lower Canada and the WM withdraws from Upper Canada • Samuel Leigh's health fails and he leaves New Zealand to return to England for medical care and rest • Jabez Bunting is elected president of the WM Conference for the first time, marking his rise to leadership • Robert Southey publishes *The Life of Wesley, and the Rise and Progress of Methodism*	**1820**

	A. WORLD HISTORY & POLITICS	B. AMERICAN HISTORY & POLITICS	C. SCIENCE, MEDICINE & TECHNOLOGY	D. DAILY LIFE, POPULAR CULTURE & ENTERTAINMENT
1820 cont.		• The Cherokee Nation adopts a representative form of government modeled on that of the US, an elected principal chief, a senate, and a house of representatives • President Monroe and Vice President Thompkins are reelected (Democratic-Republican Party)		
1821	• Forces led by Simón Bolívar decisively defeat the Spanish at the Battle of Carabobo in Venezuela, assuring the independence of the Republic of Greater Colombia • Peru achieves independence from Spain, followed by Guatemala and Santo Domingo • Napoleon dies in exile on the island of St. Helena • Greek forces capture the Turkish fortress in the Peloponnesus and massacre 10,000 Turks, beginning the Greek War of Independence against the Ottoman Empire • In the wake of the Spanish revolution, Agustín de Iturbide, commander of the royalist forces in Mexico, and Vicente Guerrero, leader of the rebels, agree to join forces to achieve independence from Spain • The last Spanish viceroy in Mexico is forced to sign the Treaty of Córdoba, marking the formal beginning of Mexican independence	• Missouri is admitted to the US as the 24th state; it is a slave state • Massachusetts and New York follow Connecticut in abolishing property ownership as a qualification for voting; most other states follow their lead by 1850 • Cherokee leader Sequoyah, also called George Guess, creates a written syllabary (alphabet) for the Cherokee language	• Michael Faraday discovers electromagnetic rotation • T. J. Seebeck discovers thermoelectricity	• The *Manchester Guardian* begins publication in England
1822	• Sherbo Island proves unhealthy and inhospitable for colonization; the ACS then purchases land (perhaps at gunpoint) farther up the coast for its colony of free blacks and moves them there • Greece declares independence from the Ottoman Empire and adopts a liberal constitution; in response, the Turks seize the Greek island of Chios and massacre 20,000 Greeks; the Turkish army then invades mainland Greece • Brazil achieves independence from Portugal • Haitian rebels seize control of the island of Hispanola and declare the Republic of Haiti • Stephen F. Austin establishes the first legal American settlement in Texas after his father receives a charter from the Spanish colonial governor to do so	• Denmark Veasey, a freed black slave and AMEC preacher, is convicted and hanged along with 35 others in Charleston, SC, when his plans to lead a slave uprising are revealed • Trapper and trader Jedediah Smith begins his exploration of the Rockies and becomes the first white man to enter California from the east and return overland • Florida is formally organized as a Territory • The US recognizes the newly independent Latin American republics	• William Church invents the first mechanical typesetting device • A. J. Fresnel perfects lenses for lighthouses	• The first gas street lights in America are installed in Boston • The *Sunday Times* is first published in London

E. EDUCATION, LITERATURE & THE FINE ARTS	F. RELIGION, THEOLOGY, PHILOSOPHY & PSYCHOLOGY	G. AMERICAN & UNITED METHODISM	H. BRITISH & WORLD METHODISM	
		– appoints John Emory as fraternal delegate to the WM Conference in Britain, thus renewing relations that had been suspended since the departure of Thomas Coke in 1804 – establishes the Kentucky Annual Conference (total now 12) – confirms establishment of the Methodist Missionary Society • The EA General Conference meets concurrently with the annual conference • Members of Zion Church and Asbury Church meet in New York to discuss formation of a new and independent denomination • Methodists in Alabama create a missionary society to work among the Chickasaw and Choctaw Indians; this is the first known MEC mission work with American Indian tribes • Nathan Bangs publishes *A Vindication of the Methodist Episcopacy*		**1820 cont.**
• Emma Hart Willard relocates the Middlebury Female Seminary (1814) to Troy, NY, where it is to be supported by the town, and renames it the Troy Female Seminary • John Constable completes his painting *The Hay Wain* • Thomas De Quincy publishes *Confessions of an English Opium Eater* • Beethoven composes his *Mass in D major (Missa Solemnis)* • French linguist Jean François Champollion deciphers Egyptian hieroglyphics using the Rosetta Stone	• Hegel publishes his *Philosophy of Right* • Henri Comte de Saint-Simon's *Industrial System* is one of the founding works of modern socialism; it advocates the abolition of private property • Charles Finney experiences conversion and begins his evangelistic career • The Basilica of the National Shrine of the Assumption of the Virgin Mary in Baltimore, also called the Baltimore Basilica, begun in 1806, is completed and dedicated [it is the first Roman Catholic cathedral in the US]	• The UBC General Conference: – meets for the first time in Ohio, indicating the movement of the denomination away from its home in Pennsylvania – seats the first two delegates whose native tongue is English, not German – takes a strong antislavery position, banning both ministers and members from slave ownership • The MEC publishes *A Collection of Hymns for the Use of the Methodist Episcopal Church*, which draws heavily on Wesley's 1780 *Collection of Hymns*; it is the first hymnal prepared specifically for Methodist use in America • The African Methodist Episcopal Zion Church (AMEZC) is formally established; Abraham Thompson, James Varick, and Leven Smith are ordained as the first elders of the AMEZC; James Varick is elected as the first superintendent [bishop] • William Capers (MEC) founds the Asbury Mission to the Lower Creek Indians in Alabama and Mississippi • James Finley (MEC) begins missionary work with the Wyandot Indians in the Ohio Territory	• The first AME missionaries are sent to Haiti	**1821**
• Schubert stops working on his *Symphony No. 8 (Unfinished)* • Hans Christian Andersen publishes *Ghost at Palnatoke's Grave*	• Schleiermacher, in *The Christian Faith*, describes religion as being based upon the "feeling of absolute dependence" that human beings have, in all their finitude, upon the Infinite, or God • The Yale University Divinity School is established	• The execution of AMEC preachers Denmark Veasey and Gullah Jack for their role in the Charleston slave revolt causes closure of all the AMEC work in South Carolina; Morris Brown takes refuge in Philadelphia with Richard Allen and soon becomes Allen's primary assistant	• The WM Conference formally changes the title of *The Methodist Magazine* (1798) to *The Wesleyan Methodist Magazine* • Daniel Coker organizes a Methodist society among freed slaves in Liberia • Walter Lawry begins WM mission work in Tonga • Samuel Leigh returns to New Zealand from England with William White; they establish the first permanent WM mission in New Zealand at Whangaroa	**1822**

	A. WORLD HISTORY & POLITICS	B. AMERICAN HISTORY & POLITICS	C. SCIENCE, MEDICINE & TECHNOLOGY	D. DAILY LIFE, POPULAR CULTURE & ENTERTAINMENT
1823	• Guatemala, El Salvador, Honduras, Nicaragua, and Costa Rica band together to form The United Provinces of Central America, or Central American Federation	• In his annual message to Congress, President Monroe proclaims the "Monroe Doctrine" stating that the American continents are no longer open to European political interference or colonization; the message to European powers is "hands off the Western world" • St. Louis, MO, is incorporated as a city	• The British medical journal *The Lancet* is first issued	• Clement Moore's poem "A Visit from St. Nicholas," better known by its first line as "The Night Before Christmas," introduces the character named "Santa Claus" to America • The death penalty is abolished in Britain for more than 100 relatively minor crimes • A schoolboy playing football at Rugby, England, ignores the established rules, picks up the ball, and dashes across the goal of the opponents, thus creating what comes to be called "rugby football"
1824	• A republic is proclaimed in Mexico; Guadalupe Victoria becomes the first president; a new constitution is adopted that opens Mexican territory to immigration, especially from the US • Britain begins its efforts to colonize Burma, provoking the first Anglo-Burmese War (to 1826) • Civil war erupts in the Ottoman Empire; the Ottoman sultan is forced to appeal to Muhammad Ali of Egypt for assistance • The US and Russia sign a treaty setting the latitude of 54°40' as the southern border of Russian territory in Alaska • The ACS colony of free blacks in Africa is named Liberia, and the main settlement is named Monrovia	• During the US presidential election, John Quincy Adams and Henry Clay start referring to themselves as National Republicans to try to distinguish themselves from the older Democratic-Republican Party • Andrew Jackson receives more popular votes than John Quincy Adams but does not have an electoral college majority, so the contested election goes to the House of Representatives	• Portland cement, produced by burning and grinding a mixture of limestone and clay or shale, is developed by Joseph Aspdin (England) • Asphalt blocks are first used for road paving on the Champs-Élysées in Paris	• The Society for the Prevention of Cruelty to Animals (SPCA), the world's first animal welfare society, is founded in London • The newspaper *Le Globe* begins publication in Paris
1825	• The Trades Union Movement in Britain is legalized by repeal of the Combination Acts of 1799 and 1800 • Tsar Alexander I of Russia dies; he is succeeded by his brother, Nicholas I, who promptly crushes an uprising by a secret Russian revolutionary society, the "Decembrists" • Russia and Britain sign a treaty delineating the boundary between Canada and Alaska; the size of Alaska is greatly reduced, and Alaskan territory is opened to Canadian traders • "God Save the Queen [or King]," first published in 1744, is adopted by Parliament as the British national anthem • Brazil and Argentina fight over the territory that becomes the independent republic of Uruguay • The Ottoman Turks subdue the Greek rebels in the Peloponnesus • Portugal recognizes the independence of Brazil	• The House of Representatives chooses John Quincy Adams (National Republican Party) instead of Andrew Jackson to be president and John C. Calhoun (Democratic-Republican Party) to be vice president • Hundreds of settlers from the US flock to Mexican territory, especially the area of Texas • Congress approves the official establishment of the Santa Fe Trail, linking St. Louis with Santa Fe and establishing St. Louis as the "gateway to the West" • The Creek Indians reject a proposed treaty ceding all of their lands in Georgia to the US	• The Erie Canal is completed and opens to traffic; running 394 miles from the Hudson River to Lake Erie, it connects the Great Lakes with the Atlantic Ocean through New York	• The Stockton-Darlington railroad in England opens as the first rail line to carry passengers • Tea roses from China are introduced in England

E. EDUCATION, LITERATURE & THE FINE ARTS	F. RELIGION, THEOLOGY, PHILOSOPHY & PSYCHOLOGY	G. AMERICAN & UNITED METHODISM	H. BRITISH & WORLD METHODISM	
• Britain's King George IV presents the royal library of George III to the British Museum • Beethoven completes his great *Missa Solemnis* • The young Franz Liszt leaves Vienna, where he has studied with Carl Czerny and Antonio Salieri, to begin his performing career in Paris; he will soon establish himself as perhaps the greatest piano virtuoso of all time • James Fennimore Cooper publishes *The Pilot* and *The Pioneers*	• Pope Pius VII dies; he is succeeded by Pope Leo XII • Daniel O'Connell establishes the Catholic Association to advocate toleration for Roman Catholics in Britain and Ireland • Richard Watson begins publication of his *Theological Institutes*, the first major work of systematic theology produced by a Methodist scholar (completed in 1828 in 6 parts)	• *Zion's Herald* begins publication as the first Methodist weekly newspaper • Jesse Walker establishes the Potawatomi Indian Mission near Peoria, IL	• Anglican priests Samuel Marsden, Nathaniel Turner, and John Hobbs arrive in New Zealand from Australia; Turner and Hobbs stay in New Zealand to establish the Church of England there; Marsden takes Leigh, whose health is failing, back to Australia; Leigh soon returns to England; William White now heads the WM mission in New Zealand • Samuel Broadbent and Thomas L. Hodgson establish the first WM mission in the Transvaal region of southern Africa	**1823**
• The (British) National Gallery is established in London • The Franklin Institute is founded in Philadelphia; its Science Museum is the first museum of applied science in the US • Beethoven completes his *Symphony No. 9 in D Minor (Choral)*, his final symphony, concluding with the immortal "Ode to Joy" for chorus and full orchestra • Schubert composes his *Quartet in D Minor (Death and the Maiden)* • Liszt makes his London debut as a concert pianist • Louisa Stanhope publishes *The Siege of Kenilworth*	• The American Sunday School Union is established in Philadelphia • Luther Rice and colleagues form the Baptist General Tract Society [later the American Baptist Publication Society and eventually the American Baptist Board of Educational Ministries]	• The MEC General Conference: – rejects a proposal for the inclusion of lay representation in General Conference – continues the suspension of the 1820 legislation mandating the election of presiding elders – commissions a catechism for young people and directs each traveling preacher to establish and promote Sunday schools on his circuit – elects Joshua Soule and Elijah Hedding as bishops; both accept election – establishes 5 new conferences: Holston, Maine, Memphis, Illinois, and Pittsburgh (total now 17) – requires each annual conference to establish a committee on missions when any mission work exists within its bounds – authorizes black preachers to travel and preach "where their services are welcome" • The Mississippi Conference establishes a mission to the Choctaw Indians	• The AMEC begins mission work in Haiti and the Dominican Republic • The MEC creates a Canadian Conference to organize mission work there • William Shaw extends WM mission work into the eastern Cape region of south Africa	**1824**
• Liszt composes his comic opera *Don Sanche or the Castle of Love* • Beethoven's *Ninth Symphony* has its first performance in England • Sir Walter Scott publishes *The Talisman* • The National Academy of Design is established in New York to "promote the fine arts in America through instruction and exhibition"	• William Ellery Channing helps "liberal" members of the Congregational church in New England to establish the American Unitarian Association in Boston • Newton Theological Institute is established in Newton, MA [it is the oldest Baptist Seminary in the US] • Charles Hodge founds the *Princeton Review* • Coleridge publishes *Aids to Reflection*	• The UBC General Conference: – revises the Confession of Faith to prohibit any minister from condemning the mode of baptism practiced by another – declares that the Lord's Supper is to be open to "all true Christians" and "all who are penitent, seeking salvation of their souls" – instructs annual conferences to elect presiding elders who are itinerate within the conferences – authorizes an annual public collection in each circuit for the support of the bishops – forms a new annual conference in Ohio (total now four) – renews fraternal relations with the MEC • Augusta College in Augusta, KY, opens for classes; established by the Ohio and Kentucky Conferences (MEC) around the nucleus of Bracken Academy (1798) and chartered in 1822, it is the only institution of higher education west of the Appalachian Mountains [it closes in 1845 after the split between the MEC and MECS] • Timothy Merritt publishes *A Christian's Manual*, a treatise on Christian Perfection	• Wesleyan Methodism spreads from Scotland to the Orkney Islands	**1825**

	A. WORLD HISTORY & POLITICS	B. AMERICAN HISTORY & POLITICS	C. SCIENCE, MEDICINE & TECHNOLOGY	D. DAILY LIFE, POPULAR CULTURE & ENTERTAINMENT
1826	• Primarily Christian groups in the Balkans begin a struggle for freedom from Ottoman Turkish rule • Persia attacks Russian possessions in the Transcaucus, provoking Russia to declare war on Persia	• Thomas Jefferson and John Adams, lifetime friends and political rivals and the only US presidents to have signed the Declaration of Independence, both die on July 4th, the 50th anniversary of the Declaration • The Creek Indians sign the Treaty of Washington, which voids all previous treaties but cedes less land to the US • The American Temperance Society (later renamed the American Temperance Union) is founded in Boston; its members "take the pledge" to refrain from drinking alcoholic beverages	• English chemist John Walker invents the sulfur friction match	• English merchant John Horniman begins selling tea in sealed, lead-lined packages
1827	• France, Britain, and Russia demand that the Ottoman Turks end their war with the Greeks; the sultan refuses • Combined French and Russian but primarily British navies destroy an Egyptian and Turkish fleet at Navarino, curtailing the expansion of Egypt and advancing Greek independence from Turkey • Russia drives Persian forces out of the Transcaucus and seizes Tabriz and Erivan (modern Armenia) • The US and Britain agree to joint occupation of the Oregon Territory	• Reconstruction of the US Capitol building in Washington, including the original dome, is completed • The Mechanics' Union of Trade Associations is formed in Philadelphia; it is the first US labor organization to unite workers in different crafts • The Cherokee Nation adopts a formal written constitution; John Ross is elected chief, and the capital is established at New Echota (Georgia) • Tensions between northern and southern states begin to grow; the northern states increasingly demand protectionist tariffs to serve their manufacturing and industrial interests; such tariffs are strenuously opposed by the southern states whose economies depend more on agriculture	• Joseph Niépce (France) produces the first permanent photographs using metal plates • George S. Ohm formulates Ohm's Law, defining electrical current potential and resistance	• Karl Baedeker (Germany) publishes his first travel guide • *Freedom's Journal*, the first newspaper wholly owned and produced by blacks in America, begins publication in New York
1828	• Russia declares war on the Ottoman Empire; Russian forces cross the Danube and capture Varna from the Turks • Russia and Persia sign the Treaty of Turkmanchai; Persia cedes Tabriz and Erivan (modern Armenia) to Russia and pays a large indemnity • With British assistance, Uruguay gains independence as a buffer state between Argentina and Brazil	• The Tariff Act of 1828, called by critics the "Tariff of Abominations," is a protective tariff levied to drive up the prices of European goods to prevent them from competing with northern industry; intended to protect industries in New England and the mid-Atlantic states, it actually harms both northern industry and southern agriculture • By now the Democratic-Republican Party has become simply the Democratic Party • Andrew Jackson is elected as president and John C. Calhoun is reelected as vice president (Democratic Party)	• The first volume of John James Audubon's 10-volume *Birds of America* is published (completed 1838) • Friedrich Wöhler's synthesis of urea begins organic chemistry	• Minstrel dancing debuts in the US with Thomas "Daddy" Rice appearing in blackface makeup as the character "Jim Crow" in a song-and-dance act • *The Boy's Own Book*, a frequently reprinted book on English boys' sports, includes a chapter on the game of "rounders," which has many resemblances to the modern game of baseball • Andrew Jackson's political opponents call him a "jackass" and he turns the name-calling to his advantage by using a donkey on his campaign posters, leading in later years to the donkey as the symbol of the Democratic Party

E. EDUCATION, LITERATURE & THE FINE ARTS	F. RELIGION, THEOLOGY, PHILOSOPHY & PSYCHOLOGY	G. AMERICAN & UNITED METHODISM	H. BRITISH & WORLD METHODISM	
• University College, London, is established • Mendelssohn's *Overture to A Midsummer Night's Dream* perfectly exemplifies early musical Romanticism • Carl Maria von Weber's opera *Oberon, King of the Fairies* has its first performance in London • William Blake's *Illustrations of the Book of Job* is published; it is his last completed work • James Fennimore Cooper publishes his novel *The Last of the Mohicans* • Quaker abolitionist Abigail Mott publishes her *Biographical Sketches and Interesting Anecdotes of Persons of Color*, which blends accounts of the lives of famous people, such as Toussaint L'Ouverture and Phillis Wheatley, with stories of the lives of "ordinary" people such as "Poor Sarah" or "Alice the Black"	• The Lutheran Theological Seminary is established in Gettysburg, PA [it is the oldest continuing Lutheran seminary in the US]	• The EA General Conference: – orders that the conduct and doctrine of all preachers are to be examined annually – urges that "wherever practicable" a parsonage should be built or bought for the pastor and his family on each charge by voluntary contributions • Publication of *The Christian Advocate* begins in New York; it is the first weekly official publication of the MEC and the forerunner of numerous other church newspapers using the name "Advocate"	• Joseph R. Stephens begins WM mission work in Sweden • The PMC establishes its first congregations in Scotland	**1826**
• Beethoven completes his *String Quartet in B Flat* • Schubert composes his song cycle *Die Winterreise* (Winter Journey) • Hector Berlioz composes his *La mort d'Orphée* (The Death of Orpheus) • Edgar Allan Poe, *Tamerlane and Other Poems*	• John Keble publishes *The Christian Year*	• The MEC forms the Sunday School Union to promote the expansion of Sunday schools • The AMEC organizes its first women's society, Daughters of the Conference • Alexander McCaine publishes his attack on Methodist polity, *The History and Mystery of Methodist Episcopacy*	• "Nonconforming" Methodists opposed to the installation of an organ in a Wesleyan Methodist chapel in Leeds withdraw to form the Protestant Methodist Connexion	**1827**
• Johann Hummel publishes *A Complete Theoretical and Practical Course of Instruction on the Art of Playing the Piano Forte* • Noah Webster publishes his *American Dictionary of the English Language* • Schubert composes his *Symphony No. 9 in C Major* (The Great)	• The British parliament repeals the 17th-century Corporation and Test Acts, which had barred non-Anglicans (Roman Catholics or Dissenters) from holding public office • Joseph Smith's *Autobiography* describes visions of the angel Moroni, which he claims led to his discovery of the golden plates containing the *Book of Mormon* • Notable publications include: – William Ellery Channing, *Likeness to God* – Heinrich Paulus, *The Life of Jesus*	• The Associated Methodist Reformers organization is founded; it convenes a General Convention of Methodist Reformers that unsuccessfully petitions the MEC General Conference regarding election of presiding elders, lay delegates, and other polity reforms • The MEC General Conference: – rescinds 1820 legislation mandating the election of presiding elders – rejects proposals for allowing lay delegates and for condemning Freemasonry – formally sanctions the cause of temperance and urges all Methodist people to embrace it – endorses the American Colonization Society and the new colony of Liberia – establishes the Methodist Bible Society and Methodist Tract Society – requires local trustees to report to their quarterly conference • The AMEC General Conference elects Morris Brown as bishop-assistant to Bishop Richard Allen • The AMEZC holds its first General Conference; Christopher Rush is elected as the second bishop of the denomination	• The Canadian Conference of the MEC becomes autonomous • The PMC holds its first Conference in Britain	**1828**

	A. WORLD HISTORY & POLITICS	B. AMERICAN HISTORY & POLITICS	C. SCIENCE, MEDICINE & TECHNOLOGY	D. DAILY LIFE, POPULAR CULTURE & ENTERTAINMENT
1829	• Serbia and Romania free themselves from Turkish rule • Russian forces capture Adrianople and other key cities from the Turks, leaving the Ottoman Empire on the verge of collapse • Russia and the Ottoman Empire conclude the Treaty of Adrianople; Russia secures control of the mouth of the Danube River and the east coast of the Black Sea; the Turks remove all their fortifications in Wallachia and Moldavia, and recognize the autonomy of Greece • The Republic of Colombia breaks apart; Venezuela and Ecuador become independent nations; the remainder (including Colombia and Panama) becomes New Grenada • The British parliament passes the Roman Catholic Relief Act, which grants complete political emancipation to Roman Catholics in Britain	• In one of the most famous speeches in US history, Daniel Webster proclaims that the US is not simply a compact of the states; instead, it is a creation of the people, who had invested the Constitution and the national government with ultimate sovereignty, and no state has the right to "nullify" a federal law, ending with the declaration "Liberty and Union, now and forever, one and inseparable" • Gold is discovered in Creek and Cherokee territory near Dahlonega, Georgia; the state of Georgia passes legislation extending its authority over the area and abolishing Cherokee tribal government • Charles Carroll, perhaps the richest American of his day, begins construction of the Baltimore and Ohio, the first railroad built in the US for the transportation of passengers and freight	• French educator Louis Braille invents a reading and writing system for the visually impaired	• The Royal Zoological Society takes over responsibility for the menagerie of animals at the Tower of London, leading to the establishment of the London Zoo at Regent's Park • Lydia Child publishes *The Frugal Housewife* • A rowing crew from Oxford University wins the first Henley Cup race with Cambridge University • The Coney Island House opens, marking the beginning of the status of Brooklyn's Coney Island as a seaside resort and amusement mecca • Cyril Demian of Vienna patents the musical instrument he calls the "Accordion," thus coining the name
1830	• Britain's King George IV dies; he is succeeded by his brother, William IV • The Mexican government tries unsuccessfully to stem the tide of settlers flooding in from Texas • France begins building its colonial empire in north and west Africa by invading (modern) Algeria • Belgium achieves independence from the Netherlands • Gibraltar becomes a British crown colony • Ferdinand I, the son of Austrian Emperor Francis I, becomes King of Hungary	• The US census reports that the population is 12,860,702: – whites: 10,532,060 (81.9%) – free blacks: 319,599 (2.5%) – slaves: 2,009,043 (15.6%) • The US national debt is $48,565,406 • Massive German immigration to the United States begins • US Congress passes the Indian Removal Act despite opposition by many Americans, most notably Tennessee Congressman and frontier hero David Crockett, and President Jackson quickly signs it into law • Richard Allen convenes the first National Negro Convention in Philadelphia for the purpose of improving the status of black Americans	• Scottish botanist Robert Brown discovers the cell nucleus in plants	• James Perry obtains a patent for his steel slit ink pen, a great improvement in writing instruments • British engineer Edwin Budding patents the first mechanical rotary lawn mower
1831	• Belgium is separated from the Netherlands, and Leopold I becomes king of Belgium • Syria, which had been part of the Ottoman Empire since 1516, is conquered and occupied by Egypt • France creates the Légion Étrangère (French Foreign Legion) to recruit foreign nationals to help control French colonial possessions in Africa • Austria crushes rebellions in Modena, Parma, and the Papal States but fails to entirely snuff out a burgeoning nationalist movement in Italy	• Nat Turner leads a slave uprising in Virginia in which 70 whites are killed; over 100 blacks are killed in a search for Turner before he is captured, tried, and executed; Virginia again tightens its laws on slavery	• James Clark Ross determines position of magnetic North Pole • Michael Faraday discovers magnetic induction • Cyrus McCormick invents the first successful horse-drawn mechanical grain harvester • British naturalist Charles Darwin sets out on the HMS *Beagle* for a five-year surveying expedition of the southern Atlantic Ocean and Pacific Ocean • A cholera pandemic, which had started in India in 1826, spreads from Russia into central Europe, reaching England and Scotland the next year • The New London Bridge across the Thames is completed and opened to traffic; the old 600-year-old London Bridge is then demolished	• Stephen Driver of Salem, MA, uses the term "Old Glory" to describe the new American flag given to him by friends for his ship; the term soon catches on as a generic term for any American flag

E. EDUCATION, LITERATURE & THE FINE ARTS	F. RELIGION, THEOLOGY, PHILOSOPHY & PSYCHOLOGY	G. AMERICAN & UNITED METHODISM	H. BRITISH & WORLD METHODISM	
• English scientist James Smithson bequeaths his fortune to the people of the United States to found an institution for the "increase and diffusion of knowledge," which results in the establishment of the Smithsonian Institution • The great Polish-born pianist and composer Frédéric Chopin gives his first concerts as a piano virtuoso in Vienna; his music signals the shift from the Classical to the Romantic era • Mendelssohn makes his conducting debut with a performance of J. S. Bach's *St. Matthew Passion* in Berlin • Fanny Hensel (sister of Felix Mendelssohn) composes her *Capriccio for Cello and Piano in A Flat Major* • *Encyclopaedia Americana*, America's first encyclopedia, is published in Philadelphia	• Alexander Campbell and his followers separate from the Baptists of Pennsylvania and Ohio; they take the name Disciples of Christ, and their revivalist teachings quickly spread into Kentucky • The General Assembly of the Cumberland Presbyterian Church (1810) is organized and meets for the first time • Pope Leo XII dies; he is succeeded by Pope Pius VIII • Coleridge publishes his essay *On the Constitution of Church and State*	• The UBC General Conference: – elects both English and German secretaries for the first time – supports annual conferences in taking action against members who join secret societies such as the Freemasons – declines an invitation to consider union with the Methodist Protestant Church, then in the process of formation • The Oneida Indian Mission (MEC) in New York is established by Daniel Barnes • The MEC annual conferences in the southern states, led by William Capers in South Carolina, begin appointing white preachers to work exclusively among the slaves of the great plantations, leading to the "Plantation Missions"	• The PMC sends its first missionaries from England to America	**1829**
• The Royal Geographic Society is established in London • Rossini's opera *William Tell* (with its famous overture) premieres in Paris, as does the *Symphonie Fantastique* of Berlioz • Alexander Pushkin publishes *Boris Godunov* (written in 1825) • Mary Shelley publishes *The Fortunes of Perkin Warbeck*	• Joseph Smith publishes *The Book of Mormon*; his followers establish the Church of Christ; the name is changed in 1838 to the Church of Jesus Christ of Latter-day Saints • Pope Pius VIII dies; he is succeeded in 1831 by Pope Gregory XVI • The interdenominational American Sunday School Union is established; Methodists provide much of the initial leadership	• The EA General Conference: – reduces the Articles of Faith adopted in 1816 from 21 to 19, omitting the articles "Of the Marriage of Preachers" and "Of the Oath of a Christian" and making minor revisions in other articles – revises and reduces the General Rules – orders that the revised *Discipline* be published in both German and English – rules that no preacher may be accepted without some proficiency in German • The General Convention of Methodist Reformers meets in Baltimore; it formally organizes and establishes The Methodist Protestant Church (MPC) and authorizes the publication of a *Discipline and Book of Hymns* for the new church • The MEC mission to the Shawnee Indians is established near Kansas City, MO • Sally Thompson is tried and expelled from the MEC by her local church in Cherry Valley, NY, for "insubordination" due to her refusal to cease preaching	• The first WM newspaper, the *Christian Advocate*, begins publication (until 1839) • Due to the effective work of Barnabas and Jane Shaw, the WM Conference provides funds for building the first Methodist chapel and mission house in Cape Town, southern Africa	**1830**
• Chopin gives his first piano concerts in Paris • Victor Hugo publishes *The Hunchback of Notre Dame* • Mary Prince's autobiographical narrative, *The History of Mary Prince, A West Indian Slave, Related by Herself*, is the earliest known firsthand account of the brutality that women suffered under slavery	• John Stuart Mill publishes *The Spirit of the Age*	• Richard Allen dies; Morris Brown assumes full responsibility as the bishop of the AMEC • Wesleyan College (later University) is established by the MEC in Middletown, CT [it is now the oldest Methodist college in the US since Augusta College (1820) was closed in 1845] • The Boston Wesleyan Association is formed; it takes over and continues publication of *Zion's Herald* (1823)	• Both the PMC and the Bible Christians send their first missionaries to Canada • Christoph Müller, a German immigrant who had been converted in England, returns to Germany, begins preaching, forms the first WM circuit in southern Germany, and is then formally appointed a missionary by the WM Missionary Society • Richard Watson publishes his *Life of John Wesley*	**1831**

	A. WORLD HISTORY & POLITICS	B. AMERICAN HISTORY & POLITICS	C. SCIENCE, MEDICINE & TECHNOLOGY	D. DAILY LIFE, POPULAR CULTURE & ENTERTAINMENT
1832	• The Reform Bill of 1832 in England redistributes seats in Parliament and almost triples the number of eligible voters; this has the effect of shifting political power from the aristocracy to the rising urban middle class • Mehemet Ali seizes control of Egypt and Syria from the Ottoman Empire, establishing a dynasty that endures until 1952; Russia offers assistance to the Ottomans	• The source of the Mississippi River is discovered in Minnesota • The New England Anti-Slavery Society is founded in Boston • The South Carolina legislature passes an "ordinance of nullification" of the 1828 "Tariff of Abominations"; based on the reasoning of the Kentucky and Virginia Resolutions of 1798–99, it is a manifesto for states' rights and a clear challenge to the power and authority of the federal government • In the face of increasingly serious disagreements with President Jackson about states' rights versus federal authority, John C. Calhoun becomes the first vice president of the US to resign; he is then elected to represent South Carolina in the US Senate • In *Worcester v. Georgia*, the US Supreme Court rules that the Cherokee Nation has sovereignty within its territory as a result of the treaties signed with the US in 1785 and 1791, declares that the Indian Removal Act of 1830 is unconstitutional, and strikes down the laws about control of Cherokee territory passed by the state of Georgia • President Jackson defies the Supreme Court decision, saying "Justice Marshall has made his decision, now let him enforce it"; Jackson orders implementation of the Indian Removal Act and authorizes a lottery for sale of tribal lands • President Jackson is reelected and Martin Van Buren is elected as vice president (Democratic Party)	• The first of three major 19th-century cholera epidemics strikes Europe and the US	• Public street-car service begins in New York City with horse-drawn trolleys
1833	• Slavery is abolished throughout the British Empire; child labor is banned in British factories • King Ferdinand VII of Spain dies; his infant daughter Isabella II is proclaimed queen at the age of 3; her mother, Maria, serves as queen-regent until 1843 • Antonio Lopez de Santa Ana is elected president of Mexico • The Ottoman Empire accepts Russian military aid against the Egyptians	• Following negotiations between President Jackson and Senator Henry Clay, Congress revises the "Tariff of Abominations" and the South Carolina legislature rescinds its "ordinance of nullification" • The town of Chicago (Illinois) is incorporated with a population of 350 • William Lloyd Garrison founds the American Anti-Slavery Society and its journal, *The Liberator* • The poem by Oliver Wendell Holmes celebrating "Old Ironsides," the USS *Constitution*, arouses such public sentiment that the ship is saved from scrapping and rebuilt as a symbol and icon of the US Navy	• John Deere invents the steel plow; it revolutionizes agriculture, making it possible to break the sod on the American Great Plains	• The *New York Sun*, the first successful penny daily paper, begins publication
1834	• The Société Française pour l'Abolition de l'Esclavage (French Society for the Abolition of Slavery) is established in Paris • The monopoly of the British East India Company for trade with China is abolished; tensions between Britain and China grow stronger	• The Indian Intercourse Act specifies all of present-day Oklahoma north and east of the Red River, as well as much of Kansas and Nebraska, as the Indian Territory	• English mathematician Charles Babbage develops the principle of the "analytical engine" (the intellectual basis for the modern computer) • Halley's Comet reappears right on schedule	• American frontier hero David Crockett publishes *A Narrative of the Life of David Crockett*, in which he makes effective use of his famous backwoods humor • The Female Moral Reform Society is organized in New York; its goal is to end urban prostitution and to protect women from sexually predatory men; its bimonthly

(cont.)

E. EDUCATION, LITERATURE & THE FINE ARTS	F. RELIGION, THEOLOGY, PHILOSOPHY & PSYCHOLOGY	G. AMERICAN & UNITED METHODISM	H. BRITISH & WORLD METHODISM	
• Mendelssohn's *Hebrides Overture* (also known as *Fingal's Cave*) has its first performance in London • Goethe completes the final version of *Faust* • French Romantic novelist Amandine Aurore Lucile Dupin, Baroness Dudevant, writing under the pseudonym George Sand, publishes her idealistic and romantic novel *Valentine*, celebrating free love unhampered by conventional marriage • Construction begins on England's National Gallery of Art in London (completed 1838)	• The Disciples of Christ (1829), founded by Alexander Campbell, joins with The Christian Connection or Church (1804), founded by Barton W. Stone, to form the Christian Church (Disciples of Christ), sometimes called the Stone-Campbell movement • The Congregational Union of England and Wales is established in the UK • John Nelson Darby, who had left the Church of England in 1830, becomes the acknowledged leader of the group known as the Plymouth Brethren, and helps establish the theology of premillennial dispensationalism • John Mason Peck and Isaac McCoy found the American Baptist Home Mission Society [now the American Baptist Board of National Ministries]	• The MEC General Conference: – establishes six new annual conferences: Troy, New Hampshire, Oneida, Alabama, Georgia, and Indiana (total now 23) – authorizes the bishops to appoint preachers to "literary institutions" (colleges or seminaries) for 2 years when asked to do so by an annual conference – elects John Emory and James O. Andrew to the episcopacy; McKendree's health is failing • Randolph-Macon College in Ashland, VA, chartered by the MEC in 1830, opens for classes	• The Liberia Mission Annual Conference is established by the MEC; it is the first conference external to the territory of the US • W. H. Rule establishes a WM mission in Gibraltar, from whence it spreads into southern Spain • Jabez Bunting becomes the secretary and mastermind of the activities of the WM Missionary Society	**1832**
• Oberlin College opens in Ohio; it is the first fully integrated and coeducational college in the US and admits women and blacks from its inception • Mendelssohn composes his lyrical and romantic *Symphony No. 4 in A Major (Italian)* • Gaetano Donizetti completes his opera *Lucretia Borgia* • Notable publications include: – Karl von Clausewitz, *On War* – Honoré de Balzac, *The Country Doctor* – Alexander Pushkin, *Eugene Onegin* – Thomas Carlyle, *Sartor Resartus*	• The remainder of Barton W. Stone's followers in the West join with "Christians" from the East in creating the General Convention of Christian Churches • John Keble's sermon "National Apostasy" marks the beginning of The Oxford Movement (or Tractarian Movement), which sought a renewal of "catholic" (or Roman Catholic) thought and practice within the Church of England; John Henry Newman edits *Tracts for the Times* • Noah Webster produces his own translation of the Bible; it is not well received • The Congregationalist Church of Massachusetts is disestablished; it was the last religious body in the US to receive any state financial support • The Reformed Presbyterian Church General Synod is established	• The UBC General Conference: – adopts a restrictive rule declaring that the General Conference "shall have no power to change the Confession of Faith or to change the rules of the *Discipline*" – stipulates that presiding elders shall be elected for one-year instead of four-year terms – limits the General Conference representation of each annual conference to two delegates for each conference, rather than two for each district – provides for the establishment of a Printing Establishment (publishing house) – authorizes publication of church newspaper *The Religious Telescope* • Jason Lee goes west to begin work among the Indian tribes in Oregon and establishes the Indian Manual Labor Training School • John Clark establishes a mission to the Chippewa Indians near Detroit • Allegheny College, originally founded in 1817, is chartered by the MEC • William Paul Quinn begins AMEC work west of the Alleghenies	• Melville Cox (MEC) is the first American Methodist missionary sent to Liberia; he dies less than a year later • Much of the autonomous Canadian Conference (MEC) merges with British Wesleyans to form the Wesleyan Methodist Church in Canada (WMCC); the remainder reorganizes in 1834 as the autonomous Methodist Episcopal Church of Canada (MECC)	**1833**
• Berlioz composes *Harold in Italy* (based in part on Byron's 1811 poem) as the result of a commission from Nicolò Paganini; Paganini evidently thought that its viola solo was insufficiently challenging and never played it	• The General Convention of Christian Churches establishes the Christian General Book Association, which thereafter meets once in four years in connection with the Convention, the same persons being delegates to both bodies	• The MPC General Conference meets for the first time: – approves the proposed constitution for the new church; extensively revises the proposed *Discipline* – recognizes 14 annual conferences with over 500 ministers and over 26,000 members – decides that the General Conference will henceforth meet every four years, *(cont.)*	• Rufus Spaulding and Samuel O. Wright, with their wives, and Sophronia Farrington (all MEC), arrive in Liberia; Farrington is the first unmarried Methodist woman missionary	**1834**

	A. WORLD HISTORY & POLITICS	B. AMERICAN HISTORY & POLITICS	C. SCIENCE, MEDICINE & TECHNOLOGY	D. DAILY LIFE, POPULAR CULTURE & ENTERTAINMENT
1834 cont.	• Civil war breaks out in Spain; Britain, France, Portugal, and Spain form an alliance in support of Spain's constitutional government • Fire destroys most of historic Westminster Palace in London, the traditional seat of the British parliament	• The Whig Party is established out of the remnants of the National Republican Party under the leadership of Daniel Webster and Henry Clay		journal, *The Advocate of Moral Reform and Family Guardian*, will eventually have 20,000 subscribers and a far larger number of actual readers
1835	• Santa Ana assumes dictatorial powers in Mexico and revokes the Constitution of 1824 • Finding British authority in the Cape Colony intolerable, the Boers (also by now known as Afrikaners) begin their "Great Trek" north into Natal and the Transvaal • The British East India Company starts the first tea plantations in Assam, India	• After revocation of the Mexican Constitution of 1824, Texans proclaim independence from Mexico and form a militia commanded by Sam Houston • Under strong pressure from the US and Georgia, the Cherokee Nation signs the Treaty of New Echota, giving up title to all Cherokee lands in the Southeast in exchange for lands in the Indian Territory west of the Mississippi • The Second Seminole War (1835–42) begins when American military forces try to enforce the Indian Removal Act in Florida • The US national debt falls to a record low of $33,733	• Samuel Colt creates the first "six-shooter" revolving pistol	• Twinings of London creates the popular tea blend known as Earl Grey, named for British Prime Minister Charles, 2nd Earl Grey
1836	• The first Anglo-Afghan War begins as a dispute about the border between British India and Afghanistan (until 1842) • The Arc de Triomphe is unveiled at the Place d'Étoile in Paris; begun in 1806 by Jean-François-Thérèse Chalgrin, the triumphal arch was originally conceived as an emblem of Napoleonic rule inspired by ancient Roman models; it is completed as a more general symbol of French patriotism	• Texas militia forces are crushed at the Alamo and Goliad, but defeat and capture Santa Ana at the Battle of San Jacinto; Texas gains its independence from Mexico and forms the Lone Star Republic • The New York Women's Anti-Slavery Society bars blacks from its membership rolls • Arkansas is admitted to the US as the 25th state; it is a slave state, making the balance 12 free states and 13 slave states • Part of the Michigan Territory is organized into the Territory of Wisconsin • Alexander Lucius Twilight of Vermont is the first black person elected to serve in a state legislature in the US • The charter of the Second Bank of the United States expires and is not renewed • Martin Van Buren is elected as president and Richard Johnson as vice president (Democratic Party)	• John Ericsson patents the screw propeller	• William H. McGuffy publishes the first *McGuffy Reader*; it becomes the most popular and influential reader textbook of all time

E. EDUCATION, LITERATURE & THE FINE ARTS	F. RELIGION, THEOLOGY, PHILOSOPHY & PSYCHOLOGY	G. AMERICAN & UNITED METHODISM	H. BRITISH & WORLD METHODISM	
• Robert Schumann establishes the journal *Neue Zeitschrift für Musik* (New Journal for Music), one of the first significant periodicals devoted entirely to musical criticism	• The Spanish Inquisition, begun by the Roman Catholic hierarchy in the 13th century, is finally abolished	instead of every seven years as had been originally decided – establishes a Board of Foreign Missions • The UBC Publishing House is established • LaRoy Sunderland's "Essay on Theological Education" marks the beginning of the movement to establish a school of theology for the training of MEC ministers • Dickinson College in Carlisle, PA, originally founded in 1783, is chartered by the MEC • The AMEC General Conference approves resolutions calling for the establishment of temperance societies and Sunday schools across the denomination	• The first Band of Hope (a temperance group for children) is formed in the PM School in Preston, England • The WM Conference sets up a Wesleyan Educational Committee charged with establishing a theological college	**1834 cont.**
• Chopin completes his *Grand Polonaise Brillante* • Samuel Sebastian Wesley (grandson of Charles Wesley) composes his *Larghetto for Organ in F Minor* • Gaetano Donizetti's opera *Lucia di Lammermoor* premieres in the Teatro San Carlo, Naples • Luigi Cherubini publishes his musical textbook, *Course in Counterpoint and Fugue* • *Memoir of James Jackson*, written by Susan Paul, is the earliest-known published narrative by an American black woman and the first account documenting the life of a free black child in the US • Hans Christian Andersen begins publication of his *Fairy Tales* (to 1845)	• Alexis de Tocqueville publishes the first volume of his classic account of *Democracy in America* (vol. 2 appears in 1840) • D. F. Strauss publishes *The Life of Jesus Critically Examined*; his critical analysis of the gospel stories, which discounts all miracles or supernatural events, results in the loss of his faculty position at the University of Tübingen • Other notable publications include: – Francis Wayland, *The Elements of Moral Science* – Wilhelm Vatke, *The Religion of the Old Testament* – Adam Clarke, *Christian Theology* – Charles Finney, *Lectures on Revivals of Religion* – Alexander Campbell, *The Christian System*	• The EA General Conference: – authorizes publication of the monthly periodical *Der Christliche Botschafter* when sufficient subscriptions have been placed; publication begins in 1836 – instructs all the preachers to organize German Sunday schools on their circuits whenever possible – establishes the Charitable Society to care for retired preachers and their widows and children – institutes quarterly conferences on each circuit • William Nast, pioneer of MEC German work, is converted • Along with her sister, Sarah Lankford, Phoebe Palmer begins holding "Tuesday Meetings for the Promotion of Holiness" at her home in New York • McKendree College is founded by the MEC in Lebanon, IL • Nicholas Snethen publishes *Lay Representation*	• The Methodist Theological Institution is established by the WM Conference in rented space in Hoxton; it is the first school established for the purpose of training WM clergy; Jabez Bunting is named as its first president • The WM Conference approves a resolution "strongly disapproving" of women preachers • The first WM weekly newspaper, *The Watchman* appears (discontinued in 1884) • William Cross and David and Margaret Cargill from Tonga begin the first WM mission work in Fiji • Fountain Pitts (MEC) visits Brazil and forms the first Methodist congregation in Rio de Janeiro	**1835**
• Georgia Female College is established in Macon, GA; it is the first women's college in the US and opens for classes in 1839 • Auditorium-style architecture is used in the construction of the Broadway Tabernacle in New York City, which serves as the city's main meeting hall until it is demolished in 1857 • Gaetano Donizetti's dramatic opera *Belisario* (Belisarius) debuts in Vienna • Notable publications include: – Charles Dickens, *The Pickwick Papers* – Hans Christian Andersen, *The Little Mermaid*	• Union Theological Seminary is established in New York City as an independent graduate school of theology committed to "solid learning, true piety, and enlightened experience" • Ralph Waldo Emerson's little volume entitled simply *Nature* symbolizes the emergence of Transcendentalism among younger Unitarians in New England • The first Mormon temple is built and dedicated by followers of Joseph Smith in Kirtland, OH • The modern deaconess movement begins in Germany when Lutheran pastor Theodor Fliedner and his wife, Friedericke Munster, open the first deaconess "motherhouse," hospital, and training center • Arthur Schopenhauer publishes *On the Will in Nature*	• The MEC General Conference meets in Cincinnati (the first meeting west of the Appalachian Mountains): – recasts constitution of the Mission Society and decides to sponsor mission work in South America and China – receives as fraternal delegates William Lord from the WM Conference in Britain and William Case from Canada – establishes 7 new annual conferences: Black River, Erie, Liberia, Michigan, New Jersey, North Carolina, and Arkansas (total now 30) – declines to elect a bishop for Africa – refuses to reverse decision of Baltimore Conference to exclude preachers who were slaveholders from office and ordination – censures New England Conference delegates Orange Scott and William Winans for "lecturing" the Conference on slavery – approves a resolution condemning "abolitionism" and stating that the Conference "disclaims any right, wish, or intention to interfere in the civil and political relations between master and slave" – approves revised edition of 1821 *Collection of Hymns* (which is published later the same year)	• Under the leadership of Jabez Bunting, the WM Conference reverses a number of the 1793 decisions: – distinguishes between the ordained ministers and the unordained preachers – receives ministers into full connexion and ordains them by the "laying on of hands" in a Conference session for the first time since Wesley's last years – allows any ordained Methodist minister to administer the sacraments when requested – permits ordained ministers to wear gowns, cassocks, bands, or surplices if they wish • Opposition to Jabez Bunting's leadership (or control) of the WM Conference in general and to the establishment of a theological college in particular leads Samuel Warren and followers to form the Wesleyan Methodist Association; it absorbs the older Protestant Methodist Association (1827) • The MEC sends John Dempster to Argentina and Justin Paulding to Brazil as missionaries • The first WM worship service is conducted in Melbourne, Australia, when the first settlers from Britain arrive there on Christmas Day	**1836**

	A. WORLD HISTORY & POLITICS	B. AMERICAN HISTORY & POLITICS	C. SCIENCE, MEDICINE & TECHNOLOGY	D. DAILY LIFE, POPULAR CULTURE & ENTERTAINMENT
1836 cont.				
1837	• Britain's King William IV dies; he is succeeded by his 18-year-old niece, Victoria, the granddaughter of George III • Buckingham Palace in London becomes the official residence of the British monarchy [it still is today] • Canadians protest against British colonial rule in both Upper Canada and Lower Canada	• In his inaugural address, President Van Buren urges the nation to "cease agitation" over slavery • Illinois is admitted to the US as the 26th state; it is a free state, making the balance 13 free states and 13 slave states • The first modern public school system in the US is created in Massachusetts • The first National Female Anti-Slavery Society convention meets in New York City • Seminole Indian leader Osceola is captured in Florida under a false flag of truce • The Panic of 1837, the culmination of a speculative boom, causes a six-year economic depression with numerous bank failures and widespread unemployment • Congress revises and standardizes US coinage laws and prescribes the mottos and devices that should be placed upon US coins	• Louis-Jacques Daguerre creates the "daguerreotype," the first photographic image that is fixed, does not fade, and needs less than thirty minutes of light exposure • Samuel Morse (US) patents the "dots-and-dashes" telegraphic code that bears his name	• Friedrich Fröbel (Germany) opens a school for very young children, which he calls a *kindergarten* ("child's garden")
1838	• After Boer (Afrikaner) settlers are massacred in Zululand, the Boer Army defeats Zulu warriors at the Battle of Blood River in southern Africa, establishing the Republic of Natalia; border skirmishes and raids continue for many years • Honduras withdraws from The United Provinces of Central America, or Central American Federation, and declares its independence • British political radical William Lovett drafts the "People's Charter," which calls for universal male suffrage, equal electoral districts, vote by ballot, annually elected parliaments, payment of members of Parliament, and abolition of the property qualifications for membership; this gives rise to the political movement called Chartism	• The US Army begins the removal of the Cherokee, Creek, Choctaw, and Chickasaw Indians from their ancestral homelands in the southern US to the Indian Territory; the "Trail of Tears" results in over 4,000 deaths • Several hundred Cherokee refuse to leave and go into hiding in the western North Carolina mountains; they become the ancestors of the eastern band of Cherokee Indians • Kentucky gives women the right to vote in local school elections but *not* in any other local or state elections; several other states soon follow this example	• German astronomer Friedrich Wilhelm Bessel makes the accurate determination of the distance of a fixed star from the earth based on parallax measurement	• The Bon Marché opens in Paris; it will quickly grow to become the world's first true department store
1839	• The British parliament rejects the Chartist petition; riots ensue in Birmingham and elsewhere, resulting in the arrest of Chartist leaders • British troops unsuccessfully invade Afghanistan • China confiscates and burns 20,000 chests of opium in Canton; Britain retaliates with a punitive expedition, initiating the First Opium War (1839–42) • The Turkish fleet is defeated by and surrenders to Egypt	• Mississippi enacts the first Married Women's Property Law in the US, which secures the right of a married woman to continue to own property (including slaves) that she had owned prior to marriage and protects such property from seizure for her husband's debts; most other states pass similar laws by the 1870s • The Spanish slave ship *Amistad*, carrying 53 slaves, is taken over in a mutiny; John Quincy Adams successfully argues their case before the US Supreme Court; they are freed by decision of the Court in 1841	• Charles Goodyear makes possible the commercial use of rubber by his discovery of the process of vulcanization • William Robert Grove develops the first primitive fuel cell, which produces electricity by combining hydrogen and oxygen • Michael Faraday publishes his *Experimental Researches in Electricity* (to 1855) • Charles Darwin publishes his account of *The Voyage of the Beagle*	• Carl August von Steinheil (Switzerland) builds the first electric clock • Abner Doubleday is widely credited with inventing the game of baseball at Cooperstown, NY • Mathew Brady opens his first photographic studio in New York

E. EDUCATION, LITERATURE & THE FINE ARTS	F. RELIGION, THEOLOGY, PHILOSOPHY & PSYCHOLOGY	G. AMERICAN & UNITED METHODISM	H. BRITISH & WORLD METHODISM	
		• The EA General Conference meets in special session to reestablish the publishing house after financial failure • Nathan Bangs edits and publishes a supplement of 90 hymns to the 1821 MEC *Collection of Hymns* • Fire destroys the Methodist Book Concern, including all inventory • Emory College is established by the MEC in Oxford, GA • The New York Conference of the AMEC resolves to send missionaries to Canada • Jarena Lee publishes the first version of her autobiography, *The Life and Religious Experience of Jarena Lee*		**1836 cont.**
• Prussia enacts a copyright law that for the first time protects performances of concert music • Berlioz composes his titanic *Grande Messe des morts (Requiem)*, which requires tremendous vocal and orchestral resources including four antiphonal brass choirs • Mendelssohn composes his *String Quartet No. 4 in E Minor* • Notable publications include: – Thomas Carlyle, *The French Revolution, A History* – Nathaniel Hawthorne, *Twice Told Tales*	• Presbyterians in the US experience a schism between "Old School" and "New School" factions; both factions claim to be the "true" Presbyterian Church in the USA (PCUSA) of 1789 • Ralph Waldo Emerson's "American Scholar" lecture at Harvard urges the development of a distinctive American intellectual tradition not derivative from and dependent on European thought • Hegel publishes his *Lectures on the Philosophy of History*	• The UBC General Conference: – adopts a formal constitution for the denomination, but then establishes a new committee to consider its revision or rewriting – provides for representation of annual conferences in the General Conference to be on a pro rata basis – adopts a constitution and elects the first officers for the Printing Establishment • The MPC publishes a new hymnal, *Hymnbook of the Methodist Protestant Church* • Indiana Asbury College is founded by the MEC in Greencastle, IN; it later becomes DePauw University • The first AMEC Congregation in New England is organized in New Haven, CT	• The MEC sends Ann Wilkins to Liberia as a missionary • The MNC sends missionaries to Upper Canada • The Ladies' Society for Promoting Female Education in China and the East (nondenominational but with significant Methodist participation) is established in the UK • Thomas Jackson publishes his edition of *The Lives of the Early Methodist Preachers* (1st ed. in 3 vols., 1837–38; 2nd ed. in 5 vols., 1846; 3rd ed. in 6 vols., 1865; 4th ed. in 6 vols. + add., 1871)	**1837**
• Greensboro College is founded in Greensboro, NC, as a college for women; it opens for classes in 1846 • Thomas Cole's landscape *Shroon Mountain, Adirondacks* symbolizes the work of the Hudson River school of American painters • Berlioz's dramatic opera *Benvenuto Cellini* premieres at the Paris Opera • Notable publications include: – Edgar Allan Poe, *The Narrative of Arthur Gordon Pym* – Charles Dickens, *Oliver Twist*	• Emerson delivers his famous "Divinity School Address" (at Harvard Divinity School), which attacks formal religion and argues for self-reliance and trust in individual spiritual experience • Karaite manuscript collector Abraham Firkovitch acquires the Leningrad Codex, a complete copy of the Old Testament dating from ca. A.D.1009; he never indicates where he obtained the codex, which is transferred to the Russian Imperial Library in St. Petersburg in 1863	• The MPC General Conference: – adopts, after much debate, a resolution determining that the subject of slavery should be left to the respective annual conferences – approves a plan for the establishment of a Book Concern or Publishing House – recognizes a new annual conference in Arkansas (total now 15) • Most congregations of the Reformed Methodist Church (1814) join the MPC; the rest continue as a separate body until 1952, when they join the Church of Christ • The EA Missionary Society is founded • William Nast organizes the first MEC German society in America • Nathan Bangs begins publication of his *History of the Methodist Episcopal Church* (4 vols., 1838–40)	• Thomas Birch Freeman, the son of a freed African slave father and an English mother, lands at Cape Coast Castle, extending WM missions in western Africa; he is regarded as the "father of Methodism" in the Gold Coast (Ghana) in 1839, Nigeria in 1841, and Dahomey (Benin) and Togoland (Togo) in 1843 • British Methodists establish the Wesleyan Proprietary Grammar School (later Wesley College) in Sheffield to educate the sons of WM laity	**1838**
• The New York Philharmonic Orchestra is founded • Liszt pioneers the solo piano recital concert, performing from memory and without assisting artists • Berlioz composes his choral symphony *Romeo and Juliet*, which he dedicates to Nicolò Paganini • Mendelssohn conducts the Leipzig Gewandhaus Orchestra in the first performance of Schubert's *Symphony No. 9 in C Major (The Great)*	• Timothy Merritt establishes *Guide to Christian Perfection* magazine; renamed *Guide to Holiness* in 1846; purchased by Phoebe Palmer and merged with *Beauty of Holiness* magazine in 1864 • Daniel A. Payne becomes the first black man to be ordained as a Lutheran minister in the US; later he becomes president of Wilberforce College and a bishop of the AMEC • Asa Mahan publishes *The Scripture Doctrine of Christian Perfection*	• The EA General Conference: – adopts a restrictive rule prohibiting any future alteration of the EA Articles of Faith – requires a two-thirds majority vote of all members of every annual conference for further constitutional revision or change – creates a system for the election of delegates to General Conference – condemns the manufacture or use of spirituous liquors by any member for any purpose other than medicinal	• Methodists around the world celebrate the centennial of Methodism, commemorating formation by John Wesley of the first Methodist Societies in Bristol and London in 1739 [there is no known commemoration anywhere in the world in 1838 of the centennial of John Wesley's "conversion" at Aldersgate] • WM mission work begins in Switzerland • The MEC opens the College of West Africa in Liberia, its first educational institution outside the US	**1839**

	A. WORLD HISTORY & POLITICS	B. AMERICAN HISTORY & POLITICS	C. SCIENCE, MEDICINE & TECHNOLOGY	D. DAILY LIFE, POPULAR CULTURE & ENTERTAINMENT
1839 cont.				
1840	• Signature of the Treaty of Waitangi formalizes British sovereignty over New Zealand, which becomes a British crown colony; the treaty guarantees the native Maori people undisturbed possession of their property • The kingdom of Hawaii is recognized as an independent country by the US and most European countries • The United Provinces of Central America, or Central American Federation, is dissolved and its remaining member states (Guatemala, El Salvador, Nicaragua, and Costa Rica) become independent republics • British forces occupy Chosun and capture Chinese forts on the Canton River • Prussia's King Frederick William III dies; he is succeeded by his son, Frederick William IV • Construction begins on Britain's new Houses of Parliament in London (completed in 1852)	• The US census reports that the population is 17,063,353: – whites: 14,189,705 (83.2%) – free blacks: 386,293 (2.3%) – slaves: 2,487,355 (14.5%) • The US national debt is $3,573,343 • The National Road (Cumberland Road), begun in 1811, is completed from Cumberland, MD, to Vandalia, IL, a distance of 680 miles along the route of what is now US 40 (I-70), at a total cost of $7 million; plans to extend it to St. Louis are scrapped due to lack of funds and the advent of the railroads • William Henry Harrison is elected as president and John Tyler as vice president (Whig Party)	• The first school of dentistry in the US is founded in Baltimore, MD • Swiss-American naturalist Louis Agassiz publishes his influential *Studies on Glaciers*, which suggests for the first time that the earth has experienced "ice ages" in which much of it was covered by glaciers and transformed by glacial action	• The first postage stamps are issued in England; the sender of a letter is now required to pay the cost of postage in advance, rather than the recipient on delivery • Anna, Duchess of Bedford, introduces afternoon tea, which becomes a lasting English ritual
1841	• The British parliament passes the Act of Union, which combines Upper Canada and Lower Canada into one province, called simply Canada, divided into two territories, West (Ontario) and East (Quebec); English becomes the official language • British forces capture and occupy Hong Kong	• President Harrison catches pneumonia at his inauguration and dies only one month later; he is the first US president to die in office and receives the first presidential state funeral in US history; Vice President Tyler becomes president	• In a report to the British Association for the Advancement of Science, paleontologist Richard Owen proposes that recent fossil discoveries indicate the existence of a previously unknown group of large reptiles, for which he coins the term *dinosaur*, meaning "terrible lizard" • British industrialist Joseph Whitworth proposes standards for screw threads, greatly simplifying the manufacturing of tools	• Prince Albert and Queen Victoria introduce the European tradition of the Christmas tree to England when they decorate the first Christmas tree at Windsor Castle with candles, candies, fruits, and gingerbread • American showman P. T. Barnum purchases Scudder's American Museum in New York City and revamps its exhibits and show to include the midget General Tom Thumb and the original Siamese twins, Chang and Eng Bunker

E. EDUCATION, LITERATURE & THE FINE ARTS	F. RELIGION, THEOLOGY, PHILOSOPHY & PSYCHOLOGY	G. AMERICAN & UNITED METHODISM	H. BRITISH & WORLD METHODISM	
• Henry Wadsworth Longfellow receives his first wide public notice with his first volume of verse, *Voices of the Night*, which contains the poem "A Psalm of Life" • Other notable publications include: – Stendhal (Marie-Henri Beyle), *The Charterhouse of Parma* – Charles Dickens, *Nicholas Nickleby* – Edgar Allan Poe, *The Fall of the House of Usher*		– prohibits the trading or ownership of slaves by any member – elects John Seybert as the first EA bishop since Jacob Albright's death in 1808 • The first German Methodist *Lagerversammlung* (camp meeting) is held near Cincinnati • The first Methodist regional historical society is founded in Baltimore • The MEC establishes the Shawnee Manual Labor School near Kansas City, MO		**1839 cont.**
• Schumann completes his great song cycle *Dichterliebe* (Poet's Love), based on verse by Heinrich Heine • Donizetti's comic opera *The Daughter of the Regiment* premieres at the Opéra Comique in Paris • Notable publications include: – Charles Dickens, *The Old Curiosity Shop* – Richard Henry Dana Jr., *Two Years Before the Mast*	• Charles Finney publishes his influential work *Views of Sanctification* • Coleridge's *Confessions of an Enquiring Spirit* is published posthumously • The Evangelical Synod of North America is founded near St. Louis by a group of Lutheran and Reformed Christians; it is long known as the German Evangelical Church Association of the West	• The MEC General Conference: – establishes four new annual conferences: Providence, Memphis, Texas, and North Ohio (total now 34) – rules that an annual conference may not withhold connectional funds from a super-annuated preacher or refuse voluntary location to a member in good standing – allows the bishops to appoint preachers to colleges or seminaries for more than two years – declines to allow the term of pastoral appointment to be extended beyond two years – permits the bishops to unite two or more circuits or stations for a quarterly conference – creates a Committee on Sunday schools and provides for the publication of Sunday school curriculum materials by the Publishing House – authorizes the bishops to decide all points of law in an annual conference – adopts a resolution stating that slaveholding is no barrier to any order or office in the church – refuses to consider proposals for lay representation, restrictions on the powers of the bishops, and the election of presiding elders • Newbury Biblical Institute (Vermont) is established by the MEC as the first American Methodist seminary [it is a forerunner of Boston University School of Theology] • The newspaper *Die Geschäftige Martha* (The Busy Martha) is established by the UBC • Primitive Methodists in America declare their independence of the British Conference and form the American Primitive Methodist Church • Morris Brown organizes the first AMEC Conference in Canada • Nathan Bangs publishes his *History of the Methodist Episcopal Church, 1766–1840* (4 vols.)	• Disagreements within the WMCC (1833) over control of Indian missions in Canada causes it to divide again into American (MEC) and British (WM) branches, with the British retaining control of the Indian missions • The WM Conference decides to split the Methodist Theological Institution (1835) into two schools, a northern one located in Manchester and a southern one located in London, and to build permanent facilities for both	**1840**
• Richard Wagner composes his first representative opera, *The Flying Dutchman*, based on a legend about a ship's captain doomed to sail forever without rest • Schumann composes his *Symphony No. 1 in B-flat Major*, which is immediately performed under the direction of his friend Felix Mendelssohn at Leipzig	• In *The Essence of Christianity*, Ludwig Feuerbach argues that worship of God is actually worship of an idealized self, and that every person "creates" God in his or her own image • Emerson publishes the first series of his *Essays* (second series, 1844)	• The UBC General Conference: – adopts the revised constitution recommended by the committee appointed in 1837 – prohibits ministers and members from joining secret societies such as the Freemasons – prohibits ministers and members from owning slaves – forbids the discussion of slavery or abolitionism in church newspapers	• The WM Mission in Sweden is abandoned because of increasing opposition from the Lutheran state church • MEC missionaries withdraw from Brazil	**1841**

	A. WORLD HISTORY & POLITICS	B. AMERICAN HISTORY & POLITICS	C. SCIENCE, MEDICINE & TECHNOLOGY	D. DAILY LIFE, POPULAR CULTURE & ENTERTAINMENT
1841 cont.	• English missionary and physician David Livingstone arrives in Africa and begins his explorations, which involve traveling an estimated 29,000 miles in Africa, adding about one million square miles to the portion of the globe known to Europeans • Joseph Roberts becomes the first black governor of Liberia			
1842	• The First Opium War (1839–42) ends with the defeat of China; through the Treaty of Nanking, China cedes the island of Hong Kong to the British and is forced to grant major commercial concessions, opening five "treaty" ports to European trade • British forces in south Africa repel attacks by the Boers (Afrikaners) and regain control of Natal • Afghan forces decimate British and Indian troops near Kabul and force the British evacuation of Afghanistan	• A Massachusetts state court decision finds that strikes to improve labor conditions are lawful and are not "criminal conspiracies" • The Second Seminole War (1835–42) ends; the Seminole, exhausted by their struggles against US military forces, cease armed conflict, but do not sign a peace treaty; some are captured and sent to the Indian Territory, others withdraw deep into the Everglades	• Crawford W. Long performs the first surgical procedures using ether as anesthetic • Italian physicist Carlo Matteucci proves that in animals an electrical current precedes every heartbeat	• The *Illustrated London News*, the first illustrated weekly newspaper, uses woodcuts and engravings for the first time, prompting the growth of illustrated journals throughout the second half of the century
1843	• Military rule is overthrown in Spain and the monarchy restored; Queen Isabella II takes the throne in her own name, having come of age • British settlers in New Zealand begin encroaching on Maori lands in violation of the Treaty of Waitangi (1840) • Britain annexes Natal to the Cape Colony in south Africa	• The US Supreme Court upholds the Fugitive Slave Act of 1793, declaring Pennsylvania's state anti-kidnapping law unconstitutional and stating that slave owners have a right to retrieve their "property"; at the same time, the Court rules that enforcement of the Fugitive Slave Law is a federal responsibility in which states are not required to assist • John C. Frémont opens a route across the Rocky Mountains and the Sierra Nevada to California • Sojourner Truth (born in slavery as Isabella Bomefree or Baumfree) begins traveling the country giving her powerful abolitionist and women's rights lectures • Congress provides funds to Samuel Morse to construct the first telegraph line in the US, from Baltimore to Washington	• British engineer Marc Brunel and his son Isambard complete construction of a tunnel (begun in 1825) under the river Thames in London; it is the first successful underwater tunnel anywhere in the world and carries pedestrian and horse-drawn traffic until 1869 when it becomes a railway tunnel; it is still in use as part of the London Underground	• The first printed Christmas cards, designed by John Calcott Horsley, appear in London • Edwin P. Christy establishes Christy's Original Band of Virginia Minstrels; it soon becomes the most famous troupe of the type in the country, performing in blackface and popularizing the songs of Stephen C. Foster, such as "Camptown Races," "Old Folks at Home (Way Down Upon the Suwannee River)," "Massa's in de Cold, Cold Ground," and "My Old Kentucky Home" • "Columbia, Gem of the Ocean" is first published and quickly becomes a popular patriotic song

E. EDUCATION, LITERATURE & THE FINE ARTS	F. RELIGION, THEOLOGY, PHILOSOPHY & PSYCHOLOGY	G. AMERICAN & UNITED METHODISM	H. BRITISH & WORLD METHODISM	
• Edgar Allan Poe introduces the first fictional detective, Auguste C. Dupin, in his short story "The Murders in the Rue Morgue"; Dupin's exploits continue in Poe's novels *The Mystery of Marie Roget* (1842) and *The Purloined Letter* (1845) • Longfellow's *Ballads* includes some of his most famous poems, such as "The Village Blacksmith": "Under a spreading chestnut tree / The village smithy stands" • Other notable publications include: – James Fennimore Cooper, *The Deerslayer* – Charles Dickens, *Barnaby Rudge* – Nikolai Gogol, *Dead Souls*	• Theodore Parker emerges as a major Transcendentalist spokesman when he delivers "A Discourse on the Transient and Permanent in Christianity" at an ordination in south Boston	– extends prohibitions against making and selling alcoholic beverages to include laymen as well as ministers – abandons the principle of pro rata representation because some conferences objected to counting their members – requires a two-thirds majority for further constitutional revision, but fails to provide a clear mechanism for voting on such revisions – authorizes annual conferences to raise funds to support missionary work for the church • *The Ladies' Repository*, the first Methodist periodical for women, begins publication • The Baltimore Conference of the AMEC makes the first report of Sunday schools in the connection		**1841 cont.**
• King Frederick William IV of Prussia creates a new order of merit for the arts and sciences; those honored include Felix Mendelssohn, Franz Liszt, and Gioacchino Rossini • Chopin composes his *Polonaise for Piano in A Flat Major (Heroic)* • Mendelssohn completes his *Symphony No. 3 (Scottish)* and composes his incidental music for Shakespeare's play *A Midsummer Night's Dream*, which includes the famous "Wedding March" • J. M. W. Turner completes his painting *Snow Storm* • Notable publications include: – Honoré de Balzac, *The Black Sheep* – William Wells Brown, *The Narrative of William W. Brown, a Fugitive Slave*	• Construction of the Cologne Cathedral resumes after a hiatus of 284 years; [it is finally completed in 1880] • Theodore Parker publishes his Transcendentalist manifesto, *A Discourse of Matters Pertaining to Religion*	• The MPC General Conference: – recognizes new annual conferences: Indiana, South Carolina, Onondaga (New York), and Mississippi (total now 19) – after much debate on the subject, adopts a compromise resolution allowing the annual conferences to make their own rules with regard to slavery – takes steps to deal with the debts of the Book Concern through a churchwide collection • Radical abolitionists led by Orange Scott, LaRoy Sunderland, and Luther Lee withdraw from the MEC because of its refusal to condemn the institution of slavery and advocate abolition • Union Theological Association of Philadelphia is formed for the education of AMEC clergy • Jason Lee's mission work in Oregon leads to the establishment by the MEC of Oregon Institute, the first institution of higher education in the West [it becomes Willamette University in 1853]	• Didsbury College opens in Manchester as the northern branch of the Methodist Theological Institution (WM)	**1842**
• Swedish composer Franz Berwald completes his *Symphony No. 1 in G Minor (Serious)* • Mendelssohn establishes the Leipzig Conservatory and serves as its first director (it is the first musical conservatory in Germany) • Charles Dickens publishes his beloved holiday story *A Christmas Carol* • Edgar Allan Poe publishes his classic tales of suspense and horror "The Pit and the Pendulum" and "The Tell-Tale Heart" • John Ruskin's controversial work *Modern Painters* argues that the works of contemporary artists such as J. M. W. Turner are "superior" to those of the "old masters" of the Renaissance	• The Church of Scotland (the "Auld Kirk") splits when 40% of the ministers and members leave to form the evangelical Free Church of Scotland • Søren Kierkegaard publishes both *Either/Or: A Fragment of Life* and *Fear and Trembling* • Other notable works include: – John Stuart Mill, *The System of Logic* – Heinrich Ewald, *History of the People of Israel*	• The EA General Conference: – decides that a second bishop is needed and names Joseph Long to serve beside John Seybert – acknowledges a growing need for ministry among English-speaking people; repeals the 1830 rule that no preacher may be accepted without some proficiency in German; orders preparation of an English hymnal and decides to start an English newspaper as soon as possible – fixes annual salaries for itinerants at $100 for single preachers and $200 for married preachers, with a $25 allowance for each child under age 14; salaries of the bishops set at the same levels – orders development of a course of study for ministers and ministerial candidates • Followers of Orange Scott, LaRoy Sunderland, and Luther Lee formally establish the Wesleyan Methodist Connection (WMC) • The Georgia Conference (MEC) assumes responsibility for Georgia Female College, renamed Wesleyan Female College; later (1917) "Female" is dropped from the name • Phoebe Palmer publishes *The Way of Holiness*	• Richmond College opens in London as the southern branch of the Methodist Theological Institution (WM) • The WM Conference authorizes the establishment of day schools throughout England • The first Methodist sanctuary in South America is dedicated in Buenos Aires • The establishment of the Free Church of Scotland creates problems for Methodism in Scotland by attracting its members in significant numbers • Thomas Birch Freeman (MEC) begins missions in Dahomey, Togo, and Benin • Methodism is introduced into Hong Kong through British soldiers stationed there after Treaty of Nanking	**1843**

	A. WORLD HISTORY & POLITICS	B. AMERICAN HISTORY & POLITICS	C. SCIENCE, MEDICINE & TECHNOLOGY	D. DAILY LIFE, POPULAR CULTURE & ENTERTAINMENT
1844	• France and the US obtain legal and commercial concessions from China on par with that of the British under the Treaty of Nanking • War breaks out between the Maoris and the British settlers in New Zealand (until 1847), resulting in loss of much land and life by the Maoris • Britain and the US agree on latitude 54°40' (as per the 1824 treaty between the US and Russia) as the boundary between Canada and the Oregon Territory	• The violently anti-immigrant, anti-Catholic American Republican Party ("Know-Nothing" Party) is established in New York • Female textile workers in Massachusetts organize the Lowell Female Labor Reform Association (LFLRA), one of the first female worker's associations; they demand better working conditions and a 10-hour workday • The US negotiates an annexation agreement with the Lone Star Republic of Texas (1836) • James K. Polk is elected as president and George Dallas as vice president (Democratic Party)	• Samuel Morse demonstrates the telegraph to the US Congress, transmitting the message "What hath God wrought!" from Washington to Baltimore	• The Young Men's Christian Association (YMCA) is founded in London by George Williams • The popular musical *The Bohemian Girl* by Michael William Balfe and Alfred Bunn has its American premiere at the Park Theatre in New York City
1845	• The great potato famine begins in Ireland when successive crops fail due to potato blight; it lasts until 1849, is the worst famine to occur in Europe during the 19th century, and results in over 1 million deaths and 1.5 million immigrants to Britain and the US • Sikh forces from the Punjab invade British territory in India • Mexico objects to the US annexation of Texas, disputes the Texas border, and severs diplomatic relations with US	• Florida is admitted to the US as the 27th state; it is a slave state, making the balance 13 free states and 14 slave states • Texas is annexed by the US, becoming the 28th state; the status of slavery there is disputed • The claim of "manifest destiny," meaning that the westward territorial expansion of the US is not only inevitable but divinely ordained, appears in newspaper editorials supporting the annexation of Texas; proponents of "manifest destiny" believe in the superiority of America's culture and form of government, which must be expanded in order to "civilize" other peoples • The US Navy School (later the Naval Academy) is established at Annapolis, MD	• E. B. Bigelow (US) constructs the first power loom for manufacturing carpets • Ascanio Sobrero (Italy) develops the explosive nitroglycerine • Stephen Perry (UK) patents the rubber band, made of vulcanized rubber, to keep letters sorted • Alexander von Humboldt's *Cosmos: A Sketch of a Physical Description of the Universe* (5 vols., 1845–62), brings together most of the scientific knowledge of the time about the earth and has been called the first textbook of geophysics	• Stiff petticoats and tightly laced corsets become fashionable for upper-class women in Europe

E. EDUCATION, LITERATURE & THE FINE ARTS	F. RELIGION, THEOLOGY, PHILOSOPHY & PSYCHOLOGY	G. AMERICAN & UNITED METHODISM	H. BRITISH & WORLD METHODISM	
• The University of Notre Dame, the premiere Roman Catholic institution of higher education in the US, is established in South Bend, IN • Alexandre Dumas publishes his popular tale of *The Three Musketeers* • J. M. W. Turner completes his painting *Rain, Steam and Speed—The Great Western Railway*	• Joseph Smith, leader of the Mormon settlement in Nauvoo, IL, is murdered by a mob with the apparent complicity of the governor of Illinois; Brigham Young becomes the leader of the Mormons • The followers of Adventist lay preacher William Miller prepare for "The Day of Atonement"—the second coming of Jesus—and are shattered when it does not happen as Miller had predicted • Baptists in the US split into northern and southern factions over the issue of slavery • Kierkegaard publishes *Philosophical Fragments* and *The Concept of Dread*	• The MEC General Conference: – following extensive debate over issues of slavery and the powers of episcopacy, votes to suspend Bishop James Andrew from the exercise of his office so long as he owns slaves; this provokes intense debate over the rights and powers of the General Conference versus those of the bishops and the annual conferences – after failure to reach a mutually acceptable compromise solution, approves a "Plan of Separation" for dividing the church into northern and southern branches – approves creation of a course of study for training of itinerant ministers extending over four years, to be prescribed by the bishops only – prohibits bishops from stationing a preacher in the same charge more than two years in six, or in the same city more than four years in succession – authorizes the creation of German Districts, and sends William Nast to Germany – establishes six new annual conferences: Germany, Vermont, North Indiana, Indian Mission, West Texas, and Florida (total now 40) • The New York Ladies' Home Missionary Society (MEC) is organized • John Dempster is named president of the Methodist Biblical Institute of Newbury, Vermont (later moved to Concord, New Hampshire) • Ohio Wesleyan College is established by the MEC in Delaware, OH • The AMEC General Conference adopts the first course of study for AMEC preachers and establishes both the Home and Foreign Missionary Societies	• The PMC begins mission work in New Zealand under the direction of Robert Ward • Wesleyan Methodists in New Zealand establish the Wesleyan Native Institution (later, Wesley College) in Auckland; it is the first institution of higher education in the country	1844
• Wagner's opera *Tannhäuser* debuts at the Dresden Hoftheater • Schumann composes his *Piano Concerto in A Minor* • Frederick Douglass publishes his autobiographical *Narrative of the Life of Frederick Douglass, an American Slave* • George Catlin's paintings, such as *An Iowa Medicine Man*, offer sympathetic and dignified portraits of American Indians • Other notable publications include: – Alexandre Dumas, *The Count of Monte Cristo* – Edgar Allan Poe, *The Raven*	• Pro-slavery Baptists in the southern US withdraw support from the Baptist Triennial Convention (1814) and form the Southern Baptist Convention • John Henry Newman converts to Roman Catholicism and publishes his *Essay on the Development of Christian Doctrine* • In his landmark work *Paul, the Apostle of Jesus Christ*, Ferdinand Christian Baur contends that only Romans, First Corinthians, and Galatians are genuinely Pauline epistles, and that the Paul of the Acts of the Apostles is a different person from the Paul of these genuine epistles • Other notable publications include: – Philip Schaff, *The Principle of Protestantism* – Frederick Engels, *The Condition of the Working Class in England* – Kierkegaard, *Stages on Life's Way*	• The UBC General Conference: – lifts the prohibition against the discussion of slavery or abolitionism in church newspapers – orders that the newspaper *Die Geschäftige Martha* (The Busy Martha) be discontinued – approves a report stating that women should not be allowed to become ministers (even though some annual conferences are moving toward licensing women to preach) – takes the first steps toward establishing educational institutions by authorizing annual conferences to found colleges – establishes a course of study for the training of ministerial candidates – continues the prohibition of the manufacture and sale of alcoholic beverages, but rejects a proposed ban on use or consumption of the same – refuses to authorize "verbal" modification of the Confession of Faith • The Methodist Episcopal Church, South (MECS) is organized at a Constitutional Convention in Louisville composed of delegates from 15 annual conferences (Kentucky, Missouri, Holston, Tennessee, North Carolina, Memphis, Arkansas, Virginia, Mississippi, Texas, Alabama, Georgia, South Carolina, Florida, and *(cont.)*	• Irish Methodists establish the Wesleyan Connexional School (later Wesley College) in Dublin as a boarding and day school for Methodist boys • Taufa'ahau of Ha'apia, a Methodist local preacher in Tonga who had been converted in 1834, is enthroned as King George Tupou I, becoming the first Methodist king anywhere in the world; he founds a dynasty of Methodist rulers	1845

	A. WORLD HISTORY & POLITICS	B. AMERICAN HISTORY & POLITICS	C. SCIENCE, MEDICINE & TECHNOLOGY	D. DAILY LIFE, POPULAR CULTURE & ENTERTAINMENT
1845 cont.				
1846	• The Mexican-American War begins when Mexico attacks Fort Texas on the Rio Grande; US military forces under Zachary Taylor defeat the Mexican army at the Battle of Palo Alto; Congress then declares the US at war with Mexico and announces the annexation of Mexican territory in the Southwest and West • Britain's protectionist Corn Law of 1815 is repealed, resulting in lower prices for grain • The British parliament passes the British Possessions Act, which gives Canada the right to establish customs duties and tariffs • British forces defeat the invading Sikh army in India; the Sikhs are forced to sign the Treaty of Lahore, ceding Kashmir to the British and paying a large financial indemnity	• American settlers in northern California launch the "Bear Flag Revolt" against Mexican rule, declaring an independent California Republic • The Wilmot Proviso, introduced in Congress by David Wilmot of Pennsylvania, attempts to ban slavery in territory gained in the Mexican War; the proviso is blocked by southerners in Congress • Iowa is admitted to the US as the 29th state; it is a free state; the balance is now 14 free states and 14 slave states, with the situation in Texas still unclear • While being rung in observance of George Washington's birthday, the Liberty Bell cracks in a way that cannot be repaired and it cannot ever again be rung normally • Michigan is the first US state to abolish capital punishment	• Elias Howe (US) invents the first mechanical sewing machine • Richard Hoe (US) patents the first rotary offset press; called the "lightning press" because of its unprecedented speed (8,000 pages per hour), it allows newspaper publishers to increase their circulation exponentially • The first observation of the planet Neptune is made based on calculations made separately by John Adams and Jean Le Verrier • The Asiatic cholera pandemic begins spreading around the world, reaching the US by 1849 and Europe and England by 1854	• The first recognized modern baseball game is played at the Elysian Fields in Hoboken, NJ, between the Knickerbockers and the New York Nine

E. EDUCATION, LITERATURE & THE FINE ARTS	F. RELIGION, THEOLOGY, PHILOSOPHY & PSYCHOLOGY	G. AMERICAN & UNITED METHODISM	H. BRITISH & WORLD METHODISM	
		Indian Mission) and attended by Bishops Soule and Andrew • Olaf Gustaf Hedstrom opens a mission to Scandinavian immigrants on the ship *John Wesley* (usually known as *Bethel Ship*) in New York harbor, leading to the establishment of Methodism in western New York, Illinois, Michigan, and Wisconsin, but also in Denmark, Norway, Sweden, and Finland through the work of returning immigrants		**1845 cont.**
• Berlioz completes his opera *The Damnation of Faust*, based on the work of Goethe • Mendelssohn's oratorio *Elijah* premieres in Birmingham, England • Schumann completes his *Symphony No. 2 in C Major* • Belgian musical instrument maker Adolphe Sax invents the first form of the instrument that bears his name, the saxophone, a hybrid of single-reed woodwinds, such as the clarinet, and keyed brass instruments, such as the trumpet • Edward Lear publishes his first volume of limericks for children, *A Book of Nonsense*	• Pope Gregory XVI dies; he is succeeded by Pope Pius IX • Brigham Young leads the majority of the Mormon community out of Illinois to a temporary settlement on the Missouri River in Nebraska • Notable publications include: –Kierkegaard, *Concluding Unscientific Postscript* – John Nevin, *The Mystical Presence*	• The MECS General Conference meets for the first time: – formally receives Bishops Soule and Andrew when they declare their adherence to the MECS; Soule becomes senior bishop – elects William Capers and Robert Paine to the episcopacy – empowers the Council of Bishops to declare any General Conference action to be unconstitutional if they deem it so – establishes a committee to oversee division of the assets of the Methodist Book Concern and the Chartered Fund as provided in the "Plan of Separation" – creates a Committee on Missions and instructs each annual conference to establish a Missionary Society – approves publication of a *Discipline* essentially identical to that of the MEC but with changes appropriate to the "situation" of the MECS – votes to send Lovick Pierce as a delegate to the 1848 MEC General Conference with a proposal for the establishment of "fraternal relations" with the MEC – appoints a committee to prepare a new hymnal for the MECS – creates 2 new annual conferences (St. Louis and Louisville) and changes boundaries of several others (total now 17) • The MPC General Conference meets in Cincinnati: – recognizes 7 new annual conferences and reorganizes several others; organizes Baltimore Colored Mission Conference – tables a resolution declaring slavery "an offense condemned by the word of God"; then adopts a resolution stating that the General Conference "does not feel authorized by the constitution to legislate on the subject of slavery" – decides that each annual conference shall have the right to employ and appoint its own ministers or preachers to serve as home missionaries • The UBC revives the newspaper *The Busy Martha* and renames it *The German Telescope* • Zilpha Elaw, the first important black female evangelist in American Methodist history, who left the MEC in 1828 to launch her own preaching ministry in the slave states, publishes her autobiography, *Memoirs of the Life, Religious Experience, Ministerial Travels, and Labours of Mrs. Zilpha Elaw, an American Female of Colour*	• The pamphlet *Fly Sheets from the Private Correspondent* appears in England, marking the beginnings of the Wesleyan Reform movement by WM ministers resentful of the power of Jabez Bunting, who along with a small group of London ministers dominated the WM Conference	**1846**

	A. WORLD HISTORY & POLITICS	B. AMERICAN HISTORY & POLITICS	C. SCIENCE, MEDICINE & TECHNOLOGY	D. DAILY LIFE, POPULAR CULTURE & ENTERTAINMENT
1847	• Zachary Taylor's army turns back a Mexican attack led by Santa Ana at Buena Vista • Another American force commanded by Winfield Scott captures the coastal city of Veracruz, then decisively defeats Mexican forces at Churubusco and Chapultepec Castle to take Mexico City, forcing Santa Ana to flee and negotiate for peace • Liberia becomes an independent republic with Joseph Roberts as its first president; it is formally recognized by Britain in 1848, by France in 1852, and by the US in 1862 • Slavery is abolished in Swedish colonies in the West Indies	• A group of California-bound settlers led by George Donner is trapped by snow in the Sierra Nevada in the winter of 1846–47, of the 87 members of the party, 41 perish from cold and starvation; some of the survivors resort to cannibalism of the dead; in the spring, rescuers from California reach the survivors and bring them to safety through what is now called Donner Pass • Atlanta, GA, is incorporated as a city	• The American Medical Association is founded in Philadelphia "to promote the science and art of medicine and the betterment of public health" • British mathematician George Boole publishes his *Mathematical Analysis of Logic* • German physicist Hermann von Helmholtz develops his theories about the conservation of energy and potential energy	• Allen Taylor (US) patents a process for manufacturing machine-stamped tin cans for food storage • Frederick Douglass starts an abolitionist newspaper, *The North Star*, in Rochester, NY • The first postage stamps are issued in the US; postal rates are still based on both weight (or number of sheets) and distance
1848	• The Mexican-American War ends with the Treaty of Guadalupe Hidalgo; the Rio Grande River is established as the border between the US and Mexico; in exchange for a payment of $15 million, Mexico cedes to the US 525,000 square miles of its territory in the Southwest and West, including most of what is now New Mexico, western Colorado, Arizona, Utah, Nevada, and California • The February Revolution in France overthrows the monarchy and establishes the French Republic; Louis Napoleon Bonaparte is elected president • The "Springtime of Nations" revolutions rock Sicily, Germany, Italy, and the Austrian Empire, but all end in failure and repression • Austrian Emperor Ferdinand I abdicates; he is succeeded by his brother, Francis Joseph I • Following a major slave revolt in the French colony of Martinique in the Caribbean, slavery is abolished in France and all its territories and all slaves are emancipated • Slavery is abolished in Danish colonies in the West Indies • Switzerland becomes a federal union of cantons under a new constitution	• The Free-Soil Party is formed to oppose the extension of slavery into the territory acquired by the US from Mexico • Utah is settled by Mormons who followed Brigham Young westward after the murder of Joseph Smith; Salt Lake City is established • Lucretia Mott and Elizabeth Cady Stanton organize the first American women's rights convention at the Wesleyan Chapel in Seneca Falls, New York, where the "Declaration of Sentiments" is signed by 68 women and 32 men • Wisconsin is admitted to the US as the 30th state; it is a free state; the balance is now 15 free states and 14 slave states, with the situation in Texas still unclear • Zachary Taylor is elected as president and Millard Filmore as vice president (Whig Party)	• The (first) Public Health Act in Britain passes following a cholera epidemic and sets up a General Board of Health in London to improve water supplies, sewage, and general sanitation • Scottish scientist William Thomson, Lord Kelvin, devises the temperature scale that bears his name • Russian engineer F. N. Semyeno drills the first modern oil well in Asia on the Aspheron Peninsula northeast of Baku (in modern Azerbaijan)	• The Associated Press news agency is established by representatives of six New York City newspapers, allowing them to pool their resources to collect news from Europe; it will grow into the world's largest news organization

E. EDUCATION, LITERATURE & THE FINE ARTS	F. RELIGION, THEOLOGY, PHILOSOPHY & PSYCHOLOGY	G. AMERICAN & UNITED METHODISM	H. BRITISH & WORLD METHODISM	
• Giuseppe Verdi composes his opera *Macbeth* • Longfellow's long narrative poem *Evangeline* tells the story of two lovers separated during the French and Indian War • Other notable publications include: – Charlotte Brontë, *Jane Eyre* – Emily Brontë, *Wuthering Heights* – Honoré de Balzac, *Cousin Bette*	• The German Evangelical Lutheran Synod of Missouri, Ohio and Other States [later called the Lutheran Church-Missouri Synod] is established • The United Presbyterian Church of Scotland is created by the merger of several Scottish Presbyterian congregations unhappy with both sides of the split of 1843 • Charles Finney publishes his *Lectures on Systematic Theology*	• The EA General Conference – reiterates that "none of our members shall be permitted to hold slaves or traffic in them under any pretext whatever" – resolves to establish "a seminary for general sciences" and sends the matter to the membership, where the proposal is rejected – authorizes publication of an English newspaper, *The Evangelical Messenger*; publication begins in 1848 – declines to act on a proposal to follow some annual conferences by banning secret society membership • The MECS begins publication of *Methodist Quarterly Review* as a counterpart to *Methodist Review*, which the MEC continues to publish • The MECS publishes its first hymnbook, *A Collection of Hymns for Public, Social and Domestic Worship* • Newbury Biblical Institute moves to Concord, NH, and is renamed Methodist General Biblical Institute • The White River Conference of the UBC gives Charity Opheral "a note of commendation" as a "pulpit speaker"; she is the first woman in any branch of American Methodism to be in effect licensed to preach, but she is not included in the list of recognized UBC preachers • The UBC establishes Otterbein College in Westerville, Ohio; it is the first college established by the UBC • The MEC begins mission work in San Francisco • The MECS publishes *Southern Ladies' Companion*	• Judson Dwight Collins and Moses C. and Jane White are the first MEC missionaries to China, beginning their work near Fuzhou (Foochow); they are supported by the direct efforts of Phoebe Palmer and her husband • More *Fly Sheet* pamphlets appear, attacking Jabez Bunting and his associates for autocracy and abuses of power • The American (MEC) and British (WM) branches of Methodism in Canada, which split in 1840, again reunite, reforming the WMCC (originally established in 1833) • The WMCC extends its mission work into the Hudson's Bay region of Canada	**1847**
• The Pre-Raphaelite Brotherhood is established in London by three students (John Everett Millais, William Holman Hunt, and Dante Gabriel Rossetti) associated with the British Royal Academy of Art • Liszt retires from public performances on the piano and moves to Weimar, Germany (near Leipzig), beginning a new phase of his career as teacher, conductor of the Weimar court orchestra, and composer • William Makepeace Thackeray completes his finest and best-known novel, *Vanity Fair* • Alexandre Dumas publishes *The Man in the Iron Mask*	• Brigham Young and his followers reestablish the Church of Jesus Christ of Latter-Day Saints in Salt Lake City, UT • John Humphrey Noyes and his followers establish the Oneida Community, a Christian Socialist society that becomes a leading example of the American Utopian movement • F. D. Maurice and Charles Kingsley establish the Christian Socialist Movement in London • Karl Marx and Frederick Engels produce their revolutionary work *The Communist Manifesto* • John Stuart Mill publishes his *Principles of Political Economy*, 2 vols. (2nd and 3rd eds. with important differences, 1849, 1852)	• The MEC General Conference: – refuses to recognize or receive Lovick Pierce as a delegate from the MECS and rejects a proposal for fraternal relations with the MECS – repudiates the "Plan of Separation" approved in 1844, adopts a resolution barring fraternal relations with the MECS, and refuses to divide the Chartered Fund and the assets of Book Concern – establishes five new annual conferences: New York East, East Maine, West Virginia, California, and Oregon; counts nine annual conferences as "lost" to the South (total now 36) – rescinds an 1840 resolution stating that slaveholding is no bar to orders or office in the church – authorizes the bishops to employ "colored" preachers but declines to organize "colored" Conferences – adopts a standard reading list for the course of study for preachers, to be supervised by the presiding elders, and with examinations to be conducted by the bishops or a committee appointed by them – moves provisions concerning membership out of the "Class Meetings" section of the *Discipline* into a new section entitled "Of Receiving Members into the Church" – makes local and located preachers amenable to the quarterly conference – appoints a committee to revise the hymnal	• Robert S. Maclay and Henry Hickok join the MEC mission in Fuzhou (Foochow) • Charles Taylor begins MECS mission work in China in the region around Shanghai and Suzhou (Suchow), near the mouth of the Yangtze River • Still more *Fly Sheet* pamphlets appear in London, becoming increasingly hostile and scurrilous	**1848**

	A. WORLD HISTORY & POLITICS	B. AMERICAN HISTORY & POLITICS	C. SCIENCE, MEDICINE & TECHNOLOGY	D. DAILY LIFE, POPULAR CULTURE & ENTERTAINMENT
1848 cont.				
1849	• Parliament ends Britain's Navigation Acts, making it possible for American clipper ships to transport China tea and other goods to British ports • The British defeat the Sikhs at Gujurat, India, and annex the Punjab region • An effort at German unification fails when King Frederick William IV of Prussia is offered but refuses the crown and title of "Emperor of the Germans" • David Livingstone crosses the Kalahari Desert and discovers Lake Ngami	• The 1848 discovery of gold at John Sutter's sawmill in the Sacramento Valley of California sets off the California gold rush, which attracts more than 100,000 prospectors called "Forty-Niners" • Harriet Tubman escapes from slavery in Maryland and begins working with the Underground Railroad, leading approximately 300 slaves to freedom during the next decade • Elizabeth Blackwell receives her M.D. degree from the Medical Institution of Geneva, New York, becoming the first woman in the US with a medical degree • Cubans begin immigrating to Florida in large numbers	• Canadian geologist Abraham Gesner perfects the technique of producing kerosene or "coal oil" from coal; it burns cleaner and is less expensive than the whale and vegetable oils then in use for lighting and does not spoil in storage	• Stephen Foster's song "O Susanna!" becomes the unofficial anthem of the California gold rush • Walter Hunt invents the safety pin • Henry Charles Harrod opens a grocery store and tea shop in London, which grows into Harrod's, one of the world's largest department stores

1850	• The Taiping Rebellion against the Ch'ing Dynasty in China, led by Hong Xiuquan, begins; it will last until the fall of "The Kingdom of Heavenly Peace" in 1864	• The US census reports that the population is 23,191,876:
		  – whites: 19,553,068 (84.3%)
		  – free blacks: 434,495 (1.9%)
		  – slaves: 3,204,313 (13.8%)
		• The US national debt is $63,452,773
		• After long and intense debate, Congress reaches agreement on the Compromise of 1850: Texas is recognized as a slave state, and the federal government assumes its debt; California is admitted to the US as the 31st state; it is a free state, making the balance 15 slave and 16 free states; the territories of New Mexico, Nevada, Arizona, and Utah are organized without any restrictions on slavery
		• The second Fugitive Slave Act requires citizens to assist in the recovery of fugitive slaves and denies a fugitive's right to a jury trial
		• Congress approves enlargement of the US Capitol building (the South Wing is completed in 1857, the North Wing in 1859, and the Dome and Rotunda in 1863)
		• Both San Francisco and Los Angeles, CA, are incorporated as cities
		• Lucy Stanton is the first black woman in the US to complete a collegiate course of study (at Oberlin College)
		• President Taylor falls ill, probably of cholera, and dies; Vice President Fillmore becomes president
			• R. W. Bunsen (Germany) invents the gas burner that comes to bear his name
			• German physicist Rudolf Clausius formulates the second law of thermodynamics, which states that entropy increases at the expense of available energy
				• Joel Houghton (US) receives the first patent for a mechanical dishwashing machine
				• P. T. Barnum arranges and promotes the enormously successful US tour of Jenny Lind, the "Swedish Nightingale," at the time the world's most famous singer
				• Austrian military bandmaster Josef Franz Wagner writes the march "Under The Double Eagle"; American bandmaster John Philip Sousa includes it in his repertoire and popularizes it in the US
				• The bowler hat comes into fashion for men in Britain
				• The British parliament passes the Public Libraries Act, establishing free public libraries across the country; it is extended to Scotland and Ireland in 1853

E. EDUCATION, LITERATURE & THE FINE ARTS	F. RELIGION, THEOLOGY, PHILOSOPHY & PSYCHOLOGY	G. AMERICAN & UNITED METHODISM	H. BRITISH & WORLD METHODISM	
		• "Zion" is officially added to the name of the African Methodist Episcopal Zion Church • The AMEC General Conference votes down a proposal to create the office of presiding elder • The EA begins publishing *The Evangelical Messenger* • The Ladies' China Missionary Society of Baltimore is organized • Phoebe Palmer publishes *Faith and Its Effects*		1848 cont.
• Asher B. Durand's painting *Kindred Spirits* depicts fellow Hudson River School painter Thomas Cole and poet William Cullen Bryant contemplating the beauty of a gorge in the Catskill Mountains • Otto Nicolai writes his opera *The Merry Wives of Windsor* • Notable publications include: – Charles Dickens, *David Copperfield* – Francis Parkman, *The Oregon Trail* – Edgar Allan Poe, *The Bells*	• Henry David Thoreau publishes his classic and influential essay on "Civil Disobedience" (originally entitled "Resistance to Civil Government") explaining why he chose to go to jail rather than to support the Mexican War (1846–48) by paying taxes; the essay advocates passive resistance to government authority, a method of protest that is later adopted by Mohandas Gandhi and Martin Luther King, Jr. • Other notable publications include: – Horace Bushnell, *God in Christ* – Kierkegaard, *The Sickness unto Death*	• The UBC General Conference: – strengthens rules against secret societies, totally prohibiting members from being Freemasons – defeats a proposal to repeal the constitution adopted in 1841 – refuses to consider revision of supplement of the Articles of Faith – prohibits the use as well as the manufacture and sale of "ardent spirits" • The MEC publishes a new version of *Hymns for the Use of the Methodist Episcopal Church*; revised 1852, tune edition 1857 • Jarena Lee publishes a revised and expanded edition of her 1836 autobiography under the new title *The Religious Experience and Journal of Mrs. Jarena Lee*	• In the wake of the "Fly Sheet" controversy, Samuel Dunn, James Everett, and William Griffith are expelled from the WM Conference; they emerge as leaders of the Wesleyan Reformers • Ludwig S. Jacoby (MEC) begins mission work in northern Germany, in the area around Bremen	1849
• Liszt arranges the first public performance of his friend Richard Wagner's romantic opera *Lohengrin* • John Ruskin publishes *The Seven Lamps of Architecture*, praising the union of architectural aesthetics and spirituality in the Gothic style • Nathaniel Hawthorne publishes his classic tale of love and adultery in colonial New England, *The Scarlet Letter* • Other notable publications include: – Sojourner Truth, *The Narrative of Sojourner Truth, a Bondswoman of Olden Time* – Ivan Turgenev, *A Month in the Country*	• F. D. Maurice and associates in Britain begin publication of the weekly paper *The Christian Socialist* • Pope Pius IX restores the Roman Catholic hierarchy in the UK, establishing 13 episcopal sees and the Archdiocese of Westminster (in London); Nicholas Wiseman is made a cardinal and appointed as the first archbishop of Westminster, the Catholic Primate of England • Notable publications include: – Kierkegaard, *Training in Christianity* – Edward Amasa Park, *Bibliotheca Sacra*	• The MECS General Conference: – establishes the book depository [publishing house] for the church in Nashville – confirms the power of the bishops to transfer preachers between annual conferences and rejects proposals to permit individual churches or charges to petition for the appointment of particular preachers – notes the rejection of Lovick Pierce by the 1848 MEC General Conference and resolves not to renew offer of fraternal relations with the MEC – approves a lawsuit against the MEC to enforce the provisions of the 1844 "Plan of Separation" calling for division of the Chartered Fund and the assets of the Book Concern – establishes the Western Virginia Annual Conference (total now 18) – transfers control of Transylvania University to the Kentucky and Louisville Conferences • Jenny Lind, the "Swedish Nightingale," is converted by the *Bethel Ship* mission • The MPC General Conference: – tries but fails to declare the term *slavery* only "an ecclesiastical question"; slavery continues to be a divisive question – approves a proposal empowering the General Conference to hear and decide appeals of church trials; the proposal is later rejected by the annual conferences – tables a recommendation that the order of deacon be abolished – provides financial support for the stationing of the presidents of the annual conferences and for their supervisory travel • The Five Points Mission (MEC) is established by Methodist women in one of the poorest parts of New York City	• Johann Conrad Link (MEC) returns from America to Stuttgart and becomes first preacher of *Die Evangelische Gemeinschaft* in Germany • John Peter Larsson (MEC), a *Bethel Ship* mission convert, returns from the US to his native Sweden and begins preaching and organizing Methodist societies • The EA launches its first mission work in Germany	1850

	A. WORLD HISTORY & POLITICS	B. AMERICAN HISTORY & POLITICS	C. SCIENCE, MEDICINE & TECHNOLOGY	D. DAILY LIFE, POPULAR CULTURE & ENTERTAINMENT
1850 cont.				
1851	• By coup d'état, Louis Napoleon becomes Emperor Napoleon III of France • The Great Exhibition of the Works of Industry of all Nations is held in London, highlighted by construction of the magnificent Crystal Palace in Hyde Park [later moved to South London]; it attracts more than 6 million visitors and is the first in a series of World's Fairs and International Exhibitions of culture and industry • Gold is discovered in Australia (New South Wales and Victoria), producing a gold rush and drawing immigrants from around the world	• Maine becomes the first state to enact a law prohibiting alcohol • Sojourner Truth delivers her "Ain't I a Woman" speech for the first time	• French scientist Jean Bernard Léon Foucault uses a large freely suspended pendulum to demonstrate the earth's rotation • Isaac Singer (US) develops the first continuous stitch sewing machine, which becomes a great commercial success • British inventor Frederick Scott Archer develops the collodion photographic process; images require only two or three seconds of light exposure and result in finely detailed glass plate negatives from which positive images can be printed	• The first YMCA in the US is established in Boston; it quickly spreads across the country • *The New York Times* begins publishing "All the News That's Fit to Print" for a penny a copy • The Reuters News Agency opens in London • The Christmas tree market is born in the US when Mark Carr hauls two sleds of evergreens from the Catskills into New York City and sells them all • Jacob Fussell opens the first ice cream factory in the US in Baltimore, MD • Stephen Foster writes "Old Folks at Home" [a.k.a. "Suwannee River"]
1852	Britain recognizes the independence of the Transvaal area of southern Africa, leading to creation of the Orange Free State and the South African Republic	• Wells, Fargo & Co. begins offering banking and financial services and transcontinental transportation for goods and people from the eastern US to California, using steamboats, wagons, and stagecoaches where railroads do not yet exist • Franklin Pierce is elected as president and William King as vice president (Democratic Party)	• Jean Bernard Léon Foucault invents the gyroscope • Swiss astronomer Rudolf Wolf discovers that intense sunspot activity coincides with increased disturbances in Earth's magnetic field	• Women's rights activist Amelia Jenks Bloomer invents a style of dress for women including full, split-legged trousers under a short skirt, which she advocates particularly for riding a bicycle; they come to be called "bloomers" • Boston physician William Channing creates the first telegraphic fire alarm system

E. EDUCATION, LITERATURE & THE FINE ARTS	F. RELIGION, THEOLOGY, PHILOSOPHY & PSYCHOLOGY	G. AMERICAN & UNITED METHODISM	H. BRITISH & WORLD METHODISM	
		• Ole Peter Petersen is appointed by the MEC as a local preacher to Norwegians in upper Iowa		**1850 cont.**
• Verdi's enormously successful opera *Rigoletto* is written to be the inaugural performance at the new La Fenice Theater in Venice • Liszt composes his *Transcendental Etudes for Piano* [a source of both great pleasure and great discomfort to almost all subsequent pianists] • Schumann completes his *Symphony No. 3 (Rhenisch)* • German American artist Emanuel Gottlieb Leutze creates one of America's iconic historical paintings, *Washington Crossing the Delaware* • Wagner publishes his treatise on *Opera and Drama*, describing his artistic ideal of the *gesamtkunstwerk* ("total work of art") • Other notable publications include two of the greatest works in the entire history of American literature: – Herman Melville, *Moby Dick* – Nathaniel Hawthorne, *The House of the Seven Gables*	• Auguste Comte begins the publication of his *System of Positive Polity* (4 vols., 1851–54) • Other notable publications include: – Arthur Schopenhauer, *Studies in Pessimism* – Horace Bushnell, *Christ in Theology*	• The EA General Conference: – defeats a proposal to allow bishops to transfer preachers across conference lines – permits preachers and congregations to introduce a period of six months probation in the reception of new members "wherever such a course should be considered beneficial" – decides to relocate the publishing house from New Berlin, PA, to Cleveland, OH • The MECS publishes *Songs of Zion: A Supplement to the Hymn Book of the Methodist Episcopal Church, South*, edited by Thomas O. Summers • As a result of the Fugitive Slave Act of 1850, many members of the AMEC emigrate to Canada • Lydia Sexton receives a license to preach from her UBC quarterly conference, which is annually renewed until her death in 1894 • Northwestern College (later University) is established in Evanston, IL, by a group of Methodist laymen • Nathan Bangs publishes The *Necessity, Nature, and Fruits of Sanctification*	• The 1851 census in the UK determines that the combined membership of all the Methodist bodies in the country is 534,000 or about 3% of the total adult population • Westminster College is founded in London by the WM Conference to train teachers for Methodist day schools • The Kingswood School moves from Bristol to new facilities in Bath • The first British WM missionaries arrive in Hong Kong • George Piercy, a WM local preacher from Britain, goes to China at his own expense and begins preaching there • John C. Link arrives in Stuttgart, Germany, as the first missionary of the EA	**1851**
• Harriet Beecher Stowe publishes her classic antislavery novel *Uncle Tom's Cabin*, which has an enormous influence on public opinion in the northern states • Nathaniel Hawthorne publishes *The Blithedale Romance*	• Representatives from all the Congregational churches in the US meet in Albany, NY, to discuss a plan of union; nothing comes out of the discussions until 1871 • John Henry Newman publishes *The Idea of a University*	• The MEC General Conference: – establishes eight new annual conferences: Wyoming, Cincinnati, North Indiana, Northwest Indiana, Southeast Indiana, Southern Illinois, California, and Arkansas (total now 44) – elects five new bishops, including Matthew Simpson – establishes a legal commission to defend against legal action by the MECS to enforce financial provisions of the "Plan of Separation" – declines to extend term of ministerial probation to four years, to sanction lay delegates, or to separate the mission work of the church into "home" and "foreign" departments – instructs the bishops to visit Liberia, to establish a mission in Italy, and to ordain a missionary bishop when the Restrictive Rule should be changed to allow it – makes the bishop the president of an annual conference • The earliest known articles about the establishment of an order of deaconess in the MEC appear in *Zion's Herald* • Black Methodists in New York and Philadelphia propose that the MEC take steps to establish mission conferences in the southern states • The AMEC General Conference defeats a motion to license women as preachers by a wide majority • The Congregational Methodist Church is formed by southern Methodists, mostly in Georgia, Alabama, and Mississippi, who break away from the MECS; the new church retains Methodist doctrine but adopts a congregational polity	• The French WM Conference is formed	**1852**

	A. WORLD HISTORY & POLITICS	B. AMERICAN HISTORY & POLITICS	C. SCIENCE, MEDICINE & TECHNOLOGY	D. DAILY LIFE, POPULAR CULTURE & ENTERTAINMENT
1853	• A US fleet under Commodore Matthew Perry enters Tokyo Bay, opening Japan to the influence of Western culture and technology; rapid modernization follows • The Crimean War begins: Britain, France, and the Ottoman Empire fight to check Russia's expansionist ambitions • Taiping rebel soldiers capture Nanjing, killing 30,000 Imperial soldiers and slaughtering thousands of civilians; Nanking becomes the movement's capital • New Zealand is granted self-government by Britain	• To settle border disputes arising from the 1848 Treaty of Guadalupe Hidalgo, the US purchases from Mexico a strip of territory in what is now southern New Mexico and Arizona, bordered on the east by the Rio Grande, on the north by the Gila River, and on the west by the Colorado River; named for James Gadsden, the US diplomat who negotiated the deal, the Gadsden Purchase adds about 30,000 square miles to the US at the cost of payment to Mexico of $10 million • The New York Exhibition of the Industry of All Nations opens; it is the first world's fair on US soil, and its central exhibition hall is modeled after the 1851 London Crystal Palace • The town of Seattle, WA, is established (incorporated 1869)	• Polish chemist Ignacy Łukasiewicz develops the techniques for refining kerosene from crude oil; kerosene continues to be called "coal oil" by many people; gasoline, which is produced as a by-product of kerosene distillation, is at first used as a cheap solvent and regarded as having no significant commercial value • Physicians Alexander Wood (Britain) and Charles Pravaz (France) independently pioneer the use of the hypodermic syringe for drug administration	• Levi Strauss, who had begun selling clothing to gold miners in 1850, fashions pants from denim fabric because of its durability, thus creating the first "blue jeans" • Stephen Foster writes "My Old Kentucky Home"
1854	• Russia annexes Kazakhstan; allied troops land in Crimea, defeat the Russians at Balaclava and Inkerman, and begin the siege of Sevastapol; Russia evacuates the Danube region • The disastrous charge of the British Light Cavalry Brigade against the Russian artillery emplacements at Balaclava during the Crimean War is immortalized by Alfred, Lord Tennyson	• The Kansas-Nebraska Act in effect repeals the Missouri Compromise of 1820, under which slavery was prohibited in both territories; it provides for Nebraska to be free but for "popular sovereignty" to determine whether Kansas will be slave or free; this removes both Kansas and Nebraska from the Indian Territory, greatly reducing its size • Conflict almost immediately breaks out between proslavery and antislavery factions in Kansas, turning the area into a battleground ("Bleeding Kansas") until 1859 • The Republican Party is established by antislavery forces strongly opposed to the extension of slavery into western territories; it absorbs the Free-Soil Party and the remnants of the Whig Party in the northern states; most southern Whigs join the Democratic Party • The first major clash between the Lakota (Sioux) Indians and the US Army occurs near Fort Laramie, Wyoming; 19 US soldiers are killed • Congress passes the Graduation Act permitting public land that has remained unsold for thirty years to be bought for as little as 12.5¢ per acre	• Isaac Singer loses a lawsuit over patent infringement to Elias Howe, marking the end of the "sewing machine war" between them • German watchmaker Heinrich Goebel invents the first form of the electric lightbulb • Another major cholera outbreak reaches England from Europe • Italian scientist Filippo Pacini isolates the bacillus that causes cholera, but his discovery remains largely unknown • Ignacy Łukasiewicz drills the first oil well in Poland to obtain crude oil for the production of kerosene • American gun makers Horace Smith and Daniel Wesson invent the revolver that bears their name, the Smith & Wesson • British mathematician George Boole publishes *An Investigation of the Laws of Thought*, in which he describes what comes to be known as Boolean algebra	• Stephen Foster writes some of his most popular nonminstrel songs, including "Jeanie With the Light Brown Hair" and "Hard Times Come Again No More" • Walter Hunt invents disposable paper collars for men's dress shirts
1855	• The Russians are forced out of Sevastapol; Austria threatens to enter the war if Russia does not accept peace terms • Tsar Nicholas I of Russia dies; he is succeeded by his son, Alexander II, who begins negotiations to end the war • David Livingstone is the first European to see the great falls on the Zambezi River in modern Zimbabwe, to which he gives the name Victoria Falls • Paris holds its first Exposition Universelle on the Champs-Élysées; it is a financial failure	• Abolitionists in New England and other parts of the North form "Emigrant Aid Societies" to send antislavery activists to Kansas where they can vote to keep it free; in Georgia and Alabama similar societies send settlers to Kansas who will vote in defense of slavery • US Army troops massacre 100 Lakota (Sioux) Indians at their encampment in Nebraska	• English metallurgist Henry Bessemer introduces the "Bessemer converter" for the refining of pig iron into steel by forcing air through the molten metal to burn away impurities	• The US Post Office shifts to the British system (1840); the sender of a letter is now required to pay the cost of postage in advance through the mandatory use of postage stamps rather than the recipient on delivery; postal rates are still based on both weight (or number of sheets) and distance • The Young Women's Christian Association (YWCA), modeled on the YMCA, is established in London

E. EDUCATION, LITERATURE & THE FINE ARTS	F. RELIGION, THEOLOGY, PHILOSOPHY & PSYCHOLOGY	G. AMERICAN & UNITED METHODISM	H. BRITISH & WORLD METHODISM	
• Verdi's great opera *Il Trovatore* (The Troubador) premieres in Rome; it includes the rousing and well-known "Anvil Chorus" • Later the same year, Verdi's *La Traviata* (The Lost One) premieres in Venice; it is not well received at first but later becomes one of his most popular operas • German immigrant Henry Engelhard Steinway establishes Steinway & Sons in New York City and crafts his first Steinway concert grand piano • *Bleak House*, by Charles Dickens, is the first British novel to feature a detective as the main character	• Ferdinand Christian Baur begins publication of his *History of the Christian Church* (5 vols., 1853–63) • Antoinette Brown (Blackwell) is the first woman to be ordained as a minister in the US (by a Congregationalist parish in New York); Luther Lee, one of the founders of the Wesleyan Methodist Connection, preaches at her ordination and later publishes the sermon "Women's Right to Preach the Gospel" • Theodore Parker condemns the "degradation of women" and endorses women's suffrage in his sermon "On the Public Function of Woman" • The first Chinese Buddhist Temple in the US is completed in San Francisco	• The UBC General Conference: – acknowledges infant baptism as valid and makes any minister who rebaptizes someone who had been baptized as a child subject to church trial – rejects a proposal for lay representation in General Conference or annual conferences as "inexpedient and unscriptural" – authorizes formal establishment of a centralized missionary society for the church – moves the publishing house to Dayton, OH • Garrett Biblical Institute is established by the MEC in Evanston, IL; John Dempster is the first president; it opens for classes in 1855 • Benigno Cardenas, a converted Roman Catholic priest, preaches the first Methodist sermon in Spanish in Santa Fe, NM	• The first ordained WM missionaries go to China from Britain and begin work around Guangzhou (Canton); they bear letters from the WM Conference officially recognizing the ministry of George Piercy (1851) • *London Quarterly Review* begins publication • Ole Peter Petersen, who was converted in New York through the Bethel Ship mission, returns as an ordained MEC minister to establish the Methodist missions in Norway • Thomas Chegwin launches a WM mission in Portugal • Ludwig S. Jacoby publishes the *Handbook of Methodism* in Germany (2nd ed. 1855, 3rd ed. 1870)	**1853**
• F. D. Maurice and his Christian Socialist associates establish the Working Men's College to provide a liberal education for working men; Maurice also founds the Working Women's College, later to become the Francis Martin College; the two institutions merge in 1964 • The Ashmun Institute, the first liberal arts college for blacks in the US, is established in rural Pennsylvania; it is renamed Lincoln University in 1866 • Berlioz composes his opera *The Birth of Christ* • Wagner completes *The Rhinegold*, the first of the four operas that comprise *The Ring of the Nibelung* • Charles Dickens publishes his novel *Hard Times* • Thoreau publishes *Walden, or Life in the Woods*, the record of the two years he spends living in partial seclusion in a hand-built cabin on Walden Pond near Concord, MA, explaining the pleasure of withdrawing for a time from social engagement • Alfred, Lord Tennyson publishes his poetic commemoration of *The Charge of the Light Brigade* • Frederick Douglass publishes his second autobiography, *My Bondage and My Freedom* • Jean-François Millet completes his painting *The Reaper*	• Pope Pius IX declares the dogma of the Immaculate Conception of the Blessed Virgin Mary to be an article of faith • William Holman Hunt completes his painting *The Light of the World*, one of the most popular artistic images of Jesus in the 19th century • Ludwig Feuerbach publishes *The Essence of Christianity* • Kierkegaard publishes *The Attack Upon Christendom*	• The US Supreme Court upholds the legality of the 1844 "Plan of Separation" between the MEC and the MECS and accordingly orders division of the assets of the Methodist Book Concern between the MEC and the MECS • The MECS General Conference: – divides Arkansas Conference into two new annual conferences, Arkansas and Ouachita; creates the Pacific Annual Conference (extending from California to New Mexico west of the Rocky Mountains) and Kansas Mission Conference (total now 21) – establishes the Southern Methodist Publishing House in Nashville – approves the constitution of the Sunday School Society – omits the section on "band-societies" from the *Discipline* • The MPC General Conference: – organizes the Oregon Mission; hears report of failure of China Mission – decides to establish the Western Methodist Protestant Book Concern in Cincinnati and to divide assets of the original Book Concern in Baltimore [this foreshadows the impending division of the MPC over slavery] – again declines to abolish the order of deacon • The AMEC issues a formal condemnation of slavery and the slave trade	• The *Christian Ambassador* (later the *Holborn Review*) is established in Britain • The MEC Missionary Society begins support for the evangelistic ministry of John Peter Larsson in Sweden • The WM missions in Australia, Tasmania, New Zealand, Tonga, and Fiji are united to form the Australasian Wesleyan Methodist Conference	**1854**
• The University of Iowa becomes the first state university in the US to admit women • Berlioz composes his *Te Deum* • Liszt gives the first performance of his *Piano Concerto No. 1*, conducted by Berlioz • Verdi composes his first "grand" opera, *Les Vêpres siciliennes* (The Sicilian Vespers), for the Paris Opera House • Richard Burton, the first non-Muslim to visit Mecca and Medina, recounts the experience of that 1853 journey in his *Pilgrimage to Mecca* • Thomas Babington Macaulay completes his *History of England* (4 vols., begun in 1849) • Walt Whitman publishes the first of many editions of his landmark volume of *(cont.)*	• Herbert Spencer publishes his *Principles of Psychology* • Isaac Hecker publishes *Questions of the Soul*	• The EA General Conference: – establishes a children's newspaper, *Der Christliche Kinderfreund* – organizes a religious tract society – orders the publication of the *History of the Evangelical Association* in both German and English – declines to act on a proposal to move toward organic union with the WMC and the UBC • Commissioners from the MEC and the MECS, meeting in Cincinnati, agree on plan for division of Chartered Fund and assets of the Book Concern	• The British WM Conference establishes an independent conference in eastern Canada • The autonomous Australasian WM Conference assumes responsibility for all South Pacific Methodist missions, including Australia, Tasmania, New Zealand, Tonga, and Fiji • Methodism is introduced to Hawaii by MEC missionaries • The first UBC missionaries, W. J. Shuey, D. K. Flickinger, and D. C. Kimbler, sail for Sierra Leone to begin UBC mission work in Africa	**1855**

	A. WORLD HISTORY & POLITICS	B. AMERICAN HISTORY & POLITICS	C. SCIENCE, MEDICINE & TECHNOLOGY	D. DAILY LIFE, POPULAR CULTURE & ENTERTAINMENT
1855 cont.				
1856	• The Treaty of Paris concludes the Crimean War (1854–56); it guarantees free access to the Black Sea; Russian expansion is checked for a time, but the Ottoman Empire goes into decline • Persia goes to war with Britain after taking Herat in Afghanistan • The Second Opium War (1856–58) begins, again pitting China against Britain and France; British and French forces besiege Canton • Tea bushes from China are planted in the area of Darjeeling, India, for the first time, and flourish there • David Livingstone completes the first crossing of the African continent by a European, traveling from the west coast to the east, and returns to England	• Proslavery and antislavery forces clash in "Bleeding Kansas"; abolitionist extremist John Brown leads a group of followers in an attack at Pottawatomie Creek, killing five proslavery men • James Buchanan is elected as president and John C. Breckinridge as vice president (Democratic Party)	• German-born British engineer William Siemens patents the open-hearth furnace, which can produce and sustain much higher temperatures than any other furnace • French metallurgist Pierre-Émile Martin develops the Siemens-Martin process for producing steel in an open-hearth furnace using scrap steel and pig iron • The world's first commercial oil refinery opens at Ploieşti, Romania • The first remains of a human species other than *Homo sapiens* are found in the Neander Valley near Düsseldorf, Germany, hence the name "Neanderthal"	• British chemist William Henry Perkin develops the first important synthetic dye, aniline purple or mauve
1857	• The Indian Mutiny begins when native Indian soldiers in the Bengal army of the East India Company revolt, claiming great abuse, triggering a widespread uprising against British rule in India • The British navy destroys the Chinese fleet; British and French forces occupy Canton • Mexico adopts a liberalizing constitution, reducing the power of the army and the Roman Catholic Church, provoking civil war between liberal and conservative forces • Britain and Persia sign a peace treaty under which Persia gives up its claim to Herat and recognizes the independence of Afghanistan	• In *Scott v. Sandford*, the US Supreme Court rules not only that Missouri slave Dred Scott did not become free by virtue of moving with his owner to a nonslave state but also that blacks, even when free, could not ever become citizens of the United States and thus have no right to sue in federal courts • The Supreme Court also rules that Congress does not have the authority to ban slavery in federal territories, holding that part of the Missouri Compromise (1820) to be unconstitutional • President Buchanan appoints Alfred Cumming to replace Mormon leader Brigham Young as governor of the territory of Utah; to avoid being replaced, Young declares martial law, forbids US troops from entering Utah, and encourages Mormons to take up arms if they do • John D. Lee leads a band of Mormon fighters in attacking a California-bound wagon train in Mountain Meadows, UT; 120 pioneers, mostly Methodists, are killed, all but the small children [Lee is tried and executed in 1877 for his role in the massacre]	• Michael Dietz invents a kerosene or "coal oil" lamp; virtually overnight kerosene replaces whale oil as the fuel of choice for illumination in America and Europe, which greatly increases the demand for oil and sends the US whaling industry, which was then producing 4 to 5 million gallons of whale oil annually, into a severe decline, arguably saving many species of whales from extinction	• The first passenger elevator begins service in a New York City department store; it is made possible by the safety brake developed by Elisha G. Otis in 1853 • "Jingle Bells" (originally "One Horse Open Sleigh") is written by James Pierpont to be sung at a Thanksgiving program at his church in Boston; it becomes one of the best-known and most commonly sung secular Christmas songs in the world, though the song itself does not mention Christmas • A group called "The Mystik Krewe of Comus" stages the first modern Mardi Gras parade in New Orleans with bands and torchlit floats

E. EDUCATION, LITERATURE & THE FINE ARTS	F. RELIGION, THEOLOGY, PHILOSOPHY & PSYCHOLOGY	G. AMERICAN & UNITED METHODISM	H. BRITISH & WORLD METHODISM	
poetry entitled *Leaves of Grass* (the final edition appears in 1892) • Longfellow's epic narrative poem *The Song of Hiawatha*, based on the legends of the Ojibway Indians, is written in the same meter as the Finnish national folk epic, *The Kalevala*		• Randolph S. Foster publishes *A Treatise on the Need of the Methodist Episcopal Church With Respect to Her Ministry*		**1855 cont.**
• Jacques Offenbach becomes director of his own opera house in Paris, Les Bouffes-Parisiennes • Wagner completes *The Valkyrie*, the second of the four operas that comprise *The Ring of the Nibelung* • Elizabeth Barrett Browning publishes her volume of poetry, *Aurora Leigh*	• Rudolf Hermann Lotze begins the publication of *Mikrokosmos* (3 vols., 1856–64)	• The MEC General Conference: – gives presiding elders authority to employ blacks as local pastors – authorizes the Book Agents to extend the clerical discount to local preachers – authorizes the election of a bishop by Liberia Annual Conference, with jurisdiction restricted to Africa – establishes 8 new annual conferences: Delaware, Detroit, Peoria, West Wisconsin, Upper Iowa, Newark, Kansas & Nebraska, and German Mission (total now 52) – divides German-language work in the US into 9 districts attached to various regular annual conferences – tables a resolution calling for the establishment of episcopal service areas – omits the section on "band-societies" from the *Discipline* – declines to act on a resolution declaring divorce to be unlawful except in the case of adultery • Wilberforce University, named for the British abolitionist leader, is established; forced to close in 1862, it is purchased and reincorporated by the AMEC in 1863, becoming the first institution of higher education in the US to be owned and operated by black Americans • The AMEC General Conference makes all elders of six years service members of General Conference; establishes time limit of two years on all pastoral appointments (circuit or station) • Peter Cartwright publishes *The Autobiography of Peter Cartwright, The Backwoods Preacher*	• The MEC Missionary Society sends William Goodfellow to reinitiate missionary work in South America • Clementina Rowe Butler and William Butler establish the first MEC mission work in India • The MEC organizes the Germany Missionary Conference • The British Methodist Episcopal Church (BMEC) is established in Canada as the result of AMEC missions begun in the 1830s • William Arthur, in *The Tongues of Fire*, gives a powerful voice to the holiness message and movement in Britain and Europe	**1856**
• The American Institute of Architects is founded in New York • Liszt completes his *Dante Symphony* • Jean-François Millet completes his painting *The Gleaners* • Charles Dickens publishes the final installment of *Little Dorritt* • Charles Baudelaire completes his great verse collection, *Fleurs du Mal*; several poems are found "damaging to public morals," and the author is fined • Other notable publications include: – Anthony Trollope, *Barchester Towers* – Gustave Flaubert, *Madame Bovary* – Thomas Hughes, *Tom Brown's Schooldays*	• David Livingstone publishes his *Missionary Travels and Researches in South Africa*, and his exploits in Africa attract worldwide attention • Other notable publications include: – Charles Finney, *Lectures to Professing Christians* – Dwight L. Moody begins his revivalist career – Francis Wayland, *Notes on the Principles and Practices of Baptist Churches*	• The UBC General Conference: – for the first time hears a formal address by the bishops reviewing the state of the church – passes a resolution that women should not be allowed to preach; however, several annual conferences go on granting preaching licenses or "notes of recommendation" to women such as Charity Opheral and Lydia Sexton – debates the doctrine of "total depravity" and adopts a compromise formulation stating that apart from grace, "man . . . is fallen from original righteousness and destitute of holiness" – defeats proposals to weaken prohibitions against secret society membership and in favor of lay representation • A group of Methodist Protestants opposed to slavery hold a convention in Cincinnati; agree to send a petition to the 1858 MPC General Conference proposing revision of the constitution to remove any suggestion that it authorizes or approves slaveholding by ministers or members	• The Australasian WM Conference establishes a mission in Samoa • Thakombau, the most powerful chieftain in Fiji, is converted and publicly baptized as a Methodist • The United Methodist Free Churches (UMFC) is formed in the UK by merger of the Wesleyan Methodist Association (1836) and most of the Wesleyan Reformers (1849) • The Wesleyan Reformers who refuse to join in the UMFC merger create the Wesleyan Reform Union • Boie Smith, another *Bethel Ship* mission convert, returns to his native Denmark to establish MEC work there • The MEC establishes a mission in northern Bulgaria	**1857**

	A. WORLD HISTORY & POLITICS	B. AMERICAN HISTORY & POLITICS	C. SCIENCE, MEDICINE & TECHNOLOGY	D. DAILY LIFE, POPULAR CULTURE & ENTERTAINMENT
1858	• Britain dissolves the East India Company and assumes direct rule of the Indian subcontinent, marking the end of the Mughal Empire • British forces recapture Delhi and Lucknow, putting an end to the Indian Mutiny • The Treaty of Tientsin concludes the Second Opium War; China agrees to open more ports to foreign trade • China cedes the north side of the Amur River to Russia through the Treaty of Aigun • Richard Burton and John Speke discover Lake Tanganyika and Lake Victoria Nyanza in Africa • David Livingstone returns to the Zambezi River region of Africa and resumes his explorations and missionary work • Prussia's King Frederick William IV goes insane; his brother William takes power as regent	• Minnesota is admitted to the US as the 32nd state; it is a free state; the balance is now 16 free states and 16 slave states • Senate candidates Abraham Lincoln and Stephen Douglas hold their memorable debates, and Lincoln gives his famous "House Divided" speech to the Illinois State Republican Convention • The Third Seminole War (1855–58) ends when Chief Billy Bowlegs and his followers are captured and removed to the Indian Territory; only about 300 Seminole remain in the Florida Everglades but they and their descendants never sign a peace treaty with the US • The US Army enters Salt Lake City, restores peace, and installs Alfred Cumming (a non-Mormon) as governor of the Utah Territory; Mormon fighters make small sporadic raids on Army camps through the winter, then fade away • Fredrick Law Olmsted completes his plan for the 843-acre Central Park in Manhattan, the first large landscaped public park in the country	• Abraham Gesner establishes the North American Kerosene Gas Light Company in New York to distribute kerosene in America • The first oil well in North America is drilled in Ontario, Canada • American pipe fitter Charles Moncky develops an adjustable wrench that soon comes to be called the "monkey wrench"	• British fashion designer Charles Frederick Worth, regarded as "the father of haute couture," opens the first great women's fashion house in Paris; the House of Worth dominates Parisian fashion until the end of the nineteenth century • Ezra Warner (US) patents the first can opener • Joseph Rechendorfer (US) patents a pencil with an attached eraser • The first YWCA in America is established in New York City
1859	• China refuses to allow foreign diplomats to enter the capital of Beijing • Austria goes to war with France and Sardinia; after suffering defeats by combined French and Sardinian forces at Magenta and Solferino, Austria agrees to sign the Treaty of Zürich; Austria keeps Venetia, and Sardinia gains Lombardy • Italian nationalist Giuseppe Garibaldi establishes the Italian National Society to promote the establishment of a united kingdom of Italy • Construction begins on the Suez Canal between the Mediterranean and Red seas, which will allow water transport from Europe to Asia without circumnavigating Africa	• Oregon is admitted to the US as the 33rd state; it is a free state; the balance is now 17 free states and 16 slave states • John Brown leads a raid on the US Army arsenal at Harper's Ferry, Virginia; he is captured by US troops commanded by Robert E. Lee, convicted of treason, and executed but is seen by radical abolitionists as a martyr • Antislavery forces finally triumph in Kansas; a territorial committee drafts and adopts an antislavery constitution, and Kansas petitions for statehood as a free state • The Comstock Lode is discovered in Nevada, beginning a gold- and silver-mining boom	• Robert Bunsen and Gustav Kirchhoff (Germany) develop the spectroscope, which splits a beam of light into its component colors • French inventor Gaston Plante develops the first practical and rechargeable lead-acid storage battery; it will find its primary application in the automobile • Charles Darwin publishes his revolutionary and controversial work, *On the Origin of Species by Means of Natural Selection*, in which he outlines his theory of evolution • Louis Agassiz publishes his *Essay on Classification*, which rejects Darwin's evolutionary theories; Agassiz sees "the divine plan of God" everywhere in nature and cannot reconcile himself to a theory that does not invoke design • The first successful oil well in the US is drilled at Titusville, PA, by Edwin L. Drake	• The Great Atlantic and Pacific Tea Company (later A&P) opens its first stores in New York, beginning the concept of the "chain store" • French acrobat Charles Blondin crosses Niagara Falls on a tightrope • Vaudeville performer Daniel Decatur Emmett composes the song "Dixie," first performed by Bryant's Minstrels at Mechanics' Hall in New York City • The Philadelphia Zoological Gardens are the first modern zoo in America • The bells of the Great Clock of Westminster, including the 13-ton hour bell named "Big Ben," ring out across London for the first time

E. EDUCATION, LITERATURE & THE FINE ARTS	F. RELIGION, THEOLOGY, PHILOSOPHY & PSYCHOLOGY	G. AMERICAN & UNITED METHODISM	H. BRITISH & WORLD METHODISM	
• The New York Symphony gives its first public concert • Jacques Offenbach's operetta *Orpheus in the Underworld* makes the "Can-Can" a popular favorite • Longfellow's narrative poem *The Courtship of Miles Standish* tells the fictional story of a famous love triangle in colonial New England • George Eliot publishes *The Sad Fortunes of the Rev. Amos Barton*	• The United Presbyterian Church of North America (UPCNA) is formed by the merger of the Associate Presbyterian Church and much of the Associate Reformed Presbyterian Church (both ca. 1755) [the ARPC Synod of the Carolinas does not merge and continues as the nucleus of the modern ARPC] • Isaac Hecker founds The Missionary Society of St. Paul the Apostle, more commonly known as the "Paulist Fathers" • Bernadette Soubirous, a 14-year-old peasant from Lourdes, France, experiences her first vision of the Virgin Mary • Horace Bushnell publishes his *Nature and the Supernatural* • Theodore Parker attacks revivalism and evangelicalism in two published sermons that become national best-sellers: *A False and True Revival of Religion* and *The Revival of Religion Which We Need*	• The MECS General Conference: – votes to substitute the words *church* and *churches* for the words *society* and *societies* throughout the *Discipline* except in the General Rules – approves and sends to the annual conferences a constitutional amendment to remove from the General Rules the prohibition forbidding "the buying and selling of men, women, and children with an intention to enslave them"; the annual conferences approve the amendment – approves a mission to Central America – encourages the formation of Sunday schools and elects a corresponding secretary for the Sunday school Society – creates the Rio Grande Mission Conference (total now 20) – approves the translation and publication in German of the *Discipline*, Book of Hymns, and Catechism • The MEC establishes the Ladies Missionary Society • The MPC General Conference: – declines the antislavery request of the petition from the 1857 Cincinnati Convention, declaring that "this General Conference has no constitutional authority to grant the prayers of said petitioners" – tables resolutions stating that "a severance from this General Conference is not a severance from the Methodist Protestant Church" and calling for the creation of a second antislavery General Conference • Antislavery Methodist Protestants break away from the MPC to form The Methodist Church [reunion occurs in 1877] • Francis Burns is elected bishop by the Liberia Annual Conference (MEC); he is the first black person elected to the episcopacy in any branch of American Methodism as well as the first person to hold the title Missionary Bishop • Mrs. M. L. Kelley (MECS) organizes a fund-raising effort for missionaries in China; this is the earliest recorded effort by MECS women in support of foreign missions	• The Ladies' China Missionary Society supports a girls' school in China, and two unmarried teachers, Sarah and Beulah Woolston, are sent there by the MEC Missionary Society • Ludwig Nippert establishes the first MEC mission in Berlin, Germany • Christian Willerup travels from the MEC mission in Norway to Copenhagen and begins the first MEC work in Denmark • The WM Women's Missionary Auxiliary begins in England • W. E. Boardman publishes *The Higher Christian Life*	**1858**
• Johannes Brahms composes his *Piano Concerto No. 1* • Charles Gounod's opera *Faust* has its first performance in Paris • The French Opera House, the first great opera house in America, is built in New Orleans • Harriett Wilson's *Our Nig: Or, Sketches from the Life of a Free Black,* is believed to be the first novel written and published in English by a black woman in the US • Charles Dickens publishes *A Tale of Two Cities:* "It was the best of times, it was the worst of times" • Other notable publications include: – George Eliot, *Adam Bede* – Alfred, Lord Tennyson, *The Idylls of the King* – Edward Fitzgerald, *The Rubáiyát of Omar Khayyám*	• Nathaniel Taylor, *Lectures on the Moral Government of God* (posthumous) • John Stuart Mill, *On Liberty* • Karl Marx, *Critique of Political Economy* • Konstantin von Tischendorf discovers Codex Sinaiticus	• The EA General Conference: – sustains charges against Solomon Neitz for publishing a volume entitled *Christian Sanctification in Accordance with the Apostolic Doctrine* that contradicts the Articles of Faith, but declines to impose any punishment on him – organizes a Board of Missions and a Board of Publication – creates a unified Sunday school and Tract Society – appoints a committee to revise the course of study for ministers and ministerial candidates • The MPC publishes a revised version of the 1837 *Hymn Book of the Methodist Protestant Church* • The MECS organizes its first Spanish-language mission in Texas • Phoebe Palmer proclaims the rights of women to preach the Gospel in her book *The Promise of the Father*	• The first Methodist Episcopal Society in Denmark is formed • Gustav Lervik begins MEC mission work in Finland • WM missionaries in southern Africa complete a project begun in 1833 to translate the Bible into Xhosa • Catherine Booth, cofounder of the Salvation Army, publishes her pamphlet "Female Ministry: Woman's Right to Preach the Gospel"	**1859**

	A. WORLD HISTORY & POLITICS	B. AMERICAN HISTORY & POLITICS	C. SCIENCE, MEDICINE & TECHNOLOGY	D. DAILY LIFE, POPULAR CULTURE & ENTERTAINMENT
1859 cont.				
1860	• British and French forces occupy Beijing, forcing China to sign a convention that establishes the right of foreign diplomatic representation in China's capital, removes most restrictions on foreign travel within China, guarantees western missionaries the right to work and even own property in China, and legalizes the opium trade, which was the catalyst for the whole dispute • War breaks out again between the Maoris and the British settlers in New Zealand; the conflict lasts until 1870 and results in the destruction of Maori power • Giuseppe Garibaldi and his supporters seize control of Sicily and Naples; Sardinian forces then join Garibaldi's to defeat the Papal army at Castelfidardo • Russia establishes the port city of Vladivostock in the southeast of Siberia on the Sea of Japan	• The US census reports that the population is 31,443,321: – whites: 26,922,537 (85.6%) – free blacks: 488,070 (1.6%) – slaves: 3,953,760 (12.6%) – other: 78,954 (0.2%) • The US national debt is $64,842,287 • The famous but short-lived Pony Express is established to deliver mail between St. Joseph, MO (the westernmost point then reached by railroad and telegraph lines) and Sacramento, CA; it cuts the time of mail delivery (20 days by stagecoach) in half • Abraham Lincoln is elected as president and Hannibal Hamlin as vice president (Republican Party)	• Louis Agassiz succeeds in his lifelong dream when the Museum of Comparative Zoology at Harvard University opens its doors; it is the first institution of its kind in the world • B. Tyler Henry (US) creates and patents the first lever-action repeating rifle; it is later produced by the Winchester Arms Co. from which it took its popular name • French engineer Jean Joseph Étienne Lenoir invents and patents what is generally regarded as the first practical internal combustion engine: a double-acting, electric spark ignition fueled by coal gas • Florence Nightingale (UK) establishes the world's first school for nurses at St. Thomas' Hospital in London • German-born American physician Abraham Jacobi, considered the founder of American pediatrics, establishes the first clinic in the US specifically for the treatment of children's diseases	• Ebenezer Butterick develops first paper dress patterns for use in the home sewing of clothing • Christmas tree ornaments made of glass first appear in Germany • The first Boys Club in the US is organized in Hartford, CT, by a group of women concerned about young boys roaming the streets; the idea soon spreads to other major cities where similar clubs are organized
1861	• A united kingdom of Italy is proclaimed when Sicily and Naples join Tuscany and Sardinia; a unified Italian parliament meets for the first time and declares Victor Emmanuel II of Sardinia as king • Britain's Prince Albert dies; Queen Victoria does not remarry • Tsar Alexander II of Russia declares the emancipation of the serfs but requires them to pay compensation to their former owners • France, Britain, and Spain combine to force Mexico to honor its debts • Prussia's King Frederick William IV dies; he is succeeded by his brother, William I	• South Carolina secedes from the US, followed by Mississippi, Florida, Alabama, Georgia, and Louisiana; they form themselves into the Confederate States of America (CSA), with its capital at Montgomery, AL; Jefferson Davis is elected as its president • Texas soon secedes from the US and joins the CSA, bringing the total to 7 states • The Civil War begins with the shelling of Fort Sumter; President Lincoln's call for all remaining states in the Union to send troops to recapture Sumter and other forts, defend the capital, and preserve the Union prompts four more states (Virginia, Arkansas, Tennessee, and North Carolina) to secede from the US and join the CSA, bringing the total to 11 Confederate states • The capital of the CSA is moved from Montgomery, AL, to Richmond, VA • The "border states" of Kentucky and Missouri are counted by the CSA as having seceded, bringing the total to 13 Confederate states, but are not regarded by the US as ever having withdrawn from the union • The first major military clash of the Civil War takes place at Manassas (Bull Run); neither army is well trained; both are shocked by the number of casualties • After the secession of the Southern states, Congress musters enough votes to admit Kansas to the US as a free state; it is counted as the 34th state • The northern half of Nebraska Territory (to the Canadian border) is separated to become the Dakota Territory • Apache chief Cochise leads Indian resistance to white settlement in the Southwest	• James Clerk Maxwell (US) demonstrates a projected color photographic image, using three different color filters • The skeleton of Archaeopteryx, a link between reptiles and birds, is discovered at Solnhofen, Germany [it is now at the British Museum in London] • Henry H. Rogers establishes the first oil refinery in the US: the Wamsutta Oil Refinery in Pennsylvania • French paleontologist Édouard Lartet publishes his *New Researches on the Coexistence of Man and of the Great Fossil Mammifers Characteristic of the Last Geological Period*, in which he develops his theory about prehistoric human habitation	• British plumber Thomas Crapper opens his shop in London; his name will later come to be synonymous with the high-quality toilets that his firm supplies • Elizabeth P. Peabody introduced Friedrich Fröbel's ideas about early childhood education to the US by establishing the first American "kindergarten" in Boston • Julia Ward Howe publishes "The Battle Hymn of the Republic," based on the tune "John Brown's Body," in the *Atlantic Monthly* • *The Chicago Times* publicizes its motto: "It is a newspaper's duty to print the news and raise hell" • The Central Park Zoo opens in New York City • British chocolate maker Richard Cadbury creates the first known heart-shaped candy box for Valentine's Day • Photographer Mathew Brady, who had secured permission from Lincoln to follow the troops, loses his equipment in the chaos following the battle of Manassas (Bull Run); he then finances a corps of field photographers who collectively provide the first extended photographic documentation of a war • Pierre and Ernest Michaux (France) create the first pedal-powered bicycle

E. EDUCATION, LITERATURE & THE FINE ARTS	F. RELIGION, THEOLOGY, PHILOSOPHY & PSYCHOLOGY	G. AMERICAN & UNITED METHODISM	H. BRITISH & WORLD METHODISM	
		• Lydia Sexton applies to the Illinois Conference to have her quarterly conference license to preach advanced to an annual conference license; the presiding bishop rules that there is no authority in the UBC for licensing a woman • The MECS establishes Trinity College in Randolph County, NC		**1859 cont.**
• Franz von Suppé's first light operetta, *The Finishing School*, debuts in Vienna • Notable publications include: – George Eliot, *The Mill on the Floss* – R. M. Potter, *The Fall of the Alamo* – Nathaniel Hawthorne, *The Marble Faun*	• Emerson publishes *The Conduct of Life* • The publication of *Essays and Reviews*, a collection of articles favorable to "modernism" by prominent intellectuals including Benjamin Jowett, Mark Pattison, and Frederick Temple (later archbishop of Canterbury), sparks a "culture war" in Victorian England • The Mormon minority who rejected leadership of Brigham Young after the murder of Joseph Smith establish the Reorganized Church of Jesus Christ of Latter-Day Saints (RLDS) under the leadership of Joseph Smith III, grandson of the prophet • The Swedish Augustana Synod (Lutheran) is established	• The MEC General Conference: – approves establishment of a theological institute in Germany – authorizes a mission conference for India – prohibits mission conferences from voting on constitutional matters – establishes four new annual conferences: Nebraska, NW Wisconsin, Central Ohio, East Maine (total now 56); Peoria changes to Central Illinois – approves a resolution favoring total abstinence and prohibition of the sale of liquor – declines to consider modification of the presiding eldership, lay delegation, or "colored" conferences • The Free Methodist Church (FMC) is founded by Benjamin T. Roberts near Rochester, NY, over issues of holiness, episcopal authority, and free pews; Roberts had been expelled for his views from the Genesee Annual Conference in 1858	• MECS missionaries Rev. and Mrs. Young J. Allen arrive in China • The UMFC begins mission work in New Zealand	**1860**
• Harriet Ann Jacobs publishes her gripping autobiography, *Incidents in the Life of a Slave Girl: Written by Herself*, which tells the story of her life as a Southern slave and her subsequent escape north to reunite with her children and freedom • Other notable publications include: – Charles Dickens, *Great Expectations* – Anthony Trollope, *Orley Farm* – George Eliot, *Silas Marner* – Mary Elizabeth Braddon, *The Octoroon*	• The northern and southern branches of the Protestant Episcopal Church split over slavery • The northern and southern branches of the "Old School" Presbyterians split over slavery; the northern branch keeps the name the Presbyterian Church in the USA (PCUSA); the southern branch forms the Presbyterian Church in the Confederate States of America (PCCSA) • Recovering from the "Great Disappointment" of Millerite Adventism (when Christ failed to return as predicted in 1844), Ellen G. H. White becomes the leading spokesperson for the Adventist cause and the founder of the Seventh-Day Adventist Church • Horace Bushnell publishes his *Christian Nurture*	• The UBC General Conference: – declines to consider proposals in favor of pro rata representation and lay representation – strengthens prohibitions against secret society membership by saying that violators should be dealt with "as in the case of other immorality" – ignores questions about slaveholding by members in Virginia and Maryland – significantly reorganizes many annual conferences and establishes several new ones • Plainfield College in Plainfield, IL, is founded by the EA [it moves to Naperville, IL, in 1870 and is renamed North Central College in 1926]	• J. Lewis Krapf and Thomas Wakefield begin UMFC mission work in Kenya, primarily around Mombassa • *Methodist Recorder* is founded in England • The WM Conference sends two missionaries to Italy to support work already begun in Florence by Bartholomeo Gualteri, a convert from Roman Catholicism	**1861**

	A. WORLD HISTORY & POLITICS	B. AMERICAN HISTORY & POLITICS	C. SCIENCE, MEDICINE & TECHNOLOGY	D. DAILY LIFE, POPULAR CULTURE & ENTERTAINMENT
1862	• Swiss philanthropist Jean Henri Dunant publishes *The Memory of Solferino*, regarding the suffering of the wounded at the 1859 Battle of Solferino during the Franco-Austrian War, leading to the establishment of the International Committee for the Relief of the Wounded (later the International Committee of the Red Cross) in 1863 and the Geneva Convention of 1864 • Otto von Bismarck is appointed as prime minister and chancellor in Prussia and begins a campaign for German unification under Prussian leadership • British and Spanish troops withdraw from Mexico; French forces remain • The kingdom of Italy begins a policy of *risorgimento* (unification) of the Italian peninsula by annexing Venice (then controlled by Austria), Rome (then occupied by French troops), and most of the Papal States • Taiping rebels in China are defeated in Shanghai and Ningpo • London hosts another Great Exhibition; over 29,000 exhibitors participate, and it attracts more than 6 million people but is still much less successful financially than the 1851 Exhibition	• Robert E. Lee takes command of the Army of Northern Virginia • Major battles occur at Shiloh, Second Manassas (Bull Run), Antietam, and Fredericksburg; though undermanned and undersupplied, Confederate armies fight Union forces to a standstill • The Confederate government enacts a military draft covering all white males between the ages of 18 and 35 • The first battle of ironclad gunships at Hampton Roads (USS *Monitor* vs. CSS *Virginia*) marks the end of the era of wooden battleships • Congress abolishes slavery in the District of Columbia and all western territories of the US • President Lincoln issues the Emancipation Proclamation, which becomes effective January 1, 1863 • The transcontinental telegraph line is completed to California, effectively ending the need for the Pony Express, which is disbanded • Denver, CO, is incorporated as a city • Congress adopts the Homestead Act, granting 160-acre tracts of land to qualified individuals (married men over age 21, excluding American Indians, blacks, and non-European immigrants) for no cost other than an $18 filing fee provided they agree to build a home, live on the land, and make improvements (such as digging a well or breaking and plowing at least 10 acres) for at least 5 years; some 270 million acres, or 10% of the total land area of the US, is claimed and settled under this act	• John Ericsson designs an ironclad, steam-powered warship for the US Navy; the USS *Monitor* features a screw propeller and a rotating gun turret • Richard J. Gatling invents the hand-cranked multibarrel machine gun that bears his name • T. S. Mort (Australia) builds the first machine-chilled cold storage unit • Jean Bernard Léon Foucault successfully measures the speed of light for the first time • London's new Westminster Bridge across the Thames is opened, replacing the 1750 structure of the same name	• The first income tax law in US history, passed by Congress in 1861 to help pay for the cost of the Civil War, is ruled by the Supreme Court to be constitutional and goes into effect • Sarah Bernhardt, one of the most popular actresses of the century, makes her debut at the Comédie Française in Paris • Stephen Foster writes his immortal "Beautiful Dreamer"
1863	• French troops occupy Mexico City and install Austrian archduke Maximilian, the younger brother of Austrian Emperor Francis Joseph I, as emperor of Mexico • Slavery is abolished in the Dutch colonies in the Caribbean • Polish nationalists launch the "January Revolution" against Russian rule, which spreads into Lithuania and White Russia • Prussia and Austria demand that the duchies of Schleswig and Holstein be ceded to them by Denmark • Ismail Pasha becomes the ruler of Egypt and initiates a policy of modernization	• Congress passes the Enrollment Act, creating a national military draft for males twenty to forty-five • Major battles occur at Chancellorsville, Gettysburg, Vicksburg, Chickamauga, and Lookout Mountain; the force of Union arms and supplies begins to prevail; Ulysses S. Grant's victory at Vicksburg gives the Union complete control of the Mississippi River; Robert E. Lee's defeat at Gettysburg forces his Confederate army back into Virginia • President Lincoln gives his immortal Gettysburg Address and designates the last Thursday in November as Thanksgiving Day • Work is completed on the new Dome of the US Capitol; the statue "Freedom" is installed on its crowning cupola • West Virginia secedes from the state of Virginia and is admitted to the US as the 35th state • Idaho Territory, covering modern Montana and Idaho, is formed out of the Dakota Territory • US Army troops commanded by the legendary Christopher "Kit" Carson force the Navajo Indians to surrender, after years of conflict with white settlers; 12,000 Navajos are forced to make the 300-mile "Long Walk" to a reservation near Fort Sumner in the Bosque Redondo of eastern New Mexico	• Jean Joseph Étienne Lenoir develops an improved version of his 1860 internal combustion engine that is fueled by gasoline and uses a primitive carburetor; he attaches it to a three-wheeled wagon that makes a historic fifty-mile road trip • The New York Medical College and Hospital for Women is established in New York City largely through the efforts of Clemence S. Lozier to make it possible for women to study medicine	• The first practical, four-wheel roller skates with metal wheels are invented by James Plimpton of Medford, MA • The first underground railroad or "subway" opens in London • The London Football Association is formed by a number of clubs devoted to the form of the game that is now called soccer • US domestic first-class (letter) postage rates become "uniform," that is, based solely on weight, regardless of distance; the cost of first-class domestic postage is set at 3¢ per half ounce • Popular songs to emerge from the Civil War include "All Quiet On The Potomac Tonight," "Just Before the Battle, Mother," "You Are Going To The Wars, Willie Boy!" "Tramp! Tramp! Tramp! (The Boys Are Marching)," and "When Johnny Comes Marching Home Again"

E. EDUCATION, LITERATURE & THE FINE ARTS	F. RELIGION, THEOLOGY, PHILOSOPHY & PSYCHOLOGY	G. AMERICAN & UNITED METHODISM	H. BRITISH & WORLD METHODISM	
• The Morrell Act grants 30,000 acres of federal land to each US state to be sold to finance new schools or colleges to teach "agriculture and mechanical arts"; 69 new "land-grant" schools are established, many with "A&M" in their names • Verdi completes his opera, *La forza del destino (The Force of Destiny)*; it debuts at the newly founded St. Petersburg Conservatory, directed by Anton Rubinstein • Berlioz completes his opera *Béatrice et Bénédict*, which debuts in Baden-Baden, Germany • Honoré Daumie paints *The Third-Class Carriage* • Charles Dodgson (better known by his pen name, Lewis Carroll) sends the hand-written manuscript of his tales about "Alice's Adventures Underground" to 10-year-old Alice Liddell • Victor Hugo publishes his powerful novel about the French Revolution, *Les Misérables*	• The northern and southern branches of the "New School" Presbyterians split over slavery; the southern branch forms the US Presbyterian Church (USPC); the northern branch adopts as its name the Presbyterian Church (PC) • The Church of England allows women to serve as unordained deacons • Alexander Crummell's sermons, collected in *The Future of Africa*, represent the "back to Africa" movement • Other notable publications include: – Samuel Wakefield, *Complete System of Christian Theology* – John William Colenso, *The Pentateuch Critically Examined*	• The MECS General Conference scheduled to meet in New Orleans is canceled because the city is occupied by Union forces • The MPC General Conference scheduled to be in Georgetown, DC, cannot fully assemble because of the war; only delegates from the East Coast can attend • The FMC holds its first General Conference • The Union Army seizes the facilities of the Methodist Book Concern in Nashville for use in federal government printing	• Thomas Crosby begins WM missionary work on Vancouver Island in British Columbia, establishing both schools and mission stations among the native Indians of the region • Mrs. J. K. Billheimer begins UBC missionary work in Sierra Leone • George F. Playter publishes *The History of Methodism in Canada: With an Account of the Rise and Progress of the Work of God Among the Canadian Indian Tribes, and Occasional Notices of the Civil Affairs of the Province*	**1862**
• The National Academy of Sciences is established in Washington, DC, to "investigate, examine, experiment, and report upon any subject of science or art" whenever called upon to do so by any department of the US government • Berlioz completes his opera *The Trojans*, which has its first performance at Théâtre-Lyrique in Paris • Édouard Manet completes his painting *Lunch in the Grass*; when it is rejected for exhibition at the Paris Salon as being too controversial and revolutionary, Manet instead exhibits it at the Salon des Refusés (established to exhibit the many works rejected by the official Salon) • Longfellow publishes *Tales of a Wayside Inn*, which includes the well-known poem "Paul Revere's Ride": "Listen my children and you shall hear / Of the midnight ride of Paul Revere" • Other notable publications include: – Edward Everett Hale, *The Man Without a Country* – Jules Verne, *Five Weeks in a Balloon*	• The General Synod of the Lutheran Church in the Confederate States of America is established; in 1866 it is renamed the United Lutheran Synod of the South • Leaders from eleven protestant denominations, including the Methodist Episcopal Church, organize the National Reform Association, whose primary mission is to amend the US Constitution to "declare the nation's allegiance to Jesus Christ" and to "indicate that this is a Christian nation"; its proposed "Christian Amendment" to the Constitution is not approved by Congress • Olympia Brown is ordained by the St. Lawrence Universalist Association • Notable publications include: – Ernest Renan, *The Life of Jesus* – John Stuart Mill, *Utilitarianism*	• The EA General Conference: – directs the Board of Missions to find ways to evangelize the newly emancipated slaves – sends another missionary to Germany and three more to the West Coast • The AMEC sends two itinerant preachers to South Carolina as missionaries to the freedmen there; this marks the beginning of the AMEC expansion into the Southern states for the first time since the closure of the AME church in Charleston, SC, in 1822 • AMEC minister [later bishop] Henry M. Turner becomes the first black chaplain to serve in the US Army • The UBC establishes a Freedman's School in Vicksburg, MS; Sarah A. Dickey and two colleagues teach there until 1865 • Wilberforce University (originally founded in 1856 but closed in 1862) is purchased and chartered by the AMEC; Daniel A. Payne becomes the first black college president in US history	• The WMMS celebrates the jubilee of WM missions, marking 50 years since the organization of the first WM Missionary Society in the Leeds District in 1813 • George Smith publishes the fourth and final edition of his *History of Wesleyan Methodism* (3 vols.)	**1863**

	A. WORLD HISTORY & POLITICS	B. AMERICAN HISTORY & POLITICS	C. SCIENCE, MEDICINE & TECHNOLOGY	D. DAILY LIFE, POPULAR CULTURE & ENTERTAINMENT
1863 cont.		• The Fort Bridger Treaty sets the boundaries of the Wind River Reservation in Wyoming for the Shoshone and Arapaho Indians • The US national debt surpasses $1 billion for the first time		
1864	• Russia crushes the Polish revolt and begins the "Russification" of Poland, resulting in severe oppression of the Polish Catholic Church by the Russian Orthodox Church • Russia annexes the Caucasus and expands in central Asia • Austria and Prussia declare war on Denmark, which is easily defeated • The Taiping Rebellion in China, which has cost an estimated 30 million lives since its beginning in 1850, ends with the fall of "The Kingdom of Heavenly Peace" and the restoration of Imperial rule • "The Geneva Convention for the Amelioration of the Condition of the Wounded and Sick of Armies in the Field" is signed by 35 nations, resulting in the establishment of the International Red Cross • Karl Marx establishes the International Working Man's Association as an international socialist organization ("The First International")	• Congress repeals the Fugitive Slave Acts of 1793 and 1850 and approves a bill authorizing equal pay, equipment, arms, and health care for black Union troops • William T. Sherman's Union army captures and burns Atlanta, then begins the March to the Sea, taking Savannah and splitting the Confederacy in half • After a series of brutal and bloody battles, including the Wilderness, Spotsylvania, and Cold Harbor, Grant's Union army forces Lee's Confederate army to take up entrenched positions at Petersburg, in defense of Richmond; Grant settles down to mount a siege • In the West, a Confederate advance by Robert Bell Hood into Tennessee results in devastating defeats at Franklin and Nashville and the complete destruction of Hood's army as a fighting force • Arlington National Cemetery is established when the US Army appropriates the grounds of Lee's mansion, Arlington House, for that purpose • In response to proposals of the National Reform Association, Congress authorizes the use of the motto "In God We Trust" on all American coinage • Nevada is admitted to the US as the 36th state • President Lincoln is reelected and Andrew Johnson is elected as vice president (Republican Party)	• Louis Pasteur develops the process that bears his name, "pasteurization," to prevent abnormal fermentation in wine and beer; it is later applied to dairy products and other foods • George Perkins Marsh, *Man and Nature; or, Physical Geography as Modified by Human Action*, demonstrates that human activity can cause dramatic and irreversible changes to the environment • Rebecca Lee Crumpler becomes the first black woman to receive an MD degree when she graduates from the New England Female Medical College	• The first day care center for children in the US is organized by the Philadelphia YMCA
1865	• Under the Treaty of Gastein, Prussia is to administer Schleswig and Austria is to administer Holstein; Lauenburg is ceded to Austria • Florence replaces Turin as the capital of the kingdom of Italy • Wellington replaces Auckland as the capital of New Zealand • War breaks out in southern Africa between the Boers (Afrikaners) of the Orange Free State and the Basuto Tribe	• President Lincoln's second inaugural address outlines his policy for Reconstruction: "with malice toward none, with charity for all" • Sherman's Union army moves north, taking Columbia, SC, then defeating the last Confederate army in the West, under Joe Johnston, at Bentonville, NC • Grant breaks the Confederate lines at Petersburg and captures Richmond; Confederate President Jefferson Davis tries to flee Richmond but is captured and imprisoned • Lee retreats from Richmond but is surrounded and forced to surrender to Grant *(cont.)*	• Claude Bernard publishes his influential *Introduction to the Study of Experimental Medicine* • Joseph Lister introduces antiseptic techniques to surgery, including the sterilization of instruments, resulting in greatly reduced mortality rates • Gregor Johann Mendel formulates principles concerning the hereditary transmission of physical characteristics in plants by crossbreeding garden peas; they come to be called "Mendel's Laws" and lay the basis for the development of the science of genetics	• Britain sets the first speed limit for automobiles at four miles per hour in an effort to reduce accidents • The Union Stockyards open in Chicago; they will become the largest in the US, establishing Chicago as the meat-packing center of the country • Tony Pastor, the "father of American vaudeville," opens a theater in New York City featuring entertainment for men only

E. EDUCATION, LITERATURE & THE FINE ARTS	F. RELIGION, THEOLOGY, PHILOSOPHY & PSYCHOLOGY	G. AMERICAN & UNITED METHODISM	H. BRITISH & WORLD METHODISM	
				1863 cont.
• Jacques Offenbach's operetta *The Beautiful Helen* (about Helen of Troy) debuts at the Paris Variétés • Notable publications include: – Jules Verne, *A Journey to the Center of the Earth* – Fyodor Dostoyevsky, *Notes from the Underground* – Elizabeth Gaskell, *Wives and Daughters* – Charles Dickens, *Our Mutual Friend* (serialized 1864–65)	• Pope Pius IX issues his *Syllabus of Errors* condemning (among other things) modernism, liberalism, socialism, rationalism, civil marriage, and secular education • Moody Church, named in honor of evangelist Dwight L. Moody, is established in Chicago • Notable publications include: – John Henry Newman, *Apologia pro Vita Sua* – Daniel D. Whedon, *The Freedom of Will*	• The New England Conference (MEC) admits John N. Mars into full connection; he is the first black elder in full connection in the MEC • The AMEC General Conference sends fraternal delegates to the MEC General Conference and considers the possibility of union with the AMEZC • The MEC General Conference: – approves a resolution approving "the measures of the Government in prosecuting the war against the rebellion" – authorizes the bishops to arrange districts and change presiding elders in the interval between conferences – grants full clergy rights for black preachers – organizes the first black mission conferences in Delaware and Washington, DC; others follow across the Southern states – organizes the Central, Northwest, and Southwest German Conferences and the India Mission Conference – for the first time includes in the *Discipline* an order for the reception of new members – approves publication of a German hymnbook – establishes annual conferences in Colorado and Nevada (total of all conferences now 58) – extends maximum length of pastoral service on a circuit from two to three years (until 1888) – rejects proposals to make presiding elders the legal advisors of the bishops in making appointments, to allow lay representation, and to elect missionary bishops • Frank B. Smith becomes the first black preacher to be admitted to full connection in an MEC annual conference (New England) • Delegates from the AMEC and the AMEZC meet in a joint convention in Philadelphia and agree on a proposal for union, but the proposal is rejected by the General Conferences of both bodies • The AMEZC begins aggressive expansion in the Southern states, forming its first southern conference in North Carolina	• The MNC opens Ranmoor College in Sheffield as its primary theological college • Wesleyan Methodist deaconess work begins in Germany • The Presbyterian Church of Wales, which has roots in Calvinistic Methodism, holds its first General Assembly	1864
• The Massachusetts Institute of Technology (MIT) admits its first class of students (15) • Schubert's *Symphony No. 8 (Unfinished)* is performed for the first time in Vienna • Wagner's opera *Tristan and Isolde* premieres in Munich • Brahms composes his *Trio for Violin, Horn and Piano* • Edvard Grieg completes his *Violin Sonata No. 1* • Frederick Edwin Church completes his painting of the *Aurora Borealis*	• Thomas Huxley (who coined the word *agnostic* to describe himself) humiliates Bishop Samuel Wilberforce in an evolution debate in England • Notable publications include: – John Stuart Mill, *Auguste Comte and Positivism* – Philip Schaff, *The Person of Christ* • The separated northern and southern branches of Protestant Episcopal Church reunite into one body, retaining the same name	• The MECS bishops and a group of preachers meet in Palmyra, MO; they issue the "Palmyra Manifesto," which proclaims the continuation of the MECS as a separate denomination and calls for the MECS General Conference to meet the following year • The UBC General Conference: – creates a Sabbath School Association for the denomination to centralize and foster the work of Christian education – reorganizes the German work of the denomination • The MEC organizes the Missouri Mission Conference	• The beginnings of the Salvation Army appear in the street ministry of William Booth, a former MNC minister, in East London; it was first known as "the Christian Mission"; the name "Salvation Army" is first used in 1878 • The EA organizes its mission in Germany into the German Conference and launches mission work in Switzerland and Alsace	1865

	A. WORLD HISTORY & POLITICS	B. AMERICAN HISTORY & POLITICS	C. SCIENCE, MEDICINE & TECHNOLOGY	D. DAILY LIFE, POPULAR CULTURE & ENTERTAINMENT
1865 cont.	• Peru declares war on Spain, which had refused to recognize Peru's independence, and forms an alliance with Chile, Bolivia, and Ecuador	at Appomattox; Johnston then surrenders to Sherman, and the Civil War comes to an end • The US national debt soars past $2.6 billion • The 13th Amendment to the US Constitution abolishes slavery • Lincoln is assassinated by Confederate sympathizer John Wilkes Booth; Vice President Johnson becomes president • Lincoln is the second president to receive a formal state funeral, but the first person to lie in state in the newly finished Rotunda of the US Capitol	• The first permanently successful telegraph cable is laid across the Atlantic Ocean • British mountaineer Edward Whymper and his party make the first successful ascent of the Matterhorn	
1866	• Prussia concludes an alliance with Italy and accuses Austria of violating the Treaty of Gastein • The brief Austro-Prussian War results in the dominance of Prussia and the exclusion of Austria from the German Confederation • By the Treaty of Vienna, Austria cedes Venice to Italy, and Prussia annexes the previously independent German states of Hannover, Hesse, Nassau, Frankfurt, and Schleswig-Holstein • The Ottoman protectorates of Moldavia and Wallachia unite in the federation of Romania • Serbia and Montenegro form a secret alliance against Prussia • The Boers (Afrikaners) in south Africa defeat the Basutos, who are forced to give up considerable territory • Japan signs a trade agreement that opens Japanese markets to the US, Britain, and France	• Congress passes the Civil Rights Act of 1866, which extends full citizenship rights to former slaves and gives the federal government the power to protect those rights; this prepares the way for the 14th and 15th Amendments • The National Labor Union convention marks the beginning of efforts to improve working conditions through legislative reform rather than through collective bargaining • Tennessee is the first of the Southern states to be readmitted to the US • The Ku Klux Klan is founded in Pulaski, TN, by Nathan Bedford Forrest; originally a social club for Confederate veterans, it quickly becomes a vehicle for Southern white resistance to Radical Reconstruction and largely disappears by the end of the 1870s with the close of the Reconstruction era • Jesse James and his brother, Frank, form an outlaw gang that carries out numerous train and bank robberies all over the American West for the next 15 years • Elizabeth Cady Stanton and Susan B. Anthony form the American Equal Rights Association, an organization for white and black women and men dedicated to the goal of universal suffrage • The Oglala Lakota (Sioux) chief Red Cloud leads his people in battle against white settlers in "Red Cloud's War"	• Charles M. Hall develops first process for producing aluminum by electrolytic action • Thomas Arlbutt invents the clinical thermometer • Thaddeus Lowe builds a factory in New Orleans to produce artificial ice for commercial use	• The American Society for the Prevention of Cruelty to Animals (ASPCA), the first animal welfare society in the US, is established in New York City • Alexander Gardner publishes his *Photographic Sketch Book of the Civil War*, which gives many Americans who were not on the battlefields or in the hospitals their first glimpse into the horror and cost of the war

E. EDUCATION, LITERATURE & THE FINE ARTS	F. RELIGION, THEOLOGY, PHILOSOPHY & PSYCHOLOGY	G. AMERICAN & UNITED METHODISM	H. BRITISH & WORLD METHODISM	
• Lewis Carroll publishes the final version of *Alice's Adventures in Wonderland* with memorable illustrations by John Tenniel • Whitman writes his memorable elegy for Abraham Lincoln, "When Lilacs Last in the Dooryard Bloom'd" • Other notable publications include: – Mary Mapes Dodge, *Hans Brinker or the Silver Skates* – P. T. Barnum, *The Humbugs of the World* – Elizabeth Gaskell, *The Life of Charlotte Brontë*	• The [southern] Presbyterian Church in the US (PCUS) is formed by union of PCCSA (Old School, 1837/1861) and USPC (New School, 1837/1862) • Samuel Crowther (Nigeria) becomes the first black bishop in the Anglican Communion	• Several congregations of the Union Church of Africans (UCA, 1813) split off to form the African Union Church; the original body then takes the name Union American Methodist Episcopal Church (UAMEC) • MEC Bishop Matthew Simpson delivers the eulogy at Abraham Lincoln's burial in Springfield, IL • The MEC establishes the Freedmen's Aid and Southern Education Society to provide aid and education to newly freed blacks in the Southern states • The AMEC organizes its first southern conference in South Carolina, embracing all of the southeastern US		**1865 cont.**
• American artist Mary Cassatt quits art school in Philadelphia and moves to Paris, where she will become a leading impressionist painter • Bedřich Smetana composes his great comic opera *The Bartered Bride* which debuts in Prague • Offenbach's operetta *Parisian Life* debuts in Paris's Palais Royale • Franz von Suppé's operetta *The Light Cavalry*, with its famous overture, debuts in Vienna • Dostoyevsky publishes *Crime and Punishment* • William Wells Brown publishes *The Negro in the American Rebellion*	• Cardinal Nicholas Wiseman, Archbishop of Westminster, in his posthumously published *Twelve Lectures on the Connexion Between Science and Revealed Religion*, argues that although modern scientific thought has repeatedly been thought to disprove Christian doctrine, further investigation has always shown that a reconstruction is possible	• American Methodism commemorates the centennial of the formation of the first Methodist society in America, in New York in 1766 [the earlier formation of a Methodist society by Robert Strawbridge in 1763 is not widely known or acknowledged at the time] • The MEC organizes the Eastern German Conference and the South Carolina, Tennessee, and Texas Mission Conferences • The MECS General Conference meets for the first time after the Civil War: – adopts the principle of equal lay and clergy representation in General and annual conferences – admits the Baltimore Conference to the MECS – receives petitions from black members to form a separate church – appoints a committee to consider proposals for creation of a separate church structure for black members – fixes maximum length of pastoral service on a circuit at four years – removes attendance at class meeting as requirement for church membership and abolishes a legal probationary period for new members – includes an order for the reception of new members in the *Discipline* • The MPC General Conference: – endures much confusion about who is entitled to sit as delegates because of the schism that led to the creation of The Methodist Church in 1858 – receives a communication from the MECS announcing its approval of lay representation and inviting the MPC to confer about possible union – approves the establishment of Western Maryland College in Westminster, MD • Helenor M. Davisson is ordained deacon by the North Indiana Conference of the MPC; she is the first woman to be ordained in any branch of Methodism • Several black congregations leave the MPC and join with the Union Church of Africans (UCA) to create the African Union Methodist Protestant (AUMP) Church • Shaw University (later Rust College) is founded by the Freedmen's Aid and Southern Education Society (MEC) • The AMEC organizes annual conferences in Georgia and Louisiana	• *Bethel Ship* mission converts Gustaf and William Bernlund return from the US to Finland and begin MEC work there	**1866**

	A. WORLD HISTORY & POLITICS	B. AMERICAN HISTORY & POLITICS	C. SCIENCE, MEDICINE & TECHNOLOGY	D. DAILY LIFE, POPULAR CULTURE & ENTERTAINMENT
1867	• The British parliament passes the British North America Act, which unites all the separate British provinces in North America to create the Dominion of Canada, marking the beginning of the modern state of Canada • The Prussian-dominated North German Confederation replaces the former German Confederation (1815) • The former Austrian Empire is transformed into Austria-Hungary, a dual monarchy in which the Austrians dominate the Czechs and Poles and the Hungarians dominate the other Slavic peoples; Francis Joseph I continues as Emperor of Austria and is crowned King of Hungary • Paris holds its second Exposition Universelle on the Champs du Mars; it has over 43,000 exhibits and attracts more than 6.8 million visitors	• The Reconstruction Act of 1867 establishes federal military control and administration in the Southern states, and provides voting rights for all citizens, including freed slaves • The Southern states hold constitutional conventions and begin the process of reconstruction under the Congressional military plan • Southern white women begin forming Confederate memorial societies to help preserve the memory of the "Lost Cause" • US Secretary of State William H. Seward negotiates the purchase of Alaska from Russia by the US—the purchase is called "Seward's Folly" by critics • Because they had supported the Confederacy, the US requires the "Five Civilized Tribes" (Cherokee, Creek, Choctaw, Chickasaw, and Seminole) to abolish slavery, grant former slaves citizenship, and allow railroads to cross their territory; the US also reserves the western half of the Indian Territory for western Indian tribes • The US signs the Medicine Lodge treaty with members of several western Indian tribes, including the Arapaho, Comanche, Cheyenne, and Kiowa, by which they agree to leave Kansas, Nebraska, and other western states for reservation lands in the Indian Territory, which is effectively reduced to the area of present-day Oklahoma; most members of those tribes ignore the treaty • Nebraska is admitted to the US as the 37th state	• Swedish chemist Alfred B. Nobel develops dynamite, a stable explosive • Joseph Monier (France) patents reinforced concrete, which he develops for making large flower pots by pouring concrete into a mold around an iron mesh frame • Alpheus Hyatt establishes the *American Naturalist* magazine • The first International Conference of the Red Cross meets in Paris	• The first bent-wire paper clip is patented by Samuel B. Fay • The Michaux brothers begin to manufacture bicycles, making them more widely available • Charles Feltman, a German butcher who immigrated to the US, opens the first hot dog stand at Brooklyn's Coney Island • Popular songs include "The Man on the Flying Trapeze" by George Leybourne and "The Moon Is Out To Night, Love" by Will S. Hays
1868	• Restoration of Meiji Emperor in Japan concludes 700 years of Shogun (military) rule, brings an end to the Samurai warrior caste and their strict Bushido code of ethics, and opens the way to Japan's modernization • Spanish revolutionaries depose Queen Isabella II from the Spanish throne and force her to flee to France; the short-lived First Spanish Republic is proclaimed • Russian troops occupy the city of Samarkand in central Asia • Diamonds are discovered in south Africa • Britain ends the transportation of convicts to Australia • Basutoland (now Lesotho) is proclaimed to be British territory	• Political opponents of President Johnson's "conservative and conciliatory" reconstruction policies persuade the House of Representatives to vote articles of impeachment against him; after a month-long trial in the Senate he is acquitted by the margin of one vote • Alabama, Arkansas, Florida, Georgia, Louisiana, North Carolina, and South Carolina are readmitted to the US and their representatives seated in Congress • The 14th Amendment to the US Constitution grants state and federal citizenship to "all persons born or naturalized in the United States" with the exception of American Indians, thus in effect overturning the 1857 Dred Scott decision of the Supreme Court; guarantees rights of all citizens to "equal protection of the laws" at both federal and state levels, thus writing the principle of equality into the *(cont.)*	• Skeletons of Cro-Magnons (first representatives of *Homo sapiens* in Europe, successor of the Neanderthals) from the Upper Paleolithic age are found in France and identified by Édouard Lartet • Christopher Sholes develops and patents the office typewriter	• The game of badminton is invented in the UK at the estate of the Duke of Baufort, Badminton Hall (hence its name) • The Lincoln Park Zoo opens in Chicago • The last public hanging in Britain takes place at Newgate Prison

E. EDUCATION, LITERATURE & THE FINE ARTS	F. RELIGION, THEOLOGY, PHILOSOPHY & PSYCHOLOGY	G. AMERICAN & UNITED METHODISM	H. BRITISH & WORLD METHODISM	
• The New England Conservatory is established • Modest Mussorgsky completes his symphonic poem *Saint John's Night on the Bare Mountain* (better known as *Night on Bald Mountain*) • Johann Strauss Jr. composes *The Blue Danube Waltz* • Charles Gounod's opera *Romeo and Juliette* debuts at the Théâtre-Lyrique in Paris • Claude Monet paints *The Beach at Sainte-Adresse* • Henrik Ibsen publishes his verse drama, *Peer Gynt*	• The first Lambeth Conference of worldwide Anglican bishops is convened to deal with the affair of Bishop John William Colenso of Natal, who had been tried and convicted of heresy by English bishops of the Church of England in 1863 for his advocacy of the modernist approach to scripture (and his belief in black equality) • The General Lutheran Council is organized in the US • The National Camp Meeting Association for the Promotion of Holiness is founded by John S. Inskip and William M. Osborn • Karl Marx publishes *Das Kapital* (*Capital*) (first English edition 1887)	• The EA General Conference: – acquits Solomon Neitz of charges that his teachings about sanctification contradict the Articles of Faith, appoints a committee to prepare an authoritative statement on the doctrine of holiness, and approves that statement, which says (in part) that sanctification can be reached in this life but may come either gradually or instantaneously – makes the general church officers *ex officio* members of General Conference – establishes the General Conference as the supreme law court of the Association and as a court of appeals for any minister who feels he has been unjustly censured – hears an address by William Nast from the MEC; responds by saying that while organic union with the MEC does not seem practical, "every effort should be made to serve the Lord cooperatively" • The Methodist General Biblical Institute (1847) is relocated to Boston by the MEC and renamed Boston Theological Seminary • Drew Theological Seminary is established by the MEC in Madison, NJ • First Methodist Church in Akron, OH, is designed with a semicircular sanctuary with curved pews on a sloping floor, with central pulpit and choir loft behind, and with Sunday school rooms opening to the auditorium; the "Akron Plan" becomes the dominant model for urban Methodist churches until the early 20th century • The MEC establishes Central Tennessee College in Nashville • The AMEC organizes annual conferences in North Carolina and Florida • Benjamin T. Tanner's *An Apology for African Methodism* is both a history of the rise and progress of the AMEC and a defense against the criticisms African Methodists were facing within American society	• Methodism in Brazil grows significantly due to immigrants from the Southern US leaving after the Civil War, including Junius Newman, who plays a key role in the expansion of Methodism in Brazil • Laws prohibiting preaching in Spanish are lifted in Argentina; John Thompson (MEC) preaches the first public sermon in Spanish	1867
• Mary Cassatt's painting *The Mandolin Player* is accepted by the Académie des Beaux-Arts for exhibition at the Paris Salon, marking her arrival as an artist • Albert Bierstadt's painting *Among the Sierra Nevada Mountains, California* gives a romantic depiction of the scenic grandeur of the American West • Brahms completes his great *German Requiem*, written in honor of his close friend Robert Schumann • Pyotr Ilich Tchaikovsky composes his *Symphony No. 1 in G Minor (Winter Dreams)* • Richard Wagner's opera *The Master Singers of Nuremberg* debuts in Munich's Hoftheater • Notable publications include: – Louisa May Alcott, *Little Women* – Horatio Alger, *Raggedy Dick*	• John Vincent develops the "uniform lesson plan" for Sunday school literature; it is adopted by the International Sunday School Association in 1872	• The MEC General Conference: – approves lay representation (limited to 2 lay delegates from each district to each annual conference by 1872) – sanctions the Freedmen's Aid and Southern Education Society as an official church agency – accepts Delaware and Washington Mission Conferences as annual conferences; James Davis (Delaware) and Benjamin Brown (Washington) become the first black preachers to be seated as delegates in a Methodist General Conference – organizes thirteen new annual conferences: Central New York, Central Pennsylvania, East German, Georgia, Holston, Louisiana, Mississippi, North Carolina, St. Louis, Tennessee, Texas, Virginia, and Wilmington (total now 71) – establishes a "Commission on Reunion" and appoints two messengers to next meeting of the MECS General Conference	• The MEC sends missionaries to France, but the mission does not succeed and is soon abandoned • The MEC missions in Germany and Switzerland are organized into the German Annual Conference; known inside Germany as the Bischöfliche Methodistenkirche (BMK) or the Methodist Church in Germany • Headingly College is established in Leeds by the WM Conference to train ministerial students after Richmond College is sold to the WM Missionary Society to be used to train missionaries for work overseas • The WM Conference opens Methodist College in Belfast, Northern Ireland • The PMC opens the Theological Institute at Sunderland	1868

	A. WORLD HISTORY & POLITICS	B. AMERICAN HISTORY & POLITICS	C. SCIENCE, MEDICINE & TECHNOLOGY	D. DAILY LIFE, POPULAR CULTURE & ENTERTAINMENT
1868 cont.		Constitution for the first time; abolishes the Three-Fifths Compromise of 1787, under which three-fifths of a state's slaves were counted as citizens for purposes of representation and taxation; but defines "citizens" and "voters" as "male" • The New England Suffrage Association is organized to advocate for the right of women to vote, which is denied to them by the 14th Amendment • Wyoming Territory is created out of parts of the Dakota, Idaho, and Utah Territories • The US Seventh Cavalry under General George A. Custer massacres Cheyenne civilians at the Washita River • The Navajo Nation signs a treaty with the US that allows them to return from their "exile" in the Bosque Redondo to their ancestral homelands and recognizes their tribal sovereignty in the area set apart as a reservation for them • The Fort Laramie Treaty between the US and the Sioux Nations (the Lakota, the Dakota, and the Nakota speaking peoples) acknowledges their right to self-determination and promises to exempt the sacred Black Hills from all white settlement forever • Ulysses S. Grant is elected as president and Schuyler Colfax as vice president (Republican Party)		
1869	• Napoleon III reintroduces parliamentary government in France • Britain, France, and Italy take control of Tunisia • The Suez Canal, begun in 1859, is officially dedicated and opened to traffic • The Hudson Bay Company, which has held a trade monopoly since 1670 in the region watered by streams flowing into Hudson Bay in Canada, transfers its territory to the Dominion of Canada • David Livingstone is the first European to reach Lake Tanganyika in Africa, traversing its entire length	• The US Supreme Court rules in *Texas v. White* that unilateral secession from the US by any state is unconstitutional • Southern states begin to elect "Redeemer" governments, replacing the biracial Republican state governments, created under Congressional reconstruction, with whites-only Democratic state governments that are generally sympathetic to the former Confederate cause and opposed to racial equality • The tracks of Central Pacific and Union Pacific railroads are joined by the ceremonial driving of the "golden spike" at Promontory Point, UT, completing the first transcontinental railroad connection; transforms western states by reducing overland travel time from Omaha to Sacramento from 4-6 months to 6 days • Susan B. Anthony and Elizabeth Cady Stanton found the National Woman Suffrage Association (NWSA) • Lucy Stone and Julia Ward Howe found the American Woman Suffrage Association (AWSA) • Wyoming Territory is formally organized and passes the first women's suffrage law in America, giving approximately 1,000 women the right to vote in local and territorial elections • Arabella Mansfield is granted permission to practice law in Iowa, making her the first female lawyer in America • John Wesley Powell and his party make the first successful passage of the Colorado River through the Grand Canyon • The first Japanese immigrants to the US arrive in California	• Russian scientist Dmitry Mendeleyev formulates his periodic law for the classification of the elements • Construction begins on the Brooklyn Bridge, which will connect Brooklyn with Manhattan across the East River; it is the first suspension bridge ever built using steel wire cable (completed in 1883)	• A plant fungus ruins the coffee crop in Ceylon (Sri Lanka) and spreads throughout the Orient and Pacific, giving a hefty boost to tea drinking; the focus of coffee production shifts to Latin and South America • The Cincinnati Red Stockings become the first all-professional baseball team and play 64 games without a loss • The first intercollegiate football game in America takes place between Rutgers and Princeton; the game resembles soccer more than modern-day American football • William F. Semple (Mt. Vernon, OH) receives a US patent for chewing gum

E. EDUCATION, LITERATURE & THE FINE ARTS	F. RELIGION, THEOLOGY, PHILOSOPHY & PSYCHOLOGY	G. AMERICAN & UNITED METHODISM	H. BRITISH & WORLD METHODISM	
		• Otis Gibson begins work with Chinese immigrants in California • Walden Seminary is founded by the Freedmen's Aid and Southern Education Society (MEC) • Annie Wittenmyer establishes The Ladies and Pastors Christian Union • The AMEC General Conference meets for the first time as a delegated conference, with both clergy and lay delegates; gives permission for annual conferences to institute office of presiding elder		**1868 cont.**
• Edvard Grieg's *Piano Concerto* has its first performance in Copenhagen • Richard Wagner's opera *The Rhinegold*, completed in 1854, has its premiere in Munich • Leo Tolstoy publishes his literary masterpiece, *War and Peace*, his epic story of the Napoleonic Wars, including the invasion of Russia in 1812 • The great American writer Mark Twain (real name, Samuel Langhorne Clemens) makes his literary debut with *The Celebrated Jumping Frog of Calaveras County, and Other Sketches* • Other notable publications include: – Matthew Arnold, *Culture and Anarchy* – R. D. Blackmore, *Lorna Doone*	• The first Vatican Council (1869–70) is convened by Pope Pius IX • The British parliament passes the Irish Church Disestablishment Bill, officially disassociating the (Anglican) Church of Ireland from the state and repealing the law that required all Irish citizens, most of whom are Roman Catholics, to pay tithes for its support • The [northern] Presbyterian Church in the USA (PCUSA) is created by the reunion of the PCUSA (Old School) (1837/1861) and the PC (New School) (1837/1862) • The Colored Cumberland PC separates from the Cumberland PC • John Stuart Mill publishes *The Subjection of Women*	• The UBC General Conference meets east of Ohio for the first time since 1817: – establishes a board of education and gives it specific instructions to establish a theological seminary for training ministers – approves a resolution requiring more stringent enforcement of the established prohibitions against secret society membership – votes to continue mission work in Africa, despite financial difficulties and personnel problems, and to open a new mission in Germany – relaxes prohibitions against the use of instrumental music and church choirs – defeats a proposal for lay representation on the grounds that there is no "widespread demand" for it – creates a Church Erection Society as an adjunct of the Missionary Society – abandons the principle of fixed salaries for itinerant preachers, making the quarterly conferences responsible for setting salaries • The Ocean Grove Camp Meeting Association is established by the MEC in New Jersey • Maggie Newton Van Cott is the first woman granted a local preacher's license by the MEC • The MEC organizes annual conferences in the South, overlapping the territory of the MECS: Lexington, Louisville, Mississippi, North Carolina, South Carolina, Tennessee, and Texas (total now 78) • The Woman's Foreign Missionary Society (WFMS) is formed by MEC women; it is the first independent missionary society for women; it begins publication of *The Heathen Woman's Friend*, the first such missionary magazine (to 1896)	• B. A. Carlson formally organizes the MEC Mission in Sweden • Thomas B. Stephenson (WM) founds National Children's Home and Orphanage in England • The MEC establishes the Methodist Episcopal Theological Seminary in Frankfurt am Main, Germany • The UBC launches a mission to Germany	**1869**

	A. WORLD HISTORY & POLITICS	B. AMERICAN HISTORY & POLITICS	C. SCIENCE, MEDICINE & TECHNOLOGY	D. DAILY LIFE, POPULAR CULTURE & ENTERTAINMENT
1869 cont.				
1870	• The brief Franco-Prussian War begins; Prussia invades France, captures and occupies Paris, deposes Napoleon III, and proclaims the establishment of the Third Republic of France • Italian troops capture Rome and proclaim the annexation of the Papal States to the kingdom of Italy • The Cortes (legislature) in Spain restores a constitutional monarchy; Queen Isabella II abdicates the throne in favor of her son, Alfonso XII • Manitoba becomes a province of the Dominion of Canada • The British parliament passes the Irish Land Act, protecting tenants from arbitrary eviction by their landlords	• The US census reports that the population is 38,558,371 – whites: 33,589,377 (87.1%) – blacks: 4,880,009 (12.7%) – other: 88,985 (0.2%) • The US national debt is $2,480,672,427 • The 15th Amendment to the US Constitution guarantees that the right of US citizens to vote "shall not be denied or abridged by the United States or by any state on account of race, color, or previous condition of servitude" • Mississippi, Texas, and Virginia are readmitted to the US • Hiram Revels (Mississippi) is the first black person to serve in the US Senate • Ada H. Kepley is the first woman in the US to receive a law degree when she graduates from the Union College of Law in Chicago • Congress declares Christmas Day to be a national holiday in the US	• Richard Leach Maddox invents the gelatin dry plate silver bromide photographic process; negatives no longer have to be developed immediately • John D. Rockefeller and associates create the Standard Oil Company of Ohio to market kerosene for home heating and lighting; it acquires or takes over a number of smaller oil companies and soon comes to dominate the American market • Although various forms of "black paper" or "carbon paper" previously existed, the firm of L. H. Rogers & Co. seizes its commercial potential and perfects the technology for its production; when the Rogers carbon paper meets the Remington typewriter (1874) a revolution in office document production occurs	• Margaret Knight invents a new machine part that automatically folds and glues paper grocery bags with square bottoms • Twinings of London begins to blend its imported tea to ensure uniformity and to establish brand name identity • William Lyman (US) patents an improved, easy-to-use can opener featuring a sharp wheel that rolls and cuts around the rim of a can • Political cartoonist Thomas Nast recalls Andrew Jackson's 1828 presidential campaign and uses a donkey as the symbol of the Democratic Party in a *Harper's Weekly* cartoon

E. EDUCATION, LITERATURE & THE FINE ARTS	F. RELIGION, THEOLOGY, PHILOSOPHY & PSYCHOLOGY	G. AMERICAN & UNITED METHODISM	H. BRITISH & WORLD METHODISM	
		• Boston Theological Seminary (1867) is reincorporated as Boston University, with the seminary becoming the Boston University School of Theology (1871) • The Reformed Zion Union Apostolic Church is established by the followers of James R. Howell who withdraw from the AMEZC • Clark and Claflin Colleges and New Orleans University are founded by the Freedmen's Aid and Southern Education Society (MEC)		**1869 cont.**
• The Metropolitan Museum of Art in New York and the Museum of Fine Arts in Boston are established • Tchaikovsky's fantasia on *Romeo and Juliet* debuts in Moscow, conducted by Nikolai Rubenstein • Richard Wagner's opera *The Valkyrie*, completed in 1857, has its premiere at the Munich Court Theatre • The first edition of *The Dictionary of American Biography* is issued • Other notable publications include: – Jules Verne, *20,000 Leagues Under the Sea* – Louisa May Alcott, *An Old Fashioned Girl* – Bret Harte, *The Luck of Roaring Camp and Other Sketches*	• Pope Pius IX promulgates the First Dogmatic Constitution on the Church of Christ, declaring the primacy and infallibility of the bishop of Rome; the discussion and approval of the constitution provoke bitter controversies (especially in Germany, Switzerland, and the Netherlands), which leads to the withdrawal from the church of those known as "Old Catholics" • Mary Baker Eddy begins instructing students in the principles of Christian Science • Notable publications include: – John Henry Newman, *The Grammar of Assent* – Albrecht Ritschl, *The Christian Doctrine of Justification and Reconciliation* (3 vols., 1870–74) – John Hunt, *Religious Thought in England from the Reformation to the End of the Last Century*	• The MECS General Conference: – seats lay (male) delegates for the first time, in numbers equivalent to clergy delegates, as voting members of the General Conference – rejects a proposal for the establishment of a theological school for training MECS ministers – approves plan for organizing its black members into an entirely separate church structure – decides to keep the Publishing House in Nashville – rejects a proposal to change the name of the denomination to "Episcopal Methodist Church" – denies any inherent and absolute veto power on the part of the bishops and outlines procedure by which the General and annual conferences have ultimate authority for approval of constitutional issues [this is an important check on the power of the bishops and a step toward the creation of a Judicial Council] – includes a revised order for the reception of new members in the *Ritual* • The MPC General Conference: – rebuffs overtures from the separatist Methodist Church (1858) for closer relationship – resolves to enter into formal fraternal relations with the MEC and MECS – adopts a revised *Ritual* and order of worship – disapproves of the ordination of women (a decision that Helenor Davisson and Pauline Martindale cheerfully ignore) – approves publication of a new hymnal, *The Voice of Praise: A Collection of Hymns for the Use of The Methodist Protestant Church* • The Colored Methodist Episcopal Church (CMEC) is formally established to provide a separate denominational organization for the black membership of the MECS; William Miles and Richard Vanderhorst are elected as the first two bishops [the denomination's name is changed to Christian Methodist Episcopal Church in 1952] • Dr. and Mrs. Otis Gibson (MEC) establish Mission House in San Francisco for Chinese workers • Thomas Harwood (MEC) is sent to New Mexico and opens a school in Cherry Valley (near Albuquerque)	• Isabella Thoburn and Clara Swain, the first WFMS (MEC) missionaries, arrive in India; other WFMS (MEC) missionaries are sent to China (1871); Mexico, South America, and Bulgaria (1874); Sierra Leone (1875); Japan (1876); Italy (1877); Malaya (1887); Korea (1888); and the Philippines (1903) • The MEC begins mission work in Austria • Methodists begin to emigrate from Britain to New Zealand in some number	**1870**

	A. WORLD HISTORY & POLITICS	B. AMERICAN HISTORY & POLITICS	C. SCIENCE, MEDICINE & TECHNOLOGY	D. DAILY LIFE, POPULAR CULTURE & ENTERTAINMENT
1871	• The Treaty of Frankfurt ends the Franco-Prussian War; France cedes the Alsace-Lorraine to Germany and agrees to pay a large financial indemnity • Germany is united as an empire under Prussian control; King William I of Prussia becomes the kaiser (Emperor) and Otto von Bismarck becomes the first chancellor of the Second Reich of Germany • Rome becomes the capital of the kingdom of Italy; the temporal authority of the Papacy is restricted to a small confined territory, which will later become Vatican City • The Cape Colony annexes Basutoland in south Africa • British Columbia becomes a province of the Dominion of Canada • The British parliament legalizes trade unions in the UK • After an eight-month inland trek from the eastern coast of Africa, American journalist Henry Stanley finds David Livingstone, who has been "missing" (out of contact) with Europe for several years, at his clinic on the shores of Lake Tanganyika: "Dr. Livingstone, I presume?"	• Congress approves the Indian Appropriations Act, which declares that Indian nations will no longer be recognized as independent powers, nullifying all treaties between the US government and Indian nations, and making Indians "wards of the nation" • Congress passes the Ku Klux Klan Act, which grants the federal government the authority to punish the denial of equal protection or privileges and immunities; President Grant then imposes martial law and suspends the writ of habeas corpus in South Carolina • Much of Chicago is destroyed in the great fire that raged for two days and nights, destroying over 17,000 buildings and causing 200 deaths • Apache chief Cochise agrees to peace terms in the Broken Arrow Treaty and moves his nation to a reservation in southern Arizona	• The American Museum of Natural History opens in New York • Simon Ingersoll (US) invents the pneumatic rock drill • Norwegian physician G. H. A. Hansen first identifies the bacillus that causes leprosy and has the dubious distinction of having his name attached to the affliction, now called "Hansen's Disease" • Richard Hoe (US) develops his "web perfecting" press system, which can produce 18,000 sheets an hour, printed on both sides, by employing a continuous roll, or "web," of paper • Charles Darwin publishes *The Descent of Man, and Selection in Relation to Sex*, which makes explicit the application of Darwin's theory of natural selection to human evolution and outlines in detail the theory of sexual selection	• The first musical and theatrical collaboration of W. S. Gilbert and Arthur Sullivan, *Thespis*, opens in London • P. T. Barnum's first traveling circus opens in Brooklyn, featuring Jumbo the elephant and a number of "freak shows" • The Rugby Football Union is organized in England by teams favoring the ball-carrying version of football and adopts the rules then in vogue at Rugby School
1872	• In an attempt to control the power of the Roman Catholic Church, Otto von Bismarck initiates the *Kulturkampf* in Germany • Russia and the Balkan nations succeed in stopping a Turkish plan for reorganization of the Ottoman Empire • Russia, Austria-Hungary, and Germany form The Three Emperors' League to preserve peace among them and to isolate France • The British parliament passes the Ballot Act, providing for voting by secret ballot for the first time • Cetshwayo becomes the last great Zulu king and war leader	• Susan B. Anthony is arrested in New York for attempting to vote for Grant in the presidential election, asserting that the 14th and 15th Amendments entitle her to do so • President Grant's administration regulates work among American Indians to various denominations, beginning government funding of social programs through churches • Yellowstone National Park is created; it is the first designated national park and the beginning of the US national park system • President Grant is reelected and Henry Wilson is elected as vice president (Republican Party)	• American engineer George Westinghouse perfects the automatic railroad air brake • The New England Hospital for Women and Children in Boston opens as a training school for nurses	• Montgomery Ward becomes the first mail-order house, starting with a one-page catalog • The Ancient Arabic Order Nobles of the Mystic Shrine for North America is established in New York; its members, known as "Shriners," are all Master Masons who are devoted to philanthropy and community service • Brewster Higley writes the words that become the popular song "Home on the Range" • The Krewe of Rex is organized in New Orleans and pioneers many elements of the modern Mardi Gras celebration, including the tradition of crowning a "King of Carnival"

E. EDUCATION, LITERATURE & THE FINE ARTS	F. RELIGION, THEOLOGY, PHILOSOPHY & PSYCHOLOGY	G. AMERICAN & UNITED METHODISM	H. BRITISH & WORLD METHODISM	
• Britain's Queen Victoria dedicates the Royal Albert Hall of Arts and Sciences in London as a memorial to her late consort • Richard Wagner completes *Young Siegfried* (later simply *Siegfried*), the third of the four operas that comprise *The Ring of the Nibelung* • Verdi's opera *Aïda* premieres in Cairo, Egypt, to great acclaim, and is received with equal enthusiasm at its European premiere at La Scala in Milan, becoming perhaps Verdi's most popular opera; the "Grand March" is a particular crowd-pleaser • Tchaikovsky completes his *String Quartet No. 1 in D* • Samuel Butler publishes *Erewhon* • Lewis Carroll publishes *Through the Looking Glass*	• The National Council of the Congregational Churches is established • Notable publications include: – Charles Hodge, *Systematic Theology* (3 vols., 1871–73) – Charles Krauth, *Conservative Reformation and Its Theology* – James F. Clarke, *Ten Great Religions*	• The EA General Conference: – repeals a statute prohibiting members from publishing books without first submitting them to a review committee – refuses to formally ban members from joining secret societies but urges preachers to "keep aloof" from them – declines to act on proposals to bring about organic union with the MEC – extends the maximum length of pastoral appointments from two to three years • Union Biblical Seminary is founded by the UBC in Dayton, OH (later becomes United Theological Seminary) • The MPC organizes the North Carolina Colored Mission Conference • Alejo Hernandez, the "Father of Methodism" in Texas and Mexico, is ordained as deacon by the MECS	• A memorial tablet with profile likenesses of John and Charles Wesley is placed in Westminster Abbey, London, in their honor • Robert Moreton is the first ordained WM missionary assigned to Portugal • Restrictions from the 1660s that prohibited Nonconformists (including Methodists) from enrolling as students at Oxford and Cambridge are finally lifted • The UMFC opens Victoria Park College in Manchester as its primary theological training center • The first Methodist worship service in Rome is held on Easter Sunday	**1871**
• James McNeil Whistler completes his famous painting entitled *Arrangement in Grey and Black: Portrait of the Painter's Mother*, better known simply as "Whistler's Mother" • Claude Monet defines and gives a name to artistic "Impressionism" in his painting *Impression, Sunrise* • Tchaikovsky composes his *Symphony No. 2 in C Minor* (*Little Russian*) • Georges Bizet writes his *L'Arlésienne Suite No. 1* from the incidental music to Alphonse Daudet's play of the same name • Notable publications include: – Thomas Hardy, *Under the Greenwood Tree* – George Eliot, *Middlemarch* – Fyodor Dostoyevsky, *The Possessed* – Mark Twain, *Roughing It*	• Friedrich Nietzsche publishes *The Birth of Tragedy* • John Tulloch publishes *Rational Theology and Christian Philosophy in England in the Seventeenth Century* (2 vols.), which focuses on the work of the Cambridge Platonists • F. D. Maurice publishes his history of *Moral and Metaphysical Philosophy* (2 vols.)	• The MEC General Conference: – seats lay (male) delegates, two from each annual conference, as voting members for the first time – makes program boards responsible to General Conference, thus establishing a general agency structure (followed by the MECS two years later) – organizes 8 new annual conferences: Northern New York and Western New York (which absorb the former Black River, Genesee, and East Genesee Conferences), Arkansas, Chicago German, Florida, Lexington, NW Iowa, and Rocky Mountain (total now 86; the MEC now almost entirely overlaps the territory of the MECS [annual conference numbers not noted after this point]) – approves the Woman's Foreign Missionary Society as an official agency of the church and reorganizes the General Mission Committee – declines to elect "colored" bishops, to change the tenure of episcopal office, or to separate "home" and "foreign" mission work – drops the word *colored* out of the *Discipline*, making all ministers eligible for leadership roles based on qualifications rather than race – instructs quarterly conferences to renew licenses to preach annually – declares that dancing, playing games of chance, attending theaters, horse races, and so on, are "imprudent conduct" and that persons guilty of them should be subject to disciplinary action – classifies bishops as "effective" (active) or "non-effective" (superannuated) for the first time • The Methodist churches receive the largest quota of funding from the federal government for the administration of American Indian schools within their (cont.)	• Southlands College is opened in Battersea by the WM Conference; it is the first teacher training college for women in the UK; Westminster College (1851) becomes all-male at this time • Trinity Hall, Southport, opens as a boarding school for the daughters of WM ministers • Gilbert Haven (MEC) visits Mexico and establishes the first Mexican MEC congregations • After the German government adopts a "Dissenter Law," Wesleyan Methodists in Germany withdraw from the state church and begin administering the sacraments; they conduct their first ordination in 1875 • Thomas Jackson publishes his edition of *The Works of the Rev. John Wesley, A.M.* (3rd ed., 14 vols.) • Luke Tyerman publishes his account of *The Life and Times of the Rev. John Wesley, M.A., Founder of the Methodists* (3 vols.)	**1872**

	A. WORLD HISTORY & POLITICS	B. AMERICAN HISTORY & POLITICS	C. SCIENCE, MEDICINE & TECHNOLOGY	D. DAILY LIFE, POPULAR CULTURE & ENTERTAINMENT
1872 cont.				
1873	• Russia annexes Uzbekistan • German troops are withdrawn from Paris, which they have occupied since 1870 • The Meiji government of Japan withdraws sanctions against Christian missionaries, although freedom of religion is not specifically granted • Spain abolishes slavery in its colony of Puerto Rico • Prince Edward Island becomes a province of the Dominion of Canada • Vienna holds an International Exposition that is the greatest up to that time; the buildings erected in the Prater, the famous Viennese park on an island in the Danube, house almost 26,000 exhibits and more than 6.5 million visitors attend	• In the "Slaughterhouse Cases" originating in Louisiana, the US Supreme Court draws a distinction between federal and state citizenship rights, holding that the 14th Amendment does not deprive any US state of its legal jurisdiction over the civil rights of its citizens or of its regulatory powers • The US informally abandons bimetallism and adopts the gold standard for its currency, although the action is not formalized until 1900 • Ellen Swallow Richards, the first woman to be admitted to the Massachusetts Institute of Technology, earns her BS degree; she becomes the first female professional chemist in the US	• Congress passes the Comstock Act, making it a federal crime to import or distribute any device, medicine, or information designed to prevent conception or induce abortion; 24 US states then enact their own versions of Comstock laws to restrict the contraceptive trade on a state level • James Clerk Maxwell publishes *Electricity and Magnetism*	• Joseph E. Glidden perfects the manufacture of barbed wire, which quickly leads to the demise of the "open range" of the West as ranchers fence in their pastures • The ice cream soda is invented when a scoop of ice cream is accidentally dropped into flavored soda water by a counter clerk at James W. Tuff's soda fountain in Philadelphia
1874	• Fiji comes under British control • Bolivia and Chile settle a dispute about the border between them • Faced with the prospect of the bankruptcy of the Ottoman Empire, European creditors agree to restructure its debt • David Livingstone dies in Africa; Henry Stanley continues the explorations of his friend, leading an expedition into the interior of Africa and following the Congo River all the way to its mouth at the Atlantic Ocean, which he reaches in 1877	• The Woman's Christian Temperance Union (WCTU) is formed; Annie Wittenmyer is its first president and Frances Willard is chosen corresponding secretary • Blanche K. Bruce, an ex-slave from Mississippi, is the first black elected to the US Senate • The US Supreme Court rules in *Minor v. Happersett* that the state of Missouri has the constitutional right to deny a woman the right to vote because the Missouri state constitution limits voting to males, holding that since the right to vote is not among the privileges guaranteed to all US citizens it is therefore not protected by the 14th Amendment • William T. Sherman leads US Army forces during the "Red River War" in Texas involving more than 14 separate battles *(cont.)*	• The first structural steel bridge is completed; engineered by James Eads, it spans the Mississippi River in St. Louis • William Blackstone builds the first mechanical clothes washing machine • Robert Wood Johnson begins to make and sell antiseptic bandages and wound dressings • E. F. Remington & Sons, better known for making firearms and sewing machines, begins the commercial production of office typewriters, using the patented design of Christopher Sholes	• The first game of lawn tennis in the US is played on the grounds of the Staten Island Cricket and Baseball Club • Henry Solomon introduces pressure-cooking methods for canning foods • A cartoon by Thomas Nash in *Harper's Weekly* establishes the elephant as the symbol of the Republican Party

E. EDUCATION, LITERATURE & THE FINE ARTS	F. RELIGION, THEOLOGY, PHILOSOPHY & PSYCHOLOGY	G. AMERICAN & UNITED METHODISM	H. BRITISH & WORLD METHODISM	
		mission fields; this policy continues until the 1892 General Conference when it is deemed a violation between the separation of church and state, but actual funding continues into the early 20th century • Cookman Institute is founded by the Freedmen's Aid and Southern Education Society (MEC) in Jacksonville, FL • The AMEC General Conference prohibits local preachers from serving on official boards		1872 cont.
• Timothy O'Sullivan's great photographs of Canyon de Chelley mark a major turning point in the development of photography as art • Brahms composes his *String Quartet No. 1* and his *Variations on a Theme by Joseph Haydn* • Verdi completes his *String Quartet in E Minor* • Claude Monet completes his painting *Poppies; near Argenteuil* • Notable publications include: –Jules Verne, *Around the World in Eighty Days* – Ambrose Bierce, *The Fiend's Delight*	• A group of conservatives withdraw from the Protestant Episcopal Church after disagreement over certain sacramental and ritualistic practices to establish the Reformed Episcopal Church • Isaac Mayer Wise establishes The Union of American Hebrew Congregations, the major organization of Reform Jews in the US • Wilhelm Wundt publishes his *Principles of Physiological Psychology* (2 vols. 1873–74)	• The UBC General Conference: – reaffirms prohibitions against secret society membership – votes to refer to the membership of the churches a proposal in favor of lay representation, triggering an argument about how such a vote should be taken, which sidetracks the issue – receives reports of progress in the Africa mission but difficulty in the German mission – decides that the centennial of the church should be observed in 1874, since Otterbein had become the pastor of an independent congregation in 1774 • Union Biblical Institute is founded at Naperville, IL, by the EA; it opens for classes in 1876; the name is later changed to Evangelical Theological Seminary • Vanderbilt University in Nashville, originally chartered in 1872, is established by the MECS after the gift of a $1-million endowment by Cornelius Vanderbilt; it opens for classes in 1875, and its theological department quickly becomes the principal seminary for training MECS ministers • The UBC's Sarah A. Dickey opens Mt. Hermon Seminary for black girls in Mississippi • Anna Howard Shaw receives a local preacher's license from the Big Rapids (MI) District of the MEC • Bennett and Wiley Colleges are founded by the Freedmen's Aid and Southern Education Society (MEC) • The MEC organizes the Florida Conference	• Kingswood School is reorganized as an upper school with Woodhouse Grove School as its junior department • William and Clementina Rowe Butler establish an MEC mission in northern Mexico • Alejo Hernandez is ordained as elder by the MECS, becoming its first Hispanic Methodist minister, and organizes the first MECS congregation in Mexico City • John Keener establishes an MECS mission in southern Mexico • Charles A. Fulwood (MECS) inaugurates the first Methodist work in Cuba • Robert S. Maclay (MEC) establishes the first Methodist mission in Japan	1873
• The University of Basel considers and rejects a proposal to admit women to doctoral programs; one of the few professors to argue and vote in favor of it was Friedrich Nietzsche • The first major exhibition of Impressionist paintings is held in Paris, including works by Claude Monet, Pierre-Auguste Renoir, Camille Pissaro, Alfred Sisley, Paul Cézanne, Édouard Manet, Edgar Degas, and Berthe Morisot • Richard Wagner completes *The Twilight of the Gods* (originally entitled *The Death of Siegfried*), the last of the four operas that comprise *The Ring of the Nibelung* • Verdi's soaring *Requiem*, composed in honor of his friend Alessandro Manzoni, is performed for the first time in Milan • Modest Mussorgsky composes his piano suite *Pictures at an Exhibition*, and his *(cont.)*	• The American Evangelical Lutheran Church (AELC) is established by Danish immigrants in Wisconsin • Frances Havergal writes her well-known hymn, "Take My Life and Let It Be" • Charles Hodge publishes *What is Darwinianism?*	• The MECS General Conference: – appoints a commission to meet with a similar commission of the MEC "to remove all obstacles to formal fraternity between the two churches"; the MEC appoints a similar commission in 1876 – organizes the German Mission Conference – frees the Board of Missions from domestic responsibilities to concentrate on overseas work and makes home missions the responsibility of the annual conferences – defeats a proposal to create a missionary agency for the women of the church – notes that the 1866 General Conference did not abolish class meetings, but made attendance a matter of conscience rather than church law – rejects calls for reunion with the MEC in favor of fraternal relations	• The Australasian WM Conference begins following the American pattern, meeting as General Conference every three years, with four annual conferences: New South Wales & Queensland, Victoria & Tasmania, South Australia & West Australia, and New Zealand • The Wesleyan Methodist Church in Canada (WMCC, 1833/1847) and the Wesleyan Methodist Conference of Eastern British America unite, along with some smaller groups, to form the Methodist Church in Canada (MCC) • James H. Rigg publishes *The Living Wesley*	1874

	A. WORLD HISTORY & POLITICS	B. AMERICAN HISTORY & POLITICS	C. SCIENCE, MEDICINE & TECHNOLOGY	D. DAILY LIFE, POPULAR CULTURE & ENTERTAINMENT
1874 cont.		against the Arapaho, Comanche, Cheyenne, and Kiowa nations, culminating in their defeat at Palo Duro Canyon in the Texas Panhandle; after their surrender, these tribes are forced onto the reservation lands in the southwestern portion of the Indian Territory set aside for them in the Medicine Lodge Treaty of 1867 • George A. Custer, commanding the US Seventh Cavalry, violates the Fort Laramie Treaty of 1868 by entering the Black Hills on a surveying expedition, during which gold is discovered on Lakota (Sioux) lands, triggering a gold rush by white explorers and settlers		
1875	• In a territorial exchange, Russia cedes the Kurile Islands to Japan, receiving Sakhalin Island in return • The Balkan Rebellion begins; Slavs in the Ottoman provinces of Bosnia and Herzegovina rebel, supported by Montenegro, Serbia, and Russia • The First Spanish Republic comes to an end with the restoration of the monarchy; King Alfonso XII, son of the deposed Isabella II, takes the throne • An independence movement begins in Ireland	• Blanche K. Bruce (Republican) of Mississippi becomes the first black senator to serve a full six-year term in the US Senate (not until 1969 did another black American serve in the US Senate) • Congress passes the Civil Rights Act of 1875, which prohibits racial discrimination on juries and in public accommodations, excluding public schools • American Express adopts the first private pension plan in American industry	• The International Bureau of Weights and Measures is established; 17 European countries adopt the metric system • The (second) Public Health Act in Britain transfers responsibility for water and sewer safety from central to local government, even in the urban areas; local authorities now must pay for all services, with the taxes now drawn from local ratepayers • The first commercial oil field in California is discovered at Pico Canyon in Los Angeles County • Heinrich Schliemann publishes the account of his archaeological excavations of Troy in *Troy and Its Remains*	• The Westminster Kennel Club is formed in New York; it holds its first dog show in 1877 • The first running of the Kentucky Derby is won by Aristides • Harvard and Yale play a football game for the first time; they use rules established by Harvard, which are similar to those of British and Canadian rugby football
1876	• Japan breaks Korean isolation by forcing a trade treaty upon Korea • Britain's Queen Victoria is declared to be Empress of India • Serbia and Montenegro declare war on the Ottoman Empire, prompting a rebellion against Ottoman rule in Bulgaria, which is quickly suppressed • A group of liberal reformers called the "Young Turks" force the Sultan of the Ottoman Empire to resign and his successor to adopt a new progressive constitution • The British occupy the city of Quetta in Pakistan as a block to southward expansion by Russia	• The US celebrates its centennial, marking the 100th anniversary of the Declaration of Independence • The "International Exhibition of Arts, Manufactures, and Products of the Soil and Mine," the first great American international exposition, is held in Philadelphia to celebrate the centennial • Lakota (Sioux) and Cheyenne Indian warriors under Crazy Horse and Sitting Bull destroy the US Seventh Cavalry, commanded by George Custer, at the Battle of the Little Bighorn • The US breaks the 1868 Fort Laramie Treaty with the Lakota, Dakota, and Nakota (Sioux) Nations and opens much of their sacred Black Hills territory to homesteading and gold mining by white settlers • The US also breaks the 1871 Broken Arrow Treaty with the Apache Nation and confiscates the Apache Reservation in *(cont.)*	• Alexander Graham Bell invents the telephone and establishes the American Telephone and Telegraph Co. (AT&T) • Robert Koch discovers anthrax bacillus • French physician Augustus Desiré Waller successfully records the first electrocardiogram of a human heart • British engineer Dougald Clerk develops the first successful two-stroke gasoline-powered internal combustion engine • German engineer Nicolaus August Otto builds the first successful four-stroke gasoline-powered internal combustion engine, called the "Otto Cycle Engine," and immediately builds it into a motorcycle	• Daniel Peter, a Swiss candy maker, develops milk chocolate by adding condensed milk to chocolate liquor • Thomas Lipton opens his first tea shop in Glasgow • Professional baseball's National League is organized • The E. Anheuser Brewing Company of St. Louis (later Anheuser-Busch) introduces Budweiser lager beer to the US market • Representatives from Harvard, Yale, Columbia, and Princeton meet to form the Intercollegiate Football Association and develop a new set of "American-style" football rules • Andrew Culver opens the Oriental Hotel, inaugurating the era of opulent hotels at Coney Island

E. EDUCATION, LITERATURE & THE FINE ARTS	F. RELIGION, THEOLOGY, PHILOSOPHY & PSYCHOLOGY	G. AMERICAN & UNITED METHODISM	H. BRITISH & WORLD METHODISM	
operatic masterpiece, *Boris Godunov*, premieres to great acclaim in Moscow • Thomas Hardy publishes *Far From the Madding Crowd*		– approves a constitutional amendment to prohibit the use of alcoholic beverages by any member; the amendment is not approved by the annual conferences • The MECS publishes revised and enlarged editions of both the 1847 *Collection of Hymns* and the 1851 *Songs of Zion* • The MPC General Conference: – abolishes the order of deacon and strikes its form of ordination from the *Discipline* – agrees to a proposal from the separatist Methodist Church (1858) for appointment of a joint commission to consider possible reunion – exchanges fraternal greetings with General Conferences of the MEC and MECS – approves creation of a theological department at Western Maryland College • Woman's Parent Mite Missionary Society (AMEC) is organized • The MEC organizes the West Texas Conference and creates a Mexican Border District • The Chautauqua Institution is established by John Vincent as (initially) an attempt to educate Methodist Sunday school teachers • The AMEC is established in the Dominican Republic		**1874 cont.**
• Construction of the Paris Opéra, begun in 1861, is finally completed • Claude Monet paints his Impressionist masterpiece *Boating at Argenteuil* • Antonín Dvořák composes his sublime *Serenade for Strings* • Tchaikovsky composes his *Piano Concerto No. 1 in B Flat Minor* • Bizet's *Carmen*, a landmark in the history of French opera due to its melodic vitality and rhythmic energy, premieres in Paris • Edvard Grieg composes his *Peer Gynt Suite* as incidental music for the Henrik Ibsen play • Camille Saint-Saëns writes his *Allegro Appassionato for Cello and Piano in B Minor* • Louisa May Alcott publishes *Eight Cousins* • William Dean Howells publishes *A Foregone Conclusion*	• Dwight L. Moody begins holding mass evangelical revival meetings in major American cities; marks a new way of "marketing" religion to the public at large • The Presbyterian Church in Canada is formed by union of four sections of Presbyterianism in Canada • Representatives of Presbyterian churches across Europe and North America meet in London to establish "The Alliance of the Reformed Churches throughout the World holding the Presbyterian System" • Hebrew Union College, the first Jewish college in the US, is established in Cincinnati as the major training center for Reformed Judaism • William Burt Pope publishes his *Compendium of Christian Theology*	• The EA General Conference: – approves a proposal from the Board of Missions to establish a mission in Japan – organizes three conferences specifically for German-speaking people • Pauline Martindale is ordained elder in the Kansas Conference of the MPC; she is the first woman to be ordained elder in full connection in any branch of American Methodism • UBC women organize the Woman's Missionary Association • The MEC Board of Church Extension creates a Department of Architecture	• George Brown extends Australasian WM missions from Samoa, Fiji, and Tonga to New Guinea • Leys School is established in Cambridge to prepare the sons of Methodists for study at Oxford or Cambridge (daughters are still barred from university) • After adoption of a "Dissenter Law" by the Swedish parliament in 1873, allowing freedom of worship, Methodists in Sweden withdraw from the state church • The EA establishes a Publishing House in Stuttgart, Germany (the ancestor of all subsequent German Methodist publishing operations)	**1875**
• The Philadelphia Museum of Art is established as a result of the Centennial International Exhibition • John Singer Sargent, who is studying art in Paris, meets and is deeply influenced by Claude Monet • The first complete production of Wagner's *The Ring of the Nibelung* (often called the Ring Cycle) opens the first Bayreuth Festival in Germany • Bedřich Smetana composes his *String Quartet No. 1 in E Minor (From My Life)* • Mark Twain publishes *The Adventures of Tom Sawyer* • Degas completes his painting of *The Ballerina*	• Felix Adler establishes the Society for Ethical Culture in New York City • What will come to be called the Niagara Bible Conference meets for the first time; it defends the verbal inspiration and inerrancy of the Bible and promotes holiness and premillennialism • The Presbyterian Church of England is created by the union of the United Presbyterian Church of Scotland (1847) with numerous Scottish and English Presbyterian congregations • Herbert Spencer begins publication of his *Principles of Sociology* (3 vols., 1876–96) • Pierre Joseph Proudhon's *What Is Property?* inaugurates the modern anarchist movement • Leslie Stephen publishes his magisterial account of *The History of English Thought in the Eighteenth Century* (2 vols.)	• The MEC General Conference: – approves the division of annual conferences along racial lines and organizes the Central Alabama and Savannah Conferences – appoints a commission to meet with a similar commission of the MECS to discuss fraternal relations between the two churches – appoints a committee to study the matter of lay delegation to annual conferences and submit a proposal to the ensuing General Conference – adopts a policy allowing for the sale of the buildings and property of abandoned churches with the proceeds going to the annual conference – issues strong pronouncements against the use of tobacco and "distilled, fermented, and vinous liquors" – declines proposal to elect presiding elders • The AMEC General Conference authorizes creation of Education and Sunday school departments	• John Ranson is the first official MECS missionary sent to Brazil, following the immigration of many MECS members there after the American Civil War • The MEC mission conferences in both Sweden and Norway are organized as annual conferences • Andrew Cartwright establishes the AMEZC mission in Liberia, later expanded to the Gold Coast (Ghana) and Nigeria • The first group of EA missionaries arrive in Japan	**1876**

	A. WORLD HISTORY & POLITICS	B. AMERICAN HISTORY & POLITICS	C. SCIENCE, MEDICINE & TECHNOLOGY	D. DAILY LIFE, POPULAR CULTURE & ENTERTAINMENT
1876 cont.		southern Arizona; Geronimo leads many Apache warriors into northern Mexico and begins raiding white settlements • Samuel Tilden (Democratic Party) receives more popular votes for president than Rutherford B. Hayes (Republican Party) but neither achieves an electoral college majority; as a result the disputed election is thrown into the House of Representatives for resolution • Colorado is admitted to the US as the 38th state		
1877	• The last Russo-Turkish War begins when Russia declares war on the Ottoman Empire; Russia invades Romania and Bulgaria • Britain annexes the South African Republic (Transvaal), which has been torn by chronic conflict between the Boers (Afrikaners) and the Zulus since the 1840s • Porfiro Diaz becomes president of Mexico, a position that he retains until 1911	• In the "Compromise of 1877," Southern congressmen agree to elect Rutherford B. Hayes as president and William Wheeler as vice president in return for promises that they will end Reconstruction and abandon Republican efforts to assure civil rights for blacks in the South; as a result, in what blacks call the "Great Betrayal," Federal troops are withdrawn from the Southern states; this leads to the collapse of the remaining Republican state governments in the South, the rise of the solid Democratic South, and the beginning of the "Jim Crow" era • Chief Joseph leads his Nez Percé Indian tribe on a 1,500-mile trek from Oregon through Idaho and Montana toward Canada before they are finally stopped by US troops 30 miles south of the Canadian border, forced to surrender, and confined to a reservation in Idaho; his legendary surrender speech has gone down in history: "Hear me, my chiefs, I am tired; my heart is sick and sad. From where the sun now stands, I will fight no more forever." • The Cheyenne people of the Northern Plains surrender to the US Army and are exiled to a reservation in the Indian Territory • A national strike by railroad workers evokes widespread sympathy, but the strike is broken by federal troops dispatched by President Hayes • Congress passes the Desert Land Act, which offers 640-acre tracts of land in parts of the West for $1.25 an acre with only 25¢ an acre down, providing that the buyer pledges to irrigate at least part of it	• Thomas Edison invents the process of recording sound by translating the vibrations of a diaphragm (a crude microphone) into the movements of a needle on a rotating wax cylinder • Robert Koch develops a technique whereby bacteria can be stained and identified	• The first tennis tournament at Wimbledon, England, is held • International cricket marks its beginning from the first "test match" during the English national cricket team's tour of Australia

E. EDUCATION, LITERATURE & THE FINE ARTS	F. RELIGION, THEOLOGY, PHILOSOPHY & PSYCHOLOGY	G. AMERICAN & UNITED METHODISM	H. BRITISH & WORLD METHODISM	
		• The AMEZC removes the word *male* from its regulations for ordination but does not actually ordain a woman as deacon until 1896 • Representatives of the MEC and the MECS meet at Cape May, NJ; they issue the "Cape May Declaration," which asserts that the MEC and the MECS are each "a legitimate branch of Episcopal Methodism in the United States, having a common origin in the Methodist Episcopal Church organized in 1784" • Anna Oliver is the first woman in the US to receive a theological degree (from Boston School of Theology) • The EA opens Union Bible Institute in Naperville, IL; later the name is changed to Evangelical Theological Seminary • The West Texas Conference (MEC) establishes Andrews Normal School, later Sam Houston College, in Houston • The Freedmen's Aid and Southern Education Society (MEC) establishes a medical department at Central Tennessee College (1867); it is the first medical school for the training of black doctors in the US [it will become Meharry Medical Center in 1900] • Matthew Simpson publishes his *Cyclopedia of Methodism*, the first major encyclopedic reference work on Methodism (revised edition 1880)		**1876 cont.**
• Howard University is established in Washington, DC • Tchaikovsky's ballet *Swan Lake* has its premiere at Moscow's Bolshoi Theatre • Degas invites Mary Cassatt to join the group of artists now known as the Impressionists • Brahms composes his *Symphony No. 2 in D* • Saint-Saëns completes his opera *Samson et Dalila* • William Morris publishes *The Decorative Arts, Their Relation To Modern Life And Progress*, which gives basic definition to the values and principles of the "Arts and Crafts" movement • Other notable publications include: – Leo Tolstoy, *Anna Karenina* – Henry James, *The American* – Anna Sewell, *Black Beauty*	• Philip Schaff publishes his great edition of *The Creeds of Christendom* (3 vols.) • Other notable publications include: – Harriet Beecher Stowe, *Footsteps of the Master* – Charles Sanders Peirce, *The Fixation of Belief*	• The UBC General Conference: – again reaffirms a policy of strict enforcement of the prohibitions against secret society membership – again resists movement toward democratization, defeating proposals for pro rata representation and lay representation in General Conference – agrees that an annual conference may admit laymen whenever two-thirds of the members favor the move – officially recognizes the Woman's Missionary Association, established in 1875 • The divided branches (1858) of the MPC reunite as the Methodist Protestant Church • Maggie Elliot is ordained as an elder in full connection by the Missouri Conference of the MPC • Anna Oliver is invited to preach at a weekly preacher's meeting in New York; the invitation is withdrawn after vehement objections spearheaded by James M. Buckley • The West Texas Conference (MEC) establishes Tillotson Collegiate and Normal Institute, later Tillotson College, in Austin • The MEC organizes the Northwest Swedish Conference • Kanichi Miyama is appointed by the MEC to work with Japanese laborers in California • The first Hispanic Methodist church building in the US is constructed by the MECS in Key West, FL	• William Taylor (MEC) brings Methodism to Chile and Peru • Emily Beekin is sent to Sierra Leone as the first missionary of the Woman's Missionary Association (UBC) • Reutlingen Theological Seminary is founded in Germany by the EA	**1877**

	A. WORLD HISTORY & POLITICS	B. AMERICAN HISTORY & POLITICS	C. SCIENCE, MEDICINE & TECHNOLOGY	D. DAILY LIFE, POPULAR CULTURE & ENTERTAINMENT
1878	• Russian and Bulgarian forces defeat the Ottoman Turks at Shipka Pass; Russia seizes Adrianople • The British fleet sails to Constantinople to support the Ottomans and halt the Russians • At the Congress of Berlin, the Ottoman Empire is forced to give up most of its European territory; Serbia, Romania, and Montenegro become independent states; Bulgaria receives broad autonomy; Bosnia and Herzegovina are annexed to the Austro-Hungarian Empire; Britain acquires control of Cyprus; Russia acquires territory around the Black Sea • War breaks out again between Britain and Afghanistan • Paris holds its third Exposition Universelle on the Champs du Mars; the Palais de Trocadéro, built for the occasion, remains a permanent structure until it is torn down in 1936; the exposition houses almost 53,000 exhibits and attracts more than 16 million visitors	• New Haven, CT, is the site of the first fully functional telephone system in the US • A Woman Suffrage Amendment is introduced in the US Congress; the wording is unchanged in 1919, when the amendment finally passes both houses • A number of Northern Cheyenne led by Dull Knife escape from their reservation in Oklahoma and head back to their homeland on the Northern Plains; although caught by US troops after six weeks, they are allowed to stay in the North and are eventually granted reservation lands in Montana	• Thomas Edison patents the first practical phonograph; sound is reproduced when a wax cylinder is rotated against a needle, which moves up and down in the grooves of the cylinder, producing vibrations that are amplified by a conical horn	• W. S. Gilbert and Arthur Sullivan's musical H.M.S. *Pinafore* opens in London • A. A. Pope manufactures the first bicycles in America • Hawaii's Princess Liliuokalani composes the song *Aloha Oe*, usually translated as "Farewell to Thee," which comes to be synonymous with Hawaiian identity
1879	• The Zulu War begins in south Africa; at the Battle of Isandhlwana, 10,000 Zulu warriors armed with spears annihilate 1,800 British soldiers, but the war ends with the defeat of the Zulu army by the British at Ulundi and the capture of Cetshwayo, breaking Zulu military power permanently • British forces seize Afghanistan, forcing the Afghans to cede control of the Khyber Pass and other key areas to the British • Bolivia rescinds Chile's access to key nitrate (guano) deposits; Chile then declares war on Bolivia and Peru, beginning the War of the Pacific (to 1884)	• Professional land developers called "boomers" begin to organize "Oklahoma colonies," or communities of white settlers, in the Indian Territory • Belva Ann Lockwood becomes the first woman to argue a case before the US Supreme Court • The first municipal electric lighting system is installed in Cleveland, OH	• Thomas Edison patents the incandescent electric lightbulb • George Westinghouse develops the first telephone substation, a "hierarchical" automated switching system that can route telephone calls to a central exchange, laying the groundwork for large telephone networks • The United States Geological Survey (USGS) is established as a research agency of the US Department of the Interior; it is responsible for mapping the geology, hydrology, and topography of the country	• W. S. Gilbert and Arthur Sullivan open *The Pirates of Penzance* in New York instead of London, thus securing US copyright and royalties • London's first telephone exchange is established • F. W. Woolworth opens his first "five and ten cent" variety store • James and John Ritty invent a "cash register" for their Ohio saloon that displays the amount of each sale and keeps a running total (a drawer to hold cash is added later) • Daniel Peter and Henri Nestlé join together to form the Nestlé Company, which soon dominates European chocolate-making
1880	• France annexes Tahiti as a colony • The Boers (Afrikaners) in the Transvaal revolt against British rule and proclaim a new republic, beginning the First Boer War • Chile captures significant coastal territory from both Bolivia and Peru • The major European nations and the US agree to recognize the independence of Morocco and to maintain equal trade access	• The US census reports that the population is 50,155,783: – whites: 43,402,970 (86.6%) – blacks: 6,580,793 (13.1%) – other: 172,020 (0.3%) • The US national debt is $2,120,415,370 • James Garfield is elected as president and Chester A. Arthur as vice president (Republican Party)	• John Milne and colleagues in Britain develop the first accurate modern seismograph	• The British Perforated Paper Company develops and markets recognizably modern toilet paper • James Bonsaak patents an automatic cigarette-making machine, making possible mass production of cigarettes

E. EDUCATION, LITERATURE & THE FINE ARTS	F. RELIGION, THEOLOGY, PHILOSOPHY & PSYCHOLOGY	G. AMERICAN & UNITED METHODISM	H. BRITISH & WORLD METHODISM	
• The University of London becomes the first major university in Britain to admit women to regular undergraduate degree studies; Cambridge follows in 1881 and Oxford in 1883 • Boston's Handel and Haydn Society gives the first American performance of Verdi's *Requiem* • Notable publications include: – Henry James, *Daisy Miller* – Thomas Hardy, *The Return of the Native*	• Pope Pius IX dies; he is succeeded by Pope Leo XIII • Charles Sanders Peirce publishes his important essay "How to Make Our Ideas Clear" in the magazine *Popular Science Monthly*; it is widely considered to mark the beginning of American Pragmatism	• The MECS General Conference: – acts to deal with the financial distress of the Publishing House – adopts a standard reading list for the course of study for preachers comparable to that established for the MEC in 1848 – organizes and recognizes the MECS Woman's Foreign Missionary Society (WFMS) – admits the former Illinois Conference of the MEC into full membership in the MECS – decides to participate in the Ecumenical Methodist Conference planned for 1881 • The MEC publishes the new *Hymnal of the Methodist Episcopal Church* • The MEC organizes the Little Rock Conference • The MPC organizes Colorado-Texas Colored Mission Conference • The CMEC General Conference recognizes "Alice Courtney, Evangelist"; this is the first record of such recognition of a female preacher	• Laymen are accepted into and seated in the British WM Conference for the first time • The sundered branches of Methodism in Ireland unite to form The Methodist Church in Ireland (MCI); it covers the entire island (including Northern Ireland) and maintains close ties to British Methodism • The EA begins mission work among German-speaking people in the Alsace-Lorraine region of France and Germany • Wesley Memorial Church in Oxford is completed and dedicated • William Booth's ministry in East London, established in 1865, formally takes the name "The Salvation Army" • Lochie Rankin goes to China as the first missionary of the WFMS (MECS)	**1878**
• The Rabelais Club is founded in London and holds a literary dinner once every two months; high-profile members included novelists Henry James, Thomas Hardy, Bret Harte, Oliver Wendell Holmes, Walter Besant, and George Du Maurier • Bedřich Smetana completes his cycle of symphonic poems entitled *Ma Vlast (My Country)*, including *The Moldau* • Tchaikovsky's opera *Eugene Onegin* premieres in Moscow • Henrik Ibsen's play *A Doll's House* premieres at Copenhagen's Royal Theatre • Henry M. Turner publishes his historical account *Emigration of the Colored People of the United States* • Other notable publications include: – Henry James, *Daisy Miller* – August Strindberg, *The Red Room*	• Mary Baker Eddy establishes the Church of Christ, Scientist, becoming the first woman to found a major religion • John Henry Newman is made cardinal by Pope Leo XIII	• The EA General Conference: – orders preparation of a new catechism, which is to be printed in both German and English – approves a proposal to change the name of the EA to "The Evangelical Church of North America"; the proposal is voted down by the annual conferences – rejects a proposal to station bishops by episcopal areas – rescinds the 1867 action making the general church officers *ex officio* members of General Conference – tightens the system for granting exhorter's licenses • Anna Oliver is recommended for ordination as deacon by the MEC New England Conference; the presiding bishop, Edward G. Andrews, declines to submit the matter to a vote of conference because, in his judgment, church law does not permit the ordination of women; from this decision Presiding Elder Lorenzo R. Thayer appeals to the following General Conference, thus creating the famous "Test Case" concerning the ordination of women • The women of the MPC establish the MPC Woman's Foreign Missionary Society (WFMS) • The MEC organizes the West and St. Louis German Conferences • The MPC organizes the Alabama-Mississippi Conference	• James M. Thoburn begins MEC work in Burma, primarily around Rangoon and in lower Burma	**1879**
• Auguste Rodin completes the sculpture for which he is best known: *The Thinker* • Offenbach's operatic masterpiece, *The Tales of Hoffmann*, including the famous "Barcarolle," remains unfinished at his death; it is orchestrated by his friend Ernest Guiraud and premieres in Paris in 1881 • Tchaikovsky completes his bombastic *1812 Overture*, commemorating Russia's victory over France in the Napoleonic Wars *(cont.)*	• Former Methodist preacher Daniel S. Warner establishes The Church of God (Anderson, IN) • The Society of Biblical Literature (SBL) is established • Albrecht Ritschl begins the publication of his *History of Pietism* (3 vols., 1880–86)	• The MEC opens Methodist Episcopal Hospital in Brooklyn, NY; it is the first of many Methodist hospitals built in the US and abroad • The MEC General Conference: – refuses to approve the ordination of women in the "Test Case" involving Anna Oliver and Anna Howard Shaw – decides that "the masculine pronouns 'he,' 'his,' and 'him,' wherever they occur in the *Discipline*, shall not be construed as *(cont.)*	• The Salvation Army spreads to the US and Australia, then throughout the world: France (1881); Canada and India (1882); Sri Lanka, Pakistan, southern Africa, and New Zealand (1883) • The WFMS (MPC) sends Harriett G. Brittan to Yokohama, Japan, as its first missionary	**1880**

	A. WORLD HISTORY & POLITICS	B. AMERICAN HISTORY & POLITICS	C. SCIENCE, MEDICINE & TECHNOLOGY	D. DAILY LIFE, POPULAR CULTURE & ENTERTAINMENT
1880 cont.				
1881	• Russia seizes control of Turkmenistan from Persia • Tsar Alexander II of Russia is assassinated; he is succeeded by his son, Alexander III, who attempts to reverse the liberalizing reforms implemented by his father and to restore the absolutism of Tsar Nicholas I • A wave of anti-Jewish pogroms in Russia and eastern Europe causes the mass emigration of eastern European Jews (2.5 million Jews settle in the US; thousands settle in Palestine) • The First Boer War ends with the defeat of British forces at Majuba Hill; Britain grants the Transvaal internal self-government • France seizes control of Tunisia from the Ottoman Empire	• President Garfield is assassinated by deranged attorney Charles J. Guiteau, a "disappointed office seeker" who blamed Garfield for his problems; Vice President Arthur becomes president • The US Supreme Court rules in *Springer v. US* that the federal income tax instituted in 1862 is constitutional • The Federation of Organized Trades and Labor Unions is organized (it will later become the American Federation of Labor)	• The second transcontinental railroad is completed across the US by the linking of the Southern Pacific Railroad with the Atchison, Topeka, and Santa Fe Railroad at Deming in New Mexico Territory • Construction begins on the Canadian Pacific Railway connecting Montreal, Quebec, with Vancouver, British Columbia, on the Pacific Coast (completed in 1865) • Austrian-born British inventor David Gestetner establishes the Gestetner Cyclograph Company to manufacture and market his stencil duplicator, which for the first time makes possible the efficient production of multiple copies of office documents, in effect serving as a "short run" printing press for individuals and groups of all sorts, enabling them to produce and distribute documents quickly and easily	• P. T. Barnum merges his circus with that of rival showman James Bailey to create the Barnum and Bailey Circus, which becomes internationally famous as "The Greatest Show on Earth" • The Fourteenth Street Theater in New York City becomes the first vaudeville theater to advertise and feature "clean, family-friendly entertainment"; it is a great success • Clara Barton founds the American Red Cross, which receives a congressional charter in 1900

E. EDUCATION, LITERATURE & THE FINE ARTS	F. RELIGION, THEOLOGY, PHILOSOPHY & PSYCHOLOGY	G. AMERICAN & UNITED METHODISM	H. BRITISH & WORLD METHODISM	
(complete with orchestrated cannon fire and cathedral bells), and his sublime *Serenade for Strings* • Brahms composes his *Academic Festival Overture* and his *Tragic Overture* • Dvořák completes his *Symphony No. 6 in D Major* • Dostoyevsky publishes his immortal *The Brothers Karamazov* • Other notable publications include: – Mark Twain, *A Tramp Abroad* – Joel Chandler Harris, *Uncle Remus, His Songs and His Sayings* – Lew Wallace, *Ben-Hur: A Tale of the Christ*		excluding women from the office of Sunday school superintendent, class leader, or steward," but the decision is declared unconstitutional by the bishops – adopts a revised "Ecclesiastical Code" relating to church trials – organizes Indian Mission Conference, Northwest Norwegian Conference, and East Tennessee Conference – approves the adoption of the International Lesson Series for use in Sunday schools • Anna Howard Shaw, having been denied ordination in the MEC, joins the MPC and is ordained elder by the MPC's New York Conference • The MPC General Conference: – seats Thomas Wells as the first black General Conference delegate – receives Mrs. J. H. Claney of the Woman's Foreign Missionary Society as the first woman to address the Conference in an official capacity – appoints delegates to the forthcoming Methodist Ecumenical Conference – moves to reorganize the Book Concern of the unified church – declines to take any action with regard to Freemasonry • The University of Southern California, founded under MEC auspices, opens for classes in Los Angeles • The MECS publishes revised editions of the separate 1874 *Collection of Hymns* and *Songs of Zion* in one volume as *The New Hymnbook* • Antonio Diaz begins MEC mission work among Hispanics in Los Angeles • AMEC missions and evangelism below the Mason-Dixon Line push its membership to over 400,000 • The WFMS (MECS) begins publication of *The Woman's Missionary Advocate* (to 1910)		**1880 cont.**
• Booker T. Washington founds the Normal and Industrial Institute for Negroes (later the Tuskegee Institute) in Tuskegee, AL • Atlanta Baptist Female Seminary, the first institution of higher education for black women, is established in Atlanta; the name is changed to Spelman Seminary in 1894 and then to Spelman College in 1924 • The Boston Symphony Orchestra is established • Brahms's *Piano Concerto No. 2* premieres in Budapest • Tchaikovsky's *Violin Concerto* debuts in Vienna • Degas exhibits *The Little Fourteen-Year-Old Dancer* at the sixth Impressionist Exhibition in Paris; the wax sculpture, wearing a real tulle skirt and horsehair wig tied with a silk ribbon, causes a scandal because of its "naturalistic" depiction of the young model • Frederick Douglass publishes the final version of his autobiography, *The Life and Times of Frederick Douglass* • Jefferson Davis publishes *The Rise and Fall of the Confederate Government*, his apologia for the "Lost Cause" • Other notable publications include: – Mark Twain, *The Prince and the Pauper* – Henry James, *The Portrait of a Lady*	• B. F. Westcott and F. J. A. Hort produce their critical edition of *The New Testament in the Original Greek* • A. A. Hodge and B. B. Warfield coauthor the article on "Inspiration (of the Bible)," defending biblical inerrancy, in *Presbyterian Review* • Horace Bushnell publishes his essay "Our Gospel a Gift to the Imagination" in *Building Eras* • Susan B. Anthony, Elizabeth Cady Stanton, and Matilda Joslyn Gage begin the publication of their landmark *History of Women's Suffrage* (3 vols., 1881–87, plus a fourth volume in 1902 and two additional volumes in 1922); the work is dedicated to their distinguished predecessor, Mary Wollstonecraft	• The UBC General Conference: – authorizes or acknowledges a number of changes in the annual conferences – approves a proposal for pro rata representation of the annual conferences in General Conference – defeats proposals to increase rigidity of laws against secret society membership – does not consider the matter of lay representation • Westminster Theological Seminary is established by the MPC in Westminster, MD, adjacent to Western Maryland College; it is formally incorporated in 1884 [it is moved to Washington and renamed Wesley Theological Seminary in 1958] • The EA establishes Schuylkill Seminary in Reading, PA • The New Congregational Methodist Church is established by a number of congregations in south Georgia, which withdraw from the MECS but do not wish to affiliate with the Congregational Methodist Church (1852) • The AMEC establishes Morris Brown College in Atlanta, GA • The AMEC begins publication of *The A.M.E. Journal*; it is the oldest journal owned and published by blacks in the world	• The first Ecumenical Methodist Conference meets in London, resulting in the formation of the World Methodist Council • The WM Conference opens Handsworth College in Birmingham, England, to provide a theological training center in the Midlands • The PMC opens Hartley College in Manchester as its primary theological college • Amanda Berry Smith begins missionary work in Liberia and Sierra Leone • The MEC organizes the Italy Mission Conference	**1881**

	A. WORLD HISTORY & POLITICS	B. AMERICAN HISTORY & POLITICS	C. SCIENCE, MEDICINE & TECHNOLOGY	D. DAILY LIFE, POPULAR CULTURE & ENTERTAINMENT
1882	• Germany, Austria-Hungary, and Italy form the Triple Alliance; in response, France, Britain, and Russia form the opposing Triple Entente, thus establishing the basic lines of division in Europe leading up to WWI • Korea signs the Treaty of Chemulpo with the US, beginning a century of friendly relations between the two nations • The Boers (Afrikaners) in south Africa begin westward expansion toward the Kalahari Desert • Britain suppresses a nationalist revolt in Egypt with a naval bombardment of Alexandria, then seizes control of Egypt from the Ottoman Empire	• Congress passes the Chinese Exclusion Act, which bars immigration to the US from China for ten years • The outlaw Jesse James is shot by a member of his own gang seeking the reward money for his death • The Hopi Indian Reservation in the southwestern US is established by President Arthur through an executive order	• Thomas Edison's Electric Illuminating Company builds the world's first electrical power generation and distribution system, providing 110 volts of direct current (DC) to customers near his laboratory in New York City • Robert Koch discovers the tuberculosis bacterium • Josef Breuer uses hypnosis to treat hysteria and begins to develop techniques of "deep psychotherapy" in collaboration with Sigmund Freud	• In Britain, the Married Women's Property Act secures to married women the right of ownership of property of all sorts in their own names • Schuyler Wheeler produces the first electric fan for domestic use • Edward Johnson, an associate of Thomas Edison, decorates a Christmas tree for the first time with electric lights • W. S. Gilbert and Arthur Sullivan's musical *Iolanthe* opens on Broadway
1883	• The eruption of Krakatoa in Indonesia is the third most violent in recorded history, following only Tambora (Indonesia, 1815) and Santorini (Greece, 1628); tsunamis caused by the explosion destroy hundreds of villages along the coast of Java and Sumatra, killing over 30,000 people; the ash cloud affects weather systems around the globe for the next year • French forces take control of the city of Hue in what is now southern Vietnam • Romania forms a secret alliance with Austria-Hungary out of fear of Russia • Paul Kruger is elected president of the South African Republic (Transvaal) • The army of Muhammad Ahmad of Sudan, believed by his followers to be Islam's long-awaited Mahdi (messianic ruler), defeats a combined British and Egyptian force near Khartoum	• The US Supreme Court declares the Civil Rights Act of 1875 unconstitutional and rules that the 14th Amendment does not apply to privately owned facilities, including hotels, restaurants, and railroads • The Pendleton Civil Service Reform Act, drafted in part as a response to President Garfield's assassination, establishes the United States Civil Service Commission and provides for the appointment of most permanent federal employees on the basis of the "merit system" rather than political party affiliation (the "spoils system") • Construction of the Northern Pacific Railroad is completed; it runs from Lake Superior to Helena, MT, where it connects with the Oregon Railway to Seattle	• The Brooklyn Bridge, begun in 1869, is completed and opened to traffic; its 1,595-foot main span is the longest in the world at the time • Hiram Maxim invents the first fully automatic machine gun; it is manufactured by Vickers Arms Co. in England • Nikola Tesla, a Croatian scientist working in Paris, develops the first brushless electrical motor, or induction motor, using alternating electrical current (AC)	• William Frederick "Buffalo Bill" Cody's touring "Wild West Show" becomes popular throughout the US; it features Annie Oakley and (for a time) Sitting Bull • The cost of first-class domestic postage in the US is set at 2¢ per half-ounce
1884	• Russian forces take control of the city of Merv in central Asia (modern Turkmenistan) and advance toward the Afghan border • Britain and France establish separate protectorates in Somalia • France establishes protectorates over Tonkin (northern Vietnam) and Annam (central Vietnam), thus controlling the entire country • At the Berlin West Africa Conference, representatives of 14 European countries and the US agree on division of authority over the lands around the Niger and Congo rivers • Otto von Bismarck proclaims a German protectorate in southwest Africa called Tanganyika; the British fear German expansion and cooperation with the Boers (Afrikaners) in south Africa, and conclude treaties with native chieftains in Bechuanaland (modern Botswana)	• New Orleans holds the World's Industrial and Cotton Centennial Exposition, commemorating the beginning of cotton exports from the US to England in 1784 • Former Union General William T. Sherman refuses the presidential nomination of the Republican Party, saying "I will not accept if nominated and will not serve if elected" • Grover Cleveland is elected as president and Thomas Hendricks as vice president (Democratic Party); they are the first Democrats elected since the Civil War	• Charles Parsons (Britain) invents the first practical steam turbine engine • Knut Faber (Denmark) discovers and isolates the tetanus bacterium • German scientist and physician Robert Koch, not knowing of the earlier (1854) work of Filippo Pacini, independently identifies and publicizes his discovery of the bacillus that causes cholera • The Prime Meridian, designated as 0° longitude, is established at Greenwich, England, and an international system of 24 time zones comes into general use, with the International Date Line being 180 degrees opposite the Prime Meridian • Hilaire Bernigaud, Comte de Chardonnet (France), receives a patent for a process of making a fiber he calls "artificial silk"; it is the world's first commercially viable synthetic fiber and is renamed as "rayon" in 1924	• Samuel A. Barnett, an Anglican clergyman, establishes Toynbee Hall, the first "settlement house," in the slums of East London; the idea is to have university men "settle" in a working-class neighborhood where they would not only help relieve poverty and despair but also learn something about the real world from the people of the slums • Dow Jones & Co. is established in New York City in 1882 and begins providing financial data including the "Dow Jones Averages" of selected stock prices to clients • Lewis E. Waterman patents his design for a refillable fountain pen • La Marcus Thompson builds the Switchback Railway, arguably the first roller coaster in America, at Coney Island • W. S. Gilbert and Arthur Sullivan's musical *The Mikado* opens in London

E. EDUCATION, LITERATURE & THE FINE ARTS	F. RELIGION, THEOLOGY, PHILOSOPHY & PSYCHOLOGY	G. AMERICAN & UNITED METHODISM	H. BRITISH & WORLD METHODISM	
• The Berlin Symphony Orchestra is established • Richard Wagner completes his final opera, *Parsifal* • Nikolay Rimsky-Korsakov's opera *The Snow Maiden* premieres in the Mariinsky Theatre, Saint Petersburg • Édouard Manet completes his painting *A Bar at the Folies-Bergère* • Notable publications include: – Robert Louis Stevenson, *The New Arabian Nights* – Theodore Roosevelt, *The Naval War of 1812*	• Friedrich Nietzsche publishes *The Gay Science* (2nd ed. 1887)	• The MECS General Conference: – creates a Board of Church Extension – notes a dramatic turnaround in the financial performance of the Publishing House • The MEC establishes a Board of Church Extension • The Woman's Home Missionary Society (WHMS) is formed by MEC women; Lucy Webb Hayes (wife of former president Rutherford B. Hayes) is elected president • Paine College is founded in Augusta, GA, as a joint venture of the MECS and the CMEC • The MPC publishes a new hymnal, *The Tribute of Praise and Methodist Protestant Hymn Book*	• In Germany, leaders of the WM, EA, and MEC missions create the Evangelical Alliance to promote cooperative ministries	1882
• The Metropolitan Opera House opens in New York with Charles Gounod's *Faust*, featuring the great soprano Christine Nilsson • American poet Emma Lazarus writes her sonnet "The New Colossus," which expresses her faith in the US as a haven for the oppressed; in 1903 it will be inscribed on the base of the Statue of Liberty • Claude Monet moves to his beloved Giverny and begins a series of paintings of the gardens and surrounding area • Other notable publications include: – Mark Twain, *Life on the Mississippi* – Robert Louis Stevenson, *Treasure Island*	• A group of American biblical scholars, including Cyrus I. Scofield, hold the first Niagara Bible Conference (annually until 1897), which pioneers the establishment of the principles of Christian fundamentalism • Notable publications include: – Julius Wellhausen, *Prolegomenon to the History of Israel* – Adolf von Harnack, *The History of Ancient Christian Literature* (3 vols., 1893–1904) – Milton S. Terry, *Biblical Hermeneutics: A Treatise on the Interpretation of the Old and New Testaments*	• The EA General Conference: – devises a plan for distribution of the profits of the publishing house: half to be distributed equally among the annual conferences, half to be distributed on the basis of sales or subscriptions originating in the annual conferences – orders the publication of extensive new Sunday school literature – urges members to strict observance of the Sabbath, even recommending that they travel to and from camp meetings on Saturday and Monday – condemns the "loose" marriage and divorce laws of some states, calls for the abolition of the liquor trade and traffic, and denounces all forms of gambling, including stock market speculation and life insurance – grants a charter to the Woman's Missionary Society, which had been established by EA women in 1880 – postpones indefinitely the "ecumenical affair" with the MEC • The MEC charters Gammon Theological Seminary, originally founded in 1875 as the theological department of Clark College • Walden Seminary (1868) is renamed Philander Smith College	• The Southern African Conference (WM) is established, uniting all WM work throughout present-day South Africa, Botswana, Lesotho, Namibia, and Swaziland, though under all-white leadership	1883
• John Singer Sargent completes his best-known portrait, *Madame X (Madame Pierre Gautreau)* • Anton Bruckner composes his *Te Deum* • The first edition of the *Oxford English Dictionary* is published • Mark Twain publishes *The Adventures of Huckleberry Finn*	• Charles Taze Russell gathers a community that incorporates as Zion's Watch Tower Tract Society; after 1931, called Jehovah's Witnesses • The Council of Roman Catholic Bishops in America imposes automatic excommunication on American Catholics who remarry after divorce • Notable publications include: – Frederick Engels, *The Origin of the Family, Private Property and the State* – Henry Boynton Smith, *System of Christian Theology*	• The MEC General Conference: – calls for the organization of Temperance Societies in the annual conferences – issues a lengthy statement on the sanctity of marriage, declaring adultery the only justification and legal basis for divorce and prohibiting ministers from remarrying divorced persons – issues a statement outlawing discrimination in worship or religious instruction on grounds of race, color, or "previous condition of servitude" – continues its refusal to allow women to be licensed to preach or ordained – authorizes the creation of central conferences for territories outside the US – organizes the Norwegian and Danish Conferences and the Indian Mission Annual Conference – officially recognizes the church's theological schools by listing them in the *Discipline* – elects William Taylor as missionary bishop for Africa	• The BC and PM congregations in Canada along with the MECC (1834) join the Methodist Church in Canada (MCC, 1874); the union now embraces all the Methodist bodies in the country except the BMEC (1856), which merges instead with the AMEC • The MEC creates the India Central Conference, Africa Mission Conference, and Finland District of Sweden Conference • An attempt to form an autonomous WM Conference in the Caribbean fails • The first Cantonese-speaking WM Conference is formed in Hong Kong • Robert S. Maclay travels from his mission in Japan to Korea and obtains permission from King Kojong for Christian missionaries to open schools and hospitals in Korea	1884

	A. WORLD HISTORY & POLITICS	B. AMERICAN HISTORY & POLITICS	C. SCIENCE, MEDICINE & TECHNOLOGY	D. DAILY LIFE, POPULAR CULTURE & ENTERTAINMENT
1884 cont.	• Britain's Representation of the People Act (also called the Third Reform Act) extends voting rights to all adult males regardless of property ownership or income • The War of the Pacific ends with the Truce of Valparaiso; Chile secures control of rich nitrate (guano) deposits at Atacama from Peru; Bolivia is left landlocked; Chile guarantees free passage of Bolivian trade goods through Chilean territory to the Pacific port of Arica		• George Eastman discovers how to apply the photographic dry-plate emulsion to a strip of paper rather than a glass plate, thus inventing photographic "film"	
1885	• The Indian National Congress, later known as the Congress Party, is formed; its aim is to secure the independence of India from Britain • Belgium's King Leopold II claims the territory of the Congo in Africa as a colony; the major powers of Europe recognize the Belgian claim, setting off their "Scramble for Africa"; by 1900, Ethiopia and Liberia will be the only remaining independent states on the African continent • King Alfonso XII of Spain dies; he is succeeded in 1886 by his posthumously born son, Alfonso XIII, whose mother, Queen Maria Christina serves as regent until 1902 • Muhammad Ahmad captures Khartoum and massacres the British and Egyptian garrison, taking control of Sudan • Russian and Afghan forces clash along the Afghan border, provoking a crisis between Russia and Britain • Germany proclaims a protectorate in east Africa after signing treaties with black tribal leaders in the area • Faced with a failing empire, the Ottoman sultan suspends the progressive constitution of 1876	• The first known celebration of Flag Day takes place in a Wisconsin public school on June 14, marking the 108th anniversary of the adoption of the Stars and Stripes as the national flag of the US in 1777 • The territory of the Navajo Nation is expanded to accommodate their growing population (it will be expanded again on a number of occasions to its present size of 16 million acres, making the Navajo reservation the largest in the US)	• The Home Insurance building in Chicago is the first modern "skyscraper"; it is 10 stories high and 138 feet tall • Louis Pasteur develops the rabies vaccine • William Stanley, working with George Westinghouse, designs a practical electrical transformer to vary alternating current (AC) voltage • Gottlieb Daimler (Germany) develops a four-stroke gasoline-powered internal combustion engine with a vertical cylinder into which gasoline is injected through a carburetor (which he patents in 1887) and a spark-induced ignition; it is usually acknowledged to be the prototype of the modern gasoline engine	• The Lever brothers begin selling wrapped bars of soap in England • Dr Pepper, America's first major soft drink, is created by Charles Alderton in Waco, TX • A group of popular songwriters and publishers gathers in New York City, forming what comes to be called "Tin Pan Alley" • The cost of a first-class postage stamp (for letters of one ounce or less delivered inside the US) is set at 2¢

E. EDUCATION, LITERATURE & THE FINE ARTS	F. RELIGION, THEOLOGY, PHILOSOPHY & PSYCHOLOGY	G. AMERICAN & UNITED METHODISM	H. BRITISH & WORLD METHODISM	
		– approves a report affirming the power of the General Conference to fix the residence of its bishops in particular cities, but does not act to do so • The WHMC (MEC) begins publication of *Woman's Home Missions* (to 1940) • Delegates from the MEC, MECS, MPC, AMEC, AMEZC, and CMEC meet in the Methodist Centennial Conference in Baltimore to celebrate the 100th anniversary of the establishment of Methodism in the US as an independent church • The MPC General Conference: – approves a proposal for organic union with the Cumberland Presbyterians, but the plan fails due to opposition from the other side – rescinds the 1880 ordination of Anna Howard Shaw by the New York Conference, ruling that it was "out of order"; however, Shaw continues to be recognized and serve as an elder in her conference – authorizes each annual conference to determine the length of pastoral appointments for its ministers – adopts a new constitution for the Board of Missions and the Woman's Foreign Missionary Society – organizes Spring Creek [TN] Colored Mission Conference • The AMEC General Conference – approves merger with the BMEC (1856) – approves licensing women to preach, but limits them to evangelistic work – establishes the AME Sunday School Union • The CMEC receives a state charter for Lane Institute (later Lane College) in Jackson, TN		**1884 cont.**
• Brahms completes his majestic *Symphony No. 4 in E Minor*, his final full-length symphonic work • Dvořák composes his *Symphony No. 7 in D Minor* • Alexander Borodin writes his *String Quartet No. 2 in D* • Vincent van Gogh completes his *Self-Portrait with a Straw Hat* • William Dean Howells publishes his most widely read novel, *The Rise of Silas Lapham* • Winslow Homer begins to paint a series of seascapes depicting human struggle against the elemental power of the ocean	• Samuel David Ferguson becomes the first black person to be ordained a bishop of the Protestant Episcopal Church • Nietzsche, in *Also sprach Zarathustra* (Thus Spoke Zarathustra), proclaims that "God is dead" • Other notable publications include: – Josiah Royce, *The Religious Aspect of Philosophy* – Henry Ward Beecher, *Evolution and Religion*	• The UBC General Conference: – establishes a church commission to prepare an amended version of the Constitution and Confession of Faith – adopts a modified, less rigorous prohibition against secret society membership – decides to open an eastern book publishing operation in Harrisburg, PA • The General Holiness Assembly adopts a formal definition of entire sanctification as "a second definite work of grace wrought by the Baptism with the Holy Spirit" • Phineas Bresee establishes the First Church of the Nazarene in Los Angeles • Lucy and Joseph Shelly Meyer start the Deaconess Movement in the MEC by establishing the Chicago Training School • Sarah Hughes is the first woman ordained in the AMEC as an itinerant deacon; the action is rescinded by the AMEC General Conference in 1889 • The WHMS (MEC) opens its first school, the Haven Industrial School in Savannah, GA • The first denominational historical society related to American Methodism is formed by the UBC • The Spanish Mission Conference (MEC) and the Mexican Frontier Conference (MECS) are organized	• Hugh Price Hughes (WM) becomes editor of the *Methodist Times* in the UK; it is part of the WM "Forward Movement" of social and political activity and reform • WM missions in the West Indies become the autonomous West Indies Conference • The first MEC churches are established in Bulgaria and the Dominican Republic • Bishop William Taylor (MEC) begins his African mission work in Kenya and Angola • Bishop James M. Thoburn (MEC) begins missions in Singapore and Malaya • Rev. and Mrs. Henry G. Appenzeller and Dr. and Mrs. William B. Scranton begin MEC mission work in Korea, accompanied by Presbyterian minister Horace G. Underwood • The Free Church of Tonga separates from the Wesleyan Methodist Mission	**1885**

	A. WORLD HISTORY & POLITICS	B. AMERICAN HISTORY & POLITICS	C. SCIENCE, MEDICINE & TECHNOLOGY	D. DAILY LIFE, POPULAR CULTURE & ENTERTAINMENT
1885 cont.				
1886	• Britain and Germany forge an agreement defining the frontier between the Gold Coast (British) and Togoland (German) in Africa • Britain annexes Upper Burma as a crown territory • Portugal claims all the territory between Angola (in west Africa) and Mozambique (in east Africa) • Spain abolishes slavery in its colony of Cuba • The first woman's suffrage bill is introduced into the British parliament; it does not pass	• The Statue of Liberty, a gift from France, is dedicated in New York Harbor • The Federation of Organized Trades and Labor Unions of the United States and Canada and The Knights of Labor merged together and formed the American Federation of Labor (AFL); Samuel Gompers is elected president • A labor union rally in Chicago's Haymarket Square turns violent and becomes a riot when a bomb explodes, killing seven policemen and prompting police to fire on the crowd, killing four and wounding many others; seven anarchists and union leaders are later convicted and four are hanged • The surrender of Geronimo marks the effective end of Apache resistance to white settlement in the Southwest, which had been almost constant since Cochise went on the warpath in 1861	• *The New York Tribune* begins regular commercial use of the linotype machine, patented by Ottmar Merganthaler (US) in 1884 • George Westinghouse forms the Westinghouse Electric Corporation and begins developing systems for AC electrical power generation and distribution in competition with the DC system of Thomas Edison • Charles Hall (US) and Paul Héroult (France) independently develop a process for extracting aluminum from bauxite ore using electrolysis, launching the modern aluminum industry • Gottlieb Daimler and Karl Benz create the world's first self-powered, four-wheeled automobile, using Daimler's gasoline engine • German-born American inventor Emile Berliner patents the flat disc phonograph, the gramophone, in which the needle moves from side to side in a groove of even depth, rather than up and down	• Coca-Cola is formulated by John S. Pemberton and first sold to the public at the soda fountain in Jacob's Pharmacy in Atlanta • Joel Cheek names his popular coffee blend "Maxwell House," after the hotel in Nashville where it is served • John Philip Sousa writes his very popular patriotic march "Semper Fidelis" • The first "Tournament of Roses" parade is held in Pasadena, CA
1887	• Britain's Queen Victoria celebrates the Golden Jubilee of her coronation in 1837 • Several women's rights organizations in Britain join together to create the National Union of Women's Suffrage Societies (NUWSS) • France merges Vietnam and Cambodia into a federation called the Indochinese Union (French Indo-China) • Britain and Germany compete for control of east Africa, particularly the island of Zanzibar • Britain annexes Zululand in south Africa in order to repress further Zulu uprisings • The Rocky Mountains Park Act becomes law in Canada, creating that nation's first national park, Banff National Park • Mexico City erects a statue of Cuauhtemoc, the Aztec leader during the Spanish conquest in 1521, representing a revival of interest in the history of the indigenous peoples of the region	• Kansas grants women unlimited rights to vote in municipal and local elections but not state elections • Susanna Medora Salter becomes the first woman elected mayor of an American town, Argonia, KS • Congress passes the Dawes Act, which initiates the allotment of land to individual Indians as their reservations are being broken up for sale; the US government retains title and generates income for the Indians from use of the land, mostly from grazing, energy, and mineral royalties; the proceeds go into a trust fund to be paid out to Indian holders of individual trust accounts • The Dawes Act also provides that the US government may make "surplus" land available for sale to whites; by 1932, whites will own two-thirds of the 138,000,000 acres that the Indians hold in 1887 • Congress passes the Interstate Commerce Act authorizing the federal government to regulate all transportation and business activity that crosses state borders, and establishes the Interstate Commerce Commission (ICC) to enforce the act • White business leaders in Hawaii, backed by an armed militia they had founded, impose the "Bayonet Constitution" on King David Kalakaua; it sharply limits his powers and consolidates the influence of wealthy whites at the expense of native Hawaiians	• Thomas Morton is credited with the first successful appendectomy in the US • Nikola Tesla, who had recently come to the US from Europe, receives several patents related to the generation and transmission of alternating current (AC) electricity, which can be transmitted over much longer distances than DC electricity without excessive power loss because "transformers" can easily step the voltage up or down as needed • George Westinghouse purchases the rights to Tesla's patents and begins to develop a system for the commercial production and transmission of AC electricity • Stockbrokers L. H. Taylor & Co. establish the first private-line telegraph service between their offices in New York and Philadelphia • Hannibal Goodwin advances the development of photographic film by putting the emulsion on a transparent celluloid base • The A. B. Dick Co. begins manufacturing and marketing the Mimeograph system for document reproduction, based on patents by Thomas Edison	• The Amateur Athletic Union (AAU) is established for teams and players in almost every amateur sport • According to tradition, observance of Groundhog Day begins in Punxsutawney, PA, home of the prognosticating groundhog "Punxsutawney Phil" • "Buffalo Bill's Wild West Show" travels to England and then tours Europe • England's George Lohmann, one of the greatest cricket players of all time, becomes the first bowler to take eight wickets in a test inning (against Australia) • Chef August Escoffier is called upon to create a special dessert to commemorate Queen Victoria's golden jubilee; he creates a simple (but simply magnificent) dish he calls "cherries jubilee," a combination of poached cherries and vanilla ice cream topped by flaming cherry brandy
1888	• The Convention of Constantinople, signed by all the major European powers, declares the Suez Canal to be neutral territory and guarantees safe passage of the ships of all nations during war or peace	• Wells Fargo becomes the country's first nationwide express company, connecting over 2,500 communities in 25 states • The Washington Monument, dedicated in 1885, is opened to the public for the first time	• Nikola Tesla develops the first electrical induction motor, based on AC electricity • George Eastman perfects his hand-held box camera, which he names the "Kodak" and markets with the slogan "You push the button, we do the rest"; it comes loaded *(cont.)*	• The "Schoolchildren's Blizzard" results in 235 deaths in the upper Great Plains; many are children on their way home from school • The great East Coast Blizzard of 1888 results in 400 deaths and as much as 5 ft of snow; damage is estimated at $20 million

E. EDUCATION, LITERATURE & THE FINE ARTS	F. RELIGION, THEOLOGY, PHILOSOPHY & PSYCHOLOGY	G. AMERICAN & UNITED METHODISM	H. BRITISH & WORLD METHODISM	
		• Maclay College of Theology is established in San Fernando, CA, by the Southern California Annual Conference of the MEC • Turner Theological Seminary is chartered by the AMEC; it opens for classes as a department of Morris Brown College in 1894		**1885 cont.**
• Anton Bruckner's *Symphony No. 7*, his breakthrough work, is performed for the first time in Vienna under the baton of Hans Richter • Camille Saint-Saëns composes his charming musical suite *The Carnival of the Animals* • Auguste Rodin completes his sculptures *The Kiss* and *The Burghers of Calais* • Georges Seurat completes his Neo-Impressionist (or Pointilist) masterpiece *A Sunday on La Grande Jatte* • Notable publications include: – Henry James, *The Bostonians* – Leo Tolstoy, *The Death of Ivan Ilyich* – Thomas Hardy, *The Mayor of Casterbridge* – Robert Louis Stevenson, *The Strange Case of Dr. Jekyll and Mr. Hyde* and *Kidnapped*	• The first international, interdenominational student Christian conference ever held meets in London, resulting in the establishment of The World Student Christian Federation (formally organized in 1895) • The American National Baptist Convention is established; it is the first national association for black Baptists • The Jewish Theological Seminary is founded in New York City through the efforts of Sabato Morais and H. Pereira Mendes as the major training center for Conservative Judaism in the US • Nietzsche publishes *Beyond Good and Evil* • Adolf von Harnack begins publication of his seminal work *The History of Dogma* (3 vols., 1886–89)	• The MECS General Conference: – takes a strong stand against the sale or use of alcoholic beverages, despite significant opposition to this as "dabbling in politics" – directs the bishops to include foreign missions fields in their visitation; declines to consider election of missionary bishops as such – appoints a committee to revise the Hymnbook • The MEC organizes the Central Missouri and Northern German Conferences	• Joseph C. Hartzell takes over the leadership of the Africa Mission Conference (MEC) • Brazilian Methodism becomes an annual conference of the MECS; Hugh C. Tucker arrives in Rio de Janeiro from Tennessee and begins 60 years in Brazil, becoming the most notable and influential foreigner in the country and receiving the highest decoration ever bestowed upon a civilian by the Brazilian government • The Switzerland Annual Conference of the MEC is separated from the German Annual Conference (or BMK, 1868); both become autonomous	**1886**
• Boston's Handel and Haydn Society gives the first American performance of Bach's *Mass in B Minor* • Verdi's historical opera *Otello* (based on Shakespeare's play *Othello*) premieres at La Scala in Milan • Melville Dewey, inventor of the "Dewey decimal system" for the classification of library books, establishes the State Library School in Albany, NY, the first library school in the US • Albert Pinkham Ryder completes his mysterious, luminous painting *Moonlight* • Arthur Conan Doyle gives the literary world its most famous detective, Sherlock Holmes, along with his friend and companion, Dr. Watson, and his nemesis, Prof. Moriarty, in "A Study in Scarlet," published in *Beeton's Christmas Annual* • Other notable publications include: – H. Rider Haggard, *She* – Thomas Hardy, *The Woodlanders*	• The Chicago Evangelization Society is established by Dwight L. Moody; after his death in 1899, the name is changed to the Moody Bible Institute • Notable publications include: – Nietzsche, *The Genealogy of Morals* – Isaac Hecker, *The Church and the Age*	• The EA General Conference: – is forced to deal with controversies about the "moral character" of some delegates and the seating of other delegates, stemming mostly from personal rivalries among key leaders – resists proposals to place limits on the episcopal form of church government – reiterates an earlier prohibition against ministers remarrying divorced persons – extend its "blue law" policies to urge members not to read the Sunday editions of newspapers or to hold interest or patronize businesses that are open on Sunday • Ella Niswonger is the first woman to graduate from the regular seminary course at Union Biblical Seminary (now United Theological Seminary) • Japanese pastor Kanichi Miyama is granted full clergy rights by the MEC; he is the first person of Asian descent to be ordained as a Methodist minister • The MPC organizes the Indian Mission Conference • The AMEC establishes Shorter College in Little Rock, AR • Minor Raymond's *Systematic Theology* describes sanctification as a "gradual process"	• Army chaplain J. H. Bateson from Britain begins WM work in northern Burma, centered near Mandalay • Isabella Thoburn founds the first Christian woman's college in Asia (Lucknow, India) • Bible Christians from Britain begin mission work in New Zealand • The Methodist Theological Seminary in Seoul, Korea, is established by Henry G. Appenzeller • James H. Rigg, *Principles of Church Organization*, expounds the particular style of Victorian British Methodism	**1887**
• Steinway & Sons makes its last square piano, deciding to focus entirely on concert grand pianos • The National Geographic Society is founded in Washington, DC	• The Church of Scotland allows the ordination of women as deacons • The American Society of Church History (ASCH) is established under the leadership of Philip Schaff	• The MEC General Conference: – refuses to seat five women elected as delegates, including Frances Willard; deciding that *laymen* means males only – creates a Constitutional Commission to consider the possibility of lay representation in annual conferences	• The AMEC General Conference formally establishes the church's work in central Africa • William Taylor takes over the work of the Congregational Church in Mozambique for the MEC	**1888**

	A. WORLD HISTORY & POLITICS	B. AMERICAN HISTORY & POLITICS	C. SCIENCE, MEDICINE & TECHNOLOGY	D. DAILY LIFE, POPULAR CULTURE & ENTERTAINMENT
1888 cont.	• Kaiser William I of Germany dies; he is succeeded briefly by his son, Friedrich III, who dies 99 days later, then by his grandson, William II • Arab tribes on the east coast of Africa resist both British and German control • Slavery is abolished and slaves emancipated in Brazil; it is the last state in the Americas to do so	• Benjamin Harrison is elected as president and Levi P. Morton as vice president (Republican Party) • Paiute Indian shaman Wovoka creates the apocalyptic Ghost Dance, which envisions the Indians being lifted up into the spirit world while the earth opens up to swallow all white men and is then restored to its natural state, before the Europeans came, to be inhabited by the Indians and the ghosts of their ancestors • The Ghost Dance spreads to other American Indian tribes and is especially embraced by the Lakota (Sioux), who begin making "ghost shirts" that they believe will protect their warriors against the bullets of US soldiers	with enough photographic film to take 100 2"-diameter round photographs; after exposure the film is returned to a laboratory where it is "developed" and printed; the camera is reloaded with film and returned with the photographs • British inventor John B. Dunlop patents his pneumatic tire for automobiles, which consists of a rubber inner tube encased in a canvas jacket with a rubber tread	• The St. Andrews Golf Club of Yonkers, NY, is established, regularizing the game of golf in the US • W. S. Gilbert and Arthur Sullivan produce their musical *The Yeomen of the Guard* in both London and New York
1889	• Britain's Naval Defense Act stipulates that the British fleet should be equal in strength to the Russian and French fleets combined • Italy concludes a "treaty of friendship and cooperation" with Ethiopia • The British South Africa Company, headed by Cecil Rhodes, receives a British royal charter granting it all the rights and powers of government in the territory of southern Africa north of the Transvaal and east of Mozambique • Paris holds its fourth Exposition Universelle to commemorate the Centennial of the French Revolution; it attracts almost 62,000 exhibitors and more than 32 million visitors. • The Eiffel Tower in Paris is completed as a part of the Centennial celebrations; it surpasses the Washington Monument as the tallest structure in the world (300 meters, or 984 feet) • The US, Britain, and Germany conclude a treaty providing for the neutrality of Samoa and establishing a joint protectorate • The first Pan-American Conference meets in Washington, DC, with the US and all Latin American nations except the Dominican Republic taking part	• Four new states are admitted to the US: North Dakota (39), South Dakota (40), Montana (41), and Washington (42) • Congress opens the western half of the Indian Territory in Oklahoma to white settlement, creating a great land rush; those who sneak into the area trying to stake claims before the official starting date are called "sooners" • The Qualla Indian Reservation is chartered in western North Carolina for the Eastern Band of Cherokee Indians • Florida establishes a poll tax that must be paid before a citizen can vote, which has the effect of disenfranchising many blacks as well as poor whites; the other Southern states soon do likewise • The South Fork Dam in Johnstown, PA, built in 1852, fails after heavy rains; the surprise flood kills over 2,200 people • The United Mine Workers of America (UMW) is formed by merging the National Progressive Union (organized 1888) and the mine locals under the Knights of Labor • The US Army grows alarmed about the spread of the Ghost Dance movement among the Lakota and sends Indian police and soldiers to the Lakota (Sioux) reservation to stop it by arresting Sitting Bull, who is killed as Lakota warriors try to protect him from arrest	• William Dickson, commissioned by Thomas Edison, builds the first motion-picture camera and names it the Kinetograph • Ivan Pavlov (Russia) begins the research that will lead him to develop his concept of "conditioned reflex" • Gottlieb Daimler builds an improved four-stroke gasoline engine with mushroom-shaped valves and two V-slant cylinders • The first long distance electric power transmission line in the US is completed, running 14 miles between a generator at Willamette Falls and downtown Portland, OR • Pioneering American journalist Nellie Bly (Elizabeth Cochrane), inspired by Jules Verne, begins an attempt to travel around the world in less than 80 days, finishing the journey in 72 days, 6 hours, and 11 minutes	• Dow Jones & Company's "Customers' Afternoon Letter" of financial and business news becomes *The Wall Street Journal* • Fabrics made of the "artificial silk" fiber later known as rayon are introduced to the public at the Paris Exposition • John Philip Sousa writes his popular "Washington Post March" • Football coach Walter Camp selects the first "All-American" football team • In the last championship boxing match of the "bare-knuckles" era, John L. Sullivan beats Jake Kilrain in a fight that lasts for 75 rounds

E. EDUCATION, LITERATURE & THE FINE ARTS	F. RELIGION, THEOLOGY, PHILOSOPHY & PSYCHOLOGY	G. AMERICAN & UNITED METHODISM	H. BRITISH & WORLD METHODISM	
• John G. Gregg introduces his system of stenography, or shorthand, in a brochure entitled "Light-Line Phonography" • The Concertgebouw of Amsterdam is established • van Gogh paints *The Yellow Chair and Sunflowers* • Paul Gauguin paints *The Vision after the Sermon: Jacob Wrestling with the Angel* • Gustav Mahler composes his *Symphony No. 1* and his song cycle *Des Knaben Wunderhorn* (The Boy's Magic Horn) • Rimsky-Korsakov composes both his *Russian Easter Overture* and his symphonic suite *Scheherazade* • Erik Satie composes his piano suite *Trois Gymnopédies* • Henry James publishes *Aspern Papers* • Richard Burton completes publication of his sensational unexpurgated 16-volume edition of *The Arabian Nights*	• Curtis Schofield's *Rightly Dividing the Word of Truth*, offers a spirited defense of premillennial dispensationalism, drawing heavily on John Darby and the Plymouth Brethren; it propels Schofield to the status of a leading figure in American fundamentalism • Mikhail Bakunin's *God and the State*, completed in 1872, is published posthumously	– sanctions the office of deaconess as a ministry of the church, but refuses to give deaconesses sacramental authority, even on the mission field – determines that new mission conferences may be organized but are not to have representation in the General Conference – extends maximum length of pastoral service on a circuit from three to five years and allows presiding elders to serve for six years – organizes the California German, Northern Pacific German, and Northwest Norwegian-Danish Missions • The MPC General Conference: – appoints a committee to consider revision of the Articles of Religion – declines to act on a proposal to license women to preach • The MECS establishes a church in Havana, Cuba • The WHMS (MEC) establishes the Immigrant Girls Home in New York City • The MPC establishes the Charleston Colored Mission Conference	• Cuban MECS missionaries from Florida organize the first Methodist church in Havana • Sarah Gorham becomes the first woman AMEC missionary • The Wesley Historical Society (WHS) is established in the UK	**1888 cont.**
• Richard Strauss composes *Death and Transfiguration* • Enrique Granados completes his first notable work, his suite of *Spanish Dances* for piano • van Gogh completes what is arguably his most famous painting, *Starry Night* • Theodore Roosevelt publishes the first of four volumes of *The Winning of the West* (1889–96) • Other notable publications include: – Mark Twain, *A Connecticut Yankee in King Arthur's Court*	• Former professional baseball player Billy Sunday begins his career as a popular and flamboyant evangelist • Charles A. Briggs, the greatest apostle of Presbyterian progressivism, publishes his volume *Whither? A Theological Question for the Times* advocating revision of the Westminster Confession of Faith • Frances Willard argues for the right of women to preach in her important volume *Woman in the Pulpit* • Other notable publications include: – Henri Bergson, *Time and Free Will*	• The UBC General Conference: – endorses the new Constitution and Confession of Faith prepared by the 1885 church commission, after they had been submitted to and approved by the annual conferences – approves a proposal for lay representation in General Conference and revises the standing rule on lay representation in annual conferences to make it mandatory instead of optional – authorizes the annual conferences to license women to preach and to ordain them to the ministry – orders the legal incorporation of the UBC in the state of Ohio • Ella Niswonger becomes the first woman to be ordained in the UBC, by the Central Illinois Conference • Objections to the adoption of the new UBC Constitution, to lay representation, and to the ordination of women by Bishop Milton Wright and a group of followers lead to their withdrawal from the UBC to establish a new denomination called "The Church of the United Brethren in Christ (Old Constitution)" • Eugenia St. John is ordained elder by the Kansas Annual Conference of the MPC • The MEC establishes the Epworth League, the first youth organization in American Methodism • The MECS publishes a new hymnal, *The Hymnbook of the Methodist Episcopal Church, South* • The New England Deaconess Home and Training School is founded in Boston • Primitivo Rodriguez begins translating and editing resources in Spanish for the MEC • Enrique Someillan becomes the first Cuban Methodist pastor in Key West • The American Primitive Methodist Church (1840) absorbs other PM congregations in Illinois and Wisconsin to form the *(cont.)*	• Methodists around the world celebrate the 150th anniversary of the formation of the first Methodist societies in 1739 • The Wesley Memorial Church is erected in Epworth as a memorial to the Wesley family • The MEC organizes the Northern German Conference, superseding the North German Mission Conference • B. A. Carlson travels from Sweden to begin MEC mission work in Russia • The first Methodist missionaries in Hungary arrive from Austria and Germany to work among German immigrants • The MEC begins mission work in Albania • The UBC begins mission work in China	**1889**

	A. WORLD HISTORY & POLITICS	B. AMERICAN HISTORY & POLITICS	C. SCIENCE, MEDICINE & TECHNOLOGY	D. DAILY LIFE, POPULAR CULTURE & ENTERTAINMENT
1889 cont.				
1890	• German Kaiser William II dismisses Otto von Bismarck as Chancellor of Germany due to a difference over policy in dealing with Russia • Britain and Portugal reach an agreement defining the boundary between Angola (Portuguese) and south Africa (British) • Cecil Rhodes becomes Prime Minister of the Cape Colony in south Africa • Britain and Germany agree to recognize the German protectorate over Madagascar, established in 1885, and the British protectorate over Zanzibar • Bananas are first planted as a cash crop in Costa Rica with such success that the "miracle fruit" quickly spreads across Central America, becoming so critical economically that the Central American countries are soon called "Banana Republics"	• The US census reports that the population is 62,947,714: – whites: 55,101,258 (87.5%) – blacks: 7,488,676 (11.9%) – other: 357,780 (0.6%); includes Indian territory and reservations for the first time • The US national debt is $1,552,140,204 • Congress passes the Sherman Antitrust Act to restrain the power of trusts and monopolies such as Standard Oil, which now controls over 80% of the gas and oil in the US • Idaho is admitted to the US as the 43rd state • Wyoming is admitted to the US as the 44th state; its state constitution is the first to guarantee women the right to vote • Sequoia and Yosemite National Parks, the second and third national parks, are created • The National American Woman Suffrage Association (NAWSA) is formed by merger of NWSA and AWSA; Frances Willard and Anna Howard Shaw are among the leaders • Jane Addams and Ellen Gates Starr establish Hull House in Chicago; it is the first "settlement house" project in the US; within a year, there are more than a hundred "settlement houses" throughout the country, mostly run by women • American soldiers attack and massacre over 200 Lakota (Sioux) men, women, and children at Wounded Knee, SD, in the last battle of the American Indian wars; the "ghost shirts" of the Lakota warriors do not stop bullets after all	• Rubber gloves are first used in surgery at Johns Hopkins Hospital, Baltimore • German engineer Wilhelm Maybach builds the first four-cylinder, four-stroke gasoline engine • Gottlieb Daimler establishes the Daimler Motoren-Gesellschaft to manufacture his automobiles; it is the world's first automotive company [this is the symbolic beginning point of the modern automobile industry and simultaneously the point at which the oil industry begins to shift its focus from the production of kerosene to the production of gasoline] • The Firth of Forth Bridge in Scotland is completed; it is the first major bridge built primarily of steel; it is at the time the longest bridge in the world at 8,276 feet and is one of the largest and strongest cantilever bridges ever built	• Robert Gaur develops the corrugated cardboard box • George Bayle creates peanut butter as a health food for people who cannot chew more solid food; the process is later patented by the Kellogg Co. • F. W. Woolworth imports the first glass Christmas tree ornaments from Germany to the US • Social reformer Jacob Riis publishes his shocking portrayal of slum life in American cities, *How the Other Half Lives*, one of the earliest social documentary books in the US
1891	• Germany, Austria-Hungary, and Italy renew the Triple Alliance; France and Russia begin negotiations with Britain about a counterbalance alliance • Belgian forces defeat the native tribes in the Congo; the Katanga Company is established to exploit the copper and other mineral resources in the region • Britain and the Netherlands agree on the boundaries of British and Dutch territory in Borneo • The Emperor of Ethiopia, Menelik II, denounces the Italian claim of a protectorate over his country • The second Pan-American Conference meets in Mexico City • More than 10,000 die in major earthquake in Japan • Russia experiences serious famine due to widespread crop failures	• Mississippi adopts a literacy test designed to keep blacks from voting; other Southern states quickly follow suit; in order not to disenfranchise illiterate whites, a "grandfather clause" allows those who could vote before 1870, or their descendants, to vote regardless of literacy or tax qualifications • The Populist Party (or Popular Party) is established by coalition of agrarian reformers in the Midwest and South; its platform calls for (among other things) the unlimited coinage of silver to increase the money supply (which hoped to ease the financial burdens of debt-ridden farmers), a graduated income tax, government ownership and management of the railroads, the direct election of US senators, and other measures designed to give farmers political and economic parity with business and industry • The Creative Act authorizes the establishment of forest reserves from publicly owned lands to be administered by the Forestry Division of the US Department of Agriculture; lands may be set aside as reserves by presidential executive order; over a million acres are immediately set aside at Yellowstone by President Harrison	• Russia begins construction of the Trans-Siberian Railroad; when completed in 1917, it is the longest continuous rail line on Earth, covering almost six thousand miles • When the California citrus industry is decimated by the cottony-cushion scale insect, ladybird beetles (ladybugs) are imported from Australia in one of the first successful experiments in biological pest control	• Asa Candler buys all rights to Coca-Cola, patents the formula, incorporates The Coca-Cola Company, and registers the "Coca-Cola" trademark • A moving stairway is constructed as a novelty ride at Coney Island; it is redesigned for the 1900 Paris Exposition and dubbed the "escalator" • Basketball (the only major sport strictly of US origin) is invented by James Naismith at the YMCA in Springfield, MA • The first cafeteria in the US is established at the YWCA in Kansas City, MO, to provide low-cost meals for working women

E. EDUCATION, LITERATURE & THE FINE ARTS	F. RELIGION, THEOLOGY, PHILOSOPHY & PSYCHOLOGY	G. AMERICAN & UNITED METHODISM	H. BRITISH & WORLD METHODISM	
		Primitive Methodist Church in the USA (PMCUSA) and holds its first General Conference • Harriett Baker is the first woman appointed to serve as the pastor of an AMEC congregation (Lebanon, PA)		**1889 cont.**
• Tchaikovsky's ballet *The Sleeping Beauty* debuts in St. Petersburg • Claude Debussy composes his *Suite Bergamasque*, which contains the very popular "Clair de Lune" • Cézanne completes his painting *The Card Players* • Thomas Wentworth Higginson and Mabel Loomis Todd publish *The Poems of Emily Dickinson*, the first collection of her poetry to appear in print, four years after her death (1886) • Henrik Ibsen publishes his memorable drama *Hedda Gabler*	• The Finnish Evangelical Lutheran Church is established in the US • The Mormon Church officially renounces the practice of polygamy • Charles Gore's *Lux Mundi* suggests that an Anglo-Catholic can accept historical and literary criticism of the Bible • William James's landmark work *The Principles of Psychology* revolutionizes the study of the discipline in the US • Other notable publications include: – James George Frazer, *The Golden Bough: A Study in Comparative Religion* (enlarged to 12 vols., 1911–15) – Hugh Price Hughes, *Social Christianity*	• The MECS General Conference: – establishes the MECS Woman's Home Missionary Society (WHMS) – organizes the Epworth League under the direction of the Sunday School Committee • The UBC begins publication of *Quarterly Review of the United Brethren in Christ*; name is changed to *United Brethren Review* in 1902; publication ceases in 1908 • The Free Methodist Church General Conference repudiates the leadership of Benjamin T. Roberts and refuses to allow the ordination of women • The MEC establishes the Chinese Methodist Missionary Society • The MEC establishes the Navajo Mission Conference • The WHMS (MEC) provides education for Hispanic children at the Harwood School in Albuquerque, the Frances DePauw School in Los Angeles, and the George O. Robinson School in San Juan, Puerto Rico	• The Wesley Deaconess Institute (WM) is founded in London by Thomas B. Stephenson • Irwin Richards (MEC) begins missionary work in Mozambique • William Booth publishes *Darkest England and the Way Out*	**1890**
• Carnegie Hall opens in New York • Claude Monet exhibits *Haystacks*, a series of 15 paintings showing the effect of light and weather on the same stacks of hay • Postimpressionist French artist Henri de Toulouse-Lautrec produces "La Goulue and Her Sister at the Moulin Rouge," the first of his famous posters depicting the personalities and facets of Parisian night life and the French world of entertainment • Gauguin, inspired by his new life in Tahiti, completes his painting *Tahitian Women* • The completed manuscript of Herman Melville's great novella *Billy Budd* is found among his papers after his death [it is not published until 1924] • Notable publications include: – Thomas Hardy, *Tess of the d'Urbervilles* – Oscar Wilde, *The Picture of Dorian Gray* – Ambrose Bierce, *In the Midst of Life*	• Pope Leo XIII issues his encyclical *Rerum Novarum (On Capital and Labor)* concerning the condition of the working classes; it condemns socialism but leaves the door open to Catholic alliance with Socialist political groups • Charles A. Briggs is appointed Professor of Biblical Studies at Union Theological Seminary in New York; his inaugural address on "The Authority of Holy Scripture" is a broadside against the verbal inspiration and inerrancy of Scripture • The first International Council of Congregational Churches is held in London • Notable publications include: – Henry Ward Beecher, *Life of Jesus Christ* – Washington Gladden, *Who Wrote the Bible?* – Samuel R. Driver, *An Introduction to the Literature of the Old Testament*	• The EA General Conference: – formally suspends Bishop Ralph Dubs, who had defected from the EA along with a group of followers to form a new denomination, The United Evangelical Church (UEC), which is committed to lay representation – rules that any preachers or members who had allied with the "dissident" group had "disentitled themselves of any of the privilege of membership" in the EA – appoints a commission to prepare a report on the issue of lay representation in the EA General Conference • The United Evangelical Church (UEC) is formed at a conference in Philadelphia; some of its members continue to try to make peace with the EA until 1894 but are not successful • The MEC organizes the California German Conference (superseding the California German Mission Conference), the New Mexico Spanish Mission Conference, and the Upper Mississippi Conference • The EA expands the Woman's Missionary Society (1883) into Woman's Home and Foreign Missionary Society • Belle Harris Bennett establishes the Scarritt Training and Bible School, Kansas City, MO	• The WM Conference officially changes the name of the organization from the Wesleyan Methodist Society to the Wesleyan Methodist Church in the UK (WMC [UK]) • The MEC in Finland is officially recognized by the national government • The second Ecumenical Methodist Conference meets in Washington, DC • AMEC Bishop Henry M. Turner establishes missions in Liberia and Sierra Leone; this marks the first extension of the AMEC outside North America • WM missionaries from southern Africa accompanying the pioneering party of Cecil Rhodes introduce Methodism from the Transvaal into Southern Rhodesia (now Zimbabwe) • J. H. Overton publishes his biography, *John Wesley*	**1891**

	A. WORLD HISTORY & POLITICS	B. AMERICAN HISTORY & POLITICS	C. SCIENCE, MEDICINE & TECHNOLOGY	D. DAILY LIFE, POPULAR CULTURE & ENTERTAINMENT
1891 cont.				
1892	• France claims the Côte d'Ivoire (Ivory Coast) as a colony and concludes a treaty with Liberia defining the border between them • Belgian forces defeat and drive Arab slaveholders and traders from east Africa out of the upper Congo • The British suppress uprisings by native African and Arabic peoples in Nyasaland (modern Malawi) • Britain claims a protectorate over the Gilbert and Ellice Islands in the Pacific	• Congress extends the Chinese Exclusion Act (1882) for another ten years • Telephone lines are completed between New York and Chicago • The US establishes Ellis Island as its official welcome and processing center for European immigrants • A magazine for young people in Boston, *The Youth's Companion*, publishes the earliest version of what comes to be called the Pledge of Allegiance • Ida B. Wells-Barnett publishes *Southern Horrors: Lynch Law in All Its Phases* and launches a nationwide campaign against lynching after the murder of three black businessmen in Memphis who were personal friends • Grover Cleveland is elected as president (for the second time; first term 1885–88) and Adlai E. Stevenson as vice president (Democratic Party)	• Rudolf Diesel (Germany) patents his internal combustion engine, which uses high compression of the fuel to ignite it, eliminating the spark plug; it requires "heavier" fuel than gasoline • The General Electric Company is established; it buys the patent rights to Thomas Edison's lightbulb and his lightbulb factory • Boll weevils enter Texas from Mexico and begin their march of infestation of cotton fields across the southern US	• W. L. Judson invents a slide fastener for clothing; it is later renamed the "zipper" • In the first prizefight to use boxing gloves and modern rules, "Gentleman Jim" Corbett defeats John L. Sullivan to become boxing's heavyweight champion
1893	• France claims a protectorate over Laos and merges it into the Indochinese Union (French Indo-China) with Cambodia and Vietnam	• When Hawaii's Queen Liliuokalani, who had come to the throne in 1891, attempts to implement a new constitution restoring the power of the monarchy, white business *(cont.)*	• The Johns Hopkins Medical School opens in Baltimore • Henry Ford builds his first automobile	• Sears, Roebuck and Company follows Montgomery Ward into the mail-order business

E. EDUCATION, LITERATURE & THE FINE ARTS	F. RELIGION, THEOLOGY, PHILOSOPHY & PSYCHOLOGY	G. AMERICAN & UNITED METHODISM	H. BRITISH & WORLD METHODISM	
		• Santiago H. Limbs begins MEC work among Spanish-speaking workers in Los Angeles • Benjamin T. Roberts, founder of the Free Methodist Church, publishes *Ordaining Women*, in which he advocates full clergy rights for women		**1891 cont.**
• Tchaikovsky composes his most popular ballet, *The Nutcracker* • Dvořák is appointed director of the National Conservatory of Music in New York City • Edvard Munch paints *The Kiss* • Childe Hassam, known as the "American Monet" for bringing the ideas of French impressionism to the US, completes his painting *Celia Thaxter in Her Garden* • Gauguin paints his brooding scene of superstitious dread *Spirit of the Dead Watching* • Joel Chandler Harris publishes *Uncle Remus and His Friends* • Rudyard Kipling publishes his volume of poetry, *Barrack-Room Ballads*, including "Gunga Din" and "The Road to Mandalay"	• Construction begins on the Cathedral of St. John the Divine (officially the Cathedral Church of Saint John the Divine in the City and Diocese of New York), the Mother Church of the Episcopal Diocese of New York [it is the largest cathedral in the US and is still not entirely complete as of 2005] • The PCUSA adopts the "Portland Deliverance," requiring ministers to subscribe to the theory of biblical inerrancy on pain of dismissal; this features prominently in the heresy trials of Charles A. Briggs (1893), Henry Preserved Smith (1894), and Arthur C. McGiffert (1900) • The American Psychological Association (APA) is founded • Martin Kähler publishes his groundbreaking work of biblical criticism, *The So-Called Historical Jesus and the Historic, Biblical Christ*	• The MEC General Conference: – establishes the University Senate to define and evaluate the educational standards of the educational institutions of the church [it is the first accrediting body of its kind in the US] – approves participation in the establishment of American University in Washington, DC, which traces its history to a letter written by George Washington expressing hope that a "national university" would be built in the nation's capital (a Congressional charter is granted in 1893; construction begins in 1896) – endorses the work of the American Bible Society and the American Sabbath Union – rejects the "diocesan model" of "districting" bishops in favor of an itinerating general superintendency – organizes the North Pacific German Mission Conference and West Norwegian-Danish Mission – approves and sends to the annual conferences the report of the Constitutional Commission concerning lay representation in annual conferences • Eugenia St. John, who had been ordained elder by the Kansas Conference of the MPC in 1889, is elected as a clergy delegate to the MPC General Conference; she is the first woman to serve in this capacity • The MPC General Conference: – votes to seat women (three lay, one clergy) for the first time as delegates to the General Conference – adopts legislation allowing each annual conference to decide whether or not to elect women as conference delegates or to ordain them as elders – hears report that the Committee on Articles of Faith appointed in 1888 could not agree on specific recommendations for revision of the Articles; votes to continue the committee for the next four years – recognizes the Young People's Society of Christian Endeavor • The MEC establishes Iliff School of Theology in Denver, CO • Trinity College (1859) is moved to Durham, NC • The AMEZC General Conference for the first time seats lay women as delegates • Delegates from the AMEC, AMEZC, and CMEC meet in Pittsburgh but fail to make any significant progress toward union • The WHMC (MECS) begins publication of *Our Homes* (to 1910)	• The independent Ethiopian Church of Mangena Mokone (ECMM) is founded by its namesake, a former WM minister in south Africa • John Scott Lidgett (WM) establishes the Bermondsey Settlement urban mission in the slums of South London • The MEC organizes the Finland Mission Conference and St. Petersburg Mission Conference in Russia	**1892**
• Dvořák composes his *Symphony No. 9* (*The New World*) • Tchaikovsky composes his *Symphony No. 6* (*Pathétique*)	• The World's Parliament of Religions meets in Chicago • The PCUSA General Assembly finds Charles A. Briggs guilty of heresy for his *(cont.)*	• The UBC General Conference: – for the first time seats lay delegates, including two women – receives report of the legal incorporation of the UBC under the 1889 constitution	• The MEC organizes the South American Conference • The PMC begins missionary work in eastern Nigeria, especially among the Efik and Igbo peoples	**1893**

	A. WORLD HISTORY & POLITICS	B. AMERICAN HISTORY & POLITICS	C. SCIENCE, MEDICINE & TECHNOLOGY	D. DAILY LIFE, POPULAR CULTURE & ENTERTAINMENT
1893 cont.	• Russia and France agree to a military alliance to remain in force so long as the Triple Alliance (Germany, Austria-Hungary, and Italy) remains • The British grant the Natal province in south Africa internal self-government and crush rebellions against the rule of the British South Africa Company in Matabeleland • New Zealand becomes the first country to grant women the right to vote in national elections • Siam (Thailand) agrees with France on a definition of its borders and renounces its historic territorial claims on Laos	leaders stage a revolt, backed by US troops, imprison Queen Liliuokalani, and petition for the annexation of Hawaii by the US (which happens in 1898) • Colorado becomes the second US state after Wyoming (1869 as territory and 1890 as state) to grant women the right to vote in state and local elections; Colorado is followed by Utah and Idaho (1896), Washington (1910), California (1911), Oregon, Kansas, and Arizona (1912), Alaska and Illinois (1913), Montana and Nevada (1914), New York (1917), Michigan, South Dakota, and Oklahoma (1918) • The World's Columbian Exposition, Chicago's first World's Fair, celebrates "the 400th anniversary of the discovery of America by Christopher Columbus" and marks the 60th anniversary of the city; it boasts more than 65,000 exhibits and attracts more than 27.5 million visitors • The American Railway Union is established to unite railway laborers in a single organization; Eugene Debs is its leader	• The U.S. Railroad Safety Appliance Act makes air brakes mandatory on all trains in the US • The Westinghouse Electrical Company, using its AC electrical system, provides the power and lighting for the World's Columbian Exposition in Chicago, the largest display of electric lighting the world has ever seen, and captures the lead in the "war of the electrical currents" with the DC electrical system of Thomas Edison and General Electric	• Hockey's first Stanley Cup championship is won by Montreal • George Ferris builds the first Ferris Wheel ride for the Chicago World's Fair; it is 250 feet tall, and has 36 cars • Other Chicago World's Fair "firsts" include Cracker Jacks, Aunt Jemima syrup, Cream of Wheat, Shredded Wheat, Pabst Beer (in bottles), Juicy Fruit chewing gum, a commemorative coin set (quarter, half dollar, and dollar) from the US Mint, and a commemorative stamp set from the US Post Office • Josephine Cochrane (US) develops the first practical dishwashing machine and establishes a company to manufacture and market it, later known as KitchenAid • The song "Happy Birthday To You," by Mildred J. Hill and Patty Smith Hill, is first published in their book *Song Stories for the Kindergarten*
1894	• Japanese troops invade and occupy Korea, Taiwan (Formosa), and southern Manchuria, provoking the Sino-Japanese War • Tsar Alexander III of Russia dies; he is succeeded by his son, Nicholas II • In prelude to the 1915 Armenian Genocide, Turkish soldiers massacre more than 200,000 Armenian Christians between 1894 and 1896 • France and Germany agree on the northern border of Cameroon • France establishes a new protectorate over Dahomey (modern Benin) in west Africa • Britain establishes a protectorate over (modern) Uganda • Alfred Dreyfus, a Jewish artillery officer in the French army, is arrested and convicted on phony charges of treason and deported to Devil's Island in French Guiana (he is exonerated in 1906); the "Dreyfus Affair" reveals the extent of anti-Semitism in France and much of the rest of Europe	• The American Railway Union launches a labor strike against the Pullman Company; the strike is eventually broken by the intervention of US Army troops; news accounts of the strike lead to a deepening awareness that there is a "labor problem" in America • The Anti-Saloon League, founded in Ohio in 1893, becomes a national organization and quickly ranks alongside the WCTU as one of the most powerful prohibition lobbies in America	• Alexandre Yersin (Switzerland) and Kitasato Shibasaburo (Japan) independently identify the organism that causes bubonic plague during an outbreak in China • London's Tower Bridge across the Thames is completed; the two 200-foot-tall towers support a moveable roadway that can be raised to allow ships to pass	• Emile Berliner's Gramophone Company, which makes phonograph records, and Eldridge Johnson's Consolidated Talking Machine Company, which makes machines for playing them, merge to firm the Victor Talking Machine Company • The Holland brothers open their Kinetoscope Parlor in New York City; it is the first commercial exhibition of movies • Milton Hershey establishes his chocolate manufacturing business • Joseph Pulitzer's newspaper, the *New York World*, publishes the first color comics in the US

E. EDUCATION, LITERATURE & THE FINE ARTS	F. RELIGION, THEOLOGY, PHILOSOPHY & PSYCHOLOGY	G. AMERICAN & UNITED METHODISM	H. BRITISH & WORLD METHODISM	
• Verdi's final opera *Falstaff* premieres at La Scala in Milan • Debussy's *String Quartet* debuts in Paris • Henry O. Tanner completes his painting of *The Banjo Lesson* • Edvard Munch paints his well-known *The Scream* • American poet Paul Laurence Dunbar, the son of former slaves and one of the first black writers to gain national prominence in the US, publishes his first volume of verse, *Oak and Ivy*, at his own expense • In "The Final Problem," Arthur Conan Doyle attempts to kill off the character Sherlock Holmes, having him fall off a cliff with his nemesis, Prof. Moriarty [the public outcry is so great that the author is finally persuaded to resurrect his detective in "The Adventure of the Empty House" in 1902] • Other notable publications include: – Stephen Crane, *Maggie: A Girl of the Streets* – Henry Blake Fuller, *The Cliff-Dwellers*, considered the first American "city novel"	1891 address at Union Theological Seminary, suspends him from the ministry, and demands that Union fire him from its faculty; Union's board of directors refuses to accept the decision, votes to "divorce" the seminary from denominational oversight, and retains Briggs on the faculty • Pope Leo XIII issues his encyclical *Providentissimus Deus (On the Study of Holy Scripture)*; it reasserts the traditional doctrine of biblical inerrancy and prohibits modern criticism that undermines this doctrine • Pope Leo XIII appoints Archbishop Francesco Satolli to be the first Apostolic Delegate to the US • The Mormon Tabernacle in Salt Lake City, UT, under construction for 40 years, is completed and dedicated • The National Camp Meeting Association for the Promotion of Holiness (1867) changes its name to the National Association for the Promotion of Holiness • Hannah Greenbaum Solomon founds the National Council of Jewish Women (NCJW) • Notable publications include: – Philip Schaff, *History of the Christian Church* – Émile Durkheim, *The Division of Labor in Society*	– endorses the establishment of the Young People's Christian Union in 1890 – removes the three-year limit on pastoral appointments that had been in place for many years, leaving the length of appointments up to the bishops and presiding elders • The women of the MPC establish the MPC Woman's Home Missionary Society (WHMS) • The MEC organizes the Central Swedish Conference and the New Mexico Spanish Mission Conference (superseding New Mexico Spanish Mission) • The MPC organizes the Arkansas-Mississippi Conference • The AMEC is formally established in Barbados • The Philadelphia Annual Conference (MEC) creates the first Methodist Layman's Association	• The first English-speaking Methodist congregation is established in Hong Kong by the WMC [UK] • Methodists in Europe organize the Central Council of the Conferences and Missions of the Methodist Episcopal Church in Europe	**1893 cont.**
• Jean Sibelius composes his symphonic poem *The Swan of Tuonela* • Debussy's enchanting *Prelude to the Afternoon of a Faun* premieres in Paris • The great tenor Enrico Caruso begins his operatic career in Naples, his hometown • Notable publications include: – Rudyard Kipling, *The Jungle Book* – H. Rider Haggard, *The People of the Mist* – Mark Twain, *The Tragedy of Pudd'nhead Wilson* – John Muir, *The Mountains of California*	• Notable publications include: – John Dewey, *The Study of Ethics* – G. T. Ladd, *A Primer of Psychology* – John Miley, *Systematic Theology*	• The MEC annual conferences fail to ratify the proposal for lay representation in annual conferences • The MECS General Conference: – hears the bishops, in their episcopal address, express formal disapproval of the Holiness movement – approves the establishment of a Commission on Federation, to meet with the MEC counterpart – establishes a General Board of Education and orders the creation of a wider range of Sunday school publications • The UEC (1891) General Conference meets for the first time: – adopts Articles of Faith and a *Discipline* based on those of the EA but providing for lay representation – creates general boards and agencies to structure the work of the new denomination – orders the production of a catechism and for hymnbooks to be printed in German and English – agrees to purchase the Evangelical Publishing Company from its private owners and to center denominational publishing operations in Harrisburg, PA • The MEC organizes the Western, Central, and Northern Swedish Conferences • The CMEC General Conference authorizes the office of "stewardess" in the church, opening the way for formal participation of women in local church leadership and in quarterly conferences, with special responsibility for assisting with the Lord's Supper, but rejects a recommendation from the bishops that women be licensed to preach • Julia Foote is ordained deacon by the AMEZC; she is the first black woman to be ordained in any branch of American Methodism (she is ordained elder in 1900)	• WM missionaries from south Africa reach what becomes Northern Rhodesia (now Zambia)	**1894**

	A. WORLD HISTORY & POLITICS	B. AMERICAN HISTORY & POLITICS	C. SCIENCE, MEDICINE & TECHNOLOGY	D. DAILY LIFE, POPULAR CULTURE & ENTERTAINMENT
1894 cont.				
1895	• The Sino-Japanese War ends with the defeat of China, which is forced to cede Taiwan and the Pescadores Islands to Japan; European powers respond with a policy they call "carving up the Chinese melon," but they force Japan to return Port Arthur to China • British forces from the Cape Colony make an unsuccessful attempt to overthrow the Boer (Afrikaner) government in the Transvaal • The European powers complete their colonization of Africa and begin extending colonies and commercial concessions into Asia • Italian troops advance into Ethiopia but are defeated at Amba Alagi	• The Cotton States International Exposition held in Atlanta is a symbol of the "New South" that is emerging after Reconstruction • Booker T. Washington makes a speech at the Atlanta Exposition in which he summarizes his concept of race relations appropriate for the times in one statement: "In all things that are purely social we can be as separate as the fingers, yet one as the hand in all things essential to mutual progress"; this is promptly labeled by critics such as W. E. B. DuBois as the "Atlanta Compromise" • The number of bison in the American West declines to less than 1,000 • NAWSA moves to distance itself from Elizabeth Cady Stanton after her publication of *The Woman's Bible* because many conservative suffragists consider her to be too radical	• Italian engineer Guglielmo Marconi invents a wireless telegraph system, marking the beginning of radio transmissions • Wilhelm Conrad Röntgen (Germany) discovers X-rays • Helium is successfully isolated by William Ramsay (England) • Louis and Auguste Lumière (France) develop a motion-picture camera • The National Medical Association is formed by a group of black physicians who believe that their interests are not being adequately represented by the American Medical Association (1847)	• The poem "America the Beautiful" by Katharine Lee Bates first appears in print; the lyrics are revised in 1904 and again in 1913, and by 1926 the lyrics are firmly associated with the tune "Materna" • The first US Open golf tournament is won by Horace Rawlins • The first wholly professional football game in the US is played in Latrobe, PA, between the Latrobe YMCA and the Jeannette Athletic Club (Latrobe won) • The first electrically lighted Christmas tree is displayed in the White House, beginning an annual tradition • *Field and Stream* magazine begins publication
1896	• Russia and Japan attempt to organize joint dominance of Korea • Ethiopian forces defeat the Italians at the Battle of Adua; Italy signs the Treaty of Addis Ababa, recognizing the independence of Ethiopia but retaining their colony in Eritreia • German Kaiser William II sends a telegram to the Boers (Afrikaners) in the Transvaal congratulating them on repelling British forces; the implication of German interference causes outrage in Britain • The Transvaal and the Orange Free State conclude a military alliance • H. H. Kitchener heads a joint British and Egyptian army in an effort to retake the Sudan • British forces defeat the Ashanti people in central Ghana • Mohandas Gandhi begins to teach *satyagraha* (Sanskrit for "truth and firmness"), a policy of passive resistance to and noncooperation with British colonial government in south Africa	• Utah is admitted to the US as the 45th state • The *Plessy v. Ferguson* decision by the US Supreme Court establishes the "separate but equal" doctrine permitting racial segregation in public facilities, including schools, as long as facilities for both races are of equal quality; this codifies the legal basis for "Jim Crow" laws enforcing racial segregation in the southern states • The National Association of Colored Women (NACW) is formed, bringing together more than 100 black women's clubs; leaders in the black women's club movement include Josephine St. Pierre Ruffin, Mary Church Terrell, and Anna Julia Cooper • Democratic presidential candidate William Jennings Bryan makes what is possibly the single most dramatic and powerful speech in American political history in opposition to the implementation of the gold standard for US currency: "You shall not crucify mankind upon a cross of gold" • William McKinley is elected as president and Garrett A. Hobart as vice president (Republican Party)	• The Westinghouse Electrical Company builds the first successful long-range power network, with AC generators at Niagara Falls producing electricity that is transmitted to Buffalo, NY, and distributed to customers there; this marks the beginning of a transition from kerosene lighting to electric lighting across the country	• The US Post Office begins rural free delivery (RFD) in West Virginia; this soon spreads to the rest of the country • William Randolph Hearst's newspaper, the *Morning Journal*, begins the first regular weekly full-color comic supplement, the *Katzenjammer Kids* • Colgate Ribbon Dental Creme is the first toothpaste to be sold in a tube • The first Olympic Games of the modern era are held in Athens, Greece, including the first running of the long-distance race called the marathon, commemorating the Greek soldier named Pheidippides who, according to legend, ran from the village of Marathon to Athens in 490 B.C. to deliver the news of a military victory

E. EDUCATION, LITERATURE & THE FINE ARTS	F. RELIGION, THEOLOGY, PHILOSOPHY & PSYCHOLOGY	G. AMERICAN & UNITED METHODISM	H. BRITISH & WORLD METHODISM	
		• Sarah Dickey is voted full clergy rights by the UBC • Turner Theological Seminary opens for classes as a department of Morris Brown College [the name is changed to honor AMEC Bishop Henry M. Turner in 1900] • A group of Methodist men in Philadelphia establish the Brotherhood of St. Paul; it is the first organization specifically for lay Methodist men		**1894 cont.**
• The London School of Economics and Political Science is established • Dvořák composes his *Cello Concerto in B Minor*, considered by many to be the greatest cello concerto ever composed • The first ever Promenade Concert is held at the Queen's Hall in London • The first complete performance of Gustav Mahler's *Symphony No. 2 (Resurrection)* takes place in Berlin • Henry O. Turner completes his painting of *Daniel in the Lion's Den* • Oscar Wilde publishes his best-known play, *The Importance of Being Earnest* • Other notable publications include: – Thomas Hardy, *Jude the Obscure* – George MacDonald, *Lilith* – H. G. Wells, *The Time Machine* – Henryk Sienkiewicz, *Quo Vadis?* – Stephen Crane, *The Red Badge of Courage*	• The American National Baptist Convention (1886) merges with two other groups of black Baptists to create the National Baptist Convention of America • Several Pentecostal church bodies in New York and New England unite to create the Association of Pentecostal Churches of America • Benjamin T. Tanner, in *The Color of Solomon—What?* argues that biblical scholars wrongly portrayed the son of David as a white man • Elizabeth Cady Stanton (et al.) publish the first volume of *The Woman's Bible* (vol. 2, 1898) • Andrew D. White publishes the first edition of *A History of the Warfare of Science With Theology in Christendom*, in which he seeks to "aid in letting the light of historical truth into that decaying mass of outworn thought which attaches the modern world to mediaeval conceptions of Christianity"	• The EA General Conference: – takes steps to reorganize the denomination after the UEC schism – declines to adopt any form of term limits on the service of bishops or presiding elders – hears but does not act on a proposal for lay representation in General Conference – creates an Evangelical Correspondence College for the education of preachers – establishes Albright Collegiate Institute (later Albright College) in Meyerstown, PA • The AMEC builds a new publishing house in Philadelphia • The New York Evangelical Training School and Settlement House is founded by Jennie Fowler Willing (MEC) to train deaconesses and serve Hell's Kitchen, an infamous New York slum	• E. R. Hendrix and C. F. Reid initiate MECS mission work in Korea • United Brethren begin mission in Japan • The Methodist Episcopal Church Congress of Europe meets for the first time in Berlin	**1895**
• The first five Nobel Prizes are established (physics, chemistry, physiology or medicine, literature, and peace) • The College of New Jersey, chartered in 1746, becomes Princeton University • Richard Strauss, inspired by Nietzsche, composes his symphonic poem *Also sprach Zarathustra* (Thus Spoke Zarathustra) • Giacomo Puccini's opera *La Bohème* (The Bohemian) debuts in Turin; it becomes one of the best-loved and most-performed operatic works of all time • W. E. B. DuBois has his doctoral dissertation, *The Suppression of the African Slave-Trade to the United States of America, 1638–1870*, published as the initial volume in the *Harvard Historical Studies* series • Rainer Maria Rilke publishes what is probably his best known book of verse, *Larenopfer* • The best of the poems of Paul Laurence Dunbar are collected in the volume *Lyrics of Lowly Life*, with an introduction by William Dean Howells • Other notable publications include: – Anton Chekhov, *The Seagull* – William Morris, *The Well at the World's End*	• The United Evangelical Lutheran Church (UELC, Danish) is established • Theodor Herzl's *The Jewish State* inaugurates the Zionist movement devoted to the creation of a Jewish national homeland in Palestine • Henri Bergson publishes *Matter and Memory*	• The MEC General Conference: – approves the appointment by the bishops of a Commission on Federation, to meet with the MECS counterpart – creates a new Constitutional Commission to reconsider the work of the 1888 Commission – denounces the alcoholic beverage industry and urges both pastors and church members to cooperate with the work of the Anti-Saloon League – proposes that the fourth Sunday in November be designated as Temperance Sunday – calls for the election of bishops without consideration of race or color – organizes the West Norwegian-Danish Conference – authorizes the Congo Mission Conference • The WFMS (MEC) replaces *The Heathen Woman's Friend* (1869) with *The Missionary Woman's Friend* (to 1940) • The MEC opens Bancroft Rest Home in Ocean Grove, NJ; it is the first retirement home for missionaries and deaconesses • The MPC General Conference: – receives an Act of Incorporation from the Maryland state legislature – indefinitely postpones proposed changes to the Articles of Religion – orders revision and publication of the Shorter Catechism – establishes Kansas City University – organizes the Chickasaw Mission Conference and the Dallas Colored Mission Conference	• The AMEC begins missionary work in southern Africa; the Ethiopian Church of Mangena Mokone decides to join the AMEC • The Wesley Guild is established by the WM Conference in Britain • The National Council of Evangelical Free Churches is established in the UK; WM leader Hugh Price Hughes is elected as the first president • The United Methodist Free Churches and the Bible Christians unite with the WM Annual Conference in New Zealand; the Primitive Methodists remain separate	**1896**

	A. WORLD HISTORY & POLITICS	**B. AMERICAN HISTORY & POLITICS**	**C. SCIENCE, MEDICINE & TECHNOLOGY**	**D. DAILY LIFE, POPULAR CULTURE & ENTERTAINMENT**
1897	• Crete proclaims union with Greece, provoking the Ottoman Empire to declare war on Greece, beginning the Greco-Turkish War • H. H. Kitchener's Anglo-Egyptian forces recapture considerable territory in Sudan • Ethiopia and France sign a treaty defining the border of Somalia • Britain makes Zululand into the province of Natal in south Africa • Germany occupies the area around Kiaochow Bay in northern China after the murder there of two missionaries from Germany • Britain's Queen Victoria celebrates the Diamond Jubilee (60 years) of her coronation in 1837 • The Zionist Organization is founded by Theodor Herzl at the First Zionist Congress in Basel, Switzerland [renamed the World Zionist Organization in 1960]; its goal is "to establish a home for the Jewish people in Palestine, secured under public law"	• Discovery of gold along the Klondike River in the Yukon Territory begins a gold rush drawing over 30,000 prospectors within the first year • The Organic Administration Act creates the National Forest system in the US, preserving forest lands "to improve and protect forests or secure favorable water flows and to furnish a continuous supply of timber for citizens of the United States"	• Ronald Ross (Great Britain) discovers that the bacillus causing malaria is carried by the Anopheles mosquito • J. J. Thomson discovers the electron and is awarded the Nobel Prize for the achievement in 1906	• The first electric-powered subway line in the US opens in Boston • Composers Scott Joplin, James Scott, and Joseph Lamb popularize ragtime, giving birth to America's popular music industry • The player piano, originally called the Pianola, is invented by Edwin Votey • Jell-O fruit-flavored gelatin appears for the first time; the first four flavors are orange, lemon, strawberry, and raspberry (lime is not introduced until 1930) • The first known published recipe for chocolate brownies appears in the Sears and Roebuck catalog • The famous editorial by F. P. Church proclaiming that "Yes, Virginia, there is a Santa Claus" is published in the *New York Sun* • The Boston Athletic Association sponsors the first Boston Marathon, held annually since then; John J. McDermott wins with a time of 2:55:10 • John Philip Sousa composes his famous patriotic march "The Stars and Stripes Forever"; it immediately becomes a staple of Fourth of July celebrations throughout the US • John Philip Sousa's band makes phonograph recordings of popular "cakewalk" and early "ragtime" tunes in addition to military marches
1898	• The sinking of the battleship USS *Maine* in Havana leads to the beginning of the Spanish-American War • US forces defeat the Spanish at Guantanamo Bay; Theodore Roosevelt leads the "Rough Riders" up San Juan Hill to victory; and the US fleet destroys much of the Spanish navy near Santiago; elsewhere, US forces capture Puerto Rico, the Philippines, and Guam • The Treaty of Paris ends the Spanish-American War; Spain gives up its claims to Cuba and cedes Puerto Rico, the Philippines, and Guam to the US; the US establishes military bases in all of them • H. H. Kitchener's Anglo-Egyptian forces capture Khartoum, driving the Mahdists out of Sudan, and move on to Fashoda on the Nile River; French forces then occupying Fashoda evacuate, avoiding a confrontation • China leases Hong Kong to Britain for 99 years • Journalist and writer Emile Zola publishes his famous open letter J'accuse! (I Accuse!) to the president of France exposing the cover-up of the 1894 Dreyfus Affair; an explosive controversy about anti-Semitism in France erupts • The British parliament passes the Reform Bill of 1898; it almost doubles the size of the British electorate by enfranchising agricultural workers and provides for virtually universal male suffrage	• President McKinley signs a Congressional resolution declaring Cuba to be independent of Spain and authorizing the use of US army and navy forces to force Spain to leave Cuba • In response the US and Spain declare war on each other, and the Spanish-American War begins • Eugeve V. Debs helps to found the Socialist Democratic Party, later the Socialist Party, in the US • The US annexes the Hawaiian Islands	• Pierre and Marie Curie discover radium; they share the 1903 Nobel Prize for Physics • Danish engineer Valdemar Poulsen demonstrates the principle of magnetic recording with a machine called the Telegraphone that can record speech magnetically on moving steel wire	• Pepsi Cola is formulated and sold for the first time • The Paris Metro subway system begins operation • Competition for subscribers and advertisers between New York newspaper tycoons Joseph Pulitzer and William Randolph Hearst gives rise to "yellow journalism," many characteristics of which, such as banner headlines, sensational stories, an emphasis on illustrations, and colored supplements, will become a permanent feature of popular newspapers in the US and Europe • Scott Joplin publishes his "Swipsy Cakewalk"
1899	• Britain recognizes all of China north of the Great Wall as being within the Russian sphere of influence • The Second Boer War begins in south Africa, sparked by the discovery of gold in the Transvaal; the Boers (Afrikaners) *(cont.)*	• Congress ratifies the Treaty of Paris and approves US participation in the International Peace Conference in The Hague • The US announces its "open door" policy with respect to China, stressing the *(cont.)*	• Dutch botanist Hugo De Vries independently replicates Mendel's discoveries about heredity in plants and proposes that units he calls "pangenes" are the carriers of hereditary traits	• A German pharmaceutical company later named Bayer AG develops and markets aspirin as a general pain reliever • Large-scale bottling of Coca-Cola begins in Chattanooga, TN, enabling nationwide (eventually worldwide) distribution

E. EDUCATION, LITERATURE & THE FINE ARTS	F. RELIGION, THEOLOGY, PHILOSOPHY & PSYCHOLOGY	G. AMERICAN & UNITED METHODISM	H. BRITISH & WORLD METHODISM	
• In commemoration of the centennial of Tennessee's statehood in 1896, a full-scale replica of the Greek Parthenon is constructed in Nashville, "The Athens of the South" • The Tate Gallery, one of the world's great art museums, opens in London • Paul Dukas composes his symphonic poem *The Sorcerer's Apprentice*, inspired by Goethe's 1797 poetic ballad of the same title • Richard Strauss composes *Till Eulenspiegel's Merry Pranks* • Debussy's orchestration of Erik Satie's *Trois Gymnopédies* (1888) premieres in Paris • Notable publications include: – Rudyard Kipling, *Captains Courageous* – Edmond Rostand, *Cyrano de Bergerac* – Bram Stoker, *Dracula* – H. G. Wells, *The Invisible Man*	• Pope Leo XIII issues the encyclical *Regimini Militantis Ecclesiae (On the Supremacy of the Church Militant)*, which condemns Protestantism as "Lutheran rebellion" • The predominantly black Church of God in Christ is established in Jackson, MS; it will grow to become one of the largest Pentecostal churches in the world • The Lutheran Free Church (LFC, Norwegian) is established in Minnesota • Notable publications include: – William James, *The Will to Believe* – Edwin Hatch and Henry A. Redpath, *Concordance to the Septuagint* (2 vols., 1897–1906) – Washington Gladden, *Social Facts and Forces: The Factory, the Labor Union, the Corporation, the Railway, the City, the Church* – Shailer Mathews, *The Social Teachings of Jesus* (revised in 1928 as *Jesus on Social Institutions*)	• The UBC General Conference: – hears reports on the progress of numerous court cases stemming from the 1889 "walk-out" of the "radicals" under Bishop Wright, who had demanded possession of the publishing house and other church properties; the UBC is determined to be the "legal" Church of the United Brethren in Christ, with the "radicals" being ordered to pay court costs – decides that the centennial celebration of 1874 had been premature and orders that the centennial of the UBC should be celebrated in 1900 and through the meeting of the 1901 General Conference – approves creation of the office of deaconess • The International Holiness Union and Prayer League is founded in Cincinnati by former MECS minister Seth Cook Rees [it is later renamed the International Holiness Church (IHC)] • The Woman's Board of Home Missions (MECS) opens the Sue Bennett Memorial School in London, KY, to bring Christian higher education to the mountain children of Appalachia • The MEC organizes the Atlanta Conference • The Independent African Methodist Church (IAMC) is established	• The WM (British) missions in southern Germany are merged with the BMK, or German Annual Conference of the MEC (1868); the BMK assumes responsibility for mission work in Austria • The MEC creates China Central Conference • Queen's College is established in Melbourne as the central theological institution of Australian Wesleyan Methodism; E. H. Sugden is the first Master • *The Proceedings of the Wesley Historical Society* are published for the first time	**1897**
• Rimsky-Korsakov's opera *Mozart and Salieri* is based upon and furthers the unfounded legend that Salieri tried to poison Mozart out of frustrated jealousy of Mozart's genius • Stephen Crane's volume *The Open Boat and Other Tales* contains some of his finest short stories • Other notable publications include: – Henry James, *The Turn of the Screw* – H. G. Wells, *The War of the Worlds*	• Henry P. Mendez, a Sephardic Jewish leader in New York City, establishes the Orthodox Union of Jews in America • John R. Mott creates the Student Volunteer Movement for Foreign Missions (and will chair it until 1928) • The first Pentecostal Holiness Congregation is formed in Goldsboro, NC • The Fire-Baptized Holiness Association is established; it ordains women and allows female presiding elders over local congregations • The Los Angeles Church of the Nazarene is formally established; its constitution recognizes the equal rights of women and men to all church offices, including the ministry • Charlotte Perkins Gilman publishes her landmark volume *Women and Economics*; it denounces women's financial dependence on men and supports day-care programs and cooperative kitchens, and is one of the foundational volumes of modern feminism • Eberhard Nestle publishes his ground-breaking critical edition of the Greek New Testament, *Novum Testamentum Graece* • Other notable publications include: – Borden Parker Bowne, *The Christian Revelation* – William N. Clarke, *An Outline of Christian Theology*	• The MEC and MECS Commissions on Federation meet jointly in Washington; an ongoing Joint Commission on Federation is established as a result • The MECS General Conference: – establishes an Educational Commission to set standards for schools and colleges – initiates the "Twentieth Century Campaign" as the church's first connectional educational campaign – refuses formal endorsement of the Women's Christian Temperance Union – forbids anyone to preach within the bounds of a charge without the permission of the preacher in charge, an action directed primarily at traveling "holiness evangelists" • The UEC General Conference: – condemns socialism but calls for alleviation of the adverse conditions that give rise to it – calls for the end of the liquor trade and traffic – goes on record as opposing the growing "passion for pleasure" in America • Mary J. Small, who had been ordained as a deacon in 1895, is the first woman to be ordained by AMEZC as an elder in full connection • AMEC women form Woman's Home and Foreign Missionary Societies • The MPC organizes the Chicago German Mission Conference	• The union of Independent Methodists in the UK (1806) formally becomes the Independent Methodist Connexion of Churches • The Ethiopian Church of Mangena Mokone (1892) is formally adopted as part of the AMEC by Bishop Henry M. Turner; Mokone becomes an AMEC elder • Josephine Campbell (MECS) opens the Carolina Institute (school for young girls) in Korea • The MECS sends Warren A. Candler and Walter R. Lambuth to Cuba to reorganize missionary work there after disruption by the Spanish-American War • The AMEC also establishes a mission in Cuba • The WM "Twentieth Century Fund" is launched in the UK; it will raise over £1 million by 1904	**1898**
• Maurice Ravel composes his *Pavane for a Dead Princess* • Debussy composes his *Three Nocturnes* (Nuages, Fêtes, and Sirènes), characterized by impressionistic harmony and texture • Jean Sibelius's *Symphony No. 1* premieres in Helsinki	• Pope Leo XIII issues his encyclical *Testem Benevolentiae (Concerning New Opinions, Virtue, Nature and Grace, With Regard To Americanism)* attempting to curb Roman Catholic "accommodation" to democratic liberalism and "Americanism"	• The EA General Conference: – approves plans for a Centennial Jubilee of the EA in 1900 – authorizes a study of the possibility of establishing a mission in China – orders the preparation of a "junior catechism" for children aged 8-12	• Bishop James M. Thoburn (MEC) begins mission work in the Philippines • The MECS mission in Cuba is reestablished; the chapel built at Matanzas is the first Protestant church building in Cuba	**1899**

	A. WORLD HISTORY & POLITICS	B. AMERICAN HISTORY & POLITICS	C. SCIENCE, MEDICINE & TECHNOLOGY	D. DAILY LIFE, POPULAR CULTURE & ENTERTAINMENT
1899 cont.	defeat the outnumbered British garrisons in several different places and besiege Ladysmith; Britain hurriedly sends reinforcements • Somalian forces raid British and Italian possessions in Ethiopia around the Red Sea • The first International Peace Conference, meeting at The Hague, establishes a permanent Court of International Justice and Arbitration, which is intended to settle conflicts among the major powers, particularly over colonial territories • A treaty signed by the US, Britain, and Germany recognizes US interests in Samoa; American Samoa is placed under the control of the US Navy	necessity of free trade for US merchants but asking the major powers to preserve China's independence and for noninterference with the free use of Chinese ports; this helps to prevent an open partition of China • The US annexes Wake Island in the Pacific, primarily for use as a cable station • Mt. Rainier National Park is established		• The American Eveready Battery Company produces the first dry-cell flashlight and uses the biblical quotation "Let There Be Light" on the cover of their 1899 catalog • Scott Joplin composes his "Original Rags" and "The Maple Leaf Rag," and ragtime music is accepted into the popular musical mainstream
1900	• Members of an antiforeigner secret society in China known as the Fists of Righteous Harmony, called the "Boxers" because of their martial arts skills, launch a rebellion against Western influence in China • The Boxers succeed in seizing Beijing and besiege foreigners there; an international (but mostly British and American) relief force reaches Beijing and routs the Boxers, then loots the capital and ransacks the Forbidden City, destroying the power of the Ch'ing dynasty • The US reaffirms but expands its "open door" China policy, and the Anglo-German Yangtze Accord maintains the "open door" policy in Chinese territory in which Britain and Germany have influence • Russia occupies all of Manchuria but fails to secure a naval base in southern Korea • Italy and Ethiopia sign a treaty defining the border between Ethiopia and the Italian colony of Eritreia • British forces begin the conquest of northern Nigeria • British forces in south Africa defeat the Boers (Afrikaners), relieving Ladysmith and Mafeking, then capturing Bloemfontein • A clear border is established between Burma and China • Paris holds its fifth Exposition Universelle; the ornate Alexander III Bridge over the Seine is constructed for the occasion; it attracts almost 80,000 exhibits and about 40 million visitors	• The US census reports that the population is 75,994,575: – whites: 66,809,196 (87.9%) – blacks: 8,833,994 (11.6%) – other: 351,385 (0.5%) • The US national debt is $2,136,961,091 • The Gold Standard Act formally discontinues the policy of bimetallism for US currency, defining the value of the dollar in terms of gold only • Hawaii becomes a territory of the US • Booker T. Washington founds the National Negro Business League • A major hurricane hits Galveston, TX, killing over 8,000 people, making it the deadliest single storm in US history • The US purchases the Danish West Indies (St. Thomas, St. John, St. Croix, and Water Island) from Denmark; they become the US Virgin Islands • The US declares Puerto Rico an unorganized territory and establishes a civil government • Both the Populist and the Democratic parties nominate William Jennings Bryan for president; he runs on a platform of anti-imperialism and free silver • President McKinley is reelected and Theodore Roosevelt is elected as vice president (Republican Party)	• Max Planck originates the theory that energy is radiated in small, discrete units, which he calls quanta; the "quantum theory" revolutionizes the understanding of atomic and subatomic processes • Karl Landsteiner first identifies blood types A, B, and O based on antigens on red blood cells (type AB discovered in 1902) • Count Ferdinand von Zeppelin builds his first airship • Wilhelm Maybach, working as a designer with the Daimler Motoren-Gesellschaft, builds the first Mercedes automobile; capable of reaching a speed of 35 mph, it represents a major turning point in automobile design and is generally regarded as the first "modern" motor car • British archaeologist Arthur Evans begins his excavation of the ruins of the ancient city of Knossos in Crete and discovers evidence of a previously unknown Bronze Age civilization to which he gives the name *Minoan*	• The "Brownie" camera, designed for Eastman Kodak by Frank Brownell, goes on the market with a retail price of one dollar, making photography widely available to the public • The Hills Bros. grocery store begins marketing roasted coffee in vacuum-sealed tins • Olympic Games: Paris
1901	• Britain's Queen Victoria dies after a reign of 82 years (the longest in British history); she is succeeded by her son, Edward VII • The Commonwealth of Australia is created by the union of the crown colonies of New South Wales, Queensland, South Australia, Tasmania, Victoria, and western Australia • Russia tries to force China into yielding control of Manchuria but encounters strong opposition from Japan, Britain, and the US	• President McKinley is assassinated by anarchist Leon Czolgosz at the Pan-American Exposition in Buffalo, NY; Vice President Roosevelt becomes president • Andrew Carnegie, J. P. Morgan, Charles Schwab, and Elbert H. Gary establish US Steel, which becomes the world's first $1 billion company • The US stock market crashes, losing 46% of value, triggering a depression that lasts into 1903 • The Army Nurse Corps is established, followed in 1908 by the Navy Nurse Corps	• Marconi successfully transmits radio signals across the Atlantic, from Cornwall, England, to a receiving station near St. John's, Newfoundland • Dutch physician Wilhelm Einthoven invents a new galvanometer, which simplifies and improves the process for producing electrocardiograms • American archaeologist Andrew E. Douglass originates the science of dendrochronology (the study of tree rings to date past events)	• The Victor Talking Machine Company establishes the Victor "Red Seal" Records label • New York becomes the first state to require automobiles to have state-issued license plates • Professional baseball's American League is organized as competition for the older National League (1876)

E. EDUCATION, LITERATURE & THE FINE ARTS	F. RELIGION, THEOLOGY, PHILOSOPHY & PSYCHOLOGY	G. AMERICAN & UNITED METHODISM	H. BRITISH & WORLD METHODISM	
• Edward Elgar completes his *Enigma Variations*, and the work has its first performance in London • Arnold Schoenberg composes his string sextet *Transfigured Night*, regarded as his first important work • American dancer Isadora Duncan makes her professional debut in Chicago, inaugurating a career that will foster the rise of modern dance • Charles Chesnutt's *The Conjure Woman* establishes him as one of the first black authors to be accepted in America's literary mainstream • Other notable publications include: – Leo Tolstoy, *Resurrection* – William Butler Yeats, *The Wind Among the Reeds*	• W. E. B. DuBois publishes *The Philadelphia Negro: A Social Study*, the first serious sociological case study of a black community in the US • Other notable publications include: – John Dewey, *The School and Society* – Thorstein Veblen, *The Theory of the Leisure Class* – Borden Parker Bowne, *The Christian Life*	– appoints another committee to study the issue of lay representation • The "Publishing House Controversy" breaks out: the US Senate approves a bill (previously approved by the House in 1889) for payment of $288,000 to the MECS for use of the facilities of the Publishing House in Nashville for federal government purposes during the Civil War; after the payment is made, the Senate appoints an investigating committee over the size of the attorney's fees involved (35%) • The AMEC establishes Payne University in Selma, AL		**1899 cont.**
• The Art Nouveau style dominates design and architecture in turn-of-the-century Paris • Boston's Symphony Hall is completed and dedicated, and proves to be one of the best musical venues ever constructed • Jean Sibelius's best-known and most significant composition, the tone poem *Finlandia*, premieres in Helsinki; it is (for a time) banned by the Russian rulers of Finland because it arouses too much patriotic fervor among the Finns • Puccini's opera *Tosca* debuts at La Scala in Milan and soon becomes a staple of the operatic repertoire • The exhibition of Monet's magnificent series of *Water Lilies* paintings makes him famous throughout France, Britain, and the US • Edward Elgar's oratorio *The Dream of Gerontius* premieres in Birmingham • L. Frank Baum takes Dorothy "off to see the wizard" in his classic and timeless story of *The Wonderful Wizard of Oz* • Other notable publications include: – Thomas Mann, *Buddenbrooks* – Joseph Conrad, *Lord Jim* – Theodore Dreiser, *Sister Carrie*	• The United Presbyterian Church of Scotland (1847) and the majority of the Free Church of Scotland (1843) unite to form The United Free Church of Scotland • Holiness teacher and former Methodist pastor Charles Fox Parham opens his Bethel Bible Institute in Topeka, KS; modern Pentecostalism begins with his formulation of the doctrine that glossolalia is the "Bible evidence" of baptism in the Holy Spirit • Notable publications include: – Sigmund Freud, *Interpretation of Dreams* – Wilhelm Wundt, *Comparative Psychology* – Adolf von Harnack, *What is Christianity?* – William James, *Principles of Psychology* – Borden Parker Bowne, *The Atonement*	• The MEC General Conference: – approves the proposals of the Constitutional Commission for revision of the constitution to give full laity rights to women and to allow equal numbers of clergy and lay delegates in annual conferences; sends the new constitution to the annual conferences for ratification – removes limits on the length of pastoral service on a circuit, leaving appointments entirely to the judgment of the bishops – again refuses to license women as preachers or to allow them to be ordained – organizes the Mobile Conference and the Japanese Mission Conference – admits the Northern Swedish Mission Conference as an annual conference • The AMEC General Conference authorizes formal incorporation of the denomination • Central Tennessee College (1867) in Nashville is renamed Walden University [which closes in 1925]; the medical department becomes independent as Meharry Medical Center • The MPC General Conference: – reorganizes the Board of Foreign Missions and the Board of Home Missions – votes to insert the word *catholic* after the word *holy* in the Apostles' Creed as used in the church • Charles W. Drees begins MEC mission work in Puerto Rico • Maclay College of Theology moves to Los Angeles, changes its name to Southern California School of Theology, and becomes part of the University of Southern California	• The MEC creates the Denmark Mission Conference [it becomes the Denmark Annual Conference in 1911] • Methodism is introduced into Hungary by F. H. Otto Melle from the BMK church in Dresden, Germany [services in the Hungarian language begin in Budapest in 1907] • The MECS mission in Cuba holds its first annual meeting • The New Testament is translated into Korean	**1900**
• Constantin Stanislavsky, founder of the Moscow Art Theatre, develops the revolutionary theory of "method acting" that comes to bear his name • Edward Elgar composes his *Pomp & Circumstance March No. 1* • Thomas Moran completes his painting *Sunset* • Booker T. Washington publishes his autobiography, *Up from Slavery* • Miles Franklin's *My Brilliant Career* is considered the first authentic Australian novel; it is published in Edinburgh	• The American Standard Version of the Bible (ASV) is published • Agnes Ozman becomes the first of Charles Parham's followers to receive the sign of Spirit baptism: glossolalia • C. Austin Miles's *New Songs of the Gospel* includes Charles A. Tindley's gospel hymn "I'll Overcome Some Day" [in the 1960s it will be transformed into the great anthem of the civil rights movement, "We Shall Overcome"] • Friedrich Nietzsche publishes *The Will to Power*, his last major work	• The UBC General Conference: – celebrates the centennial of the establishment of the UBC by William Otterbein and Martin Boehm and of the first annual conference session in 1800 – receives Ella Niswonger as the first woman to be elected as a clergy delegate – hears the bishops attack the "materialistic hypothesis of evolution" and a "destructive form of 'higher criticism'" that "waged war on the Word of God" – adopts a proposal for equal representation of clergy and lay delegates to General Conference beginning in 1905	• The third Ecumenical Methodist Conference meets in London • The UBC begins mission work in the Philippines • Bishop Joseph C. Hartzell organizes the MEC East Central Africa Mission Conference, embracing MEC work in Mozambique, Rhodesia, and the Transvaal • The MEC mission in Korea ordains the first lay preacher	**1901**

	A. WORLD HISTORY & POLITICS	B. AMERICAN HISTORY & POLITICS	C. SCIENCE, MEDICINE & TECHNOLOGY	D. DAILY LIFE, POPULAR CULTURE & ENTERTAINMENT
1901 cont.	• The Boers (Afrikaners) in south Africa wage a guerrilla war against the British, but they are gradually subdued when British forces, now under Kitchener's command, begin devastating the farms that sustain and shelter the guerrillas	• Militant prohibitionist Carry Nation receives national attention for her public saloon-smashing campaign against alcoholic beverages	• British inventor Frederick William Lanchester patents disc brakes for automobiles • Thomas Edison invents the alkaline storage battery • The Spindletop oil well "gusher" near Beaumont heralds the birth of the Texas oil industry	
1902	• The US gains control of the Panama Canal project by purchasing the rights from a French construction company • The Treaty of Vereeniging ends the Second Boer War in south Africa; Transvaal and the Orange River (formerly the Orange Free State) become British crown colonies • Russia recognizes Chinese sovereignty over Manchuria and agrees to a phased troop withdrawal but fails to carry through • King Alfonso XIII of Spain turns 16 and assumes control of the Spanish government • Australia grants women the right to vote in national elections • The eruption of Santa Maria in Guatemala ranks no. 4 on the list of most violent volcanic eruptions in recorded history	• The US ends its occupation of Cuba, which becomes independent • The US Bureau of the Census is established; it later becomes part of the Department of Commerce • Congress indefinitely extends the Chinese Exclusion Act (1882, renewed 1892), which bars immigration of Chinese workers from the Philippines • Oregon becomes the first US state to allow the use of initiative and referendum for any citizen to propose legislation • Congress passes the Reclamation Act allowing the lease or sale of public land in the West, with the revenue to be placed in a national fund to be used for constructing dams and irrigation projects; the president is given authority to retain and set aside public lands for use as national parks or recreation areas • Crater Lake National Park is the first to be created under the provisions of the Reclamation Act	• The Aswan Dam on the Nile River in Egypt is completed; it helps but is not entirely successful in controlling the annual flooding of the Nile • Willis Carrier (US) builds the first practical mechanical air-conditioning system • The fossilized remains of a Tyrannosaurus Rex are found in Montana	• L. Frank Baum adapts his novel into the musical *The Wizard of Oz*; it premieres at the Grand Opera House in Chicago and makes stars of vaudeville team members David Montgomery (the Tin Woodman) and Fred Stone (the Scarecrow), opening on Broadway the following year • Beatrix Potter writes her first *Peter Rabbit* story • Theodore Roosevelt becomes the first US president to ride in an automobile • Barnum's Animal Crackers are introduced by the National Biscuit Co. (Nabisco), which controls 70% of American cracker and cookie output • The first known 4-H Club is formed in Springfield, OH; the four Hs stand for the development of youth through the improvement of "Head, Heart, Hands, and Health" • Scott Joplin composes "The Entertainer"
1903	• The Social Democratic Labor Party in Russia splits into Bolsheviks (led by Vladimir Ilyich Lenin) and Mensheviks (led by Julius Martov) • Panama declares independence from Colombia • The US and Panama sign a treaty giving the US control of a 10-mile-wide strip of land across the Panama isthmus (which becomes the Panama Canal Zone) for a one-time payment of $10 million and an annual payment of $250,000 • The Women's Social and Political Union (WSPU) is established in the UK to advocate for women's right to vote; it is more radical than NUWSS • French-controlled territory in central Africa is organized into four colonies: Gabon, Chad, Ubangi-Shari, and Middle Congo	• Wisconsin is the first US state to hold direct primary elections • The National Women's Trade Union League (NWTUL) is established to advocate for improved wages and working conditions for women; it later becomes the nucleus of the International Ladies' Garment Workers' Union (ILGWU) • Horatio Jackson completes the first transcontinental trip by automobile, from San Francisco to New York in 65 days • Cuba becomes an American protectorate; the US secures a perpetual lease on the Guantanamo Bay Naval Station	• Orville and Wilbur Wright fly the first successful powered airplane at Kitty Hawk, NC • The American Telegraph Company is founded to manufacture Telegraphones as office dictation machines and telephone recorders	• Victor Herbert's musical *Babes in Toyland* opens on Broadway • Boston beats Pittsburgh in the first World Series between the two major baseball leagues • Ludwig Roselius (Germany) perfects the process of removing caffeine from coffee beans without destroying their flavor; he markets the decaffeinated coffee under the brand name Sanka (which is introduced to the US in 1923) • Toy maker Margarete Steiff (Germany) designs her first teddy bears • Camp King Gillette (US) invents and markets the first "safety razor" with disposable blades • Edwin Porter's groundbreaking film *The Great Train Robbery* (12 minutes long) is the first movie to achieve realistic continuous action; it pioneers innovative techniques such as the jump cut and the close-up
1904	• Construction of the Panama Canal begins under US control • Japan begins the Russo-Japanese War by launching a surprise naval attack on Port Arthur that almost obliterates the Russian *(cont.)*	• The US Supreme Court rules that citizens of Puerto Rico are not aliens and cannot be denied entry to the continental US, although they do not have full US citizenship rights	• John A. Fleming (England) patents the diode vacuum tube, which converts an alternating current to a direct current • William C. Gorgas is appointed chief sanitation officer of the Panama Canal *(cont.)*	• The first line of the New York City subway system opens in Manhattan • George M. Cohen writes "Give My Regards to Broadway" [the song finds new life along with "You're a Grand Old Flag" *(cont.)*

E. EDUCATION, LITERATURE & THE FINE ARTS	F. RELIGION, THEOLOGY, PHILOSOPHY & PSYCHOLOGY	G. AMERICAN & UNITED METHODISM	H. BRITISH & WORLD METHODISM	
• Other notable publications include: – Anton Chekhov, *The Three Sisters* – Rudyard Kipling, *Kim* – George Bernard Shaw, *Caesar and Cleopatra*	• Wilhelm Wrede's *The Messianic Secret in the Gospels* argues that even Mark's Gospel is ahistorical and was shaped by early Christian belief	– approves conversations with the MPC and the Congregational Church about possible cooperation, if not union • The MPC organizes the Baltimore-Washington Conference • The AMEC founds the Colored Deaconess Home in Roanoke, VA • The MPC publishes a revised version of *The Methodist Protestant Church Hymnal* (with tunes, readings, and ritual) • The WHMS (MEC) begins its first work with blacks at Paine Institute in Augusta, GA		**1901 cont.**
• Debussy embodies the essence of musical impressionism in his opera *Pelléas and Mélisande*, which some critics regard as a perfect fusion of music and drama • Carl Nielsen conducts the premiere of his *Symphony No. 2 (The Four Temperaments)* in Copenhagen • Monet completes his painting of *Waterloo Bridge* • Pablo Picasso paints *Two Sisters (The Meeting)* • Enrico Caruso becomes an international operatic superstar after performing in *La Bohème* at the Monte Carlo Opera and in *Rigoletto* in London's Covent Garden Theater • *The Times Literary Supplement* is launched in London • American author Owen Wister publishes his classic novel of the American West, *The Virginian* [which becomes a classic film starring Gary Cooper in 1929] • Other notable publications include: – Joseph Conrad, *The Heart of Darkness* – Arthur Conan Doyle, *The Hound of the Baskervilles* – Rudyard Kipling, *The Just-So Stories* – André Gide, *The Immoralist*	• William James publishes his classic account of *The Varieties of Religious Experience* • Benedetto Croce begins the publication of his *Philosophy of the Spirit* (1902–17) • Other notable publications include: – Washington Gladden, *Social Salvation* – Adolf von Harnack, *The Mission and Expansion of Christianity in the First Three Centuries* – Alfred Loisy, *The Gospel and the Church*	• The MECS General Conference: – finds no wrongdoing on the part of the church's Book Agents in reaching the 1899 settlement of the "Publishing House Controversy" – creates the office of deaconess [following the UBC (1897) and MEC (1888) and followed by the EA (1903) and the MPC (1908)] – establishes a Bureau of Correspondence to prepare and oversee the course of study – places local preachers entirely under the jurisdiction of the district conference • The UEC General Conference: – authorizes incorporation of the Board of Christian Extension – elects its first Editor of Sunday School and Christian Endeavor League Literature – makes numerous minor changes to the *Discipline* • The MEC organizes the Oklahoma-Nebraska Conference and the Puerto Rico Mission; Juan Vazquez becomes the first Puerto Rican to be licensed as a local preacher	• In Britain, the Primitive Methodist Connexion (1811) becomes the Primitive Methodist Church (PMC) • The Methodist Church in Australasia (MCA) is formed by merger of the United Methodist Free Churches and the Bible Christians in Australia with the Australasian WM Conference (mirroring the 1896 merger in New Zealand); the union brings together all the Methodist bodies in Australia and New Zealand with the exception of the Primitive Methodists in NZ, who continue to remain apart • Methodist work is begun in Borneo and the Solomon Islands by missionaries from Tonga, Fiji, and Samoa	**1902**
• Enrico Caruso makes his American debut with the Metropolitan Opera in New York City in Giuseppe Verdi's *Rigoletto*, opening each season there for the next 17 years • Anton Bruckner's *9th Symphony* premieres in Vienna • Picasso completes his painting of *The Old Guitarist*, which perfectly represents his "blue period" • Alfred Stieglitz begins publication of his photographic journal *Camera Work* (to 1917), which promotes modern photography as a fine art • Jack London's masterpiece *The Call of the Wild* tells the story of a dog named Buck, a family pet in California who becomes a member of a sled dog pack in the Yukon • Other notable publications include: – Henry James, *The Ambassadors* – Samuel Butler, *The Way of All Flesh*	• Pope Leo XIII dies; he is succeeded by Pope Pius X • The PCUSA makes modest revisions to the Westminster Confession of Faith, which are seen by proponents as modernizing within the mainstream of Calvinist theology and by opponents as unwarranted concessions to Arminianism • W. E. B. DuBois, in his classic work *The Souls of Black Folk*, describes the efforts of black Americans to reconcile their African heritage with their pride in being US citizens • Other notable publications include: – G. E. Moore, *Principia Ethica* – Alfred Loisy, *The Fourth Gospel* – Maurice Blondel, *History and Dogma*	• The EA General Conference: – adopts and sends to the annual conferences a plan for establishing lay representation in General Conference; the plan is approved by the annual conferences during the following quadrennium – creates a Deaconess Society for the denomination and authorizes annual conferences to form auxiliary societies – votes to establish a mission in Hunan Province, China – instructs the bishops to prepare a book on EA law – adopts stricter rules for the supervision of local church members • The first Korean immigrants to the US (including Korean Methodists) arrive in Hawaii and soon after in California • The MEC establishes the Lincoln Conference, superseding the Oklahoma-Nebraska Conference	• The Methodist Episcopal Church Congress of Europe meets for the second time in Zürich • The MEC organizes the Alaska Mission Conference • Cliff College opens in Calver, England, to train lay evangelists; it will become the center for holiness teaching in British Methodism • The autonomous WM conference in the West Indies fails; the British WM Missionary Society assumes responsibility for churches there (until 1967) • A proposed union of the Methodist, Congregational, and Presbyterian churches in New Zealand fails due to opposition by the Presbyterians	**1903**
• The London Symphony Orchestra is established • Anton Chekhov introduces modern realism to the stage through his play *The Cherry Orchard* which premieres at the Moscow Art Theatre	• Mary McLeod Bethune founds the Daytona Normal and Industrial School for Negro Girls • Max Weber publishes *The Protestant Ethic and the Spirit of Capitalism* (English translation by Talcott Parsons, 1930)	• The MEC General Conference: – declares that the new constitution submitted to the annual conferences by the 1900 General Conference has been ratified and is in effect – seats ministerial and lay delegates in equal numbers for the first time	• Methodist missions in Portugal are organized into the Igreja Evangélica Metodista Portuguesa (Evangelical Methodist Church in Portugal), which becomes an overseas conference of the WMC [UK]	**1904**

	A. WORLD HISTORY & POLITICS	B. AMERICAN HISTORY & POLITICS	C. SCIENCE, MEDICINE & TECHNOLOGY	D. DAILY LIFE, POPULAR CULTURE & ENTERTAINMENT
1904 cont.	Oriental Fleet; Japanese ground forces then attack Manchuria through Korea • Britain and France sign the Entente Cordiale, putting an end to hostilities between them • Native African tribes, the Hotentots and Heroros, rebel against German colonial rule in southwest Africa (modern Namibia) but are suppressed by 1907	• President Roosevelt pronounces the "Roosevelt Corollary" to the Monroe Doctrine, declaring that the US would prohibit any non-American intervention in Latin-American affairs and ensure that Latin-American countries met their international obligations; this leads to increasing use of military force by the US to maintain or restore the internal stability of nations in the region • The Louisiana Purchase Exposition and World's Fair is held in St. Louis, MO, to celebrate the centennial of the Louisiana Purchase; it attracts almost 20 million visitors • The steamship *General Slocum* catches fire and burns to the water line in New York's East River, killing over 1,000 people; the tragedy leads to greatly strengthened fire prevention and safety regulations for passenger ships • Roosevelt is elected as president and Charles W. Fairbanks as vice president (Republican Party) • Ida Tarbell publishes *The History of the Standard Oil Company*, an exposé of the giant oil monopoly which leads to its investigation by Congress	project; within two years he has ended a yellow fever epidemic and brought malaria under control in Panama • Invented by physicist James Dewar in 1892, the "Thermos bottle" first goes on sale for commercial and home use	and "Yankee Doodle Dandy" in the 1942 film of that title] • Cans of Campbell's Pork and Beans first appear on grocery shelves • New York tea merchant Thomas Sullivan successfully markets and popularizes the tea bag, initially used for sending one-cup samples of his teas to customers, who steeped the bags • An inspired vendor at the World's Fair in St. Louis creates the ice cream cone by wrapping a waffle into a cone shape (or so the story goes) • Victor "Red Seal" Records produces the first recordings of tenor Enrico Caruso, which become phenomenally successful • Olympic Games: St. Louis (first in the US)
1905	• Japan destroys the rest of the Russian navy in the Battle of the Tsushima Straits • The US sponsors a peace conference that brings the Russo-Japanese War to a close; under the Treaty of Portsmouth, Russia cedes Sakhalin Island and Korea to Japan, which also gains control of railroads in Manchuria • America recognizes Japanese predominance in Korea in return for a Japanese pledge not to interfere in the Philippines • Bloody Sunday demonstrations in St. Petersburg signal the start of the 1905 Russian Revolution • Tsar Nicholas II is forced to issue the October Manifesto, a sort of constitution that establishes Russia's first parliament (Duma), and the Edict of Toleration, which guarantees religious minorities the right to exist in Russia • Nicholas II falls under the spell of Rasputin, a Siberian peasant who pretended to be a healer and a prophet • The title "Prime Minister" comes into regular formal use in Britain • The Canadian provinces of Alberta and Saskatchewan are created	• Immigration to the US for the first time tops one million, mostly from northern and southern Europe • President Roosevelt establishes the US Forest Service • W. E. B. DuBois establishes the Niagara Movement, an organization of black artists and intellectuals who demand full political, civil, and social rights for all black Americans, in notable contrast to the "accommodationist" philosophy espoused by Booker T. Washington in the "Atlanta Compromise" of 1895 • Industrial Workers of the World (IWW), later known as the "Wobblies," is founded in Chicago by radical labor leaders William D. "Big Bill" Haywood, Eugene V. Debs, and Mary "Mother" Jones; over the next decade it enlists thousands of workers and organizes dozens of strikes, forcing major concessions from business and industry such as the eight-hour workday • Chicago lawyer Paul Harris founds the Rotary Club, America's first civic service club • The US Forest Service is established by Congress to administer the National Forest reserves	• Albert Einstein publishes his *Special Theory of Relativity* and makes famous the equation $E = mc^2$ • The Mexican government initiates archaeological excavations at the site of Teotihuacan, under the direction of archaeologist Leopoldo Batres; the lost Pyramid of the Sun is discovered and restored	• President Roosevelt summons college athletics leaders to a White House conference to urge reforms to reduce the number of serious injuries to football players, 18 of whom had died during the year • The first motion-picture theater in the US opens in Pittsburgh; the admission is 5¢, and so it comes to be called a "nickelodeon"; by 1910 there are an estimated 10,000 "nickelodeons" in cities across the country • The first pizzeria in the US opens in New York City • Claude Hatcher creates Chero-Cola, the ancestor of Royal Crown Cola, in Columbus, GA • *The Chicago Defender*, a black newspaper intended for the masses, begins publication

E. EDUCATION, LITERATURE & THE FINE ARTS	F. RELIGION, THEOLOGY, PHILOSOPHY & PSYCHOLOGY	G. AMERICAN & UNITED METHODISM	H. BRITISH & WORLD METHODISM	
• Puccini's opera *Madam Butterfly* draws hisses at La Scala in Milan on opening night but becomes a success after Puccini revises it (and eventually becomes his most popular work) • Béla Bartók's symphonic poem *Kossuth* premieres in Budapest, becoming his first major work to be performed • Gustav Mahler completes his song cycle *Kindertotenlieder* (Songs of the Death of Children) • Two great classics of children's literature are published: James Barrie's tale of *Peter Pan*, a boy who "won't grow up" and Edward Stratemeyer's *The Story of the Bobbsey Twins* • Other notable publications include: – Joseph Conrad, *Nostromo* – Henry James, *The Golden Bowl* – O. Henry, *Cabbages and Kings*	• Sigmund Freud publishes *The Psychopathology of Everyday Life*	– seats women as lay delegates for the first time; Annie T. Strickland (Little Rock Conference) is the first and only black woman to be seated – amends the Third Restrictive Rule to allow central conferences to elect bishops "for work among particular races and languages, or for any of our foreign missions," with their authority restricted to the group or area that elected them – reduces the majority required for passage of constitutional amendments from three-fourths to two-thirds – organizes the Philippine Islands Mission Conference – recognizes Ladies Aid Societies in the *Discipline* for the first time – approves the recommendation of the Joint Commission on Federation for publication of a common hymnal, catechism, and order of worship for the MEC and MECS; invites the AMEC, AMNEZC, and CMEC to cooperate in this venture (they decline to do so) – establishes the Chinese Mission and Indian Territory Mission • The MPC General Conference: – approves relocation of the Publishing House to larger and improved facilities in Baltimore – considers establishment of a Board of Education – organizes the Choctaw Mission Conference • Bordon Parker Bowne (Boston University) is charged with heresy for teaching doctrines "contrary to the Articles of Religion and established doctrinal standards"; all charges are dismissed after a church trial by the New York East Conference (MEC) • Minnie Jackson Goins is the first black woman to be ordained elder in the UBC (Northwest Kansas Conference)	• The MEC mission in Korea is organized as the Korea Mission Conference • The MEC begins mission work in Lithuania in 1904, mostly among German speakers	**1904 cont.**
• Isadora Duncan, who in 1903 had delivered her famous address "The Dance of the Future" in Berlin, establishes the first school of modern dance there; she is regarded as the founder of the modern dance movement • Franz Lehár's romantic musical comedy *The Merry Widow* premieres in Vienna • Richard Strauss composes his opera *Salome* • Debussy's great impressionist orchestral tone poem *La Mer* (The Sea) premieres in Paris • Henri Matisse completes his painting *Woman with a Hat* • Paul Signac advances the Neo-Impressionist tradition with his lovely canvas *Grand Canal, Venice* • Notable publications include: – Edith Wharton, *The House of Mirth* – Baroness Orczy, *The Scarlet Pimpernel* – George Bernard Shaw, *Major Barbara* – Oscar Wilde, *De Profundis*	• France adopts a law stipulating "the separation of churches and the state"; the law bars the state from officially recognizing, funding, or endorsing religious groups, thus enshrining secularism as a national principle • The American Sociological Association (ASA) is founded • The Baptist World Alliance is established as a voluntary international organization intended to promote cooperation and fellowship among Baptists around the globe • Vladimir Ilyich Lenin publishes his revolutionary treatise *Two Tactics of Social-Democracy in the Democratic Revolution* • Other notable publications include: – Shailer Mathews, *The Messianic Hopes in the New Testament* – William N. Clarke, *The Use of the Scriptures in Theology* – G. K. Chesterton, *Orthodoxy* – George Santayana, *The Life of Reason* – Wilhelm Dilthey, *Poetry and Experience* – M.-J. LaGrange, *Historical Criticism and the Old Testament* • Charles A. Tindley publishes *Soul Echoes #1*, which includes some of the greatest of his gospel hymns, such as "Stand by Me" and "We'll Understand It Better By and By" • A group of holiness MECS churches in Texas and Arkansas leave the denomination and unite to form the Holiness Church of Christ	• The UBC General Conference: – meets for the first time west of the Missouri River, in Topeka, KS – seats equal numbers of clergy and lay delegates for the first time – approves a "syllabus" projecting plans for cooperation and possibly union with the MPC and the Congregational Churches and authorizes participation in a meeting with the other bodies in 1906 – empowers the UBC churches in Canada to unite with the Congregationalists in Canada • Borden Parker Bowne's *The Immanence of God* marks the beginnings of Boston Personalism • The MEC and MECS jointly publish a new hymnbook entitled simply *The Methodist Hymnal* and establish a common order of Sunday worship and a common catechism • South Florida Mission and Hawaii Mission (MEC) are established • The MEC organizes the Pacific German Conference • The EA establishes the Evangelical Theological Seminary in Reading, PA	• The United Brethren in Germany join in cooperative ministries with the BMK • The MECS begins mission work in Panama • The MEC forms the Chilean Annual Conference and begins mission work in Java and Sumatra	**1905**

	A. WORLD HISTORY & POLITICS	B. AMERICAN HISTORY & POLITICS	C. SCIENCE, MEDICINE & TECHNOLOGY	D. DAILY LIFE, POPULAR CULTURE & ENTERTAINMENT
1906	• A British ultimatum forces the Ottoman Empire to cede the Sinai Peninsula to Egypt • Finland grants women the right to vote in national elections • Ethiopia is divided into British, French, and Italian spheres of influence • The third Pan-American Conference meets in Rio de Janeiro • Greeks in Crete rebel against Turkish rule, demanding union with Greece • The second Geneva Convention extends the principles of the first Geneva Convention (1864) to apply to naval warfare	• An earthquake and subsequent fire destroy most of San Francisco; total earthquake death toll is more than 3,000; over 200,000 are left homeless; damage is estimated at $500,000,000 (in 1906 dollars) • President Roosevelt sails to the Panama Canal Zone, becoming the first US president to travel outside the country while in office • Mary Mallon, better known as "Typhoid Mary," is held responsible and jailed for spreading typhoid fever during an epidemic in New York • Mesa Verde National Park is established • The US government files suit against Standard Oil under terms of the Sherman Antitrust Act • Upton Sinclair's novel *The Jungle*, a dramatic exposé of the American meatpacking industry, portrays the unsanitary and miserable working conditions in the Chicago stockyards, leading to an investigation by the federal government and the subsequent passage of the Pure Food and Drugs Act by Congress • US troops are called out to suppress a race riot in Atlanta, which erupts after spurious, inflammatory newspaper reports of sexual assaults by black men on white women; over four days, white mobs lynch an estimated 100 black men and assault many more	• American inventor Lee DeForest develops the triode vacuum tube, a key component in the development of radio; it will eventually be replaced by the transistor • Canadian engineer Reginald Fessenden makes the first extended radio broadcast on Christmas Eve, including a phonograph recording of Handel's "Largo" • Alois Alzheimer (Germany) describes physical abnormalities in the brain of a patient with severe dementia, thereby establishing a physiological basis for such an illness (now named Alzheimer's Disease) • Frederick Hopkins (England) concludes that a lack of vitamins causes scurvy and rickets • Norwegian explorer Roald Amundsen traverses the Northwest Passage and determines the position of the magnetic North Pole	• The Intercollegiate Athletic Association of the United States (IAAUS) is established; in 1910 it becomes the National Collegiate Athletic Association (NCAA) • W. K. Kellogg forms the Kellogg Co. and begins marketing corn flakes as a breakfast food • George C. Washington, an English chemist living in Guatemala, creates the first mass-produced instant coffee • Representatives of the Boys Club organizations of 53 US cities meet in Boston and form the Federated Boys Clubs of America
1907	• Britain and Russia sign a treaty dividing what is now Iran into respective spheres of influence • The US Navy's "Great White Fleet" sails for the Pacific in a show of maritime power, reaching Japan in 1908 • Britain grants internal self-government to the Transvaal and the Orange Free State • Britain and France agree to recognize the independence of Siam (Thailand) • New Zealand becomes a dominion within the British Empire • Honduras loses a brief but violent war with Nicaragua; US Marines are sent to Honduras to protect US nationals and business interests against revolutionary groups	• Oklahoma is admitted to the US as the 46th state • President Roosevelt approves the minting of new US gold coins bearing the motto "E Pluribus Unum" instead of "In God We Trust"; a storm of public criticism follows • The Aeronautical Division of the Army Signal Corps is established; it will eventually grow into the Army Air Corps • The Central American Peace Conference meets in Washington, DC, and agrees to establish a Central American Court of Justice • Alabama and Georgia become the first US states to adopt laws prohibiting the manufacture or sale of alcoholic beverages	• The first commercial color photographic process, called Autochrome plates, is developed by Louis and Auguste Lumière in France • J. Murray Spangler invents the first upright electrical vacuum cleaner	• Mother's Day is established in the US; it is declared a national holiday in 1914 • Florenz Ziegfeld introduces his Ziegfeld Follies, the legendary musical extravaganza • The Hamburg Zoo in Germany pioneers the use of barless, moated display areas that mimic natural habitats instead of cages • Harry C. "Bud" Fisher begins drawing Mr. A. *Mutt* (later *Mutt and Jeff*); it is the first daily comic strip • Hershey's Chocolates introduces the foil-wrapped chocolate Kiss • James Emmitt Casey and Claude Ryan establish the American Messenger Company in Seattle, WA [it will become Merchant's Parcel Delivery in 1913 and United Parcel Service (UPS) in 1919]

E. EDUCATION, LITERATURE & THE FINE ARTS	F. RELIGION, THEOLOGY, PHILOSOPHY & PSYCHOLOGY	G. AMERICAN & UNITED METHODISM	H. BRITISH & WORLD METHODISM	
• Salzburg, Austria, the birthplace of Mozart, holds the first Mozart Festival in his honor • Sergey Rachmaninoff completes his opera *Francesca Da Rimini* • Carl Nielsen composes his *String Quartet in F* • Arnold Schoenberg composes his *Chamber Symphony No. 1* • Notable publications include: – Mark Twain, *What is Man?* – Jack London, *White Fang* – Upton Sinclair, *The Jungle* – Joel Chandler Harris, *Uncle Remus and Brer Rabbit*	• Pope Pius X delivers his encyclical *Vehementer Nos (On the French Law of Separation)* condemning the 1905 French law; it asserts that the proposition that the state should be separate from the church "is absolutely false, a most pernicious error" • The Azusa Street Revival begins in Los Angeles; it will be a major catalyst to the formation of Pentecostal and Charismatic churches • The Church of God (Cleveland, TN) holds its first General Assembly • The majority of Cumberland Presbyterian churches reunite with the PCUSA, ending a division of nearly 100 years • Conservatives withdraw from the Christian Church (Disciples of Christ) (1832) to form a number of independent Churches of Christ; they have no central governing body • The Vedanta Society builds the first known Hindu temple in the US in San Francisco • Albert Schweitzer's *The Quest of the Historical Jesus: A Critical Study of its Progress from Reimarus to Wrede* concludes that the historical Jesus cannot be found in the Gospels and that "He comes to us as one unknown" • Other notable publications include: – Rudolf Kittel's landmark critical edition of the Hebrew Bible, *Biblica Hebraica* – Francis Brown, Samuel R. Driver, and Charles A. Briggs, *A Hebrew and Aramaic Lexicon of the Old Testament* – The final edition of Mary Baker Eddy's *Science and Health with Key to the Scriptures*	• The MECS General Conference: – laments a decreasing supply of ministers – authorizes unordained local preachers to baptize and perform marriages within their charge but bars them from serving Holy Communion – provides for annual conference boards of missions to employ evangelists within their boundaries – takes steps attempting to place Vanderbilt University more firmly under the control of the MECS • The UEC General Conference: – receives a fraternal delegate from the UBC who outlines the similarities between the two bodies and urges the prospect of union among the UEC, UBC, MPC, and Congregationalist Churches – declines to pursue conversations about possible union "at this time" • Representatives of the MPC, UBC, and Congregationalist Churches meet in Dayton and adopt an MPC resolution proposing "the organic union of these three bodies" under the name The United Church • The MEC organizes the East Oklahoma Mission	• The Protestant Church of Belgium merges with two Reformed churches to create the United Protestant Church of Belgium • The MEC begins mission work in Bolivia • The government of Russia formally recognizes the MEC Mission in Lithuania • Methodists and Presbyterians in Korea cooperate to establish Union Christian College in Pyongyang • Richard Green publishes *The Works of John and Charles Wesley: A Bibliography*	**1906**
• Picasso completes his painting of Les Demoiselles d'Avignon (The Ladies of Avignon), generally regarded as his first Cubist painting • Paris holds the first major exhibition of Cubist paintings • Gustav Klimt paints his best-known work, *The Kiss* • Frederick Delius's opera *A Village Romeo and Juliet* has its first performance in Berlin • Ferruccio Busoni publishes his *Sketch of a New Aesthetic of Music* • Other notable publications include: – Henry Adams, *The Education of Henry Adams* – Joseph Conrad, *The Secret Agent* – E. M. Forster, *The Longest Journey*	• President Roosevelt lays the cornerstone of the National Cathedral (officially the Cathedral Church of St. Peter and St. Paul) in Washington, DC [construction is not finally completed until 1990] • Various Baptist groups in the northern states unite to form the Northern Baptist Convention, which allows full ordination rights for women • The Church of God (Cleveland, TN) is established; Ambrose J. Tomlinson is elected general overseer [it claims to be the oldest Pentecostal body in the US, tracing its roots back to 1886] • The Pentecostal Assemblies of the World is established [it is the oldest of the "oneness" Pentecostal denominations] • The Association of Pentecostal Churches of America (1895) and the Los Angeles Church of the Nazarene (1898) unite to form the Pentecostal Church of the Nazarene • Walter Rauschenbusch publishes *Christianity and the Social Crisis*, which marks the starting point of the Social Gospel movement in America • Other notable publications include: – Henri Bergson, *Creative Evolution* –William James, *Pragmatism: A New Name for Some Old Ways of Thinking* – John Scott Lidgett, *The Christian Religion*	• The EA General Conference: – seats lay delegates for the first time – liberalizes the principle of lay representation and extends it to annual conferences – endorses efforts to organize a National Federation of the Churches of Christ in America and votes to participate in such a movement – receives a resolution from the Young People's Alliance for reunion with the UEC – appoints a Commission on Church Union to open conversations with the UEC – establishes a Commission on Evangelism – urges that temperance work be combined with education – decrees that henceforth only unfermented wine may be used in celebrating the Lord's Supper – extends the maximum length of a pastoral appointment and the term of service of presiding elders to five years • The MEC establishes the Methodist Federation for Social Service (MFSS) • The MEC organizes the Pacific Chinese Mission • Discussions about union of the MPC, UBC, and Congregationalist Churches fall apart completely • The Brotherhood of St. Paul merges with several local organizations for Methodist men to create the Methodist Brotherhood	• The United Methodist Church in the UK (UMC [UK]) is formed by the union of the UMFC (1857), the MNC (1797), and the Bible Christians (1815) • The MEC Congress of Europe meets for the third time in Copenhagen and approves a proposal to General Conference for the organization of a central conference of Europe • The Cuba Mission (MECS) is formally organized; it later becomes mission conference (1919) and then annual conference (1923) • The MEC begins its first mission work in the Baltics and renews its abandoned mission in France • The Methodist Church of Japan (Nippon Methodist Kyokwai) is formed from the separate MEC and MECS missions • The MEC opens the Florence B. Nicholson Seminary in the Philippines	**1907**

	A. WORLD HISTORY & POLITICS	B. AMERICAN HISTORY & POLITICS	C. SCIENCE, MEDICINE & TECHNOLOGY	D. DAILY LIFE, POPULAR CULTURE & ENTERTAINMENT
1908	• Huge reserves of crude oil and natural gas are discovered in the Persian Gulf region • Bosnia/Herzegovina is occupied by Austria • King Charles I of Portugal is assassinated along with his son and heir, Luis Filipe, paving the way for the Portuguese Revolution in 1910 • A strong earthquake and resulting tsunami kill 100,000 in southern Italy and Sicily • Japan and the US reach an informal agreement recognizing the right of the US to refuse Japanese workers entrance into the US • Britain enacts comprehensive social welfare legislation, including the world's first unemployment insurance scheme and a noncontributory old-age pension (the "dole") to begin at age 70 • A large meteorite explodes in the air over the remote Tunguska region of Siberia with a force estimated at 10-15 megatons (around 1,000 times greater than the atomic bomb dropped on Hiroshima in 1945); it flattens an estimated 60 million trees in over 2,150 square kilometers in an outward-radiating pattern • A revolution by the Young Turks in the Ottoman Empire forces the reinstatement of the Constitution of 1876 • The young Pu-Yi, of the Qing (Manchu) Dynasty, ascends the throne of China at the age of 3 [he will be the last emperor of China]	• Congress enacts legislation requiring that the motto "In God We Trust" appear on all US coins, and that coins minted without it be withdrawn from circulation and replaced • The US Supreme Court rules that a labor union boycott of industry falls under the provisions of the 1890 Sherman Antitrust Act and is thus illegal • Congress passes a law regulating child labor in the District of Columbia and encourages the individual states to pass similar measures • William H. Taft is elected as president and James S. Sherman as vice president (Republican Party)	• The Ford Motor Company introduces the legendary Model T; embodying Henry Ford's desire to "democratize the automobile," it sells for $850 and is available only in black; nicknamed the "Tin Lizzie," it provides practical, affordable transportation for ordinary people because of its low cost, durability, and ease of maintenance • The General Motors Corporation is formed; it will provide the first serious competition for the Ford Motor Company	• Hugh Moore invents the "Dixie Cup," originally named "Health Cup" and intended to replace the communal metal cup that had been used with water fountains • The Boy Scout movement is begun in the UK by Robert Baden-Powell • Jack Johnson becomes the first black heavyweight boxing champion • Olympic Games: London
1909	• Japanese prince Hirobumi Ito is assassinated by a group of Korean nationalists; Japan begins a 36-year occupation of Korea • Coup d'états produce new governments in Turkey and Persia • Siam (Thailand) cedes to Britain its control of much of the Malay Peninsula • Russia invades northern Persia and occupies Tabriz • An occupation force of British, French, Russian, and Italian troops withdraws from Crete after having quelled hostilities between Greeks and Turks on the island • US military forces help rebels in Nicaragua overthrow that country's dictator	• W. E. B. DuBois and Booker T. Washington establish the National Association for the Advancement of Colored People (NAACP); DuBois edits its newsletter, *The Crisis*, until 1934 • The US government opens 700,000 acres of public land in Washington, Idaho, and Montana to settlement, and passes the Enlarged Homestead Act, authorizing 320-acre homesteads in that area • The National Conservation Commission, headed by Gifford Pinchot, begins to make the first complete survey of the various resources that exist on (and under) public lands in the West	• Robert E. Peary and Matthew Henson (both US) reach the North Pole • Louis Bleriot (France) becomes the first person to cross the English Channel by airplane • Belgian-American chemist Leo H. Baekeland, the "father of plastics," begins to manufacture the first synthetic resin to have commercial application; later known as Bakelite	• Father's Day is established in the US; it is declared a national holiday in 1966 • Thomas Lipton begins blending and packaging his tea in New York • Scott Joplin publishes *The School of Ragtime: Six Exercises for Piano*, containing his explanation of ragtime style • The Whiffenpoofs, an all-male 14-member vocal ensemble, is founded at Yale University; it is the oldest collegiate a cappella group in the US and best known for its theme, "The Whiffenpoof Song": "To the tables down at Mory's . . ."
1910	• Britain's King Edward VII dies; he is succeeded by his son, George V • Japan formally annexes Korea, a control that persists until the Japanese collapse at the end of WWII (1945)	• The US census reports that the population is 91,972,266: – whites: 81,731,957 (88.9%) – blacks: 9,827,763 (10.7%) – other: 412,546 (0.4%)	• The National Museum of Natural History opens as part of the Smithsonian Institution in Washington, DC • French scientist Henri Marie Coanda builds and successfully test flies the world's first jet-propelled biplane	• The National Hockey League is established • The Boy Scouts are introduced in America

E. EDUCATION, LITERATURE & THE FINE ARTS	F. RELIGION, THEOLOGY, PHILOSOPHY & PSYCHOLOGY	G. AMERICAN & UNITED METHODISM	H. BRITISH & WORLD METHODISM	
• Arturo Toscanini makes his conducting debut at the Metropolitan Opera in New York • Arnold Schoenberg's *Book of Hanging Gardens* brings a new style to classical music, replacing harmony and tonality with dissonance • Bartók completes his *Violin Concerto No. 1* • Maurice Ravel composes his *Spanish Rhapsody* • Debussy's *Children's Corner* premieres in Paris • Alexander Scriabin composes *The Poem of Ecstasy* • Kenneth Grahame's *The Wind in the Willows*, one of the English classics of children's literature, narrates the adventures of Mole, Rat, Badger, Toad, and their friends • Other notable publications include: – Arnold Bennett, *The Old Wives' Tale* – E. M. Forster, *A Room with a View*	• Pope Pius X publishes the apostolic constitution *Sapienti consilio*, which changes the status of the American Catholic Church from that of a "missionary church" under the control of the Congregation de Propaganda Fide to that of a full member of the Roman Catholic Church • The Federal Council of Churches is formed and holds its first meeting (becomes the National Council of Churches in 1950) • The Christian Commercial Men's Association of America, later renamed Gideons International, places its first Bibles in a hotel room in Montana • The Holiness Church of Christ (1905) merges with the Pentecostal Church of the Nazarene (1907); this is regarded as marking the official foundation of the Pentecostal Church of the Nazarene as a denomination (the word *Pentecostal* is formally dropped from the name in 1919) • Andover Theological Seminary (1807) and Harvard Divinity School (1816) attempt a merger but separate again in 1931 • Philip Schaff begins work on an American edition of the German *Realencyklopädie für Theologie und Kirche*, which appears as *The New Schaff-Herzog Encyclopedia of Religious Knowledge* (12 vols., 1908–14) • Other notable publications include: – Alfred Loisy, *The Synoptic Gospels* – Adolf Deissmann, *Light from the Ancient East*	• The Bishops of the AMEC, AMEZC, and CMEC hold a joint meeting for the first time • The MEC General Conference: – adopts Methodism's first Social Creed [the MECS follows in 1914 and the MPC in 1916] – notes with approval the organization of the MFSS – removes requirement that bishops approve faculty appointments at Methodist seminaries, establishing the right of academic freedom – organizes the Pacific Swedish Mission Conference and Philippine Annual Conference – endorses the Methodist Brotherhood organization for lay men and encourages the formation of Methodist Brotherhood groups in each annual conference – substitutes the term *district superintendent* for *presiding elder* throughout the *Discipline* – removes a specific time limit on probation for membership and places responsibility for determining the "fitness" of a candidate for membership jointly upon the pastor and the official board, who must concur • The MPC General Conference: – creates the office of deaconess in the church – receives proposal of organic union from the UBC – exchanges fraternal delegations with the MEC –reaffirms the 1884 ban on divorce and on remarriage of divorced persons except in case of adultery • The UBC terminates the publication *United Brethren Review* (1890) • The MEC establishes the Mary J. Platt School for Spanish girls in Tucson, AZ	• The EA begins mission work in Riga, Latvia • The MECS begins mission work in Manchuria • The Korea Mission Conference (MEC) becomes Korea Annual Conference • The AMEC opens AME Seminary in Freetown, west Africa	**1908**
• Sergey Diaghilev establishes the Ballets Russes, beginning the era of modern ballet and his 20-year reign as ballet's leading figure • Ralph Vaughan Williams composes *A Sea Symphony* • Gustav Mahler completes his song cycle *Das Lied von der Erde* (The Song of the Earth) • Anton Webern composes his *6 Pieces for Orchestra* • Gertrude Stein publishes *Three Lives*, her influential character study of three women • Other notable publications include H. G. Wells, *Ann Veronica*	• The Association of Biblical Instructors in American Colleges and Secondary Schools is established; the name is changed to the National Association of Biblical Instructors in 1933 and to The American Academy of Religion (AAR) in 1963 •Pope Pius X establishes the Pontifical Biblical Institute in Rome • Curtis Schofield publishes *The Schofield Reference Bible, King James Version*, which becomes the standard study Bible of American evangelicals and fundamentalists (an expanded edition appears in 1917) • William James publishes *The Meaning of Truth* and *A Pluralistic Universe*	• The UBC General Conference: – elects the denomination's first full-time Secretary of Christian Stewardship – grants representation of the Women's Missionary Association on both the Board of Foreign Missions and the Board of Home Missions – acknowledges the union of UBC churches in Canada with the Congregationalists there – establishes the Otterbein Brotherhood as a men's fellowship group • Kimball School of Theology is established by the MEC in Salem, OR • The name of Union Biblical Seminary (1871) is changed to Bonebrake Theological Seminary • The MEC establishes the Italian Mission Conference • A group of MEC congregations in North Dakota withdraws to form the Northwestern Holiness Association, which becomes the Holiness Methodist Church in 1920	• The MEC is legalized in Russia • Nicolas Zamora and his followers withdraw from the MEC to form the Iglesia Evangélica Metodista en las Islas Filipinas (the Evangelical Methodist Church in the Philippines) • The MEC Mission in French North Africa (Algeria and Tunisia) is organized • Willis Hoover, inspired by the Azusa Street Revival, begins Pentecostal preaching in Chile, leading to his expulsion from the MEC and his formation of the Methodist Pentecostal Church (Iglesia Metodista Pentecostal) of Chile • Nehemiah Curnock publishes his edition of *The Journal of the Rev. John Wesley, A.M.* (8 vols., 1909–16) • W. J. Townsend, H. B. Workman, and George Eayrs publish *A New History of Methodism*	**1909**
• Igor Stravinsky completes *The Firebird* for Sergey Diaghilev's Ballets Russes • Gustav Mahler's sprawling *Symphony No. 8 in E Flat Major* (called the Symphony of a Thousand due to its requirement for eight *(cont.)*	• The World Missionary Conference at Edinburgh inaugurates the modern ecumenical movement; John R. Mott is one of the key organizers	• The MECS General Conference: – rejects a proposal to extend full laity rights to women – merges the Woman's Home and Foreign Mission Societies into the Woman's *(cont.)*	• The New Zealand Conference requests independence from the MCA; this request is approved by the MCA General Conference but also requires approval from the several annual conferences as well as *(cont.)*	**1910**

	A. WORLD HISTORY & POLITICS	B. AMERICAN HISTORY & POLITICS	C. SCIENCE, MEDICINE & TECHNOLOGY	D. DAILY LIFE, POPULAR CULTURE & ENTERTAINMENT
1910 cont.	• Russia and Japan agree to recognize separate spheres of influence in Manchuria • The British parliament unites the Cape, Natal, Transvaal, and Orange River provinces to create the Union of South Africa, which becomes a dominion within the British Empire • France unifies its several African colonies to form French Equatorial Africa • The fourth Pan-American Conference meets in Buenos Aires	• The US national debt is $2,652,665,838 • Congress passes the Mann Act, which attempts to prohibit "white slavery" by banning the interstate transportation of females for "immoral purposes" • The Mann-Elkins Act extends the power of the ICC to regulate railroads and places telephone, telegraph, and cable companies under ICC jurisdiction • Angel Island, in San Francisco Bay, becomes the primary immigration center for Asians and Pacific Islanders entering the US • Glacier National Park is established	• Thomas Edison introduces his kinetophone, which makes talking movies ("talkies") a reality • George Eastman invents the Photostat, which uses photographic techniques to make exact copies of documents on photosensitive paper • The reappearance of Halley's Comet coincides with the death of Mark Twain, as it had with his birth (in 1834)	• Camp Fire Girls of America is established as the first nonsectarian organization for girls in the US; its watchword is "WoHeLo," a word created from the first two letters of the words "work, health, love" • The first live musical radio broadcast takes place when Lee DeForest presents a Metropolitan Opera performance by Enrico Caruso as Canio in Ruggero Leoncavallo's *Pagliacci* • Victor Herbert's musical comedy *Naughty Marietta* opens on Broadway
1911	• The first known use of aircraft as an offensive weapon occurs in the Turkish-Italian War; Italy defeats the Turks and annexes Libya • After coming near to war over Morocco, Germany and France agree to recognize a French protectorate over Morocco and France cedes territory from French Equatorial Africa to Germany's control • Civil war erupts in Mexico, and US troops are sent to the Texas border to prevent it from spreading and to protect US citizens and their property • Italy and the Ottoman Empire go to war; the Italians capture and annex Tripoli • Sun Yat-Sen leads a nationalist revolution in China that overthrows the Qing (Manchu) Dynasty	• The US Supreme Court finds Standard Oil Company and American Tobacco Company to be in violation of the Sherman Antitrust Act and orders them broken up • The Triangle Shirtwaist Company fire in New York kills 146 workers and leads to demands for better safety and working conditions for garment workers • The National League on Urban Conditions Among Negroes is formed (later the name becomes the National Urban League) • The National Association Opposed to Woman Suffrage (NAOWS) is organized to oppose women having the right to vote • The Weeks Act authorizes the US government to purchase private lands for inclusion in the national forests	• Roald Amundsen (Norway) and his team cross Antarctica to reach the South Pole just one month before Robert F. Scott (US) and his team; Scott and his two companions perish on the return trip just 11 miles from their base camp • Thomas Morgan (US) proves that inherited factors are determined by genes at specific locations along a chromosome • Hiram Bingham (US) discovers ancient Incan city of Machu Picchu	• Scott Joplin publishes his ragtime opera, *Treemonisha* • Irving Berlin completes and records "Alexander's Ragtime Band," his first hit, which culminates the ragtime craze and changes the course of American popular song • The Indianapolis 500 automobile race is run for the first time • The left-wing magazine *The Masses* begins publication, addressing social issues such as the labor struggle, class war, revolution, and women's emancipation, with literary contributions from figures such as Carl Sandburg and political cartoons by artists including Pablo Picasso and Abraham Walkowitz; it is suppressed by the federal government in 1917 because of its opposition to American entry into WWI

E. EDUCATION, LITERATURE & THE FINE ARTS	F. RELIGION, THEOLOGY, PHILOSOPHY & PSYCHOLOGY	G. AMERICAN & UNITED METHODISM	H. BRITISH & WORLD METHODISM	
soloists, double choir, and augmented orchestra) has its first performance in Munich • Edward Elgar conducts the premiere of his *Violin Concerto*, with Fritz Kreisler playing the solo part • Ralph Vaughan Williams composes his *Fantasia on a Theme of Thomas Tallis* • Frederick Delius composes *The Walk to the Paradise Garden* • Notable publications include: – Gaston Leroux, *The Phantom of the Opera* – Jane Addams, *Twenty Years at Hull House*	• Publication of *The Fundamentals*, a 12-volume collection of essays by 64 British and American scholars and preachers, begins (through 1915), laying the foundation of modern Fundamentalism and stimulating the Fundamentalist-Modernist controversy • Max Weber, begins publication of *Economy and Society* (completed 1914)	Missionary Council and makes it part of the general missionary organization of the church; Belle Harris Bennett is elected president and serves until 1922 – incorporates all adult Bible classes under the General Sunday School Board – reorganizes the General Board of Missions to oversee all MECS missionary activities – adds a provision to the *Discipline* advising ministers to refrain from the use of tobacco – requires the bishops to announce all appointments to the entire annual conference in open session • The UEC General Conference: – receives fraternal delegates from the MEC and UBC – appoints representatives to meet with the Commission on Church Union created by the EA in 1907 • The MEC and MECS begin joint publication of graded church school curriculum materials • The California German Mission (MEC) becomes a full annual conference • Nellie Perkins begins work as a UBC missionary in Velarde, NM • The Joint Commission on Federation (MEC and MECS) meets in Baltimore with delegates from the MPC; they appoint a Committee of Nine to draft a proposal for a union of the three bodies	enabling legislation from the national and local governments with regard to church property (1910–13) • Augustine Léger publishes his groundbreaking *La Jeunesse de Wesley: L'Angleterre religieuse et les origines du méthodisme au XVIIe siècle*	**1910 cont.**
• Richard Strauss's operatic masterpiece, *Der Rosenkavalier* (The Knight of the Rose), premieres in Dresden • The eleventh edition of the *Encyclopedia Britannica* represents in many ways the sum of human knowledge at the beginning of the 20th century and is still widely regarded as the greatest edition of the *Britannica* ever published • Wassily Kandinsky forms the Blue Rider group, along with Franz Marc, Paul Klee, and other German expressionist artists • Edward Elgar conducts the premiere of his *Symphony No. 2* in London • Arnold Schoenberg publishes his revolutionary *Theory of Harmony* • Other notable publications include: – Edith Wharton, *Ethan Frome* – Frances Hodgson Burnett, *The Secret Garden* – Ambrose Bierce, *The Devil's Dictionary*	• The Fire Baptized Holiness Church merges into the Pentecostal Holiness Church • Notable publications include: – Evelyn Underhill, *Mysticism* – Hans Vaihinger, *The Philosophy of "As If"* – Alfred North Whitehead, *An Introduction to Mathematics* – Adolf von Harnack, *The Date of Acts and of the Synoptic Gospels* – Rufus M. Jones, *The Quakers in the American Colonies*	• The EA General Conference: – hears a report from the Commission on Church Union that discussions with the UEC are "progressing favorably" – appoints a new Commission on Church Union with enlarged powers and instructions to continue the discussions with the UEC – refers back to the Commission a request by the Canadian Conference for union with the Methodist Church in Canada – instructs the bishops to appoint fraternal delegates to the General Conferences of the UEC, the UBC, and the MEC – broadens the responsibilities of the Commission on Evangelism to include a Bureau of Literature and a Bureau of Public Service – establishes a Superannuation Fund for the care of retired ministers and their families • The bishops of the AMEC, AMEZC, and CMEC hold their second joint meeting • The Methodist Book Concern publishes *The Ladies' Aid Manual*, suggesting appropriate organization and activities for Ladies' Aid Societies • The Joint Commission on Federation meets and adopts the "Chattanooga Report," outlining principles for possible reunion; it is to be referred to the MEC and MECS General Conferences • The MECS Board of Missions begins publication of *The Missionary Voice* (to 1932), combining several previous missionary publications	• The fourth Ecumenical Methodist Conference meets in Toronto • The MEC mission in Finland is organized as the Finland Annual Conference • The Southern Congo Conference of the AMEC is established • MECS Bishop Walter R. Lambuth begins work in central Congo	**1911**

	A. WORLD HISTORY & POLITICS	B. AMERICAN HISTORY & POLITICS	C. SCIENCE, MEDICINE & TECHNOLOGY	D. DAILY LIFE, POPULAR CULTURE & ENTERTAINMENT
1912	• Pu-Yi, the last emperor of China, abdicates the throne, ending both the 267-year Qing (Manchu) Dynasty and the 2,000-year-old Imperial system • Sun Yat-sen forms the Chinese Nationalist Party and proclaims the establishment of the Republic of China • Germany, Austria-Hungary, and Italy renew the Triple Alliance • The Balkan Wars begin, resulting from ongoing territorial disputes; the Ottoman Turks are defeated by an alliance of Bulgaria, Serbia, Greece, and Montenegro; Albania declares its independence • The Soviet Communist Party begins publishing the newspaper *Pravda* (Truth) • The British parliament considers a bill allowing for "home rule" in Ireland, which is attacked as unfair to Ulster (Northern Ireland) • US Marines are sent to both Cuba and Nicaragua to protect the lives and property of US nationals	• New Mexico is admitted to the US as the 47th state, and Arizona as the 48th state • Massachusetts becomes the first state to adopt a minimum wage for working-class women and children • Alaska is organized as a US territory • New York passes a labor law establishing a 54-hour maximum work week • Congress passes legislation establishing an eight-hour workday for federal employees • When the Republican party nominates President Taft for a second term, many liberals who favored the nomination of Theodore Roosevelt withdraw to form the Progressive ("Bull Moose") Party, which becomes the first national political party to adopt a woman's suffrage plank • While campaigning in Milwaukee, WI, Roosevelt is shot and wounded by a would-be assassin • Woodrow Wilson is elected as president and Thomas R. Marshall as vice president (Democratic Party); Roosevelt receives more popular votes than President Taft; Roosevelt and Taft together have more votes than Wilson	• C. T. R. Wilson's cloud-chamber photographs lead to the detection of protons and electrons • Alfred Wegener (Germany) first proposes the idea of continental drift • The "unsinkable" luxury ocean liner *Titanic* hits an iceberg and sinks in the North Atlantic; more than 1,500 of the 2,224 persons aboard the ship die • The Florida Overseas Railroad, begun by Henry Flagler in 1904, is completed, providing an unbroken rail connection from the Florida mainland to Key West	• Jim Thorpe sets Olympic and world records in the pentathlon and decathlon; his medals and records are stripped from him when it is learned that he had played minor-league baseball for pay [both his amateur status and Olympic medals are restored posthumously by the International Olympic Committee in 1982] • W. C. Handy publishes "The Memphis Blues" and changes the course of American popular song • *Photoplay* debuts as the first magazine for movie fans • The Tour de France bicycle race is held for the first time • The Girl Scouts of America organization is founded by Juliette Gordon Low • Olympic Games: Stockholm
1913	• The Anglo-Turkish Convention determines the boundary between what is now Iraq and Kuwait • Bulgaria attacks Serbia and is defeated after Romania, Greece, and the Ottoman Empire intervene; the Ottoman Turks recapture Adrianople • South Africa passes immigration laws restricting the entry of Indians and Asians • Mohandas Gandhi is arrested and jailed for leading a resistance movement against British rule in South Africa • China recognizes the independence of Outer Mongolia • Suffragettes demonstrate in London demanding the right to vote for women • Norway grants women the right to vote in national elections	• California law makes it illegal for "aliens ineligible for citizenship" to own property; since a 1790 federal law granted naturalization only to white immigrants, Asian immigrants are now effectively barred from owning land • The 16th Amendment to the US Constitution establishes a federal income tax • The 17th Amendment to the US Constitution provides for direct popular election of senators (they were previously chosen by state legislatures) • Alice Paul and Lucy Burns organize the Congressional Union, known after 1916 as the National Women's Party • Over 5,000 supporters of women's rights stage the Woman Suffrage Parade in Washington, DC • Congress establishes the US Federal Reserve Bank and its governing board • Congress passes the Webb-Kenyon Act prohibiting the shipment of alcoholic beverages into states where their sale is illegal under state law • Congress establishes separate Departments of Labor and of Commerce, both with cabinet status • Garment workers strike in New York and Boston and win pay raises and reduced hours • Climbers reach the South Peak (true summit) of Mt. McKinley (Denali) in Alaska	• Henry Ford creates the first moving assembly line for mass production of automobiles at his Ford Motor Company plant in Detroit • Hans Wilhelm Geiger and Walther Müller (Germany) invent the "Geiger Counter" for the detection of radioactivity • Neils Bohr (Denmark), working with Ernest Rutherford (England), formulates his theory of atomic structure • William M. Burton (US) patents a process for refining oil by the thermal "cracking" of large petroleum molecules; the process produces gasoline with higher octane content than the earlier "still refining" technique • The Los Angeles Aqueduct is completed, bringing water from the Owens River across the Sierra Nevada and beginning the transformation of Los Angeles from desert town into sprawling metropolis • Industrialist Harry Brearley (England) develops "stainless steel" by adding carbon and chromium to steel	• Standard Oil opens the world's first automotive service station in Columbus, OH • The first crossword puzzle appears in the *New York World* • The US Post Office begins parcel post delivery service • The first modern income tax system in the US, passed by Congress after ratification of the 16th Amendment, goes into effect • *Darktown Follies* opens in Harlem and helps to make Harlem a black cultural center • The National Biscuit Company creates the Oreo cookie • The National Board of the YWCA creates a commission on sex education, the first organization of its kind in the country • Cecil B. DeMille makes his first notable movie, *The Squaw Man*, in a rented barn in Hollywood, CA; its success helps to ensure the future of Hollywood as the moviemaking capital of the world

E. EDUCATION, LITERATURE & THE FINE ARTS	F. RELIGION, THEOLOGY, PHILOSOPHY & PSYCHOLOGY	G. AMERICAN & UNITED METHODISM	H. BRITISH & WORLD METHODISM	
• Maurice Ravel completes his evocative, impressionistic ballet *Daphnis and Chloé*, commissioned by Sergey Diaghilev for his Ballets Russes • Debussy composes his *Images for Orchestra* • Rachmaninoff composes his *Vocalise* • Leopold Stokowski is named conductor of the Philadelphia Symphony • Gustav Mahler's *Symphony No. 9* premieres in Vienna by the Vienna Philharmonic Orchestra conducted by Bruno Walter • Frederick Delius composes his tone poem *On Hearing the First Cuckoo in Spring* • Picasso completes his painting *The Violin* • Matisse paints *The Red Studio*, a work that demonstrates his innovative use of bright colors and erratic perspective • Wassily Kandinsky publishes *Concerning the Spiritual in Art*, the first major theoretical treatise on artistic abstraction and completes his painting *The Garden of Love (Improvisation Number 27)* • Other notable publications include: – James Weldon Johnson, *The Autobiography of an Ex-Colored Man* – Thomas Mann, *Death in Venice* – Zane Grey, *Riders of the Purple Sage*	• Notable publications include: – William James, *Essays in Radical Empiricism* (posthumous) – Carl Jung, *The Theory of Psychoanalysis* – Bertrand Russell, *The Problems of Philosophy* – Émile Durkheim, *The Elementary Forms of Religious Life* – Josiah Royce, *The Sources of Religious Insight* – Walter Rauschenbusch, *Christianizing the Social Order*	• The MEC General Conference: – establishes episcopal service areas to organize the work and clarify the responsibilities of the bishops, who are henceforth expected to reside within and itinerate through the geographic area for which they are responsible, not the whole church – introduces the principle of financial apportionments – recognizes the MFSS as an executive agency of the church – gives unordained local pastors the right to baptize and marry (but not to serve Holy Communion) when they serve alone on a charge – approves resolutions seeking suppression of the liquor industry and calling for total abstinence by all Methodists – organizes the South Swedish Conference • Harry F. Ward becomes executive secretary of MFSS and serves until 1944 • The MPC General Conference: – authorizes a joint commission to explore the possibility of organic union with the UBC – empowers the commission to call a special session of the General Conference if "speedy action is advisable" • Seth Cook Rees moves to Pasadena and establishes the Pilgrim Church	• Westminster Central Hall in London is dedicated and becomes the headquarters of the WMC [UK] • The PMC establishes a new headquarters in London • The MEC begins mission work in Latvia • John Nuelsen, elected bishop in 1908, is appointed to oversee all MEC work in Europe • John Telford reedits Thomas Jackson's *The Lives of the Early Methodist Preachers* (four editions, 1837–71) under the title *Wesley's Veterans* (7 vols., 1912–14)	**1912**
• Igor Stravinsky's revolutionary *Rite of Spring* causes a near-riot at its premiere performance in Paris • George Bernard Shaw publishes *Pygmalion* • D. H. Lawrence's largely autobiographical novel *Sons and Lovers* deals with life in a small mining town • The "Armory Show" (so named for the 69th Infantry Regiment Armory in New York City where it first exhibited) is widely regarded as the most important art exhibit in the United States in the 20th century; it features over 1,300 European and American works of art covering the period from 1799 to 1913 • Marcel Proust publishes *Swann's Way*, the first volume of his *À la recherche du temps perdu* (16 vols., 1913–27), known in English as *Remembrance of Things Past* (1922–31) and widely regarded as one of the world's great literary achievements • Marc Chagall completes *In Paris Through the Window*, showing the influence of Cubism on his work	• Timothy Drew (Noble Drew Ali) establishes the Moorish Science Temple of America (MSTA) in Newark, NJ, sponsored by the Sultan of Morocco, to teach the principles of Islam to blacks in the US • Solomon Schlechter establishes the Jewish Theological Seminary in New York City and organizes the United Synagogue of Conservative Judaism • Arthur C. Headlam, et al., publish *Foundations: A Statement of Christian Belief in Terms of Modern Thought*, which represents the modernist Anglican response to *The Fundamentals* • Other notable publications include: – Edmund Husserl, *Ideas: General Introduction to Pure Phenomenology* – Alfred North Whitehead and Bertrand Russell, *Principia Mathematica* – Josiah Royce, *The Problem of Christianity* – Miguel de Unamuno, *The Tragic Sense of Life* – Sigmund Freud, *Totem and Taboo* – R. H. Charles, *The Apocrypha and Psuedepigrapha of the Old Testament* (2 vols.) – Wilhelm Bossuet, *Kyrios Christos: A History of the Belief in Christ from the Beginnings of Christianity to Irenaeus*	• The UBC General Conference: – declares that the aim of its mission program is to make its overseas fields self-supporting – approves a proposal for union with the MPC under the name The United Protestant Church; the proposal fails to win the necessary three-fourths vote in the annual conferences during the following quadrennium – authorizes full-time secretaries for the Board of Education and for Young People's Work – ties the orphanages and benevolent homes established by several annual conferences more closely to the general church • The MECS opens the Lake Junaluska Assembly in North Carolina as the "Southern Chautauqua" • The first Wesley Foundation is organized at the University of Illinois by James C. Baker (MEC) • A dispute between the Board of Trustees of Vanderbilt University and the bishops of the MECS over who can appoint University trustees results in a court case; the resulting decision of the Tennessee Supreme Court in 1914 vests control of the university with the Trustees and denies "visitorial powers" to the MECS bishops • The first Convention of Methodist Men (MEC) meets • The MEC formally organizes the Puerto Rico Mission Conference	• The Methodist Church of New Zealand/Te Haahi Weteriana o Aotearoa (MCNZ) formally becomes autonomous; the PM congregations in New Zealand join the new body • Former Methodist lay preacher William Harris, who had been converted by the MEC mission in Liberia, responds to a vision and begins preaching across Côte d'Ivoire (Ivory Coast); within two years he has baptized over 100,000 people, who are known as "Harrists," before he is expelled from the country • The UMC makes Ranmoor College (formerly the MNC, 1864) the theological college for first-year students, who then transfer to the larger Victoria Park College (formerly UMFC, 1871) for their second and third years • The WMMS celebrates the centennial of WM missions, marking 100 years since the organization of the first WM Missionary Society in the Leeds District in 1813	**1913**

	A. WORLD HISTORY & POLITICS	B. AMERICAN HISTORY & POLITICS	C. SCIENCE, MEDICINE & TECHNOLOGY	D. DAILY LIFE, POPULAR CULTURE & ENTERTAINMENT
1914	• The Panama Canal is completed and opens to shipping • The assassination by a Serbian nationalist of Archduke Francis Ferdinand, heir to the throne of Austria-Hungary, and his wife, Sophie, provokes a crisis between Austria-Hungary and Germany on the one hand, and Serbia and Russia on the other, ultimately setting off WWI, pitting the Allies—Britain, France, Italy, Russia, Serbia, and (finally) the US and Japan—against the Central powers—Austria-Hungary, Germany, and the Ottoman Empire • The South African government makes important concessions to the demands of Mohandas Gandhi, including recognition of Indian marriages and abolition of the poll tax for them; Gandhi returns to India • The British parliament passes a Home Rule Bill granting political independence to Ireland, but its implementation is delayed by the outbreak of WWI • The Fellowship of Reconciliation (FOR) is established in England as an ecumenical movement of people committed to active nonviolence as a means of political, social, and economic transformation; it becomes the International Fellowship of Reconciliation in 1919 • The name of the Russian capital is changed from St. Petersburg to Petrograd	• President Wilson proclaims the neutrality of the US when WWI begins and offers to broker peace negotiations between the warring powers • The Federal Trade Commission is created to regulate interstate commerce • The Clayton Antitrust Act restricts the use of court injunctions in labor disputes and exempts labor unions and farm organizations from the provisions of the Sherman Antitrust Act • Marcus Garvey establishes the Universal Negro Improvement Association (UNIA) in Harlem, which promotes Garvey's black nationalist agenda	• Feminist activist Margaret Sanger begins publication of *The Woman Rebel*, which provides information about birth control in defiance of social conventions and the legal restrictions of the 1873 Comstock Act and similar state statutes • A US circuit court decides a patent suit over airplane design in favor of the Wright brothers and against Glenn Curtiss • The world's first red and green traffic lights are installed in Cleveland • George Washington Carver begins experimenting with peanuts as a new cash crop for Southern farmers • The last known passenger pigeon in the US dies in the Cincinnati Zoo	• Charlie Chaplin plays the Little Tramp, his most famous character, in the film of that name • The first issue of *The New Republic* magazine is published • W. C. Handy writes his classic "St. Louis Blues" • The trench coat is designed for wear by British Army officers; it is later popularized for both men and women by French fashion designer Gabrielle "Coco" Chanel • The Smith-Lever Act formally establishes the Cooperative Extension Service at state land-grant colleges and universities, resulting in the employment of County Agents to assist family farmers and the sponsorship of 4-H clubs across the country
1915	• German submarines sink the *Lusitania*, a British passenger liner, killing 1,198 people including 112 Americans; the resulting outrage brings the US much closer to war • The Second Battle of Ypres is infamous for the first use (by Germany) of chemical weapons on the battlefield • British forces spearheaded by troops from the Australia and New Zealand Army Corps (ANZAC) unsuccessfully attempt to assault Turkish positions at Gallipoli and are forced to withdraw after suffering heavy casualties; the event is commemorated in Australia and New Zealand by ANZAC Day (April 25) • Turkish soldiers commit genocide, killing an estimated 600,000 to 1 million Armenians, beginning with 17,000 at Trebizond in eastern Turkey • The US branch of the Fellowship of Reconciliation (FOR) is established • Denmark grants women the right to vote in national elections	• The population of the US passes the 100 million mark • The US states that the loss of US lives and ships is a violation of neutrality for which Germany will be held responsible and begins providing economic and military aid to Allied nations • The Revenue Cutter Service, the Lifesaving Service, and the Steamship Inspection Bureau are merged to create the US Coast Guard • In *Guinn v. United States* the Supreme Court rules that the 15th Amendment prohibits states from establishing literacy tests as a qualification for voting in federal elections • The ICC prohibits railroad companies from also owning shipping lines on the Great Lakes • The Ku Klux Klan (KKK) is reorganized by William J. Simmons at Stone Mountain, GA, near Atlanta	• Alexander Graham Bell and his assistant Thomas Watson make the first coast-to-coast telephone call • Thomas Hunt Morgan and three students publish *The Mechanism of Mendelian Heredity*, which establishes the basis for the new science of genetics • Georges Claude (France) patents the electric neon light tube • The one millionth Model T automobile rolls off Henry Ford's assembly line	• The Louisiana YWCA holds the first interracial conference held in the South since Reconstruction • Jim Thorpe organizes the Canton Bulldogs, one of the earliest professional football teams • The first Raggedy Ann doll is created; she becomes a children's book character in 1918 • Tom Brown's band of musicians from New Orleans goes to Chicago and starts advertising itself as a "Jass Band" • Films: The technically brilliant but thoroughly racist Civil War epic by D. W. Griffith, *The Birth of a Nation*, introduces many of the techniques of modern filmmaking, including the narrative close-up and the flashback

E. EDUCATION, LITERATURE & THE FINE ARTS	F. RELIGION, THEOLOGY, PHILOSOPHY & PSYCHOLOGY	G. AMERICAN & UNITED METHODISM	H. BRITISH & WORLD METHODISM	
• Ralph Vaughan Williams composes *A London Symphony* (revised in 1921) • Charles Ives completes *Three Places in New England* • Frederick Delius composes his *Violin Sonata No. 1* • Inspired by the cubism of Picasso, Henri Matisse creates his austere, almost abstract painting *View of Notre-Dame* • Edgar Rice Burroughs introduces the world to *Tarzan of the Apes*	• The Assemblies of God, "a voluntary, cooperative fellowship," is organized at the first General Council meeting in Hot Springs, AR; women are fully accepted as ministers and Dolly Drain Simms is the first woman to be ordained • Pope Pius X dies; he will be canonized as a saint in 1954; he is succeeded by Pope Benedict XV • Notable publications include: – Sigmund Freud, *On Narcissism* – Rufus M. Jones, *Spiritual Reformers in the Sixteenth and Seventeenth Centuries*	• The MECS General Conference: – severs all relations with Vanderbilt University and approves the establishment of two new seminaries for the church, one east and one west of the Mississippi River [this leads to the foundation of Emory University in Atlanta and Southern Methodist University in Dallas, with their respective schools of theology] – adopts the Social Creed, originally adopted by the MEC in 1908 – separates its mission in Mexico and Texas into two units, the Texas Mexican Mission and the Pacific Mexican Conference – organizes the Latin District of the Florida Conference – defeats a proposal to change the wording of the Apostles' Creed from "holy catholic church" to "church of God" – again rejects proposal to extend full laity rights to women – approves the continuation of steps toward reunion with the MEC and agrees to participate in new Joint Commission on Union • The MPC General Conference meets in a special session; after much debate, some of it rancorous, it appoints a commission to meet with delegates from the UBC to explore further the basis of proposed union • The UEC General Conference: – warmly receives a fraternal delegate from the EA, who gives a very positive report about the progress of discussions of the joint EA and UEC Commission on Church Union – resolves to improve Sunday school instruction by providing teacher training classes – considers adopting graded lessons for Sunday school classes • American University in Washington, DC, admits its first class of students, including four women • First Methodist Church in Akron, OH—the first of the "Akron Plan" churches (1867)—is demolished and replaced by a traditional sanctuary in Gothic style and a separate educational building	• *The Wesleyan Methodist Magazine* (1822) in the UK is transformed into *The Magazine of the Wesleyan Methodist Church* • The MEC and MECS Boards of Mission agree to an allocation of mission work in Mexico: MECS in northern Mexico along the border with Texas and New Mexico, MEC around Mexico City and in southern Mexico	1914
• Carter G. Woodson, considered by many to be the father of "Black History," establishes the Association for the Study of Negro Life and History and publishes his first major work, *The Education of the Negro Prior to 1861* • Manuel De Falla composes *Nights in the Gardens of Spain* and *Wedded by Witchcraft* • Charles Ives composes his *Concord Sonata* • Notable publications include: – T. S. Eliot, *The Love Song of J. Alfred Prufrock* – D. H. Lawrence, *The Rainbow* – Franz Kafka, *The Metamorphosis* – Willa Cather, *The Song of the Lark* – Ford Madox Ford, *The Good Soldier*	• John R. Mott is named General Secretary of the International Committee of the YMCA [he will serve in that capacity until 1928, and from 1926 to 1937 as president of the YMCA's World Committee] • The first Masjid (Islamic mosque) in the US is built in Maine by Muslim immigrants from Albania • Controversy over control of the publishing house causes a split in the National Baptist Convention of America (1895); one group continues with that name while the other group takes the name National Baptist Convention, USA	• The EA General Conference: – following a report from the Commission on Church Union, endorses continued discussions about union with the UEC – votes to continue participation in the Federal Council of Churches – authorizes the bishops to appoint delegates to the Conference on Faith and Order called by the Protestant Episcopal Church – extends the maximum length of a pastoral appointment to seven years – establishes a budget system of financing for all denominational activities • Emory College (1836) is rechartered as Emory University; Asa Candler (then president of Coca-Cola) donates a $1-million endowment to the new university; the Candler School of Theology (MECS; named for Bishop Warren Candler) and the Emory Law School are built on a new campus in Atlanta and open for classes in 1916; the undergraduate college moves from Oxford, GA, to the Atlanta campus in 1919	• The Pentecostal Church of Scotland unites with the Church of the Nazarene (in the UK) • Methodists and Presbyterians in Korea establish Chosun Christian College in Seoul	1915

	A. WORLD HISTORY & POLITICS	B. AMERICAN HISTORY & POLITICS	C. SCIENCE, MEDICINE & TECHNOLOGY	D. DAILY LIFE, POPULAR CULTURE & ENTERTAINMENT
1915 cont.		• The Panama-Pacific International Exposition is held in San Francisco to celebrate the opening of the Panama Canal; it features 30,000 exhibitors and has about 13 million visitors		
1916	• The Battle of Jutland between British and German fleets is the largest sea battle in history, involving 148 ships, including 60 battleships and cruisers and 160,000 men; it has inconclusive results and little influence on the war • British forces suffer staggering losses (57,470 casualties in one day) in attacks on German positions in the Battle of the Somme; the battle lasts for over four months and causes over 500,000 casualties to each side; the battle of Verdun results in over 400,000 casualties to each side • Mexican revolutionary leader and bandit Pancho Villa raids American settlements in Texas and New Mexico until the US Army forces him and his band of pistoleros back into Mexico • Through the secret Sykes-Picot agreement, Britain and France make plans to divide the Middle East into separate spheres of influence • An armed uprising in Dublin on Easter Sunday seeking to create an independent Irish Republic leads to the arrest of 3,000 protesters and the execution of 15 nationalist leaders • Britain establishes the Gilbert and Ellice Islands Colony, which later becomes the nations of Kiribati and Tuvalu	• President Wilson issues an ultimatum to Germany: unless German submarine attacks on US ships cease immediately, the US will sever diplomatic relations • By executive order, Wilson designates "The Star-Spangled Banner" as the US national anthem • Wilson also declares the establishment of National Flag Day on June 14, the anniversary of the Flag Resolution of 1777 • Congress amends the Enlarged Homestead Act of 1909 to allow 640-acre stock-raising homesteads in some parts of the West • Jeannette Rankin, of Montana, is the first woman to be elected to the US House of Representatives • The US National Park Service is established as part of the Department of the Interior • Construction begins on the Stone Mountain Memorial carving near Atlanta; conceived and sponsored by the United Daughters of the Confederacy, it is intended to honor Confederate leaders Robert E. Lee, Stonewall Jackson, and Jefferson Davis; the carving of the three mounted figures is 90 feet tall and 190 feet wide; construction continues intermittently to 1928 and then halts due to lack of funds • President Wilson and Vice President Marshall are reelected (Democratic Party)	• Margaret Sanger opens the first birth control clinic in the US in New York City; she is arrested and serves a 30-day sentence for "maintaining a public nuisance"	• The Professional Golf Association is organized; Jim Barnes is the first PGA champion • Race car driver Barney Oldfield completes the first lap of over 100 miles per hour at the Indianapolis Speedway • Coca-Cola introduces the distinctive "contour bottle," which becomes one of the few packages ever granted trademark status by the US Patent Office • John Lloyd Wright develops the construction toys called Lincoln Logs • The Olympic Games are canceled due to WWI • Nathan Handwerker leaves his employer Charles Feltman's Coney Island hot dog stand to start Nathan's Famous Hot Dogs [which now calls itself the world's greatest hot dog purveyor] • Stein's Dixie Jass Band plays its first gig under its new name, the Original Dixieland Jass Band (changed in 1917 to Jazz Band)
1917	• Germany begins unrestricted submarine warfare against Allied shipping in the Atlantic • The February Revolution in Russia forces Tsar Nicholas II to abdicate, thereby ending the Romanov dynasty and the Russian Empire; then the October Revolution brings Vladimir Lenin and the Bolshevik Party, now called the Communist Party, to power in Russia • Four separate Soviet Socialist Republics (SSRs) arise in the territory of the former Russian Empire: Russia, Ukraine, Belarus, and the Transcaucasus (Armenia, Georgia, Azerbaijan)	• German submarines sink the US ship *Housatonic*, and the US immediately severs diplomatic relations with Germany; Congress then declares war on Germany • The US enters WWI, and the first American troops are sent to France under the command of John J. Pershing • Congress passes the Selective Service Act, which requires all men age 18-45 to register for military service, and the Espionage Act, which prohibits espionage for a foreign country and provides heavy penalties for those guilty of such activity • The US stock market crashes, losing about 40% of its value in four months	• The work of French physicist Paul Langévin on piezoelectricity and piezo-ceramics leads to the development of underwater sonar • American astronomer Harlow Shapley makes the first reliable measurement of the size of the Milky Way Galaxy by establishing the spatial distribution of globular clusters • Howard Krum receives a US patent for the first practical teletypewriter, which can receive telegraphic signals and automatically convert them to typed text • A 100-inch reflecting telescope is installed at Mt. Wilson Observatory in *(cont.)*	• The first op-ed page appears in the *New York Times* • The Original Dixieland Jazz Band makes the first jazz recordings for Columbia Records • The Chattanooga [TN] Bakery creates the Moon Pie • The Direct Marketing Association (DMA), a trade association for businesses interested in the marketing of goods and services directly to potential consumers, is established • The cost of a US first-class postage stamp increases to 3¢

E. EDUCATION, LITERATURE & THE FINE ARTS	F. RELIGION, THEOLOGY, PHILOSOPHY & PSYCHOLOGY	G. AMERICAN & UNITED METHODISM	H. BRITISH & WORLD METHODISM	
• The US branch of the Fellowship of Reconciliation (FOR) is established • Denmark grants women the right to vote in national elections		• Southern Methodist University School of Theology (MECS) is established in Dallas; it is renamed Perkins School of Theology in 1945 • Shaw University (1866) becomes Rust College • The MEC Book Concern begins using Abingdon Press as the name for its general trade book publications		**1915 cont.**
• Carter G. Woodson begins publication of *The Journal of Negro History* • The National Academy of Sciences in the US is expanded to include the National Research Council • A group of maverick European intellectuals in Zürich begin publishing the magazine *Dada*, which marks the beginning of "Dadaism" and the Surrealist movement, attracting artists such as Wassily Kandinsky, George Grosz, Amedeo Modigliani, Piet Mondrian, Salvador Dalí, and Joan Miró • Charles Ives finishes his *Fourth Symphony*, his defining piece • Debussy composes his *Sonata for Flute, Viola and Harp* • Notable publications include: – James Joyce, *Portrait of the Artist as a Young Man* – Franz Kafka, *The Judgment* – Carl Sandburg, *Chicago Poems*	• The Cooperative General Association of Free Will Baptists is established • Notable publications include: – Ferdinand de Saussure, *Course in General Linguistics* – John Dewey, *Democracy and Education* – Carl Jung, *Psychology of the Unconscious*	• The MEC General Conference: – mandates use of unfermented grape juice rather than wine in celebration of the Lord's Supper – establishes a permanent Commission on the Course of Study – assigns the residences of the bishops in "episcopal areas" and forms groups of contiguous annual conferences around them – approves MEC participation in a Joint Commission on Union with the MECS • The MEC bishops declare violation of the 1884 ban on remarriage of divorced persons by MEC clergy except in the case of adultery to be "an act of maladministration" and hence a punishable offence • The AMEC celebrates the centennial of its establishment as a separate denomination; publishes *The Centennial Encyclopedia of African Methodism*, edited by R. R. Wright Jr. • The Reformed New Congregational Methodist Church is established in Illinois and Indiana [now defunct] • Representatives from seven Methodist denominations (MEC, MECS, MPC, AMEC, AMEZC, CMEC, and the Methodist Church of Canada) gather in Evanston, IL, for the first Pan-Methodist Conference • The MEC and MECS begin serious conversations about the possibility of unification by reorganization; the Joint Commission on Federation (1898) is replaced by the Joint Commission on Union; the MPC stays aloof from these conversations • The MPC General Conference: – adopts the Social Creed, originally adopted by the MEC in 1908 and the MECS in 1914 – revises the *Ritual* to include an "enlargement and enrichment of the Order of Worship" and adds a form for the reception of new members	• The MEC begins mission work in Costa Rica and organizes the Bolivia Mission Conference	**1916**
• The first Pulitzer Prizes are awarded for editorial writing, reporting, history of the US, and biography or autobiography (prizes for fiction, and for drama and poetry, debut in 1918) • The first edition of *The World Book Encyclopedia* is published • The San Francisco Conservatory is established • Sergey Prokofiev composes his *Symphony No. 1 (Classical)*, which does much to establish the neoclassical style that will dominate much 20th-century music • Ottorino Respighi composes his *Ancient Airs and Dances Suite No. 1*	• The Norwegian Lutheran Church of America (NLCA) unites 90% of Norwegian Lutherans in the US and Canada • Three shepherd children near Fatima, Portugal, report visions of the Virgin Mary • Father Ed Flanagan founds Boys Town, a home for orphaned or delinquent children, in Omaha, NE • Notable publications include: – Sigmund Freud *The Origin and Development of Psychoanalysis*	• The UBC General Conference: – establishes a general Board of Administration, with a full-time general secretary, to function in the intervals between General Conferences – charges that board with the responsibility of promoting the financial plans of the church and coordinating the work of the church's several boards and agencies • The MEC establishes the Mexican Methodist Institute (later the Wesleyan Institute) in San Antonio, TX • The MEC founds the Fenton Memorial Rest Home at the Chautauqua Institute exclusively for MEC deaconesses	• Local Congregational Methodist missionary societies in Georgia, Mississippi, and Louisiana send Mattie Long as their first missionary to India	**1917**

	A. WORLD HISTORY & POLITICS	B. AMERICAN HISTORY & POLITICS	C. SCIENCE, MEDICINE & TECHNOLOGY	D. DAILY LIFE, POPULAR CULTURE & ENTERTAINMENT
1917 cont.	• British troops enter Jerusalem; Britain issues the Balfour Declaration, promising Jews a "national home" in Palestine, while reassuring the non-Jewish population of civil and religious freedom • The Netherlands and the Soviet Union grant women the right to vote in national elections • Dutch dancer Mata Hari is convicted and executed as a German spy	• The US purchases the Virgin Islands (St. Croix, St. John, and St. Thomas) from Denmark for $25 million • The US national debt exceeds $5 billion for the first time • Congress passes the Jones Act, extending the full rights of US citizenship to Puerto Ricans • Denali National Park is established in Alaska	California; it is the largest in the world at the time • The Trans-Siberian Railroad, begun in 1891, is finally completed; it runs 5,778 miles from Moscow through the Russian steppes and Siberia to the Pacific port of Vladivostok	
1918	• American troops engage in their first important battle at Château-Thierry, as they and French forces stop a German advance; the Americans then face and defeat the Germans at Aisne-Marne and Meuse-Argonne • WWI ends with the surrender of the Central powers; German kaiser William II abdicates and goes into exile; Germany's Second Reich comes to an end • The "dual monarchy" of Austria-Hungary is dissolved; Austria and Hungary become separate independent republics • Bolsheviks murder Tsar Nicholas II and his family in Russia; Vladimir Lenin becomes Chief Commissar; he nationalizes the factories, collectivizes the farms, and outlaws the church; the Russian capital is moved from Petrograd to Moscow • Civil war erupts between the Red Army of the Bolsheviks and the Mensheviks (helped by Britain, Japan, and the US) • Montenegro unites with Serbia to establish the kingdom of Serbs, Croats, and Slovenes • Finland, Estonia, Latvia, Lithuania, Ukraine, Georgia, Armenia, and Azerbaijan proclaim their independence • Great Britain and Canada grant women the right to vote in national elections; in Britain, it is limited to women over age 30 • Iceland becomes a sovereign state in union with Denmark	• The US broadens the 1917 Espionage Act providing serious penalties for any obstruction of the war effort • The US Supreme Court rules that Article I of the Constitution gives Congress the power to authorize compulsory military service (conscription) • The Sedition Act broadens the 1917 Espionage Act by prohibiting spoken or printed attacks on the US government, the Constitution, or the flag • US Socialist leader Eugene V. Debs is sentenced to 10 years in jail for protesting the government's prosecution of individuals under the Espionage and Sedition Acts • President Wilson decides he will personally attend the Paris Peace Conference	• Margaret Sanger wins an appeal of her 1916 conviction, opening the way for physicians in New York City to provide birth control information to women • John Browning (US) invents the automatic rifle, which is named after him • Albert Einstein, *Relativity: The Special and the General Theory* • The "Spanish flu," a worldwide influenza pandemic, kills an estimated 50 million people by 1920 (650,000 in the US alone)	• Daylight Saving Time (DST) is introduced in the US • The US Post Office begins the first regular airmail service between New York City and Washington, DC
1919	• The Treaty of Versailles marks the official end to WWI; the Ottoman Empire and the German Empire are dismantled; Germans are left embittered because of the humiliation and heavy reparations payments that are imposed on them – The Weimar Republic is established in Germany; Friedrich Ebert becomes its first president – France regains the Alsace-Lorraine territories seized by Germany in 1871, and Poland, Austria, and Czechoslovakia emerge as independent states – France takes control of Syria and Lebanon, which is enlarged to include Maronite Christians, Druze, and both Shiite and Sunni Muslim areas, setting the stage for later conflict	• President Wilson presents the Treaty of Versailles and the League of Nations Covenant to the Senate for ratification • The 18th Amendment to the US Constitution inaugurates the Prohibition Era; it bans the manufacture, sale, or transportation of "intoxicating liquors" • The Volstead Act, passed over Wilson's veto, provides an enforcement mechanism for the 18th Amendment by specifically prohibiting the manufacture, transportation, and sale of beverages containing more than 0.5% alcohol • The American Federation of Labor, headed by Samuel Gompers, leads a strike against US Steel; the strike is broken in 1920 but results in the abolition of the 12-hour workday in the US steel industry	• John Alcock and his fellow British aviator Arthur Brown make the first nonstop transatlantic flight, from St. John's, Newfoundland, to Ireland • Richard Byrd (US) makes the first flight over the South Pole • Ernest Rutherford creates the first artificially induced and controlled nuclear reaction • AT&T introduces the first rotary dial telephones • The YWCA convenes and finances the first International Conference of Women Physicians	• Charlie Chaplin, D. W. Griffith, Douglas Fairbanks, and Mary Pickford establish United Artists in an attempt to control their own work • Chicago becomes the center of the jazz world when it attracts artists such as Louis Armstrong and Jelly Roll Morton • The "Black Sox" World Series scandal shocks the nation; eight members of the Chicago White Sox team accept payoffs from gamblers to throw the series • American inventor Edwin George begins manufacturing gasoline-powered lawn mowers • The Radio Corporation of America (RCA) is established by AT&T and GE to develop commercial radio broadcasting and sell radio equipment made by GE and Westinghouse

E. EDUCATION, LITERATURE & THE FINE ARTS	F. RELIGION, THEOLOGY, PHILOSOPHY & PSYCHOLOGY	G. AMERICAN & UNITED METHODISM	H. BRITISH & WORLD METHODISM	
• Matisse completes his painting *The Three Sisters* • Alfred Stieglitz takes the first in his remarkable 20-year series of photographs of Georgia O'Keeffe [they are married in 1924] • Notable publications include: – W. Somerset Maugham, *Of Human Bondage* – T. S. Eliot, *Prufrock and Other Observations*	– Walter Rauschenbusch, *A Theology for the Social Gospel* – Vladimir Ilyich Lenin, *The State and Revolution*			**1917** cont.
• Bartók's *String Quartet No. 2* premieres in Budapest • Erik Satie composes his *Socrate*, based on Plato's dialogues, for four sopranos and chamber orchestra • Frederick Delius composes *A Song Before Sunrise* • Percy Grainger completes his *Country Gardens* • Fernand Léger's painting *Engine Rooms* is a glorification of modern machinery • Charles-Édouard Jeanneret (later known as "Le Corbusier") and Amédée Ozenfant publish *After Cubism*, a manifesto of the "Purist" movement in art and architecture • Other notable publications include: – Booth Tarkington, *The Magnificent Ambersons* – Willa Cather, *My Ántonia*	• The Lutheran General Synod (1820), United Synod of the South (1863), and Lutheran General Council (1867) merge to form the United Lutheran Church in America (ULCA) • Following the Bolshevik Revolution, all church property in Russia is confiscated and all religious instruction in schools is abolished • The Northern Baptist Convention votes to permit the ordination of women • Notable publications include: – Romani Guardini, *The Spirit of the Liturgy* – Oswald Spengler, *The Decline of the West* (2 vols., 1918–22)	• The MECS General Conference: – accepts a report from the bishops stating that the Apostles' Creed embodies "fixed and formal Methodist doctrine" and so cannot be changed by General Conference action without revision of the First Restrictive Rule – groups the annual conferences into "episcopal areas" with a bishop resident in each area having four-year presidential oversight – approves full laity rights for women in both General and annual conferences – establishes the Indian Mission Conference – creates a War Work Committee and urges support of the war against Germany • The bishops of the AMEC, AMEZC, and CMEC meet to discuss the possibility of organic union, but the talks collapse • The UEC General Conference: – approves a Plan of Union with the EA and sends it to the annual conferences for ratification – establishes a War Service Commission to assure the continuing relationship of the church to those entering military service – discusses the deaconess work of the church but takes no action in light of the expected reunion with the EA • The CMEC General Conference: – grants women the right to be licensed as local preachers and ordained as local deacons and elders – establishes the Connectional Women's Missionary Society, which quickly becomes the primary focus of women's activities in the church	• The WMC [UK] establishes the Epworth Press imprint for popular titles, to distinguish them from official church publications • The MECS mission in Korea is organized as the Korean Annual Conference • The MEC begins a combination of mission and relief work in France after the end of WWI	**1918**
• The Los Angeles Symphony gives its first public concert • The Juilliard School of Music is established in New York City • Edward Elgar's *Cello Concerto* premieres in London • The Ballets Russes gives the world premiere of Manuel De Falla's ballet *The Three-Cornered Hat* in London • Igor Stravinsky composes his orchestral *Firebird Suite* • Paul Klee paints *Dream Birds* • Walter Gropius founds the Bauhaus school of design in Weimar, Germany • H. L. Mencken publishes *The American Language* • Sherwood Anderson publishes his collection of short stories, *Winesburg, Ohio: A Group of Tales of Ohio Small Town Life*	• Madeline Southard, an MEC local preacher, establishes The American Association of Women Preachers (which later becomes The International Association of Women Ministers) • The word *Pentecostal* is dropped from the name of The Church of the Nazarene (1908) to separate it from groups that accepted "speaking in tongues" • Karl Barth's landmark study of *The Epistle to the Romans* (2nd ed. 1922, English translation 1933) marks the emergence of the neoorthodox movement in theology • Other notable publications include: – Martin Dibelius, *From Tradition to Gospel* – D. C. Macintosh, *Theology as an Empirical Science*	• The EA General Conference: – approves a Plan of Union with the UEC and sends it to the annual conferences for ratification – launches the "Forward Movement" for strengthening and enlarging the church – discontinues the Evangelical Correspondence College established in 1895 – establishes a committee to consider the condition of the church in postwar Germany and to render financial and spiritual assistance as needed • The centennial of the Methodist Missionary Society is celebrated by the Centenary Movement and culminates in the "Methodist World's Fair" in Columbus, *(cont.)*	• The UMC closes Ranmoor College (1864) and transfers all theological students to the larger Victoria Park College (1871) • The MECS organizes its work in Cuba into the Cuba Mission Conference	**1919**

	A. WORLD HISTORY & POLITICS	B. AMERICAN HISTORY & POLITICS	C. SCIENCE, MEDICINE & TECHNOLOGY	D. DAILY LIFE, POPULAR CULTURE & ENTERTAINMENT
1919 cont.	– Britain takes control of Egypt, Palestine, the Transjordan, and Iraq, which is put together from three separate Ottoman provinces centered in Mosul (north), Baghdad (middle), and Basra (south) • The May 4th Movement in China protests against Japanese acquisition of Chinese territory through the Treaty of Versailles; it marks the beginning of modern Chinese nationalism • Irish War of Independence results in creation of the Irish Free State (1922) • Germany, Austria, Poland, Sweden, and Czechoslovakia grant women the right to vote in national elections • The first Pan-African Congress, organized by W. E. B. DuBois, opens in Paris with fifty-seven delegates from sixteen countries and colonies • The League of Red Cross Societies is founded in Paris	• The stock market experiences a sudden postwar boom (up by 51%) followed by a long decline (back down by 46% in 1921) • The Communist Labor Party (later American Communist Party) is formed in Chicago after a split with the Socialist Party • Gov. Calvin Coolidge calls out the Massachusetts National Guard to end a strike by policemen in Boston • Congress adopts a Child Labor Tax Law providing that businesses employing children under the age of 14 will be assessed 10% of their annual profits • Grand Canyon, Zion, and Acadia National Parks are established		• Sir Barton is the first racehorse to win the Triple Crown (Kentucky Derby, Preakness, and Belmont) • The cost of a US first-class postage stamp is reduced from 3¢ to 2¢ • The Original Dixieland Jazz Band brings New Orleans jazz to England and Europe with their first international tour
1920	• The League of Nations is established by Woodrow Wilson and other world leaders; Geneva (in historically neutral Switzerland) is selected for its headquarters • Adolf Hitler helps organize the National Socialist Party (better known as the Nazi Party) in Germany • Polish leader Józef Piłsudski defends Warsaw against an invading Russian army, and Poland annexes western Ukraine and Belarus • Mohandas Gandhi, now called "Mahatma" (meaning "Great Soul") by millions, begins a campaign of civil disobedience in India, protesting British political and commercial control • The British parliament passes another Home Rule Bill for Ireland, specifying separate parliaments for Ulster (Northern Ireland) and southern Ireland • German East Africa becomes a British protectorate and is renamed Tanganyika; British East Africa is renamed Kenya and becomes a British crown colony	• The US census reports that the population is 105,710,620: – whites: 94,820,915 (89.7%) – blacks: 10,463,131 (9.9%) – other: 426,574 (0.4%) • The US national debt is $25,952,456,406 • The 19th Amendment to the US Constitution, which guarantees the right of women to vote in all elections, is ratified in time for the fall elections • President Wilson receives the Nobel Peace Prize and is infuriated when the US Senate refuses to ratify the Treaty of Versailles and the League of Nations Covenant • Congress passes the Water Power Act, establishing the Federal Power Commission to regulate the generation of electricity from hydroelectric projects on public lands and navigable streams • The NAWSA ceases to exist, but its organization becomes the nucleus of the League of Women Voters • A "red scare" sweeps the country; federal agents arrest large numbers of people suspected of being Communists, anarchists, or "labor agitators" • The American Civil Liberties Union (ACLU) is established, in large measure, to oppose the 1918 Sedition Act and its indiscriminate use to arrest "undesirables" • The Red Crescent, a Muslim charity modeled after the Red Cross, is established in Detroit • Warren G. Harding is elected as president and Calvin Coolidge as vice president (Republican Party)	• Retired American army officer John T. Thompson patents his submachine gun (the "Tommy gun") • Herman Rorschach devises the inkblot test	• Radio station KDKA in Pittsburgh begins the first regular commercial broadcasts in the US • Mamie Smith's first blues recordings become a hit, alerting record companies to the market for blues records • Earle Dickson produces the first Band-Aid • The US Post Office begins cross-country airmail flights • The Boston Red Sox sell Babe Ruth to the New York Yankees for $125,000, beginning of "The Curse of the Bambino" • Douglas Fairbanks, the first great action hero of the American cinema, stars in *The Mark of Zorro* • The National Football League is established in Canton, OH; the Akron Pros win the first league championship • The Wonder Wheel, a 150-foot-tall Ferris wheel, opens at Coney Island; it is the tallest in the world at the time • Olympic Games: Antwerp
1921	• The civil war in Russia ends with Vladimir Lenin's victory (millions have died of starvation, the population of Petrograd has dropped from 2.5 million in 1917 to 0.6 million in 1920)	• Congress adopts a joint resolution declaring the end of WWI and ratifies separate peace treaties with Germany and Austria, and Hungary	• Albert Einstein's *Meaning of Relativity* provides a semipopular account of his theory • Margaret Sanger founds the American Birth Control League, which evolves into the Planned Parenthood Federation of America in 1942	• The first NCAA-sanctioned National Collegiate Track and Field Championships are held in Chicago; athletes from 62 colleges and universities compete • The first "Miss America" beauty pageant is held in Atlantic City, NJ

E. EDUCATION, LITERATURE & THE FINE ARTS	F. RELIGION, THEOLOGY, PHILOSOPHY & PSYCHOLOGY	G. AMERICAN & UNITED METHODISM	H. BRITISH & WORLD METHODISM	
		OH; attended by thousands, it raises over $150 million for mission work in the US and abroad • The Bible Institute in Hatillo, Puerto Rico, merges with several other schools to create the Evangelical Seminary of Puerto Rico		**1919** cont.
• Maurice Ravel composes his *La Valse* and his *Sonata for Violin and Cello* • Ernest Bloch composes his *Violin Sonata No. 1* • Gustav Holst's orchestral suite *The Planets* premieres in Birmingham • Eugene O'Neill's first full-length play, *Beyond the Horizon*, is produced on Broadway and wins a Pulitzer Prize, marking the beginning of modern American drama • Agatha Christie publishes *The Mysterious Affair at Styles*, her first mystery novel featuring Inspector Poirot • Other notable publications include: – Sinclair Lewis, *Main Street* – F. Scott Fitzgerald, *This Side of Paradise* – D. H. Lawrence, *Women in Love* – Carl Sandburg, *Smoke and Steel* – George Bernard Shaw, *Heartbreak House*	• The Life and Work movement holds its first world conference • Joan of Arc is declared a Roman Catholic saint by Pope Benedict XV • The Protestant Episcopal Church in the US allows the ordination of women as deacons • Friedrich Gogarten begins publication of the journal *Between the Times* in association with Karl Barth, Emil Brunner, and Rudolf Bultmann • Other notable publications include: – Jacques Maritan, *Art and Scholasticism* – Sigmund Freud, *Beyond the Pleasure Principle*	• The Joint Commission on Unification agrees on a proposed constitution and plan of union of the MEC and MECS and submits it to the respective General Conferences • The MEC General Conference: – does not approve the plan of union with the MECS, but recommends continuation of Joint Commission on Unification – approves the issuance of the local preacher's license, the first step to ordination, to women – organizes Latin American Mission for Western Arizona and California – elects the first black bishops to serve in America: Robert E. Jones and Matthew W. Clair – orders the Board of Missions to renew its efforts among the American Indians – rejects proposals for term episcopacy and refuses to regard a retired bishop as a member of the annual conference to which he last belonged – uses the term "episcopal area" for the first time to designate the group of annual conferences for which a particular resident bishop has administrative responsibility • The MPC General Conference: – receives report that the movement toward union with the UBC has come to a halt due to failure of the UBC to "take a vote of their people" – approves funding for the president of General Conference to travel over the church during the quadrennium • Carrie Johnson is selected to head a standing committee of the Woman's Missionary Council (MECS) to study the race question and develop ways for black and white women to work together • The Upper Mississippi Conference (MEC) issues the first preaching license to a black woman, Mary E. Jones	• Methodists, Presbyterians, Moravians, and United Brethren in the Dominican Republic form the Board of Christian Work; it may be the oldest such cooperative denominational work • The MECS establishes mission work in Siberia and in what is now the Czech and Slovak Republics (former Yugoslavia) • The MEC establishes its first mission in Manchuria	**1920**
• The Cleveland Playhouse opens, becoming the first resident professional theater in the US • Ralph Vaughan Williams composes his *Mass in G Minor* and the final orchestral *(cont.)*	• The British parliament passes the Church of Scotland Act, formally recognizing the full independence of the church from the government in religious matters	• The UBC General Conference: – creates a new Department of Evangelism and a new Board of Home Missions and Church Extension	• The fifth Ecumenical Methodist Conference meets in London • The MEC establishes the Baltic and Slavic Mission, including Methodist churches in Estonia, Latvia, and Lithuania *(cont.)*	**1921**

	A. WORLD HISTORY & POLITICS	B. AMERICAN HISTORY & POLITICS	C. SCIENCE, MEDICINE & TECHNOLOGY	D. DAILY LIFE, POPULAR CULTURE & ENTERTAINMENT
1921 cont.	• Lenin enacts the New Economic Policy in the Soviet Union and annexes eastern Ukraine • Prince Hirohito comes to power in Japan as regent for his father, Emperor Yoshihito, who has become mentally ill • The Anglo-Irish Treaty establishes the Irish Free State (later the Republic of Ireland), which becomes independent in 1922; it leaves Northern Ireland as part of the United Kingdom • At the Washington Disarmament Conference, all the major European powers agree to limit naval tonnage and pledge to respect the territorial integrity of China • France and Poland sign a mutual defense pact • King Abdul Asiz ibn Saud conquers much new territory in Arabia, eliminating the rival Rashid and Shalan dynasties • Turkey recognizes Armenia to be a Soviet republic, and signs a treaty of alliance with Afghanistan • The Chinese Communist Party (CCP) is founded in Shanghai	• The Tomb of the Unknown Soldier is dedicated at Arlington National Cemetery • Congress passes the Budget and Accounting Act, which creates the Bureau of Budget • Congress repeals the 1918 Sedition Act • The Federal Highway Act of 1921 creates the Bureau of Public Roads and provides funds to help state highway agencies construct a paved system of two-lane interstate highways • The stock market experiences a period of sustained growth (the "Roaring Twenties")		• The first White Castle hamburger stand opens in Wichita, KS; the small square hamburgers cost 5¢ each • Gabrielle "Coco" Chanel introduces Chanel No. 5, which becomes the world's best-selling perfume • *Barron's*, America's premier financial weekly, is founded; its first editor is Clarence Barron • Films: Chaplin's *The Kid* and Rudolph Valentino's *The Sheik*; *The Four Horsemen of the Apocalypse*
1922	• The Union of Soviet Socialist Republics (USSR, or Soviet Union) is created from the union of the separate SSRs in Russia, Ukraine, Belarus, and the Transcaucasus (Armenia, Georgia, Azerbaijan) • The new USSR grants women the right to vote • The League of Nations gives Britain a mandate to rule Palestine and implement the 1917 Balfour Declaration; the Jewish Agency is established to represent the Jewish people and to cooperate with Britain in establishing a Jewish "national home" in Palestine • Benito Mussolini seizes power in Italy and forms a Fascist government, gradually transforming it into a dictatorship • The Reparations Commission established by the Allied powers fixes German liability for WWI at a crushing 132 billion gold marks (around $33 billion), causing hyper-inflation in Germany: by the end of the year, $1 equals four million Deutschmarks • Germany adopts "Deutschland, Deutschland Über Alles" ("Germany, Germany Above All") as its national anthem • The USSR and Germany sign a treaty mutually canceling all prewar debts and renouncing all war claims • Britain ends its protectorate over Egypt, which becomes an independent kingdom under King Fuad I • Mahatma Gandhi is arrested in India for civil disobedience and sentenced to six years in jail • Vladimir Lenin suffers an incapacitating stroke; maneuvering begins among his possible successors as leader of the USSR, including Joseph Stalin and Leon Trotsky	• The US Supreme Court unanimously upholds the constitutionality of the 19th Amendment but declares the Child Labor Law of 1919 to be unconstitutional • The Lincoln Memorial is completed and dedicated in Washington, DC • The Ku Klux Klan begins to promote anticommunism along with "white supremacy"; by the end of the 1920s it has over 4 million members nationally • Oklahoma is placed under martial law to control violence and curb Ku Klux Klan activity there • President Harding denounces the violence committed by both labor and management during bitter strikes by coal miners and railroad workers • Rebecca Felton (Georgia) is appointed to the US Senate to fill a temporary vacancy; she is the first female senator, though she serves for only 2 days	• Canadian physicians Frederick Banting and Charles Best begin the first systematic use of insulin to control diabetes • Herbert Evans (US) discovers the human growth hormone produced by the pituitary gland • Howard Carter (UK) discovers the virtually intact tomb of the Egyptian Pharaoh Tutankhamen ("King Tut")	• Country Club Plaza, the first unified shopping center in the US, opens in Kansas City, MO • *Reader's Digest* begins publication • Jazz musician Edward "Duke" Ellington moves to New York and forms a band that ultimately becomes the Duke Ellington Orchestra • Louis Armstrong leaves New Orleans for Chicago to join King Oliver's Creole Jazz Band • Films: Robert Flaherty's *Nanook of the North* is the first feature film documentary; F. W. Murnau's *Nosferatu* is the first Dracula film and is still considered one of the very best; *Toll of the Sea*, starring Anna May Wong, is Hollywood's first Technicolor film

E. EDUCATION, LITERATURE & THE FINE ARTS	F. RELIGION, THEOLOGY, PHILOSOPHY & PSYCHOLOGY	G. AMERICAN & UNITED METHODISM	H. BRITISH & WORLD METHODISM	
version of his sublime tone poem *The Lark Ascending* • Prokofiev composes his opera *The Love for Three Oranges* • Arthur Honegger composes the incidental music to Rene Morax's play *King David* • Georges Braque completes his painting *Still Life with Guitar* • Picasso completes his painting *Three Musicians* • Eugene O'Neill's Pulitzer Prize-winning play *Anna Christie* has its premiere • Luigi Pirandello completes his comedic drama *Six Characters in Search of an Author* • Edith Wharton publishes her best-known novel, *The Age of Innocence*	• The International Missionary Council (IMC) is founded; John R. Mott serves as president until 1942 • The General Conference of Original Free Will Baptists is established • The Church of Simon Kimbangu is founded in the Congo; it becomes the most successful independent church in Africa • Pittsburgh radio station KDKA broadcasts the first religious program over the airwaves from Calvary Episcopal Church • Ludwig Wittgenstein argues in his *Tractatus Logico-Philosophicus* that the aim of philosophy is "the logical clarification of thoughts" and that what cannot be talked about clearly and cogently "we must consign to silence" • The National Baptist Convention publishes *Gospel Pearls*, including songs by Charles A. Tindley, Lucie Campbell, and Thomas A. Dorsey • Other significant publications include: – Bertrand Russell, *The Analysis of Mind* – Rudolf Bultmann, *History of the Synoptic Tradition* – John A. Faulkner, *Modernism and the Christian Faith*	– clarifies the functions and responsibilities of the General Board of Administration – launches a new pension plan for the ministers of the denomination – hears an address by William Jennings Bryan attacking Darwinism and, in response, passes a resolution supporting "the basic elements of Christianity" – appoints a committee to consider and propose revisions of the *Discipline* to the succeeding General Conference • The EA establishes Red Bird Mission in the southeastern corner of Kentucky to provide education and evangelism ministries to the people of the Southern Highlands • The MEC establishes the Wesleyan Service Guild (WSG) for women employed outside the home who cannot attend meetings or participate in service projects during "business hours" • The MEC organizes the South Florida-Mississippi Conference, superceding South Florida Mission	[it becomes a mission conference in 1924 and a provisional annual conference in 1929] • The MEC creates the Africa Central Conference • The Methodist Church in Poland is established as the result of relief efforts conducted by the MECS after WWI	**1921 cont.**
• Maurice Ravel orchestrates Modest Mussorgsky's 1874 piano suite *Pictures at an Exhibition* • Ralph Vaughan Williams composes his *Pastoral Symphony* • James Joyce's controversial novel *Ulysses* is published in England; the US Post Office destroys 500 copies because it is considered obscene • Carter G. Woodson publishes his landmark textbook *The Negro in Our History* [which will go through 10 editions by 1962] • Sinclair Lewis's *Babbitt*, set in the fictional midwestern small town of Zenith, satirizes the American virtues of conformity and patriotism • Other notable publications include: – William Faulkner, *Light in August* – Hermann Hesse, *Siddhartha* – T. S. Eliot, *The Waste Land* – F. Scott Fitzgerald, *The Beautiful and Damned*	• Pope Benedict XV dies; he is succeeded by Pope Pius XI • Pius XI's first encyclical, *Ubi Arcano Dei Consilio* (On the Peace of Christ in His Kingdom), inaugurates the "Catholic Action" movement, seeking to encourage lay men and women to spread Catholic values and political ideas throughout society • The Greek Orthodox Archdiocese of North America is formally established • The International Holiness Church (1897) and the Pilgrim Church (1912) unite to form the Pilgrim Holiness Church (PHC) • Harry Emerson Fosdick's sermon "Shall the Fundamentalists Win?" is directly answered by Clarence E. Macartney's sermon "Shall Unbelief Win?" • Martin Buber argues in his classic *Ich und Du* (English translation: *I and Thou*, 1937) that there is a fundamental difference between knowledge of impersonal objects ("I-It") and knowledge of other persons ("I-Thou") • Albert Schweitzer publishes *On the Edge of the Primeval Forest: Experiences and Observations of a Doctor in Equatorial Africa*	• The MECS General Conference: – seats women (18) as lay delegates for the first time – agrees to a continuation of the Joint Commission on Unification – notes with approbation the growth of Emory University and Southern Methodist University and their respective schools of theology – establishes a program for building and maintaining hospitals across the denomination – establishes the Board of Lay Activities • The General Conferences of the UEC (1922) and the Evangelical Association (1816) meet in a special session; the two bodies reunite to form The Evangelical Church (EC) • The EC General Conference meets for the first time: – reaffirms the extensive resolution passed separately by the final EA and UEC General Conferences merging the two bodies – adopts a unified *Discipline* and slightly revised version of the *Articles of Faith* – urges ministers and members to forget past animosities – agrees to maintain two publishing houses (Cleveland, OH, and Harrisburg, PA) • Some members of the UEC opposed to reunion with the EA withdraw to establish the Evangelical Congregational Church (ECC); after prolonged litigation, the ECC secures the title to Albright College in Meyerstown, PA, and makes it the center of denominational activity • Daytona Normal and Industrial School (1904) merges with Cookman Institute (1872) to form Bethune-Cookman Institute • The faculty of the Candler School of Theology votes to allow the enrollment of women • The CMEC General Conference refuses to seat a female delegate elected by one of its annual conferences, deciding that the term *laymen* applies only to males	• The MECS establishes missions in Belgium, Czechoslovakia, and Poland-Danzig • Methodism in New Zealand celebrates its centennial • The PMC begins mission work in Guatemala • Kingswood School achieves public school status in Britain	**1922**

	A. WORLD HISTORY & POLITICS	B. AMERICAN HISTORY & POLITICS	C. SCIENCE, MEDICINE & TECHNOLOGY	D. DAILY LIFE, POPULAR CULTURE & ENTERTAINMENT
1923	• The Ottoman Empire (first established in 1290) comes to an end when the Muslim Caliphate is formally dissolved and Turkey is declared a republic; Mustafa Kemal, who in Turkish history is called Atatürk ("Father of the Turks"), becomes its first president • All Allied troops are evacuated from Constantinople; Turkey takes control of the city • Black leaders in South Africa establish the African National Congress (ANC) to oppose the discriminatory policies of the South African government and seek voting rights for blacks • French and Belgian troops occupy the Ruhr region of Germany to enforce reparations payments • Adolf Hitler attempts a coup d'état (known as the "Beer Hall Putsch") in Germany; the coup fails and Hitler is imprisoned • More than 100,000 Japanese die as the result of an earthquake that destroys half of Tokyo • Rhodesia becomes a self-governing British crown colony	• President Harding orders all US troops still in Germany to come home • Harding suffers a massive heart attack and dies; Vice President Coolidge becomes president • US Steel implements 8-hour workdays, representing a major victory for organized labor • The National Woman's Party first proposes the Equal Rights Amendment to eliminate discrimination on the basis of gender • The National Flag Conference, meeting in Washington, DC, changes the wording of the Pledge of Allegiance to specify "the flag of the United States" rather than simply "my flag" as in the original 1892 version; "of America" is added in 1924	• The Frigidaire Co. introduces the first successful self-contained electrical and mechanical refrigerator • John B. Tytus (US) invents the process for continuous hot-strip rolling of steel • John Harwood (UK) patents the self-winding wristwatch, which soon replaces the pocket watch as the timepiece preferred by most men • The duplicator machine that is commonly called the "mimeograph" is developed and marketed by Ditto, Inc.; its low cost and ease of use make it very popular, particularly in schools and churches as well as in businesses; generations of schoolkids come to know that distinctive "Ditto" smell, and its popularity gives rise to the term *ditto* as a slang term	• Harlem's Cotton Club opens; black artists such as Lena Horne and Cab Calloway perform for primarily white audiences • Jelly Roll Morton writes and records his first big hit, "King Porter Stomp" • Bessie Smith, the "Queen of the Blues," records her first song, "Down Hearted Blues," which is an immediate hit • Other notable black musicians making their first recordings include Ida Cox, Joe "King" Oliver, Louis Armstrong, and Sidney Bechet • Rin Tin Tin, the magnificent German shepherd, becomes the first canine star of the movies • The first tea plantation is established in Kenya • *Time* magazine debuts • Films: Cecil B. DeMille releases *The Ten Commandments* [take one: DeMille will remake this silent version in 1956]
1924	• After Vladimir Lenin's death, Joseph Stalin rises to power in the USSR, and the USSR adopts a constitution based on "the dictatorship of the proletariat" • The USSR expands to include new SSRs in Turkmenistan and Uzbekistan • Name of Petrograd (formerly St. Petersburg) is changed to Leningrad • Hitler is released from prison and sets about reorganizing the Nazi Party • King Abdul Asiz ibn Saud conquers Mecca and Medina, ending the Hashemite dynasty and leading to the emergence of modern Saudi Arabia in 1932 • Mahatma Gandhi is released from prison in India; Hindu-Muslim relations there remain tense • The major western powers agree to reduce the level of German reparations payments to 1 billion marks per year, rising over a four-year period to 2.5 billion marks per year	• J. Edgar Hoover is named Director of the Bureau of Investigation (which becomes the Federal Bureau of Investigation, or FBI, in 1935) • The "Teapot Dome" scandal erupts; several government officials and oil company executives are indicted for conspiracy and bribery concerning fraudulent leases of national oil reserves • Congress establishes sharply reduced quotas for immigration into the US, especially from Japan, Asia, Latin America, and Africa • The Indian Citizenship Act grants full citizenship rights for the first time to all American Indians born in the US (but not necessarily full legal equality with whites) • Over the veto of President Coolidge, Congress passes the Soldier's Bonus Bill promising to pay all WWI veterans a bonus of $1 for every day of their service • Coolidge is elected as president and Charles G. Dawes as vice president (Republican Party) • The Society for Human Rights, the country's earliest known gay rights organization, is established in Chicago	• Construction on the Wilson Dam at Muscle Shoals on the Tennessee River in Alabama, begun in 1918, is completed; its lake and locks greatly facilitate navigation • Astronomer Edwin Hubble (US) demonstrates that spiral nebulae are composed of stars like our own galaxy • AT&T sends photographs by wire in an important step toward the invention of television • Two US Army airplanes land in Seattle, Washington, completing the first round-the-world flight in 175 days • The Teletype Corporation introduces a line of teletypewriters; they become so popular that the name "Teletype" becomes synonymous with teleprinters in the US • The Computer Tabulating Recording Company of New York is reorganized as International Business Machines Corp. (IBM)	• The George and Ira Gershwin musical *Lady, Be Good!* opens on Broadway • Walt Disney creates his first animated cartoon film, *Alice's Wonderland* • *The Eveready Hour* is the first commercially-sponsored radio program • *Little Orphan Annie* makes her comic strip debut • Macy's department store sponsors its first Thanksgiving Day parade in New York City • Low-tech achievement: notebooks get spiral bindings • Films: John Ford's *The Iron Horse* • Summer Olympics: Paris • Winter Olympics (held for the first time): Chamonix-Mont-Blanc

E. EDUCATION, LITERATURE & THE FINE ARTS	F. RELIGION, THEOLOGY, PHILOSOPHY & PSYCHOLOGY	G. AMERICAN & UNITED METHODISM	H. BRITISH & WORLD METHODISM	
• Zoltán Kodály composes his *Hungarian Psalms* • Darius Milhaud composes his *Creation of the World* • Bartók completes his *Dance Suite* • Paul Hindemith composes his *String Quartet No. 3 in C* • William Walton composes his *Toccata for Violin and Piano* • Paul Klee completes his paintings *Static-Dynamic Gradation*, evidencing his preoccupation with the relationship of colors, and his *Ventriloquist and Crier in the Moor* which strikes many viewers as the quintessential "Klee" due to its humor and grotesque fantasy • Hugh Lofting, *The Voyages of Doctor Doolittle* • George Bernard Shaw, *Saint Joan*	• Pentecostal evangelist Aimee Semple McPherson begins using radio to broadcast her sermons based on the "Foursquare Gospel" message of Jesus as Savior, Healer, Baptizer, and Returning King • Asbury Theological Seminary is founded in Wilmore, KY, "to prepare and send forth a well-trained, sanctified, Spirit-filled, evangelistic ministry" [originally a part of Asbury College, the Seminary becomes fully independent in 1941] • Muslims are expelled from Greece; Christians are expelled from much of Turkey; Christianity largely disappears from Asia Minor • J. Gresham Machen publishes his theological manifesto *Christianity and Liberalism* • Other significant publications include: – Sigmund Freud, *The Ego and The Id* – George Santayana, *Skepticism and Animal Faith* – Kahlil Gibran, *The Prophet*	• The Joint Commission on Unification produces a second proposed constitution and Plan of Union of the MEC and MECS and submits it to the General Conferences • Schuylkill Seminary (1881) becomes Schuylkill College • The MECS Publishing House begins using the name Cokesbury Press for its trade book publishing department and publishes the first edition of the little brown *Cokesbury Hymnal*, which quickly becomes (and long remains) a popular favorite across the church; revised editions appear in 1928, 1938, and 1940	• Cuba Mission Conference (MECS) becomes Cuba Annual Conference • The MEC divides the Finnish-Swedish Annual Conference from the Finland Annual Conference for linguistic reasons • WMC [UK] missionary William J. Platt arrives in Côte d'Ivoire (Ivory Coast)	**1923**
• The Juilliard Graduate School opens in New York City • The Curtis Institute of Music is established in Philadelphia; it is the only major conservatory in the US to offer promising young musicians full-tuition scholarships based solely on merit • Emma Dearborn of Columbia University devises the Speedwriting Shorthand system • The first important Surrealist exhibition in Paris includes Picasso's paintings *The Dance* and *The Kiss* • Maurice Ravel's exciting *Bolero* premieres in Paris • George Gershwin's *Rhapsody in Blue*, creatively and effectively blending classical music traditions with popular music and jazz, premieres in New York • Ottorino Respighi composes his *Ancient Airs & Dances* and *The Pines of Rome* • Spanish guitarist Andrés Segovia, widely regarded as the most important classical guitarist of the 20th century, launches his international concert career in Paris • Thomas Mann publishes *The Magic Mountain* • Chilean poet Pablo Neruda publishes *Twenty Love Poems and a Song of Despair* • Herman Melville's great novella *Billy Budd*, which was found among his papers after his death in 1891, is finally published	• The Auburn Affirmation, signed by over 1,200 PCUSA ministers, defends theological freedom, denies that the Bible is without error, and declares that doctrines such as Christ's substitutionary atonement and bodily resurrection should not be made "tests for ordination or for good standing in our church" • The American Baptist Association is formally established by very conservative Baptists who had separated from the Southern Baptist Convention in 1905 • Karl Barth, in *The Word of God and the Word of Man*, asserts that "There is no way from us to God"; God is the "wholly other," totally unlike human beings, who are utterly dependent on an encounter with the divine as revealed in Jesus Christ for any understanding of ultimate reality • Other notable publications include: – Jean Piaget, *Judgement and Reasoning in the Child* – Wilbur Fisk Tillett, *Paths That Lead to God* – Shailer Mathews, *The Faith of Modernism*	• The MEC General Conference: – approves the proposed constitution and Plan of Union between the MEC and MECS by a vote of 802-13 – authorizes the ordination of women as local deacons and elders, thus giving them the right to administer the sacraments, but prohibits them from annual conference membership – establishes the Southwest Spanish Mission – rejects a proposal to discontinue use of episcopal areas for the "districting" of the bishops – begins the process of eliminating German, Swedish, and Norwegian-Danish conferences based on language and ethnicity, merging them with geographic annual conferences [the process is not completed until 1938] – reaffirms the 1884 ban on divorce and on remarriage of divorced persons except in case of adultery – rescinds prohibitions on dancing and theater attendance for church members • In the months following the MEC General Conference, 29 women are ordained as local deacons • The MECS General Conference meets in a special called session: – approves the proposed constitution and Plan of Union between the MEC and MECS by a vote of 298-74 and refers it to a vote of the annual conferences – authorizes creation of Wesley Brotherhood organizations for MECS laymen • The MPC General Conference: – receives a report of the actions of the MEC and MECS General Conferences – expresses its hope for the emergence of a united Methodism • Scarritt Bible and Training School is moved to Nashville and the name is changed to Scarritt College for Christian Workers	• William Harris, now in Liberia, sends word that his followers should join the Methodist Church, and the WMC [UK] Conference establishes the Methodist Church of Côte d'Ivoire (Ivory Coast) • Queen Salote of Tonga effects a reconciliation of the Free Church of Tonga with the Wesleyan Methodist Mission to form the Free Wesleyan Church of Tonga • The MEC creates Northern European Central Conference	**1924**

	A. WORLD HISTORY & POLITICS	B. AMERICAN HISTORY & POLITICS	C. SCIENCE, MEDICINE & TECHNOLOGY	D. DAILY LIFE, POPULAR CULTURE & ENTERTAINMENT
1924 cont.				
1925	• The name of Volgograd is changed to Stalingrad • The Geneva Protocol prohibits the use of chemical and biological weapons in warfare but does not ban their production or storage • Paul von Hindenburg becomes Reich president in Germany • Germany signs the Treaty of Locarno, agreeing to demilitarize the Rhineland and establishing fixed borders with France and Belgium • Hitler publishes *Mein Kampf*, written while he was in prison; it proclaims his hatred for democracy, his views about Aryan superiority over all other races (especially the Jews), and his vision of *lebensraum* ("living space") for the German people • Cyprus becomes a British crown colony • Reza Kahn Pahlavi becomes Shah of Iran and establishes the Pahlavi dynasty	• The "Monkey Trial" of John Scopes for teaching evolution in Cleveland, TN, pits Clarence Darrow against William Jennings Bryan and grips the nation; Bryan wins the trial and Scopes is convicted, but Darrow's withering cross-examination of Bryan is thought to have been a factor in Bryan's sudden death a week later • A. Philip Randolph establishes the Brotherhood of Sleeping Car Porters (BSCP), the first trade union for black workers • In Wyoming, Nellie Taylor Ross becomes the first woman to serve as governor of a state when she is elected to succeed her deceased husband, William Bradford Ross; Miriam Amanda "Ma" Ferguson is inaugurated governor of Texas days later • The city of Nome, AK, is saved from a major diphtheria outbreak by vaccine carried from Anchorage by dogsled relay; the event is now commemorated by the annual Iditarod Dogsled Race (first run in its modern form in 1973)	• Scottish inventor John Baird transmits the first television images in London • Leica produces the first 35mm camera • Walter P. Chrysler merges two smaller automobile companies to create the Chrysler Corporation	• The Victor Talking Machine Company switches from an acoustical/mechanical to an electrical system of recording and playback, introducing a new line of phonographs called "Victrolas" • Radio Station WSM in Nashville begins broadcasting *The WSM Barn Dance*; the name is changed in 1928 to *The Grand Ole Opry* • *The New Yorker* magazine begins publication; the editorial staff includes Dorothy Parker and Robert Benchley • Louis Armstrong forms his own group, Louis Armstrong & His Hot Five, and begins making his own jazz recordings • The musical *No, No, Nanette!* by Irving Caesar, Otto Harbach, and Vincent Youmans opens in both London and New York • Films: Chaplin's classic *The Gold Rush*; Sergey Eisenstein's *Battleship Potemkin* (which establishes the film montage technique); *The Phantom of the Opera*
1926	• The League of Nations approves the International Slavery Convention, which prohibits slavery and the slave trade around the world • Britain grants complete autonomy within the British Empire to Canada, Australia, New Zealand, South Africa, and the Irish Free State • Leon Trotsky and his followers are expelled from the Community Party in Russia, marking Joseph Stalin's complete control of power in the USSR • Following the death of Sun Yat-sen, Chiang Kai-shek becomes the leader of China's Nationalist Party • Mao Zedong rises to power as leader of the Chinese Community Party and establishes the Red Army • When Chiang Kai-shek leads a purge of Communists from the Chinese government, civil war breaks out between the Nationalist Party and the Communist Party • Emperor Yoshihito of Japan dies; his son Hirohito becomes Emperor • Fascist youth organizations are established in both Italy and Germany	• Congress refuses to allow the US to join the Court of International Justice and Arbitration (established in 1899) • Congress passes an Immigration Act, which curtails and renders nearly impossible any immigration from non-European countries; Filipinos are exempted from these restrictions because they are residents of a US territory • The Revenue Act significantly reduces the level of income and inheritance taxes and eliminates many smaller "nuisance" taxes • The Bureau of Air Commerce is established to regulate the growing civil aviation industry; its responsibilities include licensing aircraft and pilots • The Army Air Corps is formally established • Philadelphia hosts the Sesquicentennial Exposition to commemorate the 150th anniversary of the Declaration of Independence; although the exposition is an artistic and patriotic success, it is a financial failure; only about 6 million people attend • The National Council of American Indians (NCAI) is founded by Gertrude Bonnin (Zitkala-Sa)	• Richard Byrd (US) makes the first flight over the North Pole • Robert Goddard launches his first successful liquid-fuel rocket, using a mixture of gasoline and liquid oxygen • The first 16mm movie camera is produced by Kodak	• The Book-of-the-Month Club is founded and begins to sell books on a subscription basis at reduced prices; it pioneers the "negative option" system of mail-order sales by which monthly selections are automatically shipped unless club members specifically decline them • The Scholastic Aptitude Test (SAT) is administered to American students for the first time • The National Broadcasting Company (NBC) is founded by General Electric, RCA, and Westinghouse • Belgian chocolatier Joseph Draps starts the Godiva Company to compete with Hershey's and Nestlé's in the American market • Jelly Roll Morton & His Red Hot Peppers make their first recordings, including "Black Bottom Stomp" and "Sidewalk Blues" • Films: *Ben-Hur: A Tale of Christ*, costs nearly $4 million, an unheard-of price to make a movie

E. EDUCATION, LITERATURE & THE FINE ARTS	F. RELIGION, THEOLOGY, PHILOSOPHY & PSYCHOLOGY	G. AMERICAN & UNITED METHODISM	H. BRITISH & WORLD METHODISM	
		• The MEC establishes the Gulfside Assembly in Waveland, MS, as "a Chautauqua for black people in the South" • James B. Duke and his brother, Benjamin N. Duke, create the Duke Endowment; this leads to the establishment of Duke University in Durham, NC, around the older Trinity College (1859/1892); the School of Religion [now Divinity School] and Graduate School open for classes in 1926, the Medical School and hospital in 1930 • MECS men begin creating Wesley Brotherhood organizations		**1924 cont.**
• The Exposition des Arts Décoratifs et Industriels Modernes, or Art Deco Exhibition, opens in Paris • Aaron Copland completes his *Symphony for Organ/Orchestra* • Ralph Vaughan Williams composes his *Flos Campi* (Flower of the Field) for solo viola, chorus, and small orchestra, evoking passages from the Song of Songs of the Bible • Alban Berg's controversial *Wozzek* removes tonality from opera • Expatriate American poet Ezra Pound begins his *Cantos* • F. Scott Fitzgerald's novel *The Great Gatsby* exposes the moral bankruptcy of the "Roaring Twenties," especially the decadence of the rich • Other notable publications include: – Franz Kafka, *The Trial* – Theodore Dreiser, *An American Tragedy*	• The World Conference on Faith and Order meets in Lausanne • The World Conference on Life and Work meets in Stockholm • Pope Pius XI establishes the Pontifical Institute of Christian Archaeology • John Dewey publishes his *Experience and Nature*	• The Plan of Union between the MEC and MECS fails when it does not receive the approval of the required three-fourths of MECS annual conferences • The UBC General Conference: – approves proposed revisions of the *Discipline*; the expectation tithing is dropped, along with restrictions on church choirs and instrumental music; the exhortation against "conformity to the world" is watered down; the rule against electioneering at General Conference is eliminated – merges the Church Erection Society with the Home Mission Society – instructs annual conferences to pattern their organization after that of the general church – defeats a proposal to establish a unified Board of Christian Education • The MPC organizes the South Carolina Colored Mission Conference	• The United Church of Canada is created by the merger of the Methodist, Congregationalist, and most Presbyterian congregations in Canada • The MEC creates Central European Conference	**1925**
• The publication of the literary journal *Fire!!* by a new generation of black writers and artists, including Langston Hughes, Wallace Thurman, and Zora Neale Hurston, marks the full flowering of the Harlem Renaissance, for which Hughes's critical essay "The Negro Artist and the Racial Mountain" is a defining piece • Carter G. Woodson launches Negro History Week as an initiative to bring national attention to the contributions of black people throughout American history • Zoltán Kodály composes his comic opera *Háry János* • Bartók completes *The Miraculous Mandarin* • Peter Warlock composes his *Capriol Suite* • Arturo Toscanini conducts the first performance of Giacomo Puccini's unfinished opera *Turandot* at La Scala in Milan • Martha Graham, the American pioneer of the modern-dance revolt, gives her first New York performance • Georgia O'Keeffe completes her painting *Black Iris* • A. A. Milne's classic children's tale *Winnie the Pooh* introduces the world to Christopher Robin and his toy animal (cont.)	• Duse Muhammad Ali establishes an organization in Detroit known as the Universal Islamic Society, which has a strong impact on Marcus Garvey and his movement • Polish-speaking Tatar Muslim immigrants build a mosque in Brooklyn, NY; it is the oldest mosque in the US in continuous use • Rudolf Otto, in *The Idea of the Holy*, describes the apprehension of the Holy, or the "numinous," as the *mysterium tremendum et fascinans* (the mystery that at once produces both awe and fascination) • Other notable publications include: – Johannes Pedersen, *Israel: Its Life and Culture* (2 vols., 1926, 1940) – Rudolf Bultmann, *Jesus and the Word* – Harry Nelson Wieman, *Religious Experience and the Scientific Method* – D. C. Macintosh, *The Reasonableness of Christianity* – R. H. Tawney, *Religion and the Rise of Capitalism* – Will Durant, *The Story of Philosophy*	• The MECS General Conference: – responds to rejection of the 1924 Plan of Union by the annual conferences by establishing a new committee to "study the whole question" of unification "in its historic, economic, social, legal, and other aspects" and report to the 1930 General Conference – authorizes the creation of central or regional conferences in the church's mission fields, with the goal being speedy establishment of autonomous national churches – orders publication of a report by the Committee on the Spiritual State of the Church (appointed in 1922) on "doctrinal unrest" in the church • The EC General Conference: – brings all the religious education work of local churches under the supervision of local Boards of Christian Education, which are accountable to the General Conference through the (general) Board of Education – approves relocation of the Publishing House in Cleveland to "better quarters" • The CMEC General Conference votes to grant full laity rights to women, including service as Annual and General Conference delegates	• Wesley House at Cambridge University, originally founded in 1921, opens as an educational center for Methodist ministerial students [it is now part of the ecumenical Federation of Theological Colleges in Cambridge] • The Florence B. Nicholson Seminary (1907) in the Philippines becomes Union Theological Seminary and moves to new quarters in Manila; it now receives Methodist, United Brethren, Presbyterian, Disciple, and Congregationalist support • George Eayrs publishes *John Wesley, Christian Philosopher and Church Founder*	**1926**

	A. WORLD HISTORY & POLITICS	B. AMERICAN HISTORY & POLITICS	C. SCIENCE, MEDICINE & TECHNOLOGY	D. DAILY LIFE, POPULAR CULTURE & ENTERTAINMENT
1926 cont.				
1927	• Post–WWI Allied control of Germany ends; Germany's economic system collapses • Nanking falls to the Chinese Communists, but soon the Nationalists retake the city • Japan sends troops into Shantung to block a northward advance by Chinese Nationalists toward Peking (Beijing) • The US sends warships to Chinese ports to bring US citizens out of China • Allied occupation of Germany ends; the League of Nations assumes responsibility for dealing with the problem of German armaments • Oil is discovered in Iraq • US Marines are sent into Nicaragua to protect US interests during civil unrest there	• Congress creates the Federal Radio Commission (FRC) and requires broadcast licensees to operate "in the public interest" • The US Supreme Court rules that the "Teapot Dome" oil leases were fraudulent and restores oil fields to the control of the federal government • Italian American anarchists Nicola Sacco and Bartolomeo Vanzetti are executed despite worldwide protests over weak evidence about their guilt; their 1920 trial is later recognized as deeply flawed • The "Great Flood" of the Mississippi River system inundates the lower Mississippi basin, submerging New Orleans and 27,000 square miles of southern Louisiana • Construction begins on the Mt. Rushmore National Monument in the Black Hills of South Dakota	• Charles Lindbergh makes the first solo flight across the Atlantic Ocean in *The Spirit of St. Louis* • Fossil remains of "Peking man" (ca. 350,000 to 400,000 years old) are discovered by Davidson Black near Peking (Beijing), China • The Holland Tunnel under the Hudson River is completed and opens to traffic, connecting New York City with Jersey City, NJ • Margaret Sanger helps to organize the first World Population Conference in Geneva • After producing over 15 million Model T automobiles since 1908, Henry Ford's automobile factory goes off production for 18 months to switch from the Model T to the Model A; in the interval, Chrysler breaks into the low-priced-car market with the Plymouth	• The British Broadcasting Corporation (BBC) is established as a public corporation, replacing the earlier private British Broadcasting Company, Ltd. (1922) • The Columbia Broadcasting System (CBS) is founded • Jerome Kern's revolutionary *Showboat* links the Broadway musical with classical opera • Hoagy Carmichael composes the classic "Star Dust" • The country music industry begins in Bristol, TN, where Ralph Peer, the talent scout for Victor Records, records the songs of Jimmie Rodgers and the Carter Family • Legendary baseball slugger Babe Ruth hits a record 60 home runs • The Cyclone, America's first classic roller coaster, begins operation at Coney Island • Kool-Aid is marketed by Edwin Perkins; originally there are 7 flavors • The George and Ira Gershwin musical *Funny Face* opens on Broadway • The Literary Guild book club begins • Films: Popular vaudevillian Al Jolson astounds audiences with his nightclub act in *The Jazz Singer*, the first feature-length movie with recorded sound, or "talkie"
1928	• Stalin enacts the first Five-Year Plan for collectivization and rapid industrialization of the USSR • Brazil's economy collapses due to the failure of its coffee harvest • The US is among the nations who sign the Pact of Paris (also known as the Kellogg-Briand Pact), a multilateral treaty renouncing war as an instrument of national policy and agreeing to the settlement of international disputes by peaceful means; while well-intended, it is totally ineffective • The Reform Act of 1928 reduces the voting age for women in Britain from 30 to 21, putting women on equal footing with men • The Muslim Brotherhood, the grandfather of all Islamic revolutionary movements, is founded in Egypt • Egypt's King Fuad I dissolves Parliament and suspends the constitution • Britain recognizes the Chinese Nationalist government at Nanking as the legitimate government of China	• In the wake of the 1927 "Great Flood," Congress passes the Mississippi Flood Control Act, providing for levee construction, reforestation, and soil conservation to help prevent future flooding in the Mississippi Valley • Congress appropriates $32 million to enforce Prohibition and to combat "bootlegging" and "speakeasies" during the next year • President Coolidge vetoes the McNary-Haugen Bill, which was intended to provide assistance to cotton and tobacco farmers, citing the evils of price-fixing • Bryce Canyon National Park is established • Norman Thomas is the first Socialist candidate in a US presidential election • Democratic presidential candidate Al Smith calls for the repeal of the 18th Amendment • Herbert Hoover is elected as president and Charles Curtis as vice president (Republican Party) • Oscar DePriest (Illinois) becomes the first black elected to the House of Representatives from a northern state	• Alexander Fleming discovers penicillin, the most versatile and powerful antibiotic discovered to date • Werner Heisenberg's *Physical Principles of Quantum Theory* contains an explanation of his "Uncertainty Principle" • The German airship *Graf Zeppelin* makes the first aerial transatlantic crossing (from Germany to the US) carrying paying passengers • Australian pilots Charles Smith and Charles Ulm make the first flight across the Pacific • The first electric respirator (iron lung) is used at Boston's Children's Hospital to treat a child with polio • Fritz Pfleumer (Germany) develops and patents a magnetic recorder that uses paper tape coated with steel dust • The Chrysler Corporation purchases the Dodge Brothers, becoming one of the "Big Three" of the American automobile industry alongside Ford and General Motors • Kodak produces the first 16mm movie film, making amateur color motion pictures possible	• Times Square gets moving headlines in electric lights • The Carter Family records "Wildwood Flower" for the first time • Louis Armstrong records "West End Blues" and turns it into a jazz classic • Blues guitarist "Mississippi" John Hurt makes his first recordings for Okeh Records, but his career fails when the company goes out of business during the Depression • Bing Crosby has his first big hit with the Paul Whiteman band, "Ol' Man River"; his smooth, gentle singing distinguishes him from vaudeville "shouters" and gives rise to the term *crooner* • Gabrielle "Coco" Chanel designs her first tweed women's suit in a casual style stressing simplicity and comfort • Films: Walt Disney introduces Mickey Mouse to the world in the animated cartoon film *Steamboat Willie* • Summer Olympics: Amsterdam • Winter Olympics: St. Moritz

E. EDUCATION, LITERATURE & THE FINE ARTS	F. RELIGION, THEOLOGY, PHILOSOPHY & PSYCHOLOGY	G. AMERICAN & UNITED METHODISM	H. BRITISH & WORLD METHODISM	
friends Pooh, Piglet, Tigger, Kanga, Roo, Rabbit, Owl, and Eeyore • Other notable publications include: – Ernest Hemingway, *The Sun Also Rises* – Franz Kafka, *The Castle*		• Bennett College in Greensboro, NC, is reorganized by the MEC as a four-year liberal arts college for women; it is a joint venture of the WHMS and the Board of Education • The MECS organizes the California Oriental Mission • Belle C. Harmon (Montana State Conference) is the first of 12 women to be ordained as local elders in the MEC		**1926 cont.**
• The Theremin is the first entirely electronic musical instrument ever created • Bartók's *Piano Concerto No. 1* premieres in Frankfurt with the composer at the piano and Wilhelm Furtwängler conducting • Alban Berg's *Lyric Suite* premieres in Vienna • Igor Stravinsky completes his challenging opera *Oedipus Rex* • Dmitri Shostakovich composes his *Symphony No. 2 in B Major* • Matisse completes his remarkable painting *Reclining Odalisque (Harmony in Red)* • The first of the Hardy Boys stories about the fictional adventures of teenage detective brothers Frank and Joe Hardy is published • Other notable publications include: – Willa Cather, *Death Comes for the Archbishop* – Thornton Wilder, *The Bridge of San Luis Rey* – Hermann Hesse, *Steppenwolf*	• The Faith and Order movement holds its first world conference in Lausanne; this leads to the later formation of the World Council of Churches • The North American Christian Convention marks the separation of the Independent Christian Churches/Churches of Christ from the Christian Church (Disciples of Christ) because of the perceived liberalism of the latter • The International Church of the Foursquare Gospel, which grows out of the Pentecostal preaching of Aimee Semple McPherson, is formally established • Notable publications include: – Karl Barth, *The Doctrine of the Word of God: Prolegomena to Church Dogmatics* – Emil Brunner, *The Mediator* – Bertrand Russell, *Why I Am Not A Christian* – Martin Heidegger, *Being and Time* – Gabriel Marcel, *Metaphysical Journal* – Sigmund Freud, *The Future of an Illusion* – Alfred Adler, *Understanding Human Nature* – James Weldon Johnson, *God's Trombones*	• Albert Knudsen publishes *The Philosophy of Personalism*, marking the full flowering of Boston Personalism, perhaps the most distinctive school of theological thought to emerge from within American Methodism [the tradition continues in the work of L. Harold DeWolf, Edgar S. Brightman, and Peter Bertocci, all members of the faculty at Boston University School of Theology, and deeply influences Martin Luther King, Jr., when he is a student there (1951–55)]	• *The Magazine of the Wesleyan Methodist Church* (1914) in the UK becomes simply *The Methodist Magazine* • The Wesleyan Methodist Church of South Africa becomes autonomous • The AMEC dedicates Bethel Church in Capetown, South Africa • Representatives of the MEC and MECS annual conferences in Korea agree on a plan of union	**1927**
• George Gershwin completes his jazzy tone poem *An American in Paris* • Kurt Weil and Bertolt Brecht compose their *Three-Penny Opera* • Arturo Toscanini becomes music director of the New York Philharmonic • Arnold Schoenberg's *Variations for Orchestra* premieres in Berlin • Edward Hopper's painting *From Williamsburg Bridge* is a sterling example of "American realism" • D. H. Lawrence publishes his erotic classic *Lady Chatterley's Lover*, which is widely banned due to its explicit sexual content • *The Oxford English Dictionary*, begun in 1858, is finally finished, and covers over 15,000 printed pages • Other notable publications include: – A. A. Milne, *The House at Pooh Corner* – Margaret Mead, *Coming of Age in Samoa* – Erich Maria Remarque, *All Quiet on the Western Front*	• Notable publications include: – Hermann Gunkel, *Introduction to the Psalms* (to 1933) – Rudolph Carnap, *The Logical Structure of the World* – R. G. Collingwood, *Faith and Reason: A Study of the Relations Between Religion and Science*	• The MEC General Conference: – empowers the central conferences to elect their own bishops but retains the right to determine the number of bishops and their areas of episcopal responsibility – adopts the "Seminary Rule" allowing ministerial candidates to substitute a degree from an approved seminary for completion of the standard course of study readings and examinations – approves and sends to the annual conferences a constitutional amendment to allow lay representation in annual conference meetings; the amendment is rejected by vote of the annual conferences – places the Epworth League under the general work of the Board of Education – recommends that the annual conferences establish minimum salaries for all preachers and establishes a committee to study the matter of equitable apportionment of expenses and adequate support of clergy – broadens the exception clause for remarriage after divorce to apply to the innocent person in the case of adultery "or its full moral equivalent," leaving it up to the pastor to determine when this is the case; in addition, divorced persons are allowed into church membership if they are "repentant"	• The North Africa Provisional Conference (MEC) supersedes the Methodist Missions in Algeria and Tunisia • The MEC creates the Latin America Central Conference • Notable publications include Frank W. Collier, *John Wesley Among the Scientists*	**1928**

	A. WORLD HISTORY & POLITICS	B. AMERICAN HISTORY & POLITICS	C. SCIENCE, MEDICINE & TECHNOLOGY	D. DAILY LIFE, POPULAR CULTURE & ENTERTAINMENT
1928 cont.				
1929	• Stalin orders the persecution of "kulaks" (capitalist farmers) in the USSR; 15 million peasants are deported to the Arctic regions and 6.5 million die • Tadzhikistan joins the USSR • Fighting begins between Jews and Arabs in Palestine, caused by a clash at the Wailing Wall in Jerusalem • Vatican City becomes the world's smallest sovereign, independent state with signature of the Lateran Treaty by the Papacy and the Italian government, ending years of conflict between them • The third Geneva Convention, specifying rules for the treatment of prisoners of war, is signed by 125 nations • The National Revolutionary Party is established in Mexico and quickly becomes the country's ruling party • Hitler appoints Heinrich Himmler as head of the SS, or *Schutzstaffel*, the elite Nazi Party corps also known as "Black Shirts" • Britain, France, Italy, Japan, and the US sign a naval disarmament treaty • France begins construction of the Maginot Line as a defense against Germany • The Jewish Agency (1922) in Palestine is expanded to become the Jewish Agency Executive, embracing both the Zionist Organization (1897) and non-Zionist, public Jewish groups; Chaim Weizmann is elected as chairman	• Congress passes the Agricultural Marketing Act, creating the Federal Farm Board to stabilize farm prices • The US stock market crashes, losing over 40% of its value in September and October and almost 50% by November, marking the start of the Great Depression • President Hoover signs a bill authorizing a $160-million cut in the US income tax • Grand Teton National Park is established after 31 years of dispute between ranchers and conservationists • The St. Valentine's Day Massacre in Chicago, in which members of Al Capone's gang execute seven members of the rival gang of Bugs Moran with machine guns, dramatizes the intense competition for control of the illegal liquor traffic during Prohibition • The League of United Latin American Citizens, centered in Texas, is created by the merger of several earlier regional organizations to fight discrimination against Hispanics	• German physician Hans Berger records human brain wave activity using the electroencephalogram (EEG) • German mechanical engineer Andreas Stihl patents the first gasoline-powered chainsaw, which he calls "the tree-felling machine" • Robert Goddard launches the first rocket to carry scientific instruments, including a barometer, a thermometer, and a small camera	• Clarence Birdseye offers his quick-frozen foods to the public • Already-sliced Wonder Bread appears on store shelves for the first time • C. J. Grigg develops and markets the lemon-lime soda called 7UP • Paul Galvin, the head of Galvin Manufacturing Corporation, invents the first automobile radio, the "Motorola" • RCA acquires the Victor Talking Machine Company and becomes RCA-Victor, widely known by its trademarked image of the dog "Nipper" looking for the source of "His Master's Voice" in a phonograph speaker • Popeye the Sailor and Tarzan swing into the comic strips • Guy Lombardo's Orchestra plays "Auld Lang Syne" for the first time • Thomas "Fats" Waller records "Ain't Misbehavin'" • Amédé Ardoin makes the first recordings of zydeco music in Louisiana • Films: *The Broadway Melody* is the first widely distributed sound film and the first musical to win an Oscar for Best Picture; Gary Cooper has his first starring role in *The Virginian*
1930	• The Nazi party wins 107 seats in the German Reichstag (legislature), becoming the majority party and gaining a role in a coalition government • Mahatma Gandhi proclaims a new campaign of civil disobedience against British rule in India; he is imprisoned, then released in 1931 when the British make concessions • Haile Selassie becomes emperor of Ethiopia, fulfilling for many people a prophecy that becomes a cornerstone of Rastafarianism • The Union of South Africa grants women the right to vote in national elections • The name of the historic city of Constantinople is formally changed to Istanbul by the government of Turkey	• The US census reports that the population is 122,775,046: – whites: 110,286,740 (89.8%) – blacks: 11,891,143 (9.7%) – other: 597,163 (0.5%) • The US national debt is $16,185,309,831 • The Smoot-Hawley Tariff Act, intended to protect domestic farmers against foreign agricultural imports, raises US tariffs to historically high levels and cripples US trade • At President Hoover's request Congress appropriates $116 million for public works programs to deal with the unemployment of 4.5 million Americans • The US repudiates the 1904 "Roosevelt Corollary" to the Monroe Doctrine; the US will continue to protect Latin American countries from European aggression but is not responsible for their debts or other international obligations • The Japanese American Citizens League is founded in California to fight for the civil rights primarily of Japanese Americans and also for the benefit of Chinese Americans and other peoples of color	• English aviator Amy Johnson makes the first flight from England to Australia • American astronomer Clyde Tombaugh, working at the Lowell Observatory in Arizona, discovers the planet Pluto • MIT Professor Vannevar Bush builds what he calls a "differential analyzer"; it is the first analog computer • The remarkable Chrysler Building is completed in New York; its Art Deco style draws on designs used on the hubcaps of Chrysler automobiles; it is (briefly) the tallest building in the world at 1,048 feet, and its stainless steel spire is still a striking element of the New York skyline	• Duke Ellington has his first big hit with "Mood Indigo" • The George and Ira Gershwin musical *Girl Crazy* opens on Broadway, introducing Ethel Merman in the leading role and featuring the song "I Got Rhythm" • Robert Tyre Jones, Jr. (Bobby), of Atlanta, records golf's first "grand slam" [of that era], winning the British Amateur and Open titles and the US Amateur and Open titles in one year • *Blondie* (and Dagwood) joins the daily comics • *The Better Homes and Gardens Cookbook* sells the first of 15,000,000 copies • The little red "Radio Flyer" wagon is produced in New York • Uruguay wins first World Cup in soccer ("football" to most of the world) • Films: *All Quiet on the Western Front*; The Marx Brothers' *Animal Crackers*; *Hell's Angels*; *Little Caesar* (Hollywood's first gangster film)

E. EDUCATION, LITERATURE & THE FINE ARTS	F. RELIGION, THEOLOGY, PHILOSOPHY & PSYCHOLOGY	G. AMERICAN & UNITED METHODISM	H. BRITISH & WORLD METHODISM	
		• The MPC General Conference: – celebrates the centennial of the establishment of the MPC – authorizes the president to call a special session of the General Conference if conversations about church union with the MEC and MECS "are probably acceptable" – consolidates the youth work of the church under the Board of Education		**1928 cont.**
• The Museum of Modern Art opens in New York City • Prokofiev's *Symphony No. 3* premieres in Paris • William Walton composes his *Concerto for Viola and Orchestra* • Shostakovich completes his *Symphony No. 3 in E Flat Major* • Eugene O'Neill's intense and disturbing drama *Strange Interlude* is banned in Boston; when published, it becomes a national best seller and helps to transform American theater • Winston Churchill completes his 4-volume work *The World Crisis*, recounting the history of WWI • Ernest Hemingway's novel *A Farewell to Arms* portrays the suffering and tragedy of WWI through its depiction of a romance between an American lieutenant and a British nurse in Italy • Other notable publications include: – William Faulkner, *The Sound and The Fury* – Thomas Wolfe, *Look Homeward, Angel* – Virginia Woolf, *A Room of One's Own*	• Most of the Presbyterian church bodies in Scotland, including the "Auld Kirk" and The United Free Church of Scotland (1900), unite to form the Church of Scotland • Princeton Theological Seminary is reorganized under "modernist" influences; several conservative faculty members led by J. Gresham Machen resign from the Princeton faculty and establish Westminster Theological Seminary in Philadelphia • Mother Teresa begins her work among the poor in Calcutta, India • The Vienna Circle, a group of analytical philosophers led by Rudolph Carnap, publishes the philosophical manifesto, *A Scientific World-View* • Other notable publications include: – Alfred North Whitehead, *Process and Reality* – Edmund Husserl, *Ideas: General Introduction to Pure Phenomenology* – H. Richard Niebuhr, *The Social Sources of Denominationalism* – John Dewey, *The Quest for Certainty* – Georgia Harkness, *Conflicts in Religious Thought*	• The UBC General Conference: – establishes a unified Department of Christian Education, unifying the work formerly delegated to the Department of Education, Sunday school and Brotherhood work, and Christian Endeavor – supports a proposal for union with the UBC, the Reformed Church in the United States, and the Evangelical Synod of North America; the proposal is not received with enthusiasm by the annual conferences [the latter two bodies do unite in 1934] – revives the Otterbein Brotherhood as a men's fellowship group • The MEC organizes the Southwest Conference by merger of the Little Rock Conference and part of the Lincoln Conference, and the Central West Conference by a merger of the Central Missouri Conference and the other part of the Lincoln Conference • Albright Collegiate Institute (1895) merges with Schuylkill College (1923) to become Albright College, located in Reading, PA	• The Methodist Church Union Act is passed by the British parliament, providing the legal basis for the Uniting Conference of 1932 to promulgate the Deed of Union • Methodism comes to the Dutch islands of Aruba and Curaçao through WMC [UK] missionaries • Arnold Lunn publishes his biography, *John Wesley*	**1929**
• The BBC Symphony is established in London; Adrian Boult is its first director • Igor Stravinsky composes his *Symphony of Psalms* for the 50th anniversary of the Boston Symphony [in 1999, *Time* magazine names it the best piece of the century] • William Grant Still composes his groundbreaking *Afro-American Symphony* • Howard Hanson completes his *Symphony No. 2 (Romantic)* • Grant Wood completes his famous painting *American Gothic*, an image that epitomizes the virtues that he believed dignified the midwestern character • Diego Rivera begins his great mural for the National Palace in Mexico City (completed in 1935) • Carolyn Keene's teenage detective Nancy Drew starts solving mysteries in novels for girls • Notable publications include: – Dashiell Hammett, *The Maltese Falcon* – William Faulkner, *As I Lay Dying*	• The American Lutheran Church (ALC, German) is formed, merging the Joint Synod of Ohio (1818), Buffalo Synod (1845), and Texas (1851) and Iowa Synods (1854) • Pope Pius XI issues an encyclical condemning artificial birth control but tacitly legitimating the "rhythm method" • American black Muslims establish the First Muslim Mosque in Pittsburgh, PA • Notable publications include: – José Ortega y Gasset, *The Revolt of the Masses* – Sigmund Freud, *Civilization and its Discontents* – Albert Knudsen, *The Doctrine of God* – Edgar Sheffield Brightman, *The Problem of God*	• The MECS General Conference: – follows the MEC (1924) in allowing ordination of women as local deacons and elders – rejects a petition calling for full clergy rights for women, including conference membership – establishes a "Seminary Rule" comparable to that of the MEC (1928) – unites the General Sunday School Board and the Epworth League with a reorganized General Board of Christian Education – authorizes lay representation in annual conferences – considers proposals for appointment of another Commission on Unification but instead establishes a Commission on Interdenominational Relations – approves and sends to the annual conferences a constitutional amendment for the creation of a Judicial Council; it is not approved by the annual conferences – establishes Latin Mission in Florida; reorganizes Texas Mexican Mission as Texas Mexican Conference	• The Korean Methodist Church is formed as an autonomous church by union of the separate MEC and MECS annual conferences; it accepts women as clergy with full rights and admits them into full connection; it assumes responsibility for the MECS missions in Siberia and Manchuria (1908/1920) • The Methodist Church of Brazil, frustrated by absentee episcopal supervision from the US but not allowed to elect its own bishop, separates from the MECS and becomes the autonomous *Igreja Metodista Brasil*; William Tarboux is then elected as its first bishop • The separate MEC and MECS missions in Mexico (from 1914) merge to form the autonomous *Iglesia Metodista de Mexico* (Methodist Church of Mexico) • The Wesleyan Methodist Church of Bermuda becomes a Presbytery of the Maritime Conference of the United Church of Canada • The Belgium Mission of the MECS becomes the Belgium Annual Conference	**1930**

	A. WORLD HISTORY & POLITICS	B. AMERICAN HISTORY & POLITICS	C. SCIENCE, MEDICINE & TECHNOLOGY	D. DAILY LIFE, POPULAR CULTURE & ENTERTAINMENT
1930 cont.		• The US Supreme Court rules that purchasing or consuming bootleg liquor does not violate the 18th Amendment, which had only prohibited its manufacture, sale, or transportation		
1931	• The Great Depression spreads throughout Europe and into Asia; the US proposes a one-year moratorium on reparations payments to ease a severe economic crisis in Germany; Britain and France do not agree • The British parliament passes the Statute of Westminster, officially establishing the British Commonwealth of Nations as a free association of self-governing dominions united by a common allegiance to the Crown • Japan takes advantage of confusion in China and invades and occupies Manchuria, setting up a puppet state with the last Chinese emperor, Pu-Yi, as the symbolic head • Mao Zedong proclaims the establishment of the Chinese Soviet Socialist Republic under his chairmanship • King Alfonso XIII of Spain is overthrown by revolution; the Second Spanish Republic is proclaimed • Egypt and Iraq sign a friendship treaty, drawing Egypt into closer relations with other Arab countries	• The Great Depression deepens, banks fail, and millions in the US and Europe are out of work • Over President Hoover's veto, Congress passes the Veterans Compensation Act, permitting cash loans to veterans of half of the bonuses promised to them in 1924 • As a result of the work of US Treasury agent Elliott Ness and his squad, called the "Untouchables," notorious bootlegger and gangster Al Capone is convicted of tax evasion and violations of the Volstead Act and sentenced to 11 years in prison (he is freed in 1939 and dies in 1947) • The trial and conviction of nine young black men in Alabama (the "Scottsboro Boys") on fabricated charges of the rape of two white women reveals the depth of Southern racism to the world • Congress formally adopts "The Star-Spangled Banner" as the US national anthem, confirming President Woodrow Wilson's 1916 executive order	• The Empire State building in New York is completed; at 102 stories and 1,250 feet, it surpasses the Chrysler Building as the tallest in the world at the time • The George Washington Bridge connecting New York City and New Jersey across the Hudson River, begun in 1927, is completed and opens to traffic • Harold Edgerton (US) develops the stroboscope, a precisely timed flash that enables photographers to capture fast motions • Max Knott and Ernst Ruska (Germany) develop the first electron microscope	• *Dick Tracy* joins the comic strips (with his futuristic wrist radio) • Irma Rombauer's American classic, *The Joy of Cooking,* is published • The Federated Boys Clubs of America becomes the Boys Clubs of America • Films: *Frankenstein* (starring Boris Karloff); *City Lights* (Chaplain's masterpiece and his last totally silent film); *The Public Enemy*
1932	• Britain orders the dissolution of the Indian National Congress; Mahatma Gandhi is arrested and jailed and, in response, begins another campaign of civil disobedience, including personal fasting • Hindenburg beats Hitler in the German presidential election, but the Nazis win 230 Reichstag seats; Germany lifts its ban on Nazi storm troopers such as the SS • Famine grips the USSR as Stalin's Five-Year Plan fails, leading to agricultural disaster	• Congress establishes the Reconstruction Finance Corporation (RFC) in an attempt to stimulate the US economy • Thousands of WWI veterans march on Washington, demanding payment of the bonus voted by Congress (1924 and 1931); the marchers are dispersed by US Army troops commanded by Douglas McArthur using tanks and cavalry • The infant son of Charles Lindbergh is kidnapped and killed; Bruno Hauptmann is arrested for the crime in 1934, convicted in 1935, executed in 1936	• The 36-floor Philadelphia Saving Fund Society (PSFS) building is the first modern metal and glass skyscraper • American inventor Allen B. DuMont pioneers the technology of "radio detection and ranging" (radar) to locate ships, but the US military asks him not to patent the technology so it can remain a military secret • American aviator Amelia Earhart becomes the first woman to fly solo across the Atlantic Ocean	• Manhattan's Radio City Music Hall opens • Duke Ellington writes "It Don't Mean a Thing, If It Ain't Got That Swing," launching the swing era of the 1930s and 1940s • The first Krystal Restaurant opens in Chattanooga, TN • "The Puddle Family" radio show, sponsored by Procter & Gamble, comes to be known as the first "soap opera" • The cost of a US first-class postage stamp increases to 3¢

E. EDUCATION, LITERATURE & THE FINE ARTS	F. RELIGION, THEOLOGY, PHILOSOPHY & PSYCHOLOGY	G. AMERICAN & UNITED METHODISM	H. BRITISH & WORLD METHODISM	
		• The CMEC General Conference for the first time seats women (20) as lay delegates • The EC General Conference: – celebrates the erection of Albright Memorial Church in Washington, DC – eliminates the position of Secretary of Evangelism and makes other program cuts due to the economic effects of the Depression – approves organization of The Albright Brotherhood group for laymen and places it under the supervision of the Board of Christian Education – creates a Board of Public Morals and Temperance • The Woman's Missionary Council (MECS) sends Mrs. B. W. Lipscomb to organize the women of two Spanish-speaking conferences (Texas-Mexico and Western Mexico) • Dillard University is established by the MEC in New Orleans through the merger of New Orleans University (1869) with Straight College (founded by the American Missionary Association in 1868) • Kimball School of Theology (1909) in Salem, OR, is closed by the MEC, and the facilities are taken over by Willamette University (1842)		**1930 cont.**
• The Metropolitan Opera begins its continuing weekly radio broadcasts [Milton Cross will host them until 1977] • Ralph Vaughan Williams composes his last notable musical work, *Job: A Masque for Dancing* • William Walton completes his oratorio *Belshazzar's Feast* • Ferde Grofé composes his *Grand Canyon Suite* • Georgia O'Keeffe, who had first visited and fallen in love with northern New Mexico in 1929, completes her most famous western paintings, *Red, White, and Blue* and *Cow's Skull with Calico Roses* • Salvador Dalí creates his classic painting *The Persistence of Memory* • Robert Frost wins the Pulitzer Prize in Poetry for his *Collected Poems* • Other notable publications include: – William Faulkner, *Sanctuary* – Pearl S. Buck, *The Good Earth*	• The National Council of the Congregational Churches (1871) and the General Convention of the Christian Churches (1833) merge to form the General Council of Congregational Christian Churches • Karl Barth publishes his important study of Anselm, *Fides Quarens Intellectum*, arguing that Anselm's ontological argument for the existence of God must be understood from the standpoint of faith • Edwyn Hoskins publishes *The Riddle of the New Testament*	• The Association of Southern Women for the Prevention of Lynching is founded; it is led by Jessie Daniel Ames (MECS) • The Free Methodist Church General Conference completely reorganizes the denomination, creating a central Board of Administration and consolidating board and agency operations under it	• The sixth Ecumenical Methodist Conference meets in Atlanta, GA • The Methodist Church of Southern Africa is formed through a merger of the Wesleyan Methodist Church and several smaller Methodist bodies; it comprises work in Botswana, Lesotho, Mozambique, Namibia, South Africa, and Swaziland • The Methodist Theological Seminary is established in Seoul, Korea • John Telford publishes his edition of *The Letters of the Rev. John Wesley, A.M.* (8 vols.)	**1931**
• Thomas Beecham founds the London Philharmonic Orchestra • Maurice Ravel's *Piano Concerto* premieres in Paris • Benjamin Britten composes his *Sinfonietta* • Sergey Prokofiev's *Piano Concerto No. 5* premieres in Berlin • Notable publications include: – Aldous Huxley, *Brave New World* – William Faulkner, *Light in August*	• The General Association of Regular Baptist Churches is established by a group of conservative Baptist churches in the US who withdraw from the Northern Baptist Convention due to its perceived drift toward modernism or liberalism • Thomas A. Dorsey, "The Father of Gospel Music," writes and the young Mahalia Jackson records "Take My Hand Precious Lord," inaugurating a "golden age" of gospel music	• The MEC General Conference: – again approves a constitutional amendment to allow lay representation in annual conferences; this time the annual conferences vote to approve it – approves participation with the MECS and MPC in a new Joint Commission on Union – rejects proposals calling for the election of district superintendents and for their confirmation by annual conferences – votes to advocate for US membership in the League of Nations	• The Methodist Church in the UK (MC [UK]) is formed by union of the Wesleyan Methodist Church [UK] (1891), the Primitive Methodist Church (1811/1902), and the United Methodist Church [UK] (1907); the Wesleyan Reform Union (1857) and the Independent Methodists (1806/1898) remain apart • *The London Quarterly Review* and the *Holborn Review* are merged to form the *London Quarterly and Holborn Review* (LQHR)	**1932**

	A. WORLD HISTORY & POLITICS	B. AMERICAN HISTORY & POLITICS	C. SCIENCE, MEDICINE & TECHNOLOGY	D. DAILY LIFE, POPULAR CULTURE & ENTERTAINMENT
1932 cont.	• Brazil and Uruguay grant women the right to vote in national elections • The Chaco War breaks out between Bolivia (which has been landlocked since 1884) and Paraguay over control of the Choco Boreal wilderness; when the war ends in 1935, Paraguay controls most of the disputed territory but Bolivia has a corridor to the Paraguay River and thus access to the Atlantic Ocean at the Rio de la Plata • Japan invades China following the supposed murder of a Japanese Buddhist priest in Shanghai, seizing Manchuria and turning it into a dependent state called Manchukou	• Franklin D. Roosevelt is elected as president and John N. Garner as vice president (Democratic Party); Roosevelt promises a "New Deal" for the people of America • Hattie Wyatt Caraway (Arkansas) is the first woman elected to the US Senate	• British physicists John Douglas Cockcroft and Ernest Walton succeed in splitting the atom for the first time • The German firm AEG begins to manufacture the machine called the Magnetophon while BASF produces the plastic-based tape coated with iron oxide particles that it uses	• *The Atlanta Daily World*, the first black daily newspaper in modern times, begins publication • Films: Shirley Temple appears in her first full-length movie, *The Red-Haired Alibi*; *Tarzan, the Ape Man*; *Scarface*; *Grand Hotel* • Summer Olympics: Los Angeles • Winter Olympics: Lake Placid
1933	• Hitler ascends to power in Germany; the Reichstag names him Chancellor and passes laws giving him dictatorial powers • Hitler and Joseph Goebbels employ the power of radio to influence the masses with Nazi propaganda • Hitler's police force, the *Gestapo*, begins hunting down and eliminating opponents of the government and constructs the first Nazi concentration camp at Dachau • Germany and Japan withdraw from the League of Nations • Five million people in the USSR, primarily in Kazakhstan and Ukraine, die of the famine caused by Stalin's failed forced collectivization • Stalin begins a great purge of the Communist Party in the Soviet Union, imprisoning or executing many old Bolsheviks • Switzerland bans the wearing of political party uniforms in public • Catalonia is given internal self-government in Spain, leading to demands for the same by the Basques and other groups; this is a step toward the outbreak of civil war	• The Great Depression deepens still further; over 15 million Americans are now unemployed; more than 4,000 banks fail • President Roosevelt's "New Deal" program begins with the establishment of the National Recovery Administration (NRA), the Public Works Administration (PWA), and the Civilian Conservation Corps (CCC) • The US adopts a "modified gold standard," discontinues the minting and bans the circulation of gold coins, and devalues the dollar against gold, which is still used as the defining value • The Federal Deposit Insurance Corporation (FDIC) is established to provide security for the American banking system, and the Farm Credit Act helps farmers to refinance mortgages • Roosevelt begins his "Fireside Chats" on radio, bypassing hostile newspapers to talk directly to the American people • Frances Perkins is appointed Secretary of Labor by President Roosevelt, making her the first woman to serve as a member of a presidential cabinet • The 20th Amendment to the US Constitution sets new start dates for the terms of Congress and the president • The 21st Amendment to the US Constitution repeals the 18th Amendment and marks the end of Prohibition • The Tennessee Valley Authority (TVA) is created to control flooding and improve navigation on the Tennessee River and its tributaries and to produce electrical power for the entire Tennessee Valley region • The Chicago Century of Progress International Exposition and World's Fair celebrates the centennial of the city's founding; it attracts over 39 million visitors • Tuskegee Institute reports that 3,773 persons have been lynched in the US since 1888 and that three-fourths of them were black	• Wiley Post makes the first solo flight around the world in just under 8 days, stopping 11 times en route • Philo Farnsworth demonstrates the first television for potential investors by broadcasting the image of a dollar sign • Edwin Armstrong develops frequency modulation (FM), a static-free method of radio transmission	• Sally Rand's fan dance is a hit at the Chicago World's Fair • *Esquire* debuts as the first men's magazine • *Newsweek* magazine is published for the first time • The Apollo Theater opens in New York City's Harlem district; featuring live broadcasts by the orchestras of Duke Ellington and Count Basie, it becomes a mecca for black entertainers, launching the careers of Ella Fitzgerald, Sarah Vaughn, and Pearl Bailey, all of whom are winners of "Amateur Night" contests there • Leadbelly (born Huddie William Ledbetter), the great black folk and blues musician, is "discovered" in Louisiana by musicologists John and Alan Lomax; they record hundreds of his songs on portable recording equipment for the Library of Congress • America's first drive-in movie theater opens in Camden, NJ • Elmer Doolin creates Fritos brand corn chips • Hostess Twinkies are first made by the Continental Baking Company • Perry Como begins his singing career with the Freddie Carlone orchestra • H. R. Mott reformulates Chero-Cola (1905) and renames it Royal Crown Cola; it becomes an instant success in the South • Films: *King Kong*; *Dinner at Eight*; *Duck Soup*; *42nd Street*
1934	• Stalin's main advisor, Sergey Kirov, is assassinated, prompting Stalin to begin the "great purge" of the Communist Party; 2.5 million Soviet citizens are arrested and 700,000 are executed by 1937	• Dust storms ruin about 100 million acres and damage another 200 million acres of cropland in Kansas, Texas, Colorado, and Oklahoma (the "Dust Bowl"); farm families <div align="right">*(cont.)*</div>	• Enrico Fermi (US) works on the creation of new elements through the bombardment of uranium with neutrons	• Horton Smith wins the first Masters Golf Tournament • Cole Porter's musical *Anything Goes* premieres on Broadway

E. EDUCATION, LITERATURE & THE FINE ARTS	F. RELIGION, THEOLOGY, PHILOSOPHY & PSYCHOLOGY	G. AMERICAN & UNITED METHODISM	H. BRITISH & WORLD METHODISM	
– Charles Norman Hall, *Mutiny on the Bounty* – T. S. Eliot, *Selected Essays, 1917–1932* – Erskine Caldwell, *Tobacco Road*	• Karl Barth begins the publication of his *Kirchliche Dogmatik* (1932–53; English translation: *Church Dogmatics* 1936–68) • Other notable publications include: – Reinhold Niebuhr, *Moral Man and Immoral Society* – Henri Bergson, *The Two Sources of Morality and Religion* – Jacques Maritan, *The Degrees of Knowledge*	– passes resolutions opposing militarism and supporting conscientious objection to military service • The MEC and the MECS cooperate in launching a new joint periodical, *Religion in Life*, which replaces the MEC *Methodist Review* (1818) and the MECS *Methodist Quarterly Review* (1847) • The MECS Board of Missions replaces *The Missionary Voice* (1911) with *World Outlook* (to 1965) • The MPC General Conference: – approves participation with the MEC and MECS in new Joint Commission on Union – accepts proposal to participate with the MEC and MECS in Joint Hymnal Commission for creating a new common hymnal		**1932 cont.**
• Carter G. Woodson publishes *The Mis-education of the Negro* • Zoltán Kodály completes his *Dances of Galanta* • Prokofiev composes his *Lieutenant Kije Suite* • Bartók's *Piano Concerto No. 2* premieres in Frankfurt • Gertrude Stein publishes *The Autobiography of Alice B. Toklas*, which is actually the story of her own life in disguise • James Joyce's controversial novel *Ulysses* is allowed into the US • Other notable publications include: – Erskine Caldwell, *God's Little Acre* – Thomas Mann, *Joseph and His Brothers*	• Paul Tillich is dismissed from the faculty of the University of Frankfurt by Germany's Nazi government; he moves to the US and joins the faculty of Union Theological Seminary • Martin Niemoeller forms "The Pastors' Emergency League" in Germany to oppose the Nazi-sponsored German Christian Church; it gives rise to the "Confessing Church" movement • Dorothy Day founds *The Catholic Worker* newspaper and the movement of the same name; it supports pacifism and social causes • J. Gresham Machen is the founding president of the Independent Board for Presbyterian Foreign Missions, established as an alternative to the PCUSA denominational missions board • Gerhard Kittel begins the publication of his massive *Theological Dictionary of the New Testament* (10 vols., 1933–76; Vols. 5-10 edited by Gerhard Friedrich; English translation 1964–76 • Other notable publications include: – Alfred North Whitehead, *Adventures of Ideas* – Sigmund Freud, *New Introductory Lectures on Psychoanalysis*	• The UBC General Conference: – requires that within eight years all applicants for an annual conference license to preach must be college graduates "except in extraordinary cases" – decides to discontinue work in German language for ministerial candidates – takes the position that too many churches and ministers are using the realities of the Depression as an excuse for failure to meet their obligations to the denomination – approves participation in a Commission on Church Federation and Union to discuss possible merger with the EC • The National Council of Methodist Youth is formed, drawing members from both the MEC and MECS	• The Methodist Peace Fellowship is established in Britain • In Chile, the Iglesia Evangelica Pentecostal splits off from the Iglesia Metodista Pentecostal • The MC [UK] issues *The Methodist Hymn Book*	**1933**
• Paul Hindemith's operatic masterwork *Mathis der Maler* (Matthias the Painter) about the painter Mathias Grünewald and his struggles with society causes a public (*cont.*)	• The emerging "Confessing Church" movement in Germany adopts the Barmen Declaration, written by Karl Barth and Hans Asumssen, contesting the theological (*cont.*)	• The MECS General Conference: – approves participation with the MEC and MPC in new Joint Commission on Union, which meets for the first time later the same year	• An estimated 5,000 people attend the Council of Christian Pacifist Groups Conference sponsored by the WMC in Westminster Central Hall	**1934**

	A. WORLD HISTORY & POLITICS	B. AMERICAN HISTORY & POLITICS	C. SCIENCE, MEDICINE & TECHNOLOGY	D. DAILY LIFE, POPULAR CULTURE & ENTERTAINMENT
1934 cont.	• After fighting off strong attacks by the Nationalist Chinese Army, Mao leads the epic 6,000-mile "Long March" of his Red Army and its Communist supporters to remote Yunan Province • After the death of German President Hindenburg, Hitler is named Führer by the Reichstag, uniting the chancellorship and the presidency of Germany • Mahatma Gandhi formally resigns from politics; Jawaharlal Nehru becomes the leader of the Congress Party, which has been organized to replace the banned Indian National Congress • The Republic of South Africa achieves independence from Britain under a whites-only Afrikaner minority government • The USSR is admitted to the League of Nations • Cuba and Turkey grant women the right to vote in national elections	begin leaving the drought-stricken Great Plains and move west to California • Congress establishes the Federal Communications Commission (FCC); it replaces the FRC (1927) and is charged with regulating all interstate and international communications by radio, television, wire, and cable • Congress creates the Securities and Exchange Commission (SEC) to regulate the US stock market and the Federal Housing Administration (FHA) to regulate and insure mortgage loans to homeowners • Lettie Pate Whitehead becomes the first American woman to serve on the Board of Directors of a major corporation (The Coca-Cola Company) • The Tydings-McDuffie Act restricts immigration from the Philippines to 50 people annually • Notorious gangsters Clyde Barrow and Bonnie Parker are ambushed and killed by lawmen in Louisiana; John Dillinger is ambushed and killed by the FBI in front of Biograph Theater in Chicago • The Great Smoky Mountains National Park is established • Chicago holds the Century of Progress International Exposition • Elijah Muhammad (born as Elijah Poole in Sandersville, GA) becomes the head of the Nation of Islam (the Black Muslims), and takes the title "Holy Prophet and Messenger of Allah"	• Karl Popper, in *The Logic of Scientific Discovery* helps to define the modern scientific method by rejecting inductive reasoning and insisting that specific logical criteria must be met before a scientific hypothesis can be accepted as "true"	• *Flash Gordon* and *Li'l Abner* appear in the comics • Wurlitzer and Seeburg begin producing their eye-catching, coin-operated record-playing machines, which come to be called "jukeboxes" [probably from the slang term *jook*, meaning "dance"] • Benny Goodman on NBC's *Let's Dance* starts the big band swing era on radio • Paul Whiteman & His Orchestra record "Smoke Gets In Your Eyes" • Chick Webb & His Orchestra record "Stompin' At the Savoy" • Jazz singer Billie Holiday (born Eleanora Fagan, later known as "Lady Day") makes her debut at Harlem's Apollo Theater to rave reviews • Films: *Cleopatra*; *It Happened One Night*; *The Thin Man*; *Of Human Bondage*
1935	• Hitler renounces the Treaty of Versailles, introduces military conscription, and begins openly rearming Germany • Hitler begins the systematic persecution of Jews in Germany, who are deprived of citizenship and civil rights through the infamous Nuremberg Laws • Italy invades Ethiopia; the League of Nations imposes sanctions, but they have little effect • France and the USSR conclude a mutual defense agreement to protect against an unprovoked attack by Germany • The British parliament passes the Government of India Act, providing for creation of a state legislature in Delhi and separating Burma and Aiden from India • Persia is renamed Iran under Shah Reza Pahlavi • David Ben-Gurion becomes chairman of the Jewish Agency Executive	• Congress approves the Works Progress Administration (WPA), a primary element of President Roosevelt's "New Deal" initiative • Congress passes the Social Security Act, which provides for the use of contributions made by workers and employers to insure income to unemployed, retired, or disabled workers and dependent children, and the National Labor Relations Act, which provides support for organized labor and establishes the National Labor Relations Board (NLRB) • The Rural Electrification Administration (REA) is established to bring electrical power to rural areas of the country; the government also restricts public utility monopolies • The Wealth Tax Act increases income tax rates for wealthy individuals and corporations and also increases gift and estate taxes • Mary McLeod Bethune organizes the National Council of Negro Women (NCNW), a coalition of black women's groups that lobbies against job discrimination, racism, and sexism	• Construction is completed on Hoover Dam (for a time called Boulder Dam) in the Black Canyon of the Colorado River, creating Lake Mead; it is the largest dam in the world at the time, 660 feet thick at its base and 726 feet tall • Eastman Kodak introduces the Kodachrome process of color photography • Robert Watson-Watt (UK) successfully uses radar to detect airplanes	• Swing music begins to evolve and separate from jazz; clarinetist and bandleader Benny Goodman takes the name "The King of Swing"; Tommy Dorsey, Harry James, and Artie Shaw also lead popular "swing" dance bands • Ella Fitzgerald begins her singing career with the Chick Webb Orchestra • The first canned beer, "Krueger Cream Ale," is marketed by the Krueger Brewing Company of Richmond, VA • Alcoholics Anonymous (A.A.), the ancestor of many other twelve-step programs, is established by William Griffith Wilson ("Bill W.") and Robert Holbrook Smith ("Dr. Bob"); the book outlining their principles is published in 1939 • Laura Ingalls Wilder publishes *Little House on the Prairie*, a reminiscence of her family's stay in Indian Territory • Baseball slugger Babe Ruth retires with a record 714 home runs • *Your Hit Parade* appears on the radio and becomes a popular weekly show • The Downtown Athletic Club of New York establishes the annual Heisman *(cont.)*

E. EDUCATION, LITERATURE & THE FINE ARTS	F. RELIGION, THEOLOGY, PHILOSOPHY & PSYCHOLOGY	G. AMERICAN & UNITED METHODISM	H. BRITISH & WORLD METHODISM	
uproar in Germany when Wilhelm Furtwängler conducts its premiere with the Berlin Philharmonic and vigorously supports the opera in the press; the opera is banned by Nazi cultural authorities • Ralph Vaughan Williams composes his *Fantasia on Greensleeves* • Sergey Rachmaninoff's *Rhapsody on a Theme of Paganini* is premiered by the Philadelphia Symphony Orchestra, conducted by Leopold Stokowski, with the composer at the piano • Notable publications include: – Henry Miller, *Tropic of Cancer* – F. Scott Fitzgerald, *Tender Is the Night* – Evelyn Waugh, *A Handful of Dust* – Ruth Benedict, *Patterns of Culture* • George Balanchine and Lincoln Kirstein establish the School of American Ballet in New York	claims of the Nazi state; Barth is expelled from his faculty position at the University of Bonn • The Reformed Church in the United States (1747/1793) and the Evangelical Synod of North America (1840) merge to form the Evangelical and Reformed Church • The PCUSA General Assembly orders the Independent Board for Presbyterian Foreign Missions to disband and those ministers and elders of the PCUSA officially connected to it to resign immediately; J. Gresham Machen refuses to do so, resulting in his suspension from the PCUSA ministry • Emil Brunner publishes his *Nature and Grace: A Dialogue with Karl Barth*, in which he argues that human beings have never completely lost the image of God in which they were created, provoking Barth's vigorous disagreement in *No! An Answer to Emil Brunner* • John Dewey publishes *A Common Faith* • Cameron Townsend establishes the Summer Institute of Linguistics in Arkansas to train missionaries of what later will become Wycliffe Bible Translators in basic linguistic, anthropological, and translation principles (it will develop into SIL International)	– again approves and sends to the annual conferences a constitutional amendment for the creation of a Judicial Council; this time it is approved by the annual conferences (by 1938) – limits presiding elders to serving terms of no more than four years, following which they must serve four years in some other capacity before being eligible for reappointment – approves publication of a new hymnal – adopts a revised version of the "Social Creed" – tables a resolution calling for the establishment of episcopal service areas – omits the section on "class meetings" from the *Discipline* • The EC General Conference: – approves participation in a Commission on Church Federation and Union to discuss possible merger with the UBC (and the United Church of Canada) – removes the time limit (previously seven years) on pastoral appointments – orders that the Publishing House in Cleveland be closed, its property sold as soon as possible, and its operations consolidated with the Publishing House in Harrisburg, PA – eliminates a separate episcopal area for Europe • Garrett Biblical Institute (1853) merges with the Chicago Training School (1885) to create Garrett Theological Seminary • Edgar S. Brightman continues the tradition of Boston Personalism with his *Personality and Religion* • Edwin Lewis follows his 1933 essay "The Fatal Apostasy of the Modern Church" with his landmark *Christian Manifesto*, condemning modernism and liberalism and marking the emergence of Barthian neoorthodox thought within American Methodism		**1934 cont.**
• George Gershwin combines black folk idiom and Broadway musical techniques in *Porgy and Bess*, based on the novel by American writer DuBose Heyward • Allen Lane (UK) establishes Penguin Books, which pioneers low-cost paperback publication of the classics as well as modern literary works • James T. Farrell, *Studs Lonigan - A Trilogy* • Pearl S. Buck, *A House Divided* • John Steinbeck, *Tortilla Flat* • T. S. Eliot, *Murder in the Cathedral*	• The German government deports Karl Barth to his native Switzerland • Regina Jones (Berlin) becomes the first woman to be ordained as a Jewish Rabbi • The Cooperative General Association of Free Will Baptists (1916) and the General Conference of Original Free Will Baptists (1921) merge to form the National Association of Free Will Baptists; it is the major association of Baptist churches that reject Calvinist theology • Notable publications include: – R. H. Lightfoot, *History and Interpretation in the Gospels* – Reinhold Niebuhr, *An Interpretation of Christian Ethics* – Shailer Mathews, *Creative Christianity* – Oswald Chambers, *My Utmost for His Highest*	• The MEC, MECS, and MPC issue a joint book of hymns, entitled simply *The Methodist Hymnal*, including four "Orders of Worship" • The Joint Commission on Union reaches agreement on a proposed constitution and Plan of Union of the MEC, MECS, and MPC, which is then submitted to the General Conference of each body • The name of the Methodist Federation for Social Service (MFSS) is changed to the Methodist Federation for Social Action (MFSA) • *The Upper Room* magazine is established by the MECS Home Missions Board • George C. Cell publishes The *Rediscovery of John Wesley*, the first significant 20th-century study of Wesley's theology	• The French Mission Conference of the MEC fails and is disbanded	**1935**

	A. WORLD HISTORY & POLITICS	B. AMERICAN HISTORY & POLITICS	C. SCIENCE, MEDICINE & TECHNOLOGY	D. DAILY LIFE, POPULAR CULTURE & ENTERTAINMENT
1935 cont.		• The NAACP begins sponsoring campaigns against inequalities among segregated schools and initiating court cases against certain state-run law programs that are discriminatory • The Labor Day hurricane of 1935 slams into the Florida coast, killing over 400 and causing $6 million in damage; it is the first category 5 hurricane to strike the US and has the lowest barometric pressure ever recorded		Trophy, named for legendary coach John W. Heisman, to honor the most valuable college football player in the country; the first winner is Jay Berwanger from the University of Chicago • Jesse Owens, representing Ohio State University, breaks four world records at the Big Ten Conference track championships • Films: Leni Riefenstahl's *Triumph of the Will* glorifies Hitler's Nazi regime; other films include *Mutiny on the Bounty*; *The Informer*; *Top Hat*; *A Night at the Opera*
1936	• Britain's King George V dies; he is succeeded by his son, Edward VIII • Hitler and Mussolini form Berlin-Rome Axis; joined by Japan in 1940 • Francisco Franco leads a Spanish army mutiny in Morocco; it spawns fighting in Spain, which turns into the Spanish Civil War; Germany and Italy support Franco; Russia, England, and France support the government • The Transcaucasian Soviet Socialist Republic is abolished and new SSRs are created from its territory in Armenia, Georgia, and Azerbaijan; in addition, new SSRs are formed in Kazakhstan and Kyrgyzstan; all become member states of the Soviet Union • Anastasio Somoza leads a coup d'état in Nicaragua ushering in Somoza family dictatorship for more than 4 decades • Japan signs an "anticommunist" pact with Germany and later with Italy • Hitler renounces the Treaty of Locarno (1925), and German troops reoccupy the Rhineland • China declares war on Japan because of Japan's occupation of Manchuria • Sunni Muslim clerics play a prominent role in an Arab revolt against British rule in Palestine • Egypt achieves independence from Britain • Italy annexes Ethiopia, and the king of Italy, Victor Emmanuel III, takes the title Emperor of Ethiopia as Haile Selassie flees the country • London's famous Crystal Palace, dating from the Great Exhibition of 1851, is destroyed by fire	• In a series of 5-4 rulings, the US Supreme Court strikes down as unconstitutional several pieces of "New Deal" legislation, including the National Industrial Recovery Act, the Agricultural Adjustment Act, and state minimum-wage laws • Over President Roosevelt's veto, Congress passes the Adjusted Compensation Act, which provides for immediate payment of the benefits promised to WWI veterans in 1924 and 1931 • The Social Conservation and Domestic Allotment Act offers payment to farmers who practice soil conservation by taking land out of cultivation • The federal law prohibiting the dissemination of contraceptive information through the mail is modified, and birth control information is no longer classified as "obscene" • A strike against General Motors leads to recognition of the United Auto Workers union by GM • President Roosevelt and Vice President Garner are reelected (Democratic Party); they carry all but two states and win the electoral college vote 523 to 8; Congress is 80% Democratic	• The TVA completes construction of Norris Dam on the Clinch River and Wheeler Dam on the Tennessee River • Douglas DC-3 enters airline service in the US; the first modern airliner, it can reach 210 mph with 21 passengers [it becomes the most widely used airplane in history] • The San Francisco-Oakland Bay Bridge, begun in 1933, opens to traffic • Alan Turing's essay "On Computable Numbers" describes a general-purpose computer • American engineer H. W. Dudley of Bell Labs develops the first successful electronic speech synthesizer, which he calls the voice coder	• William and Ethel Stuckey open a roadside stand in Georgia to sell pecans to motorists en route to and from Florida, beginning the Stuckey's store chain • *Life* magazine is first published • *Billboard* magazine publishes its first "music hit parade" listings • Cole Porter writes and records "Begin the Beguine" • Dale Carnegie publishes *How to Win Friends and Influence People* • Films: *Modern Times*; *The Great Ziegfeld*; *Mr. Deeds Goes to Town*; *Swing Time* (features Fred Astaire and Ginger Rogers) • Summer Olympics: Berlin • Winter Olympics: Garmisch-Partenkirchen • To Hitler's great annoyance, black American track star Jesse Owens wins four Olympic gold medals, challenging Nazi beliefs in Aryan racial supremacy
1937	• Francisco Franco's followers, called Falangists, merge with Nationalists and conquer northwest Spain; the loyalist Spanish government is forced to move from Valencia to Barcelona • German planes, assisting Franco in the Spanish Civil War, bomb and destroy the city of Guernica, killing most of its residents including women and children • Japan invades China, capturing Beijing and Shanghai; Japanese troops massacre over 200,000 civilians and POWs in the "Rape of Nanking" • US/Japanese relations quickly deteriorate after Japanese aircraft attack and sink the US gunboat *Panay* • Britain's King Edward VIII abdicates the throne after 11 months in order to be able *(cont.)*	• President Roosevelt proposes a Court Reform Bill to Congress that would have allowed him to "pack" the US Supreme Court with up to six additional (and presumably more sympathetic) members; the bill is rejected by Congress • The Supreme Court reverses itself and upholds, by a 5-4 vote in the other direction, a state minimum-wage law very similar to laws it had previously overturned; shortly thereafter the Supreme Court finds both the Social Security Act and the National Labor Relations Act, two key pieces of "New Deal" legislation, to be constitutional • President Roosevelt declares the neutrality of the US in the developing conflict in Europe	• Amelia Earhart and copilot Fred Noonan disappear off New Guinea during an attempted flight around the world • The German airship *Hindenburg* explodes and burns on landing in New Jersey; video recording of the disaster is broadcast coast to coast • George Stibitz of Bell Labs invents the electrical digital calculator • French scientist Eugene Houdry develops the catalytic cracking process for refining oil, using catalysts to create chemical reactions and producing more gasoline than thermal oil refining; the "Houdry process" becomes the basis of the modern petrochemical industry	• The Glenn Miller Orchestra makes its debut in New York; its distinctive "smooth swing" sound, typified by its theme song, "In the Mood," emphasizes orchestrated arrangements over improvisation • The Count Basie Orchestra first records "One O'Clock Jump," which will become the band's signature tune • *Babes In Arms*, the first major musical by Richard Rodgers and Lorenz Hart, opens on Broadway • The Waring blender is invented by Fred Osius, one of the founders of Hamilton Beach Co. • The first issue of *Look* magazine goes on sale • Ruth Graves Wakefield, owner of the Toll House Inn near Whitman, MA, substitutes *(cont.)*

E. EDUCATION, LITERATURE & THE FINE ARTS	F. RELIGION, THEOLOGY, PHILOSOPHY & PSYCHOLOGY	G. AMERICAN & UNITED METHODISM	H. BRITISH & WORLD METHODISM	
				1935 cont.
• Bartók's masterpiece, *Music for Strings, Percussion and Celesta*, premieres in Basel • Prokofiev completes his charming musical drama *Peter and the Wolf* for orchestra and narrator and his ballet *Romeo and Juliet* • Zoltán Kodály composes his *Te Deum* • Alban Berg's *Violin Concerto* is premiered by Louis Krasner in Barcelona • Alan Hovhaness composes his *Cello Concerto* • Thomas Hart Benton completes his controversial mural, *A Social History of the State of Missouri*, combining portrayals of ordinary Americans with images drawn from American folk tales, for the state capitol building in Jefferson City, MO • Notable publications include: – Margaret Mitchell, *Gone with the Wind* – William Faulkner, *Absalom, Absalom!*	• Conservative Presbyterians led by J. Gresham Machen withdraw from the PCUSA to form the Presbyterian Church of America; the name is changed in 1939 to the Orthodox Presbyterian Church (OPC) • Pope Pius XI issues the encyclical *Vigilanti Cura* (On the Motion Picture) in which he warns the faithful against the "corrupting influence" of television and movies • Henry Havelock Ellis completes monumental studies in the *Psychology of Sex* • Other notable publications include: – A. J. Ayer, *Language, Truth, and Logic* – Arthur O. Lovejoy, *The Great Chain of Being* – Alfred Loisy, *The Origins of the New Testament* – C. S. Lewis, *The Allegory of Love* – Jacques Maritan, *True Humanism [Integral Humanism]* – John M. Keynes, *The General Theory of Employment, Interest and Money*	• The MEC General Conference: – focuses primarily on proposed Plan of Union of the MEC, MECS, and MPC – after extensive debate about the jurisdictional system and particularly the proposed Central Jurisdiction, approves the Plan of Union by a vote of 470-83 and sends it to the annual conferences, which also approve it overwhelmingly, 17,239-1,862 – passes resolutions strongly supporting total abstinence and prohibition • The MPC General Conference: – approves the proposed Plan of Union by a vote of 142-39, as do 21 of 25 annual conferences at their next sessions – empowers the president to call a special session if both the MEC and MECS give final approval to Plan of Union	• The MEC forms five separate conferences of the BMK in Germany into the Germany Central Conference; F. H. Otto Melle is the first native German to be elected bishop • The United Church of Canada allows the ordination of women • Umphrey Lee publishes *John Wesley and Modern Religion*	**1936**
• Picasso creates the memorial painting *Guernica* for the Spanish pavilion at the Paris Exposition, memorializing the horrors of the Spanish Civil War • Stuart Davis completes his jazz-inspired and distinctively American painting *Abstraction* • Ralph Vaughan Williams composes his musical setting to Irish playwright J. M. Synge's great drama *Riders to the Sea* • William Walton composes his *Crown Imperial Coronation March* for the coronation of Britain's King George VI • Carl Orff completes his vigorous secular oratorio *Carmina Burana*, based on medieval poetry • Francis Poulenc composes his *Mass in G Major*	• Pope Pius XI denounces Hitler in the encyclical *Mit brennender Sorge* (On the Church and the German Reich) • The World Conference on Faith and Order meets in Edinburgh • Mahalia Jackson has a gospel music hit with her recording of Thomas A. Dorsey's "Peace in the Valley" • World Conference on Life and Work meets in Oxford • Emil Brunner publishes *The Divine-Human Encounter* and *Man in Revolt*, both of which reflect the position of Martin Buber's *I and Thou* (1922) • Dietrich Bonhoeffer writes *The Cost of Discipleship* in which he attacks the doctrine of "cheap grace" being proclaimed by the Protestant churches in Germany	• The UBC General Conference: – hears a positive report from the Commission on Church Federation and Union on the progress of conversations about possible union with the EC – acts to set aside a major barrier to union by creating a pension program for ministers and their widows comparable to that of the EC, making participation compulsory by 1941 – revises the reading list of the course of study – exhorts, but does not require, ministerial candidates to attend Bonebrake Seminary – approves reorganization of the publishing house as The Otterbein Press • The Methodist Student Movement (MSM) is established to promote the (cont.)	• The several Methodist missions in China unite to form The Methodist Church In the Republic of China • Maximin Piette publishes *John Wesley in the Evolution of Protestantism* (translation of the original French *La Réaction de John Wesley dans l'Evolution du Protestantisme*, 1927)	**1937**

	A. WORLD HISTORY & POLITICS	B. AMERICAN HISTORY & POLITICS	C. SCIENCE, MEDICINE & TECHNOLOGY	D. DAILY LIFE, POPULAR CULTURE & ENTERTAINMENT
1937 cont.	to marry an American divorcée, Wallis Simpson; the crown then goes to his brother, George VI • The office of Prime Minister in the UK receives formal statutory recognition through the Ministers of the Crown Act; the official title is "First Lord of the Treasury and Prime Minister" • Neville Chamberlain becomes British Prime Minister and tries to secure peace in Europe through a policy of appeasement of Germany and Italy • Italy withdraws from the League of Nations • Paris holds its sixth Exposition Universelle, which attracts over 33 million visitors; the old Palais du Trocadéro (from the 1878 Exposition) is torn down and replaced by the new Palais de Chaillot	• Congress passes the Neutrality Act, prohibiting the export of munitions or war materials from the US to nations at war and the use of US ships to transport armaments into war zones • The Housing Act provides for loans to local communities for rent subsidies and the construction of low-cost housing • The Lilly Endowment, a private philanthropic foundation based in Indianapolis, is established by J. K. Lilly Sr. and his sons through gifts of stock in their pharmaceutical business, Eli Lilly and Company; it becomes one of the most important private charitable organizations in American history	• Construction of the Golden Gate Bridge in San Francisco, begun in 1933, is completed and the bridge opens to pedestrians (to vehicles in 1938)	a chopped-up bar of Nestlé semi-sweet chocolate for regular baker's chocolate in her favorite cookie recipe, thus creating the Toll House chocolate-chip cookie • Edgar Bergen and his puppet Charlie McCarthy make their radio debut on NBC • Films: French director Jean Renoir's anti-war film *The Grand Illusion* is banned in Germany and Italy; Walt Disney's first full-length animated feature, *Snow White and the Seven Dwarfs*, becomes an instant classic; other hits include *Stage Door*; *Captains Courageous*; *Lost Horizon*; and *Way Out West* (possibly the best Laurel and Hardy film)
1938	• Hitler names himself War Minister; Germany annexes Austria and threatens to annex Sudetenland (western Czechoslovakia) • British Prime Minister Neville Chamberlain proclaims the achievement of "peace in our time" after leading the negotiation of the Munich Pact by which Britain, France, and Italy agree to let Germany partition Czechoslovakia • The night of anti-Semitic riots and destruction of Jewish institutions in Germany and Austria known as *kristallnacht* ("the night of broken glass") marks the beginning of the active Nazi persecution of Jews that leads to the Holocaust • Japanese forces conquer most of China including Canton; the Chinese Nationalist Army retreats up the Yangtze River to Chunking and proclaims it the new capital; the Japanese install a puppet Chinese government in Beijing • Britain's coastal radar system, the Chain Home, goes into 24-hour operation • Franco's Nationalists bomb Barcelona and capture Lerida, effectively cutting Spain in half • Large-scale production of oil begins in Saudi Arabia and Kuwait • Sinn Fein merges into the Irish Republican Army	• President Roosevelt proposes expanded appropriations to strengthen and enlarge the US military; Congress resists • Congress passes the Fair Labor Standards Act, which establishes a minimum wage standard of $0.25 per hour for employees engaged in interstate commerce or in the production of goods for interstate commerce; it also sets the minimum age of employment and regulates the hours of work for children in the US • The Agricultural Adjustment Administration provides increased government financial support for farmers and sets up crop insurance policies • Congress establishes the House Committee on Un-American Activities to investigate the activities of Socialist, Communist, and Fascist organizations in the US • The Federal Highway Act authorizes a feasibility study for what will become the Interstate Highway System	• TVA completes construction of Pickwick Dam on the Tennessee River; 12 other dams are under construction or being planned • Ugo Cerletti and Lucio Bini (Italy) pioneer the medical use of electroconvulsive therapy (ECT), or shock therapy, for the treatment of mental illness • Chester F. Carlson invents a process for the electronic reproduction of documents or images that he names "xerography," now commonly called photocopying • DuPont chemist Wallace H. Carothers creates and patents nylon, the first completely synthetic organic polymer fiber • Hungarian-born brothers Georg and Ladislao Biro (Argentina) perfect the first practical ballpoint pen • The Overseas Highway in the Florida Keys, begun in 1935 after the Labor Day hurricane destroyed major sections of the Florida Overseas Railroad, is completed; the system of 35 bridges and causeways stretches 113 miles from mainland Florida to Key West • The Parker Dam on the Colorado River, 150 miles downstream from Hoover Dam, is completed, creating Lake Havasu	• Orson Welles broadcasts his radio adaptation of H. G. Wells's *War of the Worlds*, creating a nationwide panic as many listeners believe that aliens have landed in New Jersey • Roy Acuff joins *The Grand Ole Opry* and helps bring national recognition to the Nashville-based radio program • Thelonius Monk composes his classic jazz ballad "'Round Midnight" • Benny Goodman and his band give the first swing music concert at Carnegie Hall, marking general acceptance of the "legitimacy" of the musical genre • Irving Berlin revises his song "God Bless America," originally written in 1918; when Kate Smith sings it on Armistice Day, it creates a national sensation, resulting in proposals to make it America's national anthem • Joe Louis defeats Germany's Max Schmelling, retaining his world heavyweight boxing championship title and avenging his loss to Schmelling in 1936 • The Nestlé company of Switzerland invents freeze-dried coffee and markets it as Nescafé • Herman W. Lay begins marketing his potato chips • Prosper Montagné publishes the *Larousse Gastronomique*, a comprehensive compilation of the techniques and recipes of classic French cuisine • The first *Superman* comic book appears • Films: Shirley Temple stars in what may be her best film, *Rebecca of Sunnybrook Farm*; *Angels With Dirty Faces*; *Jezebel*; *Pygmalion*; *The Adventures of Robin Hood*
1939	• Francisco Franco's forces capture Madrid, ending the Spanish Civil War; Franco becomes dictator • Italy and Germany form the "Pact of Steel" military alliance • Stalin and Hitler sign a nonaggression pact that includes the partition of Poland between Germany and the USSR	• The US stock market begins a steep decline, losing 40% of its value by 1942 • Ironically, the European war causes a boom in the US manufacturing economy from materials orders • San Francisco hosts the Golden Gate International Exposition and World's Fair (to 1940) to celebrate the opening of its *(cont.)*	• Paul Müller recognizes that DDT (first isolated in Germany in 1874) is a powerful insecticide; DDT is used in WWII, and then worldwide, to combat diseases transmitted by insects • Pan American World Airways establishes the first regular transatlantic airline passenger service, from New York to England and France	• Lou Gehrig's record streak of consecutive baseball games played ends at 2,130 • Billy Strayhorn's great jazz ballad "Take the 'A' Train" becomes the theme song of the Duke Ellington Orchestra • Harry James forms his own big band and hires Frank Sinatra as his main vocalist; *(cont.)*

E. EDUCATION, LITERATURE & THE FINE ARTS	F. RELIGION, THEOLOGY, PHILOSOPHY & PSYCHOLOGY	G. AMERICAN & UNITED METHODISM	H. BRITISH & WORLD METHODISM	
• Notable publications include: – John Steinbeck, *Of Mice and Men* – Isak Dinesen, *Out of Africa* – Zora Neale Hurston, *Their Eyes Were Watching God* – J. R. R. Tolkien, *The Hobbit*	• Other notable publications include: – H. Richard Niebuhr, *The Kingdom of God in America* – Georges Bernanos, *The Diary of a Country Priest* – Talcott Parsons, *The Structure of Social Action*	development of young leaders in the church and society • The Board of Trustees of American University votes to admit black students, making AU one of the first universities in a segregated city to do so		**1937 cont.**
• Samuel Barber composes his *Adagio for Strings* • Aaron Copland completes his ballet *Billy the Kid* • Bartók's *Sonata for Two Pianos and Percussion* premieres in Basel • Thornton Wilder publishes his greatest drama, *Our Town*, which brings him the Pulitzer Prize • John Dos Passos publishes his *U.S.A.* trilogy containing his three novels *The 42nd Parallel* (1930), *1919* (1932), and *The Big Money* (1936) • Other notable publications include: – Elizabeth Bowen, *The Death of the Heart* – Marjorie Kinnan Rawlings, *The Yearling* – André Malraux, *Man's Hope* – George Orwell, *Homage to Catalonia*	• Conservative Presbyterians led by Carl McIntire withdraw from the PCUSA and establish the Bible Presbyterian Church • C. S. Lewis publishes *The Lion, The Witch, and The Wardrobe*, the first volume in his series of religious allegories known as *The Chronicles of Narnia* • Other notable publications include: – Jean-Paul Sartre, *Nausea* – Sigmund Freud, *An Outline of Psychoanalysis* – John Dewey, *Logic: The Theory of Inquiry* and *Experience and Education* – Gerhard von Rad, *The Problem of the Hexateuch and Other Essays*	• The MECS General Conference meets for the last time: – establishes the Judicial Council, which now begins to function for the first time – approves the Plan of Union by a vote of 434-26; it had previously been approved by its annual conferences by a vote of 7,650-1,247 – receives a unanimous opinion from the Judicial Council affirming the constitutionality of the Plan of Union and the method of its adoption – orders the election in upcoming annual conferences of clergy and lay delegates to the 1939 Uniting Conference – directs that lay delegates to annual conference be elected from each pastoral charge instead of by the district conferences – takes the same position on divorce adopted by the MEC in 1884: divorce and the remarriage of divorced persons is prohibited except in the case of adultery • The EC General Conference: – hears a report from the Commission on Church Federation and Union expressing hope for eventual union with the UBC despite "knotty problems" – amends the constitution to provide for an Administrative Council to govern the affairs of the church between sessions of the General Conference, dissolving the Commission on Finance – organizes a Board of Christian Social Action, which replaces the Board of Public Morals and Temperance (1930) – removes an eight-year time limit on the appointment of district superintendents to a given district – approves a recommendation of the bishops to join the movement to establish a World Council of Churches	• Methodists around the world celebrate the 200th anniversary of John Wesley's Aldersgate experience • J. E. Rattenbury publishes *The Conversions of the Wesleys*, in which he characterizes John's Aldersgate experience and the similar experience of Charles three days earlier as the moment of their evangelical conversions • Umphrey Lee publishes *The Historical Backgrounds of Early Methodist Enthusiasm*	**1938**
• Francis Poulenc's *Organ Concerto* premieres in Paris • Henry Miller's *Tropic of Capricorn*, published in Paris, is banned in the US as obscene • John Steinbeck's *The Grapes of Wrath*, his best-known work, provides a graphic description of the migration of an *(cont.)*	• Pope Pius XI dies; he is succeeded by Pope Pius XII • Dietrich Bonhoeffer leaves Germany for the US but decides to return to share the life of the German people under Nazi rule • The Islamic Mission Society is founded in New York City by Sheikh Dawood	• The MEC, MECS, and MPC unite to form The Methodist Church (MC); the Plan of Union has several major features: – establishes five geographical jurisdictions, plus the nongeographical Central Jurisdiction for all the black congregations and conferences	• Passage of the Methodist Church Act of 1939 by the British parliament constitutes and incorporates the Trustees for Methodist Church Purposes, enabling property and funds at all levels to be held by a group of trustees appointed by and reporting to the MC [UK] Conference	**1939**

	A. WORLD HISTORY & POLITICS	B. AMERICAN HISTORY & POLITICS	C. SCIENCE, MEDICINE & TECHNOLOGY	D. DAILY LIFE, POPULAR CULTURE & ENTERTAINMENT
1939 cont.	• WWII begins when Germany annexes the rest of Czechoslovakia, occupies Bohemia and Moravia, and invades western Poland; in response, France and Great Britain declare war on Germany • Italy invades and conquers Albania • Soviet troops invade eastern Poland and Finland, then the Baltic states (Lithuania, Latvia, and Estonia); Ukraine declares its independence • Japan continues its undeclared war in China; Japanese and Russian forces clash on the border of Mongolia; Japan demands that Britain and France cease their support of Chiang Kai-shek's Chinese Nationalist Army • Britain changes its Middle East policy, adopting a more sympathetic attitude toward the Arabs and implementing restrictions on Jewish immigration to and settlement in Palestine; David Ben-Gurion calls upon the Jewish community to resist, leading to the emergence of "fighting Zionism" • The League of Red Cross Societies moves its headquarters from Paris to historically neutral Geneva	two great bridges (The Golden Gate and the San Francisco-Oakland Bay Bridge); it attracts over 16 million visitors • The New York World's Fair celebrates "Building the World of Tomorrow" (to 1940); it attracts more than 57 million visitors • The previously separate US Lighthouse Service is merged into the US Coast Guard • The Daughters of the American Revolution organization refuses to allow black singer Marian Anderson to perform at Constitution Hall in Washington, DC; the NAACP moves her concert to the Lincoln Memorial, where over 75,000 people attend	• German engineer Hans von Ohain develops and successfully test flies the first turbojet-powered aircraft • A prototype of the first digital computer is demonstrated by John Vincent Atanasoff and Clifford Berry at Iowa State College • Western Union introduces coast-to-coast facsimile telegraph or "telefax" service, electronically transmitting and reproducing document images; "fax" machines soon replace telegraphs for most government and business purposes • Construction is completed on Frank Lloyd Wright's Fallingwater in western Pennsylvania; in 1991 the American Institute of Architects names it "the best all-time work of American architecture"	Sinatra has his first hit record with "All or Nothing At All" • Billie Holiday begins closing her night club act with the powerful and poignant antilynching ballad "Strange Fruit" • Judy Garland's recording of "Somewhere Over the Rainbow" (from the movie *The Wizard of Oz*) is forever after associated with her • Charles Dickens's *A Christmas Carol* is broadcast to a radio audience for the first time • "Rudolph, the Red-Nosed Reindeer" joins the nation's annual Christmas festivities • *Batman* first appears in his own comic book • Films: This is the single most celebrated year in the history of American cinema, with such memorable films as *Gone with the Wind*; *The Wizard of Oz*; *Mr. Smith Goes to Washington*; *Stagecoach*; *Wuthering Heights*; *Goodbye Mr. Chips*; *Of Mice and Men*; *Babes in Arms*; *Drums Along the Mohawk*; *Beau Geste*
1940	• The Tripartite Pact between Germany, Italy, and Japan creates the military alliance of Axis powers: joined later by Hungary, Romania, and Bulgaria • The Soviet Union annexes Estonia, Latvia, and Lithuania and transforms them into SSRs; they become members of the USSR along with the newly formed Karelo-Finnish and Moldavian SSRs • Norway, Denmark, Belgium, and France all fall to the German "blitzkrieg"; British troops are trapped on the beach at Dunkirk and miraculously evacuated; Britain now stands alone against Germany • Winston Churchill becomes British Prime Minister • Germany's bombing of London (the "London Blitz") begins the Battle of Britain; the Royal Air Force fends off the Luftwaffe; Churchill says of the RAF: "Never in the field of human conflict was so much owed by so many to so few" • In response to Churchill's appeals, the US begins sending "surplus" war supplies to Britain	• The US census reports that the population is 131,669,275: – whites: 118,214,870 (89.8%) – blacks: 12,865,518 (9.7%) – other: 588,887 (0.5%) • The US national debt is $42,967,531,037 • The Selective Service Act requires all men between the ages of 21 and 36 to register for military service and forbids "discrimination of any person (in the armed forces) on account of race or color" • Edward R. Murrow's live radio broadcasts during the "London Blitz," with his signature opening "This is London," electrifies radio audiences nationwide and helps to tip American sympathies toward Britain • The Alien Registration Act (or Smith Act) makes it illegal to advocate the overthrow of the US government and requires all noncitizens living in the US to register with the government • The Pennsylvania Turnpike becomes the first multilane superhighway in the US, followed soon after by the Los Angeles Freeway	• Scientists working at the University of California in Berkeley, led by Glen T. Seaborg, succeed in isolating plutonium isotopes • The Tacoma Narrows Bridge opens as the third longest suspension bridge in the world; it is nicknamed "Galloping Gertie" due to its behavior in high wind; it collapses in a wind of 42 mph only four months after it opens • A French schoolboy discovers the Lascaux caves, with their surviving Cro-Magnon art	• The first McDonald's hamburger stand opens in Pasadena, CA • WNBT, the first regularly operating television station, begins broadcasting in New York City • Cole Porter's *Panama Hattie*, featuring Ethel Merman as Hattie Maloney, is a smash Broadway hit • The Richard Rodgers and Lorenz Hart musical *Pal Joey* opens on Broadway; the score included the memorable song "Bewitched, Bothered And Bewildered" • Woody Guthrie writes "This Land is Your Land, This Land is My Land" (originally titled "God Blessed America for Me") out of irritation at the popularity of Irving Berlin's ultrapatriotic "God Bless America" • Frank Sinatra joins the Tommy Dorsey Orchestra and begins his rise to fame as a singer • Cuban bandleader Xavier Cugat records the hit song "Perfidia" with singer Miguelito Valdés, helping to popularize Latin music in the United States • M&M candy is developed for the US military as a substitute for the standard chocolate bar, which tended to melt in K-ration packages

E. EDUCATION, LITERATURE & THE FINE ARTS	F. RELIGION, THEOLOGY, PHILOSOPHY & PSYCHOLOGY	G. AMERICAN & UNITED METHODISM	H. BRITISH & WORLD METHODISM	
impoverished Oklahoma Dust Bowl family to California during the Great Depression • Other notable publications include: – John Dos Passos, *The Adventures of a Young Man* – James Joyce, *Finnegan's Wake* – Nathaniel West, *The Day of the Locust* – Ernest Hemingway, *The Snows of Kilimanjaro*	• Sigmund Freud publishes his *Moses and Monotheism* • Karen Horney's *New Ways in Psychoanalysis* dismisses Freud's notion of "penis envy" in women as nonsense	– delegates to the jurisdictional conferences the power of electing bishops and members of general boards and agencies – creates a Judicial Council to serve as the church's "supreme court" and empowers it to determine the constitutionality of actions of the General, jurisdictional, or central conferences and to hear and decide on appeals of episcopal decisions and church trials in annual conferences – continues the central conferences for organization of Methodist churches and missions outside the US; establishes Commission on Central Conferences to coordinate their activities – creates the General Board of Lay Activities to oversee all the work with laymen – merges the various women's home and foreign missionary societies and other women's groups of the three uniting churches to create the Woman's Society of Christian Service (WSCS) and the Wesleyan Service Guild (WSG), but creates racially separate WSCS and WSG units for the Central Jurisdiction – omits the section on "class meetings" from the *Discipline* – does not permit the ordination of women as elders in full connection, but allows those MP women who are already ordained elders to continue serving in that capacity – unites the deaconess offices of three predecessor churches under single administration as the Woman's Division of Christian Service, Board of Missions and Church Extension, The Methodist Church (usually called simply the Woman's Division) – organizes a new Southwest Mexican Conference for Spanish-speaking churches; it includes all of Texas and New Mexico and overlaps six English-speaking conferences	• The MEC Central European Conference becomes the MC Central and Southern European Provisional Conference • Most of the Methodist churches in France unite with the Eglise Réformée de France (French Reformed Church); the German-speaking congregations in the Alsace-Lorraine are attached to the Switzerland Annual Conference (MEC); the few remaining congregations join together to form the Eglise Evangélique Méthodiste (Evangelical Methodist Church) in France [now the United Methodist Church in France]	**1939 cont.**
• Samuel Barber composes his *Violin Concerto* • Randall Thompson composes his *Alleluia* • Igor Stravinsky completes his *Symphony in C* • Benjamin Britten writes his *Sinfonia da Requiem* • Notable publications include: – Graham Greene, *The Power and the Glory* – Ernest Hemingway, *For Whom the Bell Tolls* – Richard Wright, *Native Son* – Carson McCullers, *The Heart Is a Lonely Hunter*	• W. E. B. DuBois publishes *Dusk of Dawn: An Essay Toward an Autobiography of a Race Concept* • Other notable publications include: – Bertrand Russell, *An Inquiry into Meaning and Truth* – Carl Jung, *The Interpretation of Personality* – D. C. Macintosh, *The Problem of Religious Knowledge*	• The MC General Conference meets for the first time: – determines that the term *consecration* rather than *ordination* should be used for the recognition of newly-elected bishops – authorizes unordained local preachers (both men and women) to administer the sacraments in charges to which they are appointed – creates the Methodist Committee on Overseas Relief (MCOR) to provide emergency aid to people suffering from the war in Europe and China – establishes the Council of Secretaries to help coordinate the work of the church's general boards and agencies – elects the first members of the Judicial Council, which now begins to function – fixes the locations of the various general boards and agencies of the church, e.g. Board of Missions in New York, Board of Education in Nashville, etc. – establishes the Pacific Japanese Provisional Conference (superseding Pacific Japanese Mission), the California Oriental Mission, and the Puerto Rico Provisional Conference – affirms the "liberal" position on divorce and remarriage adopted by the MEC in 1928	• Under pressure from Japanese authorities, the Korean Methodist Church is reorganized with pro-Japanese leadership; foreign missionaries are forced to leave Korea	**1940**

	A. WORLD HISTORY & POLITICS	B. AMERICAN HISTORY & POLITICS	C. SCIENCE, MEDICINE & TECHNOLOGY	D. DAILY LIFE, POPULAR CULTURE & ENTERTAINMENT
1940 cont.		• President Roosevelt is reelected for a third term and Henry A. Wallace is elected as vice president (Democratic Party) • Benjamin Davis becomes the first black American to be promoted to the rank of General in the US Army		• The first *Bugs Bunny* cartoons appear: "Eh, what's up, Doc?" • Films: Chaplin's *The Great Dictator* parodies Hitler and Mussolini; *The Road to Singapore* is the first of a series of "road" films featuring Bob Hope, Bing Crosby, and Dorothy Lamour; Walt Disney's *Fantasia* wins awards for its creative combination of animation with classical music • Both Summer and Winter Olympics are canceled due to WWII
1941	• Hitler breaks his nonaggression pact with Stalin; Germany invades the USSR but is stopped by the Red Army outside Moscow • Italy and Germany jointly invade north Africa; the German "Afrika Corp" under Erwin Rommel advances into Libya and captures Tobruk • The German air assault on Britain intensifies, and German submarines begin unrestricted war on North Atlantic shipping • The Nazis begin to carry out the "final solution to the Jewish question"; over 33,000 Jews are killed at the Babi Yar massacre near Kiev; deportation of German Jews begins; there are massacres of Jews in Russia • Japanese aircraft launch a surprise attack on the US military base at Pearl Harbor, badly damaging or sinking 21 ships (including 8 battleships), destroying 200 aircraft, and killing or wounding over 3,000 naval and military personnel; the US aircraft carriers are at sea and not damaged • Japan declares war on the US, Britain, Canada, Australia, and New Zealand; the Japanese bomb Hong Kong and occupy Bangkok • British troops under Bernard Montgomery land in north Africa to begin a counteroffensive against Rommel's Afrika Corps • The British navy succeeds in tracking down and destroying the German battleship *Bismarck*, the pride of the German fleet, in one of the very few engagements of capital ships in the Atlantic theater during WWII • The Indochina Communist Party, led by Ho Chi Minh, combines with the Nationalist Party to form the Vietminh	• In his State of the Union message, President Roosevelt enunciates the "Four Freedoms" to which all people are entitled: freedom of speech, freedom of worship, freedom from want, and freedom from fear • Roosevelt and Churchill meet in secret off Newfoundland where they sign the Atlantic Charter, affirming that no territorial gain is sought by the US and Britain, proclaiming that self-determination is the right of all people, and providing a blueprint for the creation of the United Nations • Congress approves the Lend-Lease Act, sending 50 destroyers and other war materials to Britain in exchange for leases for military bases in Newfoundland and the British West Indies • The US "lends" the Soviet Union $1 billion worth of surplus war materials • After the Japanese attack at Pearl Harbor, Congress declares war on Japan and then on Germany and Italy • Roosevelt issues an executive order banning racial discrimination in hiring in the federal government • The Army Air Corp begins training black pilots for the 99th Fighter Squadron at Tuskegee Institute • Construction of the Mt. Rushmore National Monument, begun in 1927, is completed; the carved heads of American presidents George Washington, Thomas Jefferson, Abraham Lincoln, and Theodore Roosevelt each stand 60 feet tall • Mammoth Cave National Park is created	• The Colorado River Aqueduct is completed, bringing water from Lake Havasu, on the Colorado River, to Los Angeles, a distance of 242 miles across the Mojave Desert • Regular electronic television broadcasts begin in the US using the NTSC system (525 lines per frame, 30 frames per second) approved by the FCC as the standard for television broadcasting and reception • Legendary guitar maker Les Paul builds the first solid-body electric guitar • RCA demonstrates a new simplified electron microscope that magnifies up to 100,000 times • The radio program *King Biscuit Time* is broadcast for the first time on KFFA in Helena, AR, featuring legendary blues artists Sonny Boy Williamson and Robert Jr. Lockwood [it will go on to become the longest running daily radio broadcast in history and the most famous live blues radio program] • The DuPont Corporation invents Teflon • Motorola manufactures a two-way AM police radio	• The nation's first FM radio station, WSM-FM, begins broadcasting in Nashville • Ted Williams has a major league baseball batting average of .406 (nobody has since hit above .400) • Joe DiMaggio hits safely in 56 straight major league baseball games (a record that still stands) • The First *Wonder Woman* and *Captain America* comic books are printed • The Andrews Sisters have a hit with "Boogie Woogie Bugle Boy" • General Mills starts selling Cheerios cereal (originally named CheeriOats) • Films: Using newly developed film stocks and a wider, faster lens, Orson Welles redefines the medium of the movie with *Citizen Kane*; other notable films include *The Maltese Falcon; How Green Was My Valley; Sergeant York*

E. EDUCATION, LITERATURE & THE FINE ARTS	F. RELIGION, THEOLOGY, PHILOSOPHY & PSYCHOLOGY	G. AMERICAN & UNITED METHODISM	H. BRITISH & WORLD METHODISM	
		– rejects a proposal to extend full clergy rights to women • Each of the six jurisdictions holds its first jurisdictional conference, at which episcopal elections are now held; W. A. C. Hughes and Lorenzo King are the first two bishops elected by the racially segregated Central Jurisdiction • The Southern Methodist Church is established by members of the MECS (primarily in South Carolina, Georgia, and Florida) opposed to reunion with the MEC, which they regard as the "Yankee church" • Some members of the MPC opposed to reunion with the MEC and MECS withdraw to form a new denomination that uses the same name; a larger group establishes the Bible Protestant Church (BPC) • Georgia Harkness becomes professor of applied theology at Garrett Biblical Institute, the first woman to hold such a position in an American theological seminary • The new Methodist Publishing House (MPH) is established in Nashville, consolidating the publishing and bookselling operations of the MC; it adopts the name Abingdon-Cokesbury Press for its trade book publishing department • The MC Woman's Division begins publication of *The Methodist Woman* (to 1968) and produces its first spiritual growth study, *Jesus and Social Redemption*		**1940 cont.**
• The National Gallery of Art in Washington, DC, is officially opened by President Roosevelt • Olivier Messiaen's incredible *Quartet for the End of Time* is composed and first performed while Messiaen is in a German prisoner-of-war camp • Bartók's *String Quartet No. 6* premieres in New York City • Eugene O'Neill's play *A Long Day's Journey into Night*, debuts • Noël Coward's play *Blithe Spirit* premieres in London, satirizing the English upper class • Paul Hindemith publishes his major treatise on musical theory, *The Craft of Musical Composition* • Robert McCloskey publishes his timeless children's classic, *Make Way for Ducklings* • Other notable publications include: – Arthur Koestler, *Darkness at Noon* – James Agee, *Let Us Now Praise Famous Men*	• The Taizé Community, an ecumenical religious order, is established in France by Brother Roger (Roger Schutz) • Reinhold Niebuhr publishes his important study of *The Nature and Destiny of Man* (2 vols., 1941, 1943) • Other notable publications include: – H. Richard Niebuhr, *The Meaning of Revelation* – Charles Hartshorne, *Man's Vision of God and the Logic of Theism* – Dorothy L. Sayers, *The Mind of the Maker*	• The UBC General Conference: – expresses appreciation for the work of the Commission on Church Federation and Union but decides to delay action on the proposed union with the EC until 1945 – passes a resolution supporting both military service and conscientious objection by church members – votes to pursue membership in the World Council of Churches – reestablishes the men's organization the Otterbein Brotherhood • A US Circuit Court decision in South Carolina upholds the legality of the merger that created The Methodist Church against litigation by disaffected members of the former MECS who had formed the Southern Methodist Church in 1940 • Many MC annual conferences, meeting in the summer, pass resolutions opposing US entrance into war; following the December 7th attack on Pearl Harbor, the Council of Bishops issues a statement asserting that Christians now have "no alternative to loyal support of the nation" • The Methodist Publishing House reports net sales of over $5 million • *Motive*, the official magazine of the Methodist Student Movement (1937), begins publication under the auspices of the MC Board of Higher Education (to 1971) • Upper Room Ministries is organized as a division of the MC Board of Discipleship • The MC organizes the Latin American Provisional Conference	• Under government pressure, the Methodist Church of Japan becomes part of the new United Church of Christ in Japan (Nihon Kirisuto Kyodan) along with about 30 other Protestant church bodies; Methodist missionaries from the US and UK are forced to leave Japan	**1941**

	A. WORLD HISTORY & POLITICS	B. AMERICAN HISTORY & POLITICS	C. SCIENCE, MEDICINE & TECHNOLOGY	D. DAILY LIFE, POPULAR CULTURE & ENTERTAINMENT
1942	• The Atlantic Charter is signed by 13 nations in addition to the US and the UK • Japanese forces advance in the South Pacific; the British surrender Singapore • US forces on the Bataan peninsula and Corregidor in the Philippines surrender; over 10,000 die on the resulting Bataan Death March • US bombers led by James Doolittle, launched from an aircraft carrier, make a surprise bombing raid on Tokyo, inflicting little real damage but greatly boosting American morale • The battles of Coral Sea and Midway in the Pacific halt Japanese expansion southward and establish the dominance of naval air power over surface fleets and battleships; the Japanese lose four aircraft carriers at Midway and never fully recover • US Marines invade and capture the island of Guadalcanal, stopping any Japanese advance to the east and providing a US forward base in the Pacific • Erwin Rommel's victory over Bernard Montgomery at El Alamein drives the British out of Libya • US forces land in north Africa to join the British forces in a counterattack against Rommel's Afrika Corp • A renewed German offensive in Russia is halted at Leningrad and Stalingrad • Italy withdraws its forces from Ethiopia and its independence is restored • The Nazis begin mass executions of Jews at Auschwitz and Birkenau; 100,000 Jews from the Warsaw Ghetto are deported to the Treblinka death camp	• President Roosevelt issues an executive order relocating over 120,000 Japanese Americans to internment camps without trial due to suspicions of disloyalty to the US; most are not released until the end of WWII • Women are officially allowed to serve in noncombat roles in all branches of the US military; each service branch creates a female auxiliary or reserve organization for women: WACS (Army), WAVES (Navy), MCWR (Marines), and SPARS (Coast Guard) • A fire at the Coconut Grove nightclub in Boston kills over 500, resulting in new regulations to improve fire safety in nightclubs, restaurants, and similar venues • The Kaiser Foundation Health Plan, America's first health maintenance organization (HMO), begins in California • Congress gives official sanction to the Pledge of Allegiance by including it in the United States Flag Code • The Congress of Racial Equality (CORE) is founded as the Committee of Racial Equality by an interracial group of students in Chicago led by George Houser and James Farmer; many of them are members of the FOR in the US influenced by Gandhi's teachings on nonviolence	• The Grand Coulee Dam on the Columbia River in central Washington, begun in 1931, is completed; it is the largest concrete structure and the largest single producer of electricity in the US • Enrico Fermi produces the first controlled, self-sustaining nuclear chain reaction at the University of Chicago • The Manhattan Project, led by Robert Oppenheimer, is established to coordinate US efforts to build an atomic bomb • Alan Turing and M. H. A. Newman develop the world's first programmable computer, which is used to crack German codes during the war	• Bing Crosby records Irving Berlin's "White Christmas"; it eventually sells over 30 million copies, making it the best-selling single recording of all time • RCA Victor sprays gold paint on a copy of Glenn Miller's million-selling album *Chattanooga Choo Choo*, creating the first "gold record" • Glenn Miller joins the US Army Air Corps; he is appointed Commander of the Army Air Corps Band, which gives more than 800 performances for US servicemen overseas during the next two years • Dizzy Gillespie's recording of "A Night in Tunisia" marks the arrival of Afro-Cuban rhythms in American jazz • CBS and NBC start commercial TV transmission • Films: *Casablanca; Pride of the Yankees; Bambi; Yankee Doodle Dandy*
1943	• President Roosevelt and British Prime Minister Churchill meet at the Casablanca Conference in January; they agree that peace with Germany, Italy, and Japan will require unconditional surrender • British and American victories force Erwin Rommel to retreat from north Africa, leaving behind 90,000 German casualties or prisoners, 500 tanks, and 400 large artillery pieces • Allied troops land on the Italian mainland after conquest of Sicily; Italy surrenders; the Nazis seize Rome • Stalin allows the revival of the Russian Orthodox Church and appointment of a Patriarch to help stimulate resistance to German invasion • The Red Army counteroffensive following the battle of Stalingrad captures 110,000 German prisoners including 24 generals • The balance of air power in Europe shifts to the Allies; massive Allied bombing campaigns devastate German cities and manufacturing facilities • Roosevelt, Churchill, and Stalin meet at the Tehran Conference in November; they agree on plans for an Allied invasion of Europe in 1944; Dwight D. Eisenhower is named Supreme Commander of the Allied Expeditionary Force for that invasion, dubbed "Operation Overlord"	• The Jefferson Memorial is dedicated in Washington, DC, on the 200th anniversary of his birth • The Pentagon is completed and becomes the largest office building in the world • The Chinese Exclusion Acts of 1882 and 1902 are repealed, permitting the immigration and naturalization of Chinese people • The US national debt exceeds $100 billion for the first time	• Successful mass production of penicillin leads to widespread use as medicine and saves countless lives • Selman Waksman (US) isolates streptomycin, the first antibiotic effective in treating tuberculosis and other diseases caused by gram-negative bacteria	• Richard Rodgers and Oscar Hammerstein's *Oklahoma!* opens and changes American musical theater by combining entertainment and serious subjects • Nat "King" Cole has his first real hit with "Straighten Up and Fly Right" • The Grand Ole Opry moves into the Ryman Auditorium in Nashville, which will be its home until it moves to the newly constructed Opry House in 1974 • The American Broadcasting Company (ABC) is created when NBC is broken up during the FCC's monopoly probe into the radio network • Norman Rockwell draws The Four Freedoms cover of *The Saturday Evening Post* • Films: *For Whom the Bell Tolls; The Ox-Bow Incident; Cabin in the Sky* (Hollywood's first general release of an all-black musical)

E. EDUCATION, LITERATURE & THE FINE ARTS	F. RELIGION, THEOLOGY, PHILOSOPHY & PSYCHOLOGY	G. AMERICAN & UNITED METHODISM	H. BRITISH & WORLD METHODISM	
• Wassily Kandinsky's painting *Circle and Square* exemplifies his style of nonrepresentational or "purely abstract" art • Edward Hopper's painting *Nighthawks* depicts the loneliness and isolation of contemporary American life • Piet Mondrian's *Composition with Red, Yellow, and Blue* explores the limits of geometric abstraction, using only a few black lines and well-balanced blocks of color to create a monumental effect • Dmitri Shostakovich's *Symphony No. 7 in C (Leningrad Symphony)* honors Russian resistance against the German invasion of 1941 • Aaron Copland composes his *Fanfare for the Common Man* and *Rodeo* • Benjamin Britten composes *A Ceremony of Carols* • Kodály completes his *Missa Brevis* • Thornton Wilder wins his third Pulitzer for his play *The Skin of Our Teeth* • Other notable publications include: – Marjorie Kinnan Rawlings, *Cross Creek* – Daphne du Maurier, *Frenchman's Creek*	• The British Council of Churches is established; the MC [UK] is one of the founding members • C. S. Lewis publishes his wickedly funny classic *The Screwtape Letters* • Albert Camus publishes *The Stranger*, his novel about the endless search for meaning	• The EC General Conference: – approves a plan from the Commission on Church Federation and Union for union with the UBC and refers it to the annual conferences for ratification – establishes a Board of Church Extension, incorporating the work of the former Bureau of Architecture – adopts the first *Manual of Rituals* for the church, which significantly revises some church rites – authorizes and urges the creation of an Administrative Council in every annual conference – extends the responsibilities of the Secretary of Christian Education by naming him also Secretary of Evangelism (reviving the office that had been abolished in 1930) – approves statements by the Board of Christian Social Action on a range of issues, including condemnation of racial discrimination • The first Assembly of the WSCS and WSG (MC) meets in St. Louis, but when racially integrated accommodations cannot be secured there, it is moved to Columbus, OH • The MC creates the Methodist Youth Fellowship (MYF) by merging the former Epworth League and the Council of Methodist Youth; the MYF holds its first convention in Columbus, OH • The merged men's Brotherhood groups of the MC take the name Methodist Men (MM) • The three separate bilingual conferences (German, Swedish, and Norwegian-Danish) of the MC are dissolved and their churches incorporated into the regular annual conferences • The Fundamental Methodist Church is established by former MPC members in Missouri who withdraw from the MC	• Arthur Wilkes publishes *Mow Cop and the Camp Meeting Movement: Sketches of Primitive Methodism*	**1942**
• Duke Ellington and his orchestra play New York's Carnegie Hall for the first time, indicating his acceptance as a "serious musician," and premiere his musical suite *Black, Brown and Beige* • Aaron Copland composes *A Lincoln Portrait* • Paul Hindemith completes his *Symphonic Metamorphoses of Themes by Carl Maria von Weber* • Benjamin Britten composes his *Serenade for Tenor, Horn and Strings* • Walter Piston completes his *Symphony No. 2* • American artist "Grandma" Moses completes her painting *Sugaring Off* • *The Little Prince* by Antoine de Saint-Exupery is published; it will eventually be translated into more than 100 languages and become the third best-selling book of all time, behind the Bible and *Das Kapital* by Karl Marx • Jean-Paul Sartre's one-act play *No Exit* popularizes his existentialist philosophy: "hell is other people" • Hermann Hesse publishes *The Glass Bead Game (Magister Ludi)*	• Pope Pius XII issues his encyclical *Divino Afflante Spiritu (On Promoting Biblical Studies)*; while appearing to affirm the encyclical *Providentissimus Deus* (issued by Leo XIII in 1893), it allows room for a redefinition of the concept of inerrancy and so opens the door to historical criticism for Roman Catholic biblical scholars • The National Association of Evangelicals (NAE) is established in the US • Jean-Paul Sartre's *Being and Nothingness* provides the philosophical articulation of his existentialist philosophy, holding that recognition of one's absolute freedom of choice is the necessary condition for authentic human existence and that individuals can never escape responsibility for their decisions • Other notable publications include: – C. S. Lewis, *Mere Christianity* – Albert Knudsen, *The Principles of Christian Ethics*	• The MC Council of Bishops adopts the "Crusade for a New World Order" initiated by Bishop G. Bromley Oxnam, which helps set the stage for the formation of the United Nations	• The MC [UK] forms the Methodist Youth Department	**1943**

	A. WORLD HISTORY & POLITICS	B. AMERICAN HISTORY & POLITICS	C. SCIENCE, MEDICINE & TECHNOLOGY	D. DAILY LIFE, POPULAR CULTURE & ENTERTAINMENT
1944	• At the Dumbarton Oaks Conference the US, Britain, and the USSR propose the establishment of the United Nations • The US Army makes an amphibious landing at Anzio and Nettuno, Italy, to circumvent a German-created impasse at Monte Casino • The Allies capture Rome from the German army • The Nazis send 476,000 Hungarian Jews to the death camp at Auschwitz • Allied forces succeed in the "D-Day" landings in Normandy (June) and begin to fight their way across Belgium and France, liberating Paris and forcing the German army back to the Rhine • Germany begins using V-1 rockets to bomb England and Belgium • Germany launches a surprise counter-offensive in Belgium, resulting in the Battle of the Bulge • US naval forces defeat the Japanese at the Battle of the Philippine Sea, putting an effective end to Japan's naval air power • Soviet forces take Poland, then invade Germany from the east • The United Nations Monetary and Financial Conference at Bretton Wood, NH, lays the foundation for the reconstruction of Europe after the war; it establishes both the International Bank for Reconstruction and Development and the International Monetary Fund; both begin operations in 1947 • France grants women the right to vote in national elections • A Dutch informant leads the Gestapo to the area in an Amsterdam warehouse where Jewish diarist Anne Frank and her family have been hiding; they are placed on the last transport train to Auschwitz	• Congress passes the Serviceman's Readjustment Act (the "G.I. Bill of Rights"), which provides a large increase in medical benefits for veterans and enables over 7 million of them to further their education in colleges or trade schools • In *United States v. Ballard*, the US Supreme Court rules that no governmental agency can determine "the truth or falsity of the beliefs or doctrines" of anyone, but also holds that while freedom of belief is absolute, the freedom to act on those beliefs is not • The US Supreme Court bans the practice of "whites-only" primaries in Texas and other states, ruling that primary elections are covered by the 15th Amendment and may not be conducted by closed political parties or private associations • The Ku Klux Klan, in decline since the Great Depression, is formally disbanded • The National Congress of American Indians (NCAI) is founded to foster unity and cooperation among tribal governments for the protection of their treaty and sovereign rights • A fire breaks out during a performance of the Ringling Bros. and Barnum & Bailey circus in Hartford, CT; over 160 people are killed, most of them children • President Roosevelt is reelected for an unprecedented fourth term and Harry S. Truman is elected as vice president (Democratic Party)	• German engineers develop the V-2, the first true guided missile • The world's first undersea oil pipeline is completed between England and France • IBM constructs the first digital program-controlled calculator, the Automatic Sequence Controlled Calculator (better known as the Harvard Mark I) • IBM develops and markets the first typewriter with proportional spacing	• NBC presents the first televised network news broadcast in the US, which at the time is considered a curiosity • Glenn Miller's plane disappears on a flight from London to Paris, apparently crashing into the English Channel; no wreckage is ever found • Thelonius Monk makes his first studio recordings with the Coleman Hawkins Quartet • The Metropolitan Opera House in New York City hosts its first jazz concert, with performances by Louis Armstrong, Benny Goodman, Lionel Hampton, Artie Shaw, Roy Eldridge, and Jack Teagarden • The radio show *The Adventures of Ozzie and Harriet* makes its debut • Films: Frank Sinatra makes his movie debut with the musical *Higher And Higher*; *Going My Way* (featuring Bing Crosby and Ingrid Bergman); *Gaslight*; *Lifeboat*; *Meet Me in St. Louis*; *National Velvet* • Both Summer and Winter Olympics are canceled due to WWII
1945	• US Marines take Iwo Jima and plant the American flag on the summit of Mt. Suribachi • The Soviet Union declares war on Japan and quickly occupies Manchuria and northern Korea • At the Yalta Conference, Britain, France, the US, and the USSR agree to divide Germany, and Berlin, into four sectors, soon to become "western" and "eastern" (Soviet) sectors • Germany falls to Allied armies; the Red Army captures Berlin, and Hitler commits suicide • Japan surrenders to the Allies after the US drops atomic bombs on Hiroshima and Nagasaki • The Korean peninsula is divided into northern (Russian) and southern (US) zones of occupation along 38th parallel • The private humanitarian organization CARE is established to provide relief to survivors of WWII; it grows to become one of the largest such organizations in the world • The United Nations is organized, succeeding the League of Nations; Trygve Lie (Norway) is elected Secretary-General; the five permanent members of the UN Security Council are the US, the USSR, Britain, France, and China • Winston Churchill's Conservative Party loses the British elections; Clement Attlee becomes British Prime Minister	• President Roosevelt dies, and the entire country sits by the radio to attend his funeral; Vice President Truman becomes president • Congress officially recognizes the "Pledge of Allegiance" • Navajo Indian "code talkers" become famous in the Pacific theater, using their native language to send communications that the Japanese cannot understand • Edward R. Murrow's radio reports on the liberation of Buchenwald grip the nation • President Truman makes the difficult decision to authorize use of the newly developed atomic bomb on Japan in an effort to end the war quickly • The US national debt surpasses $250 billion • A B-25 bomber crashes into the Empire State Building, damaging the 78th and 79th floors and killing 13	• The US successfully tests the world's first nuclear weapon, the atomic bomb, in New Mexico • Arthur Clarke envisions geosynchronous communication satellites in a *Wireless World* magazine article • US Army Capt. John Mullin "liberates" two German tape recorders and starts a US industry • The Klipschorn "folded horn" speaker design dramatically improves the reproduction of recorded sound • Percy Spencer, a scientist with the Raytheon company, accidentally discovers that microwaves can heat food, leading to the invention of the microwave oven, which Raytheon brings to market in 1947 • Grand Rapids, MI, and Newburgh, NY, become the first US cities to add fluoride to drinking water to help prevent tooth decay • Grace Hopper discovers the first computer "bug," a real moth lodged in a relay of the Harvard Mark II computer; the term sticks	• Richard Rodgers and Oscar Hammerstein have another Broadway smash with *Carousel* • Jazz artist Charlie Parker records "Koko," a song that almost single-handedly gives rise to bebop jazz • Miles Davis joins Charlie Parker's Quintet and makes his own earliest jazz recordings • "Sassy" Sarah Vaughn establishes her reputation as a leading jazz singer with her recording of "Lover," performed with Dizzie Gillespie and Charlie Parker • Doris Day sings "Sentimental Journey" with the Les Brown Band, establishing her career as a popular vocalist • Earl W. Tupper invents resealable food containers, known as "Tupperware" • The metal spring toy called the "Slinky" makes its debut at Gimbel's Department Store in Philadelphia • John Johnson founds *Ebony*, the first magazine aimed at a black audience • Films: *The Lost Weekend*; *Spellbound*; *The Picture of Dorian Gray*

E. EDUCATION, LITERATURE & THE FINE ARTS	F. RELIGION, THEOLOGY, PHILOSOPHY & PSYCHOLOGY	G. AMERICAN & UNITED METHODISM	H. BRITISH & WORLD METHODISM	
• The United Negro College Fund is established to help promote the education of blacks in the US • Bartók's *Concerto for Orchestra* is performed for the first time by the Boston Symphony Orchestra conducted by Sergey Koussevitzky • Aaron Copland composes his *Appalachian Spring* dance suite for Martha Graham's dance company; the original title was "Ballet for Martha" • Leonard Bernstein completes his ballet *Fancy Free* • Prokofiev composes his opera *War and Peace* • David Diamond creates *Rounds* for string orchestra; it is his most popular composition • Ansel Adams publishes his photograph "Mount Williamson—Clearing Storm" • Notable publications include: – W. Somerset Maugham, *The Razor's Edge* – T. S. Eliot, *Four Quartets* – Tennessee Williams, *The Glass Menagerie*	• Notable publications include: – Jean-Paul Sartre, *No Exit* – Reinhold Niebuhr, *The Children of Light and the Children of Darkness* – John R. Mott, *The Larger Evangelism*	• The MC General Conference: – approves the "Crusade for Christ" as the church's first quadrennial campaign (1944–48); it raises more than $27 million to support postwar reconstruction and missionary programs, and adds 1 million members to church roles – again rejects a proposal to extend full clergy rights to women – organizes the Philippines Central Conference – makes Liberia part of the Central Jurisdiction – approves publication of the new *Book of Worship* • The AMEC General Conference merges all the women's missionary groups of the church into one body, the Women's Missionary Society • The EC organizes the Christian Service Guild for employed women • Phillips School of Theology is established by the Board of Trustees of Lane College in Jackson, TN	• The Nazarene Theological College in Manchester, England, opens for classes	1944
• The *Adagio in G Minor* of Italian composer Thomaso Albinoni (d. 1751) is reconstructed by Italian musicologist Remo Giazotto from a fragmentary manuscript found in the ruins of Dresden State Library • Benjamin Britten's opera *Peter Grimes* premieres in London, signaling the rebirth of British opera • Igor Stravinsky composes his *Symphony in Three Movements* • Marc Chagall designs the backdrops and costumes for a New York production of Igor Stravinsky's ballet *The Firebird* • Tennessee Williams's play of shattered hope, *The Glass Menagerie*, opens on Broadway • Richard Wright publishes his searing coming-of-age novel, *Black Boy* • Other notable publications include: – George Orwell, *Animal Farm*, his satire of the Russian Revolution set in a barnyard – Evelyn Waugh, *Brideshead Revisited* – James Thurber, *The Thurber Carnival* – John Steinbeck, *Cannery Row*	• Dietrich Bonhoeffer is executed by the Nazis in Germany after a failed attempt to assassinate Hitler • The Nag Hammadi papyri (a collection of 13 codices of Gnostic scriptures and commentaries written in the 2nd or 3rd century) are discovered in Egypt • Notable publications include: – Maurice Merleau-Ponty, *The Phenomenology of Perception* – Jean-Paul Sartre, *The Age of Reason*	• The UBC General Conference: – approves a plan from the Commission on Church Federation and Union for union with the EC and refers it to the annual conferences for ratification – receives reports that three major church agencies (Otterbein Press, Bonebrake Seminary, and the Otterbein Home) have all liquidated their indebtedness • The MC Board of Missions and Church Extension holds its first annual meeting • The MC organizes the California Oriental Provisional Conference, superseding California Oriental Mission • In appreciation for a series of large gifts from Joe J. Perkins and Lois Craddock Perkins of Wichita Falls, TX, the Southern Methodist University School of Theology is renamed as the Perkins School of Theology	• The MC [UK] amalgamates Hartley College and Victoria Park College to form Hartley-Victoria College in Manchester • The MC forms the Southeastern Asia Provisional Central Conference • A. W. Harrison, *The Separation of Methodism from the Church of England*	1945

	A. WORLD HISTORY & POLITICS	B. AMERICAN HISTORY & POLITICS	C. SCIENCE, MEDICINE & TECHNOLOGY	D. DAILY LIFE, POPULAR CULTURE & ENTERTAINMENT
1946	• The League of Nations transfers its functions to the UN and is disbanded • The Philippines, a United States protectorate, gains its independence • Winston Churchill gives his famous "Iron Curtain" speech, which marks the symbolic beginning of the Cold War between the western powers, primarily the US and Britain, and the Soviet Union (and later the People's Republic of China) • International Military Tribunal announces its verdicts at the Nuremberg war crimes trial • Japanese Emperor Hirohito renounces the theory of Japanese Imperial divinity and becomes a ceremonial head of state without much real power • Israeli extremists blow up British Headquarters at the King David Hotel, in Jerusalem, killing 91, including guests • Juan Perón wins Argentina's presidential election • The Vietminh launch a revolution directed against French colonial control of Indochina • Italy and Japan grant women the right to vote in national elections	• Construction of the perfect postwar American suburb begins—the planned community of Levittown, NY; when completed in 1951 it will consist of over 17,000 single-family homes, all built using standard designs and prefabricated construction techniques, along with stores, schools, parks, and churches • A tsunami caused by a strong earthquake centered near the Aleutian Islands off Alaska strikes Hawaii with 35-foot waves without warning and kills over 170 people; this prompts the establishment of the Pacific Tsunami Warning System, administered by the National Oceanic and Atmospheric Administration (NOAA) • In *Morgan vs. Virginia*, the US Supreme Court strikes down state laws that sanction segregated facilities in interstate travel by train and bus • The US adopts a nationwide telephone numbering plan • The US Atomic Energy Commission is established • Mobster Bugsy Siegal builds the Flamingo Hotel in Las Vegas, NV, beginning the development of "Sin City" as a gambling and entertainment mecca	• The University of Pennsylvania creates the ENIAC computer, containing 18,000 vacuum tubes; it uses a punched card reader as its input and output device • The US Army Signal Corps reports bouncing a radar signal off the moon and getting an echo • RCA and NBC demonstrate rival color television systems • Zoomar introduces the camera zoom lens, the invention of American Frank Back • The Photon, the first practical phototypesetting machine, is created in France by Louis Marius Moyroud and Rene Alphonse Higgonet • Vincent du Vigneaud (US) synthesizes penicillin	• Kathleen Casey, born in Philadelphia at 12:01 a.m. on January 1st, becomes the first member of the postwar "baby boom" • Benjamin Spock publishes *The Common Sense Book of Baby and Child Care*, which establishes the mode of parenting for the "baby boom" generation • Irving Berlin's *Annie Get Your Gun* opens on Broadway • Chet Atkins makes his first appearance on the Grand Ole Opry as a member of Red Foley's band and makes his first solo recording, "Guitar Blues" • Bill Monroe records "Blue Moon of Kentucky" for the first time • Frank Sinatra records "September Song" • The first US Women's Open golf tournament is won by Patty Berg • Procter & Gamble introduces Tide, the first synthetic laundry detergent • The Cannes Film Festival is held for the first time in France • Italian inventor Achilles Gaggia perfects his espresso machine • S. Truett Cathy serves the first Chick-fil-A sandwich at his restaurant in south Atlanta • The two-piece women's bathing suit called the "bikini" makes its debut at a fashion show in Paris • A branch of the Exchange National Bank in Chicago opens the first ten drive-up teller windows • The National Convention of the YWCA adopts an Interracial Charter committing it to the desegregation of its programs and facilities • Films: *It's a Wonderful Life; The Best Years of Our Lives; The Yearling; The Razor's Edge; My Darling Clementine*
1947	• Peace treaties for Italy, Romania, Bulgaria, Hungary, and Finland are signed in Paris • India and Pakistan are created as independent states within the British Commonwealth, with mainly Hindu areas allocated to India and mainly Muslim areas to Pakistan; Jawaharlal Nehru becomes the first prime minister of India, Liaquat Ali Khan becomes first prime minister of Pakistan • Competition over the disputed territory of Kashmir leads to the first war between India and Pakistan; Mahatma Gandhi pleads unsuccessfully for peace • Mao Zedong's Red Army gains the upper hand on the Nationalists in China and seizes control of Manchuria • Communists seize power by coup d'état in Hungary • The UN General Assembly votes to partition Palestine into Jewish and Arab states *(cont.)*	• President Truman's State of the Union address is the first to be televised • US Secretary of State George C. Marshall outlines the European Recovery Program, an aid program for European nations that later comes to be known as "The Marshall Plan" • President Truman proclaims the Truman Doctrine against the spread of communism, stating that the US would support "free peoples who are resisting attempted subjugation by armed minorities or by outside pressures" • Congress passes the Taft-Hartley Act to curb the power of labor unions • The National Security Act of 1947 authorizes the creation of new institutions of foreign policy and intelligence, including the National Security Council and the Central Intelligence Agency • The Army Air Corp (1922) is transformed into the US Air Force and establishes a separate and equal element of the US armed forces	• Edwin H. Land demonstrates the first "instant camera," the Polaroid Land Camera, to a meeting of the Optical Society of America; it can produce a developed photographic image in sixty seconds • Reynolds Metals Co. uses surplus aluminum from WWII to make Reynolds Wrap aluminum foil • Willard F. Libby (US) develops the carbon-14 method of radiocarbon dating • Norwegian adventurer Thor Heyerdahl makes a 101-day, 4,300-mile journey across the Pacific in the balsa wood raft Kon-Tiki, proving that sailors from South America could have reached Polynesia • The X-1 rocket plane piloted by Chuck Yeager breaks the sound barrier for the first time	• Jazz artist Charlie Parker records "Cool Blues," helping establish the popular usage of "cool" • *Meet the Press* debuts on NBC; the first news show, it will become television's longest-running program • Jackie Robinson of the Brooklyn Dodgers cracks the "color barrier" and becomes the first black player in the history of Major League Baseball • The New York Yankees beat the Brooklyn Dodgers in seven games in the first televised World Series • The Philadelphia Warriors win the first championship of the Basketball Association of America (BAA), which was organized in 1946 [it later becomes the National Basketball Association (NBA) in 1949] • French fashion designer Christian Dior introduces the feminine "New Look" in women's clothes, featuring full skirts and tight waists, in sharp contrast to the *(cont.)*

E. EDUCATION, LITERATURE & THE FINE ARTS	F. RELIGION, THEOLOGY, PHILOSOPHY & PSYCHOLOGY	G. AMERICAN & UNITED METHODISM	H. BRITISH & WORLD METHODISM	
• George Balanchine and Lincoln Kirstein establish the New York City Ballet; it moves to Lincoln Center in 1964 • Benjamin Britten composes and writes *A Young Person's Guide to the Orchestra* • Erich Korngold composes his *Cello Concerto* • Robert Penn Warren publishes *All the King's Men* (which wins the Pulitzer Prize in 1947) • Eugene O'Neill writes his memorable play *The Iceman Cometh*	• The New Testament of The Revised Standard Version of the Bible (RSV) is published; the OT follows in 1952, the Apocrypha in 1957 • The United Bible Societies (UBS) organization is established • The Norwegian Lutheran Church of America (NLCA) becomes the Evangelical Lutheran Church (ELC) • Notable publications include: – Erich Auerbach, *Mimesis* – Bertrand Russell, *History of Western Philosophy* – Harry Nelson Wieman, *The Source of Human Good* – Mary R. Beard, *Woman as Force in History: A Study in Traditions and Realities*	• The General Conferences of the EC (1922) and the UBC (1800) meet together in special session to unite in the formation of the Evangelical United Brethren Church (EUBC) • The EUBC General Conference meets for the first time: – approves a revised *Discipline*, Articles of Faith, and Ritual for the new church – restructures the boards and agencies of the EC and UBC for the new church – denies clergy rights and conference membership to women, despite the fact that women had been ordained by the UBC since 1889; UBC women who are ordained elders at the time are allowed to continue in that capacity – merges the separate women's organizations of the EC and UBC to create the Women's Society of World Service (WSWS); the Christian Service Guild remains a separate entity until 1958 – merges the men's groups—the Otterbein Brotherhood (EC) and the Albright Brotherhood (UBC)—to form the Brotherhood of the EUBC – creates a Youth Fellowship organization for young people – decides to consolidate the two publishing house operations • The Evangelical Methodist Church (EMC) is established in Memphis, TN, "to preserve the distinctive Biblical doctrines of primitive Methodism"; it is committed to the principles of "congregational connectionalism" and "evangelistic passion" • Methodist layman John R. Mott is awarded the Nobel Peace Prize • The Order of St. Luke, a liturgical and sacramental fellowship, is organized • The second Assembly of the WSCS and WSG (MC) meets • Notable publications include: – William R. Cannon, *The Theology of John Wesley, With Special Reference to the Doctrine of Justification* – Harald Lindström, *Wesley and Sanctification*	• The United Andean Indian Mission (UAIM) is established in Bolivia, Ecuador, and Peru as a cooperative effort by American Methodists and Presbyterians (both north and south) along with the UCC • Ministerial interchanges are initiated between British and American Methodist churches • British and American Methodist missions in Italy are combined to form the Chiesia Evangelica Metodista d'Italia (Evangelical Methodist Church of Italy), which remains a district of the British Methodist Church (until 1962) • The inaugural meeting of the United Nations is held in Westminster Central Hall, London • Union Theological Seminary is founded in Matanzas, Cuba, by the Methodist and Presbyterian churches in Cuba • Disaffected evangelicals in Australia withdraw from the MCA (1902) to form the Wesleyan Methodist Church of Australia	**1946**
• Paul Hindemith composes *When Lilacs Last in the Dooryard Bloom'd (Requiem for Those We Love)* for chorus and orchestra, based on the poem by Walt Whitman • Maurice Durufle completes his *Requiem* • Samuel Barber composes *Knoxville: Summer of 1915* • Charles Ives creates the final version of his *Piano Sonata No. 2, Concord, Mass., 1840–60 (Concord Sonata)* • Tennessee Williams's great play *A Streetcar Named Desire* opens on Broadway, starring Marlon Brando and Jessica Tandy; it wins the 1948 Pulitzer Prize • Anne Frank's diary is discovered by family friends in the warehouse in Amsterdam where she had hidden from the Nazis with her family for two years; it is posthumously published as *The Diary of a Young Girl*, is translated into more than 50 languages, and becomes the most widely read diary of the Holocaust	• The first of the Dead Sea Scrolls are discovered in caves near Qumran on the Dead Sea; by 1960, the remains of more than 750 documents are found • Oral Roberts launches his healing ministry with his first citywide campaign in Enid, OK • Fuller Theological Seminary is established in Pasadena, CA, with the vision of reforming Christian evangelicalism from its anti-intellectualism and social isolationism [it is now the largest multidenominational Christian seminary in the world] • The Lutheran World Federation meets for the first time in Lund, Sweden • The Conservative Baptist Association is established by fundamentalists who leave the Northern Baptist Convention following disputes over scriptural interpretation and theology; it does not consider itself a denomination, although it functions as one	• The Methodist Youth Conference in Cleveland has an attendance of over 10,000 young people • The Rural Life Convocation in Lincoln, NE, brings together 2,100 representatives to discuss the rural church and the economic basis of country life • The CMEC Women's Missionary Council begins holding quadrennial meetings • The Wesleyan Methodist Connexion (WMC, 1843) formally changes its name to the Wesleyan Methodist Church (WMC) • The WSWS (EUBC) begins publication of *World Evangel* (to 1968)	• The seventh Ecumenical Methodist Conference meets in Springfield, MA; it creates an Ecumenical Methodist Council that attempts to challenge Anglo-American domination by decentralizing world Methodism into 24 regional sections along geographic lines • The South India Province of the British Methodist Church unites with Anglicans, Presbyterians, and Congregationalists to form the Church of South India; groups related to American Methodism decline to join • The International Methodist Historical Society is established • Notable publications include W. E. Sangster, *Methodism: Her Unfinished Task*	**1947**

	A. WORLD HISTORY & POLITICS	B. AMERICAN HISTORY & POLITICS	C. SCIENCE, MEDICINE & TECHNOLOGY	D. DAILY LIFE, POPULAR CULTURE & ENTERTAINMENT
1947 cont.	with Jerusalem to be jointly occupied under UN trusteeship • The United Nations Children's Emergency Fund (UNICEF) is established • China and Argentina grant women the right to vote in national elections	• CORE and FOR sponsor the first "Freedom Ride," sending eight white and eight black men into the South to test the 1946 Supreme Court decision declaring segregation in interstate travel to be unconstitutional; this "Journey of Reconciliation" results in national attention when four of the riders are arrested in North Carolina and forced to work on a chain gang • Supreme Court Justice Hugo Black uses Thomas Jefferson's argument for a "wall of separation between church and state" as the basis for his interpretation of the establishment clause of the 1st Amendment in the case of *Everson v. Board of Education*, writing that "Neither a state nor the federal government can set up a church. . . . Neither can pass laws which aid one religion, aid all religions, or prefer one religion over another"		"practical" wartime styles, and Paris takes on international preeminence as a center of fashion • Alan Jay Lerner and Frederick Loewe's musical *Brigadoon* opens on Broadway • The children's TV program *Howdy Doody* starts a 13-year run • Films: *Gentleman's Agreement*; *Miracle on 34th Street*; *The Farmer's Daughter*; *Out of the Past*
1948	• The British Mandate in Palestine expires and British troops are withdrawn from Jerusalem; Jewish nationalists led by David Ben-Gurion declare the independence of the state of Israel; the new nation is quickly recognized by Britain, the US, and the USSR; Ben-Gurion is its first prime minister • War breaks out in the Middle East when five Arab states (Egypt, Syria, Jordan, Lebanon, and Iraq) attack Israel; they are soon defeated by the new Israeli army; an estimated 750,000 Palestinian Arabs flee from Israel and become refugees in those Arab states • Communists seize power in Czechoslovakia through a military coup d'état • The USSR blockades West Berlin; The US begins the round-the-clock Berlin Airlift to keep the city supplied • The divided portions of Korea are granted independence; in the south, Syngman Rhee becomes president of the Republic of Korea [South Korea]; in the north, Kim Il Sung becomes prime minister of the People's Democratic Republic of Korea [North Korea] • The UN General Assembly adopts the Universal Declaration of Human Rights as "a common standard of achievement for all peoples and all nations" • Mahatma Gandhi is assassinated in New Delhi by an extreme Hindu nationalist; the world mourns his death • The World Health Organization (WHO) and the General Agreement on Tariffs and Trade (GATT) are established under UN auspices • Ceylon (Sri Lanka) achieves independence and membership in the British Commonwealth • The Organization of American States (OAS) Charter is signed at Bogotá, Colombia • The United States of Indonesia is established as Dutch and Indonesian residents settle a prolonged conflict • Israel and South Korea grant women the right to vote in national elections	• President Truman issues an executive order banning racial segregation in federal employment, including all US military forces • The Hollywood Ten, a group of writers, producers, and directors called as witnesses in the House Committee's Investigation of Un-American Activities, are jailed for contempt of Congress when they refuse to disclose if they were or were not Communists • In *McCollum v. Board of Education*, the US Supreme Court finds religious instruction in public schools to be a violation of the establishment clause of the 1st Amendment and therefore unconstitutional • The States' Rights Democratic Party, known as the "Dixiecrats," led by South Carolina Gov. Strom Thurmond, splits from the Democratic Party and runs a third-party campaign; its platform opposes racial integration and wants to retain Jim Crow laws and racial segregation • Thurmond and his running mate, Mississippi governor Fielding L. Wright, carry the previously solid Democratic states of Louisiana, Mississippi, Alabama, and South Carolina, and almost deny the election to Truman • In one of the closest votes ever, Truman is elected president (having served the final 3+ years of Roosevelt's fourth term) and Alben W. Barkley as vice president (Democratic Party) • The Dixiecrats disband after the election; key leaders such as Strom Thurmond and Jessie Helms switch to the Republican Party	• The United Nations establishes the World Health Organization (WHO) • Researchers at Bell Labs invent the transistor, a solid-state electronic device consisting of a tiny piece of semiconducting material, which soon replaces the vacuum tube • Alfred Kinsey publishes *Sexual Behavior in the Human Male* (followed by *Sexual Behavior in the Human Female* in 1953) • Joseph Zimmerman Jr. creates the first telephone answering machine • George Gamow (US) puts forth the "Big Bang" theory to explain the origin of the universe • Margaret Sanger founds the International Planned Parenthood Federation	• *The Ed Sullivan Show* is broadcast for the first time (it lasts until 1971, becoming TV's longest-running variety show) • Community Antenna Television (CATV), the forerunner to cable TV, begins service • Cole Porter's Shakespearean musical, *Kiss Me Kate*, opens on Broadway • Earl Scruggs establishes the five-string banjo as a lead instrument in bluegrass music with his classic "Foggy Mountain Breakdown" • Nat "King" Cole becomes the first black singer and musician to have his own radio show • Fred Morrison creates a plastic flying disc called the Pluto Platter that becomes the basic pattern for all later Frisbees; he receives a patent for his design in 1956 • James Brunot buys the rights to a word game from its inventor Alfred M. Butts, refines the rules, changes the design, and brings Scrabble to the world • Columbia Records introduces the 33-1/3 rpm LP ("long playing") record album, which holds 25 minutes of music per side, compared to the four minutes per side of the 78 rpm record • Patti Page becomes the first artist to use the recording technique of multitrack overdubbing • Leo Fender debuts his first solid-bodied electric guitar, the Broadcaster • Perry Como hosts his first televised "Christmas Special" • Films: *Hamlet* (with Laurence Olivier); *The Treasure of the Sierra Madre*; *Red River*; *Unfaithfully Yours* • Summer Olympics: London • Winter Olympics: St. Moritz

E. EDUCATION, LITERATURE & THE FINE ARTS	F. RELIGION, THEOLOGY, PHILOSOPHY & PSYCHOLOGY	G. AMERICAN & UNITED METHODISM	H. BRITISH & WORLD METHODISM	
• Matisse publishes *Jazz*, an album of paper cutout compositions • Other notable publications include: – James Michener, *Tales of the South Pacific* – John Steinbeck, *The Pearl*	• Karl Barth returns to the faculty of the University of Bonn and gives a series of lectures, published as *Dogmatik im Grundriss* (English translation: *Dogmatics in Outline*); he also publishes *Die protestantische Theologie 19.Jahrundert* (English translation: *Protestant Theology in the Nineteenth Century*), which he had originally given as lectures at Münster in 1925 • Other notable publications include: – Theodor Adorno and Max Horkheimer, *Dialectic of Enlightenment* – Joachim Jeremias, *The Parables of Jesus* – Georgia Harkness, *Understanding the Christian Faith* – Carl F. H. Henry, *The Uneasy Conscience of Modern Fundamentalism*			**1947 cont.**
• The Aldeburgh Festival is founded in England by Benjamin Britten, Eric Crozier, and Peter Pears • Igor Stravinsky completes his *Mass* for chorus and double wind quintet • John Cage creates his *Suite for Toy Piano* • Elliott Carter composes his *Cello Sonata* • Andrew Wyeth completes his best-known painting, *Christina's World*, depicting a young neighbor unable to walk because of a childhood case of polio • Notable publications include: – Norman Mailer, *The Naked and the Dead* – Graham Greene, *The Heart of the Matter* – Alan Paton, *Cry, the Beloved Country* – W. H. Auden, *The Age of Anxiety* – Albert Camus, *The Plague*	• Communist governments in Eastern Europe begin to obstruct and persecute the church, conducting show trials of several prominent bishops • The World Council of Churches (WCC) is established, bringing together the Life and Work and the Faith and Order movements with the International Missionary Council; W. A. Visser 't Hooft (Netherlands Reformed Church) is named as the first general secretary • Rudolf Bultmann begins publication of his influential *Theology of the New Testament* (2 vols. 1948–53; English translation 1951–55) • Martin Noth publishes his *History of Pentateuchal Traditions* • Other notable publications include: – Paul Tillich, *The Protestant Era* – Charles Hartshorne, *The Divine Relativity* – Thomas Merton, *The Seven Storey Mountain* – Bertrand Russell, *Human Knowledge: Its Scope and Limits* – Georgia Harkness, *Prayer and the Common Life*	• The MC General Conference: – approves "The Advance for Christ and His Church" as the church's quadrennial campaign; goal is to increase giving by one-third to support the work of the Board of Missions and the Methodist Committee on Overseas Relief (MCOR) – establishes Commission on the Structure of Methodism Overseas (COSMOS) as replacement for Commission on Central Conferences – creates a Commission on Chaplaincy – institutes a plan for certification of Directors of Christian Education – launches a campaign for total abstinence pledges from church members – forms a Structure Study Commission to study its various boards, agencies, and commissions, with a view to eliminating duplication and achieving more efficient and economical operations – reorganizes the Southwest Mexican Conference as the Rio Grande Conference – again rejects a proposal to extend full clergy rights to women • The MC Council of Bishops objects strenuously to charges made in a report of the Congressional Committee on Un-American Activities about the "Communistic proclivities" of Methodist bishops and organizations, including the Methodist Federation for Social Action • The MC Central Jurisdiction Conference forms a committee to study ways of eliminating the jurisdiction • The EUBC becomes the first American church body to join the newly established World Council of Churches	• Sia'atoutai Theological College is established by the Free Wesleyan Church of Tonga • The Evangelical Methodist Church (EMC) in the Philippines becomes an autonomous affiliate of the MC	**1948**

	A. WORLD HISTORY & POLITICS	B. AMERICAN HISTORY & POLITICS	C. SCIENCE, MEDICINE & TECHNOLOGY	D. DAILY LIFE, POPULAR CULTURE & ENTERTAINMENT
1949	• The Soviet Union lifts its blockade of West Berlin, marking the end of the Berlin Airlift • The North Atlantic Treaty Organization (NATO) is established: members are Belgium, Canada, Denmark, France, Great Britain, Iceland, Italy, Luxembourg, the Netherlands, Norway, Portugal, and the US • The People's Republic of China (PRC) is formally established, with its capital at Beijing; Mao Zedong is Chairman of the Communist Party; Zhou Enlai heads the new government as prime minister • Chiang Kai-shek and his Nationalist supporters flee from mainland China to the island of Formosa (Taiwan); Chiang claims that the Republic of China (ROC) is the only legitimate government of China; neither the US nor the United Nations recognize the legitimacy of the PRC • Israel and Arab states agree to an armistice; Israel controls about 50% more territory than was originally allotted to it by the 1947 UN Partition Plan • India, Indonesia, and Chile grant women the right to vote in national elections • The Republic of Ireland is formally established and withdraws from the British Commonwealth; Northern Ireland remains part of the UK • Konrad Adenauer becomes chancellor of Germany • The first three Geneva Conventions (1864, 1906, and 1929) are revised and a fourth convention concerning the treatment of civilians during times of war and under occupation is added; it is signed by 190 nations	• President Truman proposes his "Point Four" program, an American foreign-aid project aimed at providing technological skills, knowledge, and equipment to poor nations throughout the world • Congress formally designates June 14th of each year as National Flag Day • Eleven leaders of the US Communist Party are found guilty of conspiring to overthrow the US government under the 1940 Smith Act and sentenced to long prison terms • Alger Hiss, a former US State Dept. official who had been accused of being a Communist spy by news writer Whittaker Chambers in 1948, is convicted on two counts of perjury • The permanent headquarters of the United Nations is established in New York City	• The Soviet Union detonates its first atomic bomb, marking the beginning of the arms race between the US and the USSR • The Electronic Delay Storage Automatic Calculator (EDSAC) developed at Cambridge University is one of the first computers to store programs in its internal memory • The "Whirlwind" computer at MIT is the first computer to operate in real time and use a video display for its output • B-50 Superfortress *Lucky Lady II* lands in Fort Worth, TX, after completing the first non-stop around-the-world flight	• Richard Rodgers and Oscar Hammerstein's Pulitzer Prize-winning *South Pacific* opens on Broadway • Hank Williams records "I'm So Lonesome I Could Cry" and makes his first appearance on the Grand Ole Opry • B. B. King makes his first blues recordings with his legendary guitar "Lucille" • Gene Autry makes "Rudolph, the Red-Nosed Reindeer" part of America's Christmas tradition • *The Goldbergs*, the first sitcom on American television, is broadcast for the first time • Procter & Gamble introduces Joy, the first synthetic dishwashing liquid • The interlocking LEGO plastic building blocks make their first appearance • The first 45 rpm "single" records are sold in the US; using the same needle as 33-1/3 LP records, they hold about 5 minutes of music per side and become very popular in jukeboxes • Films: *All the King's Men; Twelve O'Clock High; Battleground; The Third Man; White Heat*
1950	• The USSR and China form an alliance against the US and other major powers of the Western world • The Korean War, the first armed confrontation of the Cold War period, begins with a surprise attack by North Korean forces using Soviet equipment in June; in October, troops from China join the battle against US and UN forces • The US formally recognizes the government of Vietnam and quietly begins providing it with military aid and "advisors" • Passage of the Group Areas Act marks the formal establishment of *apartheid* in South Africa • The Knesset in Israel passes the Law of Return, which grants all Jews living anywhere in the world the right to immigrate to Israel • Prime ministers of the British Commonwealth issue the London Declaration, stating that the Commonwealth is based on mutual recognition of the British monarch as a symbol of their association rather than on common allegiance to the British monarch as head of state • The Council of Europe adopts the Convention for the Protection of Human Rights and Fundamental Freedoms and establishes the European Court of Human Rights to enforce it	• The US census reports that the population is 150,697,361: – whites: 134,942,028 (89.5%) – blacks: 15,042,286 (10.0%) – other: 713,047 (0.5%) • The US national debt is $257,357,352,351 • The FCC promulgates the "Fairness Doctrine," requiring broadcasters to cover important controversial issues and to provide an opportunity for contrasting views on those issues • The "Storm of the Century" in the eastern US generates heavy snow and hurricane-force winds across 22 states and claims 383 lives; damages are estimated at $70 million • The FBI begins its "Ten Most Wanted" campaign to enlist the public in identifying and locating criminals • Two Puerto Rican nationalists fail in an attempt to assassinate President Truman • The NAACP Legal Defense Fund begins a campaign against the legal doctrine that supports "separate but equal" public schools for black and white children • In *Sweatt v. Painter*, the Supreme Court rules that segregated law schools in Texas are unconstitutional, since a newly-formed black law school did not provide the same benefits to its students as the state's prestigious white law school, thus failing the "separate but equal" test	• Grace Hopper (Harvard University) develops Flow-Matic, the first computer programming language and compiler to use ordinary English words, marking a step toward COBOL (1959) • The Kodak Colorama, at the time the world's largest photograph, is exhibited at Grand Central Station; it is 18 feet wide x 60 feet high • The FCC authorizes CBS to begin commercial color TV broadcasts • Xerox photocopiers roll off the assembly line; the term *Xerox* becomes a popularly used synonym for *photocopy* • David C. Schilling (USAF) makes the first nonstop transatlantic jet flight • Richard Lawler (US) performs the first successful kidney transplant at Loyola University	• Charles Schulz introduces the *Peanuts* comic strip • *Guys and Dolls* debuts at the 46th Street Theatre; it becomes one of Broadway's longest-running shows, with 1,200 performances in 3 years • Pete Seeger has a major hit with his version of "Goodnight, Irene," first performed in the 1930s by Leadbelly • Nat "King" Cole records his memorable "Mona Lisa" • Patti Page has a huge hit with "The Tennessee Waltz" and becomes the first (and only) artist to have a no. 1 record on the Pop, R&B, and Country charts concurrently • The game show *Truth or Consequences* debuts on television • The first TV remote control, Zenith Radio's "Lazy Bones," appears • The US Post Office cuts residential postal deliveries from twice to once a day • Diner's Club pioneers the first "universal" credit card that could be used in a variety of establishments • Films: Akira Kurosawa's *Rashomon* marks a breakthrough for foreign films; *Sunset Boulevard; All About Eve; Cinderella; King Solomon's Mines; Broken Arrow*

E. EDUCATION, LITERATURE & THE FINE ARTS	F. RELIGION, THEOLOGY, PHILOSOPHY & PSYCHOLOGY	G. AMERICAN & UNITED METHODISM	H. BRITISH & WORLD METHODISM	
• Olivier Messiaen's *Turangalila Symphony*, commissioned by the Boston Symphony Orchestra, premieres under the baton of Leonard Bernstein • Edgar Varèse composes his *Dance for Burgess* • George Crumb completes his *Sonata for Violin and Piano* • Arthur Miller's great play *Death of a Salesman*, featuring the unforgettable Willy Loman, is a milestone in American drama, winning the Pulitzer Prize, the Tony Award, and the New York Drama Critics' Circle Award • Simone de Beauvoir publishes *The Second Sex*, which becomes a classic text of the feminist movement • Other notable publications include: – George Orwell, *1984* – Ralph Ellison, *Invisible Man* – Nancy Mitford, *Love in a Cold Climate*	• Billy Graham holds the first of his urban evangelistic crusades in Los Angeles • After the establishment of Communism in China, most western missionaries are expelled • Communist governments in Eastern Europe begin to obstruct the work of Christian churches and persecute church leaders, as exemplified in the trial of Cardinal Mindszenty in Hungary • Dietrich Bonhoeffer's *Ethics* is published posthumously • Simone de Beauvoir's *The Second Sex* becomes one of the foundational texts for the women's liberation movement • Other notable publications include: – Howard Thurman, *Jesus and the Disinherited* – Reinhold Niebuhr, *Faith and History* – Joseph Campbell, *The Hero with a Thousand Faces*	• The MC Structure Study Commission begins its work • The Foundation for Evangelism is incorporated; the founders include Harry Denman, the General Secretary of the General Board of Evangelism of the MC and dedicated group supporters who want to directly support evangelism ministries within The Methodist Church; the Foundation is formally organized in 1950 • The Upper Room Fellowship is established to respond to prayer requests and to manage the growing endowment fund of Upper Room Ministries; circulation of *The Upper Room* magazine is over 2 million copies per year	• Ellen Barnette and Pearl Bellinger (MC) are the first black Methodist women to serve as missionaries in India • The Methodist Church of the Republic of China moves to Taiwan along with the Nationalist government of Chiang Kai-shek • The General Conference of the Korean Methodist Church meets for the first time since WWII in what is now South Korea	**1949**
• Francis Poulenc composes his *Stabat Mater* • Walter Piston completes his *Symphony No. 4* • John Cage creates his *String Quartet* • Gian-Carlo Menotti's first full-length opera, *The Consul*, premieres • Jackson Pollock's *Autumn Rhythm* typifies his style of nonrepresentational "action" art, created by dripping and pouring paint on the canvas • Notable publications include: – Thor Heyerdahl, *Kon-Tiki: Across the Pacific by Raft*, the account of his 1947 voyage – Ray Bradbury, *The Martian Chronicles*	• Pope Pius XII proclaims the Assumption of the Virgin Mary to be an article of faith for Roman Catholics • The National Council of Churches of Christ in the USA (successor to Federal Council of Churches, 1908) is organized • The Northern Baptist Convention (1907) is renamed the American Baptist Convention • Notable publications include: – Martin Buber, *Two Types of Faith* – Simon Weil, *Waiting for God* – Albert Knudsen, *Basic Issues in Christian Thought*	• The EUBC General Conference: – approved the union and reorganization of 29 annual conferences, made necessary as a result of the 1946 union of the EC and UBC – establishes seven episcopal areas with resident bishops in the US, plus one overseas episcopal area to be supervised by the Board of Bishops without a single resident bishop – reverses the 1946 decision to consolidate the Evangelical Press (former EC) in Harrisburg and the Otterbein Press (former UBC) in Dayton and to operate them separately • The MC organizes the Oriental Provisional Conference • The third Assembly of the WSCS and WSG (MC) meets • The first Convention of the WSWS (EUBC) meets • The MC establishes the Alaska Methodist University in Anchorage • Phillips School of Theology becomes the official denominational seminary of the CMEC	• The first Methodist International House opens in London, followed by 12 others in university cities in Britain	**1950**

	A. WORLD HISTORY & POLITICS	B. AMERICAN HISTORY & POLITICS	C. SCIENCE, MEDICINE & TECHNOLOGY	D. DAILY LIFE, POPULAR CULTURE & ENTERTAINMENT
1950 cont.		• Joseph McCarthy rises to national prominence due to his charges on the floor of the US Senate of Communist infiltration of and influence on the US government		
1951	• The Korean War ends in a stalemate with a cease-fire agreement establishing a demilitarized zone (DMZ) along the 38th parallel between North and South Korea; no peace treaty is ever signed • The US and Japan sign a treaty allowing the US to maintain military bases in Japan • China occupies and then annexes Tibet • The United Nations High Commission for Refugees (UNHCR) is established • The whites-only government of South Africa begins establishing "homelands" for blacks • Winston Churchill becomes British prime minister for the second time • Libya gains its independence from Italy • France, West Germany, Italy, Belgium, Holland, and Luxembourg establish a single market for coal and steel; this may be seen as the beginning of the European "Common Market" • Australia, New Zealand, and the US sign a mutual defense pact, called the ANZUS Treaty • The Festival of Britain is held in London to celebrate the centennial of the great Crystal Palace exhibition of 1851; this time the notable buildings include the saucer-shaped Dome of Discovery and the needle-shaped Skylon	• The 22nd Amendment to the US Constitution limits presidents of the US to a maximum of two four-year terms; anyone who serves more than two years of a four-year term to which someone else had been elected president may then be elected to only one four-year term • The US Supreme Court affirms the constitutionality of the Alien Registration Act (or Smith Act) of 1940 • Ethel and Julius Rosenberg are convicted of conspiracy to commit espionage (passing nuclear secrets to the USSR) and sentenced to death; they are executed in 1953 • The Mattachine Society, the first national gay rights organization, is formed in New York City by Harry Hay • The George Washington Carver National Monument in Joplin, MO, is dedicated; it is the first National Monument to honor a black American	• UNIVAC, the first large electronic computer, is built by Remington-Rand (later Sperry-Rand) for the US Census Bureau • French physician J. Andre-Thomas invents the first heart-lung machine, allowing advanced life support during open-heart surgery • Direct-dial coast-to-coast telephone service begins in the US • Gregory Pincus, Min Chuch Chang, John Rock, and Carl Djerassi (US) develop the first oral contraceptive • Experimental Breeder Reactor Number One (EBR-I), the world's first experimental nuclear power plant, is built by the US Atomic Energy Commission in Idaho • Charles Ginsburg leads the research team at Ampex Corporation that develops the first practical videotape recorder	• One of the greatest moments in Major League Baseball history occurs when the New York Giants' Bobby Thomson hits a game-winning home run (the "shot heard around the world") in the bottom of the ninth inning to beat the Brooklyn Dodgers and win the National League pennant after being down 14 games • Alan Jay Lerner and Frederick Loewe's *Paint Your Wagon* opens on Broadway, as does Richard Rodgers and Oscar Hammerstein's *The King and I* • Tony Bennett has his first big hit with "Because of You," a ballad produced by Mitch Miller with a lush orchestral arrangement by Percy Faith • Cleveland disc jockey Alan Freed first uses the term "rock-and-roll" (or "rock-n-roll") to promote "black" rhythm and blues music to white audiences • A group called "Jackie Brenston and his Delta Cats" (actually, Ike Turner and his Kings of Rhythm) and Bill Haley and His Saddlemen (later the Comets) record different versions of "Rocket 88"; musical historians disagree about which version should be considered the first "true" rock-and-roll record • Notable TV show debuts include Edward R. Murrow's *See It Now*, *I Love Lucy*, and *The Dinah Shore Show* • The *Dennis the Menace* comic strip appears in newspapers across the US for the first time • Sundrop Cola appears on the market and quickly becomes a Southern regional favorite • Films: *The African Queen*; *A Streetcar Named Desire*; *An American in Paris*; *A Place in the Sun*
1952	• Britain's King George VI dies; he is succeeded by his daughter, Elizabeth II • Winston Churchill announces that Britain possesses nuclear weapons • Greece and Turkey become members of NATO • The People's Republic of China (mainland China) is refused entry into the UN; the Republic of China (Taiwan) retains the seat of China on the Security Council • Japan regains independence through the Treaty of San Francisco, ending the period of occupied Japan and marking the birth of modern Japan • The African National Congress (ANC), under the leadership of Nelson Mandela, launches the "Defiance Against Unjust Laws" campaign in South Africa • A coup d'état in Egypt led by Gamal Abdal Nasser overthrows King Farouk; the monarchy is abolished and a republic is declared in 1953 • A radical political group of blacks in Kenya called the "Mau Mau" begin making violent attacks on white settlers	• The McCarran-Walter Act abolishes race as an immigration criterion and sets quotas by nation • After a popular referendum, Puerto Rico becomes a self-governing commonwealth of the US, adopting its own constitution • The Voice of America increases the number and range of its broadcasts into Eastern Europe and the USSR • By executive order, President Truman establishes the top-secret National Security Agency (NSA) as the organization within the US Government responsible for communications intelligence activities • Vice presidential candidate Richard M. Nixon, after accusations of accepting illegal campaign contributions, saves his political career with his famous "Checkers speech," which is one of the first uses of television by a political figure to appeal directly to the American people • Dwight D. Eisenhower is elected as president and Richard M. Nixon as vice president (Republican Party)	• The US tests the first thermonuclear (hydrogen) bomb at Enewetak Island; it is approximately 500 times more powerful than the nuclear (atomic) bomb • The advent of Cinerama ushers in the era of wide-screen movies • The first plastic artificial heart valve is developed at Georgetown Medical Center • C. Walton Lillehei and F. John Lewis perform the first open-heart surgery at the University of Minnesota • George Jorgensen Jr., a transsexual man in Denmark, is the recipient of the first successful sex-change operation, becoming Christine Jorgensen • United Airlines makes the first official passenger flight over the North Pole from Los Angeles to Copenhagen	• The Jackie Gleason Show (*The Honeymooners*) debuts on CBS, beginning a two-decade run • Colonel Sanders sells first Kentucky Fried Chicken franchise • Lipton develops a novel four-sided "flo-thru" tea bag • Sam Phillips starts Sun Records in Memphis and gives Elvis Presley, Carl Perkins, Jerry Lee Lewis, and Johnny Cash their first recording contracts • Kitty Wells records her country classic "It Wasn't God Who Made Honky Tonk Angels" • Agatha Christie's murder-mystery play *The Mousetrap* opens at the Ambassadors Theatre in London; as of 2004, it continues next door at the St. Martin's Theatre and remains the longest continuously running play in theater history • The first issue of *Mad* magazine is published • Mr. Potato Head makes his first appearance on the toy market

E. EDUCATION, LITERATURE & THE FINE ARTS	F. RELIGION, THEOLOGY, PHILOSOPHY & PSYCHOLOGY	G. AMERICAN & UNITED METHODISM	H. BRITISH & WORLD METHODISM	
				1950 cont.
• Duke Ellington composes his musical tribute to Harlem, the *Harlem Suite* • Gian-Carlo Menotti composes *Amahl and the Night Visitors* • Heitor Villa-Lobos completes his *Concerto for Guitar and Orchestra* • George Enescu composes his *String Quartet No. 2* • John Cage creates his *Imaginary Landscape No. 4* • Matisse culminates his artistic career with the completion of the remarkable Chapel of the Rosary in Venice, for which he creates all the wall decorations, stations of the cross, furniture, stained-glass windows, even the vestments and altarcloths • Notable publications include: – Rachel Carson, *The Sea Around Us* – Herman Wouk, *The Caine Mutiny* – Marianne Moore, *Collected Poems* – J. D. Salinger, *The Catcher in the Rye*	• The World Evangelical Fellowship (later renamed the World Evangelical Alliance) is established in London • Campus Crusade for Christ is founded on the campus of UCLA by Bill Bright, a student at Fuller Theological Seminary • Paul Tillich begins publication of his *Systematic Theology* (3 vols. 1951–63); his "method of correlation" does not begin with an appeal to the Bible but with analysis of the problems of human existence and then asks how theology can provide solutions to those problems • Dietrich Bonhoeffer's friend Eberhard Bethge compiles and edits Bonhoeffer's *Letters and Papers from Prison* • Other notable publications include: – H. Richard Niebuhr's *Christ and Culture* – Talcott Parsons, *The Social System* – Hannah Arendt, *The Origins of Totalitarianism* – William Buckley, *God and Man at Yale*	• The MC Woman's Division publishes the pamphlet *States Laws on Race and Color*, compiled by Pauli Murray; copies are given to Methodist agencies and institutions and placed in 600 colleges and university libraries and in many public libraries • The Methodist Publishing House begins publication of *The Interpreter's Bible* (12 vols., 1951–57)	• The eighth Ecumenical Methodist Conference meets in Oxford; it changes the name to World Methodist Conference, organizes standing committees, and creates the World Methodist Council (successor to the Ecumenical Methodist Council) to serve as a continuing secretariat between World Methodist Conference meetings • Didsbury College is relocated from Manchester to Bristol • The MC [UK] publishes *Constitutional Practice and Discipline* for the first time • Methodists in China are forced by the Chinese government to break all ties with the West and become self-governing and self-supporting; they have no further contact with the West until 1978	**1951**
• William Walton composes his *Orb & Scepter Coronation March* for the coronation of Queen Elizabeth II • Leonard Bernstein's opera *Trouble in Tahiti* premieres at Brandeis University • John Cage makes *Water Music* with non-traditional instruments • David Tudor gives the premiere of John Cage's *4' 33"* [of silence] in Woodstock, NY • Alberto Ginastera composes his *Sonata for Piano No. 1* • Notable publications include: – Ernest Hemingway, *The Old Man and the Sea* – John Steinbeck, *East of Eden* – Flannery O'Connor, *Wise Blood* – Samuel Beckett, *Waiting for Godot*	• Sister Teresa becomes Mother Teresa and begins her charity work in Calcutta • The World Conference on Faith and Order meets in Lund • Congregationalists in Australia and New Zealand allow the ordination of women, as does the United Church of Japan • The World Fellowship of Buddhists is established • Paul Tillich, in *The Courage to Be*, argues that human existence is rooted in God as the "ground of all being" • Dorothy Day's autobiography, *The Long Loneliness*, tells the story of the Catholic Worker movement and her involvement in it • G. E. Wright publishes *God Who Acts*	• The MC General Conference: – adopts recommendations for reducing the membership of general boards and agencies – creates the Coordinating Council, directly responsible to the General Conference, to coordinate and facilitate the work of the boards and agencies – establishes Interboard Commissions on the Local Church; on Christian Social Relations; and on Cultivation, Promotion, and Publications – breaks ties with the Methodist Federation for Social Action (MFSA) because it was perceived as too radical – forms the Board of Social and Economic Relations, which then revises the Social Creed – makes "The Advance for Christ and His Church" part of the regular program of the church and establishes "General Advance Specials" giving program – again rejects a proposal to extend full clergy rights to women – recognizes that divorce "is not the answer to the problems that bring it about" and that *(cont.)*	• Maude K. Jensen, who has been a missionary in Korea since 1926, is ordained as a local elder in the MC (Central Pennsylvania Conference); she is the first woman to have her ordination recognized by the Korean Methodist Church • Notable publications include Arthur S. Yates, *The Doctrine of Assurance, With Special Reference to John Wesley*	**1952**

	A. WORLD HISTORY & POLITICS	B. AMERICAN HISTORY & POLITICS	C. SCIENCE, MEDICINE & TECHNOLOGY	D. DAILY LIFE, POPULAR CULTURE & ENTERTAINMENT
1952 cont.	• The "Great Smog" descends on London and over 4,000 people die from its effects; the word *smog* (from *smoke* plus *fog*) is coined to describe it			• The Modern Jazz Quartet (Percy Heath, Connie Kay, Milt Jackson, and John Lewis) makes its debut; performing in tuxedos and taking jazz into concert halls, the MJQ helps give it "respectability" • Films: *The Greatest Show on Earth; Singin' in the Rain; High Noon; The Quiet Man* • Summer Olympics: Helsinki • Winter Olympics: Oslo
1953	• Soviet premier Joseph Stalin dies; Georgi Malenkov is his successor as Premier • China's first Five-Year Plan (1953–57) marks the transition to socialism • Dag Hammarskjöld (Sweden) is elected UN Secretary-General after the resignation of Trygve Lie • The British government forces the creation of the Federation of Rhodesia and Nyasaland, comprising the territories of Northern Rhodesia, Southern Rhodesia, and Nyasaland (now Malawi), primarily to ensure the continuation of whites-only rule • The death of King Abdul of Saudi Arabia ushers in a period of political instability there • West Germany achieves its independence as a fully sovereign nation • Jomo Kenyatta is arrested by the British in Kenya and charged with responsibility for the Mau Mau uprising	• The State of Georgia approves the first state literature censorship board in the US • President Eisenhower issues an executive order barring gay men and lesbians from all federal jobs • Blacks in Baton Rouge, LA, organize the first bus boycott of the budding civil rights movement to protest the segregated seating system on city buses • Joseph McCarthy becomes chairman of The Senate Permanent Investigations Subcommittee; he begins holding public hearings in which many people in the business and entertainment world, as well as in government service or the military, are accused of being Communists or Communist sympathizers; those who refuse to answer the question: "Are you now, or have you ever been, a member of the Communist Party?" are blacklisted; many lose their jobs or find it impossible to get work and are harassed constantly	• The USSR announces a successful hydrogen bomb test • TWA begins nonstop transcontinental passenger service from Los Angeles to New York City • Edmund Hillary (New Zealand) and his guide Tenzing Norgay (Nepal) make the first successful ascent to the summit of Mt. Everest • James Watson (US) and Francis Crick (UK) announce the discovery of the DNA double helix • John Gibbons (US) performs the first successful open-heart surgery with the use of a heart-lung machine • With the 701, IBM starts building commercial computers • The Davis Dam and Power Plant facility is completed on the Colorado River Pyramid Canyon, creating Lake Mohave between Hoover Dam (Lake Mead) and Parker Dam (Lake Havasu)	• Cole Porter's musical *Can-Can* opens on Broadway • The first issue of *TV Guide* magazine is published in 10 cities with a circulation of 1.5 million • General Motors begins producing the Corvette, America's first true sports car • Hugh Hefner's *Playboy* magazine hits newsstands; a nude Marilyn Monroe graces the cover • Country music great Hank Williams dies at the age of 30 of an apparent heart attack that probably resulted from drug and alcohol abuse • The Platters, one of the great "doo wop" groups, have their first big hit with "Only You," followed by "The Great Pretender" • The first public color television broadcast stars the puppets Kukla, Fran, and Ollie • United Parcel Service (UPS) introduces its coast-to-coast air parcel delivery service • Golfing great Ben Hogan becomes the first person to win the Masters, US Open, and British Open tournaments in the same year • Films: *From Here to Eternity; Shane; Stalag 17; Roman Holiday; The Robe; Peter Pan*
1954	• The French base at Dien Bien Phu falls to the Vietminh army under General Vo Nguyen Giap, and France pulls out of Vietnam • The Geneva Conference partitions Vietnam at the 17th parallel into North Vietnam (communist) and South Vietnam (capitalist) • The Southeast Asia Treaty Organization (SEATO) is founded in Bangkok, Thailand; the original members are Australia, New Zealand, Pakistan, the Philippines, Thailand, Britain, France, and the US • Algeria rebels against French colonial rule and the Algerian War of Independence begins • Gamal Abdal Nasser assumes power as president of Egypt; he negotiates a treaty under which Britain withdraws from Egypt after an occupation lasting 72 years • Guatemalan President Jacobo Guzmán steps down after a CIA-sponsored military coup, triggering a bloody civil war that will last for more than 35 years	• In *Brown v. Board of Education of Topeka, Kansas*, the US Supreme Court declares that segregation in public schools violates the 14th Amendment; it overturns the "separate but equal" doctrine established in 1894 by *Plessy v. Ferguson* • The Ku Klux Klan, which had been formally disbanded in 1944, begins to experience a revival among white supremacists across the South • The White Citizens' Council movement spreads across the South; unlike the KKK, Council members supposedly choose to combat desegregation through the courts and with economic pressure rather than violence • Congress adds the words "under God" to the Pledge of Allegiance, and the words "So help me God" to the oaths of office for federal justices and judges • The US is shaken by Edward R. Murrow's TV documentary on Joseph McCarthy; the televised "Army-McCarthy" hearings show McCarthy to be a blustering bully and result in his censure by the Senate and his *(cont.)*	• The USS *Nautilus*, the world's first nuclear submarine, is launched; it revolutionizes naval warfare • Russia builds the world's first nuclear reactor to supply electricity for commercial use • The first successful kidney transplant, from one identical twin to another, is performed by Joseph Edward Murray at Peter Bent Brigham Hospital in Boston • The first version of the FORTRAN (formula translator) programming language is published by IBM • Kodak introduces Tri-X, high-speed black-and-white film • Gerald Pearson, Calvin Fuller, and Daryl Chapin of Bell Laboratories invent the first solar-powered battery, converting sunlight into electrical current • The first mass vaccination of children against polio begins in Pittsburgh, PA • The Boeing 707, the world's first "jumbo jet," makes its inaugural test flight • A meteorite weighing 4 kg crashes through the roof of a house in Sylacauga, *(cont.)*	• NBC televises the Tournament of Roses Parade in color, using the newly approved NTSC standards; it is the nation's first coast-to-coast color broadcast • The Recording Industry Association of America (RIAA) is founded to establish technical standards for and represent the trade interests of the US recording industry • Nat "King" Cole records the song that becomes his musical signature, "Unforgettable" • Bill Haley and his Comets release "Rock Around the Clock" and "Shake, Rattle and Roll," the first nationwide rock-and-roll hit records • Muddy Waters records the blues classic "Hoochie Coochie Man" • Elvis Presley cuts his first single, "That's All Right (Mama)," at the Sun Records studio in Memphis • The Modern Jazz Quartet records John Lewis's classic "Django," his tribute to jazz guitarist Django Reinhardt • *The Davy Crockett Show* premieres on TV and sets off a national craze for coonskin caps

E. EDUCATION, LITERATURE & THE FINE ARTS	F. RELIGION, THEOLOGY, PHILOSOPHY & PSYCHOLOGY	G. AMERICAN & UNITED METHODISM	H. BRITISH & WORLD METHODISM	
		the church has a responsibility to aid those who have experienced a broken marriage • The MC Woman's Division adopts a "Charter of Racial Policies" • The MC *Methodist Men Radio Hour* originates with 38 stations (400 stations by 1958) • Houston-Tillotson College is established by the MC through the merger of Tillotson College (1877) and Samuel Houston College (1876) • The University of Southern California, established in 1880, severs its ties with the MC • A split within the EMC (1946) results in the establishment of the Evangelical Methodist Church of America in Pennsylvania		**1952 cont.**
• Heitor Villa-Lobos composes his *Harp Concerto* and his *Cello Concerto No. 2* • Karlheinz Stockhausen composes his *Counterpoints*, which places pairs of instruments in sharp contrast to each other across extreme ranges of note values • Notable publications include: – James Baldwin, *Go Tell It on the Mountain* – Arthur Miller, *The Crucible* – Ray Bradbury, *Fahrenheit 451* – Saul Bellow, *The Adventures of Augie March*	• Notable publications include: – Reinhold Niebuhr, *Christian Realism and Political Problems* – Rudolf Bultmann, et al., *Kerygma and Myth*, which includes Bultmann's famous (or notorious) essay "Jesus Christ and Mythology" – Hans Conzelmann, *The Theology of St. Luke* – Friedrich Gogarten, *Demythologization and the Church* – Ludwig Wittgenstein, *Philosophical Investigations* (published posthumously) – Anders Nygren, *Agape and Eros*	• The first Conference of Methodist Men meets • The Upper Room Chapel and Museum opens in Nashville, featuring a magnificent woodcarving of Leonardo da Vinci's painting *The Last Supper* sculpted by Ernest Pellegrini that measures seventeen feet wide and eight feet high	• The Methodist Church in Taiwan is organized • Notable publications include the first volume of Martin Schmidt's *John Wesley* (German edition, 2 vols., 1953–66; English translation: *John Wesley: A Theological Biography*, 3 vols., 1962–73)	**1953**
• The completion of the Chapel of Notre-Dame-du-Haut in Ronchamp by the French architect Le Corbusier signals the emergence of a more sculptural and expressionistic modern architecture • Arnold Schoenberg's opera *Moses and Aaron* premieres in Hamburg • Arnold Bax composes his *Autumn Legend* • Virgil Thomson completes his *Concerto for Flute, Strings, Harp and Percussion* • Aram Khachaturian composes his ballet *Spartacus* • J. R. R. Tolkien begins the publication of *The Lord of the Rings* (3 vols., 1954–56) • Other notable publications include: – Tennessee Williams, *Cat on a Hot Tin Roof* – William G. Golding, *Lord of the Flies* – James Michener, *Sayonara*	• The General Assembly of the PCUS becomes the first church body in America to endorse the Supreme Court's ruling against racial segregation • Pope Pius X is canonized as a Roman Catholic saint and becomes Pope Saint Pius X • The Fellowship of Christian Athletes is established in Kansas City [it is now the largest interdenominational school-based sports organization in the world] • Black activist Malcolm X (born Malcolm Little; later known also by the religious name El-Hajj Malik El-Shabazz) becomes a key leader of the Nation of Islam, headed by Elijah Muhammad • Sun Myung Moon founds the Holy Spirit Association for the Unification of World Christianity, popularly called the Unification Church, in Seoul, Korea • George M. James, a follower of black nationalist leader Marcus Garvey, claims in his book *Stolen Legacy* that Greek philosophy was "stolen" from ancient Egyptian (cont.)	• The EUBC General Conference: – approves the relocation of Evangelical Theological Seminary (1905) to Dayton, OH, and its merger with Bonebrake Theological Seminary (1871/1909) to create United Theological Seminary – authorizes the merger of York College (founded in York, NE, in 1890 by the UBC) with Westmar College (founded in Le Mars, IA, in 1887 as Northwestern Normal School and Business College, taken over by the UEC in 1900, and renamed in 1948) under the name and on the grounds of Westmar – approves a special financial campaign for the following quadrennium designed to raise $4 million for colleges and seminaries and $1 million for home missions and church extension – changes the name of its men's work program from the Brotherhood of the EUBC to EUB Men – states that the EUBC "shall consistently regard as valid only such divorces as are granted on the ground of adultery"	• The Central Conference of Central and Southern Europe (MC) is formed and meets for the first time • Construction begins on the headquarters building for the World Methodist Council in Lake Junaluska, NC	**1954**

	A. WORLD HISTORY & POLITICS	B. AMERICAN HISTORY & POLITICS	C. SCIENCE, MEDICINE & TECHNOLOGY	D. DAILY LIFE, POPULAR CULTURE & ENTERTAINMENT
1954 cont.		fall from power; *McCarthyism* becomes a term for the practice of making public accusations of treason or disloyalty without sufficient evidence • The US Air Force Academy is established and its construction begins at Colorado Springs, CO; the first class enters at interim facilities in 1955 and graduates in 1958 • Four Puerto Rican nationalists sneak guns into the House of Representatives and open fire, wounding five congressmen • The Ellis Island immigration station is closed after 62 years as "America's front door" • Hurricane Hazel kills approximately 1,000 in Haiti, 95 in the US, and 78 in Canada	AL, and strikes Ann Hodges, badly bruising her; it is the first documented case of an object from outer space hitting a person on Earth • Guitarist Les Paul commissions Ampex to build the first eight-track tape recorder, at his own expense • The Regency TR-1, the first all-transistor radio small enough to fit into a shirt pocket, appears on the market but is not a commercial success	• Steve Allen hosts the premiere of the *Tonight* show on NBC • The Miss America beauty pageant is televised for the first time • Roger Bannister (England) becomes first person to run a sub-four-minute mile (3:59.4) • The C. A. Swanson Co. markets the first frozen "TV dinner" • The first Burger King restaurant opens in Miami; the Whopper is introduced in 1957 • The first mass-produced transistor radio goes on sale, as does the first mass-produced color television, RCA's model CT-100 • 54% of American homes have television sets; television sales revenue surpasses radio sales revenue in the US • Films: Akira Kurosawa's classic *Seven Samurai* (remade as a western, *The Magnificent Seven*, in 1960); *On the Waterfront* (in which Marlon Brando makes his screen debut); *Rear Window*; *The Caine Mutiny*; *A Star Is Born*; *Three Coins in the Fountain*; *The High and the Mighty*
1955	• Georgi Malenkov is forced to resign as Soviet Premier; Nikita Khrushchev as Communist Party Secretary becomes the unchallenged leader of the USSR • The US declares that it will defend the Republic of China (Taiwan) against any attack by the People's Republic of China (mainland China) • West Germany is admitted to NATO and the Western European Union • To counterbalance NATO, the USSR forms the Warsaw Pact with Albania, Bulgaria, Czechoslovakia, East Germany, Hungary, Poland, and Romania • Anthony Eden becomes British prime minister, succeeding Winston Churchill • Argentina ousts dictator Juan Perón • Muslim rebels revolt against French colonial rule in Algeria	• Emmett Till, a fourteen-year-old boy from Chicago, is visiting family in Mississippi when he is brutally beaten then killed for allegedly whistling at a white woman; two white men are arrested for the murder but acquitted by an all-white jury • Rosa Parks is arrested after defying both custom and law by refusing to give up her seat at the front of the "colored section" of a bus to a white passenger in Montgomery, AL; black activists form the Montgomery Improvement Association to boycott the transit system and select Martin Luther King, Jr., as their leader • The AFL and CIO merge into one combined labor organization, the AFL-CIO • The Daughters of Bilitis, a pioneering national lesbian organization, is founded in San Francisco	• The USSR successfully tests its first thermonuclear weapon • Jonas Salk (US) announces that his polio vaccine works; Salk's vaccine is followed (in 1960) by Albert Sabin's oral vaccine • British engineer Christopher Cockerell patents a design for a hovercraft • Archaeologists set 1950 as the carbon dating base year; other years are BP (before present) • Narinder Kapany (England) develops fiber optics, successfully transmitting digital information by light pulses along very thin glass fibers	• Marian Anderson becomes the first black artist to perform with the Metropolitan Opera • Walt Disney opens his Disneyland amusement park near Los Angeles • Ray Kroc opens his first McDonald's restaurant in Des Plaines, IL • The first Waffle House opens in Avondale Estates, GA • William Buckley starts *The National Review* • Frank Sinatra records his first "concept" album, *In the Wee Small Hours*, with a sustained midnight mood of loneliness and lost love • Chuck Berry rocks the airwaves with "Maybellene," his first big hit • Miles Davis plays a legendary solo on Thelonius Monk's "'Round Midnight" at the Newport Jazz Festival, bringing him to national attention for the first time • Ford brings out the Thunderbird to compete with GM's Corvette • Three long-running TV shows make their first appearances: *Gunsmoke*, *Captain Kangaroo*, and *The Lawrence Welk Show* • Country singer George Jones has his first big hit with "Why, Baby, Why?" • Films: The film *Blackboard Jungle* features Bill Haley and the Comets' "Rock Around the Clock" over the opening credits, the first use of a rock-and-roll song in a major film; other notable films include *Rebel Without a Cause*; *East of Eden*; *Mister Roberts*; *The Seven-Year Itch* (considered by many to be Marilyn Monroe's best film, with its iconic "blowing skirt" scene)
1956	• After Britain and the US withdraw financial support for the Aswan High Dam, Egyptian President Nasser nationalizes the Suez Canal; the ensuing crisis pits Egypt against an alliance between France, Britain, and Israel; the crisis is defused but not before dragging the US and the USSR to the brink of confrontation	• President Eisenhower approves a joint Congressional resolution formally declaring "In God We Trust" to be the national motto of the US; the motto, which had been used on US coinage since 1864, first appears on paper currency in 1957 • The Federal-Aid Highway Act of 1956 marks the beginning of the modern interstate highway system	• The US tests the first aerial hydrogen bomb over Bikini Atoll • The first permanent transatlantic telephone cable is completed, linking the US and Canada with Britain and Europe • The first large commercial nuclear power station begins operation at Calder Hall, Britain [it will close in 2003 after a record 47 years of operation]	• Alan Jay Lerner and Frederick Loewe's musical *My Fair Lady* begins a six-year run on Broadway, recording a total of 2,717 performances • Chet Huntley and David Brinkley bring the "star" system to television news broadcasting • The first regularly scheduled nationally broadcast rock-and-roll show, "The Rock 'n Roll Dance Party," with Alan Freed as host, premieres on the CBS radio network

E. EDUCATION, LITERATURE & THE FINE ARTS	F. RELIGION, THEOLOGY, PHILOSOPHY & PSYCHOLOGY	G. AMERICAN & UNITED METHODISM	H. BRITISH & WORLD METHODISM	
	traditions that had developed from distinctively African intellectual and cultural roots [this work is regarded as one of the foundational texts of what is later called "Afrocentrism"] • Other notable publications include Abraham Maslow, *Motivation and Personality*	• The Woman's Division is the first agency of the MC to issue a statement in support of the Supreme Court's school desegregation decision • The fourth Assembly of the WSCS and WSG (MC) meets • The second Convention of the WSWS (EUBC) meets • The name of the CMEC is formally changed from Colored Methodist Episcopal Church to Christian Methodist Episcopal Church • The Methodist Publishing House adopts Cokesbury as the trade name for its retail and mail-order sales operations and Abingdon Press as the trade name for its book publishing unit • Notable publications include: – Richard M. Cameron, *The Rise of Methodism: A Source Book* – Robert W. Burtner and Robert E. Chiles, eds., *A Compend of Wesley's Theology* (reprinted 1982 as *John Wesley's Theology: A Collection from His Works*)		**1954 cont.**
• Alan Hovhaness composes his *Symphony No. 2 (Mysterious Mountain)* • Ralph Vaughan Williams completes his *Symphony No. 8* • George Crumb creates his *Diptych for Orchestra* • Franz Waxman composes his *Sinfonietta for Strings and Timpani* • Salvador Dalí completes his painting of *The Lord's Supper* • Georgia O'Keeffe completes her painting *Black Door with Red*, one of a series of two dozen paintings inspired by her house at Abiquiu in northern New Mexico • Notable publications include: – Vladimir Nabokov, *Lolita* – Flannery O'Connor, *A Good Man is Hard to Find*	• The Bible Presbyterian Church (1938) splits into the Collingwood Synod (ongoing) and the Columbus Synod (to 1961) • Notable publications include: – Will Herberg, *Protestant-Catholic-Jew* – Herbert Marcuse, *Eros and Civilization*	• The Fellowship of Methodist Musicians is established (MC) [after 1968 the name is changed to Fellowship of United Methodists in Music and Worship Arts] • Simon P. Montgomery becomes the first black Methodist preacher to serve as the pastor of a white Methodist congregation (in Old Mystic, CT) • The MC holds a nationwide Conference on Town and Country Life • The first *Hymnario Metodista* is published by the Rio Grande Conference • The Free Methodist Church establishes its World Headquarters in Winona Lake, IN, where its publishing house had been since 1935	• Methodists in Spain become part of the Iglesia Evangélica Español (Spanish Evangelical Church) • Paula Mojzes is appointed acting District Superintendent of the Yugoslav Methodist Provisional Conference (until 1957); she is the first woman to serve in this capacity in the MC • Notable publications include Martin Schmidt, *Der junge Wesley als Heidenmissionar und Missionstheologe* (English translation: *The Young Wesley: Missionary and Theologian of Missions*, 1958)	**1955**
• Leonard Bernstein composes his operetta *Candide* • Ned Rorem completes his *Symphony No. 2* • Mario Davidovsky composes *Three Pieces for Woodwind Quartet* • Mark Rothko exemplifies abstract impressionism in his paintings *Orange and Yellow* and *Green and Tangerine on Red*	• The PCUSA grants full clergy rights to women; Margaret Towner is the first woman to be ordained by the PCUSA • Notable publications include: – Gunther Bornkamm, *Jesus of Nazareth* – H. Richard Niebuhr, *The Purpose of the Church and Its Ministry*	• The MC General Conference: – grants full clergy rights to women, including annual conference membership – adopts legislation providing framework for elimination of the Central Jurisdiction; allows voluntary transfer of churches within the Central Jurisdiction to the geographical jurisdictions within which they are located	• The ninth World Methodist Conference meets in Lake Junaluska, NC • The World Methodist Council headquarters is relocated from New York City to Lake Junaluska • The World Federation of Methodist Women is founded	**1956**

	A. WORLD HISTORY & POLITICS	B. AMERICAN HISTORY & POLITICS	C. SCIENCE, MEDICINE & TECHNOLOGY	D. DAILY LIFE, POPULAR CULTURE & ENTERTAINMENT
1956 cont.	• Fidel Castro leads the Cuban Revolution against the regime of Fulgencio Batista • Nikita Khrushchev denounces Stalin's crimes in a secret speech to the Soviet Communist Party Congress • Khrushchev tells a group of western ambassadors at a reception in Moscow that "Whether you like it or not, history is on our side. We will bury you!" • Soviet tanks and troops roll into Hungary to crush a burgeoning movement for democratic reform • Large oil reserves are discovered in both Algeria and Nigeria • Morocco and Tunisia gain independence from France and Spain; Sudan gains independence from Britain and Egypt	• Autherine Lucy, the first black student to enroll at the University of Alabama, is suspended after riots protesting her admission • The US Supreme Court rules that segregation of the city bus system in Montgomery is unconstitutional; the city acts to desegregate the bus system after being served with federal court injunctions; blacks in Montgomery then end their bus boycott • In reaction to the developing civil rights movement, the Georgia state legislature redesigns the state flag to incorporate the Confederate battle flag • Nat "King" Cole is attacked on stage in Birmingham, AL, by four members of the White Citizens' Council; he finishes the show despite minor injuries, but vows never to perform in the South again, and does not • President Eisenhower and Vice President Nixon are reelected (Republican Party)	• Gordon Murray (Toronto, Canada) performs the world's first heart valve transplant on a patient with a severely leaking aortic valve, using the main aortic valve of a male automobile accident victim • The Lake Ponchatrain Causeway opens; it is longest causeway in the world at the time (24 miles) • The first commercial videotape recorder is developed by American engineer Richard Dolby and patented by Ampex • The IBM 305 RAMAC (Random Access Method of Accounting and Control) is the first computer "hard disk" data storage device • Liquid Paper is created on the kitchen table of a Dallas secretary, Bette Graham • Felix Wankel (Germany) develops the rotary internal combustion engine that carries his name	• Elvis Presley has no. 1 hits with "Hound Dog" and "Don't Be Cruel"; he appears on *The Ed Sullivan Show* and spreads rock-and-roll to a world audience with his first film, *Love Me Tender* • Johnny Cash has his first big hit with "I Walk the Line" • Jerry Lee Lewis rocks the world with "Great Balls of Fire" • The Everly Brothers score with their first hit single, "Bye Bye Love" • Prentice Gautt becomes the first black football player at a major NCAA school (The University of Oklahoma) • Don Larsen (New York Yankees) pitches a perfect game in the 1956 World Series • Play-Doh first appears on the market • Films: Cecil B. DeMille produces a remake of his silent 1922 version of *The Ten Commandments* (it is his last film); John Ford makes his masterpiece western *The Searchers*; other films include *Around the World in 80 Days* and *The King and I* • Summer Olympics: Melbourne • Winter Olympics: Cortina d'Ampezzo
1957	• Anthony Eden resigns; Harold MacMillan becomes British prime minister • The British colonies of Ghana and Malaya achieve independence and become members of the British Commonwealth • Israel withdraws its military forces from the Sinai Peninsula; Egypt reopens the Suez Canal • The European Economic Community (EEC), better known as the Common Market, is established by the Treaty of Rome; the initial members are France, West Germany, Belgium, Luxembourg, the Netherlands, and Italy • The International Atomic Energy Agency (IAEA) is established	• Martin Luther King, Jr., Fred L. Shuttlesworth, and Charles K. Steele establish the Southern Christian Leadership Conference (SCLC), and King becomes the first president; the SCLC becomes a major force in organizing the civil rights movement • The integration of Central High School in Little Rock, AR, is enforced by US Army troops on orders of President Eisenhower after Gov. Orval Faubus defies federal court orders • The Civil Rights Act of 1957 prohibits discrimination in public places based on race, color, religion, or national origin, and establishes America's first Civil Rights Commission as an enforcement mechanism • The FBI arrests labor boss Jimmy Hoffa and charges him with bribery • The floodgates of the Dalles Dam on the Columbia River are closed, inundating Celilo Falls and its ancient Indian fisheries to create Lake Celilo	• The US conducts its first underground thermonuclear test • Britain successfully tests its first thermonuclear weapon • The USSR launches *Sputnik 1*, the first artificial satellite placed into Earth's orbit, followed by *Sputnik 2*, carrying the dog Laika, the first living animal to enter space [she does not survive] • The first commercial American nuclear power plant opens in Shippingport, PA • A flight of three American B-52 bombers completes the first round-the-world nonstop jet plane flight in 45 hours • FORTRAN III becomes the first high-level computer programming language • RCA-Victor develops the equipment and techniques for stereophonic sound recording and introduces the first "stereo" records	• With great fanfare, Ford unveils the Edsel, which proves to be one of the great flops in US automotive history • *West Side Story*, a modern retelling of the Romeo and Juliet story composed by Leonard Bernstein with lyrics by Stephen Sondheim and choreography by Jerome Robbins, debuts on Broadway and is an instant sensation • Tony Bennett's popular and critically acclaimed album *Beat of My Heart* uses well-known jazz musicians such as Herbie Mann, Nat Adderley, Art Blakey, Jo Jones, and Chico Hamilton • *Leave It to Beaver* premieres on CBS, ushering in an era of television shows that depict the "ideal" American family • Buddy Holly and the Crickets release their great rock-and-roll hit "Peggy Sue" • Althea Gibson is the first black tennis player to win a singles title at Wimbledon • The Wham-O company begins manufacturing the modern Frisbee flying disk • Miles Davis records the album *Birth of the Cool* • Dick Clark's *American Bandstand* show is broadcast for the first time on ABC [the show runs for 30 years, until 1987] • Elvis Presley purchases the Graceland mansion in Memphis and makes it his home • Films: Pat Boone stars in *April Love* (and has a hit single with the title tune); Ingmar Bergman achieves international recognition for his brooding, allegorical masterpiece, *The Seventh Seal*; other notable films include: *The Bridge on the River Kwai*; *Peyton Place*; *Sayonara*; *12 Angry Men*
1958	• A military coup d'état in France prompted by the Algerian war overthrows the government; Charles De Gaulle becomes premier; after adoption of a new constitution creating the Fifth Republic in France, de Gaulle is elected president	• The National Aeronautics and Space Administration (NASA) is established to develop space exploration and research initiatives, as well as coordinate space-related communications projects	• *Explorer 1* is the first successfully launched US spacecraft • NASA initiates Project Mercury, aimed at putting a man in space within two years • The USS *Nautilus* makes its first passage *under* the North Pole	• Eighteen-year-old Frank Camey opens the first Pizza Hut in Wichita, KS • Mahalia Jackson records "His Eye Is On The Sparrow" • *Billboard* magazine debuts its "Hot 100" chart; Ricky Nelson's "Poor Little Fool"

(cont.)

E. EDUCATION, LITERATURE & THE FINE ARTS	F. RELIGION, THEOLOGY, PHILOSOPHY & PSYCHOLOGY	G. AMERICAN & UNITED METHODISM	H. BRITISH & WORLD METHODISM	
• Marc Chagall completes *The Bible Series* consisting of 105 hand-colored etchings illustrating the Bible (66 of them had been completed between 1930 and 1939; he returned to work on them in 1952) • Aleksandr Solzhenitsyn completes *The Gulag Archipelago*, his thoroughly documented account of the Soviet police state, on which he had begun work in 1918 [it will be published in French in 1973 and in English in 1974] • Winston Churchill begins the publication of his *History of the English-Speaking Peoples* (to 1958) • John Osborne's play *Look Back in Anger* opens in London • Allen Ginsberg publishes *Howl and Other Poems* and gives voice to views of the "beat generation" about the false hopes and broken promises of American civilization • Senator and future president John F. Kennedy publishes his *Profiles in Courage*		– makes seminary education the norm for ministerial preparation by removing the "Seminary Rule" (1924), which had assumed that the course of study was the norm – institutes a plan for certification of church musicians – approves the establishment of two new seminaries (in Kansas City, MO, and Delaware, OH) • Maude K. Jensen, who had been ordained as a local elder in the MC in 1952 (Central Pennsylvania Conference), becomes the first of 27 women from 19 MC annual conferences to be received on trial and admitted as probationary members • The MC Woman's Division establishes the Brooks Howell Home as a residence for retired Woman's Division missionaries and deaconesses • The MC dissolves the Latin American Provisional Conference and the Oriental Provisional Conference, including Chinese, Korean, and Filipino churches in California • The Methodist Publishing House begins publication of *Together* magazine		**1956 cont.**
• Paul Hindemith composes his *Harmony of the World* • Toru Takemitsu composes his *Requiem for string orchestra* • Aaron Copland completes his *Orchestral Variations* • Eugene O'Neill's *A Long Day's Journey Into Night* is produced posthumously and wins both the Tony Award and Pulitzer Prize • Lawrence Durrell begins his Alexandria Quartet with *Justine* • Dr. Seuss (Theodore Geisel) gives the world two timeless classics of children's literature: *The Cat in the Hat* and *The Grinch Who Stole Christmas* • Jack Kerouac's controversial and mostly autobiographical novel *On the Road*, completed in 3 weeks and typed on one 120-foot long roll of paper, is a defining work for the postwar "beat" generation • Other notable publications include: – Nevil Shute, *On the Beach* – Ayn Rand, *Atlas Shrugged*	• The United Church of Christ (UCC) is created by the union of the General Council of the Congregational Christian Churches (1931) and the Evangelical and Reformed Church (1934) • The Evangelical Lutheran Synod is established in the US • Billy Graham's evangelistic crusade in New York runs nightly for 16 weeks and includes services in Yankee Stadium and Madison Square Garden, drawing audiences of over 2 million • *The Apocrypha of the Old Testament, Revised Standard Version*, is published • Frank L. Cross edits the first edition of the classic *Oxford Dictionary of the Christian Church* (2nd ed. 1974 by Cross and Elizabeth A. Livingstone; 3rd ed. 1997 and 4th ed. 2005 by Livingstone) – Paul Tillich, *The Dynamics of Faith* – Northrop Frye, *The Anatomy of Criticism* – Georgia Harkness, *Christian Ethics*	• The Methodist Theological School in Ohio is established in Delaware, OH; it opens for classes in 1960 • The Hinton Rural Life Center is established in Hayesville, NC, to be a retreat and resource center for small membership churches within the MC • The second Conference of Methodist Men meets • The Southern California School of Theology withdraws from the University of Southern California and moves to Claremont, CA, becoming the School of Theology at Claremont, later renamed Claremont School of Theology	• Clifford W. Towlson publishes *Moravian and Methodist*	**1957**
• Gian-Carlo Menotti founds the Festival of Two Worlds in Spoleto, Italy • Bartók's *Violin Concerto No. 1* is premiered in Basel, 50 years after it was composed • Igor Stravinsky composes his *Lamentations of Jeremiah*	• The [northern] United Presbyterian Church in the USA (UPCUSA) is formed by the merger of the PCUSA (1869) and the UPCNA (1858) • Pope Pius XII dies; he is succeeded by Pope John XXIII	• The EUBC General Conference: – reappoints a Committee on Church Federation and Union to explore the possibility of organic union with the Methodist Church – authorizes construction of a new denominational headquarters building in Dayton – adopts a declaration calling for racial integration throughout the church and for *(cont.)*	• The first Oxford Institute of Methodist Theological Studies meets • John M. Todd publishes *John Wesley and the Catholic Church*	**1958**

	A. WORLD HISTORY & POLITICS	B. AMERICAN HISTORY & POLITICS	C. SCIENCE, MEDICINE & TECHNOLOGY	D. DAILY LIFE, POPULAR CULTURE & ENTERTAINMENT
1958 cont.	• Egypt and Syria unite to form the United Arab Republic (UAR) with Egyptian president Nasser as President • Nikita Khrushchev becomes premier of the USSR • The Soviet Union agrees to loan $100 million to Egypt to finance the construction of the Aswan High Dam • China begins "The Great Leap Forward" under the leadership of Chairman Mao Zedong • The South African government tightens its apartheid policies • The Central African Republic becomes independent from France • The Brussels World's Fair attracts 42 million visitors	• The Federal Aviation Agency (later Administration) is created; the FAA replaces the 1926 Bureau of Air Commerce and has a broader mandate including development and operation of air traffic control and navigation systems for both civil and military aircraft • The US Supreme Court unanimously supports a lower court decision that public schools in Little Rock must be integrated • The State of Georgia acquires Stone Mountain and the surrounding area as a park	• The Boeing 707 begins jet transport service between the US and Europe • The first integrated circuit chip is developed by Jack Kilby of Texas Instruments (patent issued in 1959) • Earl Baaken creates the first electrical cardiac pulse generator or "pacemaker" to correct an irregular heartbeat • A British team led by Sir Vivian Fuchs completes the first crossing of the Antarctic in Snowcat Caterpillar tractors and dogsled teams in 99 days	becomes America's first "official" no. 1 pop record • The RIAA certifies Perry Como's hit single "Catch a Falling Star" as its first ever "Gold Record" (meaning that it has sold over 500,000 copies); the cast album of *Oklahoma!* featuring Gordon Macrae is the first RIAA-certified "Gold Album" • Bobby Darin records what will becomes his signature song, "Mack the Knife" (originally part of Kurt Weil's 1928 *Threepenny Opera*) • "La Bamba" by Richie Valens has unexpected success and becomes the first Latin crossover hit in rock-and-roll history • Elvis Presley is drafted into the US Army • American Express issues its first credit card, as does the Bank of America (initially called the BankAmericard, later Visa) • The modern plastic Hula Hoop is created by Richard Knerr and Arthur "Spud" Melin • The first computer-based video game is developed by William A. Higinbotham at the Brookhaven National Laboratory: "tennis for two on an oscilloscope" • The cost of a US first-class postage stamp increases to 4¢ • Films: *Cat on a Hot Tin Roof*; *Touch of Evil*; *Vertigo*; *South Pacific*
1959	• Fidel Castro enters Havana, overthrows the Batista regime, and installs a communist government; the US bans the import of Cuban sugar; in retaliation Cuba nationalizes some $850 million worth of US property and businesses; the US then severs diplomatic ties with Cuba but retains control of the Guantanamo Bay Naval Station • Mao Zedong, who was primarily responsible for the "Great Leap Forward" fiasco, formally steps down as leader of the Chinese Communist Party • Tibetans riot against Chinese occupation; the uprising is suppressed by force; the Dalai Lama escapes from Lhasa • In response to the creation of the EEC, Britain forms the European Free Trade Area (EFTA) consisting of seven members, including the Scandinavian countries and Switzerland • The Antarctic Treaty, which prohibits nuclear explosions and disposal of radioactive waste in Antarctica, is signed by 12 nations including the US and the USSR • Britain recognizes the independence of Cyprus • Libya achieves independence from Italy • Rwanda is separated from Uganda • Singapore becomes a self-governing British crown colony • Yassir Arafat founds the Palestinian National Liberation Movement, known by its Arabic acronym as Fatah (meaning in Arabic "opening" or "conquest")	• Alaska and Hawaii are admitted to the US as the 49th and 50th states respectively • The Saint Lawrence Seaway opens to shipping; jointly administered by the US and Canada, it allows oceangoing vessels to reach the Great Lakes from the Atlantic Ocean • Soviet Premier Khrushchev tours the US, meeting with President Eisenhower at Camp David • The US Supreme Court upholds an injunction issued under the 1947 Taft-Hartley Act as constitutional, ending a 116-day strike by steelworkers in Pittsburgh • The USS *George Washington* is launched as the first submarine to carry ballistic missiles • Confederate Army veteran Walter Williams, the last survivor of the more than 4 million soldiers who fought in the Civil War, dies at age 117	• NASA announces its selection of seven military pilots to become the first US astronauts: Scott Carpenter, Gordon Cooper, John Glenn, Virgil "Gus" Grissom, Walter Schirra, Alan Shepard, and Donald "Deke" Slayton are the "Mercury Seven" • The US deploys the Atlas rocket, the first intercontinental ballistic missile (ICBM) • The Lunik II probe (USSR) reaches the moon; Lunik III photographs the dark side of the moon for the first time • Magnetic ink character recognition is developed to process checks • Xerox introduces the plain-paper photocopier; the name of the company soon comes to be popularly used as a synonym for the act of making photocopies ("I need to xerox this . . .") and also for the copies made ("xeroxes") • Motorola produces the first fully transistorized two-way mobile radio	• Richard Rodgers and Oscar Hammerstein's last great musical collaboration, *The Sound of Music*, opens on Broadway • Lorraine Hansbury's *A Raisin in the Sun* is the first Broadway play by a black woman • The National Academy of Recording Arts and Sciences sponsors the first Grammy Award ceremony (for music recorded in 1958) • Miles Davis records *Kind of Blue*, perhaps the single most influential album in the history of jazz • Ornette Coleman plays a legendary and controversial concert at New York's Five Spot • Barry Gordy establishes Motown Records in Detroit • The Kingston Trio helps to establish "modern" folk music with release of their albums *From the "Hungry i"* and *The Kingston Trio at Large* • Rock-and-roll stars Buddy Holly, Richie Valens, and the Big Bopper (J. P. Richardson) are killed in an airplane crash • The comedy team of Bob and Ray is a top radio attraction • A scandal erupts when "Twenty-One" game show contestant Charles Van Doren admits to a congressional committee that he had been given questions and answers in advance • Films: *Ben-Hur*; *Some Like It Hot*; *North by Northwest*; *Suddenly Last Summer*

E. EDUCATION, LITERATURE & THE FINE ARTS	F. RELIGION, THEOLOGY, PHILOSOPHY & PSYCHOLOGY	G. AMERICAN & UNITED METHODISM	H. BRITISH & WORLD METHODISM	
• Ralph Vaughan Williams composes his *Symphony No. 9* • Alvin Ailey establishes the American Dance Theatre • Beat generation poet Lawrence Ferlinghetti publishes his most influential collection of verse, *A Coney Island of the Mind* • Lawrence Durrell continues his Alexandria Quartet with *Balthazar* and *Mountolive* • Other notable publications include: – Harold Pinter, *The Birthday Party* – John Kenneth Galbraith, *The Affluent Society* – Leon Uris, *Exodus*	• Notable publications include: – Thomas Merton, *Thoughts in Solitude* – Michael Polanyi, *Personal Knowledge: Towards a Post-Critical Philosophy* – John R. W. Stott, *Basic Christianity*	cross-racial ministerial appointments "where advisable for more effective service to multiracial congregations" – creates the position of Secretary of Stewardship within the General Council of Administration – approves a special $5 million financial campaign for the following quadrennium, of which $2 million is intended for support of the annual conferences • Sally A. Crenshaw and Nora E. Young are the first black Methodist women received into full connection in the MC (East Tennessee Conference) • *Acción Metodista* (the Spanish language adaptation of *The Methodist Story*) makes its debut; it is reorganized in 1973 as *El Intérprete* • The fifth Assembly of the WSCS and WSG (MC) meets • The third Convention of the WSWS (EUBC) meets • St. Paul School of Theology (originally named National Methodist Theological Seminary) is founded in Kansas City, MO; it opens for classes in 1961 • Westminster Theological Seminary, established by the MPC in 1881, moves to Washington and is renamed Wesley Theological Seminary • The Interdenominational Theological Center is established in Atlanta; the founding institutions include Gammon Theological Seminary (MEC/UM, 1883), Turner Theological Seminary (AMEC, 1885/1894), Phillips School of Theology (CMEC, 1944/1950), along with the Morehouse School of Religion (Baptist, 1867); Phillips relocates from Jackson, TN, to Atlanta • Elmer T. Clark publishes his edition of *The Journal and Letters of Francis Asbury* (3 vols.)		**1958 cont.**
• The US Supreme Court rules that D. H. Lawrence's erotic novel *Lady Chatterley's Lover* is not obscene and allows its publication in the US • The Solomon R. Guggenheim Museum in New York, designed by Frank Lloyd Wright, opens to the public • Elliott Carter completes his *String Quartet No. 2* • William Strunk Jr. and E. B. White publish their influential guide to good writing, *The Elements of Style* • Other notable publications include: – Boris Pasternak, *Doctor Zhivago* – Gunter Grass, *The Tin Drum* – Philip Roth, *Goodbye, Columbus* – James Michener, *Hawaii*	• Notable publications include: – Pierre Teilhard de Chardin, *The Phenomenon of Man* – John Bright, *A History of Israel* – James M. Robinson, *A New Quest of the Historical Jesus*	• The MC Department of Town and Country Work publishes *Emerging Patterns in Town and Country Methodism, Regarding Beliefs, Organization, Leadership, and Outreach*, one of the first studies to try to take seriously the changing patterns of Methodism in postwar America • The World Christian Fellowship Window is installed and dedicated in the Upper Room Chapel in Nashville • Warren Thomas Smith publishes *Thomas Coke: The Foreign Minister of Methodism*, the first modern biography of Coke	• Gusta A. Robinett, an MC missionary, is the first woman appointed by the MC as district superintendent (Medan Chinese District, Sumatra Conference in Indonesia) • Westminster College moves from London to Oxford; it is expanded and once again admits women as students • The CMEC establishes its first missions on the African continent in Ghana and Nigeria • John A. Parker publishes *A Church in the Sun: The Story of the Rise of Methodism in the Island of Grenada, West Indies*	**1959**

	A. WORLD HISTORY & POLITICS	B. AMERICAN HISTORY & POLITICS	C. SCIENCE, MEDICINE & TECHNOLOGY	D. DAILY LIFE, POPULAR CULTURE & ENTERTAINMENT
1960	• The Organization of Petroleum Exporting Countries (OPEC) is founded with Iran, Iraq, Kuwait, Saudi Arabia, and Venezuela as members; since then Qatar (1961), Indonesia (1962), Libya (1962), United Arab Emirates (1967), Algeria (1969), and Nigeria (1971) have joined the organization • American U-2 pilot Frances Gary Powers is shot down over Russia, then tried and convicted of spying • White police in South Africa open fire on a mass political demonstration, killing 69 blacks and wounding more than 180 in what comes to be known as the Sharpeville Massacre; this greatly increases the militancy of black protests against apartheid • Alienated middle- and upper-class Cubans who had once supported the Cuban revolution begin migrating to the US in large numbers, forming a vocal anti-Castro community in Miami; Castro nationalizes all US-owned business or commercial property in Cuba • The USSR and China come into conflict over Communist ideology; Nikita Khrushchev publicly attacks the policies of Mao Zedong • France grants independence to its former African colonies: Benin, Cameroon, Chad, Congo, Gabon, Guinea, Madagascar, Mali, Mauritania, Niger, Nigeria, Senegal, Togo, and Upper Volta (now Burkina Faso) • The Belgian Congo (now Democratic Republic of the Congo) becomes independent of Belgium, and Somalia and Sierra Leone become independent from Italy and Britain • Sirimavo R. D. Bandaranaike becomes the prime minister of Ceylon [now Sri Lanka], making her the first woman to serve as an elected head of state • The new city of Brasilia replaces Rio de Janeiro as the capital of Brazil	• The US census reports that the population is 179,323,175: – whites: 158,831,732 (88.6%) – blacks: 18,871,831 (10.5%) – other: 1,619,612 (0.9%) • The US national debt is $290,216,815,241 • Ninety percent of US homes have a television set; seventy million people watch the first televised presidential debate between Senator John F. Kennedy and Vice President Richard Nixon • Four black students from North Carolina A&T College start the first "sit-in" protest at a segregated Woolworth's lunch counter in Greensboro, NC, when they are refused service; the event triggers many similar nonviolent protests throughout the South • The Student Nonviolent Coordinating Committee (SNCC) is founded at Shaw University, providing young blacks with a place in the civil rights movement; SNCC later grows into a more radical organization, especially under the leadership of Stokely Carmichael (1966–67) • Revival of the KKK is formalized when the "Invisible Empire, United Klans, Knights of the Ku Klux Klan of America, Inc." is chartered in Georgia; it comes to be known as the United Klans of America (UKA); Robert Shelton becomes Imperial Wizard in 1961 • The Arctic National Wildlife Range (ANWR) is created by Congress "for the purpose of preserving unique wildlife, wilderness and recreational values" • The Multiple Use-Sustained Yield Act states that National Forests must be administered not solely for the purpose of timber production but also for outdoor recreation, range, watershed, and wildlife and fish purposes • American nightclub performer Sammy Davis Jr., who is black, marries Swedish actress May Britt; the marriage provokes intense controversy across the US because interracial marriage is still illegal in 31 out of 50 US states • John F. Kennedy is elected as president and Lyndon B. Johnson as vice president (Democratic Party)	• The US Food and Drug Administration approves the sale of Enovid, the first hormone-based oral contraceptive available in the US • France joins the "nuclear club" with the successful test of its first thermonuclear device • The first successful human coronary artery bypass (anastomosis) is performed by Robert H. Goetz at the Albert Einstein College of Medicine-Bronx Municipal Hospital Center • Ali Javan invents the first functional helium neon gas laser at MIT • The US nuclear submarine Triton goes around the world nonstop • NASA launches Tiros I, the first weather satellite; Echo I, the first communications satellite; and Transat I, the first navigation satellite • Jacques Piccard and Don Walsh in the bathyscaphe USS Trieste break a depth record when they descend to the bottom of Challenger Deep 35,820 feet below sea level in the Pacific Ocean • President Eisenhower formally dedicates the Marshall Space Flight Center in Huntsville, AL	• The availability of "the pill" (the oral contraceptive Enovid and its successors) helps to fuel the sexual revolution in America • Alan Jay Lerner and Frederick Loewe's musical Camelot opens on Broadway • Night club entertainers Frank Sinatra, Dean Martin, Joey Bishop, and Sammy Davis Jr., make up the "Rat Pack" in Las Vegas • John Coltrane forms his own quartet and becomes the voice of the New Wave movement in jazz music • The Dave Brubeck Quartet records "Take Five," the best-selling jazz single of the century • Ray Charles records his classic version of "Georgia On My Mind" • Chubby Checker's "The Twist" launches a nationwide dance craze • Luther Simjian invents the first automatic teller machine (ATM), which he calls the Bankmatic • Domino's Pizza begins home delivery service, taking orders by phone • Harold Rhodes develops the first electric piano • The Atlanta YWCA opens the first desegregated public dining facility in the city • The Parker 45 fountain pen takes replaceable individual ink cartridges • Little Debbie Snack Cakes are produced for the first time in Collegedale, TN • The Aluminum Specialty Company introduces its flagship aluminum Christmas tree, the "Evergleam" • Mattel's "Chatty Cathy" doll speaks 11 phrases in random order • Films: Alfred Hitchcock's riveting Psycho; Frederico Felini's scandalous (at the time) La Dolce Vita; the legacy film of the "Rat Pack," Ocean's Eleven; Inherit the Wind; Spartacus; Elmer Gantry; The Magnificent Seven; The Apartment • Summer Olympics: Rome • Winter Olympics: Squaw Valley
1961	• The United Arab Republic collapses after a military coup d'état in Syria; Egypt continues to use the name UAR until the death of Egyptian president Nasser in 1970 • President Kennedy orders 100 "special forces" troops to South Vietnam; this marks the beginning point of US involvement in what will become the Vietnam War • East Germany constructs the Berlin Wall to prevent East Germans from escaping to the West • The "Bay of Pigs" invasion of Cuba (by Cuban refugees backed by the US) fails • U Thant (Burma, now Myanmar) is elected UN Secretary-General after Dag Hammarskjöld is killed in a plane crash	• President Kennedy, in his inaugural address, urges all Americans to "Ask not what your country can do for you; ask what you can do for your country" • At Kennedy's urging, Congress establishes the US Peace Corps • Kennedy creates the President's Commission on the Status of Women and appoints Eleanor Roosevelt as chairwoman • The 23rd Amendment to the US Constitution grants the District of Columbia (Washington, DC) the right to vote for three electors in presidential elections • CORE and the SNCC begin sending new groups of "freedom riders" on bus trips across the South to test compliance with new laws prohibiting segregation in interstate travel facilities	• Yuri Gagarin (USSR) becomes first human to orbit the earth • Ham, a 37-pound male chimpanzee, is rocketed into space in a test of NASA's Project Mercury capsule designed to carry US astronauts into space; he survives and lives for 17 more years • Alan Shepard becomes the first American in space, completing a 15-minute suborbital hop in a Project Mercury capsule • IBM introduces the Selectric "golf ball" typewriter • The FCC approves FM stereo broadcasting; this spurs the development of FM radio • Bell Labs tests communication by light waves • Sony markets a helical scan videotape recorder	• Country music superstar Patsy Cline records two of her biggest hits, "I Fall to Pieces" and Willie Nelson's great song "Crazy," which eventually becomes the number one jukebox single of all time • Roy Orbison has a big hit with "Crying (Over You)" • Ricky Nelson makes his mark with "Hello Mary Lou" and "Travelin' Man" • The Miracles' "Shop Around" becomes Motown's first million-selling single • The Shirelles record Carole King's "Will You Still Love Me Tomorrow"

E. EDUCATION, LITERATURE & THE FINE ARTS	F. RELIGION, THEOLOGY, PHILOSOPHY & PSYCHOLOGY	G. AMERICAN & UNITED METHODISM	H. BRITISH & WORLD METHODISM	
• Krzysztof Penderecki composes his *Threnody for the Victims of Hiroshima* • Mario Davidovsky composes his *Contrastes No. 1* for string orchestra and electronic sounds • Malcolm Arnold completes his *Symphony No. 4* • Lawrence Durrell completes his *Alexandria Quartet* with *Clea* • Dr. Seuss tells the world all about *Green Eggs and Ham* • Other notable publications include: – John Updike, *Rabbit, Run* – Harper Lee, *To Kill A Mockingbird* – Flannery O'Connor, *The Violent Bear It Away* – John Barth, *The Sot-Weed Factor*	• The American Lutheran Church (ALC, 1930, German), United Evangelical Lutheran Church (UELC, Danish, 1896) and the Evangelical Lutheran Church (ELC, Norwegian, 1917/1946) merge to form The American Lutheran Church (ALC) • Eugene Carson Blake, then Stated Clerk of the UPCUSA, calls for organic union (complete merger) of the UPCUSA, the Methodist Church, the Protestant Episcopal Church, and the United Church of Christ; this results in establishment in 1962 of the Consultation on Church Union (COCU), which later expands to include the AMEC, AMEZC, CMEC, Christian Church (Disciples of Christ), and the International Council of Community Churches • Hans-Georg Gadamer's *Truth and Method* outlines his theory of hermeneutics (the science of interpretation), which focuses on the creation of meaning in the dynamic relationship between text and interpreter through the act of reading • Other notable publications include: – Jean-Paul Sartre, *Critique of Dialectical Reason* – H. Richard Niebuhr, *Radical Monotheism and Western Culture* – Thomas Merton, *The Wisdom of the Desert* – John Courtney Murray, *We Hold These Truths: Catholic Reflections on the American Proposition* – Georgia Harkness, *Divine Providence* – L. Harold DeWolf, *A Theology of the Living Church* – Daniel T. Niles, *Who Is This Jesus?*	• The MC General Conference: – merges the Board of World Peace, the Board of Temperance, and the Board of Economic and Social Relations into one new general agency, the Board of Christian Social Relations – creates the Methodist Development Fund as a national loan fund to help churches in the US obtain money for the purchase of property and the construction of new buildings – sets up the Commission on Interjurisdictional Relations to consider abolition of the Central Jurisdiction – reestablishes the Methodist Student Movement for ministry to college students – instructs COSMOS to undertake a study of the overseas structure of the MC – revises its position concerning divorce to allow the remarriage of divorced persons following "adequate preparation and counseling" • The Central Jurisdiction forms the "Committee of Five" to study ways of eliminating the jurisdiction • The AMEC General Conference grants full clergy rights to women • The Free Methodist Church celebrates the centennial of its establishment • Notable publications include: – Colin W. Williams, *John Wesley's Theology Today*, which gives a systematic interpretation of Wesley's theology with a view to its contributions to the ecumenical movement – S. Paul Schilling, *Methodism and Society in Theological Perspective* – John Deschner, *Wesley's Christology: An Interpretation*	• Methodism in the Caribbean celebrates the bicentennial of its formal establishment in Antigua • Methodist churches in Ireland, South America, South Korea, and South Africa allow the ordination of women as elders • Albert M. Lyles publishes *Methodism Mocked: The Satiric Reaction to Methodism in the 18th Century*	**1960**
• Kodály composes his *Symphony in C Major* • Krzysztof Penderecki composes his *Dimensions of Time and Silence* for orchestra and chorus • Leonard Bernstein composes his suite of *Symphonic Dances from "West Side Story"* • Marc Chagall publishes his suite of 42 luminous color lithographs illustrating *Daphnis and Chloe* • Franz Fanon's *The Wretched of the Earth* analyzes the role of class, race, national culture, and violence in the struggle for national liberation	• The Progressive National Baptist Convention is formed by black Baptists who reject the passive stance of the National Baptist Convention, USA, on civil rights issues; key leaders include Gardner C. Taylor, Martin Luther King, Jr., Ralph Abernathy, and Benjamin Mays • The Bible Presbyterian Church, Columbus Synod (1955) becomes the Evangelical Presbyterian Church (to 1965) • The Universalist Church of America (1790) merges with most congregations of the American Unitarian Association (1825) in the US to form the Unitarian Universalist Association (UUA)	• The third Conference of Methodist Men meets • All American Methodist missionaries are recalled from Cuba; many native Cuban pastors follow • The Central Jurisdiction "Committee of Five" issues a report, "The Central Jurisdiction Speaks," calling for elimination of "all forms of racial segregation and discrimination in the Methodist Church" • Julia Torres Fernandez is the first Hispanic/Latina woman to be ordained and received into full connection in the MC (Puerto Rico Provisional Conference) • Notable publications include:	• The tenth World Methodist Conference meets in Oslo, Norway • The Methodist Church of Ghana becomes autonomous • The Methodist Church in Fiji allows the ordination of women as elders • The archives of the MC [UK] and of British Methodism more broadly are established in Epworth House at City Road Chapel in London • Notable publications include: – Maldwyn Edwards, *Family Circle: A Study of the Epworth Household in Relation to John and Charles Wesley* – John C. Bowmer, *The Lord's Supper in Methodism, 1791–1960* – V. H. H. Green, *The Young Mr. Wesley: A Study of John Wesley and Oxford*	**1961**

	A. WORLD HISTORY & POLITICS	B. AMERICAN HISTORY & POLITICS	C. SCIENCE, MEDICINE & TECHNOLOGY	D. DAILY LIFE, POPULAR CULTURE & ENTERTAINMENT
1961 cont.	• Stalingrad is renamed as Volgograd, reversing the 1925 change of names • The farthing coin, used since the 13th century, ceases to be legal tender in the UK • Former Nazi party leader Adolf Eichmann, captured in Argentina in 1960, goes on trial in Jerusalem; he is convicted of crimes against humanity and executed by hanging in 1962 in the only death sentence ever imposed by an Israeli court • The international human rights organization Amnesty International is founded in London	• Amendments to the Fair Labor Standards Act of 1938 extend its coverage to employees in large retail and service enterprises as well as to local transit, construction, and gasoline service station employees; the minimum wage is set at $1.00 per hour • The US severs all diplomatic relations with Cuba • Charlayne Hunter-Gault and Hamilton Holmes become the first black students to attend the University of Georgia	• Jack Lippes develops the contraceptive intrauterine device (IUD) • Three workers are killed by an accident at the experimental SR-1 nuclear reactor in Idaho • Neil Armstrong sets a world speed record of 6,587 km/h (4,093 mph) in the X-15 rocket plane	• Roger Maris hits 61 home runs, breaking Babe Ruth's record (60) from 1927 • Ernie Davis, from Syracuse University, is the first black football player to win the Heisman Trophy • Julia Child publishes *Mastering the Art of French Cooking*; it will be a best seller for years • The Country Music Hall of Fame is established in Nashville; the first inductees are Jimmie Rodgers, Fred Rose, and Hank Williams • Films: *West Side Story*; *The Guns of Navarone*; *Breakfast at Tiffany's*; *Splendor in the Grass*; *Judgment at Nuremberg*; *The Misfits*; *The Hustler*
1962	• The Cuban missile crisis brings the world to the brink of nuclear war; the US declares a naval blockade of Cuba; a military confrontation between the US and the USSR is narrowly averted when the Soviets withdraw their missiles from Cuba • President Kennedy orders an immediate build-up of US troops in Thailand due to Communist attacks in Laos and movement toward the Thailand border • Nelson Mandela is imprisoned in South Africa for activities against apartheid laws • Algeria, Burundi, Jamaica, Rwanda, Trinidad and Tobago, Uganda, and Western Samoa all become independent from their formal colonial masters • Fighting breaks out between China and India along their border • The United Nations General Assembly passes a resolution condemning South Africa's racist apartheid policies and calls for all UN member states to cease military and economic relations with South Africa	• James Meredith becomes the first black student to attend the University of Mississippi, despite strenuous opposition by Governor Ross Barnett; President Kennedy dispatches federal marshals to enforce a court order for Meredith's admission; during the ensuing riots, 2 people are killed and 160 federal marshals are wounded • The US Supreme Court orders the state of Tennessee to redraw its legislative districts, holding that having districts with wildly unequal numbers of people, as Tennessee did, violated the "equal protection" provision of the 14th Amendment • The US Supreme Court rules that a state-composed prayer, even if nondenominational in nature, represents government sponsorship of religion and so violates the establishment clause of the 1st Amendment • Illinois becomes the first state in the US to decriminalize homosexual acts between consenting adults in private • Seattle hosts the World's Fair, with the futuristic Space Needle as its symbol; it attracts 9.5 million visitors • Daniel K. Inouye (Hawaii) is the first person of Asian heritage elected to the US Senate • First Lady Jacqueline Kennedy takes television viewers on a visual tour of the White House, the first time TV has been used for such a purpose	• John Glenn, in *Freedom 7*, becomes the first American to orbit the earth • AT&T's *Telstar*, the first international communication satellite, is placed in orbit • NASA's *Mariner 2*, the first interplanetary space probe, reaches Venus and sends back radio signals • Rachel Carson's gripping novel *Silent Spring* helps to create a worldwide awareness of the dangers of environmental pollution and leads to a ban on the use of DDT and similar pesticides • The Space Needle, constructed for the World's Fair in Seattle, is the tallest structure in the US west of the Mississippi River at 605 feet • AT&T and the Bell System demonstrate the first commercial touch-tone phones at the Seattle World's Fair • Britain and France sign an agreement to develop the Concorde supersonic airliner	• Stephen Sondheim's musical *A Funny Thing Happened on the Way to the Forum* opens on Broadway • Barbara Streisand makes her Broadway debut in *I Can Get It For You Wholesale* • Johnny Carson takes over as the host of *The Tonight Show* • The Beatles replace drummer Pete Best with Ringo Starr, then release their first hit single in Britain, "Love Me Do"/"P.S. I Love You" • Chubby Checker's "The Twist" becomes the only song in US history to reenter the charts and hit #1 for a second time • Wilt Chamberlain sets an NBA single-game scoring record with 100 points • Sam Walton opens the first Wal-Mart store in Rogers, AR • Helen Gurley Brown's *Sex and the Single Girl* suggests that sex outside of marriage is an attractive option for single career women • The TV show *That Girl*, starring Marlo Thomas as a single young actress trying to "make it" in New York, shatters conventional sitcom stereotypes about women • The Pittsburgh Brewing Company begins selling its Iron City Beer in the first self-opening pull-tab "pop-top" cans • Andy Warhol paints his iconic portrait of Marilyn Monroe; soon after she is found dead at her home of a drug overdose • Edward Albee's *Who's Afraid of Virginia Woolf?* opens on Broadway • Films: Sean Connery brings James Bond to the screen for the first time in *Dr. No*; other notable films include *Lawrence of Arabia*; *The Manchurian Candidate*; *To Kill a Mockingbird*; *The Miracle Worker*; *The Longest Day*
1963	• A radio and telegraph "Hot Line" is established between the US and the USSR to prevent possible accidents • The US and the USSR sign the Limited Test Ban Treaty, which prohibits underwater, atmospheric, and outer space nuclear tests (more than 100 countries have ratified the treaty since 1963) • Winston Churchill becomes the first honorary US citizen when President Kennedy bestows that honor on him	• George Wallace ends the inaugural address for his second term as governor of Alabama by proclaiming "segregation now . . . segregation tomorrow . . . segregation forever" • When Wallace fulfills his campaign pledge to block desegregation of the University of Alabama by "standing in the schoolhouse door," President Kennedy federalizes the Alabama National Guard to enforce a US Circuit Court desegregation order • During civil rights protests in Birmingham, Eugene "Bull" Connor, the Commissioner of Public Safety orders the *(cont.)*	• Valentina Tereshkova (USSR) becomes the first woman in space • Kodak introduces the first "point-and-shoot" camera, the Instamatic • Sony offers an open-reel videotape recorder for home use • Philips introduces the Musicassette (the cassette tape) at the Berlin Funkausstellung • The US nuclear submarine *Thresher* sinks under mysterious circumstances 220 miles east of Cape Cod; all 129 sailors aboard are lost • NASA launches *Mercury 9*, the last mission of the program	• Betty Friedan's *The Feminine Mystique* galvanizes the modern women's rights movement • *The French Chef*, starring Julia Child, appears on public TV • The US Post Office introduces the ZIP code system (ZIP + four is added in 1983) • The all-white Mississippi State University basketball team sneaks out of town in the middle of the night despite protests from the governor and state police of Mississippi to play a team from Loyola University that features four black starters

E. EDUCATION, LITERATURE & THE FINE ARTS	F. RELIGION, THEOLOGY, PHILOSOPHY & PSYCHOLOGY	G. AMERICAN & UNITED METHODISM	H. BRITISH & WORLD METHODISM	
• Joseph Heller's memorable novel *Catch-22* establishes the use of its title in popular language to describe a no-win situation • Other notable publications include: – Tennessee Williams, *Night of the Iguana* – John Steinbeck, *The Winter of Our Discontent* – Walker Percy, *The Moviegoer* – Muriel Spark, *The Prime of Miss Jean Brodie* – Robert Heinlein, *Stranger in a Strange Land* – Irving Stone, *The Agony and the Ecstasy*	• The Orthodox Churches join the World Council of Churches • The New Testament of The New English Bible (NEB) is published; the OT follows in 1970 • Other notable publications include: – Wolfhart Pannenberg, et al., *Revelation as History* – Schubert Ogden, *Christ Without Myth* – Thomas Szasz, *The Myth of Mental Illness* – John Howard Griffin, *Black Like Me*	– Richard M. Cameron, *Methodism and Society in Historical Perspective* – Walter G. Muelder, *Methodism and Society in the Twentieth Century*		**1961 cont.**
• Marc Chagall creates the 12 magnificent stained glass windows of the Hadassah Hospital in Jerusalem • The first performance of Benjamin Britten's *War Requiem* takes place in Coventry Cathedral, which has been rebuilt after its destruction by German bombs during WWII • Francis Poulenc's *Gloria* is premiered by the Boston Symphony Orchestra • Edgar Varèse composes his *Nocturnal* • Dmitri Shostakovich finishes his *Symphony No. 13 in B Flat Minor (Babi-Yar)* • Krzysztof Penderecki composes his *Stabat Mater* • Leonard Bernstein publishes his educational and informative *Young People's Concerts for Reading and Listening* (a book and record combination), adapted from his television show of the same name (revised edition 1970) • Aleksandr Solzhenitsyn publishes his novel *One Day in the Life of Ivan Denisovich*, which is based on his own experiences as a political prisoner in the USSR • Other notable publications include: – Philip K. Dick, *The Man in the High Castle* – Ken Kesey, *One Flew Over the Cuckoo's Nest* – James Baldwin, *Another Country* – Anthony Burgess, *A Clockwork Orange* – Doris Lessing, *The Golden Notebook*	• Second Vatican Council, opened by Pope John XXIII and closed by Pope Paul VI in 1965, ushers in an era of *aggiornamento* ("updating") in Roman Catholicism, leading to such reforms as celebration of the Mass in local languages rather than only in Latin • The Lutheran Church in America (LCA) results from a merger of the Swedish Augustana Synod (1860), the American Evangelical Lutheran Church (AELC, Danish, 1874), the Finnish Evangelical Lutheran Church (1890), and the United Lutheran Church in America (ULCA, German, Slovak, and Icelandic, 1918) • The Consultation on Church Union (COCU) is formally established after conversations beginning in 1960 • Because of his hostility to the Roman Catholic Church, Cuban revolutionary leader Fidel Castro is excommunicated by Pope John XXIII • The Full Gospel Fellowship is established in Dallas to support Pentecostal ministry • Thomas Kuhn publishes his landmark study *The Structure of Scientific Revolution*, articulating his theory of gradual incremental change followed by sudden "paradigm shifts" • Other notable publications include: – Karl Barth, *Evangelical Theology: An Introduction* – Chinua Achebe, *Things Fall Apart* – Erich Fromm, *Beyond the Chains of Illusions* – Viktor Frankl, *Man's Search for Meaning* – Charles Hartshorne, *The Logic of Perfection* – Thomas Merton, *New Seeds of Contemplation* – Abraham Heschel, *The Prophets* (2 vols.)	• The EUBC General Conference: – hears an address by Charles C. Parlan of the MC describing the prospects for church union – authorizes the Committee on Church Federation and Union to proceed with its work on the assumption of union – approves a consolidation of the Confession of Faith of the former UBC and the Articles of Religion of the former EC into a single new Confession of Faith of the EUBC; action subsequently ratified by the annual conferences – establishes a new organization for the Board of Publication and names one publisher to head both the Evangelical Press (former EC) in Harrisburg and the Otterbein Press (former UBC) in Dayton – revises the statement of the *Discipline* on divorce and remarriage to allow a "more realistic and more redemptive ministry" – rejects a proposal to go on record as being opposed to capital punishment • The sixth Assembly of the WSCS and WSG (MC) meets • The fourth Convention of the WSWS (EUBC) meets • The MC Woman's Division adopts a "New Charter for Racial Policies" [it is later approved by the 1964 General Conference] • The journal *Methodist History* is established as the official historical journal of the MC • Notable publications include: – Herbert E. Stotts and Paul Deats Jr., *Methodism and Society: Guidelines for Strategy* – Lycurgus M. Starkey, *The Work of the Holy Spirit: A Study in Wesleyan Theology*	• The Methodist Church of Nigeria becomes autonomous, merging the WM districts of western Nigeria and the PM districts of eastern Nigeria • The Chiesia Evangelica Metodista d'Italia (Evangelical Methodist Church of Italy) becomes an autonomous overseas conference of the MC [UK] • The second Oxford Institute of Methodist Theological Studies meets	**1962**
• Leonard Bernstein composes his *Symphony No. 3 (Kaddish)* for orchestra, mixed chorus, boys' choir, speaker, and soprano solo • Maurice Sendak publishes his prize-winning illustrated children's book, *Where the Wild Things Are* • Jessica Mitford's *The American Way of Death* provides a blistering critique of unscrupulous practices of the American funeral industry	• Eight white religious leaders in Alabama (Methodist bishops Nolan Harmon and Paul Hardin; Episcopal bishops Charles Carpenter and George Murray; Roman Catholic bishop Joseph A. Durick; rabbi Milton Grafman; Baptist minister Earl Stallings; and Presbyterian minister Edward Ramage) publish an open letter criticizing George Wallace's defiance of federal laws and court orders on integration, incurring the wrath of Klansmen and other defenders of white supremacy; then they publish a second open letter criticizing Martin *(cont.)*	• The MC Woman's Division dedicates the Church Center for the United Nations; the 12-story building directly across from the main UN building provides office and meeting space for religious and other nongovernmental organizations connected with the work of the UN • A group of 28 Methodist pastors in the Mississippi Conference issue the landmark "Born of Conviction" declaration, condemning racism and affirming the statement of the Church's Social Creed that "all men *(cont.)*	• The Methodist Church of Ceylon becomes autonomous • The Methodist Church of the Ivory Coast becomes autonomous	**1963**

	A. WORLD HISTORY & POLITICS	B. AMERICAN HISTORY & POLITICS	C. SCIENCE, MEDICINE & TECHNOLOGY	D. DAILY LIFE, POPULAR CULTURE & ENTERTAINMENT
1963 cont.	• Alec Douglas-Home becomes British prime minister • Ludwig Erhard becomes chancellor of Germany • Levi Eshkol becomes prime minister in Israel • Ayatollah Ruhollah Khomeini is exiled from Iran by the Shah; Khomeini goes to Najaf, Iraq, where he studies with Ayatollah Bakr Sadr; together they develop the ideology of revolutionary Shiite Islam; Bakr Sadr then founds the underground movement Al Dawa (The Call) • Kenya and Zanzibar achieve independence from Britain; Zanzibar unites with Tanganyika to form Tanzania • The Organization of African Unity (OAU) is created by the newly independent nations of Africa • The independent Federation of Malaysia is formed through the merging of the former British colonies of Malaya and Singapore with North Borneo (renamed Sabah) and Sarawak • South Vietnamese President Ngo Dinh Diem is assassinated following a military coup (probably with US complicity); General Duong Van Minh takes over leadership of South Vietnam	use of fire hoses and police dogs on black demonstrators; televised images of this brutality result in greatly increased sympathy for the civil rights movement around the world • Medgar Evers is shot and killed in Jackson, MS; he is one of the first martyrs of the civil rights movement • President Kennedy delivers his "Ich bin ein Berliner" speech in West Berlin • Harvey Gantt is the first black student to enter Clemson College in South Carolina, the last US state to hold out against integration of its colleges and universities • The US Supreme Court rules that Bible reading and recitation of the Lord's Prayer as official exercises in public schools are unconstitutional • Congress passes the Equal Pay Act, making it illegal for employers to pay a woman less than a man would receive for the same job • The March on Washington brings 200,000 people to the Lincoln Memorial, where Martin Luther King, Jr., delivers his immortal "I Have a Dream" speech • A bomb explodes at the Sixteenth Street Baptist Church in Birmingham, killing four young black children • Malcolm X establishes the Organization of Afro-American Unity in Detroit • Construction resumes on the Stone Mountain Memorial carving of Robert E. Lee, Stonewall Jackson, and Jefferson Davis (begun in 1916, suspended in 1928 due to lack of funds) • President Kennedy is shot and killed during a motorcade in Dallas; Vice President Johnson is sworn in as president in the airplane bringing Kennedy's body back to Washington • Lee Harvey Oswald is arrested and charged with Kennedy's assassination; while in police custody he is shot and killed by Dallas nightclub owner Jack Ruby • President Kennedy is buried in Arlington National Cemetery after the first televised state funeral in US history		• The Beatles have their first megahits in the US with "Please Please Me," "She Loves You," "Love Me Do," "I Want To Hold Your Hand," and "(With Love) From Me To You" [in early 1964 they hold the top 5 positions on the Billboard 100 singles chart, an achievement never equaled since] • Louis Armstrong records his version of "Hello, Dolly"; it eventually reaches no. 1 on the pop charts in 1965, displacing the Beatles at the time • Patsy Cline, considered by many to be country music's all-time greatest female singer, is killed in an airplane crash • The Whisky a Go-Go night club in Los Angeles, the first disco in the US, opens • The Beach Boys define the California "surf music" sound with their hit "Surfin' U.S.A." • Peter, Paul, and Mary sing Bob Dylan's "Blowin' in the Wind" at the 1963 March on Washington • Inspired by the 1928 recordings of blues guitarist "Mississippi" John Hurt, folk musicologist Tom Hoskins locates him in Mississippi and invites him to the Newport Folk Festival, where he is a sensation and his career is reborn • Barbra Streisand earns both fame and critical acclaim for her portrayal of Fanny Brice in the Broadway musical *Funny Girl* • James Brown's album *Live at the Apollo* is considered by many critics to be one of the greatest live recordings in popular music history • TV news "comes of age" in covering the assassination of President Kennedy; for the first time, TV broadcasts run 24 hours a day • The cost of a US first-class postage stamp increases to 5¢ • Films: *Lilies of the Field* (for which Sidney Poitier is the first black actor to win an Oscar); *Charade; Hud; Cleopatra; How the West Was Won; The Birds*
1964	• Nikita Khrushchev is replaced as leader of the USSR by Leonid Brezhnev • US military forces deployed in South Vietnam increase to more to 21,000 • North Vietnamese torpedo boats reportedly attack US ships in the Gulf of Tonkin; Congress approves Gulf of Tonkin resolution authorizing the president to take "all necessary measures" to win in Vietnam, allowing for the war's expansion; the US begins bombing North Vietnam • The Federation of Rhodesia and Nyasaland is dissolved; Nyasaland becomes independent as Malawi, and Kenneth Kaunda is elected president; Northern Rhodesia becomes independent as Zambia, and Hastings Banda becomes prime minister; Southern Rhodesia changes its name to Rhodesia, and Ian Smith becomes prime minister • Nelson Mandela and seven others are sentenced to life imprisonment in South Africa and sent to the Robben Island prison	• The Council of Federated Organizations (COFO), a network of civil rights groups that includes the NAACP, CORE, and SNCC, launches a drive to register black voters during what becomes known as "Freedom Summer" • Three civil rights workers, Michael Schwerner, Andrew Goodman, and James Chaney, are murdered in Mississippi; the FBI arrests and charges eighteen men with the crime but state prosecutors refuse to try the case, claiming lack of evidence • President Johnson signs the Civil Rights Act of 1964, which prohibits discrimination of all kinds based on race, color, religion, sex, or national origin, and establishes the Equal Employment Opportunity Commission (EEOC) to investigate complaints and impose penalties • Byron De La Beckwith is tried twice in Mississippi for the 1963 murder of Medgar Evers; both trials resulting in hung juries *(cont.)*	• China joins the nuclear club by testing its first atomic weapon • NASA's *Ranger 7* spacecraft transmits the first close-up pictures of the Moon • IBM brings out the MT/ST (Magnetic Tape/Selectric Typewriter); a forerunner of personal computer word processing, it can store and retrieve data using magnetic tape • Dartmouth University's John Kemeny and Thomas Kurtz develop Beginner's All-purpose Symbolic Instruction Code (BASIC) • Douglas Engelbart creates a working prototype of the computer mouse at the Stanford Research Institute (patent issued in 1970) • US Surgeon General Luther Terry issues a report stating that smoking tobacco is causally related to lung cancer • The Chesapeake Bay Bridge-Tunnel is completed between southeastern Virginia and the Delmarva Peninsula; the entire *(cont.)*	• Two of the greatest musicals in the history of Broadway open the same year: Harold Prince's *Fiddler on the Roof*, originally starring Zero Mostel in the title role [3,243 performances before closing in 1972], and Jerry Herman's *Hello, Dolly!*, originally starring Carol Channing [2,844 performances before closing in 1970] • *Peyton Place* premieres on ABC and is the first prime-time soap opera • Merv Griffin creates and hosts the game show *Jeopardy* • John Coltrane records his incandescent masterpiece album *A Love Supreme* • The Beatles appear for the first time in the US on *The Ed Sullivan Show*; the TV audience is estimated at 73 million people, or about 40% of the entire US population • Bob Dylan's "The Times They Are A-Changin'" becomes the anthem for an entire generation

E. EDUCATION, LITERATURE & THE FINE ARTS	F. RELIGION, THEOLOGY, PHILOSOPHY & PSYCHOLOGY	G. AMERICAN & UNITED METHODISM	H. BRITISH & WORLD METHODISM	
• Other notable publications include: – James Baldwin, *The Fire Next Time* – E. P. Thompson, *The Making of the English Working Class* – John le Carré, *The Spy who Came in from the Cold* – Morris West, *The Shoes of the Fisherman* – Barbara Tuchman, *The Guns of August*	Luther King, Jr., and his followers for their civil disobedience and defiance of state laws, to which King responds with his famous "Letter from a Birmingham Jail" and then the book *Why We Can't Wait* (1964) • The World Conference on Faith and Order meets in Montreal • The Roman Catholic Church accepts cremation as an approved funeral practice • Pope John XXIII issues the encyclical *Pacem in Terris (Peace on Earth)* calling for an end to the nuclear arms race • The Lutheran Free Church (LFC, Norwegian, 1897) joins the ALC (1960) • Pope John XIII dies; he is succeeded by Pope Paul VI • The General Assembly of the PCUS approves the ordination of women; the action is sustained by a vote of presbyteries • Hannah Arendt's controversial book *Eichmann in Jerusalem* speaks of "the eerie banality of evil" • Other notable publications include: – H. Richard Niebuhr, *The Responsible Self* (posthumous) – John A. T. Robinson, *Honest to God*	are brothers" and that "man is infinite worth as a child of God"; the hostility they experience as a result forces most of them to leave Mississippi within the year		**1963 cont.**
• The National Academy of Sciences (1863) and the National Research Council (1913) are augmented by the establishment of the National Academy of Engineering • Mario Davidovsky creates his *Synchronisms No. 2* for flute, clarinet, violin, cello, and tape and his *Synchronisms No. 3* for cello and electronic sound • George Crumb composes his *Four Nocturnes (Night Music II) for Violin and Piano* • Benjamin Britten's *Curlew River: A Parable for Church Performance* premieres in England • Notable publications include: – Saul Bellow, *Herzog* – Marshall McLuhan, *Understanding Media*, in which he first describes the "global village"	• Pope Paul VI and Patriarch Athenagoras meet in Jerusalem; it is the first meeting between a Roman Catholic pontiff and a Greek Orthodox patriarch since 1439; they simultaneously lift the mutual excommunications that had been in place since the Great Schism of 1054 • Pope Paul VI celebrates mass in Italian instead of Latin in Rome, thus implementing one of the most significant changes of the Second Vatican Council • The Vatican condemns the female contraceptive pill • The Committee of Southern Churchmen is established and begins publication of the journal *Katelegete* (Be Ye Reconciled) • Malcolm X breaks with Elijah Muhammad and the Nation of Islam and forms his own movement, the Muslim Mosque, Inc. • Notable publications include: – Schubert Ogden, *The Reality of God* – Emil Brunner, *Truth as Encounter* – Herbert Marcuse, *One-Dimensional Man*	• The MC General Conference: – imposes a new organizational structure for the General Board of Missions; the Woman's Division is renamed the Women's Division and much of the administrative responsibility for its missions program is assigned to the National and World Divisions of the Board – dissolves the Pacific Japanese Provisional Conference – approves the transfer of the first black conferences from the Central Jurisdiction into a regional jurisdiction: Delaware and Washington Conferences into the Northeastern Jurisdiction, and Lexington Conference into the North Central Jurisdiction – rejects a proposal to do away with the ordination of deacons, which would have made the diaconate an *office* instead of an *order* of ministry	• The Methodist Churches of Samoa, Upper Burma, Indonesia, and Sri Lanka become autonomous • Lim Swee Beng is the second woman and first national appointed by the MC as district superintendent (Malacca District, Malaysian Chinese Conference) • The autonomous Methodist Conference of Fiji and Rotuma is established • Notable publications include: – Dow Kirkpatrick, ed., *The Doctrine of the Church* [papers from the second Oxford Institute of Methodist Theological Studies, 1962] – V. H. H. Green, *John Wesley*	**1964**

	A. WORLD HISTORY & POLITICS	B. AMERICAN HISTORY & POLITICS	C. SCIENCE, MEDICINE & TECHNOLOGY	D. DAILY LIFE, POPULAR CULTURE & ENTERTAINMENT
1964 cont.	• Harold Wilson becomes British prime minister • Sayyid Qutb, the leader of the Islamic Brotherhood, publishes *Signposts* (or *Milestones*) in Egypt; it becomes a basic intellectual text for subsequent radical Islamists, including Osama bin Laden • The Palestine Liberation Organization (PLO) is established; it is dedicated to the establishment of an independent Palestinian state in the region historically known as Palestine; Yassir Arafat's Fatah movement is the largest constituent party • Faisal ibn Abdul Aziz becomes king of Saudi Arabia after forcing his brother Saud from the throne • Jawaharlal Nehru dies; Lal Bahadur Shastri succeeds him as head of the Congress Party and prime minister in India • François "Papa Doc" Duvalier is elected president of Haiti in 1957 and proclaims himself president for life	[thirty years later he is tried again and convicted] • The New York World's Fair commemorates the 300th anniversary of the establishment of the city; it attracts more than 51 million visitors from 62 nations • Martin Luther King, Jr., is awarded the Nobel Peace Prize for his work in the civil rights movement • The 24th Amendment to the US Constitution eliminates the poll tax in federal elections; the poll tax had been instituted in eleven Southern states after Reconstruction to make it difficult for poor blacks to vote • The US Supreme Court orders the state of Alabama to redraw its legislative districts, establishing a clear standard by holding that the equal protection clause of the 14th Amendment required that "as nearly as is practicable one man's vote" must "be worth as much as another's" • The Warren Commission issues its report saying that Lee Harvey Oswald acted alone and that no conspiracy was involved in the assassination of President Kennedy • Margaret Chase Smith (Maine) becomes the first woman nominated for president of the United States by a major political party (Republican) • Johnson is elected as president and Hubert H. Humphrey as vice president (Democratic Party), receiving a record 64% of the popular vote	complex is 17.6 miles long, and cuts 95 miles off the journey between Virginia Beach and Wilmington, DE • The Verrazano Narrows Bridge from Brooklyn to Staten Island is opened; with a total length of 6,690 feet and a main span of 4,260 feet, it is at the time the world's longest suspension bridge • IBM develops SABRE, the first computerized airline reservation tracking system, for American Airlines • Robert Moog designs the first electronic synthesizer	• Roy Orbison's single "Oh, Pretty Woman" breaks the Beatles' stranglehold on the Top 10, soaring to no. 1 on the Billboard charts • The Motown Sound reigns as The Supremes have four no. 1 hits including "Baby Love," and The Temptations record their classic "My Girl" • The Rolling Stones release their eponymous debut album • Brazilian guitarist João Gilberto's recording of Antonio Carlos Jobim's "The Girl from Ipanema" with vocalist Astrud Gilberto and American jazz saxophonist Stan Getz makes bossa nova music popular around the world • Buffalo wings are invented at the Anchor Bar in Buffalo, NY • The Ford Motor Company introduces the Mustang, and Porsche AG introduces the Porsche 911 • Indiana Governor Matthew E. Welsh declares the song "Louie, Louie" by the Kingsmen to be "pornographic" • Films: *A Hard Day's Night; Mary Poppins; Dr. Strangelove; My Fair Lady; Becket; Zorba the Greek; The Umbrellas of Cherbourg; Seven Days in May* • Summer Olympics: Tokyo • Winter Olympics: Innsbruck
1965	• India and Pakistan again go to war over Kashmir • The US begins a massive military buildup in South Vietnam, increasing its troop strength there from 17,000 to 184,000 by year's end • The USSR responds to the US buildup in South Vietnam by beginning to fund, arm, and train the North Vietnamese Army • The Treaty of Brussels creates the European Community (EC), superceding the EEC (1957) and establishing the foundation for the development of the later European Union (EU) • Winston Churchill dies at his home in London • Attempting to prevent black majority rule and preserve apartheid, Prime Minister Ian Smith unilaterally declares the independence of Rhodesia from the UK • Cuba and the US formally agree to start an airlift for Cubans who want to go to the US (by 1971, 250,000 Cubans take advantage of this program) • The British parliament passes the Race Relations Act, which prohibits discrimination on the basis of race in public places such as restaurants and on public transportation • The Beatles are appointed Members of the British Empire (MBE) by Queen Elizabeth II; the honor causes some controversy	• The Selma-to-Montgomery march for voting rights for black Americans ends in violence on "Bloody Sunday" on the Edmund Pettus Bridge and with the murder of civil rights worker Viola Liuzzo • Malcolm X is assassinated while addressing a rally of the Organization of Afro-American Unity in New York City; the men later convicted of the crime have connections with the Nation of Islam, leading to speculation that the assassination was ordered by Elijah Muhammad or his associates • Riots break out in the Watts section of Los Angeles, marking the beginning of violent racial unrest in a number of US cities, including Cleveland and Chicago (1966) and Detroit (1967) • Congress establishes the Medicare and Medicaid Programs and creates the National Endowment for the Arts (NEA) and the National Endowment for the Humanities (NEH) • Congress approves the Immigration and Naturalization Act, eliminating the quota system for immigration established in 1924 based on religion, race, and place of origin • Congress passes the Voting Rights Act, abolishing literacy tests and other such requirements that tended to restrict black voting • Hurricane Betsy causes flooding that breaches the levee system and inundates much of New Orleans • In *Griswold v. Connecticut*, the US Supreme Court strikes down the last state law prohibiting the use of contraceptives by married couples • César Chávez organizes United Farm Workers and leads a strike against grape growers in California • Many younger black Americans begin using the term *Afro-American* to describe themselves	• Digital Equipment introduces the PDP-8, the world's first computer to use integrated circuit technology • The Gateway Arch in St. Louis is completed; standing on the banks of the Mississippi River, the 630-foot-tall stainless steel arch commemorates the westward expansion of the US • Russian cosmonaut Aleksei Leonov, leaving his spacecraft *Voskhod 2* for 12 minutes, becomes the first person to "walk" in space • NASA has a busy year: – *Ranger 8* crashes into the lunar surface after successfully photographing possible landing sites for the Apollo astronauts – *Gemini 3* carries the first two-person crew into Earth's orbit – *Mariner 4* flies by Mars and returns the first close-up images of the red planet – Astronaut Ed White makes the first US space walk during *Gemini 4* – *Gemini 6* and *Gemini 7* perform the first controlled rendezvous in Earth's orbit • US racer Craig Breedlove sets a new land speed record of 600.601 mph	• Dr. Robert Cade at the University of Florida develops Gatorade, a drink to help athletes replenish fluids and minerals • Fashion model Jean Shrimpton shocks the world when she appears in public wearing a *very* short skirt; almost overnight, the "miniskirt" becomes fashionable around the globe • Paul McCartney writes and the Beatles record "Yesterday" • The Beatles perform in Shea Stadium; it is the first rock concert to be held in a venue of that size and sets new world records for attendance (over 55,000) and for revenue • The Byrds' version of Bob Dylan's "Mr. Tambourine Man" and their "Turn, Turn, Turn" help to create a new form: "folk-rock" • The Rolling Stones hit the top of the charts with their signature single "(I Can't Get No) Satisfaction" • Bob Dylan electrifies the Newport Folk Festival with his raucous performance of "Like a Rolling Stone" on an electric guitar with The Band and follows that with his album *Highway 61 Revisited* • James Brown, the "Godfather of Soul," lets the world know that "Papa's Got a Brand New Bag" • Bill Cosby, starring in *I Spy*, becomes the first black actor to headline a television show • The musical *The Man of La Mancha*, loosely based on the classic novel *Don Quixote* by Miguel Cervantes, opens on Broadway [it records 2,328 performances before closing in 1971] • Films: *The Sound of Music*, starring Julie Andrews (an instant hit, it remains one of the most popular musicals ever filmed); *Doctor Zhivago; Ship of Fools; The Spy Who Came in from the Cold*

E. EDUCATION, LITERATURE & THE FINE ARTS	F. RELIGION, THEOLOGY, PHILOSOPHY & PSYCHOLOGY	G. AMERICAN & UNITED METHODISM	H. BRITISH & WORLD METHODISM	
		• Notable publications include: – Albert C. Outler, ed., *John Wesley* (originally part of The Library of Protestant Thought series of Oxford University Press) – E. S. Bucke, general editor, *The History of American Methodism* (3 vols.)		**1964 cont.**
• Andy Warhol's *Campbell's Soup Can* paintings establish him as one of the major figures of the "pop art" movement • Leonard Bernstein composes his *Chichester Psalms* for chorus and orchestra • Leopold Stokowski conducts the first complete performance of Charles Ives's *Symphony No. 4* by the American Symphony Orchestra more than ten years after the composer's death • György Ligeti completes his *Requiem* for soprano and mezzo-soprano solo, mixed chorus, and orchestra • Steve Reich composes *It's Going to Rain*, his first serialist work • *The Autobiography of Malcolm X* (written with the assistance of Alex Haley), completed before his death, is published shortly afterward • Frank Herbert's *Dune* wins the first ever Nebula Award for "best science fiction novel of the year" • Other notable publications include: – John Fowles, *The Magus* – Sylvia Plath, *Ariel*	• Pope Paul VI: – promulgates *Dei Verbum*, the Dogmatic Constitution on Divine Revelation of the Second Vatican Council; this authoritative statement of modern Roman Catholic doctrine concerning Holy Scripture affirms the encyclical *Divino Afflante Spiritu* of Pius XII and encourages Roman Catholic scholars to provide more vernacular versions of the Bible – announces that the Second Vatican Council has decided that Jews are not collectively responsible for the killing of Christ – becomes the first pope to visit the US and to address the United Nations • Mother Teresa's order, the Missionaries of Charity, spreads across the globe after Pope Paul VI authorizes its expansion • The Reformed Presbyterian Church General Synod (1833) and the Evangelical Protestant Church (1961) merge to form the Reformed Presbyterian Church Evangelical Synod • Rachel Henderlite becomes the first woman to be ordained in the PCUS • Andover Theological Seminary (1807) and Newton Theological Institute (1825) merge to become Andover Newton Theological School • The charismatic and Pentecostal movements begin to make significant headway in Latin and South America • Notable publications include: – Wolfhart Pannenberg, *Jesus-God and Man* – Harvey Cox, *The Secular City: Secularization and Urbanization in Theological Perspective* – Roland Barthes, *Elements of Semiology*	• The fourth Conference of Methodist Men meets • The Wesleyan Theological Society is established as "a fellowship of Wesleyan Holiness scholars" • The Methodist Student Movement holds its last national conference • The Methodist Higher Education Foundation (MHEF) is established to help provide funds for the education of Methodist college and seminary students • The MC Board of Missions begins publication of *New World Outlook*, which replaces the older *World Outlook* (1932)	• The Methodist Church of Lower Burma becomes autonomous • The Methodist Church in Zambia unites with two others to form the United Church of Zambia • The third Oxford Institute of Methodist Theological Studies meets • Notable publications include the first volume of Rupert Davies and Gordon Rupp, eds., *A History of the Methodist Church in Great Britain* (4 vols., 1965–88)	**1965**

	A. WORLD HISTORY & POLITICS	B. AMERICAN HISTORY & POLITICS	C. SCIENCE, MEDICINE & TECHNOLOGY	D. DAILY LIFE, POPULAR CULTURE & ENTERTAINMENT
1966	• The US begins bombing around Haiphong and Hanoi, North Vietnam, marking a major escalation of the air war • Mao Zedong regains control of the Chinese Communist Party, publishes *Quotations from Chairman Mao*, and launches the Cultural Revolution, with the emergence of the Red Guard; as a result, China is further alienated from the Soviet Union • Indira Gandhi, the daughter of Jawaharlal Nehru, becomes Prime Minister of India • Sayyid Qutb is executed in Egypt on orders from Egyptian president Nasser • Kurt Georg Kiesinger becomes chancellor of Germany • Botswana and Lesotho achieve independence from Britain	• The National Organization for Women (NOW) is founded; Betty Friedan is the first president • Stokeley Carmichael gives his "Black Power" speech and popularizes the slogan "Black is Beautiful" • The militant Black Panther Party is founded by Huey P. Newton and Bobby Seale in Oakland, CA • Amendments to the Fair Labor Standards Act of 1938 extend its coverage to a wide range of workers; the minimum wage is increased to $1.40 per hour for covered nonfarm workers, $1.00 for farm workers • The US Department of Transportation (DOT) is established; it incorporates the older Bureau of Public Roads, which is renamed the Federal Highway Administration (FHWA) • In *Miranda v. Arizona*, the US Supreme Court further defines the due process clause of the 14th Amendment and establishes "Miranda rights" (the right to remain silent, etc.) • The Freedom of Information Act (FOIA) establishes the legal right of access to government information by US citizens • The US Supreme Court, in *Harper v. Virginia Board of Elections*, eliminates the poll tax as a qualification for voting in any election; a poll tax was still in use in Alabama, Mississippi, Texas, and Virginia in state and local elections	• The USSR's *Luna 9* and NASA's *Surveyor 1* both make successful soft landings on the lunar surface • The USSR's *Luna 10* is the first satellite to be placed into lunar orbit • NASA's *Gemini 10* sets a world altitude record of 474 miles • NASA's *Lunar Orbiter 1*, the first US spacecraft to orbit another world, is launched • The Houston Astrodome is completed; a structural marvel, it seats over 50,000 people, is the first ballpark in the world to have a roof over its playing field, and is the forerunner of all the domed stadiums that will follow • Regular hovercraft passenger service begins over the English Channel [it is discontinued in 2000 due to the opening of the Chunnel]	• Maulana Karenga, professor of black studies at California State University in Long Beach, adapts Kwanza, an African harvest festival, into Kwanzaa (December 26 through January 1), a holiday for black Americans that celebrates family, community, and culture • A basketball team from Texas Western College (now the University of Texas at El Paso) that starts five black players beats an all-white team from the University of Kentucky to win the NCAA national championship, breaking a major color barrier in college sports • Two of the most significant albums in rock music history are released: *Revolver* by the Beatles and *Pet Sounds* by the Beach Boys • Paul Simon and Art Garfunkel release their breakthrough album, *Sounds of Silence* • John Lennon tells reporters that the Beatles are "more popular than Jesus," touching off a firestorm of controversy that results in the burning of Beatles records in the "Bible Belt" of the US • Jimi Hendrix redefines the rock guitar with the release of "Purple Haze" • The Jefferson Airplane with Grace Slick and Big Brother and the Holding Company with Janis Joplin give legendary concerts at the Fillmore Auditorium in San Francisco • The Beatles play what turns out to be their very last live concert at Candlestick Park in San Francisco; they will never again perform in public as a group • Herb Alpert & the Tijuana Brass set a world record by placing five albums simultaneously on Billboard's pop album chart • The first episode of *Star Trek* is broadcast on TV • Buckminster Fuller introduces the world to his geodesic sphere • The musical *Cabaret*, starring Joel Grey as the Emcee, opens on Broadway • Films: *Who's Afraid of Virginia Woolf?*; *The Sand Pebbles*; *Born Free*; *Fantastic Voyage*
1967	• US forces attack the Vietcong in the Mekong River delta, but suffer heavy losses; the US begins peace talks with Hanoi in Paris • In the Six-Day War, Israel defeats combined armies from several Arab nations and occupies the West Bank, the Gaza Strip, the Golan Heights, the Sinai Peninsula, and East Jerusalem; the Suez Canal comes under Israeli control and is closed to shipping (until 1975) • France blocks a bid by England to join the European Community (EC), as it had previously done in 1961 with regard to the EEC • Britain overturns Victorian-era laws that made homosexuality illegal	• The population of the US passes the 200 million mark • The 25th Amendment to the US Constitution clarifies the line of succession to the presidency and establishes rules for a president who becomes unable to perform his duties while in office • The eighteen men arrested for the 1964 murder of three civil rights workers in Mississippi are tried in federal court for violating civil rights laws; seven of them are convicted but receive short prison sentences; the others are acquitted • The "hippie" counterculture blossoms during the "Summer of Love" in San Francisco; the rest of the country experiences the "Long Hot Summer" of racial unrest and antiwar protests	• China conducts its first thermonuclear weapon test • NASA successfully tests its *Saturn V* rocket (the "Moon Rocket" designed for the Apollo program) • NASA's *Apollo 1* spacecraft catches fire on the launch pad, killing astronauts Virgil "Gus" Grissom, Roger Chaffee, and Ed White; these are the first deaths in America's space program • Christiaan Barnard (South Africa) performs world's first heart transplant operation • Cicely Saunders opens St. Christopher's Hospice in South London as the first modern hospice • Texas Instruments develops the first hand-held calculator	• The Beatles release their groundbreaking album *Sgt. Pepper's Lonely Hearts Club Band*, the first creative "concept album" of the rock-and-roll era • Aretha Franklin is acclaimed "The Queen of Soul" after she records "I Never Loved A Man (The Way I Love You)" and "Respect" • The Jefferson Airplane embody San Francisco's psychedelic rock in the album *Surrealistic Pillow* featuring Grace Slick's vocals on two classic tracks, "White Rabbit" and "Somebody to Love" • The Rolling Stones appear on *The Ed Sullivan Show*; at Sullivan's request, they change their lyrics from "Let's spend the night together" to "Let's spend some time together"

E. EDUCATION, LITERATURE & THE FINE ARTS	F. RELIGION, THEOLOGY, PHILOSOPHY & PSYCHOLOGY	G. AMERICAN & UNITED METHODISM	H. BRITISH & WORLD METHODISM	
• The "new" Metropolitan Opera House at Lincoln Center, designed by architect Wallace K. Harrison, opens with the world premiere of Samuel Barber's *Antony and Cleopatra* • Malcolm Arnold composes his *Fantasy for Solo Flute* • Roger Sessions composes his *Symphony No. 6* • The US Supreme Court rules that John Cleland's banned 1759 novel *Memoirs of a Woman of Pleasure [Fanny Hill]* does not meet the legal standard for obscenity and allows its publication in the US • Robert Venturi publishes *Complexity and Contradiction in Architecture*, a major statement of the postmodern movement in American architecture • Other notable publications include: – Jacqueline Susann, *Valley of the Dolls* – Jean Rhys, *Wide Sargasso Sea* – Truman Capote, *In Cold Blood* – Shusaku Endo, *Silence*	• Pope Paul VI and Arthur Michael Ramsey, the Archbishop of Canterbury, meet in Rome; it is the first official meeting for 400 years between the Roman Catholic and Anglican Churches • The Vatican announces the abolition of *Index Librorum Prohibitum* (Index of Forbidden Books) • The Church of Scotland allows the ordination of women as priests (ordination of women as deacons has been permitted since 1888) • The International Society for Krishna Consciousness (ISKCON) is founded in India by A. C. Bhaktivedanta Swami Prabhupada and soon reaches Europe and the US; devotees are often called "Hare Krishnas" after the mantra that they sing or chant • Eugene Carson Blake (UPCUSA) is named General Secretary of the World Council of Churches • The American Bible Society produces *Good News for Modern Man: The New Testament in Today's English Version* (TEV); the OT appears in 1976 • *The Jerusalem Bible* (JB), an English counterpart to a French translation, is the first complete Roman Catholic Bible translated into English from the original languages • Other notable publications include: – Peter Berger, *The Social Construction of Reality* – Schubert Ogden, *The Reality of God* – John Hick, *Evil and the God of Love* – Thomas J. J. Altizer, *The Gospel of Christian Atheism* – Martin Luther King, Jr., *Strength to Love* – Langdon Gilkey, *Shantung Compound*	• American Methodism commemorates the bicentennial of the formation of the first Methodist Society (in New York, 1766); the theme is "Forever Beginning" • The MC General Conference meets in special session concurrently with the EUBC General Conference: – approves the Plan of Union of the MC and the EUBC to create The United Methodist Church and sends it to the annual conferences for ratification – sets 1972 as the target date for elimination of all forms of structural segregation within the church – creates the Council of Central Conferences in Europe • The MEC publishes a new version of *The Methodist Hymnal* (with tunes, readings, and ritual) • The EUBC General Conference: – approves the Plan of Union of the EUBC and the MC to create The United Methodist Church and sends it to the annual conferences for ratification – reorganizes the Board of Missions under a single executive officer – expresses concern over the Vietnam War and the need for "strengthening the moral values" of American servicemen in Vietnam – supports continued participation in COCU and the NCC – upholds the denomination's traditional statement on temperance – encourages local churches to study an NCC document on US policy toward Communist China • The seventh Assembly of the WSCS and WSG (MC) meets • The fifth Convention of the WSWS (EUBC) meets • COSMOS hosts a consultation (in Green Lake, WI) on the international structure of the church • The CMEC General Conference grants full clergy rights to women; Vergie J. Gant becomes the first woman to be ordained elder by the CMEC (North Arkansas Conference) • Notable publications include: – Frank Baker, ed., *A Union Catalogue of the Publications of John and Charles Wesley* – Robert W. Monk, *John Wesley: His Puritan Heritage* (2nd ed. 1999)	• The eleventh World Methodist Conference meets in London • Bilateral ecumenical dialogue begins between the World Methodist Council and the Roman Catholic Church (still ongoing) • The AMEC begins work in England • Notable publications include: – Dow Kirkpatrick, ed., *The Finality of Christ* [papers from the third Oxford Institute of Methodist Theological Studies, 1965] – T. B. Shepherd, *Methodism and the Literature of the Eighteenth Century*	**1966**
• One of Pablo Picasso's last works, the 50-foot-tall welded steel sculpture *Head of a Woman*, is completed as a gift to the city of Chicago and stands in front of Chicago's Civic Center; its semiabstract form is initially quite controversial but it soon becomes a city landmark • Morton Subotnick uses an electronic synthesizer to create *Silver Apples of the Moon*, the first full-length LP of electronic music • George Crumb composes his *Echoes of Time and the River (Echoes II) for Orchestra* • Notable publications include: – William Styron, *The Confessions of Nat Turner* – Thornton Wilder, *The Eighth Day*	• The General Convention of the Protestant Episcopal Church in the US makes official the long-standing custom of dropping the word "Protestant" and takes the name the Episcopal Church in the USA (ECUSA) • The UPCUSA adopts the Confession of Faith of 1967, which is the first new Presbyterian confession of faith in three centuries • The Catholic Charismatic Renewal movement has its beginnings among students and faculty of Duquesne University in Pittsburgh • Albania declares itself the world's first officially atheist state	• Stimulated by Charles W. Keysor's 1966 article "Methodism's Silent Minority," Methodist evangelicals launch the Good News Movement as a "forum for scriptural Christianity" within the MC • Margaret Henrichsen becomes the first woman to serve as an MC district superintendent in the US (Maine Annual Conference) • Noemi Diaz becomes the first Hispanic/Latina woman in the US to be received into full connection in the MC (New York Annual Conference) • The last session of the Central Jurisdiction (MC) meets in Nashville; L. Scott Allen becomes the 14th and last bishop elected by the Central Jurisdiction	• The Methodist Church of Sierra Leone becomes autonomous • The Methodist Church in Kenya becomes autonomous as Kenya gains its political independence from Great Britain • The Methodist Church of the Caribbean and the Americas (MCCA) is established; with headquarters in Antigua, it covers Guyana, Honduras, Jamaica, Haiti, the Leeward Islands, Panama, Costa Rica, the South Caribbean, and (after 1968) the Bahamas • The MC [UK] merges Didsbury College (1842/1951) with Headingly College (1868) to form Wesley College, Bristol	**1967**

	A. WORLD HISTORY & POLITICS	B. AMERICAN HISTORY & POLITICS	C. SCIENCE, MEDICINE & TECHNOLOGY	D. DAILY LIFE, POPULAR CULTURE & ENTERTAINMENT
1967 cont.	• The Ibo people of Nigeria proclaim the Republic of Biafra; Nigeria launches military attacks to regain control of the region • Anastasio Somoza rises to power as president of Nicaragua • Greek and Turkish Cypriots fight on Cyprus; Turkey threatens an invasion of Cyprus and war with Greece; the UN intervenes and arranges a settlement • Montreal hosts the Expo '67 World's Fair to celebrate the centennial of Canada's confederation, as well as Montreal's 325th anniversary; more than 50 million people attend from 70 different nations	• Carl Stokes is the first black person to be elected as mayor of a major US city (Cleveland, OH) • In *Loving v. Virginia*, the US Supreme Court rules that prohibiting interracial marriage is unconstitutional; sixteen states that still banned interracial marriage at the time are forced to revise their laws • Puerto Rico votes to retain its commonwealth status over either statehood or independence • Congress passes the Public Broadcasting Act, authorizing the creation of the Corporation for Public Broadcasting (CPB) and the Public Broadcasting System (PBS)	• Amana markets the first successful microwave oven for the home, the "Radarange" • *The Queen Elizabeth II* cruise liner is launched	• The Monkees become the best-selling group of 1967, outselling the Beatles and the Rolling Stones combined [go figure!] • *Rolling Stone* and *New York Magazine* debut, spawning the popularity of special-interest and regional magazines • The Grateful Dead release their self-titled first album • James Brown's single "Cold Sweat" is widely recognized as the first "funk music" recording, emphasizing rhythm over melody and harmony and pointing toward the later emergence of rap music • The Green Bay Packers defeat the Kansas City Chiefs in the first Superbowl football game • Films: A great year at the movies, including *The Graduate* (with its soundtrack provided by Simon and Garfunkel); *In the Heat of the Night; Guess Who's Coming to Dinner; Bonnie and Clyde; Cool Hand Luke; In Cold Blood; The Dirty Dozen*
1968	• The Nuclear Nonproliferation Treaty (NPT) is signed; it calls for halting the spread of nuclear weapons capabilities [by 1986, more than 180 countries have ratified it] • Soviet troops crush the "Prague Spring" democratic movement in Czechoslovakia • The US has almost 525,000 troops in Vietnam; in the surprise Tet Offensive, Vietcong guerrillas launch coordinated attacks on Saigon, Hue, and several provincial capitals; American soldiers kill 300 Vietnamese villagers in the My Lai massacre • A Vietcong officer is executed by South Vietnamese National Police Chief Nguyen Ngoc Loan; the execution is videotaped and does much to sway public opinion against the war • President Johnson commits the US to a nonmilitary solution of the war when he announces that he will not seek reelection and orders a halt to the bombing of North Vietnam • Saddam Hussein seizes power in Iraq; he comes from a Sunni religious sect but the Baathist ideology of his regime is avowedly secular • PLO sympathizers hijack an El Al (Israeli) airliner; after generating much publicity, the hijackers release all the captives unharmed • The "troubles" begin between Catholic Nationalists and Protestant Unionists, bringing the British Army to Northern Ireland	• The National Advisory Commission on Civil Disorders (the Kerner Commission) issues a report saying that "our nation is moving toward two societies, one black, one white—separate and unequal" • President Johnson signs the Civil Rights Act of 1968, which outlaws discrimination in the sale, rental, or financing of housing • The USS *Pueblo* is captured by North Korea; the crew is eventually released but the vessel is not • Martin Luther King, Jr., is assassinated on the balcony of his room at the Lorraine Hotel in Memphis, provoking riots in Washington, Baltimore, and Chicago; James Earl Ray is eventually convicted of his murder • President Johnson declines to run for a second full term • Presidential candidate Robert F. Kennedy is assassinated in a Los Angeles hotel by Sirhan Sirhan, an Israeli-born Arab immigrant, apparently in revenge for Kennedy's support of Israel • Violent demonstrations by antiwar protesters erupt at the Democratic National Convention in Chicago • The American Indian Movement (AIM) is founded by American Indian activists • The US Supreme Court strikes down an Arkansas state law that had prohibited the teaching of evolution in public schools • The EEOC rules that sex-segregated help-wanted ads in newspapers are illegal; this ruling is upheld in 1973 by the US Supreme Court, opening the way for women to apply for higher-paying jobs hitherto open only to men • The Gun Control Act outlaws mail-order sales of rifles and shotguns, specifies persons who are banned from possessing certain guns, including drug users, and restricts shotgun and rifle sales • The US discontinues the redemption of the paper currency known as "silver certificates" for actual silver	• *Apollo 8* with three astronauts loops around the moon and returns to Earth • Douglas Engelbart and colleagues at the Stanford Research Institute stage a 90-minute public demonstration of a networked computer system; this marks the public debut of the computer mouse (which Englebart patents in 1970), hypertext, and video teleconferencing • Oil is discovered on the North Slope of Alaska	• The rock musical *Hair* opens on Broadway and in London • New Jersey police confiscate 30,000 copies of John Lennon and Yoko Ono's *Two Virgins* album at Newark Airport, saying that the cover, which features a nude photo of the two artists, is "pornographic" • "Sittin' On the Dock of the Bay" becomes Otis Redding's last and biggest hit when it is released after his untimely death in 1967 • James Brown releases the popular but controversial single "Say It Loud, I'm Black and I'm Proud" • Johnny Cash records his legendary live album *Johnny Cash at Folsom Prison* • *60 Minutes* premieres on CBS, beginning its reign as the longest-running prime-time news show • McDonald's introduces the double-decker Big Mac • The cost of a US first-class postage stamp increases to 6¢ • Films: *2001: A Space Odyssey; Romeo and Juliet; The Lion in Winter; Yellow Submarine; Rosemary's Baby* • Summer Olympics: Mexico City • Winter Olympics: Grenoble • Tommie Smith and John Carlos, two black American track stars, cause an uproar at the Summer Olympics in Mexico City when they raise their black-gloved fists in a "Black Power" salute from the podium during the playing of the American national anthem after winning the gold and bronze medals in the 200 meter sprint; they are suspended from the US Olympic team and expelled from the Olympic Village

E. EDUCATION, LITERATURE & THE FINE ARTS	F. RELIGION, THEOLOGY, PHILOSOPHY & PSYCHOLOGY	G. AMERICAN & UNITED METHODISM	H. BRITISH & WORLD METHODISM	
– Gabriel García Márquez, *Cien años de soledad* (One Hundred Years of Solitude) – Chaim Potok, *The Chosen* – William Manchester, *Death of a President*	• With the publication of his groundbreaking study *Writing and Difference*, Jacques Derrida pioneers the method of literary criticism known as deconstruction • Other notable publications include: – Paul Ricoeur, *The Symbolism of Evil* – Philip Rieff, *The Triumph of the Therapeutic* – Thomas Merton, *Mystics and Zen Masters*	• Anticipating the 1968 merger of the MC and EUBC, the Rio Grande Conference votes to continue as a separate unit after merger		**1967 cont.**
• Morton Subotnick creates his album *The Wild Bull*, a dark work of electronic music inspired by an ancient Sumerian poem of mourning • John Tavener composes his cantata *The Whale* • Notable publications include: – Norman Mailer, *Armies of the Night* – Gore Vidal, *Myra Breckinridge* – John Updike, *Couples*	• Pope Paul VI issues the encyclical *Humanae Vitae* (On the Regulation of Birth), which reasserts opposition to artificial birth control, sparking dissent in the US and Europe • The Conference of Roman Catholic bishops from the southern hemisphere meets in Medellin, Colombia, marking a new openness toward social reform • The Christian Church (Disciples of Christ) (1832) reorganizes to provide for local, regional, and national governing bodies under a General Assembly with an ongoing Administrative Committee; many congregations that reject the reorganization withdraw to form a new fellowship named the Christian Churches and Churches of Christ • Notable publications include: – Jürgen Habermas, *Knowledge and Human Interests* – Rupert Davies, *Religious Authority in an Age of Doubt* – Mary Daly, *The Church and the Second Sex* – James F. Gustafson, *Christ and Moral Life*	• The MC (1939) and the EUBC (1946) unite to form The United Methodist Church (UMC); the Plan of Union eliminates the Central Jurisdiction • The Uniting Conference: – appoints a Theological Study Commission and a Social Principles Study Commission to consider and recommend revisions of the new church's doctrinal standards and social principles – appoints a Structure Study Commission to consider and recommend an organizational plan for the new church's general boards and agencies – creates the Program Council to coordinate the work of the general boards and agencies pending the recommendations of the Structure Study Commission – separates *The Book of Discipline* from *The Book of Resolutions*; the Social Principles appear in both – creates the General Commission on Religion and Race (GCRR) and the General Commission on Archives and History (GCAH) – discontinues the positions of local deacon and local elder; individuals holding those positions at the time continue to be recognized as such – merges the former women's organizations under the names Woman's Society of Christian Service (WSCS) and Wesleyan Service Guild (WSG) – merges the former men's organizations to create the United Methodist Men (UMM) – merges the former youth organizations to create the United Methodist Youth Fellowship (UMYF) – confirms 1972 as the target date for elimination of all forms of segregation within the church – establishes the Ministerial Education Fund (MEF) to help support the education of persons for ordained ministry	• The Methodist churches in Malaysia-Singapore, Pakistan, Bolivia, Chile, Cuba, and Kenya become autonomous • The United Evangelical Church of Ecuador becomes autonomous • The Methodist Church in Germany (BMK) merges with the German EUB Church to create the Evangelische-methodistischen Kirche (EMK), which is also known as the Germany Central Conference of the UMC • The Methodist Episcopal Theological Seminary in Frankfurt am Main merges with Reutlingen Theological Seminary to form the Theologisches Seminar der EMK [at first it occupies the old buildings in Frankfort but, in 1971, moves to new and renovated buildings in Reutlingen] • *London Quarterly and Holborn Review* (1932) is merged with the Anglican *Church Quarterly Review* (established in 1875), to form *The Church Quarterly*; the new journal is not a success and disappears in 1971 • John A. Newton publishes *Susanna Wesley and the Puritan Tradition in Methodism*	**1968**

	A. WORLD HISTORY & POLITICS	B. AMERICAN HISTORY & POLITICS	C. SCIENCE, MEDICINE & TECHNOLOGY	D. DAILY LIFE, POPULAR CULTURE & ENTERTAINMENT
1968 cont.		• George Wallace makes a third-party bid for the presidency (American Independent Party) running on antidesegregation issues; he receives 13.5% of the popular vote • Richard M. Nixon is elected as president and Spiro T. Agnew as vice president (Republican Party)		
1969	• Yassir Arafat becomes chairman of the PLO • President Nixon announces the Vietnam peace offer and begins troop withdrawals; Vietcong guerillas form the Provisional Revolutionary Government in South Vietnam • The Portuguese fight nationalist rebels in Angola, Mozambique, and Portuguese Guinea (Guinea-Bissau) • Charles de Gaulle resigns the French presidency; Georges Pompidou is elected as his successor • Willy Brandt becomes chancellor of Germany • In Spain, Francisco Franco names Prince Juan Carlos as his successor as head of state • Golda Meir becomes prime minister of Israel	• An estimated 1 million Americans, including 50 members of Congress, participate in the "Vietnam Moratorium," a series of antiwar demonstrations and peace rallies held across the country • Congress approves a resolution endorsing President Nixon's efforts to achieve "peace with justice"; this is the first major Vietnam policy declaration by Congress since the 1964 Gulf of Tonkin resolution • California becomes the first state to adopt a "no fault" divorce law, which allows couples to divorce by mutual consent [by 1985 every state has adopted a similar law] • Shirley Chisholm, of New York, becomes the first black woman elected to Congress • The largest antiwar rally in US history brings an estimated 500,000 people to march for peace in Washington, DC • The Stonewall Riots in New York City transform the gay rights movement into a widespread protest for equal rights and acceptance and prompts formation of the Gay Liberation Front • Hurricane Camille kills 256 in the US and causes damages estimated at $6.9 billion along the Gulf Coast	• *Apollo 11* lands on the surface of the moon; Neil Armstrong takes "one small step for man, one giant leap for mankind" • The world's first supersonic airliner, the Concorde, makes its first test flights • The US bans use of DDT as a pesticide • James Watson publishes *The Double Helix: A Personal Account of the Discovery of the Structure of DNA*	• The Woodstock rock concert and festival is an iconic moment in American popular culture: the performers include Janis Joplin, The Who, Joan Baez, Jefferson Airplane, Sly and the Family Stone, and Crosby, Stills, Nash and Young; it is highlighted by the renegade version of "The Star-Spangled Banner" by Jimi Hendrix • The Beatles release *Abbey Road*, which many music historians consider to be the single most significant rock album ever recorded • The Who, led by incandescent guitarist Pete Townshend, record the first full-length rock opera, *Tommy* • Another British rock group, Led Zeppelin, pioneers "heavy metal" rock music in their self-titled album • King Crimson's *In the Court of the Crimson King* is a pioneering album in the development of "program rock" music; similar albums are released by The Moody Blues and Procol Harum • Miles Davis's *Bitches Brew* is widely considered the first successful full-fledged fusion of jazz with rock-and-roll • Elvis Presley's live performances break all attendance records in Las Vegas, and he has great success with his songs "In The Ghetto" and "Suspicious Minds" • The first Cracker Barrel Old Country Store opens on Interstate 40 in Lebanon, TN • David Reuben publishes *Everything You Always Wanted to Know About Sex (But Were Afraid to Ask)* • The Children's Television Workshop introduces *Sesame Street* on public television • Films: *Midnight Cowboy* (the first X-rated film to win an Oscar for Best Picture); *Butch Cassidy and the Sundance Kid*; *The Wild Bunch*; *Easy Rider*
1970	• President Gamal Abdal Nasser of Egypt dies; he is succeeded by Anwar Sadat • The Vietnam War escalates with a secret US invasion of Cambodia intended to destroy North Vietnamese sanctuaries • Civil divorce is legalized in Italy • Edward Heath becomes British prime minister	• The US census reports that the population is 203,211,926: – whites: 177,748,975 (87.5%) – blacks: 22,580,289 (11.1%) – other: 2,882,662 (1.4%) • The US national debt is $389,158,403,690	• The Aswan High Dam on the Nile River in Egypt is completed, harnessing the annual floods of the Nile and producing 10 billion kilowatt-hours of electricity annually • The US deploys the first missile with multiple independently targetable reentry vehicles (MIRVs), the *Minuteman III*	• The University of Southern California football team, led by black fullback Sam Cunningham, decimates the all-white team of the University of Alabama; as a result, the legendary Alabama coach Paul "Bear" Bryant begins recruiting black players, breaking a major color barrier in the South

E. EDUCATION, LITERATURE & THE FINE ARTS	F. RELIGION, THEOLOGY, PHILOSOPHY & PSYCHOLOGY	G. AMERICAN & UNITED METHODISM	H. BRITISH & WORLD METHODISM	
		– organizes the church outside North America into seven central conferences: Africa, Congo, West Africa, Northern Europe, Germany, Central and Southern Europe, and Philippines – empowers the central conferences to elect their own bishops but mandates that elected bishops serve four-year terms rather than for life – establishes The United Methodist Publishing House (UMPH) in Nashville • A group of EUBC members opposed to the merger withdraws to form the Evangelical Church of North America • Roy Nichols becomes the first black person elected as UMC bishop by a regional jurisdictional conference • The Wesleyan Methodist Church (1843/1947) and the Pilgrim Holiness Church (1922) merge to form the Wesleyan Church		**1968 cont.**
• Molefi Kete Asante is the founding editor of the *Journal of Black Studies* • Olivier Messiaen composes his enormous *The Transfiguration of our Lord Jesus Christ* • Walter (later Wendy) Carlos demonstrates the serious musical potential of an electronic synthesizer by using one to perform the music of Johann Sebastian Bach for the album *Switched-On Bach* • Peter Maxwell Davies composes his *St. Thomas Wake* • Notable publications include: – Philip Roth, *Portnoy's Complaint* – David Halberstam, *The Best and the Brightest* – John Fowles, *The French Lieutenant's Woman* – Mario Puzo, *The Godfather*	• James H. Cone's groundbreaking *Black Theology and Black Power* is a landmark work in the development of black liberation theology • Other notable publications include: –Claude Lèvi-Strauss, *The Raw and the Cooked* – John B. Cobb Jr., *God and the World* – Langdon Gilkey, *Naming the Whirlwind: The Renewal of God-Language* – Elizabeth Kübler-Ross, *On Death and Dying* – Peter Berger, *A Rumor of Angels: Modern Society and the Rediscovery of the Supernatural*	• Black Methodists for Church Renewal (BMCR) is officially formed • The Latin American Methodist Action Group (LAMAG) is organized; Elias Galvan is its first president • The first National Congress of United Methodist Men meets • The UMC formally organizes the Puerto Rico Annual Conference • The UMC Women's Division begins publication of *Response*, incorporating *The Methodist Woman* (1940) and *World Evangel* (1947), and produces the spiritual growth study *The Inner Life*	• The Protestant Church of Belgium is formed by union of Methodist and Evangelical Protestant churches • The Methodist Church in Argentina becomes autonomous as Iglesia Evangelica Metodista Argentina (IEMA); Carlos Gattinoni becomes its first bishop • The Council of Evangelical Methodist Churches in Latin America and the Caribbean (CIEMAL) is created to be the connectional body for mission and unity among the Methodist churches in Argentina, Bolivia, Brazil, Chile, Costa Rica, Cuba, Colombia, Dominican Republic, Ecuador, El Salvador, Guatemala, Honduras, Mexico, Nicaragua, Panama, Paraguay, Peru, Puerto Rico, Uruguay, and Venezuela, as well as the Methodist Church in the Caribbean and the Americas (MCCA) • The MC [UK] terminates publication of *The Methodist Magazine* (1927), ending a line of Methodist periodicals in the UK beginning with Wesley's *Arminian Magazine* (1777) • The fourth Oxford Institute of Methodist Theological Studies meets	**1969**
• The Institute of Medicine (US) is established and joins the National Academy of Sciences (1863), the National Research Council (1913), and the National Academy of Engineering (1964) under the umbrella of the National Academies, bringing together committees of experts in all *(cont.)*	• Elizabeth Platz (LCA) becomes the first female Lutheran pastor ordained in North America; one month later, Barbara Andrews (ALC) becomes the second	• The UMC General Conference meets in special session to further the work of organizing the UMC: – receives progress reports from the Theological Study Commission, Social Principles Study Commission, and Structure Study Commission	• Handsworth College (1881) is closed by the MC [UK] • The Church of North India is established after years of preparation, uniting the Anglican Church, the United Church of Northern India (Congregationalist and Presbyterian), the Methodist Church *(cont.)*	**1970**

	A. WORLD HISTORY & POLITICS	B. AMERICAN HISTORY & POLITICS	C. SCIENCE, MEDICINE & TECHNOLOGY	D. DAILY LIFE, POPULAR CULTURE & ENTERTAINMENT
1970 cont.	• Hafez al-Assad, a Baathist from the minority Alawite sect, seizes power in Syria • Salvador Allende of Chile becomes the first freely elected Marxist president in the Western Hemisphere • Flooding kills 500,000 people in East Pakistan • Fiji, Samoa, and Tonga join the British Commonwealth • Members of the PLO hijack four international jetliners and hold the passengers hostage until West Germany, Switzerland, and Britain release seven PLO members being held for earlier hijackings • King Hussein of Jordan declares military rule in response to a coup attempt by Fatah guerillas from the PLO, supported by Syria, resulting in the expulsion of thousands of Palestinians and forcing Yassir Arafat to relocate the headquarters of the PLO to Lebanon • Osaka, Japan, hosts the Expo '70 World's Fair, the first modern international fair held in the Orient; 110 pavilions are erected and more than 64 million people attend	• Four students are killed at Kent State University (Ohio) and two students are killed at Jackson State University (Mississippi) by National Guard units after Vietnam War protests • A peaceful antiwar rally held at the Ellipse in Washington, DC, is attended by about 280,000 people including about 10 members of Congress • In *Schultz v. Wheaton Glass Co.*, a US Court of Appeals rules that jobs held by men and women need to be "substantially equal" but not "identical" to fall under the protection of the Equal Pay Act • Congress establishes the Environmental Protection Agency (EPA) • The first annual Lesbian and Gay Pride March in the US takes place in New York and four other cities, commemorating the 1969 Stonewall Riots • Anna Mae Hays, Chief of the Army Nurse Corps, is promoted to the grade of brigadier general, becoming the first woman in the history of the US Army to attain general officer rank • The Stone Mountain Memorial carving, on which work resumed in 1963, is dedicated by Vice President Agnew (some work on it continues until 1972)	• "Houston, we have a problem": NASA's *Apollo 13* astronauts barely make a safe return to Earth in their failing spacecraft • The first jumbo jet, the Boeing 747, enters regular airline service with twice the capacity of any previous jetliner • The second Los Angeles Aqueduct is completed, doubling the flow of water from the Eastern Sierras to Los Angeles • Corning Glass creates optical glass fiber • Centronics introduces the first dot matrix printer • The US Department of Defense creates ARPANET, the first broadband electronic data communications network and the forerunner of the Internet	• *Monday Night Football* debuts on ABC and becomes an instant institution • The Beatles break the hearts of fans around the world when they break up as a group; *Let It Be* is their final album together • George Harrison releases his solo triple album *All Things Must Pass*, which includes his lead no. 1 single, "My Sweet Lord" • James Taylor releases his first album, *Sweet Baby James*, which includes the hit single "Fire and Rain" • Simon & Garfunkel's *Bridge Over Troubled Water* is their last album together • Carlos Santana's recording of Tito Puente's "Oye Como Va" marks the popular advent of Latin rock • Crosby, Stills, Nash, and Young commemorate the Kent State Massacre with their chilling "Four Dead in Ohio," which becomes an anthem of the antiwar movement • National Public Radio (NPR) is founded with 90 public radio stations as charter members • Films: *Patton*; *M*A*S*H*; *Five Easy Pieces*; *Love Story*; *Little Big Man*
1971	• India and Pakistan again go to war following a political crisis in what was then East Pakistan and the flight of millions of Bengali refugees to India • Pakistan is subdivided when its eastern section breaks away and declares independence to form Bangladesh • Congress bars the use of combat troops but not air power in Laos and Cambodia; South Vietnamese troops, with US air cover, fail in a thrust into Laos; many American ground forces are withdrawn from Vietnam combat • The United Nations General Assembly withdraws recognition of the Republic of China (Taiwan), recognizes the People's Republic of China (mainland China) as the sole legitimate government of China and gives it China's seat (one of the five permanent seats) on the UN Security Council • The British government begins a policy of "internment" (imprisonment without trial) to combat terrorism in Northern Ireland • Switzerland becomes the last nation in Europe to grant women the right to vote in national elections • The environmental activist group Greenpeace is founded in Vancouver, Canada • Idi Amin becomes president of Uganda after leading a military coup deposing Milton Obote • Six small sheikdoms in the Persian Gulf region merge to form the United Arab Emirates • When François "Papa Doc" Duvalier dies, power in Haiti passes to his son, Jean-Claude "Baby Doc" Duvalier	• The 26th Amendment to the US Constitution reduces the legal voting age in the US from 21 to 18 • William F. Calley is convicted of murder for his role in the 1968 My Lai massacre in Vietnam • Publication of the Pentagon Papers reveals the secret government study of decision-making about the Vietnam War • In *Swann v. Charlotte-Mecklenburg Board of Education*, the US Supreme Court upholds busing as a legitimate means for achieving integration of public schools • The US suspends the free exchange of US gold for foreign-held dollars and devalues the dollar • Civil rights activist Jesse Jackson leaves the staff of the SCLC and establishes his own Chicago-based organization known as People United to Save [later: Serve] Humanity (PUSH) • A revolt at the maximum-security prison in Attica, NY, ends when state police and National Guard troops storm the facility; 42 are killed, including 10 hostages • Charles Manson and three female "family members" are found guilty of the 1969 murder of actress Sharon Tate and three friends	• The USSR launches *Salyut I*, the first space station, and makes the first space docking • NASA's *Mariner 9* becomes the first space probe to orbit another planet (Mars) • NASA's *Apollo 15* astronauts David Scott and Jim Irwin are the first humans to drive a Lunar Rover Vehicle (LRV) across the surface of the moon • Gilbert Hyatt at Micro Computer Co. patents the microprocessor chip • Intel develops and produces its first microprocessor chip, the 4004, using Hyatt's design	• The groundbreaking rock musical *Jesus Christ, Superstar*, by Andrew Lloyd Webber and Tim Rice, changes the face of musical theater when it debuts on Broadway • *Godspell*, a musical by Stephen Schwartz based on the Gospel of Saint Matthew, opens in both London and New York • Singer and songwriter Carol King releases her *Tapestry* album; it proves to be one of the most popular albums ever recorded • The Southern rock group the Allman Brothers Band makes one of the most famous live albums in rock history, *Live at the Fillmore East*, showcasing the band's unique mixture of jazz, classical music, hard rock, and blues • *Ms. Magazine* is first published as a sample insert in *New York* magazine; 300,000 copies are sold out in 8 days; the first regular issue is published in July 1972 • The radio news show *All Things Considered* is broadcast for the first time on National Public Radio • Starbucks opens its first store in Seattle's Pike Place public market • The first Hard Rock Cafe opens in London • A ban on TV advertisements for tobacco products goes into effect in the US • Walt Disney World opens in Orlando, FL • The cost of a US first-class postage stamp increases to 8¢ • Films: *A Clockwork Orange*; *The French Connection*; *The Last Picture Show*; *Bananas*; *Carnal Knowledge*; *Dirty Harry*; *Fiddler on the Roof*; *Klute*; *McCabe and Mrs. Miller*; *Shaft*

E. EDUCATION, LITERATURE & THE FINE ARTS	F. RELIGION, THEOLOGY, PHILOSOPHY & PSYCHOLOGY	G. AMERICAN & UNITED METHODISM	H. BRITISH & WORLD METHODISM	
areas of scientific and technological endeavor who serve pro bono to address critical national issues and give advice to the federal government and the public • Arthur Bliss composes his *Concerto for Cello and Orchestra* • Joseph Kosuth's *One and Three Chairs* represents the modern "conceptual art" movement by juxtaposing a real chair with a photograph of a chair and a written dictionary definition of a chair • Robert Smithson's "earthworks" project *Spiral Jetty*, built out of rock and earth in the Great Salt Lake in Utah, exemplifies the "environmental art" movement • Notable publications include: – James Dickey, *Deliverance* – Erich Segal, *Love Story* – Maya Angelou, *I Know Why the Caged Bird Sings* – Albert Speer, *Inside the Third Reich* – Dee Brown, *Bury My Heart at Wounded Knee: An Indian History of the West*	• The World Alliance of Reformed Churches (Presbyterian and Congregational) is formed by the merger of the separate Alliance of the Reformed Churches and International Congregational Council • Pope Paul VI names Spanish mystic Teresa of Avila the first woman "Doctor of the Church" • The Orthodox Church in America becomes independent of the Russian Orthodox Church [it has roots going back to the work of Russian monks in Alaska as early as 1794] • Troy D. Perry establishes the Universal Fellowship of Metropolitan Community Churches to affirm and minister to homosexual persons • Notable publications include: – Brevard S. Childs, *Biblical Theology in Crisis* – Paulo Friere, *Pedagogy of the Oppressed* – James H. Cone, *A Black Theology of Liberation* – Robert Bellah, *Beyond Belief: Essays on Religion in a Post-Traditional World*	– deals with the dissolution of the Central Jurisdiction and revises the quadrennial budget to make more funds available to aid that process – establishes the Minority Group Self Determination Fund, to be administered by the General Commission of Religion and Race – sets up a $1 million scholarship fund for minority students, to be administered by the General Board of Education – gives the United Methodist Council on Youth Ministry authority for administration of the Youth Service Fund – adjourns prematurely due to lack of a quorum when many white delegates leave early rather than confront black demonstrators • National American Indian Committee, now Native American International Caucus (NAIC), is formed • National Federation of Asian American United Methodists (NFAAUM) is formed • The eighth Assembly of the WSCS and WSG (UMC) meets • COSMOS sponsors a second consultation (in Atlantic City, NJ) on the international structure of the church • The Good News Movement holds its first national convocation in Dallas; more than 1,600 people attend • The CMEC celebrates the centennial of its founding and establishes its national headquarters in Memphis, TN • Frank Baker publishes *John Wesley and the Church of England*	(British and Australian Conferences), the Council of Baptist Churches in Northern India, the Church of the Brethren in India, and the Disciples of Christ • The United Church of Pakistan is created by union of Methodists with Anglicans, Presbyterians, Lutherans, and other Protestant bodies • Jurgen Weissbach publishes *Der neu Mensch in theologischen Denken John Wesleys*	**1970 cont.**
• The Kennedy Center for the Performing Arts opens in Washington, DC, with the premiere of Leonard Bernstein's *Mass* • The Rothko Chapel, a nondenominational chapel in Houston, TX, is not only a chapel but also a major work of modern art; the interior walls are fourteen black but color-hued paintings by Mark Rothko intended to create a meditative space • Morton Feldman's best-known musical composition is inspired by and written to be performed in Rothko Chapel; it too is called *Rothko Chapel* • Steve Reich composes his first minimalist masterpiece, *Drumming* • Notable publications include: – Wallace Stegner, *Angle of Repose* – Herman Wouk, *The Winds of War* – Sylvia Plath, *The Bell Jar* – John Gardner, *Grendel*	• The World Council of Churches merges with the World Council of Christian Education, which has roots in the 18th-century Sunday school movement • The National Association for the Promotion of Holiness (1893) changes its name to the Christian Holiness Association • Sun Myung Moon expands the Unification Church (1954) to the US; his mostly young followers are often called "Moonies" by critics of the movement • The *New American Standard Version of the Bible* (NASV) is published • Kenneth Taylor completes his *Living Bible*, which he had begun in 1962 • Other notable publications include: – James M. Robinson and Helmut Koester, *Trajectories Through Early Christianity* – John Rawls, *A Theory of Justice* – Jaroslav Pelikan, *The Christian Tradition: A History of the Development of Doctrine* (5 vols., 1971–89) – Thomas Merton, *Contemplation in a World of Action* – B. F. Skinner, *Beyond Freedom and Dignity*	• Methodists Associated Representing the Cause of Hispanic Americans (MARCHA) is formed • Homer Noley joins the staff of the Board of Global Ministries, becoming the first Native American to serve on a general board or agency staff • The "cross and flame" insignia of the UMC, formally adopted in 1968, is registered with the United States Patent and Trademark Office as a service mark and collective membership mark; it may be used "by any official agency of the Church, including local churches, to identify the work, program, and materials of The United Methodist Church" • Publication of *motive* magazine is terminated	• The twelfth World Methodist Conference meets in Denver, CO; it establishes the World Methodist Evangelism Division of the World Methodist Council • The "Denver Report" of the Joint Commission between the Roman Catholic Church and the World Methodist Council is published • Other notable publications include Dow Kirkpatrick, ed., *The Living God* [papers from the fourth Oxford Institute of Methodist Theological Studies, 1969]	**1971**

	A. WORLD HISTORY & POLITICS	B. AMERICAN HISTORY & POLITICS	C. SCIENCE, MEDICINE & TECHNOLOGY	D. DAILY LIFE, POPULAR CULTURE & ENTERTAINMENT
1972	• President Nixon makes a historic trip to China, initiating an era of better bilateral relations • The US and the USSR sign the first Strategic Arms Limitation Treaty (known as SALT I) and also the Antiballistic Missile (ABM) Treaty, which bans the development or deployment of missile defense systems • Kurt Waldheim is elected UN Secretary-General • On "Bloody Sunday" British troops kill 13 unarmed protesters in Londonderry, Northern Ireland; the IRA responds with intensified attacks on British forces and their Protestant supporters; Britain imposes direct rule • Nixon responds to the North Vietnamese drive across the DMZ by ordering mining of North Vietnam ports and heavy bombing of the Hanoi-Haiphong area • "Black September" terrorists from the PLO invade the Olympic Village in Munich, killing two members of the Israeli team and taking nine more hostage; in an ensuing battle, all nine Israeli hostages are killed, along with five of the terrorists and one German policeman; the Olympics continue after 36 hours "to defy terrorism" • Japan normalizes diplomatic relations with the People's Republic of China (mainland China) after breaking ties with the Republic of China (Taiwan) • The widely published photo of a young Vietnamese girl running naked down a highway after an American napalm bomb attack on her village is one of the most indelible images of the Vietnam War • The "Black September" group hijacks a Lufthansa airliner and demands the release of three of their PLO comrades being held for the massacre of Israeli athletes at the Olympic games in Munich • Idi Amin becomes the "Butcher of Uganda," unleashing death squads to eliminate his political opponents, especially members of the Acholi and Langi ethnic groups, who had formed Milton Obote's support base; the number of civilians killed by the Amin regime is disputed but may have been as high as 500,000 • The Council of Europe adopts the "Ode to Joy" from the final movement of Beethoven's *9th Symphony* as Europe's official anthem; an official arrangement for orchestra is written by Herbert von Karajan	• The Watergate scandal begins to unfold when five men are arrested for breaking into the national headquarters of the Democratic Party • The Equal Rights Amendment (ERA), first proposed in 1923, is passed by Congress and sent to the states for ratification • In *Eisenstadt v. Baird*, the US Supreme Court rules that the constitutional right to privacy includes an unmarried person's right to use contraceptives • Enforcement responsibility for the 1968 Gun Control Act is given to the Dept. of the Treasury's Alcohol and Tobacco Tax Division of the Internal Revenue Service; the organization replaces *tax* with *firearms*, nearly doubles in size, and becomes the Bureau of Alcohol, Tobacco and Firearms (ATF) • In *Dunn v. Blumstein*, the US Supreme Court declares that lengthy residence requirements for voting in state and local elections are unconstitutional and suggests that 30 days is an ample period • Hurricane Agnes causes 117 deaths (50 in PA) and causes damage estimated at over $8.6 billion • George Wallace is shot at a political rally in Maryland while campaigning for the Democratic Party presidential nomination; he survives but is paralyzed below the waist • President Nixon's "Southern strategy" succeeds in drawing conservative white voters in the South away from their traditional allegiance to the Democratic Party, the strategy stems from the 1948 "Dixiecrat" rebellion, the success of Barry Goldwater in capturing five Deep South states (Louisiana, Mississippi, Alabama, Georgia, and South Carolina) in 1964, and the hostility of many white southerners to the civil rights movement • Nixon and Vice President Agnew are reelected (Republican Party) by an electoral college majority of 521 to 17 in the most one-sided presidential election since 1936	• Swiss scientist Jean F. Borel discovers that the class of drugs called cyclosporines suppress the activity of the body's immune system; the discovery helps decrease the rejection of transplanted organs • Larry Roberts writes the first e-mail management program to list, selectively read, file, forward, and respond to messages • EMI of Great Britain introduces a commercial CAT scanner, a giant step forward in medical imaging • NASA's *Apollo 17* is the last of its moon landing missions • Hewlett-Packard markets the HP-35, the world's first scientific pocket calculator (with trigonometric and exponential functions); the price is $395 • The production of a recombinant DNA molecule, marking the birth of modern molecular biology, is announced by David A. Jackson, Robert H. Symons, and Paul Berg	• Sales of color TV sets in the US surpass sales of black-and-white TV sets for the first time • The musical *Grease* opens on Broadway • The controversial and risqué off-Broadway musical comedy revue *Oh! Calcutta!* features one or more performers in either a state of undress, simulating sex, or both, in every scene • *M*A*S*H* premieres on CBS; *Sanford and Son* begins on NBC • Home Box Office (HBO), the first pay cable TV network, begins broadcasting • Pong, the first really successful commercial video game, makes its debut • The Rolling Stones release *Exile on Main Street*, considered by many to be their greatest album ever • Paul McCartney's new band, Wings, makes its live debut • The Nitty Gritty Dirt Band makes its landmark album *Will the Circle Be Unbroken* featuring a new generation of country and bluegrass musicians collaborating with traditional artists including Mother Maybelle Carter, Earl Scruggs, Roy Acuff, Doc and Merle Watson, Jimmy Martin, and Junior Huskey • Roberta Flack records "The First Time Ever I Saw Your Face" • Elton John pioneers the "glam rock" style with his hit single "Crocodile Rock" • The Miami Dolphins complete the only undefeated season in NFL history (17-0) by defeating the Washington Redskins in Super Bowl VII • Vincent Marotta and Samuel Glazer invent the Mr. Coffee machine • The Opryland USA country music theme park opens in Nashville • Alex Comfort publishes *The Joy of Sex: A Cordon Bleu Guide to Lovemaking* • Films: *The Godfather; Play it Again, Sam; Deliverance; Cabaret; Cries and Whispers* • Summer Olympics: Munich • Winter Olympics: Sapporo • American swimmer Mark Spitz wins an incredible record seven gold medals at the Summer Olympics in Munich

E. EDUCATION, LITERATURE & THE FINE ARTS	F. RELIGION, THEOLOGY, PHILOSOPHY & PSYCHOLOGY	G. AMERICAN & UNITED METHODISM	H. BRITISH & WORLD METHODISM	
• The Joffrey Ballet debuts the *Deuce Coupe Ballet*, set entirely around music by The Beach Boys • In response to pressure from younger members, the Association for the Study of Negro Life and History, founded by Carter G. Woodson in 1915, changes its name to the Association for the Study of Afro-American Life and History • Bobby Fischer defeats Boris Spassky in a chess match at Reykjavík, Iceland, and becomes the first American chess world champion • Notable publications include: – Eugene Genovese, *Roll, Jordan, Roll* – Richard Adams, *Watership Down* – Isaac Asimov, *The Gods Themselves*	• The United Reformed Church of England and Wales is created by merger of the Congregational Church of England and Wales with the Presbyterian Church of England • The American Baptist Convention (1950) is reorganized as the American Baptist Churches in the USA • Philip A. Potter (Methodist Church, US) is named General Secretary of the World Council of Churches • Lois Stair is the first woman to be elected moderator of the General Assembly, UPCUSA • Sally Preisand is the first woman to be ordained as a rabbi in the Reformed Jewish tradition in the US (by Hebrew Union College) • Notable publications include: – James A. Sanders, *Torah and Canon* – Mildred Bangs Wynkoop, *A Theology of Love* – Gordon Kaufman, *God the Problem* – John Howard Yoder, *The Politics of Jesus* – Henri J. M. Nouwen, *The Wounded Healer: Ministry in Contemporary Society*	• The UMC General Conference: – adopts the report of the Structure Study Commission and reorganizes church boards and agencies into four "superboards": General Board of Church and Society (GBCS) for *advocacy*, General Board of Discipleship (GBOD) for *nurture*, General Board of Global Ministries (GBGM) for *outreach*, and General Board of Higher Education and Ministry (GBHEM) for *vocation* – creates the General Council of Ministries (GCOM) as the successor to the Program Council for coordinating the work of the general agencies; it is intended to serve as an "interim General Conference" with authority to act for the UMC between General Conference sessions – creates the General Council on Finance and Administration (GCFA) for financial coordination of the work of the general agencies and to monitor their personnel and employment policies – establishes the General Commission on the Status and Role of Women (COSROW) – mandates establishment of a Council on Ministries and a Council on Finance and Administration in every annual conference – adopts the report of the Theological Study Commission on "Doctrine and Doctrinal Statements and the General Rules" as Part II of the *Discipline* – adopts a statement concerning "The Ministry of All Christians" and creates a new diaconal ministry category for full-time lay professionals, which is related to the annual conference but stands outside the itinerant ordained ministry [this is a move toward the establishment of a permanent diaconate in 1996] – adopts the report of the Social Principles Study Commission as the new UMC Social Principles document after major revision, including the addition of a statement that homosexuality is "incompatible with Christian teaching" – explicitly states through the new Social Principles that "we recognize divorce and the right of divorced persons to remarry" – dissolves COSMOS (created in 1948); establishes the new Committee on Central Conference Affairs – approves legislation authorizing autonomy for the Puerto Rico Annual Conference – merges all of the women's organizations in the UMC to form one inclusive organization with the name United Methodist Women (UMW) • The UMC Judicial Council rules that it is unconstitutional for GCOM to serve as an "interim General Conference," holding that the church's programmatic work is accountable only and directly to the General Conference and thereby removing a primary reason for the creation of GCOM • Wilbur Choy becomes the first Asian American to be elected bishop of the UMC	• Proposals for an Anglican-Methodist reunion in Britain collapse; the proposals are approved by the British Methodist Conference but fail to gain the required majority in the General Synod of the Church of England • Methodist churches in Algeria and Tunisia unite with other Protestant churches to form the Église Protestante d'Algerie, now part of the Switzerland/France Annual Conference (UMC) • Hong Kong Provisional Annual Conference is granted autonomy and becomes The Methodist Church, Hong Kong • Richmond College, London, is closed • Girls are admitted to Kingswood School for the first time • Conservative members of the Methodist Church in Ireland who oppose a perceived shift toward liberalism and modernism withdraw, forming the Fellowship of Independent Methodist Churches in Ireland in 1973 • In the face of declining enrollment and financial pressure, the MC [UK] decides to close Hartley-Victoria College in Manchester and to consolidate theological training at Wesley College in Bristol • Ole E. Borgen publishes *John Wesley on the Sacraments: A Theological Study*	**1972**

	A. WORLD HISTORY & POLITICS	B. AMERICAN HISTORY & POLITICS	C. SCIENCE, MEDICINE & TECHNOLOGY	D. DAILY LIFE, POPULAR CULTURE & ENTERTAINMENT
1973	• The Yom Kippur War begins when Egypt and Syria open a coordinated surprise attack against Israel; it ends with a cease-fire agreement under UN Resolution 338; Egypt regains control of the Suez Canal • Gush Emunim ("Block of the Faithful") is formed in Israel to establish Jewish settlements in the occupied territories • The first Arab oil embargo produces worldwide fuel shortages and dramatic price increases when OPEC doubles the price of crude oil, resulting in long lines for gasoline and short tempers in the US and Europe • The Paris Peace Accords are signed by North Vietnam, South Vietnam, and the US, ending the longest war in American history and resulting in the withdrawal of all US combat forces from South Vietnam • Britain, Ireland, and Denmark join the European Community (EC), which is now on its way to becoming the European Union (EU) • A US-supported military coup overthrows the elected Marxist government in Chile and installs Augusto Pinochet as president • British Honduras, which had been granted self-government by Britain in 1964, changes its name to Belize	• Congress stuns President Nixon when it votes to override his veto of the War Powers Act, which limits presidential powers to commit US forces abroad without specific congressional approval • The special Senate Watergate Committee holds public hearings that implicate President Nixon in a cover-up attempt; Nixon refuses to release subpoenaed tapes, citing "executive privilege" • In its *Roe v. Wade* decision, the US Supreme Court establishes a woman's right to safe and legal abortion, overriding the antiabortion laws of many states • American Indian Movement activists stage a protest at the site of the 1890 Wounded Knee massacre on the Pine Ridge Reservation in South Dakota, resulting in a 71-day standoff with FBI agents and the National Guard • Marian Wright Edelman founds the Children's Defense Fund, an organization that lobbies for children's rights and welfare • Spiro T. Agnew resigns as vice president over charges of tax evasion and corruption; Gerald Ford becomes the first vice president appointed under the provisions of the 25th Amendment • The US stock market begins a long decline, losing 45% of its value over the next two years	• Vinton Cerf and Robert Kahn create the Transmission Control Protocol and Internet Protocol (TCP/IP), which makes possible the development of the Internet • Martin Cooper develops the first working prototype of a cellular telephone, the Motorola Dyna-Tac • The US Department of Defense develops the Global Positioning System (GPS), which can determine exact location and altitude by use of triangulation by a network of satellites • The World Trade Center in New York City is completed; the "twin towers" are the tallest buildings in the world at the time: tower one is 1,368 feet; tower two is 1,362 feet; both are 110 stories • Use of DDT as an insecticide in the US is banned • IBM develops the first true sealed hard disk drive for personal computers; its two platters can each store 30 MB of data, hence it is called the "30-30" drive, leading to its nickname, the "Winchester" • NASA launches the *Skylab* space station into Earth's orbit • NASA's *Pioneer 10*, launched in 1972, makes the first close approach to and transmits photographs of Jupiter [it eventually crosses the orbit of Pluto in 1983, becoming the first artificial object to leave the solar system] • The current London Bridge across the Thames is dedicated; it is the third structure to bear the name and replaces the "New London Bridge" of 1831 • The American Psychiatric Association removes homosexuality from its official diagnostic manual, *The Diagnostic and Statistical Manual of Mental Disorders*, second edition (DSM II)	• The Federal Express Company (FedEx) begins its delivery services • Nolan Ryan strikes out a record 383 batters in a single season of baseball • Billie Jean King defeats Bobby Riggs in the tennis match dubbed the "Battle of the Sexes," which is watched by over 50 million people around the world • Secretariat, possibly the greatest racehorse in history, claims the Triple Crown, winning each race in record time and the final race (Belmont Stakes) by the still-record margin of 31 lengths • The UCLA men's college basketball team wins a record seventh straight NCAA title • The Boston Women's Health Book Collective publishes *Our Bodies Our Selves: A Book by and for Women* • The "Summer Jam at Watkins Glen" rock festival brings 600,000 to see The Allman Brothers Band, The Band, and the Grateful Dead • The blues-rock band ZZ Top gains national attention with the release of its album *Tres Hombres* • Stephen Sondheim's musical *A Little Night Music* opens on Broadway; the score includes the memorable song "Send in the Clowns," made famous by Barbara Streisand's recording • Pink Floyd releases the album *The Dark Side of the Moon* • KISS performs their first concert, at the Coventary Club in Queens, NY • Elton John releases his album *Goodbye Yellow Brick Road*, containing the memorable single "Candle in the Wind" dedicated to the memory of Marilyn Monroe • Lifetime sales of the Volkswagen Beetle, first produced in Germany in 1938, exceed those of the Ford Model-T (15 million) • Films: *The Harder They Come*, starring reggae singer Jimmy Cliff, stimulates an interest in reggae music; other films include *American Graffiti; The Exorcist; Sleeper; Last Tango in Paris; The Sting*
1974	• OPEC ends its embargo against the United States, Europe, and Japan; fuel supplies and prices gradually return to "normal" levels • Egypt and Israel sign an agreement for disengagement of military forces • Both sides in Vietnam accuse each other of frequent violations of the cease-fire agreement • Harold Wilson becomes British prime minister for the second time • Valéry Giscard d'Estaing is elected president of France • Helmut Schmidt becomes chancellor of Germany • Yitzhak Rabin becomes prime minister of Israel • In an indication of growing international opposition to apartheid, South Africa is suspended from the United Nations General Assembly	• The Supreme Court rules unanimously that President Nixon's claim of "executive privilege" over White House tapes is void and orders their release to investigators • The House Judiciary Committee approves three articles of impeachment against Nixon, charging him with obstruction of justice, abuse of power, and contempt of Congress • Nixon resigns the presidency rather than face impeachment by the full House of Representatives; Vice President Ford becomes the only person to serve as president without having been elected to either office; Ford then pardons Nixon for any and all crimes • The Equal Credit Opportunity Act prohibits discrimination in consumer credit practices on the basis of sex, race, marital status, religion, national origin, age, or receipt of public assistance	• India conducts its first test thermonuclear explosion • The skeleton of "Lucy" is discovered in Africa; the almost complete hominid skeleton is over 3 million years old; she was 3½ feet tall, had adult teeth, a small brain, and walked upright • Xerox develops the Alto workstation at its legendary Palo Alto Research Center (PARC), complete with a monitor, a graphical user interface, a mouse, and an Ethernet card for networking; it has 128 (expandable to 512) kilobytes of main memory and a hard disk with a removable 2.5 megabyte cartridge, all housed in a cabinet about as big as a small refrigerator • BBN opens Telenet, the first public packet data service (a commercial version of ARPANET) • Motorola creates the Pageboy I, the first mass-market pager • The Sears Tower in Chicago is completed; at 110 stories and 1,454 feet, it is the tallest building in the world at the time	• Patti Smith releases what is considered to be the first punk rock single, "Hey Joe," paving the way for bands such as the Sex Pistols, the Clash, the Ramones, Blondie, and Talking Heads • "Hip-hop," an umbrella term that embraces a number of related cultural practices, such as rap music, break dancing, and graffiti, along with certain fashion styles and slang, begins to spread across the nation from its home in the South Bronx • *People* magazine debuts, with Mia Farrow gracing the cover • Hank Aaron breaks Babe Ruth's record by hitting home run No. 715; he retires in 1976 with a record 755 home runs • In one of the greatest fights of all time, Muhammad Ali defeats George Foreman in the "Rumble in the Jungle" to retain his heavyweight boxing crown • Garrison Keillor hosts the first live broadcast of *A Prairie Home Companion* on Minnesota Public Radio and NPR (until 1987)

E. EDUCATION, LITERATURE & THE FINE ARTS	F. RELIGION, THEOLOGY, PHILOSOPHY & PSYCHOLOGY	G. AMERICAN & UNITED METHODISM	H. BRITISH & WORLD METHODISM	
• The magnificent Sydney Opera House in Australia hosts its first performance • The Musée National Message Biblique Marc Chagall (National Museum of the Marc Chagall Biblical Message) is opened in Nice, France, exhibiting hundreds of his biblical art works, featuring his Biblical Message Cycle, a collection of 17 enormous canvases inspired by the Old Testament • Benjamin Britten composes *Death in Venice* • Steve Reich composes Music for *Mallet Instruments, Voices and Organ*, in which he explores the minimalist musical techniques of augmentation and phrase shifting • Carl Orff's opera *De Temporum Fine Comoedia* (A Play of the End of Time), his final work, premieres at the Salzburg Music Festival under the baton of Herbert von Karajan • Tristan Murial founds the Ensemble l'Itinéraire and begins to establish the theoretical and technical bases of what would later come to be known as "spectral music" • Notable publications include: – Kurt Vonnegut Jr., *Breakfast of Champions* – Thomas Pynchon, *Gravity's Rainbow* – Graham Greene, *The Honorary Consul*	• The Presbyterian Church in America (PCA) separates from the [southern] PCUS • The RSV Committee publishes The Common Bible with the Apocrypha/Deuterocanonical Books, which has an international endorsement by Roman Catholics, Greek Orthodox, and Protestant denominations • The International Bible Society publishes the New Testament of the New International Version of the Bible (NIV) • Mary Daly publishes her feminist theological manifesto, *Beyond God the Father: Towards a Philosophy of Women's Liberation* • Other notable publications include: – Frank M. Cross, *Canaanite Myth and Hebrew Epic* – Gustavo Gutiérrez, *A Theology of Liberation* – Vine Deloria Jr., *God Is Red: A Native View of Religion* – John Hick, *God and the Universe of Faiths* – Ernst Becker, *The Denial of Death* – Juan Luis Segundo, *A Theology for Artisans of a New Humanity* (5 vols., 1973–74)	• The UMPH publishes the *Himnario Metodista*, the first full Spanish-language hymnal for the UMC, based on the earlier hymnal of Rio Grande Conference • The ninth Assembly of United Methodist Women meets [it is the first Assembly to meet under the banner of the newly-created UMW but is numbered continuously with the previous Assemblies of the WSCS and WSG] • The AMEC Council of Bishops holds a national theological summit on "The Nature and Mission of the Church" • Bernard Semmel publishes *The Methodist Revolution*	• The Evangelical Methodist Church of Costa Rica becomes autonomous but affiliates with the UMC • The fifth Oxford Institute of Methodist Theological Studies meets • In New Zealand, Maori Methodism becomes largely autonomous within the MCNZ • The Seminario Juan Wesley is established by the Iglesia Metodista de Mexico • The Fellowship of Independent Methodist Churches (FIMC) breaks away from the Methodist Church in Ireland; the FIMC has roots in the strong opposition of the Irish Methodist Revival Movement (ca. 1970) to ecumenism (especially to cooperation with Roman Catholics) and to theological liberalism	**1973**
• György Ligeti composes his *San Francisco Polyphony for Orchestra* • Philip Glass completes his *Music in 12 Parts* (1971–74), which presents a summary of minimalist compositional techniques • Carl Bernstein and Bob Woodward give their account of the unfolding Watergate scandal in *All the President's Men* • Shelby Foote completes his massive three-volume *The Civil War: A Narrative History*, called by some "an American Iliad" • Other notable publications include: – Studs Terkel, *Working* – Annie Dillard, *Pilgrim at Tinker Creek* – Erica Jong, *Fear of Flying* – John le Carré, *Tinker, Tailor, Soldier, Spy*	• Eleven Episcopal women (known as the "Philadelphia Eleven"), including Susan Hiatt and Carter Heyward, are "irregularly" ordained to the priesthood in Philadelphia by three retired bishops of the ECUSA; the action is not sanctioned by the official ECUSA hierarchy • Students, faculty, and staff from the LCMS Concordia Seminary, St. Louis, walk out to form Concordia Seminary in Exile, later Christ Seminary Seminex • The International Congress on World Evangelism is held in Lausanne, Switzerland • Notable publications include: – Jacques Ellul, *The Technological Society* – Juliet Mitchell, *Psychoanalysis and Feminism* – Paul Ricoeur, *The Conflict of Interpretations: Essays in Hermeneutics* – Jürgen Moltmann, *A Theology of Hope* – J. Deotis Roberts, *A Black Political Theology* – Hans Küng, *On Being a Christian*	• The Puerto Rico Annual Conference votes to become autonomous but retain affiliation with the UMC • Garrett-Evangelical Theological Seminary (1934) is formed from the merger of Garrett Theological Seminary and Evangelical Theological Seminary (1873) • *The Encyclopedia of World Methodism* (2 vols.), compiled under the general editorship of Nolan Harmon, is published; it is the most comprehensive reference work on Methodism ever produced • Other notable publications include: – James P. Brawley, *Two Centuries of Methodist Concern: Bondage, Freedom, and Education of Black People* – Frederick A. Norwood, *The Story of American Methodism*	• The British Methodist Conference authorizes the ordination of women as elders • Publication of *The Epworth Review* begins in Britain • Dow Kirkpatrick publishes *The Holy Spirit* [papers from the fifth Oxford Institute of Methodist Theological Studies, 1973]	**1974**

	A. WORLD HISTORY & POLITICS	B. AMERICAN HISTORY & POLITICS	C. SCIENCE, MEDICINE & TECHNOLOGY	D. DAILY LIFE, POPULAR CULTURE & ENTERTAINMENT
1974 cont.	• The Irish Republican Army claims responsibility for planting a bomb that explodes at the Houses of Parliament in London, damaging Westminster Hall	• In *Corning Glass Works v. Brennan*, the US Supreme Court rules that employers cannot justify paying women lower wages because that is what they traditionally received under the "going market rate" • The US minimum wage is increased to $2.00 per hour for nonfarm workers, $1.60 for farm workers • In the deadly "Super Tornado Outbreak," a series of 148 twisters strike within 16 hours across 13 states, 330 are killed and over 5,000 are injured in a damage path covering more than 2,500 miles • Spokane, WA, hosts the Expo '74 World's Fair, the first to have an environmental theme		• The Grand Ole Opry moves out of the historic Ryman Auditorium in downtown Nashville to its new home, Opryland • The Miller Brewing Company introduces Miller Lite, the first "lite" (low-calorie) beer • *Creative Computing*, the first magazine for home computer users, is founded • The fantasy tabletop role-playing game "Dungeons & Dragons" (abbreviated as D&D) is published • The cost of a US first-class postage stamp increases to 10¢ • Films: *The Conversation*; *Chinatown*; *The Godfather, Part II*; *Blazing Saddles*; *Thunderbolt and Lightfoot*; *Lenny*
1975	• North Vietnam invades South Vietnam; the US evacuates its embassy as Saigon falls; more than 140,000 Vietnamese refugees flee the country as the Provisional Revolutionary Government (PRG) takes control • Phnom Penh, Cambodia, falls to the Khmer Rouge, who set up a government (the "Pol Pot" regime) that engages in genocidal policies leading to the death by execution or starvation of an estimated 1.7 million people, constituting 21% of Cambodia's population • Portugal grants independence to its African colonies, including Angola, Mozambique, the Cape Verde Islands, and Guinea-Bissau • In Spain, Franco dies and the monarchy is restored; Prince Juan Carlos becomes king • King Faisal of Saudi Arabia is assassinated; he is succeeded by his half brother Prince Khalid ibn Abdul Aziz; however, Kahlid is in poor health and his half brother, Crown Prince Fahd, becomes the power behind the throne • The Suez Canal, which has been closed to shipping since 1967, is formally reopened to shipping	• The fall of Saigon triggers a large wave of Vietnamese, Lao, and Hmong immigration to the US • Teamsters Union leader Jimmy Hoffa, who had suspected links to organized crime, disappears and his body is never found • The US begins selling some of its gold reserves on the international market; this helps to make gold more of a commodity than a standard in the international monetary system • FBI agents and American Indian Movement activists confront each other at Wounded Knee on the Pine Ridge Reservation in South Dakota; one Indian and two agents are killed • Elijah Muhammad, head of the Nation of Islam, dies; he is succeeded by his son, Wallace D. Muhammad, who moderates the black nationalism and separatism of the organization • The *Edmund Fitzgerald*, the largest ore carrier on the Great Lakes, sinks without a trace during a fierce winter storm on Lake Superior, killing all 29 crew members; the tragedy is memorialized in Gordon Lightfoot's touching ballad "The Wreck of the Edmund Fitzgerald" • The US makes it legal for citizens to own, buy, sell, or trade gold, but as a commodity only, not as currency	• The Altair 8800, the first personal computer, is introduced; it is sold both fully assembled or in a "do it yourself" kit form • Bill Gates (then a Harvard freshman) and Paul Allen establish a company called Micro-Soft, later changed to Microsoft • Gordon Moore articulates what comes to be known as "Moore's Law" concerning the pace of development in computer technology: that the number of transistors on computer chips of the same size would double every 18 months • The CN Tower, built in Toronto by the Canadian National Railway, is completed; at 1,815 feet it is the world's tallest freestanding structure, though much of it is a hollow shaft without occupied floors	• *A Chorus Line* opens on Broadway and changes the course of musical theater by doing away with fancy costumes and elaborate sets and introducing an element of gritty realism not seen before [it runs for 6,137 performances before closing in 1990] • *The Wiz*, a new version of the classic *The Wizard of Oz* story, opens on Broadway • *Saturday Night Live* premieres on NBC • HBO becomes the first TV network to broadcast its signals via satellite when it shows the "Thrilla From Manila" boxing match between Muhammad Ali and Joe Frazier • John Walker (New Zealand) is the first person to run a mile in under 3:50 • The Falls City Brewing Company of Louisville, KY, introduces the "stay-tab" can; unlike older "pull-tab" cans, the tabs stay connected to the can once opened • The Camp Fire Girls organization goes coed, allowing boys to join and changing its name to Camp Fire USA with the motto "Today's kids, tomorrow's leaders" • The Sex Pistols play their first concert at St. Martin's School of Art in London • Bob Marley has an international hit with the single "No Woman, No Cry," followed by the album *Rastaman Vibration*, establishing Reggae music in the US market • Bruce Springsteen releases his breakout album *Born to Run*, rocketing him to international success • Fleetwood Mac catapults into stardom with their self-titled album featuring the hit singles "Say You Love Me" by Christine McVie and "Rhiannon (Will You Ever Win)" by Stevie Nicks • The cost of a US first-class postage stamp increases to 13¢ • Films: Stephen Spielberg makes his directing debut with *Jaws*, which becomes the highest-grossing film to date; other major films include *One Flew Over the Cuckoo's Nest*; *Monty Python and the Holy Grail*; *Nashville*

E. EDUCATION, LITERATURE & THE FINE ARTS	F. RELIGION, THEOLOGY, PHILOSOPHY & PSYCHOLOGY	G. AMERICAN & UNITED METHODISM	H. BRITISH & WORLD METHODISM	
				1974 cont.
• Beverly Sills makes her Metropolitan Opera debut • Claude Bolling and Jean-Pierre Rampal compose and play their *Suite for Flute and Jazz Piano* • Witold Lutosławski completes his extended orchestral song *The Spaces of Sleep* • Notable publications include: – Saul Bellow, *Humboldt's Gift* – E. L. Doctorow, *Ragtime* – Michael Shaara, *The Killer Angels*	• Elizabeth Ann Seton, who established the Sisters of Charity in the US in 1809 becomes the first American to be canonized as a saint by the Roman Catholic Church • Willow Creek Community Church is established outside Chicago by Bill Hybels; it becomes the model for emerging American "megachurches" by creating numerous small groups to focus on different needs within the larger congregation [by 2005 it has over 20,000 members] • Notable publications include: – Hans Frei, *The Identity of Jesus Christ: The Hermeneutical Bases of Dogmatic Theology* – José Míguez Bonino, *Doing Theology in a Revolutionary Situation* – James H. Cone, *God of the Oppressed* – Stanley Hauerwas, *Character and the Christian Life: A Study in Theological Ethics*	• Affirmation caucus is formed; it advocates for full clergy and laity rights for gay and lesbian persons • The Good News Movement issues "The Junaluska Affirmation of Scriptural Christianity for United Methodists" • Publication of the modern critical edition of *The Works of John Wesley* commences; begun as "The Oxford Edition of the Works of John Wesley" (Clarendon Press, 1975–83), it is continued as "The Bicentennial Edition of the Works of John Wesley" (Abingdon Press, 1984–); the first volume is *The Appeals to Men of Reason and Religion and Certain Related Open Letters*, edited by Gerald R. Cragg • Albert C. Outler publishes *Theology in the Wesleyan Spirit*	• The MC [UK] publishes the *Methodist Service Book*, a revision of the 1936 Book of Offices	1975

	A. WORLD HISTORY & POLITICS	B. AMERICAN HISTORY & POLITICS	C. SCIENCE, MEDICINE & TECHNOLOGY	D. DAILY LIFE, POPULAR CULTURE & ENTERTAINMENT
1976	• The deaths of Zhou Enlai (January) and Mao Zedong (September) bring change to China; Mao's widow Jiang Qing and her three principal associates, the radical clique most closely associated with Mao and the Cultural Revolution, are denounced as the "Gang of Four"; Hua Guofeng assumes the positions of party chairman and premier • The election of a National Assembly paves the way for the reunification of North and South Vietnam • White police in South Africa kill 575 people during mass protests in Soweto township; the resulting riots and confrontations spread across the country and greatly increase racial tensions • Syrian troops occupy war-torn Lebanon, ostensibly to prevent Palestinian and Lebanese leftist groups from defeating Christian militia forces • The Parti Québécois (PQ) comes to power in Quebec with the goal of creating a sovereign state that is independent of Canada • James Callaghan becomes British prime minister • Earthquakes in Italy, Bali, Turkey, China, and the Philippines result in 780,000 deaths • Israeli commandos rescue 103 hostages from a French airliner that had been hijacked by Palestinian terrorists and flown to Entebbe, Uganda	• The US celebrates the bicentennial of the Declaration of Independence • Congress authorizes the admission of women to all of the US service academies • The Consolidated Rail Corporation (Conrail) is created to take over operation of six bankrupt northeastern railroads • The US Supreme Court strikes down as unconstitutional a Missouri statute requiring a married woman to get her husband's consent before obtaining an abortion • Walter F. Mondale (Democrat) and Robert J. (Bob) Dole (Republican) take part in the first televised debate between candidates for vice president • The US and the USSR sign a treaty limiting the size of underground nuclear test explosions • The US vetoes the admission of Vietnam to the United Nations, claiming it has not done enough to account for American servicemen missing in action • James Earl (Jimmy) Carter Jr., is elected as president and Walter F. Mondale as vice president (Democratic Party)	• Cray Research, Inc. introduces the Cray-1, the world's first "supercomputer" • Intel releases the 8086 microprocessor chip • Steve Jobs and Stephen Wozniak establish Apple Computer and create the first popular personal computer, the Apple I • Alan Shugart develops the 5.25-inch "floppy disk" which quickly becomes an industry standard for personal computers • NASA's *Viking 1* and *Viking 2* become the first spacecraft to land on the surface of Mars • British Airways and Air France begin using the Concorde supersonic airliner in regular passenger service • The first known outbreak of the Ebola virus in Zaire causes hundreds of deaths due to severe and untreatable hemorrhaging • An outbreak of pneumonia kills 29 at an American Legion convention in Philadelphia; caused by a previously unknown bacterium, the illness is called legionellosis or Legionnaire's disease	• The risqué musical *Oh! Calcutta!* (1972) is revived on Broadway [it runs for 5,959 performances before closing in 1989] • Paul McCartney and Wings start their "Wings over America" tour in Fort Worth, TX • The hit single "Anarchy in the UK" by the Sex Pistols and the self-titled album by the Ramones exemplify the alienation, isolation, and antisocial frustration characteristic of punk rock • Grandmaster Flash and the Furious Five, one of the first multimember "rapping crews," are stars at the early hip-hop shows in the Bronx and Harlem; they pioneer many of the techniques used in later hip-hop music, including deejaying, needle-dropping, scratching, and sampling • The RIAA establishes the Platinum Record award for albums that have sold over 1 million copies; the first RIAA-certified Platinum album is *The Eagles: Their Greatest Hits 1971–1975* [the best-selling album of the 20th century, selling 26 million copies in the US alone] • Sony's Betamax and JVC's VHS battle for dominance of the home VCR market [the Betamax format will lose in the marketplace, despite being technically superior] • Barbara Walters is the first woman to anchor a network newscast in the US • Satellite TV dishes begin to appear in American yards • United Parcel Service (UPS) now offers delivery services within all 48 contiguous states and Hawaii • Films: *Rocky; Taxi Driver; Network; All the President's Men* • Summer Olympics: Montreal • Winter Olympics: Innsbruck
1977	• Two Boeing 747 airliners collide on the ground on the island of Tenerife, killing 583 people in the worst civil airline accident in history; as a consequence of the accident, sweeping changes are made to international airline regulations and to airplanes; all control towers and pilot crews for international flights are now required to communicate in English using standard phrases • Menachem Begin becomes prime minister in Israel • Egypt's president Sadat becomes the first Arab leader to visit Israel • Ayatollah Ruhollah Khomeini is expelled from Iraq by Saddam Hussein; he goes into exile in Paris • Protocols are added to the 1949 Geneva Conventions concerning the protection of victims of both national and international armed conflicts	• In January, for the first time in recorded history, snow falls in Miami, FL • President Carter signs the Panama Canal Treaty, agreeing to return control of the canal to Panama at the end of 1999 • Carter issues a presidential pardon to 10,000 draft resisters from the Vietnam era • Carter declares that his administration will make "human rights" an explicit dimension of US foreign policy • The State Department lifts bans on travel by US citizens to Cuba, Vietnam, Cambodia, and North Korea • The US extends the zone it claims as "territorial waters" to 200 miles • Residents are evacuated from Love Canal, near Niagara Falls, NY, because their homes are built on a toxic waste dump that is leaking dangerous chemicals • The US Supreme Court rules that states are not required to spend Medicaid funds on elective abortions • Singer and actress Anita Bryant leads a successful effort to overturn a Dade County, FL, ordinance that prohibited discrimination on the basis of sexual orientation, becoming a national symbol of opposition to homosexuality; the fallout from her (cont.)	• South Africa tests its first full-scale nuclear device • The Alaska oil pipeline, begun in 1975, is completed, running 800 miles from Prudhoe Bay on Alaska's North Slope to the port of Valdez • NASA launches the *Voyager I* and *Voyager II* space probes [by 2005, both are well beyond the orbit of Pluto and still returning scientific data to earth] • The first US space shuttle, *Enterprise*, makes its first suborbital test flights • Apple Computer develops the Apple II, the first PC with color video display • AT&T Bell Labs begins testing of a prototype cellular phone service in Chicago, Washington DC, and Baltimore • The Big Ear, a radio telescope operated by The Ohio State University as part of the SETI project, receives a radio signal from deep space; the signal has the expected earmarks of potential nonterrestrial and nonsolar system origin; it lasts for 72 seconds, then fades, and is never again detected • Lockheed-Martin's top-secret "stealth" fighter aircraft makes its first flight (it will become the F-117A Nighthawk) • 2060 Chiron, first of the outer solar system asteroids known as "Centaurs," is discovered by astronomer Charlie Kowal	• The musical *Annie*, based on Harold Gray's "Little Orphan Annie," with music by Charles Strouse and lyrics by Martin Charnin, opens on Broadway [it records 2,377 performances before closing in 1981] • The TV miniseries *Roots*, based on Alex Haley's 1976 novel, mesmerizes the nation and draws an audience of 130 million • Elvis Presley is found dead in Graceland, his home in Memphis, from an apparent drug overdose • Paul Simon records his album *Still Crazy After All These Years* • Jimmy Buffett's album *Changes in Latitudes, Changes in Attitudes* includes "Margaritaville," the biggest single of his career • The Clash headline the gala opening of the London music club, The Roxy, ironically symbolizing the "mainstreaming" of punk rock • The Home Shopping Network (HSN) originates the electronic retailing industry • Films: *Saturday Night Fever*, starring John Travolta, ignites a craze for disco music and dancing across the US; other films include *Star Wars; Close Encounters of the Third Kind; Annie Hall; New York, New York*

E. EDUCATION, LITERATURE & THE FINE ARTS	F. RELIGION, THEOLOGY, PHILOSOPHY & PSYCHOLOGY	G. AMERICAN & UNITED METHODISM	H. BRITISH & WORLD METHODISM	
• Negro History Week, originally established by Carter G. Woodson in 1926, celebrates its 50th anniversary by renaming and expanding into Black History Month • Philip Glass composes his avant-garde opera *Einstein on the Beach* • Steve Reich composes his most seminal work, *Music for 18 Musicians* • Henryk Górecki composes his *Symphony No. 3 (Symphony of Sorrowful Songs)* • Alex Haley publishes the novel *Roots: The Saga of an American Family*, tracing his family back to an African ancestor named Kunta Kinte, who was captured by slave traders in 1767 • Bruno Bettelheim publishes *The Uses of Enchantment: The Meaning and Importance of Fairy Tales*, interpreting the classic fairy tales of the Grimm Brothers in terms of Freudian psychology, sometimes in an overly literal way • Argentinean writer Manuel Puig publishes his novel *Kiss of the Spider Woman*	• The Association of Evangelical Lutheran Churches (AELC) splits from the Lutheran Church-Missouri Synod • Carl F. H. Henry begins publication of his *God, Revelation, and Authority* (6 vols., 1976–84), one of the classic works of modern evangelical theology • The ECUSA General Convention passes a resolution declaring that "no one shall be denied access" to ordination into the three orders of ministry (deacons, priests, or bishops) on the basis of gender • Anglican Church of Canada ordains women for the first time as priests • Michel Foucault begins the publication of his *History of Sexuality* (3 vols., 1976–84), demonstrating how people in western societies came to understand themselves as sexual beings • Other notable publications include: – Ernesto Cardenal, *The Gospel in Solentiname*, which provides an account of the way in which the Bible is read and interpreted in the "base communities" of Latin America – Karl Rahner, *Foundations of Christian Faith: An Introduction to the Idea of Christianity*	• The UMC General Conference: – seats women (10) as elected clergy delegates for the first time – establishes the General Commission on the Status and Role of Women (GCSRW) as a permanent standing commission – approves the Ethnic Minority Local Church (EMLC) emphasis as missional priority of the UMC; continues as such until 1988 – approves a Study Committee on Native American Ministries; grants voting privileges to Oklahoma Indian Mission Conference – creates the National Youth Ministry Organization (NYMO) to replace United Methodist Council on Youth Ministry (UMCYM) – expands the MEF to cover training for both diaconal and ordained ministry – creates the category of local pastor for persons who are appointed to serve as pastors in local churches but who are not ordained and authorizes them to administer the sacraments in the charge to which they are appointed – prohibits the use of UMC funds for the support of gay or lesbian organizations – revises the language in the *Discipline* about "same-sex marriage" from "not recommended" to "not recognized" • Harry V. Richardson publishes *Dark Salvation: The Story of Methodism as It Developed Among Blacks in America*	• The thirteenth World Methodist Conference meets in Dublin, Ireland • The Methodist Church Union Act of 1929 is repealed by the British parliament and replaced by the Methodist Church Act of 1976, which provides the legal foundation upon which the present constitutional structure of the MC [UK] rests • The archives of the MC [UK] are transferred from City Road Chapel in London to the John Rylands University Library in Manchester • The "Dublin Report" of the Joint Commission between the Roman Catholic Church and the World Methodist Council is published	1976
• Gian-Carlo Menotti founds the annual Spoleto Festival USA music festival in Charleston, SC, as the companion to the Festival of Two Worlds in Spoleto, Italy (1958) • Toru Takemitsu composes his orchestral poem *A Flock Descends Into the Pentagonal Garden* • Arvo Pärt completes his *Cantus in Memoriam Benjamin Britten* • Notable publications include: – Toni Morrison, *Song of Solomon* – Larry McMurtry, *Terms of Endearment*	• The Sacred Congregation for the Doctrine of Faith rules out the possibility of the admission of women to the Roman Catholic priesthood because women lack a "natural resemblance which must exist between Christ and his ministers" • Pope Paul VI abolishes the automatic excommunication imposed in 1884 on American Catholics who remarry after divorce • Jacqueline Means is the first woman ordained as priest in the ECUSA with official sanction; the priests who were irregularly ordained in 1974 are "regularized"; over 100 women are ordained in the ECUSA by the end of the year • Notable publications include: – John Hick, *The Myth of God Incarnate* – Thomas J. J. Altizer, *The Self-Embodiment of God* – Paul Ricoeur, *The Rule of Metaphor: Multidisciplinary Studies of the Creation of Meaning in Language* – Ronald J. Sider, *Rich Christians in an Age of Hunger*	• A Foundation for Theological Education (AFTE) is established by Edmund Robb and Albert C. Outler; dedicated to "strengthening the classical Christian witness within The United Methodist Church through theological education," it begins awarding John Wesley Fellowships to UM students pursuing doctoral studies in religion • The United Methodist Renewal Services Fellowship (UMRSF) is created as an outgrowth of the interdenominational Conference on Charismatic Renewal; it later takes the "working name" of Aldersgate Renewal Ministries (ARM) • The second National Congress of United Methodist Men meets • Bilateral ecumenical dialogue begins between the UMC and US Lutheran churches	• The MCA unites with the Congregational and Presbyterian churches in Australia to form The Uniting Church in Australia • The Free Wesleyan Church of Tonga (The Methodist Church in Tonga/Siasi Uesiliana Tau'ataina 'o Tonga) becomes autonomous • The sixth Oxford Institute of Methodist Theological Studies meets • Kenya Methodist University opens as a local initiative of the Methodist Church in Kenya • The World Methodist Council gives the first World Methodist Peace Award to Saidie Patterson for her work in Northern Ireland	1977

	A. WORLD HISTORY & POLITICS	B. AMERICAN HISTORY & POLITICS	C. SCIENCE, MEDICINE & TECHNOLOGY	D. DAILY LIFE, POPULAR CULTURE & ENTERTAINMENT
1977 cont.		political activism has a devastating effect on her entertainment career • A 25-hour electrical blackout in New York City results in looting and other disorder—and, nine months later, in a bumper crop of babies		
1978	• President Carter meets with Egyptian president Anwar Sadat and Israeli prime minister Menachem Begin at Camp David; Sadat and Begin sign the Camp David Accords, ending a 30-year conflict between Egypt and Israel; the formal Egypt-Israel Peace Treaty is signed at the White House in March 1979 • Deng Xiaoping emerges as the effective leader of China; he repudiates Mao Zedong's Cultural Revolution and begins the period of "The Four Modernizations" of China • Vietnam angers China by signing a treaty of friendship and cooperation with the Soviet Union and then by invading China's ally Cambodia in an effort to bring down the Khmer Rouge regime of Pol Pot • The mass murder/suicide of 900 followers of Jim Jones (including 270 children) takes place at their Jonestown compound in Guyana, where they had moved in 1977 from the Peoples Temple in San Francisco • King Juan Carlos ratifies Spain's first democratic constitution in half a century	• Two separate storms, both called the "Blizzard of 1978" batter the country, one in the Great Lakes and Ohio Valley, the other in New England, each producing 2-4 feet of snow and winds of over 100 mph in some places; together they claim 87 lives, leave thousands homeless, and cause over $1 billion in damage • The United States Airline Deregulation Act dismantles government control of the airline industry, leading in the short term to increased competition and lower fares, but ultimately to radical changes as established carriers are challenged by new lower-cost "no frills" carriers • The Foreign Intelligence Surveillance Act (FISA) prescribes procedures that law enforcement or intelligence agencies (including the FBI and the NSA) must follow for requesting judicial authorization for the electronic surveillance and/or physical search of persons or groups suspected of espionage or terrorist activities directed against the US or its citizens • In *Regents of the University of California v. Bakke*, the US Supreme Court rules that race may be one of the factors considered in university admissions decisions but that the use of quotas in such affirmative action programs is not permissible • Louis Farrakhan breaks with Wallace D. Muhammad and forms a new organization that assumes the original name, the Nation of Islam, and reasserts the principles of black nationalism and separatism; Wallace Mohammad's organization takes the name the Muslim American Society • Congress formally takes the US off the gold standard internationally; the dollar is now backed by the "full faith and credit" of the US government, rather than US gold reserves • The US minimum wage is increased to $2.65 per hour	• The US cancels development of the neutron bomb, the purpose of which was to kill people without damaging structures • The New River Gorge bridge in West Virginia is completed; at a total length of 4,224 feet with a central span of 1,770 feet, it is the world's longest steel single-arch bridge, and at a height of 876 feet it is also the second tallest bridge in the US • Epson introduces the TX-80, the first successful dot matrix printer for personal computers • Dan Bricklin and Bob Frankston invent VisiCalc, the first electronic spreadsheet • Louise Brown, the first "test tube baby" to result from artificial insemination, is born in Manchester, England	• The Blues Brothers (John Belushi and Dan Aykroyd) make their first appearance on *Saturday Night Live* • Kenny Rogers records his album *The Gambler* featuring the single by the same title • The Eagles release their album *Hotel California* featuring the single by the same title • The musical revue *Ain't Misbehavin'*, featuring music by Thomas "Fats" Waller, opens on Broadway • Larry L. King's musical *The Best Little Whorehouse in Texas* has its off-Broadway opening in New York; it is so successful it moves to Broadway in 1979 • The Big Band and Jazz Hall of Fame is established; the first class of inductees includes Louis Armstrong, Duke Ellington, Benny Goodman, Glenn Miller, and Ella Fitzgerald • The rock group Van Halen's self-titled debut album is widely regarded as a milestone in rock music, marking the group as a force in "heavy metal" rock • The cost of a US first-class postage stamp increases to 15¢ • Films: *The Buddy Holly Story*; *The Deer Hunter*; *Grease*; *Animal House*; *Days of Heaven*; *Coming Home*
1979	• The US and the USSR sign the second Strategic Arms Limitation Treaty (SALT II), which limits each side's arsenals and restricts weapons development and modernization • The Iranian Revolution deposes Shah Reza Pahlavi, who flees to the US; Ayatollah Ruhollah Khomeini takes power; 63 Americans are taken hostage at the American Embassy in Tehran • Vietnamese forces overthrow the Khmer Rouge regime in Cambodia and install a new government; Khmer Rouge forces retreat into Thailand and wage guerrilla war • China invades Vietnam but soon withdraws after its forces sustain shockingly high casualties	• The US establishes formal diplomatic ties with mainland China for the first time since the Communist takeover in 1949 • President Carter signs an executive order creating the Federal Emergency Management Agency (FEMA), which is charged with coordinating all disaster relief efforts in the US at the federal level • The US suspends Iranian oil imports and freezes Iranian assets in the US in retaliation for the taking of US hostages in Tehran • Robert Woodruff (who was then president of Coca-Cola) and his brother George make a gift of approximately $105 million to Emory University; it is at the time the largest single gift made to a single educational institution in the nation's history	• The *Skylab* space station falls out of Earth's orbit and disintegrates on reentry into the atmosphere • Sony produces the Walkman, the first portable personal stereo • Sony and Philips collaborate on the development of the noise-free compact disc (CD), which marks the beginning of the end for the vinyl record • WordStar becomes the first commercially successful word processing program • The nuclear power plant at Three Mile Island, PA, experiences an accident that results in partial meltdown of the reactor core	• Stephen Sondheim's musical *Sweeney Todd* opens on Broadway, combining sophisticated lyrics and music with a darkly comic plot about "the demon barber of Fleet Street" • Andrew Lloyd Webber and Tim Rice's musical *Evita* opens on Broadway, featuring the memorable tune "Don't Cry for Me, Argentina" • The Sugar Hill Gang releases the first commercial rap hit, "Rapper's Delight," bringing rap off the New York streets and into the popular music scene • The veteran rock group Pink Floyd releases their signature album, *The Wall* • The "new wave" band Blondie has its first hit in the US with "Heart of Glass"

E. EDUCATION, LITERATURE & THE FINE ARTS	F. RELIGION, THEOLOGY, PHILOSOPHY & PSYCHOLOGY	G. AMERICAN & UNITED METHODISM	H. BRITISH & WORLD METHODISM	
				1977 cont.
• The new East Building of the National Gallery of Art, designed by I. M. Pei, opens to the public • Krzysztof Penderecki completes his opera *Paradise Lost* (based on the book by John Milton) • Marc Chagall begins work on the 12 magnificent blue stained glass windows of St. Stephen's Church in Mainz, Germany, completing them in 1984 just before his death at the age of 97; he intended them to be a visible sign of friendship between France and Germany and also between Jews and Christians • Notable publications include: – Herman Wouk, *War and Remembrance* – Donald L. Coburn, *The Gin Game*, which wins the Pulitzer Prize for drama	• Pope Paul VI dies; he is succeeded by Pope John Paul I, who lives only three weeks after his election; Cardinal Karol Joseph Wojtyla (Poland) is then elected as pope and takes the name Pope John Paul II; he is the first non-Italian Pope in 450 years, and at age 58, he is the youngest Pope to be elected since Pius IX in 1846 • The Lambeth Conference of the Anglican communion accepts female ordination as an option at the discretion of the local province • Conservatives opposed to the ordination of women by the ECUSA form a number of separatist groups, including the Anglican Catholic Church, the American Episcopal Church, and the Anglican Episcopal Church of North America • Conservatives within the United Church of Christ establish United Church People for Biblical Witness • The complete *New International Version of the Bible* (NIV) is published; a revised edition appears in 1984 • Other notable publications include: – Phyllis Tribble, *God and the Rhetoric of Sexuality* – Richard J. Foster, *Celebration of Discipline: The Path to Spiritual Growth* – Hans Küng, *Does God Exist? An Answer for Today* – Walter Brueggemann, *The Prophetic Imagination* – E. Brooks Holifield, *The Gentlemen Theologians: American Theology in Southern Culture, 1795–1860*	• The tenth Assembly of United Methodist Women meets • The UMC Women's Division adopts "A Charter for Racial Justice Policies in an Interdependent Global Community" [it is later approved by the 1980 General Conference] • Upper Room Ministries begins its sponsorship of the Walk to Emmaus movement • Robert G. Tuttle Jr. publishes *John Wesley: His Life and Theology*	• The Protestant Church of Belgium merges with two Reformed churches to create the United Protestant Church of Belgium • The World Methodist Council gives the World Methodist Peace Award to Anwar Sadat for his leadership in bridging the strained relationship between Egypt and Israel	1978
• Samuel Barber composes his *Third Essay for Orchestra* • Peter Shaffer's play *Amadeus* speculates about the relationship between W. A. Mozart and his "rival" Antonio Salieri • Other notable publications include: – V. S. Naipaul, *A Bend in the River* – William Styron, *Sophie's Choice* – Norman Mailer, *The Executioner's Song* – Frederick Buechner, *The Book of Bebb*	• The ECUSA publishes a new Book of Common Prayer; the first revision of the American prayer book since 1928, it provides more contemporary usage and idioms and is not embraced by some conservative congregations • The Vatican strips Hans Küng of the authority to teach as part of a Roman Catholic faculty • Baptist preacher Jerry Falwell founds The Moral Majority, marking the emergence of the "New Christian Right" in America • Mother Teresa receives the Nobel Peace Prize for her life's work among the poor in India • Notable publications include: – Richard Rorty, *Philosophy and the Mirror of Nature*	• Pan-Methodist dialogue begins among the UMC, AMEC, AMEZC, and CMEC • Notable publications include: – Thomas E. Lenhart and Frederick A. Norwood, *Native American Methodists: A Reading List* – John H. Graham, *Black United Methodists: Retrospect and Prospect*	• Bilateral ecumenical dialogue begins between the World Methodist Council and the Lutheran World Federation (until 1984) • The Chiesa Evangelica Metodista d'Italia (Evangelical Methodist Church of Italy) enters into covenant union with the Chiesa Evangelica Valdese (Waldensian Evangelical Church) • The World Methodist Council does not give a World Methodist Peace Award	1979

	A. WORLD HISTORY & POLITICS	B. AMERICAN HISTORY & POLITICS	C. SCIENCE, MEDICINE & TECHNOLOGY	D. DAILY LIFE, POPULAR CULTURE & ENTERTAINMENT
1979 cont.	• Nicaraguan dictator Anastasio Somoza is overthrown and replaced by the leftist Frente Sandinista de Liberación Nacional (FSLN) or Sandinista party with assistance from the Castro regime in Cuba; supporters of the deposed dictator called "Contras" because of their opposition to the Sandinista regime begin an armed resistance • The US breaks off diplomatic relations with the Republic of China (Taiwan) and establishes diplomatic relations with the People's Republic of China (mainland China); Deng Xiaoping travels to the US and meets President Carter in the White House • The Soviet Union invades Afghanistan; Pakistan supports the Afghan resistance, while India implicitly supports Soviet occupation • Saddam Hussein becomes president of Iraq • After numerous provocations and border disputes, Tanzania invades Uganda and forces Idi Amin from power; he goes into exile in Saudi Arabia • Margaret Thatcher, the "Iron Lady," becomes British prime minister; she is the first (and to date only) woman to hold that office	• George Wallace calls civil rights leader John Lewis, repenting of his segregationist rhetoric and asking forgiveness for his past actions; Lewis and many other black leaders whom Wallace contacts accept his apology • The Department of Education is established at the cabinet level • Congress approves a $1.5 billion federally guaranteed loan to the Chrysler Corporation; it is the largest corporate "bailout" in US history • The US minimum wage is increased to $2.90 per hour		• The California Music Festival at the LA Memorial Coliseum features performances by Aerosmith, The Boomtown Rats, Cheap Trick, Ted Nugent, and Van Halen • The Entertainment and Sports Programming Network (ESPN) is launched, offering "All Sports, All The Time" • The radio news show *Morning Edition* begins on National Public Radio • Films: *Apocalypse Now; Alien; Kramer vs. Kramer; The China Syndrome; All That Jazz; The Muppet Movie*
1980	• At President Carter's request the Senate suspends ratification of the SALT II treaty in view of the Soviet invasion of Afghanistan • After years of armed conflict, the whites-only government of Rhodesia accepts the principle of majority rule; after the subsequent election, Robert Mugabe becomes prime minister and the country is renamed Zimbabwe; it then becomes a member of the British Commonwealth • Indira Gandhi becomes prime minister of India for second time • Ayatollah Bakr Sadr is killed in Iraq on the orders of Saddam Hussein • Iraq launches war against Iran; the conflict lasts until a 1989 cease-fire; more than 1 million people are killed • Workers strike in Poland; the independent unions form a national federation, Solidarity, led by Lech Walesa • "O Canada" becomes the official Canadian national anthem • The death of Marshall Josip Tito in Yugoslavia ushers in an era of political instability that eventually results in the disintegration of the country • The "Mariel Boatlift" occurs when Castro allows a mass exodus of refugees from Cuba's Mariel Harbor; over 125,000 Cubans reach the shores of the US aboard thousands of small boats or rafts, overwhelming the Coast Guard and Immigration officials • The Sendero Luminoso (Shining Path), a radical Maoist political organization begun by Abimael Guzmán (a.k.a. "Chairman Gonzalo") in the late 1960s, begins using violent means to overthrow the Peruvian government • Daniel Ortega becomes president of the Sandinista government of Nicaragua	• The US census reports that the population is 226,545,805: – whites: 188,371,622 (83.1%) – blacks: 26,495,025 (11.7%) – other: 11,679,158 (5.2%) • The US national debt is $930,210,000,000 (rounded to millions) • Attempt by US military forces to free American hostages in Tehran ends in disaster • In *Stone v. Graham*, the US Supreme Court finds posting of the Ten Commandments in public schools to be unconstitutional • The eruption of Mt. St. Helens in Washington State kills 19 and causes billions of dollars in property damage; it ranks fifth on the list of most violent volcanic eruptions in recorded time • The US minimum wage is increased to $3.10 per hour • At President Carter's order, the US boycotts the Summer Olympics in Moscow because of Russia's invasion of Afghanistan • The Alaska National Interest Lands Conservation Act (ANILCA) enlarges the area of the Arctic National Wildlife Range, designates much of the original range as wilderness under the 1964 Wilderness Act, and renames the whole area the Arctic National Wildlife Refuge (ANWR) • Congress responds to the 1977 Love Canal incident by establishing the EPA "Superfund" through a special tax on the chemical and petroleum industries, creating a trust fund to pay for the cleanup of abandoned or uncontrolled hazardous waste sites • John B. Anderson makes a third-party bid for the presidency (Independent Party) with Patrick J. Lahey as his running mate	• IBM hires Microsoft to create an operating system and to develop versions of BASIC, FORTRAN, COBOL, and Pascal for the PC being developed by IBM; Microsoft buys the rights to a simple operating system manufactured by Seattle Computer Products and uses it as a template; IBM allows Microsoft to keep the marketing rights to the operating system, called DOS • Apple Computer releases the Apple III • The World Health Organization (WHO) announces the global eradication of smallpox three years after the last known case	• Harry Warren's *42nd Street: The Song and Dance Fable of Broadway* opens on Broadway [it runs for 3,486 performances before closing in 1989] • Ted Turner launches CNN, the first all-news television network • Former Beatle John Lennon is murdered by a deranged fan in New York • The Police have the no. 1 single of the year in Britain with "Don't Stand So Close To Me"; Blondie has the no. 1 single of the year in the US with "Call Me" • The NCAA begins administering women's athletics programs • The video game Pac-Man is released • The stage version of Victor Hugo's immortal *Les Misérables* opens in Paris; the English version opens in London in 1985 and in New York in 1987 • Films: *The Empire Strikes Back; Ordinary People; Airplane!; Raging Bull* • Summer Olympics: Moscow • Winter Olympics: Lake Placid • The US hockey team stuns the world by defeating the USSR and then Finland to complete the "Miracle on Ice" and win the gold medal at the 1980 Winter Olympics

E. EDUCATION, LITERATURE & THE FINE ARTS	F. RELIGION, THEOLOGY, PHILOSOPHY & PSYCHOLOGY	G. AMERICAN & UNITED METHODISM	H. BRITISH & WORLD METHODISM	
	– Thomas C. Oden, *Agenda for Theology* – Edward Schillebeeckx, *Jesus: An Experiment in Christology* – Jon Sobrino, *Christology at the Crossroads: A Latin American Approach* – Elaine Pagels, *The Gnostic Gospels* – Norman K. Gottwald, *The Tribes of Yahweh: A Sociology of the Religion of Liberated Israel, 1250–1050 BCE* – Philip Hallie, *Lest Innocent Blood Be Shed: The Story of the Village of Le Chambon and How Goodness Happened There*			**1979 cont.**
• Peter Maxwell Davies composes his most popular opera, *The Lighthouse* • Krzysztof Penderecki composes his *Symphony No. 2 (Christmas)* • Philip Glass completes his opera *Satyagraha* about the early life of Mahatma Gandhi and his experiences in South Africa • Tristan Murial composes his spectral symphony *Gondwana* • Molefi Kete Asante's book *Afrocentricity: The Theory of Social Change* coins and popularizes the term *Afrocentrism*, meaning "centered or focused on Africa or African peoples, especially in relation to historical or cultural influence" • Notable publications include: – Stanley Fish, *Is There a Text in This Class?* – Salman Rushdie, *Midnight's Children* – Umberto Eco, *The Name of the Rose* – Madeleine L'Engle, *A Ring of Endless Light*	• Roman Catholic Archbishop Oscar Romero is assassinated in El Salvador while celebrating mass • The General Assembly of the Church of the Nazarene adopts a resolution affirming the service of women in leadership roles in the church • Rick Warren establishes the Saddleback Church in California; it grows to be one of the first megachurches in the US [by 2005 it has over 20,000 members] • Notable publications include: – Robert Bellah, *Varieties of Civil Religion* – Thomas J. J. Altizer, *Total Presence: The Language of Jesus and the Language of Today* – George M. Marsden, *Fundamentalism and American Culture* – Robert E. Cushman, *Faith Seeking Understanding*	• The UMC General Conference: – establishes the General Commission on Christian Unity and Interreligious Concerns (GCCUIC) – creates a churchwide special program called Peace with Justice and assigns it to the General Board of Church and Society – adds language to the *Social Principles* affirming "the sanctity of the marriage covenant that is expressed in love, mutual support, personal commitment, and shared fidelity between a man and a woman" – adopts "A Charter for Racial Justice Policies in an Interdependent Global Community" – grants voting rights to delegates from the Oklahoma Indian Mission Conference • Marjorie Matthews becomes the first woman to be elected bishop of the UMC; she is the first woman in any major Protestant denomination to hold such an office • Frederick P. Brooks Jr. delivers an address at the Good News Convocation suggesting a "loving division" of the UMC into "two independent bodies, each unified by its own theological integrity" • GBHEM and the UMPH establish and assume joint responsibility for the publication of *Quarterly Review*, which replaces *Religion in Life* (1932) • The "Women in New Worlds" conference produces two volumes of important essays: *Women in New Worlds: Historical Perspectives on the Wesleyan Tradition*, vol. 1, ed. Hilah F. Thomas and Rosemary Skinner Keller (1981), vol. 2, ed. Rosemary Skinner Keller, Louise L. Queen, and Hilah F. Thomas (1982)	• The Evangelical Episcopal Church is formed in Burundi with J. Alfred Ndoricimpa as its first bishop; it emerges from the US-based World Gospel Church, an international group with Wesleyan theological roots • The World Methodist Council gives the World Methodist Peace Award to Abel Hendricks for his courageous opposition to apartheid in South Africa	**1980**

	A. WORLD HISTORY & POLITICS	B. AMERICAN HISTORY & POLITICS	C. SCIENCE, MEDICINE & TECHNOLOGY	D. DAILY LIFE, POPULAR CULTURE & ENTERTAINMENT
1980 cont.		• Ronald Reagan is elected as president and George H. W. Bush as vice president (Republican Party) • The term *African American* begins to displace the older term *Afro-American* and to be used in parallel with similar terms, such as *Hispanic American* and *Asian American*, particularly in academic and governmental circles		
1981	• The Iranian hostage crisis ends; the hostages are released but not before President Reagan is formally sworn into office as president • Israeli Air Force planes attack and destroy a nuclear power plant in Iraq • Egyptian president Anwar Sadat is assassinated by Islamic militants inspired by the 1966 execution of Sayyid Qutb, then leader of the Islamic Brotherhood; Hosni Mubarak succeeds Sadat as president • François Mitterrand is elected president of France • Greece joins the European Community (EC) • Britain's Prince Charles, heir to the throne, marries Lady Diana Spencer in St. Paul's Cathedral, London; the royal wedding is watched around the world, and millions fall in love with Princess Diana	• The Professional Air Traffic Controllers Organization (PATCO) goes on strike; President Reagan orders all the striking controllers fired and replaced • Reagan is shot in the chest by John Hinckley, Jr., but survives the attempted assassination • Reagan appoints Sandra Day O'Connor to the US Supreme Court, making her its first woman justice • Reagan authorizes the CIA to pursue "pertinent" intelligence information inside the US • The US Supreme Court rules that the exclusion of women from the military draft is not unconstitutional • Over 9,700 immigrants are naturalized as US citizens in Los Angeles; it is the largest such ceremony ever held • The US minimum wage is increased to $3.35 per hour	• BITNET, a cooperative network based at the City University of New York, begins with the first connection to Yale; it provides academics with electronic mail and listserv servers to distribute information, as well as file transfers • IBM releases the first IBM PC and MS-DOS 1.0 • Hayes releases the Smartmodem 1200 with transfer rates of 1,200 bits per second • The Osborne 1 is the first portable computer; it weighs 24 pounds and comes with a 5" screen, two 5¼-inch floppy disk drives, modem, and battery pack • NASA successfully launches and lands the first reusable spacecraft, the space shuttle *Columbia* • Stephen and Amanda Mays, the first "test-tube twins," are born in Cambridge, England • Bruce Reitz of Stanford University performs the first successful heart-lung transplant; cyclosporine is experimentally used to combat rejection	• Andrew Lloyd Webber's magical musical *Cats*, based on *Old Possum's Book of Practical Cats* by T. S. Eliot, opens in London's West End; it will go on to be produced in ten different languages, in twenty different countries, and in over 250 major cities, including New York, Tokyo, Vienna, Budapest, Buenos Aires, Helsinki, Singapore, and Seoul • *Dreamgirls*, the award-winning Broadway musical by Henry Krieger and Tom Eyen about a black all-girl singing trio from Chicago called "The Dreams" who become music superstars, opens on Broadway • Paul Simon and Art Garfunkel perform together in a "reunion concert" in New York's Central Park attended by an estimated 500,000 fans • The Music Television (MTV) network goes on the air running around-the-clock music videos; the first clip is entitled "Video Killed the Radio Star," featuring a band called the Buggles • The Black Entertainment Television (BET) network begins broadcasting • The Irish rock band U2 makes its first US television appearance on the *Tomorrow* show with Tom Snyder • The cost of a US first-class postage stamp increases to 18¢ in March, then 20¢ in November • Films: *Chariots of Fire; Raiders of the Lost Ark; Body Heat; Gallipoli; The French Lieutenant's Woman*
1982	• The radical Shiite Islamic group Hezbollah ("Party of God") emerges as a major force in Lebanon • Israel invades Lebanon in an attempt to oust Hezbollah and the PLO; after Lebanese President Bashir Gemayel is assassinated, his militia massacres hundreds of Palestinians at the Sabra and Shatila refugee camps; Israeli forces do nothing to stop the attacks; US Marines are deployed to stop the carnage but are withdrawn after their barracks is bombed; the PLO relocates its headquarters to Tunisia • Soviet Premier Leonid Brezhnev dies; he is followed by a series of weak Soviet leaders • Javier Pérez de Cuéllar (Peru) is elected UN Secretary-General	• The Equal Rights Amendment, approved by Congress in 1972, dies when it fails to secure ratification in the necessary 38 states by the constitutional deadline (10 years after passage by Congress); it has never been revived • Congress extends the Voting Rights Act of 1965 for another 25 years despite the opposition of the Reagan administration • Wisconsin becomes the first state to outlaw discrimination on the basis of sexual orientation • A federal court rules against a "balanced" treatment of "creation science" versus "evolution science" in Arkansas public schools, finding that "creation science" is not science	• The FCC authorizes commercial cellular phone service in the US • The Commodore 64 becomes the best-selling computer of all time • Dr. Barney Clark becomes the first recipient of the Jarvik-7, the first permanent artificial heart • AIDS (Acquired Immune Deficiency Syndrome) is first named as such; the Centers for Disease Control announce that sexual contact or infected blood can transmit AIDS; the US begins formal tracking of all known AIDS cases	• Andrew Lloyd Webber's musical *Cats* opens on Broadway [it will become the second-longest running show in Broadway history with 7,485 performances before closing in 2000] • Andrew Lloyd Webber and Tim Rice's musical *Joseph and the Amazing Technicolor Dreamcoat*, first produced in 1972, finally opens on Broadway • David Letterman's *Late Night* show debuts on NBC • Michael Jackson releases his album *Thriller* [it sells more than 25 million copies, becoming the biggest-selling album in history until being surpassed in 1999 by *The Eagles: Their Greatest Hits 1971–1975*]

E. EDUCATION, LITERATURE & THE FINE ARTS	F. RELIGION, THEOLOGY, PHILOSOPHY & PSYCHOLOGY	G. AMERICAN & UNITED METHODISM	H. BRITISH & WORLD METHODISM	
		• Other notable publications include: – John H. Graham, *Black United Methodists: Retrospect and Prospect* – Stanley Ayling, *John Wesley*		**1980 cont.**
• The John D. and Catherine T. MacArthur Foundation establishes the MacArthur Fellowships program to support talented individuals "who have shown extraordinary originality and dedication in their creative pursuits and a marked capacity for self-direction"; popularly called "genius grants," each fellowship is an unrestricted, five-year award with a stipend of $500,000 [by the end of 2005, 707 fellows have been named] • The "New Spirit in Painting" exhibition at the Royal Academy in London showcases Neo-Expressionist works • Steve Reich composes his orchestral and vocal work *Tehillim* (Psalms) • Stanislaw Skrowaczewski composes his *Clarinet Concerto* • Leonard Bernstein composes his *Halil, Nocturne for Solo Flute, Piccolo, Alto Flute, Percussion, Harp and Strings* • Notable publications include: – Toni Morrison, *Tar Baby* – John Kennedy Toole, *A Confederacy of Dunces* – Frederick Buechner, *Godric* – Sylvia Plath, *The Collected Poems*	• Pope John Paul II is shot and critically wounded by Mehmet Ali Ağca, a Turkish gunman; the Pope survives the attack, and two years later visits his assailant in prison and personally pardons him • The "Third Wave of the Spirit" movement is launched at Fuller Theological Seminary by the classroom ministry of John Wimber • The [new] Evangelical Presbyterian Church (EPC) separates from the [northern] UPCUSA to avoid being part of the impending merger [1983] of UPCUSA and PCUS • The Institute on Religion and Democracy (IRD) is established "to reform the social and political witness of the American churches, while also promoting democracy and religious freedom at home and abroad"; it soon becomes the institutional host and primary sponsor for conservative "renewal" movements within mainline US denominations, establishing the "watchdog" programs UM Action, Presbyterian Action, and Episcopal Action • James W. Fowler publishes his pathbreaking work on faith development, *Stages of Faith: The Psychology of Human Development and the Quest for Meaning* • Other notable publications include: – James Gustafson, *Ethics from a Theocentric Perspective* (2 vols., 1981, 1984) – David Tracy, *The Analogical Imagination: Christian Theology and the Culture of Pluralism* – Stanley Hauerwas, *A Community of Character: Toward a Constructive Christian Social Ethic* – Alasdair C. MacIntyre, *After Virtue: A Study in Moral Theory* – Gordon Kaufman, *The Theological Imagination: Constructing the Concept of God*	• The UMC and US Lutherans release a common statement concerning baptism • The third National Congress of United Methodist Men meets • The United Methodist Men Foundation is established to create an endowment agency to fund scouting and other United Methodist Men's ministries • Frank Whaling publishes *John and Charles Wesley: Selected Writings and Hymns*	• The fourteenth World Methodist Conference meets in Honolulu, HI; it establishes the World Methodist Evangelism Institute at Candler School of Theology; George Morris is named as the first director • The "Honolulu Report" of the Joint Commission between the Roman Catholic Church and the World Methodist Council is published • The World Methodist Council gives the World Methodist Peace Award to Lord Donald Soper (UK) for his outspoken opposition to the arms race • Theodore Runyon publishes *Sanctification and Liberation: Liberation Theologies in the Light of the Wesleyan Tradition* [papers from the sixth Oxford Institute of Methodist Theological Studies, 1977]	**1981**
• Toru Takemitsu composes his *Rain Coming* for chamber orchestra and *Rain Spell* for flute, clarinet, harp, piano, and vibraphone • Arvo Pärt completes his *Passion of Our Lord Jesus Christ According to John* • Notable publications include: – Alice Walker, *The Color Purple* – Thomas Keneally, *Schindler's List*	• The Reformed Presbyterian Church Evangelical Synod (1965) joins the Presbyterian Church in America (PCA, 1973) • The landmark document *Baptism, Eucharist, and Ministry* is approved by the World Council of Churches and celebrated with the ecumenical Lima Liturgy • The Islamic Society of North America (ISNA) is established in Plainfield, IN, as an umbrella organization for many active Islamic groups seeking to further the cause of Islam in the US • Notable publications include: – Sallie McFague, *Metaphorical Theology: Models of God in Religious Language*	• The eleventh Assembly of United Methodist Women meets • The UMC General Commission on Archives and History opens its permanent headquarters, the United Methodist Archives and History Center, at Drew University • The Foundation for Evangelism launches its E. Stanley Jones Professor of Evangelism initiative, with the goal of having endowed professorships of evangelism at all UMC seminaries • Upper Room Ministries sponsors the first Academy of Spiritual Formation in Nashville • The CMEC assigns a full-time bishop to supervise its African mission work	• The seventh Oxford Institute of Methodist Theological Studies meets • The World Methodist Council gives the World Methodist Peace Award to Kenneth Mew for his work for reconciliation in Zimbabwe • The World Methodist Evangelism Institute holds its first International Evangelism Seminar at Candler School of Theology; the 10-day seminar focuses on the theme "Wesleyan Evangelism for Our World" and is attended by 66 delegates from 32 countries	**1982**

	A. WORLD HISTORY & POLITICS	B. AMERICAN HISTORY & POLITICS	C. SCIENCE, MEDICINE & TECHNOLOGY	D. DAILY LIFE, POPULAR CULTURE & ENTERTAINMENT
1982 cont.	• Britain fights off an invasion of the Falkland Islands by Argentina • Spain becomes a member of NATO • Helmut Kohl becomes chancellor of Germany • King Khalid of Saudi Arabia dies and is succeeded by his half-brother, Crown Prince Fahd • A new constitution is ratified in Canada by all provinces except Quebec, where a French-Canadian separatist movement has been active since the 1960s	• The Vietnam Veterans Memorial ("The Wall"), designed by Maya Ying Linn, is dedicated; the sculpture of soldiers by Frederick Hart is added in 1984 • Knoxville, TN, hosts the World's Fair; the theme is "Energy Turns the World" and exhibitors include advocates of nuclear energy and of solar power		• Nigerian musician King Sunny Ade releases the album *Juju Music* in the US, igniting an interest in "worldbeat" (or "ethnopop") music • *USA Today* is launched as a national newspaper • Films: *E. T.: The Extra-Terrestrial; Gandhi; 48 Hours; Tootsie; Blade Runner; The Best Little Whorehouse in Texas*
1983	• The US invades the Caribbean island of Grenada after a coup by Marxist faction, partly prompted by concerns over the island's ties with Cuba • The USSR shoots down a South Korean airliner that had crossed into Soviet territory, killing 269 people • Terrorists in Lebanon attack US Embassy, bomb US and French military barracks, over 350 killed; all western forces withdrawn the following year • Yitzhak Shamir becomes prime minister in Israel • Drought in Ethiopia brings famine to millions • Civil war erupts in Sudan between southern, non-Arab, primarily Christian populations against the northern, primarily Muslim, Arab-dominated government • South Africa amends its constitution creating a tricameral parliament with three racially separate chambers: one for whites, one for Asians, and one for "Coloureds"; blacks are still excluded • Former Nazi Klaus Barbie ("The Butcher of Lyon") is extradited from Bolivia to France to stand trial for crimes committed under the Nazi regime during WWII; he is convicted and given a life sentence	• President Reagan proposes the Strategic Defense Initiative (SDI; better known as "Star Wars") to protect the US from incoming ballistic missiles • Reagan describes the Soviet Union as an "evil empire" and defends his policy of providing financial and military aid to the "Contra" rebels fighting against the leftist Sandinista government in Nicaragua • Sally K. Ride becomes the first American woman to be sent into space • The third Monday in January is designated as a national holiday honoring Dr. Martin Luther King, Jr. • Harold Washington is sworn in as the first African American mayor of Chicago	• Name server protocols developed at University of Wisconsin mean that Internet users are no longer required to know the exact path to other systems • NASA's *Pioneer 10* becomes first spacecraft to leave the solar system • The meter is redefined as the distance traveled by light in a vacuum in 1/299,792,458 second • Dian Fossey (US) publishes *Gorillas in the Mist* about her work with mountain gorillas in Rwanda • Lockheed-Martin's F-117A Nighthawk, the world's first "stealth" fighter aircraft, enters operational service with the US Air Force • "Crack" cocaine is developed in the Bahamas and soon appears in the US, quickly becoming a national scourge	• More than 125 million viewers tune in to the last episode of M*A*S*H • Merv Griffin creates the *Wheel of Fortune* game show • The British rocker Sting and his group, the Police, release their biggest hit album, *Synchronicity*, which includes Sting's Grammy-winning song "Every Breath You Take" • The debut album of Metallica, *Kill 'Em All*, is often considered the first purely "thrash metal" album • Merle Haggard's duet album with Willie Nelson, *Pancho & Lefty*, is an enormous critical and popular success and does much to revitalize the careers of both singers • Stevie Ray Vaughan's *Texas Flood* is more popular than any blues album since the late 1960s and helps establish country-blues as an important genre • Billy Joel's breakthrough album *An Innocent Man*, compiled as a tribute to the doo-wop music of the 1960s, contains his big hits "Uptown Girl" and "Tell Her About It" • ZZ Top reaches new heights of popularity with their album *Eliminator* • Films: *The Big Chill; Terms of Endearment; Return of the Jedi; The Right Stuff*
1984	• Indian prime minister Indira Gandhi is assassinated by two of her own Sikh bodyguards, who claimed to be avenging the insult heaped upon the Sikh nation after she ordered an assault upon Sikh militants occupying the "Golden Temple" in Amritsar; her son, Rajiv Gandhi, is sworn in as head of the Congress party and prime minister • Iraq uses mustard gas and nerve gas to repel an attack by 100,000 Iranian soldiers • Britain signs an agreement to return Hong Kong to Chinese rule in 1997 • Shimon Peres becomes prime minister in Israel • Liechtenstein becomes the last country in Europe to give women the right to vote • The USSR boycotts the Summer Olympics in Los Angeles as "payback" to the US for its boycott of the 1980 Moscow games • The US establishes full, formal diplomatic relations with the Vatican	• Sex discrimination in the admission policies of organizations such as the Jaycees is forbidden by the US Supreme Court, opening many previously all-male organizations to women • The nonpartisan National Political Congress of Black Women is founded by Shirley Chisholm to address women's rights issues and encourage women to vote • The CIA directs the mining of harbors in Nicaragua; Congress votes to cut off funding used to pressure the leftist Sandinista government by supporting the "Contras" • A US Circuit Court rules that AT&T has an illegal monopoly on telecommunications and orders "Ma Bell" to be broken up into six separate regional "Baby Bells" • Geraldine Ferraro is the first woman in American history to be chosen as the nominee for vice president on a major party ticket (Democratic Party) • President Reagan and Vice President Bush (Republican Party) are reelected by an overwhelming electoral college majority of 525 to 13, the largest margin since 1972, losing only in the District of Columbia and in Minnesota, the home state of Walter Mondale, the Democratic nominee	• American astronaut Bruce McCandless II takes the first untethered space walk using a backpack with nitrogen jets • The Domain Name System (DNS) is introduced for the Internet • US and French medical researchers announce the discovery of the HIV virus • The Macintosh computer is launched by Apple Computers with one of the most famous TV commercials in history; it is the first personal computer with a successful GUI (graphic user interface) • The CD-ROM player enters the consumer electronics marketplace • The 3.5-inch diskette first appears, and soon displaces the older 5.25-inch "floppy disk" as the industry standard for personal computers • Hewlett-Packard introduces the LaserJet, the first widely available laser printer, and the ThinkJet, the first inkjet printer for personal computers with replaceable ink cartridges	• Stephen Sondheim's *Sunday in the Park with George*, his most eclectic work to date, opens (by his choice) off-Broadway • Andrew Lloyd Webber's rock musical *Starlight Express* opens at the Apollo Victoria Theatre in London where it runs for 7,406 performances [it becomes the third highest selling musical of all time, behind *Cats* and *The Phantom of the Opera*] • The National Minimum Drinking Age Act requires all states to raise their minimum age for legal purchase and public possession of alcohol to 21 • Bill Cosby stars on *The Cosby Show* on NBC, resurrecting the TV sitcom formula • Chrysler begins building a new type of vehicle: the "minivan" • Madonna's album *Like a Virgin*, including the hit single "Material Girl," makes her a major star • Bruce Springsteen rocks the country with his album *Born in the USA* • Tipper Gore spearheads the establishment of the Parents Music Resource Center (PMRC) to educate parents about "alarming trends" in popular music, claiming that rock music encourages or glorifies violence, *(cont.)*

E. EDUCATION, LITERATURE & THE FINE ARTS	F. RELIGION, THEOLOGY, PHILOSOPHY & PSYCHOLOGY	G. AMERICAN & UNITED METHODISM	H. BRITISH & WORLD METHODISM	
	– Marjorie Hewitt Suchocki, *God, Christ, Church: A Practical Guide to Process Theology* – Desmond Tutu, *Crying in the Wilderness* – Cornel West, *Prophesy Deliverance!: An Afro-American Revolutionary Christianity* – Carter Heyward, *The Redemption of God: A Theology of Mutual Relations* – Carol Gilligan, *In a Different Voice: Psychological Theory and Women's Development*	• The UMC Women's Division opens the Alma Mathews House in the Greenwich Village section of New York City as a meeting place and guest house • Naomi P. F. Southard is the first Japanese woman and Mamie Ming Yan Ko and Mochie Lam are the first Chinese women to be received into full connection in the UMC (California-Nevada Conference)		**1982 cont.**
• Leonard Bernstein completes his opera *A Quiet Place* • Notable publications include: – William Kennedy, *Ironweed* – Marion Zimmer Bradley, *The Mists of Avalon*	• The Presbyterian Church, USA [PCUSA] is formed by the merger of the [northern] UPCUSA (1958) and the [southern] PCUS (1865), ending a separation between northern and southern Presbyterians that dates back to 1861 • Elisabeth Schüssler Fiorenza publishes *In Memory of Her: A Feminist Reconstruction of Christian Origins* • Charles Hartshorne publishes *Omnipotence and Other Theological Mistakes*	• Colleen Kyung Seen Chun is the first Korean woman received into full connection in the UMC (California-Pacific Conference) • Earl Kent Brown publishes *Women of Mr. Wesley's Methodism*	• The MC [UK] issues a new hymnal, *Hymns and Songs* • The PM Church in Guatemala becomes autonomous • The MCNZ General Conference makes a formal commitment to bilingualism and biculturalism • No World Methodist Peace Award is given	**1983**
• The Association for the Study of Afro-American Life and History (1915/1972) quietly changes its name to the Association for the Study of African American Life and History • Molefi Kete Asante establishes and chairs the Department of African American Studies at Temple University; it is the first African American Studies PhD program in the US • John Steinbeck's *Of Mice and Men* is removed from Tennessee public schools when the School Board Chair promises to remove all "filthy books" from public school curricula and libraries • Steve Reich composes *The Desert Music* • Krzysztof Penderecki composes his *Polish Requiem*, which is an expansion of his earlier *Lacrimosa* (1980) • Philip Glass completes his opera *Akhnaten*, a powerful vocal and orchestral composition sung in Akkadian, biblical Hebrew, and Ancient Egyptian • Toru Takemitsu composes his *riverrun* for piano and orchestra	• Radical Polish Roman Catholic priest Jerzy Popieluszko, a key figure in the Solidarity movement, is murdered by Polish secret police • The group United Church People for Biblical Witness (1978) broadens its purpose, adopts the "Dubuque Declaration," and changes its name to the Biblical Witness Fellowship to oppose the "theological surrender" of the UCC to the "moral and spiritual confusion of contemporary culture" • The Southern Baptist Convention votes to prohibit the ordination of women and bans their service in pastoral offices • George A. Lindbeck publishes his influential study *The Nature of Doctrine: Religion and Theology in a Postliberal Age* • Other notable publications include: – James H. Cone, *For My People: Black Theology and the Black Church* – Rosemary Radford Ruether, *Sexism and God-Talk: Toward a Feminist Theology* – Geoffrey Wainwright, *Doxology: A Systematic Theology*	• The bicentennial of the establishment of the Methodist Episcopal Church in America is celebrated; the official bicentennial slogan is "Proclaiming Grace and Freedom" • The Good News Movement launches the Mission Society for United Methodists as a "supplemental mission agency" within the UMC • The UMC General Conference: – alters the Social Principles to indicate opposition to imply that "abortion on demand" is morally wrong while continuing to support abortion when medically necessary – adopts a requirement that all UMC clergy practice "celibacy in singleness and fidelity in marriage" – prohibits ordination or appointment of "self-avowed practicing homosexual persons" as ministers – appoints the Committee on Our Theological Task to consider revision or replacement of the 1972 statement on Doctrine and Doctrinal Standards [Part II of the *Discipline*]	• The previously independent Evangelical Episcopal Church (1980) is accepted into full membership in the UMC as the Burundi Annual Conference; Bishop J. Alfred Ndoricimpa is accepted as a bishop of the UMC • The first UMC congregation is established in Bangladesh • The World Methodist Evangelism Institute holds its second International Evangelism Seminar • The World Methodist Council gives the World Methodist Peace Award to Tai-Young Lee for her work for human rights in Korea • The report issued at the conclusion of the bilateral dialogue between World Methodist Council and Lutheran World Federation recommends steps toward closer fellowship between Lutheran and Methodist churches, including pulpit exchanges and mutual Eucharistic hospitality • David Hempton publishes *Methodism and Politics in British Society, 1750–1850*	**1984**

	A. WORLD HISTORY & POLITICS	**B. AMERICAN HISTORY & POLITICS**	**C. SCIENCE, MEDICINE & TECHNOLOGY**	**D. DAILY LIFE, POPULAR CULTURE & ENTERTAINMENT**
1984 cont.	• An explosion at an American-owned chemical plant in Bhopal, India, causes a leak of toxic gas; over 3,000 people are killed immediately and as many as 100,000 are injured, some 15,000 of whom will later die as a result	• After Reagan's reelection, Jesse Jackson begins building what he calls a "Rainbow Coalition" to oppose the policies of the Reagan administration		drug use, suicide, criminal activity, etc. and seeking the censorship and/or rating of music • Prince's "When Doves Cry" is the first single in more than 20 years to hit no. 1 on both the pop and R&B charts • Films: Gregory Nava's riveting film *El Norte (The North)* tells the story of a Guatemalan brother and sister who flee to the US when their father is murdered and their mother lost as a result of the conflict in their native land; other notable films include *Amadeus* (based on Peter Shaffer's 1979 play); *The Killing Fields*; *Ghostbusters*; *The Terminator* • Summer Olympics: Los Angeles • Winter Olympics: Sarajevo
1985	• Mikhail Gorbachev becomes president of the USSR, removes foreign minister Andrei Gromyko, and launches a campaign of *glasnost* ("openness") and *perestroika* ("restructuring"); he unilaterally halts deployment of Soviet missiles in Europe • Castro agrees to take back about 2,500 criminals and mentally ill refugees who entered the US during the 1980 "Mariel Boatlift" • The Italian passenger liner *Achille Lauro* is attacked by Abu Nidal guerillas from the Palestine Liberation Front, resulting in the death of Jewish-American passenger Leon Klinghoffer • Associated Press newsman Terry Anderson is taken hostage by Hezbollah partisans in Lebanon (he is not released until December 1991) • The Greenpeace vessel *Rainbow Warrior* is bombed and sunk in the harbor of Auckland, New Zealand, by agents of the French government to prevent protests of French nuclear tests in the South Pacific • Groups of Abu Nidal guerillas open fire in the airports of Rome and Vienna; 18 people are killed, another 120 are injured	• Retired US Navy officer Arthur Walker is sentenced to life in prison for selling classified military documents to the Soviet Union • US Navy intelligence analyst Jonathan Jay Pollard is arrested for giving classified information on Arab nations to Israel; he is eventually convicted and sentenced to life in prison • In *Wallace v. Jaffree* the US Supreme Court strikes down an Alabama law requiring one minute of silence before school to allow "meditation or voluntary prayer" as an unconstitutional violation of the establishment clause of the 1st Amendment • Philadelphia police drop an explosive device into the headquarters of the radical group MOVE to end a standoff; the resulting fires kill 11 MOVE members and destroy 61 homes, leaving 250 people homeless • The US Supreme Court, in a 5-4 decision, bans public school teachers from teaching in parochial schools while on the public payroll	• The USDA approves the sale of the first genetically altered food products • The Food and Drug Administration approves a blood test for HIV, used since then for screening all blood donations in the US • Scientists discover a hole in the ozone layer over Antarctica • The Asian tiger mosquito is found in the US for the first time in Houston, TX • Steve Wozniak leaves Apple Computers to start a new firm focused on home video; Steve Jobs is forced out of the company by its Board • Microsoft releases the Windows 1.0 operating system • American naturalist Dian Fossey is found murdered in Rwanda near where she had studied and tried to protect the mountain gorillas • British scientists report the discovery of a huge hole in the earth's ozone layer over Antarctica	• The "Live Aid" concert raises money for African famine relief through sales of "We Are the World," recorded by a "who's who" list of popular musicians • Cameron Mackintosh's English version of *Les Misérables* opens in London's Queen's Theatre [it is still playing at the end of 2005] • Pete Rose breaks Ty Cobb's record of 4,191 hits to become professional baseball's all-time hits leader • The wreck of the *Titanic* is located in the North Atlantic at a depth of about 13,000 feet • Media tycoon Rupert Murdock launches the FOX television network • Discovery Communications begins offering educational and real-world cable TV programming on the Discovery Channel (and soon on a family of related channels) • The RIAA agrees to put labels on records containing what the PMRC sees as "explicit content"; the label becomes known as the "Tipper sticker"; many record stores (notably, Wal-Mart) refuse to sell albums with the label, and others limit the sale of those albums to minors • Coca-Cola releases "New Coke" on the 99th anniversary of the original; it is *not* a success; the old formula is quickly reintroduced as "Coca-Cola Classic" • The first *Calvin and Hobbes* comic strip is published • United Parcel Service (UPS) offers its Next-Day Air service to any address in the 48 contiguous states, Hawaii, and Puerto Rico • The cost of a US first-class postage stamp increases to 22¢ • Films: Stephen Spielberg brings Alice Walker's *The Color Purple* to the screen and launches the career of Oprah Winfrey; *Sweet Dreams* starring Jessica Lange memorializes the life and career of country music legend Patsy Cline; other films include *Prizzi's Honor*; *Back to the Future*; *Brazil*; *Out of Africa*; *Kiss of the Spider Woman*
1986	• Spain and Portugal join the European Community (EC) • Corazon Aquino becomes Philippine president after Ferdinand Marcos flees due to unrest	• The Martin Luther King, Jr., national holiday is observed for the first time on the third Monday of January • The Iran-Contra scandal breaks; the White House is forced to reveal secret deals to sell weapons to Iran and use the proceeds *(cont.)*	• The space shuttle *Challenger* explodes shortly after takeoff, killing all seven astronauts on board • An explosion at the nuclear power plant at Chernobyl in the USSR spreads radiation across Europe, causing the death of *(cont.)*	• *The Oprah Winfrey Show* hits national television • The Rock-and-Roll Hall of Fame, designed by acclaimed architect I. M. Pei, opens in Cleveland, OH; the first class of performers to be inducted includes Chuck Berry, James Brown, Ray Charles, Sam Cooke, Fats *(cont.)*

E. EDUCATION, LITERATURE & THE FINE ARTS	F. RELIGION, THEOLOGY, PHILOSOPHY & PSYCHOLOGY	G. AMERICAN & UNITED METHODISM	H. BRITISH & WORLD METHODISM	
• Notable publications include: – August Wilson, *Ma Rainey's Black Bottom* (his first major drama) – Gore Vidal, *Lincoln: A Novel*		• Reacting to the legislation on homosexuality adopted by General Conference, activists from the Affirmation caucus establish the Reconciling Congregations Program • Judith Craig and Leontine Kelly become the second and third women to be elected bishops of the UMC; Kelly is the first African American woman bishop • Elias Galvan is the first Hispanic American and Roy Sano the first Asian American to be elected bishop • Notable publications include: – Richard P. Heitzenrater, *The Elusive Mr. Wesley* (2 vols.; 2nd edition in 2 vols., 2003) – Richard E. Brantley, *Locke, Wesley, and the Method of English Romanticism*		**1984 cont.**
• Celebrations are held around the world of the 300th anniversaries of the births of Handel and Bach • Toru Takemitsu composes the memorable score for Akira Kurosawa's film *Ran* • György Ligeti completes his *Études* for piano • Witold Lutosławski composes his *Symphony No. 3* • John Rutter composes his *Requiem* • Notable publications include: – John Irving, *The Cider House Rules* – Garrison Keillor, *Lake Wobegon Days* – Margaret Atwood, *The Handmaid's Tale* – Larry McMurtry, *Lonesome Dove* – Orson Scott Card, *Ender's Game*	• Emilio Castro (Evangelical Methodist Church of Uruguay) is named General Secretary of the World Council of Churches • The first regular quadrennial International Conference of Reformed Churches (ICRC) meets in Scotland; subsequent meetings are held in Canada (1989), the Netherlands (1993), Korea (1997), the US (2001), and South Africa (2005) • Hans Urs von Balthasar begins publication of *The Glory of the Lord: A Theological Aesthetics* (7 vols., 1985–90) • Other notable publications include: – Robert Bellah, et al., *Habits of the Heart: Individualism and Commitment in American Life* – Rosemary Radford Ruether, *Woman Church: Theology and Practice* – E. P. Sanders, *Jesus and Judaism* – Brevard S. Childs, *The New Testament as Canon* – Jaroslav Pelikan, *Jesus Through the Centuries: His Place in the History of Culture* – F. E. Peters, *The Children of Abraham: Judaism/Christianity/Islam*	• The UMC, AMEC, AMEZC, and CMEC form the Commission on Pan-Methodist Cooperation and begin to discuss cooperation and possible union • The fourth National Congress of United Methodist Men meets • The UMC Hispanic Women's Consultation holds its first meeting • The UMC and US Lutherans begin a second round of bilateral ecumenical dialogues • Notable publications include: – Theodore Runyon, ed., *Wesleyan Theology Today: A Bicentennial Theological Consultation* – Russell E. Richey and Kenneth E. Rowe, eds., *Rethinking Methodist History: A Bicentennial Historical Consultation* – Richard P. Heitzenrater, *Diary of an Oxford Methodist: Benjamin Ingham, 1733–1734*	• The Protestant Methodist Church of Côte d'Ivoire (Ivory Coast) becomes autonomous and severs its ties to the British Methodist Conference • A group of churches leave the Methodist Church of Korea and form the Reformed Methodist Church of Korea; in 1990 it becomes a provisional conference and later a full annual conference of the Free Methodist Church • The World Methodist Council gives the World Methodist Peace Award to former US President Jimmy Carter for his leadership in the causes of peace and global human rights • Bilateral ecumenical dialogue begins between the World Methodist Council and the World Alliance of Reformed Churches (until 1987) • M. Douglas Meeks publishes *The Future of the Methodist Theological Traditions* [papers from the seventh Oxford Institute of Methodist Theological Studies, 1982]	**1985**
• *The Academic American Encyclopedia* is available on CD-ROM; it is the first reference work published in this medium • Paul Schoenfield composes his *Café Music for Piano Trio*	• Desmond Tutu is elected Anglican Archbishop of Cape Town, South Africa • Pope John Paul II visits a Jewish synagogue in Rome; it is the first such visit by a pope in recorded history	• The twelfth Assembly of United Methodist Women meets, celebrating the centennial era of women's organizations in the UMC and ancestor denominations	• The fifteenth World Methodist Conference meets in Nairobi, Kenya • The World Methodist Council gives the World Methodist Peace Award to Sir Alan and Lady Winifred Walker (Australia) for their lifelong work in evangelism and as emissaries of peace	**1986**

	A. WORLD HISTORY & POLITICS	B. AMERICAN HISTORY & POLITICS	C. SCIENCE, MEDICINE & TECHNOLOGY	D. DAILY LIFE, POPULAR CULTURE & ENTERTAINMENT
1986 cont.	• Human rights activist Anatoly Shcharansky is released by the Soviet Union and leaves the country • Swedish prime minister Olof Palme is assassinated; the case is never satisfactorily resolved • A fire devastates Hampton Court Palace in England • La Belle discotheque in West Berlin, a known hangout for US soldiers, is bombed, killing 3 and injuring 230 people; Libya is held responsible • In retaliation, US warplanes bomb targets in Libya , including Tripoli, killing at least 100 people and injuring many more • The dictatorship of Jean-Claude "Baby Doc" Duvalier in Haiti ends when he flees to France after months of protest, but years of instability and unrest follow • The World Exposition in Vancouver, British Columbia, Canada, opens	to support the opposition of the Contras to the Sandinista regime in Nicaragua • In *Meritor Savings Bank v. Vinson*, the US Supreme Court finds that sexual harassment is a form of illegal job discrimination • Steve Jobs founds NeXT to create computers and software for college students and also spends $10 million to purchase LucasFilms' animation division, which he renames Pixar • The US national debt climbs past the $2 trillion mark for the first time	8,000 people, damaging the health of untold numbers, and rendering vast areas of Ukraine and Belarus uninhabitable; it is the world's worst nuclear accident • The Soviet Union launches the *Mir* space station • Halley's Comet reappears on schedule, 76 years after its last appearance in 1910 [it will return again in 2062] • The first PC virus, named "Brain," starts to spread	Domino, the Everly Brothers, Buddy Holly, Jerry Lee Lewis, Little Richard, and Elvis Presley; the first nonperformers honored are producer Sam Phillips and disc jockey Alan Freed • Metallica releases their heavy metal masterpiece album, *Master of Puppets* • The black rap group Run-DMC and the white hard-rock band Aerosmith collaborate on the single "Walk This Way," which is the first rap record to be widely popular across the nation • Pete Rose retires from professional baseball with records for most games played (3,562), most at-bats (14,053), most hits (4,286), and most singles (3,315) • McDonald's and Burger King stop frying their food in beef tallow and start releasing nutritional and ingredients information • HBO becomes the first satellite network to encrypt its signal to prevent unauthorized viewing • Country music superstar Dolly Parton opens her Dollywood theme park in Pigeon Forge, TN • Films: *'Round Midnight*, featuring music by Dexter Gordon and a supporting cast of jazz legends such as Herbie Hancock, Freddie Hubbard, and Wayne Shorter, provides an authentic portrait of the Paris jazz scene of the 1950s; other notable films include *Platoon; The Mission; My Beautiful Launderette; Nine and 1/2 Weeks; Top Gun; A Room With A View*
1987	• President Reagan challenges Soviet president Gorbachev to "tear down this wall" and open Eastern Europe to political and economic reform • Reagan and Gorbachev sign the Intermediate-Range Nuclear Forces (INF) Treaty , the first arms-control agreement to reduce the superpowers' nuclear weapons • Yitzhak Shamir becomes prime minister in Israel for the second time • Severe flooding in Bangladesh leaves millions homeless • The Islamic fundamentalist movement Harakat Al-Muqawama Al-Islamia (known as Hamas, meaning "zeal" or "fervor" in Arabic), originally an offshoot of the Egyptian Islamic Brotherhood, is established with the stated goal of destroying the state of Israel and creating a single, Islamic state in historic Palestine; it soon becomes a major force in launching the Palestinian Intifada ("uprising") against Israel's occupation of the West Bank and Gaza Strip • The total human population of the world reaches an estimated five billion (5,000,000,000) people	• "Black Monday" (October 19) on Wall Street: the stock market loses nearly a quarter of its value in the largest one-day drop in history and initiates a world stock market crash; this marks the beginning of the end of the "dot-com bubble" • The US Supreme Court strikes down Louisiana's "Creationism Act" as unconstitutional; the statute prohibited the teaching of evolution in public schools unless it was accompanied by instruction in "creation science"; the court finds that laws requiring the teaching that a supernatural being created humans improperly endorses religion • The Tower Commission, established to investigate the Iran-Contra Affair, rebukes President Reagan for not controlling his national security staff but finds no firm evidence that he had known of the diversion of funds to the Contras • The FCC rescinds the "fairness doctrine," which had required radio and television stations to "fairly" present controversial issues	• Prozac is first prescribed in the US, revolutionizing the treatment of depression • The FDA approves the use of the drug AZT for the treatment of AIDS • Richard Branson and Per Lindstrand complete the first hot-air balloon flight across the Atlantic Ocean, from Maine to Ireland (2,790 miles) • The Sunshine Skyway, which stretches almost 6 miles across Tampa Bay between Bradenton and St. Petersburg, FL, is the world's longest cable-stayed concrete bridge; the central span is 1200 feet wide and 190 feet high • Hewlett-Packard unveils the PaintJet, the first color printer for personal computer use • Microsoft releases the Windows 2.0 operating system, designed to resemble IBM's OS/2 Presentation Manager	• Cameron Mackintosh's English version of *Les Misérables* opens on Broadway [it runs for 6,680 shows before closing in 2003] • Paul Simon launches a tour in support of his 1986 album *Graceland*, bringing South African music and musicians such as Ladysmith Black Mambazo to the world stage • The rap group Public Enemy becomes widely known for its controversial lyrics and creative backing tracks • The Irish rock band U2 releases its best album to date, *The Joshua Tree* • The radio news show *Weekend Edition* begins on National Public Radio • Aretha Franklin is the first woman inducted into the Rock-and-Roll Hall of Fame • Carol King is inducted into the Songwriters Hall of Fame • Bryan Adams's "Heat of the Night" becomes the first single to be commercially released in the US on cassette; cassette singles become known as "cassingles" • Garrison Keillor terminates his radio show *A Prairie Home Companion* after a 13-year run • "Hard rock" band Guns N' Roses releases its debut album, *Appetite for Destruction* • Tipper Gore publishes her book *Raising PG Kids in an X-Rated Society* • Films: *Fatal Attraction; Hope and Glory; Full Metal Jacket; Dirty Dancing; The Last Emperor*

E. EDUCATION, LITERATURE & THE FINE ARTS	F. RELIGION, THEOLOGY, PHILOSOPHY & PSYCHOLOGY	G. AMERICAN & UNITED METHODISM	H. BRITISH & WORLD METHODISM	
• Rudolf Brucci completes his opera *Gilgamesh*, based on the ancient Sumerian epic • Elliott Carter composes his *String Quartet No. 4* • Harrison Birtwistle's acclaimed opera *The Mask of Orpheus* premieres in London • Notable publications include: – John le Carré, *A Perfect Spy* – Pat Conroy, *The Prince of Tides* – Tom Clancy, *Red Storm Rising* – Orson Scott Card, *Speaker for the Dead*	• Holly Haile Smith is the first Native American woman to be ordained in the PCUSA • Václav Havel publishes *Living in Truth*	• The bishops of the UMC issue their pastoral letter "In Defense of Creation" opposing any use of nuclear weapons • The UMC General Board of Global Ministries establishes Korean American missions in all five UMC jurisdictions • Upper Room Ministries begins publishing *Weavings*, a bimonthly journal that seeks to promote informed, committed spiritual growth • Notable publications include: – James V. Heidinger, ed., *Basic United Methodist Beliefs: An Evangelical View* – John R. Tyson, *Charles Wesley on Sanctification: A Biographical and Theological Study*		**1986 cont.**
• John Adams composes his opera *Nixon in China* about the 1972 visit of Richard Nixon to China where he met with Mao Zedong and other Chinese officials • Joan Tower composes her *Fanfare for the Uncommon Woman* (a response to Aaron Copland's 1942 *Fanfare for the Common Man*) • John Harbison composes his cantata *Flight into Egypt* • August Wilson's play *Fences* (completed in 1985) wins both the Pulitzer Prize and the Tony Award • White American historian Martin Bernal sets out the central claims of Afrocentrism in his controversial work *Black Athena: The Afroasiatic Roots of Classical Civilization* (2 vols., 1987–91) • Guatemalan human rights activist Rigoberta Menchú Tum publishes her autobiography, *I, Rigoberta Menchú*, which recounts the oppression of indigenous people in Guatemala [she receives the Nobel Peace Prize for her work in 1992] • Other notable publications include: – Molefi Kete Asante, *The Afrocentric Idea* – Toni Morrison, *Beloved* – Tom Wolfe, *The Bonfire of the Vanities* – Tom Clancy, *Patriot Games* – Robert Ludlum, *The Bourne Supremacy*	• The Evangelical Lutheran Church in America (ELCA) is formed by merger of the Association of Evangelical Lutheran Churches (AELC, 1976), The American Lutheran Church (ALC, 1960), and the Lutheran Church in America (LCA, 1962) • Christ Seminary Seminex merges with the Lutheran School of Theology at Chicago • The Alliance of Baptist Churches is established by congregations and individuals who have separated from the Southern Baptist Convention in the wake of the conservative-moderate conflict of the 1980s • Sexual and financial scandals involving televangelist superstar Jim Bakker lead to his resignation as head of the "Praise the Lord" (PTL) ministry • Other notable publications include: – John Hick and Paul Knitter, eds., *The Myth of Christian Uniqueness* – Sallie McFague, *Models of God: Theology for an Ecological, Nuclear Age*	• The UMW launches the Campaign for Children • A national conference of UM college students meets; it is called the "Jubilee Conference" to commemorate the 50th anniversary of the Methodist Student Movement and gives rise to an annual Student Forum • The UMC and US Lutherans release a common statement concerning episcopacy • The Men's Section of the UMC General Board of Discipleship is raised to full Division status, placing the UMM on par with the UMW • The UMPH launches *Disciple: Becoming Disciples Through Bible Study*, which has an enormous impact across the church • Rose Mary Denman of New Hampshire loses clergy credentials as a result of a church trial after declaring that she is a lesbian • The CMEC holds the first national CME Convocation; it is a general connectional meeting for the entire denomination • Versie P. Easter is the first woman appointed to serve as presiding elder in the CMEC • A group of 48 conservative UM clergy, led by William H. Hinson, draft and sign "The Houston Declaration" affirming the primacy of scripture, the use of traditional trinitarian language ("Father, Son, and Holy Spirit") for God, and the UMC ban against the ordination of persons practicing homosexuality • The Bicentennial Edition of Wesley's *Sermons* is completed (4 vols., 1984–87) • Other notable publications include Betty M. Jarboe, *John and Charles Wesley: A Bibliography*	• The Methodist Church in Kenya becomes autonomous • The World Methodist Evangelism Institute holds its third International Evangelism Seminar • The eighth Oxford Institute of Methodist Theological Studies meets • The report issued at the conclusion of bilateral dialogue between the World Methodist Council and the World Alliance of Reformed Churches concludes that classical doctrinal issues ought not to be seen as obstacles to unity between Methodists and Reformed and urges national and local conversation and cooperation • The World Methodist Council gives the World Methodist Peace Award to Woodrow Seals (US) and Bert Bissell (UK) for their devotion to peace and reconciliation • Notable publications include: – Michel Weyer, *Die Bedeutung von Wesleys Lehrpredigten fur die Methodisten* – Martin Schmidt, *John Wesley: Leben und Werk* (3 vols.,1987–88)	**1987**

	A. WORLD HISTORY & POLITICS	B. AMERICAN HISTORY & POLITICS	C. SCIENCE, MEDICINE & TECHNOLOGY	D. DAILY LIFE, POPULAR CULTURE & ENTERTAINMENT
1988	• The Soviet Union begins to withdraw from Afghanistan • Iraqi forces attack the Kurdish town of Halabja with chemical weapons, killing more than 5,000 • Iran and Iraq sign a cease-fire agreement • Jordan's King Hussein separates the West Bank from Jordan and cedes control of the unoccupied West Bank to the PLO • The PLO formally renounces terrorism and accepts Israel's right to exist within pre-1967 borders but continues to protest Israel's occupation of the West Bank and the Gaza Strip • Prime ministers Rajiv Gandhi (India) and Benazir Bhutto (Pakistan) conclude a pact not to attack each other's nuclear facilities • Pan Am Flight 103 explodes over Lockerbie, Scotland; Libyan agents are implicated in the explosion • Nationalist demonstrations and strikes take place in Albania, Poland, the Baltics, and the Caucasus • A major earthquake in Armenia kills 80,000 people and leaves 500,000 homeless • The National People's Congress in China moves to reform the country's economic system by introducing private enterprise • A repressive military junta seizes power in Burma and renames the country Myanmar	• Congress overrides President Reagan's veto to pass the Civil Rights Restoration Act, which extends federal antidiscrimination laws to cover private institutions that receive federal funds • Congress approves legislation banning discrimination against federal workers infected with HIV • George H. W. Bush is elected as president and J. Danforth Quayle as vice president (Republican Party) • Jesse Jackson holds a news conference during which he urges all Americans to use the term *African American* to refer to black Americans; use of the term *African American*, which had been advocated by Malcolm X and others as early as the 1960s, becomes increasingly common after this time	• The Seikan Tunnel is completed, linking the main Japanese island of Honshu with the northern island of Hokkaido; it is the longest railroad tunnel in the world (33.4 miles in length, 14.3 miles of which lie up to 800 feet under the Tsugaru Strait) • World Health Organization begins World AIDS Day to focus attention on fighting the disease • The Cellular Technology Industry Association (CTIA) is formed to establish standards for cellular phone manufacturers and service providers • In testimony before Congress, NASA scientist James Hansen sounds a warning about the dangers of global warming and the "greenhouse effect" • Use of the "morning-after" birth control drug RU486 is approved by the governments of France and China	• Andrew Lloyd Webber's *The Phantom of the Opera* opens on Broadway; it will go on to become the longest-running show in Broadway history [7,480 shows by the end of 2005 and still counting] • Smoking is banned on all US airline flights of 2 hours or less • The Rush Limbaugh Show is nationally syndicated on AM "talk radio" stations [by the end of 2005 its audience is estimated at between 14 and 20 million listeners per week, making it the largest radio talk show audience in the US] • Rap music performers Dr. Dre, Easy E, and Ice Cube form the group Niggaz with Attitude (N.W.A) and play a leading role in the development of the rap style known as "gangsta rap" for its violence and anger • Michael Jackson purchases a ranch in Santa Ynez, CA, that he calls "Neverland" • The cost of a US first-class postage stamp increases to 25¢ • Films: *Gorillas in the Mist* (based on the life and work of Dian Fossey); *Die Hard*; *Rain Man*; *Bull Durham*; *The Unbearable Lightness of Being*; *Babette's Feast* • Summer Olympics: Seoul • Winter Olympics: Calgary
1989	• A million demonstrators gather in Tiananmen Square in Beijing, demanding more democratic freedom; the demonstrations provoke the Chinese government, resulting in a military crackdown that leaves thousands dead or badly wounded • The USSR withdraws from Afghanistan; Afghan warlords then turn on each other, and the country sinks into chaos • The USSR holds the first free elections since 1917, resulting in defeat and great embarrassment for the Communist Party, and the subsequent dissolution of the Soviet Union • The East German government resigns, leading to the fall of the Berlin Wall and the reunification of East and West Germany in 1990 • The communist governments of Bulgaria, Czechoslovakia, and Romania disintegrate; Romanian dictator Nicolae Ceauşescu is executed • The regime of Augusto Pinochet in Chile ends; Patricio Aylwin is elected president • Emperor Hirohito of Japan dies; his first son, Akihito, becomes emperor	• President Bush signs law to make a payment of $20,000 to each survivor of the Japanese internment camps of the WWII period • The oil supertanker *Exxon Valdez* runs aground in Alaska's Prince William Sound, creating the largest crude oil spill (more than 11 million gallons) in US history • Hurricane Hugo claims 86 lives (57 in the US) and causes property damage estimated at over $9.7 billion • An opinion poll conducted by ABC News and *The Washington Post* finds that 66% of the black Americans surveyed prefer the term *black*, 22% prefer the term *African American*, 10% like both terms equally, and 2% have no opinion • Colin Powell becomes the first African American to serve as chairman of the Joint Chiefs of Staff	• NASA's *Voyager II* space probe, launched in 1977, has a "close encounter" with Neptune, sending back valuable information about the planet and its moons • Jaron Lanier coins the term *virtual reality* (VR) and establishes VPL Research, the first company to make and sell VR equipment • Intel releases the 486DX microprocessor, with more than 1 million transistors and multitasking capabilities • Tim Berners-Lee, working at the Conseil Européen pour la Recherche Nucléaire (CERN) in Switzerland, proposes a distributed information system, based on "hypertext," as a way of linking related pieces of information stored on computers; this is generally considered the beginning of the World Wide Web • The Toronto SkyDome is completed; it is the first domed stadium to have a completely retractable roof	• Nintendo introduces the Game Boy handheld computer game device • The first commercial direct broadcast satellite (DBS) service, Sky Television, is launched in Britain • *The Simpsons* debuts on the Fox network and becomes an instant hit • Black female rapper Queen Latifah releases her first album, *All Hail the Queen*, including the single "Ladies First," celebrating the contributions of black women to the struggle for black liberation in America and around the world; it becomes a rap classic • Kareem Abdul-Jabbar (born Lew Alcindor) retires after 20 seasons of professional basketball as the all-time leader in over 20 categories, including games played (1,560) and points scored (38,387; avg. 24.6 per game) • After a two-year hiatus, Garrison Keillor is back on the air with a new radio show, *The American Radio Company* • The "hard rock" band Mötley Crüe reaches its peak popularity with the release of its album *Dr. Feelgood*

E. EDUCATION, LITERATURE & THE FINE ARTS	F. RELIGION, THEOLOGY, PHILOSOPHY & PSYCHOLOGY	G. AMERICAN & UNITED METHODISM	H. BRITISH & WORLD METHODISM	
• The unfinished *Symphony No. 10* by Beethoven is premiered by London's Royal Philharmonic Society, over 100 years after its commission by them • Philip Glass composes *Fall of the House of Usher* • Takashi Yoshimatsu composes his *Concerto for Bassoon "Unicorn Circuit"* • António Chagas Rosa composes his *Piano Sonata*, his first notable work • John Tavener completes *The Akathist of Thanksgiving*, written in celebration of the millennium of the Russian Orthodox Church • Notable publications include: – Alfred Uhry, *Driving Miss Daisy* – Stephen Hawking, *A Brief History of Time* – Margaret Atwood, *Cat's Eye* – Umberto Eco, *Foucault's Pendulum* – Gabriel García Márquez, *Love in the Time of Cholera* – Doris Lessing, *The Fifth Child*	• The Jewish Publication Society publishes *Tanakh: The Holy Scriptures, The New JPS Translation According to the Traditional Hebrew Text* (NJPS) • The Lambeth Conference of the Anglican communion decides to allow the consecration of women as bishops at the discretion of the local province • The ECUSA elects Barbara Harris as Suffragan Bishop of Massachusetts; she is the first woman to be elected and consecrated as a bishop in the Anglican communion	• The UMC General Conference: – adopts "The Sacred Circle of Life: A Native American Vision" as a comprehensive plan for Native American ministries – adopts a replacement for the 1972 statement on Doctrine and Doctrinal Standards [Part II of the *Discipline*] – approves the publication of a new *Hymnal* for the UMC – sets a 12-year limit on executive positions in all general church agencies, effective January 1, 2001 – creates a Committee to Study Homosexuality, which is charged to present a report to the subsequent General Conference – approves the establishment of Africa University in Zimbabwe • The UMC Women's Division in cooperation with the Children's Defense Fund launches the Campaign for Children • The office of deaconess in the Methodist tradition celebrates its 100th anniversary • Lois V. Glory-Neal is the first Native American woman to be received into full connection in the UMC (Oklahoma Indian Mission Conference) • Scarritt Graduate School is closed due to low enrollment; the UMC Woman's Division purchases the property and renovates the buildings to create the Scarritt-Bennett Center, an independent conference, retreat, and educational institution • The UMPH establishes the Kingswood Books program as a special imprint of Abingdon Press for scholarly works in all areas of Wesleyan and Methodist studies • Notable publications include S T Kimbrough, Jr., and Oliver Beckerlegge, eds., *The Unpublished Poetry of Charles Wesley*, vol. 1 (vol. 2, 1990; vol. 3, 1992)	• Methodists around the world celebrate the 250th anniversary of John Wesley's Aldersgate experience; Queen Elizabeth II attends the commemorative service at St. Paul's Cathedral in London • The MC [UK] begins annual publication of volume 2 of *Constitutional Practice and Discipline* • The Methodist diaconal order succeeds the office of deaconess in the MC [UK]; it is open to both women and men, but deacons are still regarded as "lay" ministers rather than as ordained ministers • The World Methodist Council gives the World Methodist Peace Award to Gordon Wilson for his work for peace and reconciliation in Northern Ireland	**1988**
• The controversial glass Pyramide du Louvre, designed by architect I. M. Pei to be the new main entrance of the Louvre Museum and occupying the central courtyard, opens to the public • Leonard Bernstein composes his *Missa Brevis* for mixed chorus and countertenor solo with percussion • John Tavener's *The Protecting Veil* is premiered by cellist Steven Isserlis and the London Symphony Orchestra at the 1989 Proms • Salman Rushdie's novel *Satanic Verses* is published and sparks immediate controversy; Iran's Ayatollah Khomeini pronounces a death sentence (*fatwa*) on Rushdie, who goes into hiding • Other notable publications include: – Wendy Wasserstein, *The Heidi Chronicles* – Anne Tyler, *Breathing Lessons* – Kazuo Ishiguro, *The Remains of the Day* – Amy Tan, *The Joy Luck Club* – Tom Clancy, *The Cardinal of the Kremlin* – Ken Follett, *The Pillars of the Earth*	• The New Revised Standard Version of the Bible (NRSV) is published • Evangelist and Christian political activist Pat Robertson establishes the Christian Coalition • A group of conservative Presbyterian evangelicals establish Presbyterians for Renewal • Notable publications include: – John Hick, *An Interpretation of Religion: Human Responses to the Transcendent* – Rebecca S. Chopp, *The Power to Speak: Feminism, Language, God* – Jacqueline Grant, *White Women's Christ and Black Women's Jesus* – Cain Hope Felder, *Troubling Biblical Waters: Race, Class and Family* – Stanley Hauerwas and William H. Willimon, *Resident Aliens: Life in the Christian Colony* – J. Philip Wogaman, *Christian Moral Judgment*	• Chautauqua Institution is designated a National Historic Landmark • The UMC publishes *The United Methodist Hymnal*, including a new Psalter and revised liturgies for baptism, the Lord's Supper, weddings, and funerals • The fifth International Congress of United Methodist Men meets • The Good News Movement launches the Renew Network for Christian Women as a "support network for evangelical, orthodox women" and a "voice for renewal and accountability" on the part of the UMC Woman's Division • Notable publications include: – Thomas A. Langford, ed., *Doctrine and Theology in The United Methodist Church* – Richard P. Heitzenrater, *Mirror and Memory: Reflections on Early Methodism* – Robert E. Cushman, *John Wesley's Experimental Divinity: Studies in Methodist Doctrinal Standards* – W. Stephen Gunter, *The Limits of 'Love Divine': John Wesley's Response to Antinomianism and Enthusiasm* – Kenneth J. Collins, *Wesley on Salvation: A Study in the Standard Sermons* – Gregory S. Clapper, *John Wesley on Religious Affections*	• The UMC opens the Centre Méthodiste de Formation Théologique in Lausanne, Switzerland, for the education of French-speaking Methodist students in France and Switzerland • No World Methodist Peace Award is given by the World Methodist Council • Notable publications include Henry D. Rack, *Reasonable Enthusiast: John Wesley and the Rise of Methodism*	**1989**

	A. WORLD HISTORY & POLITICS	B. AMERICAN HISTORY & POLITICS	C. SCIENCE, MEDICINE & TECHNOLOGY	D. DAILY LIFE, POPULAR CULTURE & ENTERTAINMENT
1989 cont.	• Vietnam withdraws its military forces from Cambodia; leading to the election of a new Cambodian government in 1993 • US military forces invade Panama and capture Manuel Noriega, who previously had been indicted in the US on drug trafficking charges • Denmark becomes the first country in the world to legalize same-sex civil unions			• Garth Brooks rockets to the top of the country music world with his self-titled debut album, including the smash singles "If Tomorrow Never Comes" and "The Dance" • The Indigo Girls release their breakout self-titled album, including the single "Closer to Fine" • Films: Spike Lee's *Do the Right Thing* features the rap hit "Fight the Power" by Public Enemy; other films include *Driving Miss Daisy*; *Field of Dreams*; *When Harry Met Sally*; *Glory*; *Cinema Paradiso*
1990	• Boris Yeltsin is elected president of the Russian Federation; his government effectively replaces the central government of the Soviet Union as the primary power in Russia • Helmut Kohl is elected chancellor of the reunified Germany • Lech Walesa is elected president of Poland • Lithuania declares its independence from the Soviet Union, soon followed by Estonia and Latvia • Iraq invades and occupies most of Kuwait; the US imposes sanctions • F. W. De Klerk, president of South Africa, lifts restrictions against the African National Congress (ANC) and 33 other antiapartheid organizations and releases Nelson Mandela from prison after 27 years • John Major becomes British prime minister • Namibia achieves independence from South Africa and becomes a member of the British Commonwealth • The Sandinista regime in Nicaragua loses power after a democratic election	• The US census reports that the population is 248,709,873: – whites: 199,686,070 (80.3%) – blacks: 29,986,060 (12.0%) – other: 19,037,743 (7.7%) • The US national debt is $3,233,313,451,777 • The Americans with Disabilities Act (ADA) offers new protections and guarantees of rights for disabled Americans • Douglas Wilder is the first African American elected as governor of a US state (Virginia) • In response to the *Exxon Valdez* disaster, Congress passes the Oil Pollution Act of 1990, which requires the Coast Guard to strengthen its regulations on oil tank vessels and oil tank owners and operators • President Bush signs the Clean Air Act, which requires significant changes in the energy and automotive industries to reduce air pollution • The minimum wage is increased to $3.80 per hour • Congress passes the Children's Television Act for children's programming • Television Marti joins Radio Marti in sending US propaganda to Cuba	• The space shuttle *Discovery* deploys the Hubble Space telescope • Symantec launches Norton AntiVirus, one of the first commercially successful computer antivirus programs • IBM sells its Selectric division, a sign of the passing of the age of typewriters • Microsoft releases the Windows 3.0 operating system • The FDA approves the use of the surgically implanted contraceptive Norplant	• The first broadcast of the PBS documentary *The Civil War*, created by Ken Burns, produces an overwhelming response and makes a national celebrity of Civil War historian Shelby Foote • Paul Simon releases the album *Rhythm of the Saints* • Neil Young, Elton John, Kris Kristofferson, Willie Nelson, John Mellencamp, Guns N' Roses, and Jackson Browne perform at the Farm Aid IV concert in Indiana • Garth Brooks's album *No Fences*, with what becomes his signature song, the blue collar anthem "Friends in Low Places," hits no. 1 on the Billboard country music chart and no. 3 on the pop chart • The Fender Stratocaster guitar that Jimi Hendrix used to perform his famous version of "The Star Spangled Banner" at Woodstock sells at auction in London for $295,000 • The "vocal" duo Milli Vanilli admits to lip-synching hits such as "Girl You Know It's True" and have their Grammy award revoked • *Seinfeld* debuts on NBC • Recognizing that girls are a part of their cause, the national Boys Clubs of America changes the organization's name to Boys & Girls Clubs of America • Wal-Mart becomes the largest retailer in America • Films: *Goodfellas*; *Pretty Woman*; *Dances with Wolves*; *Ghost*; *The Hunt for Red October*
1991	• Mikhail Gorbachev resigns as the last president of the USSR, which is dissolved; the former member states of the Soviet Union become autonomous; the Cold War era comes to an end • Twelve member states of the former USSR (Azerbaijan, Armenia, Belarus, Georgia, Kazakhstan, Kyrgyzstan, Moldova, Russia, Tajikistan, Turkmenistan, Uzbekistan, and Ukraine) join together to create the Commonwealth of Independent States (CIS) • Russia (formally the Russian Federation) continues the membership of the former USSR in all United Nations organizations, including the Security Council; the other members of the CIS are admitted to the UN as separate states (Belarus and Ukraine had been members since 1945) • The city of Leningrad reverses the change of 1924 and takes back its old name, St. Petersburg	• After two years of debates, vetoes, and threatened vetoes, President Bush finally signs the Civil Rights Act of 1991, which strengthens existing civil rights laws and provides for the award of financial damages in cases of intentional employment discrimination • The National Civil Rights Museum opens at the site of the Lorraine Motel in downtown Memphis, where Martin Luther King, Jr., was assassinated in 1968 • The US minimum wage is increased to $4.25 per hour • An unnamed late-season hurricane in the North Atlantic labeled the "Perfect Storm" creates 10- to 30-foot waves and causes extensive erosion and flooding along the Atlantic seaboard • Racial riots erupt in Los Angeles after television news broadcasts film footage of the beating of black motorist Rodney King by four white LA police officers	• Data is transmitted through optical fiber cables at 32 billion bits per second • An x-ray photograph is taken of the human brain recalling a word • Philips introduces the Compact Disc Interactive (CD-I) player for music and video • The gigantic Itaipu Dam on the Upper Parana River at the Brazil-Paraguay border is completed; the 4.8-mile-long complex of concrete and rockfill dams contains 18 electrical generators that provide 25% of Brazil's energy supply and 78% of Paraguay's energy supply • Richard Branson and Per Lindstrand complete the first hot-air balloon flight across the Pacific Ocean, from Japan to Canada (6,700 miles) • The first major cholera epidemic in more than a century breaks out in South America, killing around 1,000 people and making 100,000 more ill	• Claude-Michel Schönberg's musical *Miss Saigon* opens on Broadway [it runs for 4,092 performances before closing in 2001] • Wal-Mart enters the international market for the first time with the opening of Club Aurrera in Mexico City • CNN dominates news coverage worldwide during the Gulf War • The grunge rock band Nirvana explodes into the mainstream with their no. 1 album *Nevermind* and its lead single "Smells Like Teen Spirit"; Nirvana's lead singer, Kurt Cobain, uncomfortably finds himself being described as the "spokesman of a generation" and Nirvana as the "flagship band" of Generation X • Pearl Jam joins the grunge rock revolution with the release of their album *Ten*, dealing with dark subjects like depression, suicide, loneliness, and murder

E. EDUCATION, LITERATURE & THE FINE ARTS	F. RELIGION, THEOLOGY, PHILOSOPHY & PSYCHOLOGY	G. AMERICAN & UNITED METHODISM	H. BRITISH & WORLD METHODISM	
				1989 cont.
• Takashi Yoshimatsu composes his *Symphony No. 1 (Kamui-Chikap)* • August Wilson's play *The Piano Lesson*, completed in 1987, garners his second Pulitzer Prize for drama • Laura Esquivel's remarkable novel *Like Water for Chocolate* is published simultaneously in Spanish and English • Other notable publications include: – Michael Crichton's blockbuster novel, *Jurassic Park* – Robert Ludlum, *The Bourne Ultimatum* – Tom Clancy, *Clear and Present Danger* – John Kenneth Galbraith, *A Tenured Professor*	• Construction of the National Cathedral in Washington, DC, begun in 1907, is finally completed; it is the sixth largest cathedral in the world and second in the US after New York's Cathedral of St. John the Divine • Bill McCartney, then football coach at the University of Colorado, plays a leading role in the establishment of Promise Keepers, a ministry that is "designed to ignite and unite men to become passionate followers of Jesus Christ" • Notable publications include: – Thomas C. Oden, *After Modernity, What?* – Gustavo Gutiérrez, *The Truth Shall Make You Free* – Judith Plaskow, *Standing Again at Sinai: Judaism from a Feminist Perspective* – C. Eric Lincoln and Lawrence H. Mamiya, *The Black Church in the African American Experience* – Molefi Kete Asante, *Kemet, Afrocentricity, and Knowledge*	• The thirteenth Assembly of United Methodist Women meets • Fifty women serve as district superintendents in the UMC • UMC bishops issue the pastoral letter "Vital Congregations—Faithful Disciples" to encourage and support church growth • The Reconciling Congregations Program (1984) is formally incorporated as a not-for-profit organization • The South Carolina Conference makes the UMC's first cross-racial pastoral appointments • Faced with financial pressure and declining enrollment, Westmar College (1954) agrees to merge with Teikyo University of Tokyo, Japan, to form Teikyo-Westmar University, prompting the UMC to sever all ties with the institution [it closes permanently in 1997] • Notable publications include: – Theodore W. Jennings Jr., *Good News to the Poor: John Wesley's Evangelical Economics* – Randy L. Maddox, ed., *Aldersgate Reconsidered* – Donald A. Thorsen, *The Wesleyan Quadrilateral: Scripture, Tradition, Reason & Experience as a Model of Evangelical Theology*	• The UMC renews mission work in Bulgaria, Albania, Latvia, Lithuania, Estonia, and Russia • The World Methodist Evangelism Institute holds its fourth International Evangelism Seminar • The World Methodist Council gives the World Methodist Peace Award to Mikhail Gorbachev (USSR) for his initiatives in introducing *glasnost* ("openness") and *perestroika* ("restructuring") and allowing religious freedom in the former Soviet Union • L. Elbert Wethington establishes the Wesley Heritage Foundation as a means of producing a Spanish edition of the major writings of John Wesley • Sela Taufatofue Manu is the first female Methodist minister in Tonga • Notable publications include M. Douglas Meeks, ed., *What Should Methodists Teach? Wesleyan Tradition and Modern Diversity* [papers from the eighth Oxford Institute of Methodist Theological Studies, 1987]	**1990**
• The 200th anniversary of Mozart's death spurs musical tributes around the world; one of the largest is at Lincoln Center in New York • American philanthropist Walter Annenberg gives his stunning collection of over 50 Impressionist and Postimpressionist paintings to the Metropolitan Museum of Art in New York; the value of the gift is set at over $1 billion • New York's Carnegie Hall celebrates its 100th anniversary • Joan Tower composes her *Concerto for Orchestra* • Mario Davidovsky composes his *Simple Dances* for flute, two percussion, piano, and cello • Witold Lutosławski completes his *Chantefleurs et Chantefables* • Douglas Coupland's novel *Generation X: Tales for an Accelerated Culture*, popularizes the use of the term	• Moderate Baptists form the Cooperative Baptist Fellowship in reaction to the increasingly conservative movement of the Southern Baptist Convention • Notable publications include: – Wolfhart Pannenberg, *Systematic Theology* (3 vols., 1991–96) – Stanley Hauerwas, *After Christendom: How the Church is to Behave if Freedom, Justice and a Christian Nation are Bad Ideas* – Cain Hope Felder, *Stony the Road We Trod: African American Biblical Interpretation* – Pamela D. Couture, *Blessed Are the Poor? Women's Poverty, Family Policy, and Practical Theology*	• The Taskforce of United Methodists on Abortion and Sexuality (or Lifewatch), a voluntary group of UMC clergy, laity, and scholars opposed to abortion, issues the Durham Declaration, calling the church "to a scriptural, theological, and pastoral approach to abortion" • The UMC General Commission on Religion and Race sponsors the publication of *Breaking Down Walls, Building Bridges: Education Against Racism* (ed. Evelyn Fitzgerald), which provides documentation of the GCRR "pilot project" on racism being tested in seminaries across the church • Other notable publications include: – Homer Noley, *First White Frost: Native Americans and United Methodism* – Justo L. González, ed., *Each in Our Own Tongue: A History of Hispanic United Methodism*	• The sixteenth World Methodist Conference meets in Singapore • "The Apostolic Tradition: Report of the Joint Commission Between the Roman Catholic Church and the World Methodist Council, Fifth Series, 1986–1991" is published • The World Methodist Council gives the World Methodist Peace Award to Barbel Bohley for her leadership in the struggle for peace and freedom in East Germany • Manfred Marquardt publishes *Praxis und Prinzipien der Sozialethic John Wesleys* (English translation: *John Wesley's Social Ethics: Praxis and Principles*, 1992)	**1991**

	A. WORLD HISTORY & POLITICS	B. AMERICAN HISTORY & POLITICS	C. SCIENCE, MEDICINE & TECHNOLOGY	D. DAILY LIFE, POPULAR CULTURE & ENTERTAINMENT
1991 cont.	• Croatia and Slovenia declare independence from Yugoslavia; the communist government of Albania falls • President F. W. de Klerk announces the abolition of apartheid laws in South Africa • The US and the United Nations launch Operation Desert Storm to liberate Kuwait from occupation by Iraq; the ground war lasts only four days; Shiites in southern Iraq and Kurds in the north rise against Saddam Hussein but receive no US support and are slaughtered • The Strategic Arms Reduction Treaty (START) between the US and the four nuclear states of the former USSR (Russia, Belarus, Kazakhstan, and Ukraine) calls for dramatic reductions of long-range nuclear weapons by both sides • The League of Red Cross Societies (1919) becomes the International Federation of Red Cross and Red Crescent Societies			• The alternative rock band Smashing Pumpkins releases the blockbuster album *Gish* • Rap music crosses into the mainstream with the success of M. C. Hammer and 2 Live Crew • Garth Brooks's third album, *Ropin' the Wind*, has advance orders of 4 million copies and enters both the country and pop album charts at no. 1; it produces hit singles "What She's Doing Now" and "The River" • Will Smith appears on primetime TV in the sitcom *The Fresh Prince of Bel-Air* • The EuroDisney amusement park complex opens near Paris; critics see this as a prime example of "American cultural imperialism" • The cost of a US first-class postage stamp increases to 29¢ • Films: *The Silence of the Lambs; Thelma & Louise; Bugsy; City Slickers; Fried Green Tomatoes*
1992	• President Bush and Russian president Yeltsin meet at Camp David and formally declare an end to the Cold War • The breakup of Yugoslavia results in war among Serbs, Croats, and Muslims; Serbian nationalists begin "ethnic cleansing" of Muslims in Bosnia; tens of thousands are killed, and more than 1 million are forced to leave their homes through 1996 • Hindu nationalists destroy a mosque in Ayodhya, India • Boutros Boutros-Ghali (Egypt) is elected UN Secretary-General • The UN Conference on Environment and Development, better known as the "Earth Summit," meets in Rio de Janeiro • Yitzhak Rabin becomes prime minister in Israel for the second time • The North American Free Trade Agreement (NAFTA) is signed by Mexico, Canada, and the US • Osama bin Laden is exiled from Saudi Arabia, takes refuge in Sudan, and begins organizing the terrorist network known as al-Qaeda ("The Base") • Britain's Prince Charles and Princess Diana are separated; their divorce is finalized in 1996 • The Greek oil tanker *Aegean Sea* runs aground off the coast of Spain and spills over 21 million gallons of crude oil • The Expo '92 World's Fair in Seville, Spain, with the theme "The Age of Discoveries," commemorates the 500th anniversary of Christopher Columbus's first voyage to America in 1492	• The 27th Amendment to the US Constitution stipulates that changes in compensation for the services of the senators and representatives shall not take effect until after a subsequent election • In *Planned Parenthood v. Casey*, the US Supreme Court reaffirms the validity of a woman's right to abortion under *Roe v. Wade*; the case successfully challenged Pennsylvania's 1989 Abortion Control Act, which sought to reinstate restrictions previously ruled unconstitutional • Hurricane Andrew leaves 26 dead and more than 100,000 homes destroyed or damaged; with total US damages estimated at $34.9 billion, it is at the time the most costly hurricane in US history • The Birmingham Civil Rights Institute opens in Birmingham, AL • In a 5-4 decision, the US Supreme Court rules that the establishment clause of the 1st Amendment prohibits clergy from offering prayers as part of a public school graduation ceremony • William J. (Bill) Clinton is elected as president and Albert A. Gore Jr. as vice president (Democratic Party) • The third-party presidential candidacy of H. Ross Perot appeals to a broad spectrum of voters who feel angry and alienated from their government; Perot receives 19% of the popular vote, the most of any third-party candidate since Teddy Roosevelt in 1912, probably taking more votes from Bush than from Clinton • Carol Moseley-Braun, of Illinois, becomes the first African American woman elected to the US Senate	• There are 900 million television sets in use around the world; 201 million are in the US • Sony introduces the Mini-Disc, a recordable magneto-optical disc • Kodak introduces the Photo CD, the first method of storing digital images to become available to the general public • The Michelangelo computer virus, originating in Europe, disables computers worldwide; it is the first virus to command international attention • Development of the text-based browser opens the World Wide Web for general use; new Web terms: *HTTP* and *URL* • Microsoft introduces the Windows 3.1 operating system • The Georgia Dome in Atlanta is completed; with a diameter of 840 feet, it has the largest cable-supported fabric roof in the world • Representatives of 172 nations convene the Earth Summit in Rio de Janeiro to address issues of environmental protection and sustainable development	• The tap-dancing musical comedy *Crazy For You* by Ken Ludwig, featuring music by George and Ira Gershwin, opens on Broadway [it runs for 1,622 performances] • Johnny Carson hosts *The Tonight Show* for the last time; he has ruled late-night television for 20 years • Compact discs surpass cassette tapes as the preferred medium for recorded music • AOL reports it has 200,000 subscribers • Rock guitar legend Eric Clapton wins the Grammy for his touching ballad "Tears in Heaven," which he wrote after the death of his four-year-old son, Conor • *The Chronic* by Dr. Dre is the first real blockbuster hip-hop album, marking the beginning of the mainstream dominance of hip-hop, as well as the influence of the West Coast "G Funk" rap style • John Gray publishes his "war-of-the sexes" bestseller *Men Are from Mars, Women Are from Venus* • Films: Spike Lee produces his controversial *Malcolm X*; Woody Allen makes *Husbands and Wives*; other notable films include *Unforgiven; Basic Instinct; Scent of a Woman; The Crying Game; A River Runs Through It* • Summer Olympics: Barcelona • Winter Olympics: Albertville

E. EDUCATION, LITERATURE & THE FINE ARTS	F. RELIGION, THEOLOGY, PHILOSOPHY & PSYCHOLOGY	G. AMERICAN & UNITED METHODISM	H. BRITISH & WORLD METHODISM	
• Other notable publications include – Amy Tan, *The Kitchen God's Wife* – John Grisham, *The Firm* – A. S. Byatt, *Possession: A Romance*		– Artemio R. Guillermo, ed., *Churches Aflame: Asian Americans and United Methodism* – Grant S. Shockley, ed., *Heritage and Hope: The African-American Presence in United Methodism* – Ted A. Campbell, *John Wesley and Christian Antiquity: Religious Vision and Cultural Changes* – Russell E. Richey, *Early American Methodism* – Susan M. Eltscher, *Women in the Wesleyan and United Methodist Traditions: A Bibliography* – C. Jarrett Gray, Jr., *The Racial and Ethnic Presence in American Methodism: A Bibliography*		**1991 cont.**
• The United Nations Educational, Scientific, and Cultural Organization (UNESCO) launches a five-year project to photograph the world's most important cultural and natural wonders before they are further damaged by natural disasters or armed conflicts • Mona Van Duyn is the first woman selected as US Poet Laureate • Arvo Pärt completes his *Berlin Mass* for chorus, organ, and string orchestra • William Mathias composes his *Flute Concerto* • David McCullough's biography *Truman* helps to burnish the reputation of former US president Harry Truman • Other notable publications include: – Susan Sontag, *The Volcano Lover* – Daniel Boorstin, *The Creators* – Gail Sheehy, *Silent Passage* – Toni Morrison, *Jazz* – James Michener, *Mexico* – Robert James Waller, *The Bridges of Madison County* – Michael Ondaatje, *The English Patient*	• Pope John Paul II acknowledges the Vatican's error in the condemnation of Galileo; later the same year, the pope is diagnosed as having Parkinson's disease • Maria Jepsen is the first woman elected bishop by the Lutheran Church in Germany • April Ulring Larson is the first woman elected bishop in American Lutheranism • Women are ordained as priests in the Anglican Churches of South Africa and Australia • Worshipers celebrate the first Russian Orthodox Easter in Moscow in 74 years • Notable publications include: – Elizabeth Johnson, *She Who Is: The Mystery of God in Feminist Theological Discourse* – Carol A. Newsom and Sharon H. Ringe, eds., *The Women's Bible Commentary* – Elisabeth Schüssler Fiorenza, *But She Said: Feminist Practices of Biblical Interpretation* – N. T. Wright, *The New Testament and the People of God* – Justo L. González, *Out of Every Tribe and Nation: Christian Theology At the Ethnic Roundtable* – Walter Wink, *Engaging the Powers: Discernment and Resistance in a World of Domination*	• A group of 80 UMC clergy and laity associated with the Good News Movement issues "The Memphis Declaration," calling on United Methodists "to live more faithfully as the body of Jesus Christ" by "confessing, proclaiming and living the Apostolic faith" • The UMC General Conference: – authorizes publication of a new *Book of Worship* – creates the Joint Committee on International Ministries with Women, Children and Youth – launches the National Plan for Hispanic Ministry – receives but does not approve the report of the Committee to Study Homosexuality, instead recommending that it be studied across the denomination during the next quadrennium – adds to the *Discipline* the statement that "all persons, regardless of age, gender, marital status or sexual orientation, are entitled to have their human and civil rights ensured" • Hae Jong Kim becomes the first Korean American to be elected bishop of the UMC • The UMC General Board of Discipleship holds a National Conference on "Black Men in Crisis" • The Puerto Rico Annual Conference begins an 8-year period of transition to autonomous status as The Methodist Church of Puerto Rico (through 2004); this is the first instance of an autonomous body related to the UMC within the territory of the US • Notable publications include: – Gayle C. Felton, *This Gift of Water: The Practice and Theology of Baptism Among Methodists in America* – Henry H. Knight III, *The Presence of God in the Christian Life: John Wesley and the Means of Grace* – Justo L. González, ed., *Voces: Voices from the Hispanic Church* – James S. Thomas, *Methodism's Racial Dilemma: The Story of the Central Jurisdiction*	• Africa University, established by the UMC in Old Mutare, Zimbabwe, opens for classes • The Nigeria Annual Conference (UMC) is formed; its roots go back to the EA mission begun in 1906 • The separate conferences of the EMK in the former East and West Germany are united; the unified church begins mission work in Albania • The Methodist Church in Russia is formally reestablished when the First UMC in Moscow and First UMC in St. Petersburg are legally registered • The second round of bilateral ecumenical dialogue begins between the World Methodist Council and the World Alliance of Reformed Churches (until 1996) • Bilateral ecumenical dialogue begins between the World Methodist Council and the Anglican Consultative Council (until 1996) • The World Methodist Council gives the World Methodist Peace Award to Zdravko Beslov for his leadership of Methodism in Bulgaria during the communist era • Kathleen Richardson is the first woman to be elected as president of Conference by the MC[UK] • The ninth Oxford Institute of Methodist Theological Studies meets	**1992**

	A. WORLD HISTORY & POLITICS	B. AMERICAN HISTORY & POLITICS	C. SCIENCE, MEDICINE & TECHNOLOGY	D. DAILY LIFE, POPULAR CULTURE & ENTERTAINMENT
1993	• The European Community (EC) formally becomes the European Union (EU) with ratification of the 1991 Treaty of European Union (Maastricht Treaty); full members are Austria, Belgium, Denmark, Finland, France, Germany (originally West Germany), Great Britain, Greece, Ireland, Italy, Luxembourg, the Netherlands, Portugal, Spain, and Sweden • Russian president Boris Yeltsin suspends the Supreme Soviet and uses the army to quell the ensuing revolt; a new constitution is adopted with a State Duma replacing the Supreme Soviet • The "Black Hawk Down" disaster in Mogadishu, Somalia, results in the withdrawal of US peace-keeping forces; UN mission continues until 1995 • The US and Russia conclude the second Strategic Arms Reduction Treaty (START II), which is intended to eliminate heavy intercontinental ballistic missiles (ICBMs) and all other multiple-warhead (MIRV) ICBMs; the treaty is approved by the US Senate in 1996 and by the Russian Duma in 2000 • South Africa adopts a new constitution guaranteeing equal rights to citizens of all races • Israel and the PLO conclude the Oslo Accords, agreeing to the gradual withdrawal of Israeli forces from parts of the Gaza Strip and West Bank, affirming the right of Palestinians to self-government in those areas and establishing a framework for further negotiations • The Chemical Weapons Convention (CWC) augments the 1925 Geneva Protocol by banning the production, storage, and use of chemical weapons; it goes into effect in 1997 • Eritreia achieves independence from Ethiopia after thirty years of intermittent civil war	• Janet Reno becomes the first woman to serve as US Attorney General when she is appointed to that post by President Clinton • The US military adopts the "Don't Ask, Don't Tell" policy, permitting homosexuals to serve in the military but banning homosexual activity • After a 51-day standoff with federal agents, the Branch Davidian compound in Waco, TX, burns to the ground, killing leader David Koresh and 80 cult members • A bomb explodes under the World Trade Center in New York, killing six and injuring hundreds; a group of Islamic terrorists is caught and convicted • Congress passes and President Clinton signs the "motor voter" law, allowing citizens to register to vote when they get or renew a driver's license • More than 80 women are sexually assaulted at the notorious "Tailhook Convention" of US Navy personnel in Las Vegas • President Clinton elevates the status of the Federal Emergency Management Agency (FEMA), making its director a member of his cabinet • Puerto Rico again votes to retain its commonwealth status over either statehood or independence (previous: 1967) • Both the Vietnam Women's Memorial and the United States Holocaust Memorial Museum are dedicated in Washington, DC • The winter "Superstorm" paralyzes the eastern seaboard, causing the deaths of some 270 people; record snowfalls (with rates of 2 to 3 inches per hour) and high winds causes $3 billion to $6 billion in damage • Massive flooding of the Mississippi River and tributaries causes $10 billion damage, especially in the upper Mississippi Valley	• Astronauts from the space shuttle *Endeavour* successfully install new optical devices to correct the performance of the $3 billion Hubble Space Telescope • Construction of the English Channel Tunnel (or Chunnel), begun in 1988, is completed, enabling the first direct rail from Britain to France and the rest of Europe • The Avid Media Composer system makes it possible to edit films digitally at the "real-time" viewing rate of 24 frames per second • Apple introduces the first "portable digital assistant" (PDA) device, the Newton • Nokia develops technology to send text messages between mobile phones • Intel creates the Pentium microprocessor chip • A "graphical user interface" (GUI) named Mosaic is developed for the World Wide Web • Microsoft introduces the Windows NT operating system, which for the first time provides 32-bit multitasking	• Tony Kushner's play *Angels in America* makes its Broadway debut, examining the history of the HIV-AIDS epidemic since the 1980s • Nolan Ryan retires from baseball with a record 5,714 strikeouts • Sears Roebuck ends publication of its "big book" mail-order catalog after 93 years • Queen Latifah releases her *Black Reign* album, including the single, "U.N.I.T.Y.," in which she denounces the sexist attitudes and the violence against women characteristic of "gangsta rap" • Whitney Houston's single "I Will Always Love You" spends 14 weeks at the top of the charts, becoming the longest running no. 1 single of all time [to date] • Nirvana's final studio album, *In Utero*, is released • The career of the hip-hop group The Wu-Tang Clan begins with the release of *Enter the Wu-Tang: 36 Chambers* • Garrison Keillor moves his popular radio show back to Minnesota and resumes using its original name, *A Prairie Home Companion* • Rapper Snoop Dogg releases his album *Doggystyle*, which becomes the first debut rap album ever to enter the charts at no. 1, helping to fuel the ascendance of the West Coast "G Funk" rap style • Oprah Winfrey interviews Michael Jackson during a prime-time special; it is Jackson's first interview in 15 years • After 11 years on NBC, David Letterman signs with CBS for $16 million • Films: Stephen Spielberg's *Jurassic Park* grosses a record $725 million in 16 weeks; other notable films include *Schindler's List*; *Gettysburg*; *The Fugitive*; *The Piano*; *Sleepless in Seattle*; *Like Water for Chocolate*; *Philadelphia*
1994	• Nelson Mandela is elected as the first black president of South Africa, defeating incumbent F. W. De Klerk; South Africa rejoins the British Commonwealth • Kim Il Sung dies and his son, Kim Jong Il, takes over leadership of North Korea • Tribal, ethnic, and political conflict leads to genocide in Rwanda as Hutu militants kill more than 500,000 Tutsis and send more than 1 million more fleeing to refugee camps in Zaire, Tanzania, and Burundi • Israel and the PLO sign an agreement transferring authority over most aspects of life in the Gaza Strip and the unoccupied West Bank to the newly-created Palestinian National Authority (PNA) • Key leaders of Serbia, Bosnia, and Croatia sign a peace agreement in Dayton, OH • Russian forces invade the breakaway province of Chechnya • Norway rejects membership in the EU	• Republicans win a majority in the House of Representatives; Newt Gingrich becomes Speaker, and introduces the "Contract with America" • The Violence Against Women Act tightens federal penalties for sex offenders, funds services for victims of rape and domestic violence, and provides for special training of police officers • The Brady Handgun Violence Prevention Act imposes, on an interim basis, a five-day waiting period and background check before a licensed gun importer, manufacturer, or dealer can sell or deliver a handgun to an unlicensed individual • A major earthquake kills 50 people and causes widespread damage to Los Angeles, particularly to its bridges and freeways • Byron De La Beckwith is tried and convicted in Mississippi for the 1963 murder of Medgar Evers • The American Indian Trust Reform Management Act requires the Interior Department to account for all the money contributed to the fund since the Dawes Act of 1887	• China begins construction of the gigantic Three Gorges Dam; when completed in 2009, it will be the largest concrete dam in the world, stretching more than one mile across the Yangtze River and rising 600 feet above the valley floor; it will also be the world's largest hydroelectric project, surpassing Brazil's Itaipu Dam • Real Audio allows audio listening across the Internet in near real time; radio stations begin opening websites for "streaming" audio broadcasts • Netscape is founded by Marc Andreesen and James H. Clark; Netscape Navigator is given away free, soon gaining 75% of the world browser market • The first mass-marketing campaigns using e-mail are launched, soon making the term *spam* part of the internet vocabulary • Microsoft releases the Windows 3.11 for Workgroups operating system • Vice President Al Gore makes a speech in which he coins the term "Information Superhighway"	• The stage version of Walt Disney's musical *Beauty and the Beast* opens on Broadway [it records 4,803 performances by the end of 2005 and is still running] • Andrew Lloyd Webber's musical *Sunset Boulevard* opens on Broadway; it runs for 977 performances • DirecTV, the first high-powered direct broadcast satellite (DBS) system, is established; it is the first North American DBS service • *ER* and *Friends* debut on NBC • Students taking the SAT may use calculators for the math exam • Kurt Cobain, lead singer for the group Nirvana, commits suicide • The US Postal Service issues an Elvis Presley commemorative stamp • Veteran rock-and-roll groups The Rolling Stones and Pink Floyd launch concert tours that each take in more than $100 million • *Baseball*, Ken Burns's epic 9-part, 18½-hour documentary about "America's favorite pastime," is broadcast on PBS

E. EDUCATION, LITERATURE & THE FINE ARTS	F. RELIGION, THEOLOGY, PHILOSOPHY & PSYCHOLOGY	G. AMERICAN & UNITED METHODISM	H. BRITISH & WORLD METHODISM	
• The Louvre Museum in Paris opens its Richelieu Wing, adding 70% to its exhibition space • The Norman Rockwell Museum, originally founded in 1969, opens in its new quarters in Stockbridge, MA, to honor the work of "America's most popular artist" • John Adams composes his *Violin Concerto* • David Diamond completes his *Symphony No. 11*, his last work • Notable publications include: – Annie Proulx, *The Shipping News* – Stephen Ambrose, *Band of Brothers* – Stephen King, *Nightmares and Dreamscapes*	• Konrad Raiser (Evangelical Church in Germany) is named General Secretary of the World Council of Churches • Mary McLeod is elected and consecrated by the ECUSA as bishop of Vermont, becoming the first woman to head a diocese of the ECUSA • The second Parliament of the World's Religions is held in Chicago, commemorating the centennial of the first World Parliament of Religions • Joel Belvarluis, ed., *A Sourcebook for the Community of Religions*, prepared for the Parliament, becomes a standard textbook in religion classes • Other notable publications include: – Cornel West, *Race Matters* – C. S. Song, *Jesus and the Reign of God* – Thomas J. J. Altizer, *The Genesis of God: A Theological Genealogy* – Diana L. Eck, *Encountering God: A Spiritual Journey from Bozeman to Banaras* – John Hick, *God and the Universe of Faiths* – Stephen L. Carter, *The Culture of Disbelief: How American Law and Politics Trivialize Religious Devotion* – Stanley Hauerwas, *Unleashing the Scripture: Freeing the Bible from Captivity to America*	• The Sixth International Congress of United Methodist Men meets • Participation by UM women in the first ecumenical feminist Re-Imagining Conference in Minneapolis sparks controversy and charges of "paganism" and "goddess worship" from conservative and evangelical critics • The UMPH publishes Carlton Young, ed., *Companion to The United Methodist Hymnal* (with historical articles, commentary, and biographies) • Other notable publications include: – Woodie W. White, ed., *Our Time Under God Is Now: Reflections on Black Methodists for Church Renewal* (commemorating the 25th anniversary of BMCR) – Russell E. Richey, Kenneth E. Rowe, and Jean Miller Schmidt, eds., *Perspectives on American Methodism: Interpretive Essays* – Paul W. Chilcote, *She Offered Them Christ: The Legacy of Women Preachers in Early Methodism* – Kenneth J. Collins, *A Faithful Witness: John Wesley's Homiletical Theology*	• The MC [UK] recognizes two orders of ordained ministry, "presbyterial" and "diaconal"; members of the diaconal order are no longer regarded as "lay" ministers • The World Methodist Evangelism Institute holds its fifth International Evangelism Seminar at Cliff College, England • No World Methodist Peace Award is given • Notable publications include Manfred Marquardt and Walter Klaiber, *Gelebte Gnade: Grundriss einer Theologie der Evangelische-Methodistischen Kirche* (English translation: *Living Grace: An Outline of United Methodist Theology*, 2001)	**1993**
• The "Three Tenors" concerts, featuring Luciano Pavarotti, Plácido Domingo, and José Carreras, are enormously successful • Oliver Knussen completes his *Horn Concerto* • Tristan Muriel creates his musical meditation *The Spirit of the Dunes* • The last novel of Albert Camus, *The First Man*, is finally published 34 years after his death • Other notable publications include: – John Updike, *Brasil* – Gore Vidal, *United States: Essays, 1952–1992* – Tom Clancy, *The Debt of Honor* – James Michener, *Recessional* – James Redfield, *The Celestine Prophecy*	• The Church of England ordains its first women priests at Bristol Cathedral; 32 women are ordained • The Southern Baptist Convention reconsiders its 1984 position and decides to leave the ordination of women to the discretion of local congregations • Notable publications include: – Rebecca S. Chopp and Mark Lewis Taylor, eds., *Reconstructing Christian Theology* – Theodore W. Jennings Jr., *Loyalty to God: The Apostles' Creed in Life and Liturgy*	• The fourteenth Assembly of United Methodist Women meets • Susie Stanley convenes the first Wesleyan/Holiness Women Clergy Conference, which becomes a biannual event • Randy L. Maddox publishes *Responsible Grace: John Wesley's Practical Theology*	• The UMC establishes the Baltic Methodist Theological Seminary in Tallinn, Estonia, with instruction in Estonian, Russian, and English • The World Methodist Council gives the World Methodist Peace Award to Elias Chacour for his efforts to enable Palestinians and Israelis to live together • Notable publications include: – M. Douglas Meeks, ed., *The Portion of the Poor: Good News to the Poor in the Wesleyan Tradition* [papers from the ninth Oxford Institute of Methodist Theological Studies, 1992] – Tim Macquiban, ed., *Methodism in Its Cultural Milieu: Proceedings of the Centenary Conference of the Wesley Historical Society in Conjunction with the World Methodist Historical Society* (1993)	**1994**

	A. WORLD HISTORY & POLITICS	B. AMERICAN HISTORY & POLITICS	C. SCIENCE, MEDICINE & TECHNOLOGY	D. DAILY LIFE, POPULAR CULTURE & ENTERTAINMENT
1994 cont.		• Former president Richard M. Nixon dies; five other US presidents (Clinton, Bush, Reagan, Carter, and Ford) attend his funeral; Billy Graham delivers the primary eulogy • Former president Ronald Reagan announces publicly that he has Alzheimer's disease and withdraws from public life • In midterm elections, the Republican Party wins majorities in both the House of Representatives and the Senate for the first time in 40 years	• The White House establishes a webpage, and Congress provides internet access for all congressional offices	• Films: *Forrest Gump; Pulp Fiction; Speed; The Shawshank Redemption; The Lion King* • Winter Olympics: Lillehammer (held this year to establish a two-year rotation between Summer and Winter Olympics)
1995	• The US restores full diplomatic relations with Vietnam • The World Trade Organization (WTO) is established with 125 members; it is the successor to GATT (1948) • Yitzhak Rabin is assassinated in Israel; Shimon Peres becomes prime minister for the second time • King Fahd of Saudi Arabia suffers a crippling stroke; his brother, Crown Prince Abdullah, becomes the de facto ruler of the country • Jacques Chirac is elected president of France • Bosnian Serb forces overrun a UN-designated "safe area" in Srebrenica, Bosnia; over 7,000 Bosnian men and boys are massacred • The first US and UN troops are sent to Bosnia for peacekeeping missions; they bomb Serb positions in Bosnia to force Serb fighters to withdraw; fighting is ended by peace treaty in December • Austria, Finland, and Sweden become members of the EU • Cameroon and Mozambique become members of the British Commonwealth • Members of the Aum Shinrikyo sect release sarin neurotoxin into the subway system in Tokyo; 12 die and over 5,000 are injured	• The Korean War Memorial is dedicated in Washington, DC • A truck bomb destroys the Murrah Federal Building in Oklahoma City, OK, killing 168 people; Timothy McVeigh is convicted of the crime in 1997 and executed in 2001 • Congress passes budget legislation that includes a provision to allow drilling in the Arctic National Wildlife Refuge (ANWR); citing a desire to protect biological and wilderness values, President Clinton vetoes the bill • A budget standoff between President Clinton and Republicans in Congress led by Speaker of the House Newt Gingrich results in the partial shutdown of the US government • A Senate committee begins investigating the "Whitewater Affair," concerning allegedly questionable real estate dealings by President and Mrs. Clinton in Arkansas • Louis Farrakhan and his Nation of Islam organize the "Million Man March" in Washington to draw attention to the social problems of African Americans	• Subscription-based services such as CompuServe, America Online, and Prodigy begin to provide "dial-up" Internet access to individual customers using modems and home computers • Kodak introduces the DC40, the first digital camera marketed to average consumers • Saquinavir, the first protease inhibitor (which reduces the ability of AIDS to spread to new cells) is approved by the FDA • Craig Venter and Hamilton Smith announce the decoding of the entire DNA sequence of a living organism • Microsoft releases the Windows 95 operating system	• Online commerce takes a leap forward when Amazon.com and eBay.com open for business • EchoStar Communications launches the EchoStar I satellite and the DISH Network • Cal Ripken Jr. breaks Lou Gehrig's baseball "Iron Man" record of 2,130 consecutive games; his record streak began on May 30, 1982, and ends on Sept. 19, 1998, after 2,632 games • Former sports hero and celebrity O. J. Simpson is acquitted on charges of murder in a trial that preoccupies much of America • *The Beatles Anthology* television miniseries airs on ABC; the first installment ends with the music video "Free As a Bird," the first new Beatles recording since their breakup in 1970 • *The Beatles Anthology 1* CD is released simultaneously; a record 450,000 copies are sold in its first day of release • Jerry Garcia dies of a heart attack; the remaining members of the Grateful Dead choose to disband the group • The cost of a US first-class postage stamp increases to 32¢ • Films: Pixar creates *Toy Story*, the first feature-length movie made entirely with computerized animation; *Babe; Braveheart; The Bridges of Madison County; Leaving Las Vegas*
1996	• The Comprehensive Test Ban Treaty (CTBT) agreement, which bans all nuclear tests both above and below the earth's surface, is signed by the US, Britain, France, Russia, and 90 other countries • Russia signs a peace treaty with the leaders of a revolt in the province of Chechnya • Benjamin Netanyahu becomes prime minister in Israel • Boris Yeltsin is reelected president of the Russian Federation • Yassir Arafat is elected the first president of the Palestinian National Authority (PNA) • Radical Islamists known as the Taliban seize power in Afghanistan; they give shelter to Osama bin Laden and al-Qaeda • Al Jazeera, an independent satellite station in Qatar, begins broadcasting and revolutionizes journalism in the Arab world • The US launches air attacks on radar and missile installations in Iraq in retaliation for Iraqi attacks on Kurdish-held cities in northern Iraq	• The US minimum wage is increased to $4.75 per hour • The US Supreme Court rules the "Communications Decency Act" to be unconstitutional • President Clinton signs the "Electronic Freedom of Information Act Amendments of 1996," which updates the 1966 FOIA for the electronic age, specifying that it applies to government records maintained in electronic format • Congress passes and President Clinton signs the Welfare Reform Act, which is intended to replace welfare with "workfare" and which within a year will reduce the national welfare roles by 1.5 million people • Theodore Kaczinski, the "Unabomber," is arrested • The US Supreme Court strikes down the long-standing male-only admission policy of the Virginia Military Institute because it "denies to women, simply because they are women, full citizenship stature" • The Centennial Olympic Games in Atlanta are marred by a pipe bomb explosion which kills one person and injures more than 100	• Archaeologists locate and begin excavating the original site of the first settlement at Jamestown, VA • NASA's *Galileo* space probe transmits historic and scientifically valuable images of the moons of Jupiter • Dolly the sheep is born at the Roslin Institute in Scotland; she is the first mammal to be cloned with DNA taken from an adult cell • Broadcasters and television and PC manufacturers agree on a standard for HDTV (high-definition digital television) • The FOX network launches FOX News Channel, a 24-hour news channel in direct competition with CNN • The Google search engine is developed by Sergey Brin and Larry Page • Apple Computers buys Pixar and appoints Steve Jobs as its interim CEO; Jobs begins to transform Apple from a computer company to a media company, cutting a deal with Disney Enterprises to distribute its next five major films	• Jonathan Larson's musical drama *Rent* opens on Broadway [it records 4,024 performances by the end of 2005 and is still running] • IBM's Deep Blue computer beats chess grandmaster Garry Kasparov • The Broadway musical *Bring in da Noise, Bring in da Funk* explores and celebrates African American history through dance and music • Country music star Garth Brooks surpasses Elvis Presley as the music industry's all-time top-selling solo performer • *The Beatles Anthology 2* and *The Beatles Anthology 3* CDs are released • Canadian singer Alanis Morissette achieves success in the US and Europe with her album *Jagged Little Pill* • The Dave Matthews Band releases the album *Crash*, the record that puts them on the map, featuring the hit singles "Crash Into Me" and "So Much to Say" • Long-time talk show host Phil Donahue retires • Thirteen-year-old country singer Leanne Rimes causes a sensation when she records "Blue," originally written for Patsy Cline

E. EDUCATION, LITERATURE & THE FINE ARTS	F. RELIGION, THEOLOGY, PHILOSOPHY & PSYCHOLOGY	G. AMERICAN & UNITED METHODISM	H. BRITISH & WORLD METHODISM	
				1994 cont.
• Installation artists Christo and Jean-Claude drape the historic German Parliament building in Berlin with layers of silver-colored fabric, creating the "Wrapped Reichstag" exhibit; it lasts for one month and draws over 1 million visitors • The Metropolitan Museum of Art in New York City celebrates its 125th anniversary with a retrospective exhibition featuring its architecture • The Smithsonian Institution in Washington launches a $100 million fund-raising campaign • The New York City Ballet premieres Jerome Robbins's *West Side Story Suite*, based on Leonard Bernstein and Stephen Sondheim's 1957 musical • The Joffrey Ballet moves from New York City to Chicago where it is promised greater financial support • Paintings by Pablo Picasso and Vincent Van Gogh sell at auction for more than $20 million each • Notable publications include: – Günter Grass, *A Wide Field* – Richard Ford, *Independence Day* – Michael Crichton, *The Lost World* – T. C. Boyle, *The Tortilla Curtain* – Nicholas Evans, *The Horse Whisperer*	• Notable publications include: – Rebecca S. Chopp, *Saving Work: Feminist Practices of Theological Education* – Benjamin R. Barber, *Jihad vs. McWorld: How Globalism and Tribalism Are Reshaping the World* – Van A. Harvey, *Feuerbach and the Interpretation of Religion* – Harvey Cox, *Fire from Heaven: The Rise of Pentecostal Spirituality and the Reshaping of Religion in the Twenty-first Century*	• Over 800 people from across the UMC, clergy and laity, gather in Atlanta to launch the Confessing Movement "for the renewal and reform of The United Methodist Church" • Notable publications include: – Richard P. Heitzenrater, *Wesley and the People Called Methodists* – James T. Campbell, *Songs of Zion: The African Methodist Episcopal Church in the United States and South Africa* – John B. Cobb Jr., *Grace and Responsibility: A Wesleyan Theology for Today* – William J. Abraham, *Waking from Doctrinal Amnesia: The Healing of Doctrine in The United Methodist Church* – Scott J. Jones, *John Wesley's Conception and Use of Scripture*	• The UMC establishes the Theological Seminary of the United Methodist Church in Russia in Moscow • No World Methodist Peace Award is given • Notable publications include S T Kimbrough, Jr., ed., *Methodism in Russia and the Baltic States: History and Renewal*	**1995**
• John Singer Sargent's painting *Cashmere* sells at auction for over $11 million, by far the most ever paid for any work by an American artist • The re-creation of Shakespeare's Globe Theater (from Stratford-upon-Avon, 1599–1614) opens in London • Harper Lee's novel, *To Kill a Mockingbird*, is removed from an advanced placement high school English reading list in Lindale, TX, because it "conflicts with the values of the community" • White American classicist Mary Lefkowitz publishes *Not Out of Africa: How Afrocentrism Became an Excuse to Teach Myth as History*, which disputes most of the assertions made by proponents of Afrocentrism such as Molefi Kete Asante (1980) and Martin Bernal (1987) • Other notable publications include: – Margaret Atwood, *Alias Grace* – Stephen Ambrose, *Undaunted Courage: Meriwether Lewis, Thomas Jefferson, and the Opening of the American West*	• The Vatican joins the internet revolution when it establishes a website (www.vatican.va/) • Conservative Episcopalians establish the American Anglican Council to "affirm Biblical authority and Christian orthodoxy within the Anglican Communion" • Conservative Lutherans establish the WordAlone Network, which is devoted to "building an evangelical confessional Lutheran future in America" • The Institute on Religion and Democracy (IRD) sponsors creation of the Association for Church Renewal (ACR), an umbrella group for more than 30 groups including The American Anglican Council, the WordAlone Network (Lutheran), the Biblical Witness Fellowship (UCC), Presbyterians for Renewal, and Good News and the Confessing Movement (UMC) • Thomas D. Jakes Sr. establishes The Potter's House in Dallas [by 2005 it has over 28,000 members and is the largest primarily African American congregation in the US]	• UMC bishops launch the Episcopal Initiative on Children and Poverty • The UMC General Conference: – adopts *By Water and the Spirit: A United Methodist Understanding of Baptism* as an official statement of church teaching – creates new designations for church membership, "baptized members" and "professing members"; only the latter are to be counted for most statistical and financial purposes – approves a reordering of the church's ministry by creating deacon and elder as separate and distinct orders of ordained ministry, each with its own distinctive purpose, powers, and responsibilities – adds to the *Social Principles* the statement that "ceremonies that celebrate homosexual unions shall not be conducted by our ministers and shall not be conducted in our churches" – establishes the new General Commission on United Methodist Men (GCUMM) – sets "Strengthening the Black Church for the 21st Century" as a quadrennial mission initiative	• The seventeenth World Methodist Conference meets in Rio de Janeiro, Brazil • The Evangelical Methodist Church in Portugal (Igreja Evangélica Metodista Portuguesa) becomes autonomous • The AMEC General Conference recognizes annual conferences in Angola and Uganda • The MC [UK] conference offices move out of Westminster Central Hall • "The Word of Life: A Statement on Revelation and Faith: Report of the Joint Commission for Dialogue Between The Roman Catholic Church and The World Methodist Council, Sixth Series, 1992–1996" is published • "Sharing in the Apostolic Communion: The Report of the Anglican-Methodist International Commission to the World Methodist Council and the Lambeth Conference" is published • The World Methodist Council gives the World Methodist Peace Award to Stanley Mogoba for his work in bringing reconciliation to South Africa	**1996**

	A. WORLD HISTORY & POLITICS	B. AMERICAN HISTORY & POLITICS	C. SCIENCE, MEDICINE & TECHNOLOGY	D. DAILY LIFE, POPULAR CULTURE & ENTERTAINMENT
1996 cont.	• England returns the Stone of Scone, the symbol of Scottish monarchy, to Scotland after holding it for 700 years under the English coronation chair • A massive truck bomb explodes outside Khobar Towers, an apartment complex in Saudi Arabia housing military personnel from the United States, Britain, and France, killing 19 and injuring more than 200 soldiers	• TWA flight 800 explodes in flight over Long Island, killing all 230 people on board • The US national debt surpasses $5 trillion • Clinton and Gore are reelected as president and vice president (Democratic Party)	• Palm Computing, Inc. releases the Palm Pilot, the first handheld PDA (personal digital assistant) to achieve real popularity and commercial success	• The revival of the musical comedy *Chicago* (originally 1975–77) opens on Broadway [it records 3,802 performances by the end of 2005 and is still running] • Britain's Spice Girls release their debut album, *Spice*, which sells an unprecedented 1.8 million copies in Britain alone • Tupac Shakur, considered to be the greatest and most inspirational rap star ever, is killed in a drive-by shooting [he remains the highest selling rap/hip-hop artist ever, having sold 67 million albums worldwide] • The Macarena, based on Latin rhythms, becomes a worldwide but short-lived dance craze • Films: *The English Patient; Jerry Maguire; Shine; Independence Day; Emma; Fargo* • Summer Olympics: Atlanta (the centennial games of the modern era of the Olympics)
1997	• Kofi Annan (Ghana) is elected UN Secretary-General • Britain returns control of Hong Kong to China, ending 155 years of British rule • Rebels in Zaire overthrow the current government and change the name of the country to Democratic Republic of the Congo • Radical Islamic militants in Egypt attack tourists in the Valley of the Kings, killing 70; a major government crackdown follows • Tony Blair becomes British prime minister • The death of Diana, Princess of Wales, in an auto accident results in worldwide mourning • Deng Xiaoping, who had in 1989 "retired" from political office in China but continued to run the country from behind the scenes, dies; Jiang Zemin, who had been general secretary since 1989 and president since 1993, assumes full power in China • Israel turns over to the Palestinian Authority most of the West Bank city of Hebron but approves the establishment of new Jewish settlements in East Jerusalem	• Proposition 209 is enacted in California, resulting in a state ban on all forms of affirmative action • Madeleine Albright is sworn in as US Secretary of State; she is the first woman in this position as well as the highest-ranking woman in the US government • The Franklin Delano Roosevelt Memorial is dedicated • Thirty-nine members of Heaven's Gate cult in California commit mass suicide • Oregon passes a "Death with Dignity Act," becoming the first US state to legalize physician-assisted suicide by terminally ill people [the US Supreme Court upholds this law as constitutional in January 2006] • US tobacco companies agree to pay states for medical costs of some tobacco-related illnesses to settle court cases against them • The US minimum wage is increased to $5.15 per hour	• NASA's *Pathfinder* lands on the surface of Mars and its *Sojourner* rover carries out the first mobile exploration of another planet; the NASA *Pathfinder* website, which is running real-time images sent from the *Pathfinder* on Mars, receives more than 100 million hits during its first four days, setting a new popularity record and requiring NASA to set up 25 mirror pages to handle the traffic • Apple reinvigorates its computer lines with the release of the colorful and popular iMac • Britain's Caroline Hamilton heads the first all-woman expedition to the North Pole; she is also one of five women to reach the South Pole in 2000 • Jeanne Calmet (France) dies at the age of 122; she has lived longer than any other person in history with documentation to prove her age • The second "Earth Summit" meets in Kyoto, Japan; it adopts the Kyoto Protocol on global climate change and control of greenhouse gases	• The theatrical version of Walt Disney's *The Lion King*, with music by Elton John and lyrics by Tim Rice, opens on Broadway [it records 3,394 performances by the end of 2005 and is still running] • The CNBC TV network, an alliance between Dow Jones and NBC Universal, is founded • Tiger Woods is the youngest person ever to win the Masters golf tournament, and he does so by the widest margin in history (12 strokes) • Elton John performs a revised version of his 1973 song "Candle in the Wind" at the funeral of Britain's Princess Diana; it becomes the most successful pop single in history, selling more than 30 million copies, with all profits going to charity, resulting in John's knighthood by Queen Elizabeth in 1998 • Wal-Mart becomes the largest employer in the US with 680,000 "associates"; total sales for the year reach $105 billion • The rock band Phish, long famous for their improvisational concerts, records the live album *Slip Stitch and Pass* in Hamburg, Germany • IBM's Deep Blue computer defeats chess grandmaster Garry Kasparov in their second six-game showdown, winning the tie-breaking game in only 62 minutes • J. K. Rowling's *Harry Potter and the Philosopher's Stone* is published in the UK; it comes to the US in 1998 as *Harry Potter and the Sorcerer's Stone* and ignites a craze for the young wizard • Films: *Titanic* is the most expensive film ever made at the time, costing between $250 and $300 million to produce and market, but will become the highest-grossing film of all time, raking in more than $580 million domestically; other films include *L.A. Confidential; Good Will Hunting; The Full Monty; Men in Black; Amistad*

E. EDUCATION, LITERATURE & THE FINE ARTS	F. RELIGION, THEOLOGY, PHILOSOPHY & PSYCHOLOGY	G. AMERICAN & UNITED METHODISM	H. BRITISH & WORLD METHODISM	
– Terry McMillan, *How Stella Got Her Groove Back* – John Berendt, *Midnight in the Garden of Good and Evil*	• Miroslav Volf publishes his award-winning work *Exclusion & Embrace: A Theological Exploration of Identity, Otherness, and Reconciliation* • Other notable publications include: – James W. Fowler, *Faithful Change: The Personal and Public Challenges of Postmodern Life* – Jürgen Moltmann, *The Coming of God: Christian Eschatology* – Larry L. Rasmussen, *Earth Community, Earth Ethics* – Richard Hays, *The Moral Vision of the New Testament* – N. T. Wright, *Jesus and the Victory of God* – Kathleen Norris, *The Cloister Walk*	– approves a constitutional amendment allowing annual conferences flexibility to "create structures unique to their mission, other mandated structures notwithstanding" • The United Methodist Student Movement (UMSM) is established under the sponsorship of the General Board of Higher Education and Ministry (GBHEM) • The UMPH publishes a Spanish language hymnal, *Mil Voces Para Celebrar*, and a new hymnal supplement, *The Faith We Sing* • Other notable publications include: – Karen B. Westerfield Tucker, ed., *The Sunday Service of the Methodists: Twentieth-Century Worship in Worldwide Methodism* – Charles Yrigoyen and Susan E. Warrick, eds., *Historical Dictionary of Methodism* (2nd ed., 2005) – Russell E. Richey, *The Methodist Conference in America* – Alice G. Knotts, *Fellowship of Love: Methodist Women Changing American Racial Attitudes, 1920–1968* – James E. Kirby, Russell E. Richey, and Kenneth E. Rowe, *The Methodists* (includes a bibliographic essay and biographical dictionary		**1996 cont.**
• John Tavener composes *Eternity's Sunrise*, based on poetry by William Blake, and dedicates it to the memory of Britain's Princess Diana • Wynton Marsalis wins the Pulitzer Prize in Music for his oratorio on slavery, *Blood on the Fields* • Maya Angelou's memoir *I Know Why the Caged Bird Sings* is removed from the ninth-grade English curriculum in Anne Arundel County, MD, because it "portrays white people as being horrible, nasty, stupid people" • Notable publications include: – Philip Roth, *American Pastoral* – Charles Frazier, *Cold Mountain* – John Grisham, *The Partner* – Thomas Pynchon, *Mason & Dixon* – Mitch Albom, *Tuesdays With Morrie*	• Mother Teresa dies in India and is mourned around the world • Notable publications include: – Michel Foucault, *The Archaeology of Knowledge* – James L. Kugel, *The Bible As It Was* – Geoffrey Wainwright, *For Our Salvation: Two Approaches to the Work of Christ* – Henry H. Knight III, *A Future for Truth: Evangelical Theology in a Postmodern World* – Charles Marsh, *God's Long Summer: Stories of Faith and Civil Rights*	• The UMC General Board of Global Missions launches the Millennium Fund for Mission • The seventh International Congress of United Methodist Men meets • Notable publications include: – Dennis M. Campbell, Russell E. Richey, and William B. Lawrence, eds., *Connectionalism: Ecclesiology, Mission, and Identity* (United Methodism and American Culture, vol. 1) – Samuel J. Rogal, *A Biographical Dictionary of 18th Century Methodism* (10 vols. by 2000) – Thomas Edward Frank, *Polity, Practice, and the Mission of The United Methodist Church* (updated edition 2002) – Kenneth J. Collins, *The Scripture Way of Salvation: The Heart of John Wesley's Theology* – W. Stephen Gunter, et al., *Wesley and the Quadrilateral: Renewing the Conversation*	• The MCNZ accepts the ordination of homosexual persons; some members and congregations withdraw as a result • The World Methodist Evangelism Institute holds its sixth International Evangelism Seminar • The 1997 World Methodist Peace Award is given to the Community of St. Egidio, a volunteer service group organized along the lines of Catholic lay movements in Renaissance, Italy • The tenth Oxford Institute of Methodist Theological Studies meets	**1997**

	A. WORLD HISTORY & POLITICS	B. AMERICAN HISTORY & POLITICS	C. SCIENCE, MEDICINE & TECHNOLOGY	D. DAILY LIFE, POPULAR CULTURE & ENTERTAINMENT
1998	• The US launches missile attacks on targets in Sudan and Afghanistan following terrorist attacks on US embassies in Kenya and Tanzania • The Russian economy collapses, producing the worst political and humanitarian crisis there since the demise of the Soviet Union • The signature of the "Good Friday Agreement" marks movement toward an end of the "troubles" in Northern Ireland • The British parliament passes the Government of Wales Act 1998, which establishes the National Assembly for Wales • Both India and Pakistan test nuclear weapons for the first time • Political protests become riots in Indonesia and force the resignation of long-time president Suharto • Gerhard Schröder becomes chancellor of Germany • Osama bin Laden proclaims "Jihad against Jews and Crusaders"; al-Qaeda bombs US embassies in Kenya and Tanzania, killing 224 • NATO gives Yugoslavian president Slobodan Milošević an ultimatum: either Yugoslavia withdraws its troops from Kosovo and takes steps toward peace, or it will face NATO air strikes • The European Court of Human Rights (often referred to informally as the "Strasbourg Court") is instituted	• A massive ice storm, caused by El Niño, strikes New England, southern Ontario, and Quebec, resulting in widespread power failures, severe damage to forests, and a number of deaths • Smoking is banned in all California bars and restaurants • The US House of Representatives votes to impeach President Clinton on charges of perjury and obstruction of justice in the wake of the Monica Lewinsky affair; he is the second president in US history to be formally impeached; the US Senate acquits him after a trial in 1999 • For the third time since becoming a US Commonwealth in 1952, Puerto Rico votes to retain its commonwealth status over either statehood or independence (previous: 1967 and 1992) • Washington National Airport is renamed Ronald Reagan Washington National Airport • Matthew Shepard, a Wyoming college student, dies after being badly beaten and tied to a fence; he becomes a symbol of victims of gay-bashing, sparking public reflection on homophobia	• Former astronaut John Glenn, aboard the space shuttle *Discovery*, at age 77 becomes the oldest human ever to fly in space • Construction begins on the International Space Station as NASA celebrates its 40th anniversary • NASA's *Lunar Prospector* spacecraft is launched into orbit around the moon and its *Athena* probe finds evidence of frozen water in permanently shadowed craters near the moon's poles • The Petronis Towers 1 and 2 in Kuala Lumpur, Malaysia, become the tallest buildings in the world, only 88 stories but 1,483 feet tall due to 110-foot decorative spires • Japanese engineers complete the Akashi Kaikyo Bridge; it is the longest suspension bridge in the world, stretching 12,828 feet with a central span of 6,527 feet • The FDA approves Viagra (sildenafil), the first oral drug treatment for male impotence • Dow Corning Co. agrees to a $3.2 billion settlement for tens of thousands of women claiming injury from manufacturer's silicone breast implants	• The revival of the 1966 musical *Cabaret* opens on Broadway [it runs for 2,377 performances before closing in 2004] • An estimated 76 million viewers watch the last episode of *Seinfeld* • *Sex and the City* premieres on HBO • Mark McGwire (70) and Sammy Sosa (66) both break the 1961 home run record of Roger Maris (61) • Phish holds its Millennium Celebration on the Big Cypress Seminole Indian Reservation in the Florida Everglades; 85,000 people show up for two nights of music culminating with a seven-and-a-half hour second set beginning at midnight and ending at sunrise; the band breaks up a few months later, feeling they have nothing left to accomplish musically • Perennial pop favorite James Taylor wins the best pop album Grammy award for his *Hourglass* • J. K. Rowling publishes the second volume in the Harry Potter series, *Harry Potter and the Chamber of Secrets* • Teenage sensation Britney Spears releases her debut album *Baby One More Time*, which includes the hit single of the same title and "(You Drive Me) Crazy" • Films: *Saving Private Ryan*; *Shakespeare in Love*; *Gods and Monsters*; *The Thin Red Line*; *The Horse Whisperer* • Winter Olympics: Nagano
1999	• NATO launches an intensive air campaign against Serbia over the killing and deportation of ethnic Albanians in Kosovo; Serbs agree to withdraw troops • Boris Yeltsin resigns as president of Russia and is replaced by Vladimir Putin • Russian troops reenter the "rebel" province of Chechnya • Hurricane Mitch devastates Central America, leaving an estimated 10,000 people dead in Honduras and Guatemala • NATO expands as Poland, Hungary, and the Czech Republic are admitted to membership • Military coup brings General Pervez Musharraf to power in Pakistan • The euro (EUR or €) becomes legal tender in twelve of the fifteen countries that form the European Union; Britain chooses to retain the pound • The US and China sign a historic trade agreement • Ehud Barak becomes prime minister of Israel • Nelson Mandela chooses not to run for a second term as president of South Africa; he is succeeded by Thabo Mbeki • Australians vote down a proposal to replace Queen Elizabeth II as head of state with a president chosen by Parliament • War erupts in Kosovo after Serbian forces loyal to Yugoslavian president Milošević begin killing and deporting ethnic Albanians; NATO forces launch an intensive air campaign against the Serbs; Milošević finally agrees to withdraw Serbian troops from Kosovo	• A school shooting incident at Columbine High School in Littleton, CO, leaves 14 students (including the 2 shooters) and 1 teacher dead and 23 others wounded • "Antiglobalization" riots break out in Seattle, WA, when an estimated 40,000 people from a wide variety of groups gather to protest against a meeting of the World Trade Organization, causing $2 to 3 million in property damage • The Edwards Dam on the Kennebec River in Maine, built in 1837, is the first dam in the US to be removed for environmental reasons, allowing Atlantic salmon to travel upstream to spawn • Jack Kevorkian, known as "Doctor Death," is convicted of murder for assisting terminally ill patients in committing suicide by administering lethal drug injections • The US Senate refuses to ratify the 1996 Comprehensive Test Ban Treaty; conservative critics claim that it compromises US national security • The US formally transfers ownership of the Panama Canal Zone to Panama in accordance with the 1977 Panama Canal Treaty	• The *Ikonos* satellite can detect an object on Earth as small as a card table • NASA is embarrassed when its *Mars Climate Orbiter* is lost due to miscommunication between programmers about English vs. metric measurements used in calculating its flight path • The world worries about the turn of the millennium and the "Y2K bug"; great sums are spent to ensure that computers don't suddenly stop working on January 1, 2000 • Archaeological excavations in Kenya unearth stone tools dated at 2.3 million years old, more than 700,000 years older than any similar tools previously found • The European Union expresses serious concerns about genetically modified foods from the US • Home video games expand with the Sega Dreamcast 128-bit operating system • The First Internet Bank of Indiana, the first full-service bank available only on the Net, opens for business • Microsoft releases the Windows 2000 operating system	• The 450-foot tall London Eye, a giant observation wheel located in the Jubilee Gardens, is built as part of London's millennium celebrations • White rapper Eminem (Marshall Mathers) wins a Grammy for his best-selling album *The Shady Slim LP*, produced by Dr. Dre • The Red Hot Chili Peppers release their most popular album, *Californication* • The Backstreet Boys release the album *Millennium*, which sets a record for most albums sold in the first week of release with 1.13 million copies • *The Sopranos* premieres on HBO • Wayne Gretzky retires from professional ice hockey as the all-time NHL leader in points (2,857), goals (894), and assists (1,963) • The Women's National Basketball Association (WNBA) is founded; it will become the most successful women's professional sports organization • The cost of a US first-class postage stamp increases to 33¢ • J. K. Rowling publishes the third volume in the Harry Potter series, *Harry Potter and the Prisoner of Azkaban* • Films: *American Beauty*; *The Talented Mr. Ripley*; *October Sky*; *The Matrix*; *The Cider House Rules*; *Star Wars: Episode I—The Phantom Menace*

E. EDUCATION, LITERATURE & THE FINE ARTS	F. RELIGION, THEOLOGY, PHILOSOPHY & PSYCHOLOGY	G. AMERICAN & UNITED METHODISM	H. BRITISH & WORLD METHODISM	
• Edward Elgar's unfinished *Symphony No. 3*, completed by Anthony Payne, is performed for the first time at the Royal Festival Hall in London • Notable publications include: – Alice McDermott, *Charming Billy* – Tom Wolfe, *A Man in Full* – Tom Brokaw, *The Greatest Generation* – John Irving, *A Widow for One Year* – Tom Clancy, *Rainbow Six*	• Soulforce is established; it is a national and ecumenical network of individuals and groups "committed to research, teach, and apply the principles of nonviolence as taught and lived by Gandhi and King on behalf of sexual and gender minorities" • Notable publications include: – William J. Abraham, *Canon and Criterion in Christian Theology: From the Fathers to Feminism* – Walter Wink, *The Powers That Be: Theology for a New Millennium* – Kathleen Norris, *Amazing Grace: A Vocabulary of Faith*	• The UMC, AMEC, AMEZC, and CMEC all approve establishment of a Pan-Methodist Commission on Union • The Confessing Movement holds its first annual national conference in Tulsa, OK • The UMC Judicial Council rules that the statement added to the *Social Principles* by the 1996 General Conference prohibiting clergy from performing "homosexual unions" has the force of church law despite its placement in the *Social Principles* • The fifteenth Assembly of United Methodist Women meets • The Women's Division adopts guidelines for the formation of teen women and college/university women units of United Methodist Women • Notable publications include: – Dennis M. Campbell, Russell E. Richey, and William B. Lawrence, eds., *The People(s) Called Methodist: Forms and Reforms of Their Life* (United Methodism and American Culture, vol. 2) – Kenneth E. Rowe, ed., *United Methodist Studies: Basic Bibliographies* (4th ed.) – Theodore R. Weber, *Politics in the Order of Salvation: Transforming Wesleyan Political Ethics* – Theodore Runyon, *The New Creation: John Wesley's Theology Today* – Randy L. Maddox, ed., *Rethinking Wesley's Theology for Contemporary Methodism* – John H. Wigger, *Taking Heaven by Storm: Methodism and the Rise of Popular Christianity in America*	• The MC [UK] receives all existing members of Methodist Diaconal Order into full conference connexion • The World Methodist Council gives the World Methodist Peace Award to Kofi Annan, Secretary General of the United Nations, for his work with that organization • The Wesley Heritage Foundation sponsors publication of the works of John Wesley in Spanish: *Obras de Wesley*, following the pattern of Wesley's own publications, is a 14-volume set that includes sermons, doctrinal treatises, Bible commentaries, faith and works spirituality, journals, and letters (Justo L. González, gen. ed.) • IDC Publishers produces *The People Called Methodists: A Documentary History of the Methodist Church in Great Britain and Ireland on Microfiche*, a collection that includes a vast array of primary sources (letters, diaries, journals, pamphlets, periodicals, tracts, monographs, and minutes) covering the period from 1738 to 1932	1998
• The Seattle Art Museum returns a painting by Henri Matisse to the family of a Jewish art collector from whom the canvas had been taken by the Nazis in 1941 • The Metropolitan Opera premieres John Harbison's *The Great Gatsby*, based on the classic novel by F. Scott Fitzgerald • George Bellows's painting *Polo Crowd* sells at auction for more than $27 million, a record for a work by an American artist • Ernest Hemingway's 100th birthday is marked by the publication of an unfinished novel, *True at First Light*, edited by his son, Patrick • Other notable publications include: – John Papajohn, *The Hyphenated American: The Hidden Injuries of Culture* – J. M. Coetzee, *Disgrace* – Seamus Heaney, *Beowulf* – Toni Morrison, *Paradise* – Joanne Harris, *Chocolat* – John le Carré, *Single & Single*	• The third Parliament of the World's Religions is held in Cape Town • The Lutheran World Federation and the Catholic Church reach a measure of agreement on a divisive theological issue dating back to the 16th century; the Joint Declaration on the Doctrine of Justification states that "we are saved by God's grace through faith alone rather than by our own efforts" but leaves open questions about the spiritual significance of human "good works" • After 902 years, Winchester Cathedral in England allows an all-girl choir to sing evensong • Notable publications include: – Lamin Sanneh, *Abolitionists Abroad: American Blacks and the Making of Modern West Africa* – Desmond Tutu, *No Future Without Forgiveness*	• Jimmy Creech (member of Nebraska Conference) is charged with violating UMC law by officiating at same-sex union services; Creech, who had already undergone a clergy trial in 1998 for similar charges, is found guilty in 1999 and loses his clergy credentials • Over 900 members of the Confessing Movement meet in Indianapolis and adopt "The Indianapolis Affirmation," which speaks to a number of issues to come before the 2000 General Conference; it includes the recommendation that "If there are clergy and laity or local churches who cannot abide by and remain true to the teachings of Scripture and our doctrine, we encourage General Conference to provide for an exit process with pension, property, and without penalty" • Notable publications include: – Dennis M. Campbell, Russell E. Richey, and William B. Lawrence, eds., *Doctrines and Discipline: Methodist Theology and Practice* (United Methodism and American Culture, vol. 3) – Dennis M. Campbell, Russell E. Richey, and William B. Lawrence, eds., *Questions for the Twenty-First Century Church* (United Methodism and American Culture, vol. 4) – Jean Miller Schmidt, *Grace Sufficient: A History of Women in American Methodism, 1760–1939* – Ted A. Campbell, *Methodist Doctrine: The Essentials* – Kenneth J. Collins, *A Real Christian: The Life of John Wesley*	• The MC [UK] Conference meets for the first time with separate diaconal and presbyterial sessions and issues the ecclesiological report *Called to Love and Praise* • The *Methodist Worship Book*, superseding the 1975 *Service Book*, is published • Westminster College is absorbed by Oxford Brooks University • The World Methodist Council gives the World Methodist Peace Award to the Grandmothers of the Plaza de Mayo in Buenos Aires, Argentina, for their protest against the violence and death then occurring in their country	1999

	A. WORLD HISTORY & POLITICS	B. AMERICAN HISTORY & POLITICS	C. SCIENCE, MEDICINE & TECHNOLOGY	D. DAILY LIFE, POPULAR CULTURE & ENTERTAINMENT
2000	• The population of the world passes the 6 billion mark • Yugoslavian president Slobodan Milošević is deposed then handed over to a UN trial on war crimes charge • After enduring increasingly sophisticated attacks by Hezbollah fighters for years, Israel withdraws its military forces from southern Lebanon, ending a long occupation • Agents of al-Qaeda launch a suicide bomb attack on the USS *Cole* in the harbor of Aden, Yemen, blowing a 40 x 40 foot hole in her hull, killing 17 US sailors, and injuring 39 more • Britain's beloved "Queen Mum" (more formally known as Her Majesty Queen Elizabeth The Queen Mother) celebrates her 100th birthday • The Russian nuclear submarine *Kursk* sinks in the Barents Sea; the entire 118-man crew perishes • A summit between the leaders of North Korea and South Korea highlight a year of improving relations between two countries that are technically still at war • Britain lifts a long-standing ban on the service of homosexuals in the armed forces • Peruvian president Alberto Fujimori flees to his native Japan when allegations of corruption in his government begin to emerge	• The US census reports that the population is 281,421,906: – whites: 194,552,774 (69.1%) – blacks: 33,947,837 (12.0%) – other: 52,921,295 (18.9%) • The US national debt is $5,674,178,209,886 • Microsoft founder Bill Gates, who has become the richest man in the world, creates the Bill and Melinda Gates Foundation as a private charitable organization devoted to the promotion of global health and education • Scores of "dot com" companies fail, causing a crash of the US stock market • Six-year-old Elian Gonzalez, who had been rescued at sea in 1999 after his mother died attempting to reach the US with him, is returned to his father in Cuba despite the efforts of anti-Castro relatives in Florida to gain custody and keep him in the US • Vermont becomes the first state in the country to give legal recognition to civil unions between gay or lesbian couples • In *Santa Fe v. Doe*, the US Supreme Court rules that permitting student-initiated and student-led prayer at public school football games violates the establishment clause of the 1st Amendment • Despite receiving 500,000 fewer popular votes than Vice President Gore and his running mate, Joseph Lieberman (Democratic Party), George W. Bush is elected as president and Richard B. Cheney as vice president (Republican Party) after the US Supreme Court, by a 5-4 decision, rules against a manual recount of disputed ballots in certain Florida counties, giving Bush/Cheney an electoral college majority • Condoleezza Rice is the first woman, and the first African American, to serve as National Security Adviser	• NASA is embarrassed again when its *Mars Polar Lander* is destroyed on impact with the Martian surface • Doomsday predictions of the Y2K computer disaster throughout the world prove inaccurate; the new millennium arrives glitch-free • Work is completed on decoding and mapping the human genetic code (DNA) or human genome • The first official crew boards the International Space Station • 21.8 million people have died of AIDS since the late 1970s; infections rise in Eastern Europe, Russia, India, Africa, and Southeast Asia; scientists note the spread of drug-resistant strains of HIV • NASA reports that the Antarctic ozone hole in the atmosphere is the largest ever recorded, three times the size of the US • A Concorde supersonic airliner crashes on takeoff from Paris, killing all 113 people aboard; all Concorde service between Europe and North America is suspended following the crash	• "Reality TV" mania hits the US with the success of shows such as *Who Wants to Be a Millionaire?* and *Survivor*, which create "real-life" situations filled with stress and tension with which contestants must cope • The Internet transforms the world of popular music; the Recording Industry Association of America (RIAA) takes legal action against Napster and other companies offering music over the Internet for download without any fees or royalty payments; Napster agrees to stop distributing copyrighted music for free, then teams up with industry giant Bertelsmann to provide material for a fee • The last original *Peanuts* comic strip is published when the creator, Charles Schulz, dies • Tiger Woods wins the US Open, the British Open, and the PGA Championship, becoming the first person since Ben Hogan (1953) to win three major golf tournament titles in one year • J. K. Rowling publishes the fourth book in the Harry Potter series, *Harry Potter and the Goblet of Fire* • U2 releases the album *All That You Can't Leave Behind*, including the hit single "Beautiful Day" • Rap star Eminem releases *The Marshall Mathers LP*; it becomes the fastest-selling rap album in history and later receives a Grammy award for Best Rap Album but provokes intense criticism from gay rights and women's advocacy groups, which condemn it as homophobic and misogynistic • The five-member "boy band" 'N Sync releases its debut album *No Strings Attached*, which sells 800,000 copies in the first two weeks and more than 2.4 million copies in the first year, more than doubling the previous record for first-album sales • Films: *Crouching Tiger, Hidden Dragon; Erin Brockovich; Gladiator; Chicken Run; O Brother, Where Art Thou?* • Summer Olympics: Sydney

E. EDUCATION, LITERATURE & THE FINE ARTS	F. RELIGION, THEOLOGY, PHILOSOPHY & PSYCHOLOGY	G. AMERICAN & UNITED METHODISM	H. BRITISH & WORLD METHODISM	
• The Tate Modern, a new art museum, opens in London in the converted Bankside Power Station • To commemorate the 250th anniversary of Johann Sebastian Bach's death, the International Bach Academy in Stuttgart, Germany, commissions and premieres four new passions, one for each Gospel, each by a different composer and in a different style: – Tan Dun's ritualistic *Water Passion After St. Matthew* features the sounds of ancient Chinese stringed instruments, a western chamber choir, percussion in the style of Beijing opera, and parts written for cellist Yo-Yo Ma and country fiddler Mark O'Connor – Osvoldo Golijov's vibrant and vital *La Pasión Según San Marcos*, sung in Spanish, is infused with the spirit of Afro-Cuban music and Brazilian rhythms (bossa nova, tango, rumba, and flamenco) – Wolfgang Rihm's dark and spellbinding *Deus Passus: Fragments of a St. Luke Passion* uses a delicate, impressionistic musical palette and employs not only biblical texts but also texts from German poets and parts of the Stabat Mater – Sophia Gubaidulina's sonically incandescent, apocalyptic *Johannes-Passion* is emphatically Russian in spirit, featuring a chorus, orchestra and soloists from the Kirov Opera, led by Valery Gergiev • Peter Maxwell Davies composes his *Symphony No. 8 (Antarctic)* • Arvo Pärt composes *Silouan's Song*, for cello and piano • John Tavener composes his *Song of the Cosmos* • Notable publications include: – Margaret Atwood, *The Blind Assassin* – Rosamunde Pilcher, *Winter Solstice* – Linda Grant, *When I Lived in Modern Times* – Sidney Poitier, *The Measure of a Man: A Spiritual Autobiography*	• As part of his observance of the holy year marking the start of the third Christian millennium, Pope John Paul II publicly repents for the church's past and present acts of intolerance and injustice toward Jews, women, indigenous peoples, and others • The Southern Baptist Convention overturns its 1994 decision to leave the ordination of women to the discretion of local congregations, declaring that "while both men and women are gifted for service in the church, the office of pastor is limited to men as qualified by Scripture"; women who currently hold ordination credentials are allowed to retain them, but no additional women will be ordained • Bruce Wilkinson's inspirational book *The Prayer of Jabez: Breaking Through to the Blessed Life* becomes an international success, selling over 9 million copies and receiving the Evangelical Christian Publishers Association's "Book of the Year" award; it also attracts serious theological criticism for its unambiguous advocacy of the "gospel of prosperity" • Other notable publications include: – Mark Juergensmeyer, *Terror in the Mind of God: The Global Rise of Religious Violence* – Karen Armstrong, *The Battle for God: Fundamentalism in Judaism, Christianity and Islam* – Sallie McFague, *Life Abundant: Rethinking Theology and Economy for a Planet in Peril*	• The UMC bishops continue the Episcopal Initiative on Children and Poverty • The UMC General Conference: – rejects a proposal to create a Global Conference to replace the General Conference as the church's top legislative body, with the General Conference becoming one of several geographic central conferences – continues the denomination's prohibition of rebaptism and rejects a service of dedication of infants as an alternative to baptism – refuses to consider proposals to let congregations leave the UMC with their property or to affiliate formally with unofficial caucuses – reaffirms the church's position that homosexual behavior is "incompatible with Christian teaching" – moves the 1996 statement prohibiting clergy from performing "homosexual unions" from the *Social Principles* to the "chargeable offenses" section of the *Discipline* – establishes the Fund for Theological Education in Post-Communist Europe to support the training of UM clergy there – authorizes GBHEM to develop procedures for certification in several specialized ministries: Christian Education, Youth Ministry, Music, Camp and Retreat Ministry, Spiritual Formation, Evangelism, and Older Adult Ministry – reaffirms the need to pursue full participation of all women in the denomination and outlines a vision for working toward that goal – approves publication of a bilingual Korean-English hymnal – approves a resolution of repentance for racism in the church – renews "Strengthening the Black Church for the 21st Century" as a mission initiative – forms the Task Force on Global Pensions to deal with the pension inequities among UMC clergy around the globe, particularly in the central conferences • The UMC, AMEC, AMEZC, and CMEC establish a Commission on Pan-Methodist Cooperation and Union, superseding two previous commissions • The Reconciling Congregations Program changes its name to Reconciling Ministries Network • The Good News Movement, the Confessing Movement, and the Institute on Religion and Democracy cooperate to form the Coalition for United Methodist Accountability (CUMA) • The AMEC elects Vashti McKenzie as the first female bishop in its 213-year history • Notable publications include: – Russell E. Richey, Kenneth E. Rowe, and Jean Miller Schmidt, eds., *The Methodist Experience in America: A Sourcebook* – John E. Harnish, *The Orders of Ministry in The United Methodist Church* – James E. Kirby, *The Episcopacy in American Methodism* – Kenneth J. Collins, *A Real Christian: The Life of John Wesley* – Sondra Matthaei, *Making Disciples: Faith Formation in the Wesleyan Tradition*	• The Baltic Mission Center in Tallinn, Estonia, is opened and dedicated by the UMC in Estonia; it is intended to provide training for a new generation of church leaders for service across the former Soviet Union • The World Methodist Council gives the World Methodist Peace Award to Nelson Mandela, former president of South Africa, honoring his role as a "symbol of freedom, justice and peace" for the last half of the 20th century • The UMC is reorganized and reestablished in Uganda • The Wesleyan Methodist Church of New Zealand is formed by conservatives who leave the MCNZ because of their opposition to the ordination of homosexuals • The United Church of Pakistan ordains its first women deacons • Notable publications include: – John A. Vickers, ed., *A Dictionary of Methodism in Britain and Ireland* – M. Douglas Meeks, ed., *Trinity, Community, and Power: Mapping Trajectories in Wesleyan Theology* [papers from the tenth Oxford Institute of Methodist Theological Studies, 1997]	**2000**

	A. WORLD HISTORY & POLITICS	B. AMERICAN HISTORY & POLITICS	C. SCIENCE, MEDICINE & TECHNOLOGY	D. DAILY LIFE, POPULAR CULTURE & ENTERTAINMENT
2001	• The military attack on Afghanistan by the US and its allies quickly topples the Taliban regime but fails to capture Osama bin Laden • The war crimes trial of Slobodan Milošević, former president of Serbia and Yugoslavia, begins in The Hague; he is charged with crimes against humanity in Croatia and Kosovo and with genocide in Bosnia • Ariel Sharon becomes prime minister in Israel; the level of violence in the Israeli-Palestinian conflict increases dramatically as the second Intifada erupts • Portugal approves same-sex civil unions but limits adoption rights to opposite-sex couples • A US reconnaissance plane is forced to land in China after a midair collision with a Chinese fighter jet; the crew is held by Chinese authorities for 11 days; angry diplomatic exchanges take place between Washington and Beijing • Laws that permit marriage for same-sex couples and grant same-sex couples adoption rights come into effect in the Netherlands	• Terrorists attack the US on September 11: the north and south towers of the World Trade Center in New York City and the Pentagon in Washington, DC, are hit by separate commercial airliners hijacked by Islamic militants; both towers of the World Trade Center collapse; over 3,000 people are killed and many thousands more injured; a fourth hijacked airliner crashes in rural Pennsylvania after passengers apparently attack the hijackers • Congress passes an Authorization for Use of Military Force (AUMF) giving President Bush the power to use "all necessary and appropriate force against those nations, organizations, or persons he determines planned, authorized, committed, or aided" the 9/11 terrorist attacks • The US identifies Islamic militant Osama bin Laden's al-Qaeda network as responsible for the attacks; President Bush declares a "War on Terror" • Congress passes the USA Patriot Act, which significantly increases the surveillance and investigative powers of law enforcement agencies inside the US but does not set aside the provisions of FISA (1977) • Congress approves the creation of the Department of Homeland Security, which absorbs some of the functions of 22 different government agencies, including FEMA • The US accuses Saddam Hussein of developing "weapons of mass destruction" (WMDs) and threatens an invasion of Iraq • Timothy McVeigh is executed for the 1995 bombing of the Murrah Federal Building in Oklahoma City, OK • Former Klansman Thomas Blanton Jr. is convicted and sentenced to life in prison for the 1963 bombing of the Sixteenth Street Baptist Church in Birmingham, as is his associate Bobby Frank Cherry in a separate trial in 2002	• President Bush announces that he will permit federal funding of research on stem cells from human embryos, but only those cells that have already been extracted • Robert Tools becomes the first person to be equipped with an entirely self-contained artificial heart, the battery-powered mechanical AbioCor • The National Academy of Sciences reports an increase in global warming and reaffirms the view that human activity is largely responsible • The US Geological Survey predicts that the city of New Orleans may be under water by the year 2100 due to subsidence (the natural sinking of land), wetland loss, predicted sea-level rise, and an absence of proper restoration programs • Microsoft releases the Windows XP operating system in Home and Professional versions • The Mir space station, launched by the USSR in 1986, falls out of orbit into the South Pacific • Apple brings its portable digital music player, the iPod, to the market, changing the digital music world forever	• The "America: A Tribute to Heroes" benefit concert is organized in the aftermath of the 9/11 attacks on the World Trade Center and The Pentagon to raise money for the victims and their families, particularly but not limited to the New York City firefighters; the concert is simulcast by over 35 network and cable channels, and features a "who's who" cast of performers • *The Producers*, adapted for the stage by Mel Brooks from the 1968 film, opens on Broadway [it is still running at the end of 2005 with almost 2,000 performances] • Tiger Woods wins the Masters golf tournament, completing the "Tiger Slam" by holding all four major tournament titles at the same time; critics complain that it is not the same as the 1930 "grand slam" of Bobby Jones since he does not win all four titles [of this era] in the same calendar year • Barry Bonds sets a major league record with 71 home runs in one season • The TV show *American Idol* debuts, combining features of "amateur hour" talent shows with reality-based TV, and becomes enormously successful • The "girl group" Destiny's Child releases the album *Survivor*, including the controversial hit single "Bootylicious" • Ken Burns's remarkable 10-part, 19-hour series *Jazz*, telling the story of the development of "America's music," is broadcast on PBS • The new Country Music Hall of Fame and Museum opens in Nashville • The cost of a US first-class postage stamp increases to 34¢ • Films: *The Lord of the Rings: The Fellowship of the Ring*; *Shrek*; *A Beautiful Mind*; *Black Hawk Down*; *Pearl Harbor*; *Harry Potter and the Sorcerer's Stone*; *Monsters, Inc.*
2002	• Russia formally becomes an ally of NATO • US and Russia sign the Strategic Offensive Reduction Treaty (SORT), designed to reduce the number of deployed strategic nuclear weapons on each side to between 1,700 and 2,200 each by the year 2012 • Israel invades the Gaza Strip and the West Bank; Palestinian suicide bombings increase • Bomb attacks on tourist areas on the Indonesian resort island of Bali kill more than 200; the regional extremist group Jemaah Islamiah, which has links to al-Qaeda, is widely blamed • Zimbabwe is suspended from membership in the British Commonwealth, then withdraws formally in 2003 • The Bahamian-flagged oil tanker *Prestige*, carrying about 20 million gallons of heavy fuel oil, splits in two in rough weather and sinks off the coast of Spain • The trial of Slobodan Milošević on charges of crimes against humanity opens at The Hague	• President Bush labels Iraq, Iran, and North Korea an "axis of evil" and declares that the US will wage war against states that develop weapons of mass destruction • The Enron Corporation declares bankruptcy, the largest in US history to date; revelations of corporate accounting shenanigans prompt congressional investigations • John Allen Muhammad and his teenage cohort, Lee Boyd Malvo, are found guilty of a series of sniper shootings in which ten people are killed and three wounded in Virginia and Maryland; they are linked to similar shootings in several other states; Muhammad is sentenced to death, Malvo to life in prison • President Bush announces that the US is unilaterally withdrawing from the 1972 ABM Treaty and advocates the development of a missile defense shield for the US	• Scientists at the State University of New York at Stony Brook create the first synthetic virus • American inventor Dean Kamen unveils the Segway Human Transport • The highly infectious Severe Acute Respiratory Syndrome (SARS) virus suddenly appears in China and causes worldwide concern; by early 2003 cases are identified in Singapore, Vietnam, Hong Kong, Taiwan, and Toronto, Canada; some isolated cases also appear in the US and Europe • The National Academy of Sciences issues a report opposing human reproductive cloning but strongly supporting therapeutic cloning using embryonic stem cells to help search for cures for such illnesses as Parkinson's Disease and diabetes • The UN announces that the rising death toll from AIDS could reach 65 million by 2020 if efforts to prevent its spread are not dramatically increased	• Paul McCartney and U2 perform during the halftime show for Super Bowl XXXVI; the performance becomes a tribute to the victims of the 9/11 terrorist attack • The "Concert For George" is held at the Royal Albert Hall in London as a memorial to George Harrison on the first anniversary of his death to benefit the Material World Charitable Foundation; directed by Eric Clapton, the performers include Paul McCartney, Ringo Starr, Clapton, Jeff Lynne, Ravi Shankar, and Billy Preston • The cost of a US first-class postage stamp increases to 37¢ • Films: *The Lord of the Rings: The Two Towers*; *Chicago*; *Gladiator*; *My Big Fat Greek Wedding*; *The Quiet American*; *The Pianist*; *Harry Potter and the Chamber of Secrets*; *Star Wars: Episode II—Attack of the Clones* • Winter Olympics: Salt Lake City

E. EDUCATION, LITERATURE & THE FINE ARTS	F. RELIGION, THEOLOGY, PHILOSOPHY & PSYCHOLOGY	G. AMERICAN & UNITED METHODISM	H. BRITISH & WORLD METHODISM	
• African American violinist Regina Carter becomes the first nonclassical artist ever allowed to play Nicolò Paganini's famous violin "The Cannon" (an Italian national treasure made by Guarneri del Gesu in 1743) when she records the album *Paganini: After a Dream* • Notable publications include: – Laura Hillenbrand, *Seabiscuit: An American Legend* – John le Carré, *The Constant Gardener* – Amy Tan, *The Bonesetter's Daughter* – Stephen King, *Dreamcatcher* – John Grisham, *A Painted House* – Yann Martel, *Life of Pi*	• Notable publications include: – Stanley Hauerwas, *With the Grain of the Universe: The Church's Witness and Natural Theology* – A. K. M. Adam, ed., *Postmodern Interpretations of the Bible: A Reader* – Daniel L. Migliore, *Faith Seeking Understanding: An Introduction to Christian Theology* – Diana L. Eck, *A New Religious America: How a "Christian Country" Has Now Become the World's Most Religiously Diverse Nation*	• The eighth International Congress of United Methodist Men meets • The UMC Judicial Council rules that the central conferences have jurisdiction over adaptations of *The Book of Discipline* except for matters protected by the UMC constitution • The UMC begins the third round of bilateral dialogue with the Evangelical Lutheran Church in America (ELCA) • Representatives of the AMEZC and CMEC meet to discuss the possibility of union • UMPH publishes *Come, Let Us Worship* (*The Korean-English United Methodist Hymnal*) • Other notable publications include: – Paul Chilcote, ed., *Her Own Story: Autobiographical Portraits of Early Methodist Women* – Nathan O. Hatch and John H. Wigger, eds., *Methodism and the Shaping of American Culture* – Theodore R. Weber, *Politics in the Order of Salvation: New Directions in Wesleyan Political Ethics* – Bryan P. Stone and Thomas Jay Oord, eds., *Thy Nature and Thy Name Is Love: Wesleyan and Process Theologies in Dialogue* – John R. Tyson and Kenneth J. Collins, eds., *Conversion in the Wesleyan Tradition* – William C. Kostlevy, ed., *Historical Dictionary of the Holiness Movement*	• The eighteenth World Methodist Conference meets in Brighton, England • The World Methodist Evangelism Institute holds its seventh International Evangelism Seminar • The World Methodist Council gives the World Methodist Peace Award to Joe Hale, the retiring General Secretary of the World Methodist Council, in recognition of "his valiant leadership as a proponent of peace and ecumenical unity throughout the world" • Christina Le Moignan and Ann Leck are elected (respectively) as president and vice president of Conference by the MC[UK]; it is the first time both positions have been filled by women simultaneously	**2001**
• The Bibliotheca Alexandrina, named after the ancient library of Alexandria, formally opens in Egypt • *The Journal of Negro History* (1916) is renamed *The Journal of African American History* • George Crumb composes his *Eine Kleine Mitternachtmusik* (A Little Midnight Music) for piano • Notable publications include: – Peter Jennings, *In Search of America* – Diane McWhorter, *Carry Me Home: Birmingham, Alabama: The Climactic Battle of the Civil Rights Revolution* – Tracy Chevalier, *The Girl with the Pearl Earring*	• The Roman Catholic Church is rocked by accusations of sexual abuse by priests and cover-ups by the hierarchy around the world; the controversy leads to the resignation of several bishops, including Bernard Cardinal Law of Boston, and to costly financial settlements with victims; the US Conference of Catholic Bishops issues a Charter for the Protection of Children and Young People • After more than forty years, the members of the Consultation on Church Union (COCU, 1960) agree to stop "consulting" and start more fully living their Christian unity by establishing a new relationship known as Churches Uniting in Christ (CUIC) • Rick Warren, the founding and senior pastor of Saddleback Church, creates a phenomenon with the publication of his book *The Purpose-Driven Life: What on Earth Am I Here For?* [by the end of 2005 it has sold over 25 million copies and been translated into over 50 languages]	• The UMC begins formal bilateral dialogue with the Episcopal Church in the US (ongoing) • The sixteenth Assembly of United Methodist Women meets • The GCCUIC (UMC) initiates dialogue with representatives of the Muslim Public Affairs Council in the US (ongoing) • Notable publications include: – Scott J. Jones, *United Methodist Doctrine: The Extreme Center* – Richard P. Heitzenrater, ed., *The Poor and the People Called Methodists* – S T Kimbrough, Jr., ed., *Orthodox and Wesleyan Spirituality*	• Churches in Cambodia, Honduras, and the Côte d'Ivoire (Ivory Coast) are formally approved as "mission churches" by the UM Board of Global Ministries • The World Methodist Council gives the World Methodist Peace Award to Boris Trajkovski, president of the Republic of Macedonia, for his efforts to bring peace to his region of the Balkans • The eleventh Oxford Institute of Methodist Theological Studies meets • Notable publications include David Carter, *Love Bade Me Welcome: A British Methodist Perspective on the Church*	**2002**

	A. WORLD HISTORY & POLITICS	B. AMERICAN HISTORY & POLITICS	C. SCIENCE, MEDICINE & TECHNOLOGY	D. DAILY LIFE, POPULAR CULTURE & ENTERTAINMENT
2002 cont.	• The euro (EUR or) becomes the sole currency in twelve of the fifteen countries that form the European Union • Britain celebrates the Golden Jubilee of the coronation of Queen Elizabeth II in 1952 • Hu Jintao succeeds Jiang Zemin as general secretary of the Community Party in China and becomes president in 2003			
2003	• The second Gulf War begins when US and British forces invade Iraq to topple the regime of Saddam Hussein; the major fighting is soon over, but resistance by insurgent fighters continues • Israel besieges the compound of Yassir Arafat in Romallah and engages in targeted assassinations of key Palestinian militant leaders; Palestinian rocket attacks and suicide bombings escalate • Israel completes the construction of the first section of a security barrier intended to separate Israeli and Palestinian areas; the proposed route does not follow the "Green Line" and arouses controversy • At the end of 2003, over 120 countries have ratified or acceded to the Kyoto Protocol concerning greenhouse emissions; the US has refused to do so because the Protocol does not impose restrictions on China or India • North Korea withdraws from the Nuclear Nonproliferation Treaty and restarts its nuclear reactors • Yugoslavia formally changes its name to Serbia and Montenegro • Belgium extends civil marriage to same-sex couples	• In the most important affirmative action decision since the 1978 *Bakke* case, the US Supreme Court upholds the University of Michigan Law School's admissions policy, ruling that race can be one of many factors considered by colleges when selecting their students; however, the Court also holds that race may not blindly be given extra weight in that process • Alabama Supreme Court Chief Justice Roy Moore refuses to comply with a federal court order to remove a 2.5-ton monument of the Ten Commandments placed by Moore's order in the Rotunda of the Alabama Judicial Building in 2001; the Alabama Court of the Judiciary removes Moore from office, and the monument is then removed from the building; in 2004, the US Supreme Court declines to hear an appeal of the lower court decision • The US Supreme Court rules in *Lawrence v. Texas* that sodomy laws in the US are unconstitutional • The Massachusetts Supreme Judicial Court strikes down the heterosexuals-only restriction in the state's marriage law • After years of protests, US military forces vacate the island of Vieques, Puerto Rico, which it has used as an artillery and bombing range since the 1940s • An opinion poll conducted by ABC News and *The Washington Post* finds that 48% of African Americans now prefer that term, 35% favor the term *black*, and 17% like both terms equally (this indicates a significant shift since the similar poll by the same organizations in 1989)	• The space shuttle *Columbia* disintegrates on reentry into the earth's atmosphere, killing everyone on board • The Wilkinson Microwave Anisotropy Probe (WMAP) produces a high-resolution map that captures the oldest light in the universe, called the cosmic microwave background, which is the remnant of the Big Bang • NASA loses contact with *Pioneer 10*, launched 31 years ago and now well out of the solar system and into deep space, when its internal power supply finally fails • An investigation of the 2000 crash of a Concorde supersonic airliner reveals serious safety and design flaws; all the remaining Concorde airliners are retired from service • The 120-million-year-old fossil of a previously unknown species of flying dinosaur that had four wings is discovered in northeastern China • Three fossilized skulls originally found in Ethiopia in 1997 are identified as the oldest known remains of modern humans; the skulls are estimated to be about 160,000 years old (more than 50,000 years earlier than any previously known human remains); scientists call the new human subspecies *Homo sapiens idaltu* (*idaltu* means "elder" in the Afar language of Ethiopia)	• *Les Misérables*, which opened on Broadway in 1987, finally closes after 6,680 performances as the third longest-running show in the history of Broadway • *Wicked*, a musical touted as "the untold story of the witches of Oz" and loosely based on the best-selling novel *Wicked: The Life and Times of the Wicked Witch of the West* by Gregory Maguire, opens on Broadway, featuring music and lyrics by Stephen Schwartz • The Recording Industry Association of America (RIAA) begins filing lawsuits against individuals for allegedly distributing copyrighted music files over peer-to-peer networks • Apple launches the iTunes Music Store, an online store selling music tracks for download over the Internet on a per-title basis through its iTunes application • Many large US Internet retailers begin collecting state sales taxes on all purchases • The group Black Eyed Peas have their first big hit with "Where Is The Love?" featuring Justin Timberlake • Beyoncé Knowles releases her debut solo album, *Dangerously in Love*, including the hit single, "Crazy in Love" • Simon and Garfunkel begin their "Old Friends" US reunion tour, twenty years after their 1983 world tour • After a three-year hiatus, J. K. Rowling is back in print with the fifth volume in the Harry Potter series, *Harry Potter and the Order of the Phoenix* • Films: *The Lord of the Rings: The Return of the King*; *Cold Mountain*; *Master and Commander*; *Mystic River*; *The Last Samurai*; *Seabiscuit*
2004	• NATO expands to 26 members with the admission of Bulgaria, Estonia, Lithuania, Latvia, Romania, Slovakia, and Slovenia • The European Union expands to 25 members with the admission of Estonia, Latvia, Lithuania, Poland, the Czech Republic, Slovakia, Hungary, Slovenia, Cyprus, and Malta; Bulgaria, Romania, and Turkey have pending applications for EU membership • Both Shiite and Sunni radicals in Iraq engage in increasingly violent attacks against American and British forces and Iraqi nationals perceived as "collaborating with the occupiers" • Commuter train bombings in Madrid, Spain, kill more than 190 people and injure (cont.)	• The National WWII Memorial is completed and dedicated in Washington, DC • Controversies over same-sex marriages or civil unions bubble around the US; the first same-sex marriages (as distinct from civil unions) take place in Massachusetts; Connecticut passes a state law authorizing same-sex civil unions (but not marriages); eleven other states approve constitutional amendments to prohibit same-sex marriages or civil unions • Publication of *The 9/11 Commission Report: Final Report of the National Commission on Terrorist Attacks Upon the United States* provokes much discussion in the US	• NASA successfully lands two rovers on the surface of Mars; they find evidence that Mars once had running water on its surface • NASA's *Cassini*, launched from Kennedy Space Center in 1997, becomes the first spacecraft to be successfully placed into orbit around Saturn • *SpaceShipOne*, the world's first privately financed reusable spacecraft, designed by Burt Rutan and piloted by Michael Melville, wins the $10 million Ansari X-Prize by making two successful manned suborbital flights • *The Queen Mary II* is launched; it is the largest cruise liner ever built, twice the size of the famous *Queen Elizabeth II*	• Francis Joyon (France) becomes the fastest world solo navigator, sailing around the globe in 73 days, over 20 days faster than the previous record • An estimated 51 million TV viewers watch the last episode of *Friends* • *Desperate Housewives* premieres on TV and becomes an immediate sensation • U2 releases the highly acclaimed album *How to Dismantle an Atomic Bomb*, which debuts at no. 1 in 32 countries, including the US, Canada, Britain, and the band's native Ireland; it sells 840,000 units in the US in its first week

E. EDUCATION, LITERATURE & THE FINE ARTS	F. RELIGION, THEOLOGY, PHILOSOPHY & PSYCHOLOGY	G. AMERICAN & UNITED METHODISM	H. BRITISH & WORLD METHODISM	
	• Other notable publications include: – Jonathan Sacks, *The Dignity of Difference: How to Avoid the Clash of Civilizations* – Charles Kimball, *When Religion Becomes Evil* – Bruce Feiler, *Abraham: A Journey to the Heart of Three Faiths* – Stephen R. Haynes, *Noah's Curse: The Biblical Justification of American Slavery* – Philip Jenkins, *The Next Christendom: The Coming of Global Christianity*			**2002 cont.**
• John Adams wins the Pulitzer Prize in Music for his composition *On the Transmigration of Souls* • Arvo Pärt composes his *In the Beginning* for chorus and orchestra • Leonardo Balada composes his *Ebony Fantasies* cantata for choir and orchestra • The 15th edition of the venerable *Chicago Manual of Style*, the "bible" of style and usage for the publishing world, appears • Other notable publications include: – Molefi Kete Asante, *Erasing Racism: The Social Survival of the American Nation* – Mitch Albom, *The Five People You Meet in Heaven* – John Grisham, *The King of Torts*	• The Roman Catholic Church in the US copes with scandal concerning the sexual abuse of children by priests and the cover-up of the abuse by the hierarchy • The Episcopal Church in the US (ECUSA) confirms an openly homosexual priest (Eugene Robinson, Diocese of New Hampshire) as bishop and permits same-sex marriages in local dioceses, producing tensions with more conservative churches within the worldwide Anglican communion • Mother Teresa is beatified (first step toward sainthood) by Pope John Paul II • Dan Brown's novel *The Da Vinci Code* is a worldwide best seller [36 million copies in print as of the end of 2005] and has been translated into 44 languages; his speculations about the Holy Grail legend and the role of Mary Magdalene in the history of Christianity are considered historically inaccurate by most scholars and heretical by many Christians • Jaroslav Pelikan and Valerie Hotchkiss publish their important critical edition of *Creeds and Confessions of Faith in the Christian Tradition* (4 vols.) • Other notable publications include: – N. T. Wright, *The Resurrection of the Son of God* – Susan Neiman, *Evil in Modern Thought: An Alternative History of Philosophy* – Stephen Prothero, *American Jesus: How the Son of God Became a National Icon* – Lamin Sanneh, *Whose Religion Is Christianity? The Gospel Beyond the West*	• Formal complaints are filed against Bishop Joseph Sprague for "dissemination of doctrines contrary to the established standards of doctrine" of the UMC in the wake of a public address at Iliff School of Theology and publication of his book *Affirmations of a Dissenter*; the complaints are dismissed after review by a panel of the North Central College of Bishops • The Confessing Movement establishes the annual Epworth Institute for UM clergy under age 45 • The Bicentennial Edition of Wesley's *Journal and Diaries* is completed (8 vols., 1988–2003) • Other notable publications include: – Richard P. Heitzenrater, *The Elusive Mr. Wesley* (revised edition in one volume) – Kenneth J. Collins, *John Wesley: A Theological Journey* – Scott J. Jones, *The Evangelistic Love of God & Neighbor: A Theology of Witness and Discipleship*	• Methodists around the world celebrate the 300th anniversary of John Wesley's birth • The MC [UK] and the Church of England sign a covenant drawing them into a new relationship of shared life and mission, building on local and regional expressions of unity between the two churches, and pledging them "to work to overcome the remaining obstacles to the organic unity of our two churches, on the way to the full visible unity of Christ's Church" and toward a time when "the fuller visible unity of our churches makes possible a united, interchangeable ministry" • Leaders of the MCNZ forge an agreement concerning homosexuality that "acknowledges the diversity of the church, the integrity of differing beliefs, and respects differences" • The autonomous Protestant Methodist Church of Côte d'Ivoire (Ivory Coast) becomes a mission of the UMC and takes the name Eglise Methodiste Unie Côte d'Ivoire • The World Methodist Council gives the World Methodist Peace Award to Casimira Rodriguez Romero for her work with domestic workers in Bolivia and throughout Latin America	**2003**
• Arvo Pärt composes his choral meditation *Da Pacem Domine* (On the Peace of God) • Philip Glass completes his *Symphony No. 7 (Toltec)* for orchestra and chorus • Notable publications include: – John le Carré, *Absolute Friends* – Stephen King, *Song of Susannah* – Philip Roth, *The Plot Against America* – Richard A. Clarke, *Against All Enemies: Inside America's War on Terror*	• The third Parliament of the World's Religions meets in connection with the Universal Forum of Cultures in Barcelona, Spain • Samuel Kobia (Methodist Church in Kenya) is named as General Secretary of the World Council of Churches • The Presbyterian Church (USA) rejects a proposal to allow the ordination of homosexual clergy and acceptance of homosexuals as lay church officers • A commission of the worldwide Anglican Communion appointed by the Archbishop of Canterbury rebukes the ECUSA for causing "pain and confusion" within the Communion and urges a moratorium on the ordination of gay clergy and the blessing of same-sex unions	• Karen Dammann (Pacific Northwest Conference) is acquitted in a church trial on charges of "practices declared by the UMC to be incompatible with Christian teachings" • The UMC Judicial Council determines that it does not have the authority to review the decision in the Dammann case • UMC bishops continue the Episcopal Initiative on Children and Poverty • The UMC General Conference: – eliminates the General Council on Ministries (GCOM), leaves the General Council on Finance and Administration (GCFA) intact, and establishes a 47-member "Connectional Table" to guide the work of the general agencies	• The Eglise Methodiste Unie Côte d'Ivoire (Ivory Coast) is accepted into full membership in the UMC, bringing one million new members into the UMC; it will by 2012 become a new annual conference within the West Africa Central Conference but will be authorized to elect its own bishop • The World Methodist Council gives the World Methodist Peace Award to Millard Fuller (US) for his work with Habitat for Humanity • The MCNZ approves the ordination of homosexuals but restricts their appointment to welcoming congregations • Methodists and Anglicans in New Zealand begin conversations about possible union	**2004**

	A. WORLD HISTORY & POLITICS	B. AMERICAN HISTORY & POLITICS	C. SCIENCE, MEDICINE & TECHNOLOGY	D. DAILY LIFE, POPULAR CULTURE & ENTERTAINMENT
2004 cont.	• more than 1,400 others; Spanish authorities conclude that al-Qaeda is behind the bombings; Spain decides to pull its troops out of Iraq • After the death of Yassir Arafat, Mahmoud Abbas is selected as the new chairman of the PLO and subsequently elected as president of the PNA; the level of Israeli-Palestinian violence decreases • The world is shocked by photos and videos of US soldiers abusing detainees in the Abu Ghraib prison in Iraq • The Sudanese Civil War leads to genocidal destruction in the Darfur region • Libya voluntarily dismantles its nuclear weapons program • Britain and New Zealand pass legislation allowing for formal same-sex civil unions with all the social, tax, pension, and inheritance rights as married couples • A very powerful (magnitude 9.2) undersea earthquake centered near the coast of Sumatra triggers a massive tsunami that devastates costal areas in 13 countries all around the Indian Ocean; waves over 100 feet high in places kill over 250,000 people, injure millions more, and cause untold billions of property damage; it is the largest natural disaster in recorded history and prompts comparably large relief efforts	• Michael Moore's controversial documentary, *Fahrenheit 9/11*, which is harshly critical of the Bush administration's handling of the war in Iraq and the "war on terrorism," wins the *Palme d'Or* (the top prize) at the Cannes Film Festival • Four major hurricanes hit Florida and adjacent areas within six weeks: Charley (Aug. 13) kills 34; Frances (Sept. 5) kills 38; Ivan (Sept. 16) kills 52 in the US, 66 in the Caribbean; Jeanne (Sept. 26) kills 28; total damages from the 4 hurricanes are estimated to exceed the cost of Andrew (1992) • Former president Ronald Reagan dies at the age of 93; he is accorded a formal state funeral in Washington • President Bush and Vice President Cheney are reelected (Republican Party)	• Taipei 101 (Taiwan) becomes the tallest building in the world: 101 stories, 1,670 feet (almost 1/3 mile) • Astronomers announce the discovery of the most distant object ever identified in our solar system, a planetoid that is named Sedna; it is the largest object discovered since Pluto in 1930	• U2 signs a deal with Apple Computer allowing the single "Vertigo" to be used in a widely aired television commercial for the special U2 Edition of Apple's iPod music player • The pace of music downloads over the internet steadily increases; Apple's iTunes online music store sells its 200,000,000th song • Brian Wilson, one of the original Beach Boys, completes and releases the album *Smile*, 37 years after its original planned release as the follow-up to the Beach Boys' album *Pet Sounds* • Kenny Leon's revival production of Lorraine Hansberry's *A Raisin in the Sun* opens on Broadway • Ken Burns's documentary film *Unforgivable Blackness: The Rise and Fall of Jack Johnson*, portraying the life of the heavyweight-boxing champion, is broadcast on PBS • Films: Mel Gibson's *The Passion of the Christ* attracts huge audiences and creates huge controversy due to its highly graphic depiction of the death of Jesus; other major films include *Million Dollar Baby*; *Beyond the Sea* (the Bobby Darin story); *Sideways*; *Ray*; *The Aviator*; *Hotel Rwanda*; *Finding Neverland*; *Harry Potter and the Prisoner of Azkaban* • Summer Olympics: Athens
2005	• The car-bombing murder of former Lebanese prime minister Rafiq Hariri touches off massive protests that lead to the withdrawal of all Syrian troops from Lebanon, ending a 30-year occupation • Suicide bombers linked to al-Qaeda set off explosions on London's Underground and a double-decker bus, killing 52 and injuring over 70 people	• The case of Terri Schiavo stirs national debate about the "right to die" as her husband and her parents clash about removal of her feeding tube because of severe brain damage that had left her in a permanent vegetative state • Hurricane Katrina batters the Gulf Coast, killing over 2,000 people, destroying over 200,000 homes and causing incalculable *(cont.)*	• NASA's *Cassini* spacecraft sends its *Huygens* probe safely to the surface of Titan, the largest moon of Saturn • The space shuttle *Discovery* completes NASA's first shuttle mission since the disintegration of the *Columbia* on reentry in 2003 • The World Meteorological Organization reports that 2005 is the warmest year for *(cont.)*	• *Les Misérables* celebrates its 20th anniversary performance at London's Queen's Theatre, overtaking Andrew Lloyd Webber's *Cats* as the longest running West End musical ever • *Monty Python's Spamalot*, a musical comedy based on the 1975 film *Monty Python and the Holy Grail*, opens on Broadway

E. EDUCATION, LITERATURE & THE FINE ARTS	F. RELIGION, THEOLOGY, PHILOSOPHY & PSYCHOLOGY	G. AMERICAN & UNITED METHODISM	H. BRITISH & WORLD METHODISM	
	• Notable publications include: – O. C. Edwards Jr., *A History of Preaching* – Desmond Tutu, *God Has a Dream: A Vision of Hope for Our Time*	– creates a Division on Ministries with Young People within the General Board of Discipleship – adopts *This Holy Mystery: A United Methodist Understanding of Holy Communion* as an official statement of church teaching – amends the *Discipline* to specify a list of "chargeable offenses" related to homosexuality that could result in a church trial – approves a resolution that no annual conference funding may be provided "to any gay caucus or group" or used "to promote the acceptance of homosexuality" – approves a $4 million Global Education Fund; continues special funding for Africa University – votes to expand the UMC media campaign ("Open Hearts. Open Minds. Open Doors.") over the next four years – approves Central Conference Pension Initiative (CCPI) to provide retirement benefits to clergy and lay employees in some of the central conferences – approves a concordat agreement between the UMC and the now fully autonomous Methodist Church of Puerto Rico – passes a "Resolution on Church Unity" (by a vote of 869-41) after hearing reports of conversations about an "amicable separation" of the church over "irreconcilable differences" relating to homosexuality • The UAMEC (1813/1865) joins the UMC, AMEC, AMEZC, and CMEC in the Commission on Pan-Methodist Cooperation and Union • After General Conference, Irene Elizabeth "Beth" Stroud (Eastern Pennsylvania Conference) is charged with violating church law by being a "self-avowed practicing homosexual"; a church trial finds her guilty and revokes her ministerial credentials • The Young Adult Seminarian Network is established under the sponsorship of GBHEM • The Western Jurisdiction elects Minerva Carcaño as the UMC's first Latina bishop • A UMC congregation is established for the first time in Mongolia • Notable publications include: – Thomas Edward Frank and Russell E. Richey, *Episcopacy in the Methodist Tradition: Perspectives and Proposals* – Ted A. Campbell and Michael T. Burns, *Wesleyan Essentials in a Multicultural Society* – Michael E. Lodahl, *God of Nature and of Grace: Reading the World in a Wesleyan Way* – Joerg Rieger and John Vincent, eds., *Methodist and Radical: Rejuvenating a Tradition*	• Notable publications include: – M. Douglas Meeks, ed. *Wesleyan Perspectives on the New Creation* [papers from the eleventh Oxford Institute of Methodist Theological Studies, 2002] – Patrick Streiff, *Methodism in Europe: 19th & 20th Century* (published by the Baltic Methodist Theological Seminary) – Clive Marsh, et al., eds., *Unmasking Methodist Theology*	**2004 cont.**
• John Harbison's *Milosz Songs* is premiered by the New York Philharmonic with soprano Dawn Upshaw, for whom the work is written • Installation artists Christo and Jean-Claude deck New York's Central Park with 7,503 orange "gates" for a period of 16 days	• Billy Graham, at the age of 86, announces that his June crusade in New York, the 417th of his long evangelistic career, will be his last • Pope John Paul II dies; he is succeeded by Cardinal Joseph Ratzinger (Germany), who takes the name Pope Benedict XVI • The Vatican rules that homosexual men should not be admitted to Roman Catholic *(cont.)*	• The Affirmation Caucus celebrates its 30th anniversary at the "Hearts On Fire" event at Lake Junaluska, NC, which is also the eighth national convocation of the Reconciling Ministries Network; critics object to the fact that it meets at Junaluska Assembly • Ed Johnson (Virginia Conference) is suspended from ministry by his annual *(cont.)*	• The Methodist Church in Cambodia becomes autonomous three years after it originated in the union of separate mission efforts of the Korean Methodist Church, the Methodist Mission of Singapore, the World Federation of Chinese Methodist Churches, the United Methodist mission unit of France and Switzerland, and the United Methodist General Board of Global Ministries	**2005**

	A. WORLD HISTORY & POLITICS	B. AMERICAN HISTORY & POLITICS	C. SCIENCE, MEDICINE & TECHNOLOGY	D. DAILY LIFE, POPULAR CULTURE & ENTERTAINMENT
2005 cont.	• After complicated negotiations following a very close election, Angela Merkel becomes the first woman to serve as chancellor of Germany • Israel unilaterally withdraws from the Gaza Strip, where the Palestinian Authority assumes political control and dismantles some West Bank settlements • The Constitutional Court of South Africa finds restrictions on same-sex marriage in South Africa to be unconstitutional • A severe earthquake rocks the Kashmir region between India and Pakistan, killing over 80,000 and leaving as many as three million people homeless • Laws authorizing same-sex civil unions are approved in Canada, Spain, and Switzerland • Ellen Johnson-Sirleaf of Liberia becomes Africa's first elected woman president • Iraq approves a new federal constitution, then holds free, democratic multiparty elections for its first permanent national assembly in the post-Saddam era	property damage; the levees in New Orleans fail, flooding much of the city; it is by far the most costly natural disaster in US history • All levels of government (federal, state, and local) are blamed for failures in responding to those affected by Hurricane Katrina, but the Federal Emergency Management Agency (FEMA) receives the greatest amount of criticism for its disastrous performance • In a pair of 5-4 decisions, the US Supreme Court rules that the Ten Commandments displays in two Kentucky courthouses violate the establishment clause of the 1st Amendment but also rules that the biblical laws can be displayed in a historical context, as they are in a frieze in the Supreme Court building itself • Edgar Ray Killen is convicted on charges of manslaughter on the 41st anniversary of the Mississippi civil rights murders of 1964 • When Rosa Parks, called "the Mother of the Civil Rights Movement," dies at the age of 92, she becomes the second African American and the first woman to lie in state in the Rotunda of the US Capitol • A federal judge finds that biology textbook stickers in a Georgia public school district stating that "Evolution is a theory, not a fact" violate the 1st Amendment • A federal judge in Pennsylvania prohibits a public school district there from teaching "intelligent design" in biology classes, saying that it is "creationism in disguise" • The US Senate again defeats proposals to allow oil drilling in the Arctic National Wildlife Refuge (ANWR) • President Bush acknowledges that he has signed executive orders authorizing the electronic surveillance of US citizens by the NSA without court orders, claiming presidential authority to do so despite the restrictions of FISA (1978) • The US national debt reaches $7,932,709,661,723	the Northern Hemisphere and the second warmest for the world since records began in 1861; Arctic sea ice shrinks to record low amounts and several major glaciers retreat by several miles • The number of Internet users around the world reaches an estimated one billion • Fears of a pandemic of avian flu ("bird flu") spread around the world as more and more isolated incidents of the disease are reported • Surgeons in France perform the world's first partial face transplant, grafting a nose, lips, and chin onto a 38-year-old woman who had been disfigured by a dog bite • South Korean scientist Hwang Woo-suk announces that he has successfully produced new human stem cell lines from a cloned human embryo; he is subsequently forced to resign from his university position when an investigation reveals that he falsified the research data on which his claim is based • Apple unveils the video version of the iPod, hoping to do for digital video what the original iPod did for digital audio • Lockheed-Martin's F-22 Raptor, the second-generation "stealth" fighter aircraft of the US Air Force, enters operational service	• Oprah Winfrey opens her musical production of *The Color Purple*, based on Alice Walker's 1982 novel, on Broadway • Mariah Carey makes a career comeback with the release of *The Emancipation of Mimi*, which debuts at no. 1 and goes 5X platinum in less than a year • Lance Armstrong (US) wins the Tour de France for a record seventh consecutive year at the age of 33 and announces his retirement from competitive bicycle racing • The US Congress holds hearings in response to accusations of widespread use of steroids by Major League Baseball players, including home-run kings Barry Bonds and Mark McGwire • Tiger Woods wins the Masters golf tournament for the fourth time, joining Jack Nicklaus (6) and Arnold Palmer (4) as the only golfers ever to do so and becoming the only golfer other than Nicklaus to win all four major tournaments twice • The phenomenal growth of the Wal-Mart chain means that 90% of the US population lives within 15 miles of a Wal-Mart store; over 100 million Americans (about one-third of the entire US population) shop at Wal-Mart each week; Wal-Mart's annual sales equal 2% of the entire US economy • J. K. Rowling publishes the sixth volume in the Harry Potter series, *Harry Potter and the Half-Blood Prince* • The US finally gets a woman president, at least on TV, as *Commander in Chief* scores big with viewers • Films: Peter Jackson's version of *King Kong*; *Walk the Line*; *Good Night, and Good Luck*; *Brokeback Mountain*; *Syriana*; *The Chronicles of Narnia: The Lion, The Witch and The Wardrobe*; *Harry Potter and the Goblet of Fire*; *Star Wars: Episode III—The Revenge of the Sith*

E. EDUCATION, LITERATURE & THE FINE ARTS	F. RELIGION, THEOLOGY, PHILOSOPHY & PSYCHOLOGY	G. AMERICAN & UNITED METHODISM	H. BRITISH & WORLD METHODISM	
• Notable publications include: – Molefi Kete Asante, *Rhetoric, Race, and Identity: The Architecton of Soul* – Joan Didion, *The Year of Magical Thinking* – John Irving, *Until I Find You* – E. L. Doctorow, *The March*	seminary training or ordained to the priesthood • Notable publications include: – Reza Aslan, *No God But God: The Origins, Evolution, and Future of Islam* – Jim Wallis, *God's Politics: Why the Right Gets It Wrong and the Left Doesn't Get It* – Jimmy Carter, *Our Endangered Values: America's Moral Crisis* – Bruce Feiler, *Where God Was Born: A Journey by Land to the Roots of Religion* – Kenneth J. Collins, *The Evangelical Moment: The Promise of an American Religion*	conference after refusing admission to church membership to an admittedly gay man; the UMC Judicial Council orders his reinstatement and issues a decision stating that the *Discipline* "invests discretion in the pastor-in-charge to make the determination of a person's readiness to affirm the vows of membership" and that the pastor is "solely responsible" for making such a determination • The 2004 conviction of Beth Stroud, which had been overturned by an appeals panel, is reinstated when the decision of the appeals panel is reversed by the UMC Judicial Council • The ninth International Congress of United Methodist Men meets • The UMC Council of Bishops and the ELCA Churchwide Assembly both approve an Agreement for Interim Eucharistic Sharing between the ELCA and the UMC • UMPH terminates the publication of *Quarterly Review* after GBHEM announces its decision to cease supporting the journal • Notable publications include: – Dennis M. Campbell, Russell E. Richey, and William B. Lawrence, eds., *Marks of Methodism: Theology in Ecclesial Practice* (United Methodism and American Culture, vol. 5) – Lester Ruth, ed., *Early Methodist Life and Spirituality: A Reader* – D. Stephen Long, *John Wesley's Moral Theology: The Quest for God and Goodness* – John A. Vickers, ed., *The Journals of Dr. Thomas Coke* – W. Stephen Gunter and Elaine Robinson, eds., *Considering the Great Commission: Evangelism and Mission in the Wesleyan Spirit*	• The United Methodist Church in Côte d'Ivoire (Ivory Coast) elects Benjamin Boni as its first bishop • The World Methodist Council gives the World Methodist Peace Award to Bishop Lawi Imathiu (Kenya) for his outspoken opposition to human rights abuses by former Ugandan dictator Idi Amin and his stance against apartheid in South Africa • Notable publications include: – Kenneth Cracknell and Susan J. White, *An Introduction to World Methodism* – Angela Shier-Jones, *A Work in Progress: Methodists Doing Theology*	**2005 cont.**

List of Works and Sources Consulted

General Reference—Published Works

Cullen, Jim. *The Art of Democracy: A Concise History of Popular Culture in the United States*. New York: Monthly Review Press, 1996.

The Encyclopædia Britannica 2006 Ultimate Reference Suite DVD. Copyright 2006 by Encyclopedia Britannica, Inc.

Gribetz, Judah, ed., *The Timetables of Jewish History: A Chronology of the Most Important People and Events in Jewish History*. New York: Simon & Schuster, 1993.

Grun, Bernard. *The Timetables of History: A Horizontal Linkage of People and Events*. Fourth rev. ed. New York: Simon & Schuster, 2005.

Hellemans, Alexander, and Bryan Bunch, eds. *The Timetables of Science: A Chronology of the Most Important People and Events in the History of Science*. New York: Simon & Schuster, 1988.

Humphries, Christian, and Francis Adlington, eds. *World History: People, Dates & Events*. Second ed. London: Philip's, 2002.

Microsoft Encarta 2006 Premium Reference Library DVD. Copyright 1999–2005 by Microsoft Corporation.

O'Neill, Mary, ed. *Chambers History Factfinder*. Edinburgh: Chambers Harrap Publishers Ltd., 2005.

Scordato, Ellen, ed. *The New York Public Library Desk Reference*. Fourth ed. New York: Hyperion, 1989.

Stearns, Peter N., ed. *The Encyclopedia of World History: Ancient, Medieval, and Modern, Chronologically Arranged*. Sixth ed. Boston and New York: Houghton Mifflin, 2001. Updated and revised edition of the classic reference work originally compiled and edited by William L. Langer. Includes CD-ROM.

Teeple, John B., ed. *Timelines of World History*. London & New York: DK Publishing, 2002.

Urdang, Laurence, ed. *The Timetables of American History, Millennial Edition*. New York: Simon & Schuster, 1996.

General Reference—Web-based Resources

American Experience Online (produced for Public Broadcasting Service by the WGBH Educational Foundation, Boston): http://www.pbs.org/wgbh/amex/index.html.

American History from AmericanHeritage.com: http://www.americanheritage.com.

Answers Corporation: Online Encyclopedia, Thesaurus, Dictionary definitions and more: http://www.answers.com.

Best of History Web Sites (an award-winning site developed by Thomas Daccord, founder of The Center for Teaching History With Technology, that contains links to more than 1,200 history-related websites "that have been reviewed for quality, accuracy, and usefulness"): http://besthistorysites.net.

Digital History (a project of the University of Houston, in connection with the Chicago Historical Society, the Gilder Lehrman Institute of American History, and The Museum of Fine Arts, Houston): Mintz, S. (2003). *Digital History*. Retrieved 2006 from http://www.digitalhistory.uh.edu.

History Matters (a project of the American Social History Project/Center for Media and Learning of the City University of New York and the Center for History and New Media at George Mason University): http://www.historymatters.gmu.edu.

The History Place ("a private, independent, Internet-only publication . . . owned and published by Philip Gavin," Boston): http://www.historyplace.com/index.html.

Information Please: Online dictionary, Internet encyclopedia, atlas, and almanac reference (Pearson Education): http://www.infoplease.com.

Internet Modern History Sourcebook (part of the Internet History Sourcebooks Project located at the History Department of Fordham University, New York): http://www.fordham.edu/halsall/mod/modsbook.html.

The Media History Project of the School of Journalism and Mass Communication, College of Liberal Arts, University of Minnesota: http://www.mediahistory.umn.edu/index2.html.

On This Day ("a showcase of some of the most significant . . . stories broadcast by BBC News since 1950"): http://news.bbc.co.uk/onthisday/default.stm.

The Religious Movements Homepage Project at the University of Virginia: http://religiousmovements.lib.virginia.edu/home.htm.

Social Science History: Time Line for the History of Science and Social Science (a resource of Middlesex University, London, by Andrew Roberts): http://www.mdx.ac.uk/www/study/sshtim.htm.

The Stanford Encyclopedia of Philosophy (a project of the Center for the Study of Language and Information, Stanford University : http://plato.stanford.edu.

The Timeline of Art History of the Metropolitan Museum of Art: http://www.metmuseum.org/toah/splash.htm?HomePageLink=toah_l.

Wikipedia, The Free Encyclopedia: http://www.wikipedia.org.

The World Factbook (produced by the Central Intelligence Agency of the United States): http://www.cia.gov/cia/publications/factbook/index.html.

History of Christianity

Chadwick, Owen. A History of Christianity. New York: St. Martin's Press, 2000.

Chidester, David. Christianity: A Global History. San Francisco: HarperSanFrancisco, 2000.

Cross, Frank L. ed., The Oxford Dictionary of the Christian Church. Third ed. Revised by Elizabeth A. Livingstone. Oxford: Oxford University Press, 1997.

Ellingson, Mark. Reclaiming Our Roots: An Inclusive Introduction to Church History. Volume 2: From Martin Luther to Martin Luther King, Jr. Harrisburg, Pa.: Trinity Press International, 1999.

Hannah, John D. Charts of Modern and Postmodern Church History. Grand Rapids: Zondervan, 2004.

McManners, John, ed. The Oxford Illustrated History of Christianity. Oxford & New York: Oxford University Press, 1992.

Mead, Frank S., Samuel S. Hill, and Craig D. Atwood, eds. Handbook of Denominations in the United States. Twelfth edition. Nashville: Abingdon, 2006.

Noll, Mark A. The Old Religion in a New World: The History of North American Christianity. Grand Rapids: Eerdmans, 2002.

Piepkorn, Arthur Carl. Profiles in Belief: The Religious Bodies of the United States and Canada. Three volumes. New York: Harper & Row, 1977.

Spickard, Paul R., and Kevin M. Cragg. A Global History of Christians: How Everyday Believers Experienced Their World. Grand Rapids: Baker Academic, 1994.

"This Week in Christian History" (produced by Christianity Today International): http://www.christianitytoday.com/history/features/twich.

Walton, Robert C. Chronological and Background Charts of Church History. Grand Rapids: Zondervan, 1986.

"What Happened this Day in Church History" (produced by the Christian History Institute): http://chi.gospelcom.net/DAILYF/daily.php.

History of Methodism

Braithwaite, Joan A., ed. *Methodism in the Caribbean: 200 Years Plus and Moving On*. Barbados: Methodist Church in the Caribbean and the Americas, 1998.

Bucke, Emory S., ed. *History of American Methodism*. 3 vols. Nashville: Abingdon, 1964.

Campbell, James T. *Songs of Zion: The African Methodist Episcopal Church in the United States and South Africa*. New York: Oxford University Press, 1995.

Cracknell, Kenneth, and Susan J. White. *An Introduction to World Methodism*. Cambridge: Cambridge University Press, 2005.

Curts, Lewis, supervisor. *The General Conferences of the Methodist Episcopal Church from 1792 to 1896*. Cincinnati: Curts & Jennings; New York: Eaton & Mains, 1900.

Davies, Rupert E., A. Raymond George, and E. Gordon Rupp, eds. *A History of the Methodist Church in Great Britain*. 4 vols. London: Epworth, 1965–1988.

Forsaith, Peter. Methodist Heritage website: http://www.forsaith-oxon.demon.co.uk/methodist-heritage.

Frank, Thomas Edward. *Polity, Practice, and the Mission of The United Methodist Church, 2006 Edition*. Nashville: Abingdon, 2006.

General Board of Global Ministries, The United Methodist Church—Country Profiles and Mission Profiles: http://gbgm-umc.org/country_profiles/index.cfm

General Board of Global Ministries, The United Methodist Church—United Methodist History: http://gbgm-umc.org/umhistory.

General Commission on Archives and History, The United Methodist Church—Resources: http://www.gcah.org/resources.htm.

González, Justo L., ed. *Each in Our Own Tongue: A History of Hispanic United Methodism*. Nashville: Abingdon, 1991.

Graham, J. H. *Black United Methodists: Retrospect and Prospect*. New York: Vantage Press, 1979.

Guillermo, Artemio R., ed. *Churches Aflame: Asian Americans and United Methodism*. Nashville: Abingdon, 1991.

Harmon, Nolan B., gen. ed. *Encyclopedia of World Methodism*. 2 vols. Nashville: The United Methodist Publishing House, 1974.

Heitzenrater, Richard P. *Wesley and the People Called Methodists*. Nashville: Abingdon, 1995.

Hempton, David. *Methodism: Empire of the Spirit*. New Haven & London: Yale University Press, 2005.

Holt, Ivan Lee. *The Methodists of the World*. New York: The Board of Missions and Church Extension of The Methodist Church, 1950 .

Kimbrough, S T, Jr., ed. *Methodism in Russia and the Baltic States*. Nashville: Abingdon, 1995.

Kirby, James E., Russell E. Richey, and Kenneth E. Rowe. *The Methodists: Student Edition*. Westport, Conn.: Praeger, 1998.

Lakey, Othal Hawthorne. *The History of the C.M.E. Church*. Rev. ed. Memphis: The C.M.E. Publishing House, 1996.

Lakey, Othal Hawthorne, and Betty Beene Stephens. *God In My Mama's House: The Women's Movement in the C.M.E. Church*. Memphis: The C.M.E. Publishing House, 1994.

Ledbetter, Anna, and Roma Wyatt, eds. *The World Methodist Council Handbook of Information, 2002–2006*. Lake Junaluska, N.C.: The World Methodist Council, 2003.

McKenna, David L. *A Future with a History: The Wesleyan Witness of the Free Methodist Church*. Indianapolis: Light and Life Communications, 1997.

Noley, Homer. *First White Frost: Native Americans and United Methodism*. Nashville: Abingdon, 1991.

Norwood, Frederick A. *The Story of American Methodism: A History of the United Methodists and Their Relations*. Nashville: Abingdon, 1974.

Peterson, P. A. *History of the Revisions of the Discipline of the Methodist Episcopal Church, South*. Nashville: Publishing House of the M.E. Church, South, 1889.

Richardson, Harry V. *Dark Salvation: The Story of Methodism as It Developed Among Blacks in America*. Garden City, N.Y.: Anchor/Doubleday, 1976.

Richey, Russell E., Kenneth E. Rowe, and Jean Miller Schmidt, eds. *The Methodist Experience in America: A Sourcebook*. Vol. 2. Nashville: Abingdon, 2000.

Schmidt, Jean Miller. *Grace Sufficient: A History of Women in American Methodism, 1760–1939*. Nashville: Abingdon, 1999.

Sherman, David. *History of the Revisions of the Discipline of the Methodist Episcopal Church*. New York: Nelson & Phillips, 1874.

Shockley, Grant S. *Heritage and Hope: The African American Presence in United Methodism*. Nashville: Abingdon, 1991.

Simpson, Matthew, ed. *Cyclopedia of Methodism, Embracing Sketches of Its Rise, Progress, and Present Condition, with Biographical Notices and Numerous Illustrations*. Rev. ed. Philadelphia: Louis H. Evers, 1880.

Streiff, Patrick Ph. *Methodism in Europe: 19th and 20th Century*. Tallinn, Estonia: The Baltic Methodist Theological Seminary, 2003.

Talbert, Marilyn Magee. *The Past Matters: A Chronology of African Americans in The United Methodist Church*. Nashville: Discipleship Resources, 2005.

Thompson, Patricia J. *Courageous Past—Bold Future: The Journey Toward Full Clergy Rights for Women in The United Methodist Church*. Nashville: General Board of Higher Education and Ministry, The United Methodist Church, 2006.

Tigert, Jno. J. *A Constitutional History of American Episcopal Methodism*. Fifth ed., rev. and enl. Nashville: Publishing House of the M.E. Church, South, 1913.

Vickers, John A., ed. *A Dictionary of Methodism in Britain and Ireland*. Peterborough, England: Epworth Press, 2000.

Walls, William J. *The African Methodist Episcopal Zion Church: Reality of the Black Church*. Charlotte, N.C.: A.M.E. Zion Publishing House, 1974.

Westerfield Tucker, Karen B. *American Methodism Worship*. Oxford: Oxford University Press, 2001.

Wright, R. R., ed. *Encyclopedia of the African Methodist Episcopal Church*. Second ed. Philadelphia: n.p., 1947.

Yrigoyen, Charles, Jr., and Susan E. Warrick, eds. *Historical Dictionary of Methodism*. Second ed. Lanham, Md.: Scarecrow Press, 2005.